# The Legal Environment ot Business

BLAW 2013 | Sam M. Walton College of Business | University of Arkansas

Cross / Miller

Author: Frank B. Cross, Roger LeRoy Miller

 CENGAGE

Australia • Brazil • Mexico • Singapore • United Kingdom • United States

The Legal Environment of Business: BLAW 2013 | Sam M. Walton College of Business | University of Arkansas, Cross / Miller

The Legal Environment of Business: Text and Cases
Frank B. Cross, Roger LeRoy Miller

©2018 Cengage Learning. All rights reserved.

For product information and technology assistance, contact us at **Cengage Learning Customer & Sales Support, 1-800-354-9706.**

For permission to use material from this text or product, submit all requests online at **www.cengage.com/permissions.** Further permissions questions can be emailed to **permissionrequest@cengage.com.**

This book contains select works from existing Cengage learning resources and was produced by Cengage learning Custom Solutions for collegiate use. As such, those adopting and/or contributing to this work are responsible for editorial content accuracy, continuity and completeness.

Compilation © 2017 Cengage Learning

ISBN: 978-1-337-69280-9

**Cengage Learning**
20 Channel Street
Boston, MA 02210
USA

Cengage Learning is a leading provider of customized learning solutions with employees residing in nearly 40 different countries and sales in more than 125 countries around the world. Find your local representative at: **www.cengage.com.**

Cengage Learning products are represented in Canada by Nelson Education, Ltd.

For your course and learning solutions, visit **www.cengage.com.**

Purchase any of our products at your local college store or at our preferred online store **www.cengagebrain.com.**

Visit our custom book building website at **www.compose.cengage.com.**

Printed at CLPDC, USA, 04-18

# Brief Contents

# Chapter 1

# CHAPTER

# Law and Legal Reasoning

One of the most important functions of law in any society is to provide stability, predictability, and continuity so that people can know how to order their affairs. If any society is to survive, its citizens must be able to determine what is legally right and legally wrong. They must know what sanctions will be imposed on them if they commit wrongful acts. If they suffer harm as a result of others' wrongful acts, they must know how they can seek compensation. By setting forth the rights, obligations, and privileges of citizens, the law enables individuals to go about their business with confidence and a certain degree of predictability.

Although law has various definitions, they all are based on the general observation that **law** consists of *enforceable rules governing relationships among individuals and between individuals and their society.* These "enforceable rules" may consist of unwritten principles of behavior established by a nomadic tribe. They may be set forth in a law code, such as the Code of Hammurabi in ancient Babylon (c. 1780 B.C.E.) or the law code of one of today's European nations. They may consist of written laws and court decisions created by modern legislative and judicial bodies, as in the United States. Regardless of how such rules are created, they all have one thing in common: they establish rights, duties, and privileges that are consistent with the values and beliefs of their society or its ruling group.

In this introductory chapter, we first look at an important question for any student reading this text: How does the legal environment affect business decision making? We next describe the major sources of American law, the common law tradition, and some basic schools of legal thought. We conclude the chapter with sections offering practical guidance on several topics, including how to find the sources of law discussed in this chapter (and referred to throughout the text) and how to read and understand court opinions.

## 1–1 Business Activities and the Legal Environment

Laws and government regulations affect almost all business activities—from hiring and firing decisions to workplace safety, the manufacturing and marketing of products, business financing, and more. To make good business decisions, a basic knowledge of the laws and regulations governing these activities is beneficial—if not essential.

Realize also that in today's business world, a knowledge of "black-letter" law and what conduct can lead to legal **liability** is not enough. Businesspersons must develop critical thinking and legal reasoning skills so that they can evaluate how various laws might apply to a given situation and determine the best course of action. Businesspersons are also expected to make ethical decisions. Thus, the study of business law necessarily involves an ethical dimension.

## 1–1a Many Different Laws May Affect a Single Business Decision

As you will note, each chapter in this text covers specific areas of the law and shows how the legal rules in each area affect business activities. Although compartmentalizing the law in this fashion promotes conceptual clarity, it does not indicate the extent to which a number of different laws may apply to just one decision. Exhibit 1–1 illustrates the various areas of the law that may influence business decision making.

■ **EXAMPLE 1.1** When Mark Zuckerberg started Facebook as a Harvard student, he probably did not imagine all the legal challenges his company would face as a result of his business decisions.

- Shortly after Facebook was launched, others claimed that Zuckerberg had stolen their ideas for a social networking site. Their claims involved alleged theft of intellectual property, fraudulent misrepresentation, and

**EXHIBIT 1–1  Areas of the Law That Can Affect Business Decision Making**

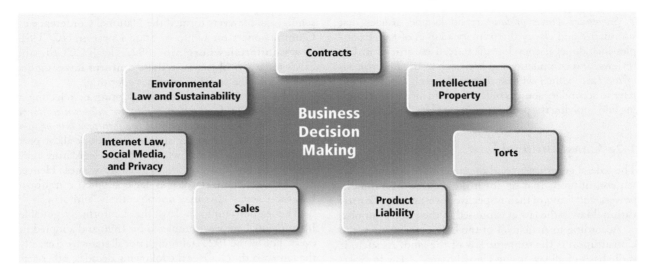

violations of partnership law and securities law. Facebook ultimately paid $65 million to settle those claims out of court.

- Facebook has been sued repeatedly for violating users' privacy (and federal laws) by tracking their Web site usage and by scanning private messages for purposes of data mining and user profiling. A class-action suit filed in Europe alleges that Facebook's data-use policies violate the law of the European Union. Facebook might have to pay millions in damages in this case.
- Facebook's business decisions have also come under scrutiny by federal regulators, such as the Federal Trade Commission (FTC). The company settled a complaint filed by the FTC alleging that Facebook had failed to keep "friends" lists and other user information private. ■

### 1–1b  Ethics and Business Decision Making

Merely knowing the areas of law that may affect a business decision is not sufficient in today's business world. Today, business decision makers need to consider not just whether a decision is legal, but also whether it is ethical.

*Ethics* generally is defined as the principles governing what constitutes right or wrong behavior. Often, as in several of the claims against Facebook discussed above, disputes arise in business because one party feels that he or she has been treated unfairly. Thus, the underlying reason for bringing some lawsuits is a breach of ethical duties (such as when a partner or employee attempts to secretly take advantage of a business opportunity).

Throughout this text, you will learn about the relationship between the law and ethics, as well as about some of the types of ethical questions that arise in business. For instance, all of the new unit-ending *Application and Ethics* features include an *Ethical Connection* section that explores the ethical dimensions of a topic treated within the unit. We have also included *Ethical Questions* for each unit, as well as within the critical thinking sections of many of the cases presented in this text. *Ethics Today* features, which focus on ethical considerations in today's business climate, appear in selected chapters, including this chapter. *A Question of Ethics* case problem is included at the end of every chapter to introduce you to the ethical aspects of specific cases involving real-life situations.

## 1–2  Sources of American Law

American law has numerous sources. Often, these sources of law are classified as either primary or secondary.

*Primary sources of law*, or sources that establish the law, include the following:

1. The U.S. Constitution and the constitutions of the various states.
2. Statutory law—including laws passed by Congress, state legislatures, or local governing bodies.
3. Regulations created by administrative agencies, such as the Federal Trade Commission.
4. Case law and common law doctrines.

We describe each of these important sources of law in the following pages.

*Secondary sources of law* are books and articles that summarize and clarify the primary sources of law. Examples include legal encyclopedias, treatises, articles in law reviews, and compilations of law, such as the *Restatements of the Law* (which will be discussed later). Courts often refer to secondary sources of law for guidance in interpreting and applying the primary sources of law discussed here.

## 1–2a Constitutional Law

The federal government and the states have separate written constitutions that set forth the general organization, powers, and limits of their respective governments. **Constitutional law** is the law as expressed in these constitutions.

According to Article VI of the U.S. Constitution, the Constitution is the supreme law of the land. As such, it is the basis of all law in the United States. A law in violation of the Constitution, if challenged, will be declared unconstitutional and will not be enforced, no matter what its source. Because of its importance in the American legal system, we present the complete text of the U.S. Constitution in Appendix B.

The Tenth Amendment to the U.S. Constitution reserves to the states all powers not granted to the federal government. Each state in the union has its own constitution. Unless it conflicts with the U.S. Constitution or a federal law, a state constitution is supreme within the state's borders.

## 1–2b Statutory Law

Laws enacted by legislative bodies at any level of government, such as statutes passed by Congress or by state legislatures, make up the body of law known as **statutory law.** When a legislature passes a statute, that statute ultimately is included in the federal code of laws or the relevant state code of laws.

Statutory law also includes local **ordinances**—regulations passed by municipal or county governing units to deal with matters not covered by federal or state law. Ordinances commonly have to do with city or county land use (zoning ordinances), building and safety codes, and other matters affecting the local community.

A federal statute, of course, applies to all states. A state statute, in contrast, applies only within the state's borders. State laws thus may vary from state to state. No federal statute may violate the U.S. Constitution, and no state statute or local ordinance may violate the U.S. Constitution or the relevant state constitution.

**Uniform Laws** During the 1800s, the differences among state laws frequently created difficulties for businesspersons conducting trade and commerce among the states. To counter these problems, a group of legal scholars and lawyers formed the National Conference of Commissioners on Uniform State Laws, or NCCUSL (**www.uniformlaws.org**), in 1892. The NCCUSL still exists today. Its object is to draft **uniform laws** (model statutes) for the states to consider adopting.

Each state has the option of adopting or rejecting a uniform law. *Only if a state legislature adopts a uniform law does that law become part of the statutory law of that state.* Note that a state legislature may adopt all or part of a uniform law as it is written, or the legislature may rewrite the law however the legislature wishes. Hence, even though many states may have adopted a uniform law, those states' laws may not be entirely "uniform."

The earliest uniform law, the Uniform Negotiable Instruments Law, was completed by 1896 and adopted in every state by the 1920s (although not all states used exactly the same wording). Over the following decades, other acts were drawn up in a similar manner. In all, more than two hundred uniform acts have been issued by the NCCUSL since its inception. The most ambitious uniform act of all, however, was the Uniform Commercial Code.

**The Uniform Commercial Code** One of the most important uniform acts is the Uniform Commercial Code (UCC), which was created through the joint efforts of the NCCUSL and the American Law Institute.[1] The UCC was first issued in 1952 and has been adopted in all fifty states,[2] the District of Columbia, and the Virgin Islands.

The UCC facilitates commerce among the states by providing a uniform, yet flexible, set of rules governing commercial transactions. Because of its importance in the area of commercial law, we cite the UCC frequently in this text. We also present Article 2 of the UCC in Appendix C. From time to time, the NCCUSL revises the articles contained in the UCC and submits the revised versions to the states for adoption.

## 1–2c Administrative Law

Another important source of American law is **administrative law,** which consists of the rules, orders, and decisions of administrative agencies. An **administrative agency** is a federal, state, or local government agency established to perform a specific function. Administrative law and procedures constitute a dominant element in the regulatory environment of business.

---

1. This institute was formed in the 1920s and consists of practicing attorneys, legal scholars, and judges.
2. Louisiana has not adopted Articles 2 and 2A (covering contracts for the sale and lease of goods), however.

Rules issued by various administrative agencies now affect almost every aspect of a business's operations. Regulations govern a business's capital structure and financing, its hiring and firing procedures, its relations with employees and unions, and the way it manufactures and markets its products. Regulations enacted to protect the environment also often play a significant role in business operations.

**Federal Agencies** At the national level, the cabinet departments of the executive branch include numerous **executive agencies.** The U.S. Food and Drug Administration, for instance, is an agency within the U.S. Department of Health and Human Services. Executive agencies are subject to the authority of the president, who has the power to appoint and remove their officers.

There are also major **independent regulatory agencies** at the federal level, such as the Federal Trade Commission, the Securities and Exchange Commission, and the Federal Communications Commission. The president's power is less pronounced in regard to independent agencies, whose officers serve for fixed terms and cannot be removed without just cause.

**State and Local Agencies** There are administrative agencies at the state and local levels as well. Commonly, a state agency (such as a state pollution-control agency) is created as a parallel to a federal agency (such as the Environmental Protection Agency). Just as federal statutes take precedence over conflicting state statutes, federal agency regulations take precedence over conflicting state regulations.

## 1–2d Case Law and Common Law Doctrines

The rules of law announced in court decisions constitute another basic source of American law. These rules include interpretations of constitutional provisions, of statutes enacted by legislatures, and of regulations created by administrative agencies.

Today, this body of judge-made law is referred to as **case law.** Case law—the doctrines and principles announced in cases—governs all areas not covered by statutory law or administrative law and is part of our common law tradition. We look at the origins and characteristics of the common law tradition in some detail in the pages that follow.

See Concept Summary 1.1 for a review of the sources of American law.

---

### Concept Summary 1.1

**Sources of American Law**

| | |
|---|---|
| **Constitutional Law** | • Law as expressed in the U.S. Constitution or state constitutions.<br>• The U.S. Constitution is the supreme law of the land.<br>• State constitutions are supreme within state borders to the extent that they do not conflict with the U.S. Constitution. |
| **Statutory Law** | • Statutes (including uniform laws) and ordinances enacted by federal, state, and local legislatures.<br>• Federal statutes may not violate the U.S. Constitution.<br>• State statutes and local ordinances may not violate the U.S. Constitution or the relevant state constitution. |
| **Administrative Law** | • The rules, orders, and decisions of federal, state, and local administrative agencies. |
| **Case Law and Common Law Doctrines** | • Judge-made law, including interpretations of constitutional provisions, of statutes enacted by legislatures, and of regulations created by administrative agencies. |

---

## 1–3 The Common Law Tradition

Because of our colonial heritage, much of American law is based on the English legal system. Knowledge of this tradition is crucial to understanding our legal system today because judges in the United States still apply common law principles when deciding cases.

### 1–3a Early English Courts

After the Normans conquered England in 1066, William the Conqueror and his successors began the process of unifying the country under their rule. One of the means they used to do this was the establishment of the king's courts, or *curiae regis*.

Before the Norman Conquest, disputes had been settled according to the local legal customs and traditions in various regions of the country. The king's courts sought to establish a uniform set of customs for the country as a whole. What evolved in these courts was the beginning of the **common law**—a body of general rules that applied throughout the entire English realm. Eventually, the common law tradition became part of the heritage of all nations that were once British colonies, including the United States.

**Courts of Law and Remedies at Law** The early English king's courts could grant only very limited kinds of **remedies** (the legal means to enforce a right or redress a wrong). If one person wronged another in some way, the king's courts could award as compensation one or more of the following: (1) land, (2) items of value, or (3) money.

The courts that awarded this compensation became known as **courts of law,** and the three remedies were called **remedies at law.** (Today, the remedy at law normally takes the form of monetary **damages**—an amount given to a party whose legal interests have been injured.) This system made the procedure for settling disputes more uniform. When a complaining party wanted a remedy other than economic compensation, however, the courts of law could do nothing, so "no remedy, no right."

**Courts of Equity** When individuals could not obtain an adequate remedy in a court of law, they petitioned the king for relief. Most of these petitions were decided by an adviser to the king, called a *chancellor,* who had the power to grant new and unique remedies. Eventually, formal chancery courts, or **courts of equity,** were established. *Equity* is a branch of law—founded on notions of justice and fair dealing—that seeks to supply a remedy when no adequate remedy at law is available.

**Remedies in Equity** The remedies granted by the equity courts became known as **remedies in equity,** or equitable remedies. These remedies include specific performance, injunction, and rescission. *Specific performance* involves ordering a party to perform an agreement as promised. An *injunction* is an order to a party to cease engaging in a specific activity or to undo some wrong or injury. *Rescission* is the cancellation of a contractual obligation. We will discuss these and other equitable remedies in more detail in later chapters.

As a general rule, today's courts, like the early English courts, will not grant equitable remedies unless the remedy at law—monetary damages—is inadequate. ■ **EXAMPLE 1.2** Ted forms a contract (a legally binding agreement) to purchase a parcel of land that he thinks will be perfect for his future home. The seller **breaches** (fails to fulfill) this agreement. Ted could sue the seller for the return of any deposits or down payment he might have made on the land, but this is not the remedy he really wants. What Ted wants is to have a court order the seller to perform the contract. In other words, Ted will seek the equitable remedy of specific performance because monetary damages are inadequate in this situation. ■

**Equitable Maxims** In fashioning appropriate remedies, judges often were (and continue to be) guided by so-called **equitable maxims**—propositions or general statements of equitable rules. Exhibit 1–2 lists some important equitable maxims.

The last maxim listed in the exhibit—"Equity aids the vigilant, not those who rest on their rights"—merits special attention. It has become known as the equitable doctrine of **laches** (a term derived from the Latin *laxus,* meaning "lax" or "negligent"), and it can be used as a defense. A **defense** is an argument raised by the **defendant** (the party being sued) indicating why the **plaintiff** (the suing party) should not obtain the remedy sought. (Note that in equity proceedings, the party bringing a lawsuit is called the **petitioner,** and the party being sued is referred to as the **respondent.**)

The doctrine of laches arose to encourage people to bring lawsuits while the evidence was fresh. What constitutes a reasonable time, of course, varies according to the circumstances of the case. Time periods for different types of cases are now usually fixed by **statutes of limitations.** After the time allowed under a statute of limitations has expired, no action (lawsuit) can be brought, no matter how strong the case was originally.

**EXHIBIT 1–2  Equitable Maxims**

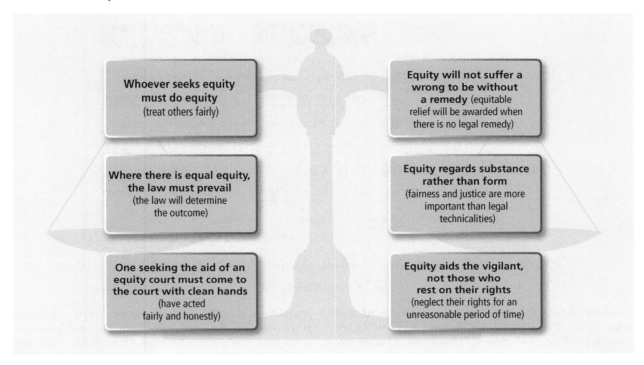

## 1–3b Legal and Equitable Remedies Today

The establishment of courts of equity in medieval England resulted in two distinct court systems: courts of law and courts of equity. The courts had different sets of judges and granted different types of remedies. During the nineteenth century, however, most states in the United States adopted rules of procedure that resulted in the combining of courts of law and equity. A party now may request both legal and equitable remedies in the same action, and the trial court judge may grant either or both forms of relief.

The distinction between legal and equitable remedies remains relevant to students of business law, however, because these remedies differ. To seek the proper remedy for a wrong, you must know what remedies are available. Additionally, certain vestiges of the procedures used when there were separate courts of law and equity still exist. For instance, a party has the right to demand a jury trial in an action at law, but not in an action in equity. Exhibit 1–3 summarizes the procedural differences (applicable in most states) between an action at law and an action in equity.

## 1–3c The Doctrine of *Stare Decisis*

One of the unique features of the common law is that it is *judge-made* law. The body of principles and doctrines that form the common law emerged over time as judges decided legal controversies.

**Case Precedents and Case Reporters** When possible, judges attempted to be consistent and to base their decisions on the principles suggested by earlier cases. They sought to decide similar cases in a similar way, and they considered new cases with care because they knew that their decisions would make new law. Each interpretation became part of the law on the subject and thus served as a legal **precedent.** A precedent is a decision that furnishes an example or authority for deciding subsequent cases involving identical or similar legal principles or facts.

In the early years of the common law, there was no single place or publication where court opinions, or written decisions, could be found. By the fourteenth century, portions of the most important decisions from each year were being gathered together and recorded in *Year Books*, which became useful references for lawyers and judges. In the

**EXHIBIT 1–3** Procedural Differences between Actions at Law and Actions in Equity

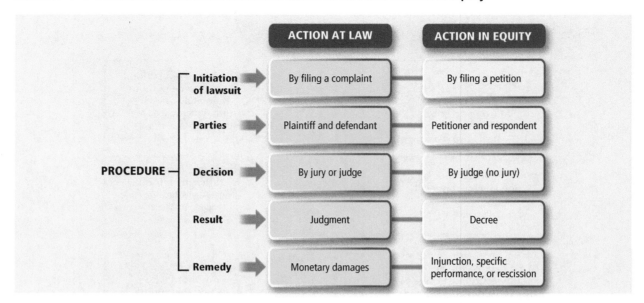

| | | ACTION AT LAW | ACTION IN EQUITY |
|---|---|---|---|
| | Initiation of lawsuit | By filing a complaint | By filing a petition |
| | Parties | Plaintiff and defendant | Petitioner and respondent |
| PROCEDURE | Decision | By jury or judge | By judge (no jury) |
| | Result | Judgment | Decree |
| | Remedy | Monetary damages | Injunction, specific performance, or rescission |

sixteenth century, the *Year Books* were discontinued, and other forms of case publication became available. Today, cases are published, or "reported," in volumes called **reporters,** or *reports*—and are also posted online. We describe today's case reporting system in detail later in this chapter.

### *Stare Decisis* and the Common Law Tradition

The practice of deciding new cases with reference to former decisions, or precedents, became a cornerstone of the English and American judicial systems. The practice formed a doctrine known as ***stare decisis,***[3] a Latin phrase meaning "to stand on decided cases."

Under the doctrine of *stare decisis*, judges are obligated to follow the precedents established within their jurisdictions. The term *jurisdiction* refers to a geographic area in which a court or courts have the power to apply the law. Once a court has set forth a principle of law as being applicable to a certain set of facts, that court must apply the principle in future cases involving similar facts. Courts of lower rank (within the same jurisdiction) must do likewise. Thus, *stare decisis* has two aspects:

1. A court should not overturn its own precedents unless there is a compelling reason to do so.
2. Decisions made by a higher court are binding on lower courts.

**Controlling Precedents** Precedents that must be followed within a jurisdiction are called *controlling*

*precedents.* Controlling precedents are a type of binding authority. A **binding authority** is any source of law that a court must follow when deciding a case. Binding authorities include constitutions, statutes, and regulations that govern the issue being decided, as well as court decisions that are controlling precedents within the jurisdiction. United States Supreme Court case decisions, no matter how old, remain controlling until they are overruled by a subsequent decision of the Supreme Court or changed by further legislation or a constitutional amendment.

**Stare Decisis and Legal Stability** The doctrine of *stare decisis* helps the courts to be more efficient because, if other courts have analyzed a similar case, their legal reasoning and opinions can serve as guides. *Stare decisis* also makes the law more stable and predictable. If the law on a subject is well settled, someone bringing a case can usually rely on the court to rule based on what the law has been in the past. See this chapter's *Ethics Today* feature for a discussion of how courts often defer to case precedent even when they disagree with the reasoning in the case.

Although courts are obligated to follow precedents, sometimes a court will depart from the rule of precedent if it decides that the precedent should no longer be followed. If a court decides that a ruling precedent is simply incorrect or that technological or social changes have rendered the precedent inapplicable, the court might rule contrary to the precedent. Cases that overturn precedent often receive a great deal of publicity.

■ **CASE IN POINT 1.3** The United States Supreme Court expressly overturned precedent in the case of

---

3. Pronounced *ster*-ay dih-*si*-ses.

## ETHICS TODAY

### *Stare Decisis* versus Spider-Man

Supreme Court Justice Elena Kagan, in a recent decision involving Marvel Comics' Spider-Man, ruled that, "What we can decide, we can undecide. But *stare decisis* teaches that we should exercise that authority sparingly." Citing a Spider-Man comic book, she went on to say that "in this world, with great power there must also come—great responsibility."[a] In its decision in the case—*Kimble v. Marvel Entertainment, LLC*—the Supreme Court applied *stare decisis* and ruled against Stephen Kimble, the creator of a toy related to the Spider-Man figure.[b]

#### Can a Patent Involving Spider-Man Last Super Long?

A patent is an exclusive right granted to the creator of an invention. Under U.S. law, patent owners generally possess that right for twenty years. Patent holders can license the use of their patents as they see fit during that period. In other words, they can allow others (called *licensees*) to use their invention in return for a fee (called *royalties*).

More than fifty years ago, the Supreme Court ruled in its *Brulotte* decision that a licensee cannot be forced to pay royalties to a patent holder after the patent has expired.[c] So if a licensee signs a contract to continue to pay royalties after the patent has expired, the contract is invalid and thus unenforceable.

At issue in the *Kimble* case was a contract signed between Marvel Entertainment and Kimble, who had invented a toy made up of a glove equipped with a valve and a canister of pressurized foam. The patented toy allowed people to shoot fake webs intended to look like Spider-Man's. In 1990, Kimble tried to cut a deal with Marvel Entertainment concerning his toy, but he was unsuccessful. Then Marvel started selling its own version of the toy.

When Kimble sued Marvel for patent infringement, he won. The result was a settlement that involved a licensing agreement between Kimble and Marvel with a lump-sum payment plus a royalty to Kimble of 3 percent of all sales of the toy. The agreement did not specify an end date for royalty payments to Kimble, and Marvel later sued to have the payments stop after the patent expired, consistent with the Court's earlier *Brulotte* decision.

A majority of the Supreme Court justices agreed with Marvel. As Justice Kagan said in the opinion, "Patents endow their holders with certain super powers, but only for a limited time." The court further noted that the fifty-year-old *Brulotte* decision was perhaps based on what today is an outmoded understanding of economics. That decision, according to some, may even hinder competition and innovation. But "respecting *stare decisis* means sticking to some wrong decisions."

#### The Ethical Side

In a dissenting opinion, Supreme Court Justice Samuel A. Alito, Jr., said, "The decision interferes with the ability of parties to negotiate licensing agreements that reflect the true value of a patent, and it disrupts contractual expectations. *Stare decisis* does not require us to retain this baseless and damaging precedent. . . . *Stare decisis* is important to the rule of law, but so are correct judicial decisions."

In other words, *stare decisis* holds that courts should adhere to precedent in order to promote predictability and consistency. But in the business world, shouldn't parties to contracts be able to, for example, allow a patent licensee to make smaller royalty payments that exceed the life of the patent? Isn't that a way to reduce the yearly costs to the licensee? After all, the licensee may be cash-strapped in its initial use of the patent. Shouldn't the parties to a contract be the ones to decide how long the contract should last?

**Critical Thinking** *When is the Supreme Court justified in not following the doctrine of* stare decisis?

---

a. "Spider-Man," Amazing Fantasy No. 15 (1962), p. 13.
b. 576 U.S. __, 135 S.Ct. 2401, 192 L.Ed.2d 463 (2015).
c. *Brulotte v. Thys Co.*, 379 U.S. 29, 85 S.Ct. 176 (1964).

---

*Brown v. Board of Education of Topeka*.[4] The Court concluded that separate educational facilities for whites and blacks, which it had previously upheld as constitutional,[5] were inherently unequal. The Supreme Court's departure from precedent in this case received a tremendous amount of publicity as people began to realize the ramifications of this change in the law. ∎

Note that a lower court will sometimes avoid applying a precedent set by a higher court in its jurisdiction by

4. 347 U.S. 483, 74 S.Ct. 686, 98 L.Ed. 873 (1954).
5. See *Plessy v. Ferguson*, 163 U.S. 537, 16 S.Ct. 1138, 41 L.Ed. 256 (1896).

distinguishing the two cases based on their facts. When this happens, the lower court's ruling stands unless it is appealed to a higher court and that court overturns the decision.

**When There Is No Precedent** Occasionally, courts must decide cases for which no precedents exist, called *cases of first impression.* For instance, as you will read throughout this text, the Internet and certain other technologies have presented many new and challenging issues for the courts to decide.

■ **EXAMPLE 1.4** Google Glass is a Bluetooth-enabled, hands-free, wearable computer. A person using Google Glass can take photos and videos, surf the Internet, and do other things through voice commands. Many people expressed concerns about this new technology. Privacy advocates claimed that it is much easier to secretly film or photograph others with wearable video technology than with a camera or a smartphone. Indeed, numerous bars and restaurants, among others, banned the use of Google Glass to protect their patrons' privacy. Police officers were concerned about driver safety. A California woman was ticketed for wearing Google Glass while driving. But the court dismissed this case of first impression because it was not clear whether the device had been in operation at the time of the offense. ■

In deciding cases of first impression, courts often look at **persuasive authorities**—legal authorities that a court may consult for guidance but that are not binding on the court. A court may consider precedents from other jurisdictions, for instance, although those precedents are not binding. A court may also consider legal principles and policies underlying previous court decisions or existing statutes. Additionally, a court might look at issues of fairness, social values and customs, and public policy (governmental policy based on widely held societal values). Today, federal courts can also look at unpublished opinions (those not intended for publication in a printed legal reporter) as sources of persuasive authority.[6]

## 1–3d *Stare Decisis* and Legal Reasoning

In deciding what law applies to a given dispute and then applying that law to the facts or circumstances of the case, judges rely on the process of **legal reasoning.** Through the use of legal reasoning, judges harmonize their decisions with those that have been made before, as the doctrine of *stare decisis* requires.

Students of business law and the legal environment also engage in legal reasoning. For instance, you may be asked to provide answers for some of the case problems

that appear at the end of every chapter in this text. Each problem describes the facts of a particular dispute and the legal question at issue. If you are assigned a case problem, you will be asked to determine how a court would answer that question, and why. In other words, you will need to give legal reasons for whatever conclusion you reach.[7] We look next at the basic steps involved in legal reasoning and then describe some forms of reasoning commonly used by the courts in making their decisions.

**Basic Steps in Legal Reasoning** At times, the legal arguments set forth in court opinions are relatively simple and brief. At other times, the arguments are complex and lengthy. Regardless of the length of a legal argument, however, the basic steps of the legal reasoning process remain the same. These steps, which you can also follow when analyzing cases and case problems, form what is commonly referred to as the *IRAC method* of legal reasoning. IRAC is an acronym formed from the first letters of the words *Issue, Rule, Application,* and *Conclusion.* To apply the IRAC method, you ask the following questions:

1. **Issue**—*What are the key facts and issues?* Suppose that a plaintiff comes before the court claiming *assault* (words or acts that wrongfully and intentionally make another person fearful of immediate physical harm). The plaintiff claims that the defendant threatened her while she was sleeping. Although the plaintiff was unaware that she was being threatened, her roommate heard the defendant make the threat. The legal issue is whether the defendant's action constitutes the tort of assault, given that the plaintiff was unaware of that action at the time it occurred. (A tort is a wrongful act. As you will see later, torts fall under the governance of civil law rather than criminal law.)

2. **Rule**—*What rule of law applies to the case?* A rule of law may be a rule stated by the courts in previous decisions, a state or federal statute, or a state or federal administrative agency regulation. In our hypothetical case, the plaintiff **alleges** (claims) that the defendant committed a tort. Therefore, the applicable law is the common law of torts—specifically, tort law governing assault. Case precedents involving similar facts and issues thus would be relevant. Often, more than one rule of law will be applicable to a case.

3. **Application**—*How does the rule of law apply to the particular facts and circumstances of this case?* This step is often the most difficult because each case presents a unique set of facts, circumstances, and parties.

---

6. See Rule 32.1 of the Federal Rules of Appellate Procedure.

7. See Appendix A for further instructions on how to analyze case problems.

Although cases may be similar, no two cases are ever identical in all respects. Normally, judges (and lawyers and law students) try to find **cases on point**—previously decided cases that are as similar as possible to the one under consideration.

4. **Conclusion**—*What conclusion should be drawn?* This step normally presents few problems. Usually, the conclusion is evident if the previous three steps have been followed carefully.

**There Is No One "Right" Answer** Many people believe that there is one "right" answer to every legal question. In most legal controversies, however, there is no single correct result. Good arguments can usually be made to support either side of a legal controversy. Quite often, a case does not involve a "good" person suing a "bad" person. In many cases, both parties have acted in good faith in some measure or in bad faith to some degree. Additionally, each judge has her or his own personal beliefs and philosophy. At least to some extent, these personal factors shape the legal reasoning process. In short, the outcome of a particular lawsuit before a court cannot be predicted with certainty.

### 1–3e The Common Law Today

Today, the common law derived from judicial decisions continues to be applied throughout the United States. Common law doctrines and principles, however, govern only areas *not* covered by statutory or administrative law. In a dispute concerning a particular employment practice, for instance, if a statute regulates that practice, the statute will apply rather than the common law doctrine that applied before the statute was enacted. The common law tradition and its application are reviewed in Concept Summary 1.2.

**Courts Interpret Statutes** Even in areas governed by statutory law, judge-made law continues to be important because there is a significant interplay between statutory law and the common law. For instance, many statutes essentially codify existing common law rules, and regulations issued by various administrative agencies usually are based, at least in part, on common law principles. Additionally, the courts, in interpreting statutory law, often rely on the common law as a guide to what the legislators intended. Frequently, the applicability of a newly enacted statute does not become clear until a body of case law develops to clarify how, when, and to whom the statute applies.

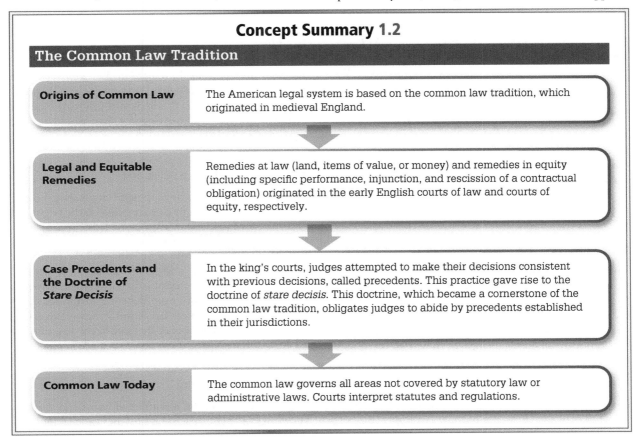

## Concept Summary 1.2

### The Common Law Tradition

| | |
|---|---|
| **Origins of Common Law** | The American legal system is based on the common law tradition, which originated in medieval England. |
| **Legal and Equitable Remedies** | Remedies at law (land, items of value, or money) and remedies in equity (including specific performance, injunction, and rescission of a contractual obligation) originated in the early English courts of law and courts of equity, respectively. |
| **Case Precedents and the Doctrine of *Stare Decisis*** | In the king's courts, judges attempted to make their decisions consistent with previous decisions, called precedents. This practice gave rise to the doctrine of *stare decisis*. This doctrine, which became a cornerstone of the common law tradition, obligates judges to abide by precedents established in their jurisdictions. |
| **Common Law Today** | The common law governs all areas not covered by statutory law or administrative laws. Courts interpret statutes and regulations. |

Clearly, a judge's function is not to *make* the laws—that is the function of the legislative branch of government—but to interpret and apply them. From a practical point of view, however, the courts play a significant role in defining the laws enacted by legislative bodies, which tend to be expressed in general terms. Judges thus have some flexibility in interpreting and applying the law. It is because of this flexibility that different courts can, and often do, arrive at different conclusions in cases that involve nearly identical issues, facts, and applicable laws.

**Restatements of the Law Clarify and Illustrate the Common Law** The American Law Institute (ALI) has published compilations of the common law called *Restatements of the Law,* which generally summarize the common law rules followed by most states. There are *Restatements of the Law* in the areas of contracts, torts, agency, trusts, property, restitution, security, judgments, and conflict of laws. The *Restatements,* like other secondary sources of law, do not in themselves have the force of law, but they are an important source of legal analysis and opinion. Hence, judges often rely on them in making decisions.

Many of the *Restatements* are now in their second, third, or fourth editions. We refer to the *Restatements* frequently in subsequent chapters of this text, indicating in parentheses the edition to which we are referring. For instance, we refer to the third edition of the *Restatement of the Law of Contracts* as simply the *Restatement (Third) of Contracts.*

# 1–4 Schools of Legal Thought

How judges apply the law to specific cases, including disputes relating to the business world, depends in part on their philosophical approaches to law. Thus, the study of law, or **jurisprudence,** involves learning about different schools of legal thought and how the approaches to law characteristic of each school can affect judicial decision making.

## 1–4a The Natural Law School

An age-old question about the nature of law has to do with the finality of a nation's laws. What if a particular law is deemed to be a "bad" law by a substantial number of the nation's citizens? Must they obey that law? According to the **natural law** theory, a higher, or universal, law exists that applies to all human beings. Each written law should reflect the principles inherent in natural law. If it does not, then it loses its legitimacy and need not be obeyed.

The natural law tradition is one of the oldest and most significant schools of jurisprudence. It dates back to the days of the Greek philosopher Aristotle (384–322

B.C.E.), who distinguished between natural law and the laws governing a particular nation. According to Aristotle, natural law applies universally to all humankind.

The notion that people have "natural rights" stems from the natural law tradition. Those who claim that a specific foreign government is depriving certain citizens of their human rights, for instance, are implicitly appealing to a higher law that has universal applicability.

The question of the universality of basic human rights also comes into play in the context of international business operations. U.S. companies that have operations abroad often hire foreign workers as employees. Should the same laws that protect U.S. employees apply to these foreign employees? This question is rooted implicitly in a concept of universal rights that has its origins in the natural law tradition.

## 1–4b The Positivist School

*Positive law,* or national law, is the written law of a given society at a particular time. In contrast to natural law, it applies only to the citizens of that nation or society. Those who adhere to **legal positivism** believe that there can be no higher law than a nation's positive law.

According to the positivist school, there are no "natural rights." Rather, human rights exist solely because of laws. If the laws are not enforced, anarchy will result. Thus, whether a law is "bad" or "good" is irrelevant. The law is the law and must be obeyed until it is changed—in an orderly manner through a legitimate lawmaking process. A judge who takes this view will probably be more inclined to defer to an existing law than would a judge who adheres to the natural law tradition.

## 1–4c The Historical School

The **historical school** of legal thought emphasizes the evolutionary process of law by concentrating on the origin and history of the legal system. This school looks to the past to discover what the principles of contemporary law should be. The legal doctrines that have withstood the passage of time—those that have worked in the past—are deemed best suited for shaping present laws. Hence, law derives its legitimacy and authority from adhering to the standards that historical development has shown to be workable. Followers of the historical school are more likely than those of other schools to strictly follow decisions made in past cases.

## 1–4d Legal Realism

In the 1920s and 1930s, a number of jurists and scholars, known as *legal realists,* rebelled against the historical approach to law. **Legal realism** is based on the idea that law is just one of many institutions in society and that it is shaped by social forces and needs. Because the law is a human enterprise, this school reasons that judges should take social and economic realities into account when deciding cases.

Legal realists also believe that the law can never be applied with total uniformity. Given that judges are human beings with unique personalities, value systems, and intellects, different judges will obviously bring different reasoning processes to the same case. Female judges, for instance, might be more inclined than male judges to consider whether a decision might have a negative impact on the employment of women or minorities.

Legal realism strongly influenced the growth of what is sometimes called the **sociological school,** which views law as a tool for promoting justice in society. In the 1960s, for instance, the justices of the United States Supreme Court helped advance the civil rights movement by upholding long-neglected laws calling for equal treatment for all Americans, including African Americans and other minorities. Generally, jurists who adhere to this philosophy of law are more likely to depart from past decisions than are jurists who adhere to other schools of legal thought.

Concept Summary 1.3 reviews the schools of jurisprudential thought.

## 1–5 Classifications of Law

The law may be broken down according to several classification systems. One system, for instance, divides law into substantive law and procedural law. **Substantive law** consists of all laws that define, describe, regulate, and create legal rights and obligations. **Procedural law** consists of all laws that outline the methods of enforcing the rights established by substantive law.

Note that many statutes contain both substantive and procedural provisions. ■ **EXAMPLE 1.5** A state law that provides employees with the right to *workers' compensation benefits* for on-the-job injuries is a substantive law because it creates legal rights. Procedural laws establish the method by which an employee must notify the employer about an on-the-job injury, prove the injury, and periodically submit additional proof to continue receiving workers' compensation benefits. ■

Other classification systems divide law into federal law and state law, private law (dealing with relationships between private entities) and public law (addressing the relationship between persons and their governments), and national law and international law. Here we look at still another classification system, which divides law into

---

### Concept Summary 1.3

**Schools of Jurisprudential Thought**

| | |
|---|---|
| **Natural Law School** | One of the oldest and most significant schools of legal thought. Those who believe in natural law hold that there is a universal law applicable to all human beings. |
| **Positivist School** | A school of legal thought centered on the assumption that there is no law higher than the laws created by the government. |
| **Historical School** | A school of legal thought that stresses the evolutionary nature of law and looks to doctrines that have withstood the passage of time for guidance in shaping present laws. |
| **Legal Realism** | A school of legal thought that advocates a less abstract and more realistic and pragmatic approach to the law and takes into account customary practices and the circumstances surrounding the particular transaction. |

civil law and criminal law. We also explain what is meant by the term *cyberlaw*.

## 1–5a Civil Law and Criminal Law

**Civil law** spells out the rights and duties that exist between persons and between persons and their governments, as well as the relief available when a person's rights are violated. Typically, in a civil case, a private party sues another private party who has failed to comply with a duty. (Note that the government can also sue a party for a civil law violation.) Much of the law that we discuss in this text is civil law, including contract law and tort law.

**Criminal law,** in contrast, is concerned with wrongs committed *against the public as a whole.* Criminal acts are defined and prohibited by local, state, or federal government statutes. Criminal defendants are thus prosecuted by public officials, such as a district attorney (D.A.), on behalf of the state, not by their victims or other private parties. Some statutes, such as those protecting the environment or investors, have both civil and criminal provisions.

## 1–5b Cyberlaw

The use of the Internet to conduct business has led to new types of legal issues. In response, courts have had to adapt traditional laws to situations that are unique to our age. Additionally, legislatures at both the federal and the state levels have created laws to deal specifically with such issues.

Frequently, people use the term **cyberlaw** to refer to the emerging body of law that governs transactions conducted via the Internet. Cyberlaw is not really a classification of law, though, nor is it a new *type* of law. Rather, it is an informal term used to refer to both new laws and modifications of traditional laws that relate to the online environment. Throughout this book, you will read how the law in a given area is evolving to govern specific legal issues that arise in the online context.

# 1–6 How to Find Primary Sources of Law

This text includes numerous references, or *citations,* to primary sources of law—federal and state statutes, the U.S. Constitution and state constitutions, regulations issued by administrative agencies, and court cases. A **citation** identifies the publication in which a legal authority—such as a statute or a court decision or other source—can be found. In this section, we explain how you can use citations to find primary sources of law. Note

that in addition to being published in sets of books, as described next, most federal and state laws and case decisions are available online.

## 1–6a Finding Statutory and Administrative Law

When Congress passes laws, they are collected in a publication titled *United States Statutes at Large.* When state legislatures pass laws, they are collected in similar state publications. Most frequently, however, laws are referred to in their codified form—that is, the form in which they appear in the federal and state codes. In these codes, laws are compiled by subject.

***United States Code*** The *United States Code* (U.S.C.) arranges all existing federal laws by broad subject. Each of the fifty-two subjects is given a title and a title number. For instance, laws relating to commerce and trade are collected in Title 15, "Commerce and Trade." Each title is subdivided by sections. A citation to the U.S.C. includes both title and section numbers. Thus, a reference to "15 U.S.C. Section 1" means that the statute can be found in Section 1 of Title 15. ("Section" may be designated by the symbol §, and "Sections," by §§.)

In addition to the print publication, the federal government provides a searchable online database at **www .gpo.gov**. It includes the *United States Code,* the U.S. Constitution, and many other federal resources. (Click on "Libraries" and then "Core Documents of Our Democracy" to find these resources.)

Commercial publications of federal laws and regulations are also available. For instance, Thomson Reuters publishes the *United States Code Annotated* (U.S.C.A.). The U.S.C.A. contains the official text of the U.S.C., plus notes (annotations) on court decisions that interpret and apply specific sections of the statutes. The U.S.C.A. also includes additional research aids, such as cross-references to related statutes, historical notes, and library references. A citation to the U.S.C.A. is similar to a citation to the U.S.C.: "15 U.S.C.A. Section 1."

**State Codes** State codes follow the U.S.C. pattern of arranging law by subject. They may be called codes, revisions, compilations, consolidations, general statutes, or statutes, depending on the preferences of the states.

In some codes, subjects are designated by number. In others, they are designated by name. ■ **EXAMPLE 1.6** "13 Pennsylvania Consolidated Statutes Section 1101" means that the statute can be found in Title 13, Section 1101, of the Pennsylvania code. "California Commercial Code Section 1101" means that the statute can be found under the subject heading "Commercial Code" of the California code in Section 1101. Abbreviations are often used. For example, "13 Pennsylvania Consolidated Statutes Section 1101" is abbreviated "13 Pa. C.S. § 1101," and "California Commercial Code Section 1101" is abbreviated "Cal. Com. Code § 1101." ■

**Administrative Rules** Rules and regulations adopted by federal administrative agencies are initially published in the *Federal Register,* a daily publication of the U.S. government. Later, they are incorporated into the *Code of Federal Regulations* (C.F.R.). The C.F.R. is available online on the government database (**www.gpo.gov**).

Like the U.S.C., the C.F.R. is divided into titles. Rules within each title are assigned section numbers. A full citation to the C.F.R. includes title and section numbers. ■ **EXAMPLE 1.7** A reference to "17 C.F.R. Section 230.504" means that the rule can be found in Section 230.504 of Title 17. ■

## 1–6b Finding Case Law

Before discussing the case reporting system, we need to look briefly at the court system. There are two types of courts in the United States, federal courts and state courts. Both systems consist of several levels, or tiers, of courts. *Trial courts*, in which evidence is presented and testimony given, are on the bottom tier. Decisions from a trial court can be appealed to a higher court, which commonly is an intermediate *court of appeals*, or *appellate court*. Decisions from these intermediate courts of appeals may be appealed to an even higher court, such as a state supreme court or the United States Supreme Court.

**State Court Decisions** Most state trial court decisions are not published in books (except in New York and a few other states, which publish selected trial court opinions). Decisions from state trial courts are typically filed in the office of the clerk of the court, where the decisions are available for public inspection. (Increasingly, they can be found online as well.)

Written decisions of the appellate, or reviewing, courts, however, are published and distributed (in print and online). As you will note, most of the state court cases presented in this textbook are from state appellate courts. The reported appellate decisions are published in volumes called *reports* or *reporters,* which are numbered consecutively. State appellate court decisions are found in the state reporters of that particular state. Official reports are published by the state, whereas unofficial reports are published by nongovernment entities.

**Regional Reporters.** State court opinions appear in regional units of the West's National Reporter System, published by Thomson Reuters. Most lawyers and libraries have these reporters because they report cases more quickly and are distributed more widely than the state-published reporters. In fact, many states have eliminated their own reporters in favor of the National Reporter System.

The National Reporter System divides the states into the following geographic areas: *Atlantic* (A., A.2d, or A.3d), *North Eastern* (N.E. or N.E.2d), *North Western* (N.W. or N.W.2d), *Pacific* (P., P.2d, or P.3d), *South Eastern* (S.E. or S.E.2d), *South Western* (S.W., S.W.2d, or S.W.3d), and *Southern* (So., So.2d, or So.3d). (The *2d* and *3d* in the preceding abbreviations refer to *Second Series* and *Third Series*, respectively.) The states included in each of these regional divisions are indicated in Exhibit 1–4, which illustrates the National Reporter System.

**Case Citations.** After appellate decisions have been published, they are normally referred to (cited) by the name of the case and the volume, name, and page number of the reporter(s) in which the opinion can be found. The citation first lists the state's official reporter (if different from the National Reporter System), then the National Reporter, and then any other selected reporter. (Citing a reporter by volume number, name, and page number, in that order, is common to all citations. The year that the decision was issued is often included at the end in parentheses.) When more than one reporter is cited for the same case, each reference is called a *parallel citation.*

Note that some states have adopted a "public domain citation system" that uses a somewhat different format for the citation. For instance, in Wisconsin, a Wisconsin Supreme Court decision might be designated "2016 WI 40," meaning that the case was decided in the year 2016 by the Wisconsin Supreme Court and was the fortieth decision issued by that court during that year. Parallel citations to the *Wisconsin Reports* and the *North Western Reporter* are still included after the public domain citation. ■ **EXAMPLE 1.8** Consider the following case citation: *Summerhill, LLC v. City of Meridan,* 162 Conn.App. 469, 131 A.3d. 1225 (2016). We see that the opinion in this case can be found in Volume 162 of the official *Connecticut Appellate Court Reports,* on page 469. The parallel citation is to Volume 131 of the *Atlantic Reporter, Third Series,* page 1225. ■

When we present opinions in this text, in addition to the reporter, we give the name of the court hearing the case and the year of the court's decision. Sample citations to state court decisions are explained in Exhibit 1–5.

**EXHIBIT 1–4** National Reporter System—Regional/Federal

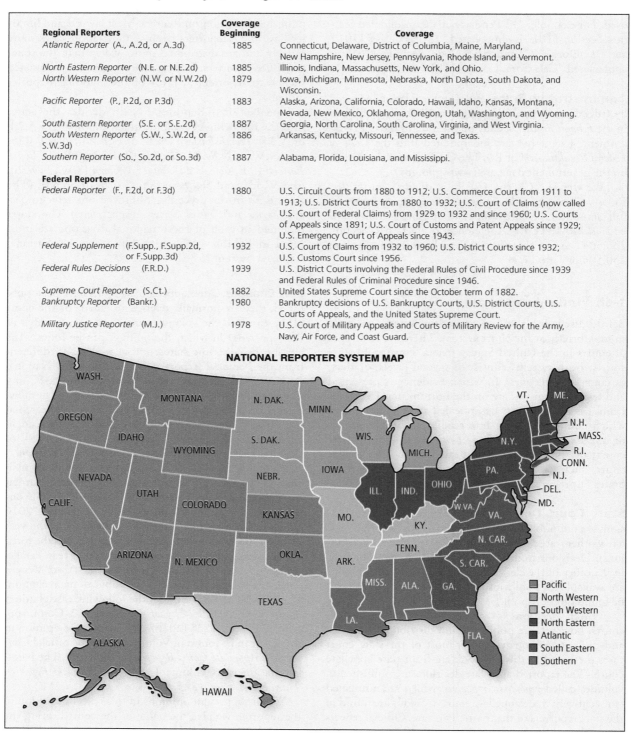

| Regional Reporters | Coverage Beginning | Coverage |
|---|---|---|
| *Atlantic Reporter* (A., A.2d, or A.3d) | 1885 | Connecticut, Delaware, District of Columbia, Maine, Maryland, New Hampshire, New Jersey, Pennsylvania, Rhode Island, and Vermont. |
| *North Eastern Reporter* (N.E. or N.E.2d) | 1885 | Illinois, Indiana, Massachusetts, New York, and Ohio. |
| *North Western Reporter* (N.W. or N.W.2d) | 1879 | Iowa, Michigan, Minnesota, Nebraska, North Dakota, South Dakota, and Wisconsin. |
| *Pacific Reporter* (P., P.2d, or P.3d) | 1883 | Alaska, Arizona, California, Colorado, Hawaii, Idaho, Kansas, Montana, Nevada, New Mexico, Oklahoma, Oregon, Utah, Washington, and Wyoming. |
| *South Eastern Reporter* (S.E. or S.E.2d) | 1887 | Georgia, North Carolina, South Carolina, Virginia, and West Virginia. |
| *South Western Reporter* (S.W., S.W.2d, or S.W.3d) | 1886 | Arkansas, Kentucky, Missouri, Tennessee, and Texas. |
| *Southern Reporter* (So., So.2d, or So.3d) | 1887 | Alabama, Florida, Louisiana, and Mississippi. |

| Federal Reporters | | |
|---|---|---|
| *Federal Reporter* (F., F.2d, or F.3d) | 1880 | U.S. Circuit Courts from 1880 to 1912; U.S. Commerce Court from 1911 to 1913; U.S. District Courts from 1880 to 1932; U.S. Court of Claims (now called U.S. Court of Federal Claims) from 1929 to 1932 and since 1960; U.S. Courts of Appeals since 1891; U.S. Court of Customs and Patent Appeals since 1929; U.S. Emergency Court of Appeals since 1943. |
| *Federal Supplement* (F.Supp., F.Supp.2d, or F.Supp.3d) | 1932 | U.S. Court of Claims from 1932 to 1960; U.S. District Courts since 1932; U.S. Customs Court since 1956. |
| *Federal Rules Decisions* (F.R.D.) | 1939 | U.S. District Courts involving the Federal Rules of Civil Procedure since 1939 and Federal Rules of Criminal Procedure since 1946. |
| *Supreme Court Reporter* (S.Ct.) | 1882 | United States Supreme Court since the October term of 1882. |
| *Bankruptcy Reporter* (Bankr.) | 1980 | Bankruptcy decisions of U.S. Bankruptcy Courts, U.S. District Courts, U.S. Courts of Appeals, and the United States Supreme Court. |
| *Military Justice Reporter* (M.J.) | 1978 | U.S. Court of Military Appeals and Courts of Military Review for the Army, Navy, Air Force, and Coast Guard. |

**NATIONAL REPORTER SYSTEM MAP**

■ Pacific
■ North Western
■ South Western
■ North Eastern
■ Atlantic
■ South Eastern
■ Southern

**EXHIBIT 1–5  How to Read Citations**

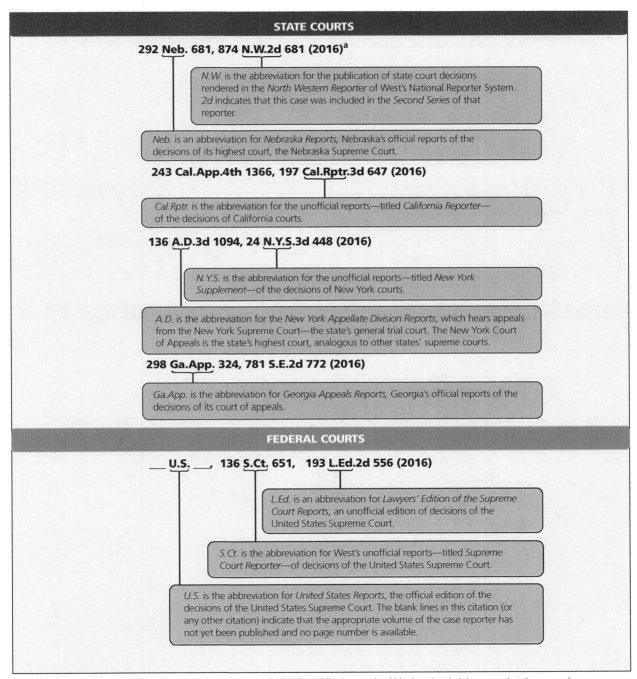

## STATE COURTS

**292 Neb. 681, 874 N.W.2d 681 (2016)[a]**

*N.W.* is the abbreviation for the publication of state court decisions rendered in the *North Western Reporter* of West's National Reporter System. *2d* indicates that this case was included in the *Second Series* of that reporter.

*Neb.* is an abbreviation for *Nebraska Reports,* Nebraska's official reports of the decisions of its highest court, the Nebraska Supreme Court.

**243 Cal.App.4th 1366, 197 Cal.Rptr.3d 647 (2016)**

*Cal.Rptr.* is the abbreviation for the unofficial reports—titled *California Reporter*— of the decisions of California courts.

**136 A.D.3d 1094, 24 N.Y.S.3d 448 (2016)**

*N.Y.S.* is the abbreviation for the unofficial reports—titled *New York Supplement*—of the decisions of New York courts.

*A.D.* is the abbreviation for the *New York Appellate Division Reports*, which hears appeals from the New York Supreme Court—the state's general trial court. The New York Court of Appeals is the state's highest court, analogous to other states' supreme courts.

**298 Ga.App. 324, 781 S.E.2d 772 (2016)**

*Ga.App.* is the abbreviation for *Georgia Appeals Reports,* Georgia's official reports of the decisions of its court of appeals.

## FEDERAL COURTS

**___ U.S. ___, 136 S.Ct. 651, 193 L.Ed.2d 556 (2016)**

*L.Ed.* is an abbreviation for *Lawyers' Edition of the Supreme Court Reports*, an unofficial edition of decisions of the United States Supreme Court.

*S.Ct.* is the abbreviation for West's unofficial reports—titled *Supreme Court Reporter*—of decisions of the United States Supreme Court.

*U.S.* is the abbreviation for *United States Reports*, the official edition of the decisions of the United States Supreme Court. The blank lines in this citation (or any other citation) indicate that the appropriate volume of the case reporter has not yet been published and no page number is available.

**a.** The case names have been deleted from these citations to emphasize the publications. It should be kept in mind, however, that the name of a case is as important as the specific page numbers in the volumes in which it is found. If a citation is incorrect, the correct citation may be found in a publication's index of case names. In addition to providing a check on errors in citations, the date of a case is important because the value of a recent case as an authority is likely to be greater than that of older cases from the same court.

Continued

**EXHIBIT 1–5  How to Read Citations—Continued**

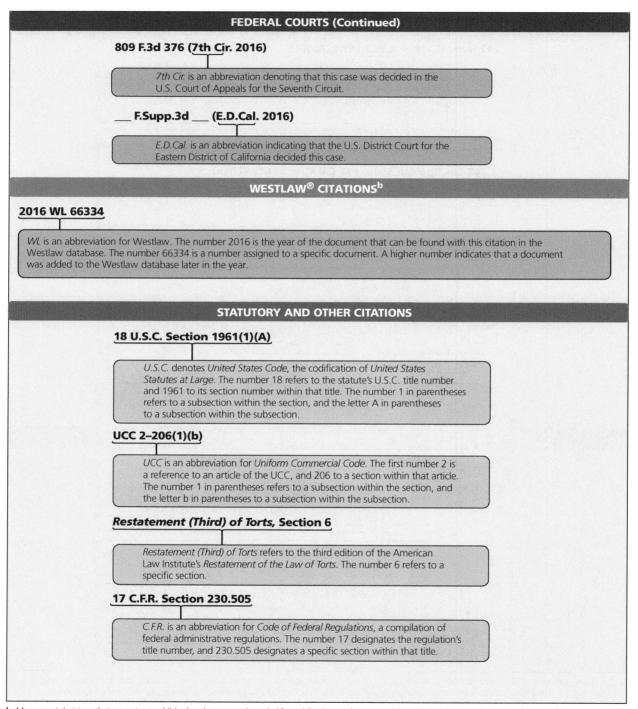

### FEDERAL COURTS (Continued)

**809 F.3d 376 (7th Cir. 2016)**

> *7th Cir.* is an abbreviation denoting that this case was decided in the U.S. Court of Appeals for the Seventh Circuit.

**___ F.Supp.3d ___ (E.D.Cal. 2016)**

> *E.D.Cal.* is an abbreviation indicating that the U.S. District Court for the Eastern District of California decided this case.

### WESTLAW® CITATIONS[b]

**2016 WL 66334**

> *WL* is an abbreviation for Westlaw. The number 2016 is the year of the document that can be found with this citation in the Westlaw database. The number 66334 is a number assigned to a specific document. A higher number indicates that a document was added to the Westlaw database later in the year.

### STATUTORY AND OTHER CITATIONS

**18 U.S.C. Section 1961(1)(A)**

> *U.S.C.* denotes *United States Code*, the codification of *United States Statutes at Large*. The number 18 refers to the statute's U.S.C. title number and 1961 to its section number within that title. The number 1 in parentheses refers to a subsection within the section, and the letter A in parentheses to a subsection within the subsection.

**UCC 2–206(1)(b)**

> *UCC* is an abbreviation for *Uniform Commercial Code*. The first number 2 is a reference to an article of the UCC, and 206 to a section within that article. The number 1 in parentheses refers to a subsection within the section, and the letter b in parentheses to a subsection within the subsection.

**Restatement (Third) of Torts, Section 6**

> *Restatement (Third) of Torts* refers to the third edition of the American Law Institute's *Restatement of the Law of Torts*. The number 6 refers to a specific section.

**17 C.F.R. Section 230.505**

> *C.F.R.* is an abbreviation for *Code of Federal Regulations*, a compilation of federal administrative regulations. The number 17 designates the regulation's title number, and 230.505 designates a specific section within that title.

**b.** Many court decisions that are not yet published or that are not intended for publication can be accessed through Westlaw, an online legal database.

**Federal Court Decisions** Federal district (trial) court decisions are published unofficially in the *Federal Supplement* (F.Supp. or F.Supp.2d), and opinions from the circuit courts of appeals (reviewing courts) are reported unofficially in the *Federal Reporter* (F., F.2d, or F.3d). Cases concerning federal bankruptcy law are published unofficially in the *Bankruptcy Reporter* (Bankr. or B.R.).

The official edition of the United States Supreme Court decisions is the *United States Reports* (U.S.), which is published by the federal government. Unofficial editions of Supreme Court cases include the *Supreme Court Reporter* (S.Ct.) and the *Lawyers' Edition of the Supreme Court Reports* (L.Ed. or L.Ed.2d). Sample citations for federal court decisions are also listed and explained in Exhibit 1–5.

**Unpublished Opinions** Many court opinions that are not yet published or that are not intended for publication can be accessed through Thomson Reuters Westlaw® (abbreviated in citations as "WL"), an online legal database. When no citation to a published reporter is available for cases cited in this text, we give the WL citation (such as 2016 WL 145734, which means it was case number 145734 decided in the year 2016). In addition, federal appellate court decisions that are designated as unpublished may appear in the *Federal Appendix* (Fed. Appx.) of the National Reporter System.

**Old Case Law** On a few occasions, this text cites opinions from old, classic cases dating to the nineteenth century or earlier. Some of these are from the English courts. The citations to these cases may not conform to the descriptions just presented because the reporters in which they were originally published were often known by the names of the persons who compiled the reporters.

# 1-7 How to Read and Understand Case Law

The decisions made by the courts establish the boundaries of the law as it applies to almost all business relationships. It thus is essential that businesspersons know how to read and understand case law.

The cases that we present in this text have been condensed from the full text of the courts' opinions and are presented in a special format. In approximately two-thirds of the cases (including the cases designated as *Classic* and *Spotlight*), we have summarized the background and facts, as well as the court's decision and remedy, in our own words. In those cases, we have included only selected excerpts from the court's opinion ("In the Language of the Court"). In the remaining one-third of the cases (labeled "Case Analysis"), we have provided a longer excerpt from the court's opinion without summarizing the background and facts or decision and remedy.

The following sections provide useful insights into how to read and understand case law.

## 1-7a Case Titles and Terminology

The title of a case, such as *Adams v. Jones*, indicates the names of the parties to the lawsuit. The *v.* in the case title stands for *versus*, which means "against." In the trial court, Adams was the plaintiff—the person who filed the suit. Jones was the defendant.

If the case is appealed, however, the appellate court will sometimes place the name of the party appealing the decision first, so the case may be called *Jones v. Adams* if Jones appealed. Because some appellate courts retain the trial court order of names, it is often impossible to distinguish the plaintiff from the defendant in the title of a reported appellate court decision. You must carefully read the facts of each case to identify the parties.

The following terms, phrases, and abbreviations are frequently encountered in court opinions and legal publications.

**Parties to Lawsuits** The party initiating a lawsuit is referred to as the *plaintiff* or *petitioner*, depending on the nature of the action. The party against whom a lawsuit is brought is the *defendant* or *respondent*. Lawsuits frequently involve more than one plaintiff and/or defendant.

When a case is appealed from the original court or jurisdiction to another court or jurisdiction, the party appealing the case is called the **appellant.** The **appellee** is the party against whom the appeal is taken. (In some appellate courts, the party appealing a case is referred to as the *petitioner*, and the party against whom the suit is brought or appealed is called the *respondent*.)

**Judges and Justices** The terms *judge* and *justice* are usually synonymous and represent two designations given to judges in various courts. All members of the United States Supreme Court, for instance, are referred to as justices. Justice is the formal title often given to judges of appellate courts, although this is not always true. In New York, a justice is a judge of the trial court (called the Supreme Court), and a member of the Court of Appeals (the state's highest court) is called a judge.

The term *justice* is commonly abbreviated to J., and *justices*, to JJ. A United States Supreme Court case might refer to Justice Sotomayor as Sotomayor, J., or to Chief Justice Roberts as Roberts, C.J.

**Decisions and Opinions** Most decisions reached by reviewing, or appellate, courts are explained in written **opinions.** The opinion contains the court's reasons for its decision, the rules of law that apply, and the judgment. You may encounter several types of opinions as you read appellate cases, including the following:

- When all the judges (or justices) agree, a *unanimous opinion* is written for the entire court.
- When there is not unanimous agreement, a **majority opinion** is generally written. It outlines the views of the majority of the judges deciding the case.
- A judge who agrees (concurs) with the majority opinion as to the result but not as to the legal reasoning often writes a **concurring opinion.** In it, the judge sets out the reasoning that he or she considers correct.
- A **dissenting opinion** presents the views of one or more judges who disagree with the majority view.
- Sometimes, no single position is fully supported by a majority of the judges deciding a case. In this situation, we may have a **plurality opinion.** This is the opinion that has the support of the largest number of judges, but the group in agreement is less than a majority.
- Finally, a court occasionally issues a ***per curiam* opinion** (*per curiam* is Latin for "of the court"), which does not indicate which judge wrote the opinion.

## 1–7b Sample Court Case

To illustrate the various elements contained in a court opinion, we present an annotated court opinion in Exhibit 1–6. The opinion is from an actual case that the United States Court of Appeals for the Eleventh Circuit decided in 2016.

**Background of the Case** In December 1955, on a bus in Montgomery, Alabama, Rosa Parks refused to give up her seat to a white man in violation of the city's segregation law. This "courageous act" sparked the modern civil rights movement. Parks's role in "the most significant social movement in the history of the United States" has been chronicled in books and movies, and featured on mementoes, some of which are offered for sale by Target Corp. The Rosa and Raymond Parks Institute for Self Development is a Michigan firm that owns the right to use Parks's name and likeness for commercial purposes. The Institute filed a suit in a federal district court against Target, alleging misappropriation in violation of the Institute's right of publicity. The court dismissed the complaint. The Institute appealed to the U.S. Court of Appeals for the Eleventh Circuit, arguing that Target's sales of books, movies, and other items that depict or discuss Rosa Parks and the modern civil rights movement violated Michigan law.

**Editorial Practice** You will note that triple asterisks (* * *) and quadruple asterisks (* * * *) frequently appear in the opinion. The triple asterisks indicate that we have deleted a few words or sentences from the opinion for the sake of readability or brevity. Quadruple asterisks mean that an entire paragraph (or more) has been omitted.

Additionally, when the opinion cites another case or legal source, the citation to the case or source has been omitted, again for the sake of readability and brevity. These editorial practices are continued in the other court opinions presented in this book. In addition, whenever we present a court opinion that includes a term or phrase that may not be readily understandable, a bracketed definition or paraphrase has been added.

**Briefing Cases** Knowing how to read and understand court opinions and the legal reasoning used by the courts is an essential step in undertaking accurate legal research. A further step is "briefing," or summarizing, the case.

Legal researchers routinely brief cases by reducing the texts of the opinions to their essential elements. Generally, when you brief a case, you first summarize the background and facts of the case, as the authors have done for most of the cases presented in this text. You then indicate the issue (or issues) before the court. An important element in the case brief is, of course, the court's decision on the issue and the legal reasoning used by the court in reaching that decision.

Detailed instructions on how to brief a case are given in Appendix A, which also includes a briefed version of the sample court case presented in Exhibit 1–6.

**EXHIBIT 1-6  A Sample Court Case**

| | |
|---|---|
| This section contains the citation—the name of the case, the name of the court that heard the case, the year of the decision, and reporters in which the court's opinion can be found. | **Rosa and Raymond Parks Institute for Self Development v. Target Corporation**<br><br>United States Court of Appeals, Eleventh Circuit,<br><br>812 F.3d 824 (2016). |

This line provides the name of the judge (or justice) who authored the court's opinion.

*ROSENBAUM*, Circuit Judge:

* * * *

In December 1955, on a bus in Montgomery, Alabama, Parks refused to give up her seat to a white man in violation of the city's segregation law.

[Rosa] **Parks's courageous act** inspired the Montgomery Bus Boycott and served as the **impetus** for the **modern Civil Rights Movement,** transforming the nation. In response to Parks's arrest, for 381 days, 42,000 African–Americans boycotted Montgomery buses, until the United States Supreme Court held the Montgomery segregation law unconstitutional and ordered desegregation of the buses.

An *impetus* is a stimulus or a spark.

The *modern civil rights movement* (1954–1964) included mass demonstrations in which participants sought equality in public and private life at national, state, and local levels, as well as an end to state and local segregation and discrimination in schools, in the workplace and at the polls. The movement culminated in the enactment of two federal Civil Rights acts in 1957 and 1964.

Parks's refusal to **cede** ground in the face of continued injustice has made her among the most revered heroines of our national story; her role in American history cannot be over-emphasized. Indeed, the United States Congress * * * has credited Parks with "igniting the most significant social movement in the history of the United States."

To *cede* is to yield or surrender.

So it is not surprising that authors would write about Parks's story and artists would celebrate it with their works. The commemoration and dissemination of Parks's journey continues to entrench and embolden our pursuit of justice. And it is in the general public interest to relentlessly preserve, spotlight, and recount the story of Rosa Parks and the Civil Rights Movement—even when that interest allegedly conflicts with an individual **right of publicity.**

A *right of publicity* is a person's right to the use of his or her name and likeness for a commercial purpose.

I.

The court divides the opinion into three sections. The first section summarizes the factual background of the case.

The Rosa and Raymond Parks Institute for Self Development (the "Institute") is a Michigan * * * corporation that owns the name and likeness of the late Rosa Parks * * * .

Continued

**EXHIBIT 1–6  A Sample Court Case—Continued**

Target Corporation ("Target"), a national retail corporation headquartered in Minneapolis, Minnesota, operates more than 1,800 retail stores across the United States.

Target offered [for sale] seven books about Parks * * * , the * * * movie *The Rosa Parks Story,* and a * * * plaque that included * * * a picture of Parks.

* * * *

*Misappropriation* is the use of a person's name or likeness without his or her consent for a commercial purpose. This is commonly referred to as a violation of the individual's right of publicity.

* * * The Institute filed the underlying complaint in [a federal district court]. The Institute alleged claims for * * * **misappropriation** * * * for Target's sales of all items using the name and likeness of Rosa Parks.

Generally, the Institute complained that * * * Target had unfairly and "without the Institute's prior knowledge, or consent, used Parks's name, likeness, and image to sell products * * * for Target's own commercial advantage." * * * The district court dismissed the complaint, and this appeal followed.

The second major section of the opinion responds to the plaintiff's appeal.

**II.**

* * * In this case we apply * * * the **substantive law** of Michigan.

* * * *

*Substantive law* is law that defines the rights and duties of persons with respect to each other. A federal court exercising jurisdiction based on diversity of citizenship—as in this case, where the two corporate parties are "citizens" of different states—applies the substantive law of the state in which the court sits (except in cases governed by federal law or the United States Constitution).

Michigan's common-law right of publicity is founded upon the interest of the individual in the exclusive use of his own identity, in so far as it is represented by his name or likeness, and in so far as the use may be of benefit to him or to others. This * * * privacy right guards against the appropriation of the commercial value of a person's identity by using without consent the person's name, likeness, or other *indicia*

*Indicia* is a synonym for indications or signs.

of identity for the purpose of trade.

Privacy rights, however, are not absolute. * * * Individual rights must yield to the

*Qualified privilege* gives someone a limited right to act contrary to another person's right without the other person's having legal recourse for the act.

**qualified privilege** to communicate on matters of public interest.

* * * *

* * * The privilege attaches to matters of general public interest and extends

In this context, *bona fide* means sincerely and honestly.

to all communications made ***bona fide*** upon any subject matter where the party

**EXHIBIT 1-6  A Sample Court Case—Continued**

communicating has an interest or a [legal, moral, or social] duty to a person having a corresponding interest or duty.

* * * *

Of course, it is beyond dispute that Rosa Parks is a figure of great historical significance and the Civil Rights Movement a matter of legitimate and important public interest. And it is **uncontested** that * * * the * * * books * * * and the movie are all *bona fide* works * * * discussing Parks and her role in the Civil Rights Movement.

Here, *uncontested* can mean unchallenged or accepted, as well as evident or obvious.

Similarly, the plaque depicts images and mentions dates and statements related to Parks and the Civil Rights Movement, in an effort to convey a message concerning Parks, her courage, and the results of her strength. Indeed, all of the works in question communicate information, express opinions, recite grievances, and protest claimed abuses on behalf of a movement whose existence and objectives continue to be of the highest public interest and concern.

* * * *

* * * The Institute has not articulated any argument as to why Michigan's qualified privilege for matters of public concern would not apply to these works, in light of the conspicuous historical importance of Rosa Parks. Nor can we conceive of any.

* * * Indeed, it is difficult to conceive of a discussion of the Civil Rights Movement without reference to Parks and her role in it. And Michigan law does not make discussion of these topics of public concern contingent on paying a fee. As a result, [the] books, the movie, and the plaque find protection in Michigan's qualified privilege protecting matters of public interest.

**[III.]**

In the third major section of the opinion, the court states its decision.

In short, the district court did not err in dismissing the Institute's complaint. The district court's order is **AFFIRMED.**

To *affirm* is to validate, to give legal force to.

## Reviewing: Law and Legal Reasoning

Suppose that the California legislature passes a law that severely restricts carbon dioxide emissions from automobiles in that state. A group of automobile manufacturers files suit against the state of California to prevent the enforcement of the law. The automakers claim that a federal law already sets fuel economy standards nationwide and that fuel economy standards are essentially the same as carbon dioxide emission standards. According to the automobile manufacturers, it is unfair to allow California to impose more stringent regulations than those set by the federal law. Using the information presented in the chapter, answer the following questions.

1. Who are the parties (the plaintiffs and the defendant) in this lawsuit?
2. Are the plaintiffs seeking a legal remedy or an equitable remedy?
3. What is the primary source of the law that is at issue here?
4. Where would you look to find the relevant California and federal laws?

**Debate This** . . . *Under the doctrine of* stare decisis, *courts are obligated to follow the precedents established in their jurisdiction unless there is a compelling reason not to. Should U.S. courts continue to adhere to this common law principle, given that our government now regulates so many areas by statute?*

## Terms and Concepts

| | | |
|---|---|---|
| administrative agency 4 | defendant 6 | *per curiam* opinion 20 |
| administrative law 4 | defense 6 | petitioner 6 |
| allege 10 | dissenting opinion 20 | plaintiff 6 |
| appellant 19 | equitable maxims 6 | plurality opinion 20 |
| appellee 19 | executive agency 5 | precedent 7 |
| binding authority 8 | historical school 12 | procedural law 13 |
| breach 6 | independent regulatory agency 5 | remedy 6 |
| case law 5 | jurisprudence 12 | remedy at law 6 |
| case on point 11 | laches 6 | remedy in equity 6 |
| citation 14 | law 2 | reporter 8 |
| civil law 14 | legal positivism 12 | respondent 6 |
| common law 6 | legal realism 13 | sociological school 13 |
| concurring opinion 20 | legal reasoning 10 | *stare decisis* 8 |
| constitutional law 4 | liability 2 | statute of limitations 6 |
| court of equity 6 | majority opinion 20 | statutory law 4 |
| court of law 6 | natural law 12 | substantive law 13 |
| criminal law 14 | opinion 20 | uniform law 4 |
| cyberlaw 14 | ordinance 4 | |
| damages 6 | persuasive authority 10 | |

## Issue Spotters

1. Under what circumstances might a judge rely on case law to determine the intent and purpose of a statute? (See *Sources of American Law.*)

2. After World War II, several Nazis were convicted of "crimes against humanity" by an international court. Assuming that these convicted war criminals had not disobeyed any law of their country and had merely been following their government's orders, what law had they violated? Explain. (See *Schools of Legal Thought.*)

• **Check your answers to the Issue Spotters against the answers provided in Appendix D at the end of this text.**

## Business Scenarios

**1–1. Binding versus Persuasive Authority.** A county court in Illinois is deciding a case involving an issue that has never been addressed before in that state's courts. The Iowa Supreme Court, however, recently decided a case involving a very similar fact pattern. Is the Illinois court obligated to follow the Iowa Supreme Court's decision on the issue? If the United States Supreme Court had decided a similar case, would that decision be binding on the Illinois court? Explain. (See *The Common Law Tradition*.)

**1–2. Sources of Law.** This chapter discussed a number of sources of American law. Which source of law takes priority in the following situations, and why? (See *Sources of American Law*.)

**(a)** A federal statute conflicts with the U.S. Constitution.

**(b)** A federal statute conflicts with a state constitutional provision.

**(c)** A state statute conflicts with the common law of that state.

**(d)** A state constitutional amendment conflicts with the U.S. Constitution.

**1–3. *Stare Decisis.*** In this chapter, we stated that the doctrine of *stare decisis* "became a cornerstone of the English and American judicial systems." What does *stare decisis* mean, and why has this doctrine been so fundamental to the development of our legal tradition? (See *The Common Law Tradition*.)

## Business Case Problems

**1–4. Spotlight on AOL—Common Law.** AOL, LLC,  mistakenly made public the personal information of 650,000 of its members. The members filed a suit, alleging violations of California law. AOL asked the court to dismiss the suit on the basis of a "forum-selection clause" in its member agreement that designates Virginia courts as the place where member disputes will be tried. Under a decision of the United States Supreme Court, a forum-selection clause is unenforceable "if enforcement would contravene a strong public policy of the forum in which suit is brought." California courts have declared in other cases that the AOL clause contravenes a strong public policy. If the court applies the doctrine of *stare decisis*, will it dismiss the suit? Explain. [*Doe 1 v. AOL LLC*, 552 F.3d 1077 (9th Cir. 2009)] (See *The Common Law Tradition*.)

**1–5. Business Case Problem with Sample Answer— Reading Citations.** Assume that you want to read the entire  court opinion in the case of *Equal Employment Opportunity Commission v. Autozone, Inc.*, 809 F.3d 916 (7th Cir. 2016). Refer to the subsection entitled "Finding Case Law" in this chapter, and then explain specifically where you would find the court's opinion. (See *How to Find Primary Sources of Law*.)

- **For a sample answer to Problem 1–5, go to Appendix E at the end of this text.**

**1–6. A Question of Ethics—The Common Law Tradition.** *On July 5, 1884, Dudley, Stephens, and Brooks— "all able-bodied English seamen"—and a teenage English boy were cast adrift in a lifeboat following a storm at sea. They had no water with them in the boat, and all they had for sustenance were two one-pound tins of turnips. On July 24, Dudley proposed that one of the four in the lifeboat be sacrificed to save the others. Stephens agreed with Dudley, but Brooks refused to consent—and the boy was never asked for his opinion. On July 25, Dudley killed the boy, and the three men then fed on the boy's body and blood. Four days later, a passing vessel rescued the men. They were taken to England and tried for the murder of the boy. If the men had not fed on the boy's body, they would probably have died of starvation within the four-day period. The boy, who was in a much weaker condition, would likely have died before the rest. [*Regina v. Dudley and Stephens*, 14 Q.B.D. (Queen's Bench Division, England) 273 (1884)] (See The Common Law Tradition.)*

**(a)** The basic question in this case is whether the survivors should be subject to penalties under English criminal law, given the men's unusual circumstances. Were the defendants' actions necessary but unethical? Explain your reasoning. What ethical issues might be involved here?

**(b)** Should judges ever have the power to look beyond the written "letter of the law" in making their decisions? Why or why not?

## Legal Reasoning Group Activity

**1–7. Court Opinions.** Read through the subsection in this chapter entitled "Decisions and Opinions." (See *How to Read and Understand Case Law*.)

**(a)** One group will explain the difference between a concurring opinion and a majority opinion.

**(b)** Another group will outline the difference between a concurring opinion and a dissenting opinion.

**(c)** A third group will explain why judges and justices write concurring and dissenting opinions, given that these opinions will not affect the outcome of the case at hand, which has already been decided by majority vote.

# Answers to the *Issue Spotters*

**1.** *Under what circumstances might a judge rely on case law to determine the intent and purpose of a statute?* Case law includes courts' interpretations of statutes, as well as constitutional provisions and administrative rules. Statutes often codify common law rules. For these reasons, a judge might rely on the common law as a guide to the intent and purpose of a statute.

**2.** *Assuming that these convicted war criminals had not disobeyed any law of their country and had merely been following their government's orders, what law had they violated? Explain.* At the time of the Nuremberg trials, "crimes against humanity" were new international crimes. The laws criminalized such acts as murder, extermination, enslavement, deportation, and other inhumane acts committed against any civilian population. These international laws derived their legitimacy from "natural law."

Natural law, which is the oldest and one of the most significant schools of jurisprudence, holds that governments and legal systems should reflect the moral and ethical ideals that are inherent in human nature. Because natural law is universal and discoverable by reason, its adherents believe that all other law is derived from natural law. Natural law therefore supersedes laws created by humans (national, or "positive," law), and in a conflict between the two, national or positive law loses its legitimacy.

The Nuremberg defendants asserted that they had been acting in accordance with German law. The judges dismissed these claims, reasoning that the defendants' acts were commonly regarded as crimes and that the accused must have known that the acts would be considered criminal. The judges clearly believed the tenets of natural law and expected that the defendants, too, should have been able to realize that their acts ran afoul of it. The fact that the "positivist law" of Germany at the time required them to commit these acts is irrelevant. Under natural law theory, the international court was justified in finding the defendants guilty of crimes against humanity.

# Sample Answers for *Business Case Problems with Sample Answer*

**Problem 1–5.** *Reading Citations.* The court's opinion in this case—*Equal Employment Opportunity Commission v. Autozone, Inc.,* 809 F.3d 916 (7th Cir. 2016)—can be found in Volume 809 of *Federal Reporter, Third Series* on page 916. The U.S. Court of Appeals for the Seventh Circuit issued this opinion in 2016.

# Chapter 2

# CHAPTER

# Court Procedures

American and English courts follow the *adversarial system of justice*. Although parties are allowed to represent themselves in court (called *pro se* representation),[1] most parties to lawsuits hire attorneys to represent them. Each lawyer acts as his or her client's advocate. Each lawyer presents his or her client's version of the facts in such a way as to convince the judge (or the judge and jury, in a jury trial) that this version is correct. Most of the judicial procedures that you will read about are rooted in the adversarial framework of the American legal system.

1. This right was definitively established in *Faretta v. California*, 422 U.S. 806, 95 S.Ct. 2525, 45 L.Ed.2d 562 (1975).

## 3–1 Procedural Rules

The parties to a lawsuit must comply with the procedural rules of the court in which the lawsuit is filed. Although people often think that substantive law determines the outcome of a case, procedural law can have a significant impact on a person's ability to pursue a legal claim. Procedural rules provide a framework for every dispute and specify what must be done at each stage of the litigation process.

Procedural rules are complex, and they vary from court to court and from state to state. There is a set of federal rules of procedure as well as various sets of rules for state courts. Additionally, the applicable procedures will depend on whether the case is a civil or criminal proceeding. All civil trials held in federal district courts are governed by the **Federal Rules of Civil Procedure (FRCP)**.[2]

### 3–1a Stages of Litigation

Broadly speaking, the litigation process has three phases: pretrial, trial, and posttrial. Each phase involves specific procedures, as discussed throughout this chapter. Although civil lawsuits may vary greatly in terms of complexity, cost, and detail, they typically progress through the stages charted in Exhibit 3–1.

2. The United States Supreme Court has authority to establish these rules, as spelled out in 28 U.S.C. Sections 2071–2077. Generally, though, the federal judiciary appoints committees that make recommendations to the Supreme Court. The Court then publishes any proposed changes in the rules and allows for public comment before finalizing the rules.

To illustrate the procedures involved in a civil lawsuit, we will use a simple hypothetical case. The case arose from an automobile accident, which occurred when a car driven by Antonio Carvello, a resident of New Jersey, collided with a car driven by Jill Kirby, a resident of New York. The accident took place at an intersection in New York City. Kirby suffered personal injuries, which caused her to incur medical and hospital expenses as well as lost wages for four months. In all, she calculated that the cost to her of the accident was $500,000.[3] Carvello and Kirby have been unable to agree on a settlement, and Kirby now must decide whether to sue Carvello for the $500,000 compensation she feels she deserves.

### 3–1b Hire an Attorney

As mentioned, rules of procedure often affect the outcome of a dispute—a fact that highlights the importance of obtaining the advice of counsel. The first step taken by almost anyone contemplating a lawsuit is to seek the guidance of a licensed attorney.

In the hypothetical Kirby-Carvello case, assume that Kirby consults with a lawyer. The attorney will advise her regarding what she can expect in a lawsuit, her probability of success at trial, and the procedures that will be involved. If more than one court would have jurisdiction over the matter, the attorney will also discuss the advantages and disadvantages of filing in a particular court. In addition, the attorney will indicate how long it will take

3. For simplicity, we are ignoring damages for pain and suffering and for permanent disabilities, which plaintiffs in personal-injury cases often seek.

## EXHIBIT 3–1  Stages in a Typical Lawsuit

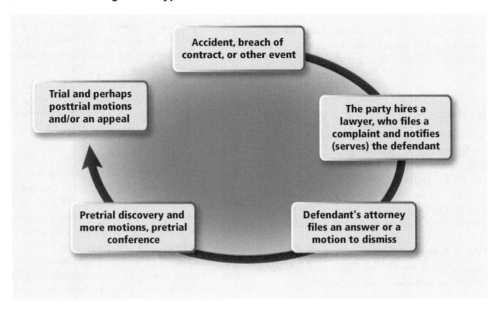

to resolve the dispute through litigation in a particular court and provide an estimate of the costs involved.

The attorney will also inform Kirby of the legal fees that she will have to pay in an attempt to collect damages from the defendant, Carvello. Attorneys base their fees on such factors as the difficulty of the matter at issue, the attorney's experience and skill, and the amount of time involved. In the United States, legal fees range from $200 to $700 per hour or even higher (the average fee is between $200 and $450 per hour). The client normally must also pay various expenses related to the case (called "out-of-pocket" costs), such as court filing fees, travel expenses, and the costs of expert witnesses and investigators.

**Types of Attorneys' Fees**  For a particular legal matter, an attorney may charge one type of fee or a combination of several types.

1. *Fixed fees* may be charged for the performance of such services as drafting a simple will.
2. *Hourly fees* may be charged for matters that will involve an indeterminate period of time. The amount of time required to bring a case to trial, for instance, probably cannot be precisely estimated in advance.
3. *Contingency fees* are fixed as a percentage (usually 33 percent) of a client's recovery in certain types of lawsuits, such as a personal-injury lawsuit.[4] If the

---
4. Contingency-fee arrangements are typically prohibited in criminal cases, divorce cases, and cases involving the distribution of assets after death.

lawsuit is unsuccessful, the attorney receives no fee, but the client will have to reimburse the attorney for all out-of-pocket costs incurred.

Because Kirby's claim involves a personal injury, her lawyer will likely take the case on a contingency-fee basis. In some cases, the winning party may be able to recover at least some portion of her or his attorneys' fees from the losing party.

**Settlement Considerations**  Once an attorney has been retained, the attorney is required to pursue a resolution of the matter on the client's behalf. Nevertheless, the amount of resources an attorney will spend on a given case is affected by the time and funds the client wishes to devote to the process.

If the client is willing to pay for a lengthy trial and one or more appeals, the attorney may pursue those actions. Often, however, after learning of the substantial costs that litigation entails, a client may decide to pursue a settlement of the claim. Attempts to settle the case may be ongoing throughout the litigation process.

Another important consideration in deciding whether to pursue litigation is the defendant's ability to pay the damages sought. Even if Kirby is awarded damages, it may be difficult to enforce the court's judgment if the amount exceeds the limits of Carvello's automobile insurance policy. (We will discuss the problems involved in enforcing a judgment later in this chapter.)

# 3–2 Pretrial Procedures

The pretrial litigation process involves the filing of the *pleadings*, the gathering of evidence (called *discovery*), and possibly other procedures, such as a pretrial conference and jury selection.

## 3–2a The Pleadings

The *complaint* and *answer* (and other legal documents discussed below) are known as the **pleadings.** The pleadings inform each party of the other's claims, reveal the facts, and specify the issues (disputed questions) involved in the case. Because the rules of procedure vary depending on the jurisdiction of the court, the style and form of the pleadings may be different from those shown in this chapter.

**The Plaintiff's Complaint** Kirby's action against Carvello commences when her lawyer files a **complaint**[5] with the clerk of the appropriate court. Complaints can be lengthy or brief, depending on the complexity of the case and the rules of the jurisdiction. The complaint contains statements or allegations concerning the following:

1. *Jurisdiction.* Facts showing that the particular court has subject-matter and personal jurisdiction.
2. *Legal theory.* The facts establishing the plaintiff's claim and basis for relief.
3. *Remedy.* The remedy (such as an amount of damages) that the plaintiff is seeking.

Exhibit 3–2 illustrates how a complaint in the Kirby-Carvello case might appear. The complaint asserts facts indicating that the federal district court has subject-matter jurisdiction because of diversity of citizenship. It then gives a brief statement of the facts of the accident and alleges that Carvello negligently drove his vehicle through a red light, striking Kirby's car. The complaint alleges that Carvello's actions caused Kirby serious personal injury and property damage. The complaint goes on to state that Kirby is seeking $500,000 in damages. (In some state civil actions, the plaintiff need not specify the amount of damages sought.)

**Service of Process.** Before the court can exercise personal jurisdiction over the defendant (Carvello)—in effect, before the lawsuit can begin—the court must have proof that the defendant was notified of the lawsuit. Formally notifying the defendant of a lawsuit is called **service of process.**

The plaintiff must deliver, or serve, a copy of the complaint and a **summons** (a notice requiring the defendant to appear in court and answer the complaint) to the defendant. The summons notifies Carvello that he must file an answer to the complaint within a specified time period (twenty days in the federal courts) or suffer a default judgment against him. A **default judgment** in Kirby's favor would mean that she would be awarded the damages alleged in her complaint because Carvello failed to respond to the allegations. A typical summons is shown in Exhibit 3–3.

**Method of Service.** How service of process occurs depends on the rules of the court or jurisdiction in which the lawsuit is brought. Under the Federal Rules of Civil Procedure, anyone who is at least eighteen years of age and is not a party to the lawsuit can serve process in federal court cases. In state courts, the process server is often a county sheriff or an employee of an independent company that provides process service in the local area.

Usually, the server hands the summons and complaint to the defendant personally or leaves it at the defendant's residence or place of business. In some states, process can be served by mail if the defendant consents (accepts service). When the defendant cannot be reached, special rules provide for alternative means of service, such as publishing a notice in the local newspaper.

In some situations, courts allow service of process via e-mail, as long as it is reasonably calculated to provide notice and an opportunity to respond. Today, some judges have even allowed defendants to be served legal documents via social media, as discussed in this chapter's *Digital Update* feature.

In cases involving corporate defendants, the summons and complaint may be served on an officer or on a *registered agent* (representative) of the corporation. The name of a corporation's registered agent can usually be obtained from the secretary of state's office in the state where the company incorporated its business (and, frequently, from the secretary of state's office in any state where the corporation does business).

**Waiver of Formal Service of Process.** In many instances, the defendant is already aware that a lawsuit is being filed and is willing to waive (give up) her or his right to be served personally. The Federal Rules of Civil Procedure (FRCP) and many states' rules allow defendants to waive formal service of process, provided that certain procedures are followed.

In the Kirby case, for example, Kirby's attorney could mail to defendant Carvello a copy of the complaint, along with "Waiver of Service of Summons" forms for

---

5. Sometimes, the document filed with the court is called a *petition* or a *declaration* instead of a complaint.

**EXHIBIT 3–2  A Typical Complaint**

```
              IN THE UNITED STATES DISTRICT COURT
           FOR THE SOUTHERN DISTRICT OF NEW YORK


                                            CIVIL NO. 9-1047

  JILL KIRBY
                       Plaintiff,

  v.                                          COMPLAINT

  ANTONIO CARVELLO

                       Defendant.
```

The plaintiff brings this cause of action against the defendant, alleging as follows:

1. This action is between the plaintiff, who is a resident of the State of New York, and the defendant, who is a resident of the State of New Jersey. There is diversity of citizenship between the parties.
2. The amount in controversy, exclusive of interest and costs, exceeds the sum of $75,000.
3. On September 10th, 2017, the plaintiff, Jill Kirby, was exercising good driving habits and reasonable care in driving her car through the intersection of Boardwalk and Pennsylvania Avenue, New York City, New York, when the defendant, Antonio Carvello, negligently drove his vehicle through a red light at the intersection and collided with the plaintiff's vehicle.
4. As a result of the collision, the plaintiff suffered severe physical injury, which prevented her from working, and property damage to her car.

WHEREFORE, the plaintiff demands judgment against the defendant for the sum of $500,000 plus interest at the maximum legal rate and the costs of this action.

By _*Joseph Roe*_____

Joseph Roe
Attorney for Plaintiff
100 Main Street
New York, New York

1/3/18

Carvello to sign. If Carvello signs and returns the forms within thirty days, formal service of process is waived.

Moreover, under the FRCP, defendants who agree to waive formal service of process receive additional time to respond to the complaint (sixty days, instead of twenty days). Some states provide similar incentives to encourage defendants to waive formal service of process and thereby reduce associated costs and foster cooperation between the parties.

**The Defendant's Response** Typically, the defendant's response to the complaint takes the form of an **answer.** In an answer, the defendant either admits or denies each of the allegations in the plaintiff's complaint and may also set forth defenses to those allegations.

Under the federal rules, any allegations that are not denied by the defendant will be deemed by the court to have been admitted. If Carvello admits to all of Kirby's allegations in his answer, a judgment will be entered for

**EXHIBIT 3–3  A Typical Summons**

```
                    UNITED STATES DISTRICT COURT
              FOR THE SOUTHERN DISTRICT OF NEW YORK

                                           CIVIL ACTION, FILE NO. 9-1047
    JILL KIRBY

                       Plaintiff,
                                                    SUMMONS
    v.

    ANTONIO CARVELLO

                       Defendant.



    To the above-named Defendant:

    You are hereby summoned and required to serve upon Joseph Roe,
    plaintiff's attorney, whose address is 100 Main Street, New York, NY, an
    answer to the complaint which is herewith served upon you, within 20 days
    after service of this summons upon you, exclusive of the day of service.
    If you fail to do so, judgment by default will be taken against you for
    the relief demanded in the complaint.


    C. H. Hynek                         January 3, 2018
    CLERK                               DATE



    John Dolan
    BY DEPUTY CLERK
```

Kirby. If Carvello denies Kirby's allegations, the matter will proceed further.

**Affirmative Defenses.** Carvello can also admit the truth of Kirby's complaint but raise new facts to show that he should not be held liable for Kirby's damages. This is called raising an **affirmative defense.**

Defendants in both civil and criminal cases can raise affirmative defenses. For example, Carvello could assert Kirby's own negligence as a defense by alleging that Kirby was driving negligently at the time of the accident. In some states, a plaintiff's contributory negligence operates as a complete defense. In most states, however, the plaintiff's own negligence constitutes only a partial defense.

**Counterclaims.** Carvello could also deny Kirby's allegations and set forth his own claim that the accident occurred as a result of Kirby's negligence and therefore she owes Carvello for damage to his car. This is appropriately called a **counterclaim.** If Carvello files a counterclaim, Kirby will have to submit an answer to the counterclaim.

### 3–2b Dismissals and Judgments before Trial

Many actions for which pleadings have been filed never come to trial. The parties may, for instance, negotiate a settlement of the dispute at any stage of the litigation process. There are also numerous procedural avenues for disposing of a case without a trial. Many of them involve one or the other party's attempts to get the case dismissed through the use of various motions.

A **motion** is a procedural request submitted to the court by an attorney on behalf of her or his client. When a motion is filed with the court, the filing party must also send to, or personally serve, the opposing party a *notice of*

## DIGITAL UPDATE — Using Social Media for Service of Process

Historically, when process servers failed to reach a defendant at home, they attempted to serve process at the defendant's workplace, by mail, and by publication. In our digital age, does publication via social media qualify as legitimate service of process?

### Can You Serve a Divorce Summons Through a Private Message on a Facebook Account?

Facebook has well over 1.6 billion active users per month. Assume that a man has a Facebook account and so does his spouse. He has moved out and is intentionally avoiding service of a divorce summons. Even a private investigator has not been able to deliver that summons. What to do? According to a New York state court ruling, the lawyer for the woman can serve the divorce summons through a private message from her Facebook account. "The past decade has . . . seen the advent and ascendancy of social media. . . . Thus, it would appear that the next frontier in the developing law of the service of process over the Internet is the use of social media sites as forums through which a summons can be delivered."[a]

### An Increasing Use of Social Media for Service of Process

More and more courts are allowing service of process via Facebook and other social media. One New York City family court judge ruled that a divorced man could serve his ex-wife through her active Facebook account. She had moved out of the house and provided no forwarding address. A Dallas district judge authorized service of process via social media, and other judges in that state have agreed with the ruling. A bill pending in the Texas state legislature would allow service via social media whenever a plaintiff can authenticate the social media account. Other states are considering similar legislation.

### Not All Courts Agree, Though

In spite of these examples, the courts have not uniformly approved of using social media to serve process. In one federal district court case, the court pointed out the relative simplicity of creating a fake Facebook account and the court's resulting inability to verify the true owner of that account.[b] In another case, involving the Federal Trade Commission (FTC), the court did allow service of process via Facebook, but noted that "if the FTC were proposing to serve the defendants only by means of Facebook, as opposed to using Facebook as a supplemental means of service, a substantial question would arise whether that service comports with due process."[c]

**Critical Thinking** *In our connected world, is there any way a defendant could avoid service of process via social media?*

a. *Baido v. Blood-Dzraqu*, 48 Misc.3d 309, 5 N.Y.S.3d 709 (2015).

b. *Fortunato v. Chase Bank USA*, 2011 WL 5574884 (S.D.N.Y. 2011) and 2012 WL 2086950 (S.D.N.Y. 2012).

c. *FTC v. PCCare247, Inc.*, 2013 WL 841037 (S.D.N.Y. 2013).

---

*motion.* The notice of motion informs the opposing party that the motion has been filed. **Pretrial motions** include the motion to dismiss, the motion for judgment on the pleadings, and the motion for summary judgment, as well as the other motions listed in Exhibit 3–4.

**Motion to Dismiss** Either party can file a **motion to dismiss** asking the court to dismiss the case for the reasons stated in the motion. Normally, though, it is the defendant who requests dismissal.

A defendant can file a motion to dismiss if the plaintiff's complaint fails to state a claim for which relief (a remedy) can be granted. Such a motion asserts that even if the facts alleged in the complaint are true, they do not give rise to any legal claim against the defendant. For example, if the allegations in Kirby's complaint do not constitute negligence on Carvello's part, Carvello can move to dismiss the case for failure to state a claim. Defendant Carvello could also file a motion to dismiss on the grounds that he was not properly served, that the court lacked jurisdiction, or that the venue was improper.

If the judge grants the motion to dismiss, the plaintiff generally is given time to file an amended complaint. If the judge denies the motion, the suit will go forward, and the defendant must then file an answer. Note that if Carvello wishes to discontinue the suit because, for example, an out-of-court settlement has been reached, he can likewise move for dismissal. The

**EXHIBIT 3–4** Pretrial Motions

| Motion to Dismiss | A motion (normally filed by the defendant) that asks the court to dismiss the case for a specified reason, such as lack of personal jurisdiction or failure to state a claim |
|---|---|
| Motion to Strike | A defendant's motion asking the court to strike (delete or remove) certain paragraphs from the complaint to better clarify the issues in dispute |
| Motion to Make More Definite or Certain | A motion by the defendant when the complaint is vague that asks the court to compel the plaintiff to clarify the cause of action |
| Motion for Judgment on the Pleadings | A motion by either party asking the court to enter judgment in his or her favor based on the pleadings because there are no facts in dispute |
| Motion to Compel Discovery | A motion asking the court to force the nonmoving party to comply with a discovery request |
| Motion for Summary Judgment | A motion asking the court to enter a judgment in his or her favor without a trial |

court can also dismiss a case on its own motion. In the following case, one party filed a complaint against two others, alleging a breach of contract. The defendants filed a motion to dismiss on the ground that the venue was improper. The court denied the motion, and the defendants appealed.

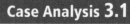

**Case Analysis 3.1**

# Espresso Disposition Corp. 1 v. Santana Sales & Marketing Group, Inc.

Florida Court of Appeal, Third District, 105 So.3d 592 (2013).

### In the Language of the Court

CORTIÑAS, J. [Judge]

\* \* \* \*

Espresso Disposition Corporation 1 and Rowland Coffee Roasters, Inc. (collectively "Appellants") seek review of the trial court's order denying their motions to dismiss [Santana Sales & Marketing Group, Inc.'s ("Appellee's")]

third amended complaint. Appellants claim that the trial court erred in denying their motions to dismiss because the plain and unambiguous language in the parties' \* \* \* agreement contains a mandatory forum selection clause [a provision in a contract designating the court, jurisdiction, or tribunal that will decide any disputes arising under the contract]

requiring that all lawsuits brought under the agreement shall be in Illinois.

Espresso Disposition Corporation 1 and Santana and Associates entered into the \* \* \* agreement in 2002. The agreement provides for a mandatory forum selection clause in paragraph 8. The provision states:

**Case 3.1 Continued**

The venue with respect to any action pertaining to this Agreement shall be the State of Illinois. The laws of the State of Illinois shall govern the application and interpretation of this Agreement.

However, Appellee filed a lawsuit against Appellants alleging a breach of the agreement in Miami–Dade County, Florida. In fact, Appellee filed four subsequent complaints—an initial complaint, amended complaint, second amended complaint, and third amended complaint—after each and every previous pleading's dismissal was based upon venue as provided for in the agreement's mandatory forum selection clause. Appellee's third amended complaint alleges the forum selection clause was a mistake that was made at the time the agreement was drafted. Additionally, Appellee attached an affidavit [a sworn statement] which states that, in drafting the agreement, Appellee * * * copied a form version of an agreement between different parties, and by mistake, forgot to change the venue provision from Illinois to Florida. In response, Appellants filed their motions to dismiss the third amended complaint, which the trial court denied.

Florida appellate courts interpret a contractual forum selection clause under a *de novo* standard of review. [The courts review the issue anew, as if the lower courts had not ruled on the issue.] Likewise, as the trial court's order denying appellant's motion to dismiss is based on the interpretation of the contractual forum selection clause, this court's standard of review is *de novo*. Therefore, the narrow issue before this court is whether the * * *

agreement provides for a mandatory forum selection clause that is enforceable under Florida law.

Florida courts have long recognized that forum selection clauses such as the one at issue here are presumptively valid. *This is because forum selection clauses provide a degree of certainty to business contracts by obviating [preventing] jurisdictional struggles and by allowing parties to tailor the dispute resolution mechanism to their particular situation. Moreover, forum selection clauses reduce litigation over venue, thereby conserving judicial resources, reducing business expenses, and lowering consumer prices.* [Emphasis added.]

Because Florida law presumes that forum selection clauses are valid and enforceable, the party seeking to avoid enforcement of such a clause must establish that enforcement would be unjust or unreasonable. Under Florida law, the clause is only considered unjust or unreasonable if the party seeking avoidance establishes that enforcement would result in no forum at all. There is absolutely no set of facts that Appellee could plead and prove to demonstrate that Illinois state courts do not exist. Illinois became the twenty-first state in 1818, and has since established an extensive system of state trial and appellate courts. Clearly, Appellee failed to establish that enforcement would be unreasonable since the designated forum—Illinois—does not result in Appellee's having "no forum at all."

Further, as we have said on a number of occasions, if a forum selection clause unambiguously mandates that litigation be subject to an agreed upon forum, then it is error for the trial court to ignore the clause. Generally, the clause

is mandatory where the plain language used by the parties indicates exclusivity. Importantly, if the forum selection clause states or clearly indicates that any litigation must or shall be initiated in a specified forum, then it is mandatory. Here, the agreement's plain language provides that the venue for any action relating to a controversy under the agreement * * * "shall be the State of Illinois." The clear language unequivocally renders the forum selection clause mandatory.

Appellee would have us create an exception to our jurisprudence on mandatory forum selection clauses based on their error in cutting and pasting the clause from another agreement. Of course, the origin of "cutting and pasting" comes from the traditional practice of manuscript-editing whereby writers used to cut paragraphs from a page with editing scissors, that had blades long enough to cut an 8½ inch-wide page, and then physically pasted them onto another page. Today, the cut, copy, and paste functions contained in word processing software render unnecessary the use of scissors or glue. However, what has not been eliminated is the need to actually read and analyze the text being pasted, especially where it is to have legal significance. Thus, in reviewing the mandatory selection clause which Appellant seeks to enforce, we apply the legal maxim "be careful what you ask for" and enforce the pasted forum.

Accordingly, we reverse [the] trial court's denial of the motions to dismiss Appellee's third amended complaint on the basis of improper venue, and remand for entry of an order of dismissal.

**Legal Reasoning Questions**

**1.** Compare and contrast a motion to dismiss with other pretrial motions. Identify their chief differences.

**2.** Why did the appellants in this case file a motion to dismiss?

**3.** What is the effect of granting a motion to dismiss?

**Motion for Judgment on the Pleadings** At the close of the pleadings, either party may make a **motion for judgment on the pleadings.** This motion asks the court to decide the issue solely on the pleadings without proceeding to trial.

The judge will grant the motion only when there is no dispute over the facts of the case and the sole issue to be resolved is a question of law. For example, in the Kirby-Carvello case, if Carvello had admitted to all of Kirby's allegations in his answer and had raised no affirmative defenses, Kirby could file a motion for judgment on the pleadings.

In deciding a motion for judgment on the pleadings, the judge may consider only the evidence contained in the pleadings. In contrast, in a motion for summary judgment, discussed next, the court may consider evidence outside the pleadings, such as sworn statements and other materials that would be admissible as evidence at trial.

**Motion for Summary Judgment** Either party can file a **motion for summary judgment,** which asks the court to grant a judgment in that party's favor without a trial. The motion can be made before or during the trial. As with a motion for judgment on the pleadings, a court will grant a motion for summary judgment only if no facts are in dispute and the only question is how the law applies to the facts. In determining whether no facts are in contention, the court considers the evidence in the light most favorable to the other party.

To support a motion for summary judgment, a party can submit evidence obtained at any point before the trial that refutes the other party's factual claim. The evidence may consist of **affidavits** (sworn statements by parties or witnesses) or copies of documents, such as contracts, e-mails, and letters obtained through the course of discovery (discussed next).

Of course, the evidence must be *admissible* evidence—that is, evidence that the court would allow to be presented during the trial. As mentioned, the use of additional evidence is one feature that distinguishes the motion for summary judgment from the motion to dismiss and the motion for judgment on the pleadings.

On appeal of a court's grant or denial of a motion for summary judgment, the appellate court engages in *de novo* review—that is, it applies the same standard that the trial court applied. In the following case, an appellate court took a fresh look at the evidence that had been presented with a motion for summary judgment granted by the lower court.

### Case 3.2

## Lewis v. Twenty-First Century Bean Processing

United States Court of Appeals, Tenth Circuit, __ F.3d __, 2016 WL 66334 (2016).

**Background and Facts** Twenty-First Century Bean Processing hired Anthony Lewis, a forty-seven-year-old African American male, for a warehouse position, subject to a thirty-day probationary period. At the end of the period, Twenty-First Century evaluated Lewis's performance to determine whether he would remain an employee. The employer decided not to retain Lewis, who then filed a suit in a federal district court against Twenty-First Century. Lewis alleged discrimination on the basis of race and age in violation of Title VII of the Civil Rights Act and the Age Discrimination in Employment Act. Twenty-First Century filed a motion for summary judgment. As evidence, the employer presented proof concerning Lewis's job performance during the probationary period. The court granted the motion. Lewis appealed.

### In the Language of the Court
Robert E. *BACHARACH*, Circuit Judge.
\* \* \* \*

*When a plaintiff alleges discrimination but offers no direct evidence of discrimination, the plaintiff bears the initial burden to establish a* prima facie *case of discrimination.* [This requires a showing that (1) the plaintiff is a member of a protected class—a person defined by certain criteria, including race or age; (2) the plaintiff applied and was qualified for the job at issue; (3) the plaintiff was rejected by the employer; and (4) the employer filled the position with someone not in a protected class.] *If a plaintiff*

**Case 3.2 Continued**

*establishes a* prima facie *case, the burden shifts to the defendant to articulate a * * * nondiscriminatory reason for its actions.* If the defendant satisfies that burden, the employee would bear the burden to prove the defendant's actions were discriminatory, which the employee could do by showing defendant's proffered reason is a pretext for illegal discrimination. [Emphasis added.]

* * * *

Mr. Lewis alleges age discrimination under the Age Discrimination in Employment Act. * * * Mr. Lewis had not presented any direct evidence of discrimination [and] the court determined that Mr. Lewis had not established a *prima facie* case because he had failed to provide evidence that his work was satisfactory. In our view, that conclusion was proper. Therefore, we affirm the district court's grant of summary judgment to Twenty-First Century on the age discrimination claim.

* * * *

Mr. Lewis also alleges race discrimination under Title VII of the Civil Rights Act. Again finding no direct evidence of discrimination, * * * the court assumed without deciding that Mr. Lewis had established a *prima facie* case of race discrimination. Thus, the burden shifted to Twenty-First Century to show a nondiscriminatory reason for terminating Mr. Lewis.

As evidence of a non-discriminatory purpose, Twenty-First Century pointed out that Mr. Lewis had missed too many work days, slept at work, used his personal cellphone at work, and reacted argumentatively when warned about his cellphone usage. After finding that any one of these policy violations could serve as a nondiscriminatory reason for the firing, the court placed the burden on Mr. Lewis to show * * * that Twenty-First Century's explanation was pretextual [not legitimate]. The district court concluded that Mr. Lewis was unable to meet this burden, and we agree.

**Decision and Remedy** *The U.S. Court of Appeals for the Tenth Circuit affirmed the lower court's summary judgment. Of the twenty-five work days in the probationary period, Lewis was absent for four days, found sleeping twice, and seen several times texting and talking on his personal phone. When informed that this use of a phone was against company policy, Lewis argued with his superior.*

**Critical Thinking**

- **Legal Environment** *Should motions for summary judgment and other pretrial motions be abolished so that all lawsuits proceed to trial? Why or why not?*
- **What If the Facts Were Different?** *Suppose that at this stage of the litigation, Twenty-First Century had not been able to provide evidence in support of its asserted reason for Lewis's firing. What would have been the result? Why?*

## 3–2c Discovery

Before a trial begins, the parties can use a number of procedural devices to obtain information and gather evidence about the case. Kirby, for example, will want to know how fast Carvello was driving. She will also want to learn whether he had been drinking, was under the influence of medication, and was wearing corrective lenses if required by law to do so while driving.

The process of obtaining information from the opposing party or from witnesses prior to trial is known as **discovery.** Discovery includes gaining access to witnesses, documents, records, and other types of evidence.

In federal courts, the parties are required to make initial disclosures of relevant evidence to the opposing party. A court can impose sanctions on a party who fails to respond to discovery requests.

Discovery prevents surprises at trial by giving both parties access to evidence that might otherwise be hidden. This allows the litigants to learn as much as they can about what to expect at a trial before they reach the courtroom. Discovery also serves to narrow the issues so that trial time is spent on the main questions in the case. The following case shows how vital discovery can be to the outcome of litigation.

**Case 3.3**

# Brothers v. Winstead

Supreme Court of Mississippi, 129 So.3d 906 (2014).

**Background and Facts** Phillips Brothers, LP (limited partnership), Harry Simmons, and Ray Winstead were the owners of Kilby Brake Fisheries, LLC (limited liability company), a catfish farm in Mississippi. For nearly eight years, Winstead operated a hatchery for the firm. During this time, the hatchery had only two profitable years. Consequently, Winstead was fired. He filed a suit in a Mississippi state court against Kilby Brake and its other owners, alleging a "freeze-out." (A freeze-out occurs when a majority of the owners of a firm exclude other owners from certain benefits of participating in the firm.)

The defendants filed a counterclaim of theft. To support this claim, the defendants asked the court to allow them to obtain documents from Winstead regarding his finances, particularly income from his Winstead Cattle Company. The court refused this request. A jury awarded Winstead more than $1.7 million, and the defendants appealed.

## In the Language of the Court

WALLER, Chief Justice for the Court.

\* \* \* \*

During discovery, Winstead produced his tax returns from 2006 to 2009, which showed substantial income as coming from the Winstead Cattle Company. The only other income listed on Winstead's tax returns was from Kilby Brake \* \* \* . Winstead had also produced [other documents showing income] from a fish farmer named Scott Kiker, which did not appear on his tax returns. [The documents supposedly involved income from sales of cattle.] Kilby Brake's theory was the entries for "cattle" represented income from sales of Kilby Brake fish Winstead was brokering and thus, it sought to compel [discovery] of all of the Winstead Cattle Company's financial records. Winstead [testified] in his deposition and again at trial that the Winstead Cattle Company did no actual business, and it was simply his hunting camp. The trial court denied Kilby Brake's motion to compel discovery into Winstead's finances.

\* \* \* [Winstead was questioned about the forms he] had produced in discovery showing income from Kiker. Winstead testified that he would often act as a middle man if he knew of a farmer who was in need of fish and another who had fish for sale, taking a commission for brokering the deal.

\* \* \* \*

\* \* \* Kiker testified that he had received a load of fish from Kilby Brake [but that] there was no paperwork on the transaction [and] that he sold this load of fish, gave Winstead a commission and did not pay Kilby Brake for the sales.

*From the evidence noted above, we find the trial court's refusal to allow both discovery into the finances of Winstead and questions concerning Winstead Cattle Company on his tax return prevented Kilby Brake and the jury from finding out whether Winstead was selling fish from Kilby Brake and disguising it on his income tax returns* \* \* \* . Importantly, the decisions by the trial court denied Kilby Brake the ability to present its case as to what happened to the fish. The record shows there were years in which Winstead received substantial income from brokering fish sales, almost $20,000 in one year. He [testified] that Winstead Cattle Company did no business and was simply his hunting camp, yet it made significant amounts of money. [Emphasis added.]

**Decision and Remedy** *The Mississippi Supreme Court reversed the lower court's decision to deny discovery of information concerning Winstead's outside finances, especially regarding income from Winstead Cattle Company. The state supreme court remanded the case for a new trial.*

## Critical Thinking

- **Ethical** *Does Winstead have an ethical duty to comply with the defendants' discovery request? Discuss.*
- **Legal Environment** *Did the defendants have a legitimate basis to make a discovery request for information regarding Winstead's outside income? Explain.*

**Discovery Rules** The FRCP and similar state rules set forth the guidelines for discovery activity. Generally, discovery is allowed regarding any matter that is relevant to the claim or defense of any party. Discovery rules also attempt to protect witnesses and parties from undue harassment, and to prevent privileged or confidential material from being disclosed. Only information that is relevant to the case at hand—or likely to lead to the discovery of relevant information—is discoverable.

If a discovery request involves privileged or confidential business information, a court can deny the request and can limit the scope of discovery in a number of ways. For instance, a court can require the party to submit the materials to the judge in a sealed envelope so that the judge can decide if they should be disclosed to the opposing party.

**Depositions** Discovery can involve the use of depositions. A **deposition** is sworn testimony by a party to the lawsuit or by any witness, recorded by an authorized court official. The person deposed gives testimony and answers questions asked by the attorneys from both sides. The questions and answers are recorded, sworn to, and signed. These answers, of course, will help the attorneys prepare their cases.

Depositions also give attorneys the opportunity to ask immediate follow-up questions and to evaluate how their witnesses will conduct themselves at trial. In addition, depositions can be employed in court to **impeach** (challenge the credibility of) a party or a witness who changes his or her testimony at the trial. Finally, a deposition can be used as testimony if the witness is not available at trial.

**Interrogatories** Discovery can also involve **interrogatories**—written questions for which written answers are prepared and then signed under oath. The main difference between interrogatories and written depositions is that interrogatories are directed to a party to the lawsuit (the plaintiff or the defendant), not to a witness. The party usually has thirty days to prepare answers.

The party's attorney often drafts the answers to interrogatories in a manner calculated to give away as little information as possible. Whereas depositions elicit candid answers not prepared in advance, interrogatories are designed to obtain accurate information about specific topics, such as how many contracts were signed and when. The scope of interrogatories is also broader because parties are obligated to answer questions, even if that means disclosing information from their records and files. As with discovery requests, a court can impose sanctions on a party who fails to answer interrogatories.

■ **CASE IN POINT 3.1** Ronald J. Hass (doing business as Valley Corp. and R. J. Hass Corp.) was a contractor who built a home for Ty and Karen Levine. Probuilders Specialty Insurance Co. provided commercial liability insurance for the contractor. Later, when the Levines sued Hass and his company for shoddy and incomplete work, Hass blamed the subcontractors. Probuilders provided Hass with legal representation, but the Levines won a judgment for more than $2 million. Then Probuilders sued Hass and his company, claiming that he had made misrepresentations to them regarding the facts of the case and seeking to avoid paying the judgment. Hass filed a counterclaim against Probuilders.

A dispute arose between Probuilders and Hass concerning discovery. Hass refused to respond fully to interrogatories and other discovery requests, and refused to give a deposition. Probuilders filed a motion to compel, and the court ordered Hass to respond to the discovery requests. Although Probuilders sent letters specifying what was needed, Hass continued to be evasive. The court imposed sanctions on Hass more than once. Ultimately, the court found that Hass had acted willfully and in bad faith, and recommended that his answers and counterclaim against Probuilders be dismissed.[6] ■

**Requests for Admissions** One party can serve the other party with a written request for an admission of the truth of matters relating to the trial. Any fact admitted under such a request is conclusively established as true for the trial. For example, Kirby can ask Carvello to admit that his driver's license was suspended at the time of the accident. A request for admission shortens the trial because the parties will not have to spend time proving facts on which they already agree.

**Requests for Documents, Objects, and Entry upon Land** A party can gain access to documents and other items not in her or his possession in order to inspect and examine them. Carvello, for example, can gain permission to inspect and copy Kirby's car repair bills. Likewise, a party can gain "entry upon land" to inspect the premises.

**Requests for Examinations** When the physical or mental condition of one party is in question, the opposing party can ask the court to order a physical or mental examination by an independent examiner. If the court agrees to make the order, the opposing party can obtain the results of the examination. Note that the court will

---

6. *Probuilders Specialty Insurance Co. v. Valley Corp.*, 2012 WL 6045753 (N.D.Cal. 2012).

make such an order only when the need for the information outweighs the right to privacy of the person to be examined.

**Electronic Discovery** Any relevant material, including information stored electronically, can be the object of a discovery request. The federal rules and most state rules (as well as court decisions) specifically allow individuals to obtain discovery of electronic "data compilations." Electronic evidence, or **e-evidence,** consists of all computer-generated or electronically recorded information, such as e-mail, voice mail, tweets, blogs, social media posts, spreadsheets, documents, and other data stored electronically.

E-evidence can reveal significant facts that are not discoverable by other means. Computers, smartphones, cameras, and other devices automatically record certain information about files—such as who created the file and when, and who accessed, modified, or transmitted it—on their hard drives. This information is called **metadata,** which can be thought of as "data about data." Metadata can be obtained only from the file in its electronic format—not from printed-out versions.

■ **EXAMPLE 3.2** In 2012, John McAfee, the programmer responsible for creating McAfee antivirus software, was wanted for questioning in the murder of his neighbor in Belize. McAfee left Belize and was on the run from police, but he allowed a journalist to come with him and photograph him. When the journalist posted photos of McAfee online, some metadata were attached to a photo. The police used the metadata to pinpoint the latitude and longitude of the image and subsequently arrested McAfee in Guatemala. ■

**E-Discovery Procedures.** The Federal Rules of Civil Procedure deal specifically with the preservation, retrieval, and production of electronic data. Although traditional interrogatories and depositions are still used to find out whether e-evidence exists, a party usually must hire an expert to retrieve the evidence in its electronic format. The expert uses software to reconstruct e-mail, text, and other exchanges to establish who knew what and when they knew it. The expert can even recover computer files that the user thought had been deleted.

**Advantages and Disadvantages.** Electronic discovery has significant advantages over paper discovery. Electronic versions of documents, e-mail, and text messages can provide useful—and often quite damaging—information about how a particular matter progressed over several weeks or months. E-discovery can uncover the proverbial smoking gun that will win the lawsuit. But it is also

time consuming and expensive, especially when lawsuits involve large firms with multiple offices. Indeed, many firms are finding it difficult to fulfill their duty to preserve electronic evidence from a vast number of sources.

A party that fails to preserve e-evidence may find itself at such a disadvantage that it will settle a dispute rather than continue litigation. ■ **CASE IN POINT 3.3** Advanced Micro Devices, Inc. (AMD), sued Intel Corporation, one of the world's largest microprocessor suppliers, for violating antitrust laws. Immediately after the lawsuit was filed, Intel began collecting and preserving the electronic evidence on its servers and instructed its employees to retain documents and e-mails related to competition with AMD. Nevertheless, many employees saved only copies of the e-mails that they had received and not e-mails that they had sent. In addition, Intel did not stop its automatic e-mail deletion system, causing other information to be lost. In the end, although Intel produced data equivalent to "somewhere in the neighborhood of a pile 137 miles high" in paper, its failure to preserve e-discovery led it to settle the dispute.[7] ■

## 3–2d Pretrial Conference

After discovery has taken place and before the trial begins, the attorneys may meet with the trial judge in a **pretrial conference,** or hearing. Usually, the conference consists of an informal discussion between the judge and the opposing attorneys after discovery has taken place. The purpose is to explore the possibility of a settlement without trial and, if this is not possible, to identify the matters in dispute and to plan the course of the trial. In particular, the parties may attempt to establish ground rules to restrict the number of expert witnesses or discuss the admissibility or costs of certain types of evidence.

## 3–2e The Right to a Jury Trial

The Seventh Amendment to the U.S. Constitution guarantees the right to a jury trial for cases at law in *federal* courts when the amount in controversy exceeds $20. Most states have similar guarantees in their own constitutions (although the threshold dollar amount is higher than $20).

The right to a trial by jury need not be exercised, and many cases are tried without a jury. In most states and in federal courts, one of the parties must request a jury, or the judge presumes the parties waive this right. If there

---

7. *In re Intel Corp. Microprocessor Antitrust Litigation*, 2008 WL 2310288 (D.Del. 2008).

is no jury, the judge determines the truth of the facts alleged in the case.

### 3–2f  Jury Selection

Before a jury trial commences, a panel of jurors must be selected. Although some types of trials require twelve-person juries, most civil matters can be heard by six-person juries. The jury selection process is known as **voir dire.**[8] In most jurisdictions, attorneys for the plaintiff and the defendant ask prospective jurors oral questions to determine whether they are biased or have any connection with a party to the action or with a prospective witness. In some jurisdictions, the judge may do all or part of the questioning based on written questions submitted by counsel for the parties.

During *voir dire*, a party may challenge a certain number of prospective jurors *peremptorily*—that is, ask that an individual not be sworn in as a juror without providing any reason. Alternatively, a party may challenge a prospective juror *for cause*—that is, provide a reason why an individual should not be sworn in as a juror. If the judge grants the challenge, the individual is asked to step down. A prospective juror, however, may not be excluded by the use of discriminatory challenges, such as those based on racial criteria or gender.

See Concept Summary 3.1 for a review of pretrial procedures.

## 3–3  The Trial

Various rules and procedures govern the trial phase of the litigation process. There are rules governing what kind of evidence will or will not be admitted during the trial, as well as specific procedures that the participants in the lawsuit must follow. For instance, a trial judge may instruct jurors not to communicate with anyone about the case or order reporters not to use social media to comment on the case while in the courtroom.

### 3–3a  Opening Statements

At the beginning of the trial, both attorneys are allowed to make **opening statements** setting forth the facts that they expect to prove during the trial. The opening statement provides an opportunity for each lawyer to give a

brief version of the facts and the supporting evidence that will be used during the trial. Then the plaintiff's case is presented. In our hypothetical case, Kirby's lawyer would introduce evidence (relevant documents, exhibits, and the testimony of witnesses) to support Kirby's position.

### 3–3b  Rules of Evidence

Whether evidence will be admitted in court is determined by the **rules of evidence.** These are a series of rules that the courts have created to ensure that any evidence presented during a trial is fair and reliable. The Federal Rules of Evidence govern the admissibility of evidence in federal courts.

**Evidence Must Be Relevant to the Issues**  Evidence will not be admitted in court unless it is relevant to the matter in question. **Relevant evidence** is evidence that tends to prove or disprove a fact in question or to establish the degree of probability of a fact or action. For instance, evidence that the defendant was in another person's home when the victim was shot would be relevant, because it would tend to prove that the defendant was not the shooter.

**Hearsay Evidence Is Not Admissible**  Generally, hearsay is not admissible as evidence. **Hearsay** is testimony someone gives in court about a statement made by someone else who was not under oath at the time of the statement. Literally, it is what someone heard someone else say. If a witness in the Kirby-Carvello case testified in court concerning what he or she heard another observer say about the accident, for example, that testimony would be hearsay. Admitting hearsay into evidence carries many risks because, even though it may be relevant, there is no way to test its reliability.

### 3–3c  Examination of Witnesses and Potential Motions

Because Kirby is the plaintiff, she has the burden of proving that her allegations are true. Her attorney begins the presentation of Kirby's case by calling the first witness for the plaintiff and examining, or questioning, the witness. (For both attorneys, the types of questions and the manner of asking them are governed by the rules of evidence.) This questioning is called **direct examination.**

After Kirby's attorney is finished, the witness is subject to **cross-examination** by Carvello's attorney. Then Kirby's attorney has another opportunity to question the witness in *redirect examination*, and Carvello's

---

**8.** Pronounced *vwahr deehr.* These verbs, based on Old French, mean "to speak the truth." In legal language, the phrase refers to the process of questioning jurors to learn about their backgrounds, attitudes, and similar attributes.

# Concept Summary 3.1

## Pretrial Procedures

**The Pleadings**
- *The plaintiff's complaint*—The plaintiff's statement of the cause of action and the parties involved, filed with the court by the plaintiff's attorney. After the filing, the defendant is notified of the suit through service of process.
- *The defendant's response*—The defendant's response to the plaintiff's complaint may take the form of an answer, in which the defendant admits or denies the plaintiff's allegations. The defendant may also raise an affirmative defense and/or assert a counterclaim.

**Pretrial Motions**
- *Motion to dismiss*—See Exhibit 3–4.
- *Motion for judgment* on the pleadings—May be made by either party and will be granted only if no facts are in dispute and only questions of law are at issue.
- *Motion for summary judgment*—See Exhibit 3–4.

**Discovery**
The process of gathering evidence concerning the case, which may involve the following:
- *Depositions* (sworn testimony by either party or any witness).
- *Interrogatories* (in which parties to the action write answers to questions with the aid of their attorneys).
- Requests for admissions, documents, examinations, or other information relating to the case.
- Requests for electronically recorded information, such as e-mail, text messages, voice mail, and other data.

**Pretrial Conference**
- A pretrial hearing, at the request of either party or the court, to identify the matters in dispute after discovery has taken place and to explore the possibility of settling the dispute without a trial. If no settlement is possible, the parties plan the course of the trial.

**Jury Selection**
- In a jury trial, the selection of members of the jury from a pool of prospective jurors. During a process known as *voir dire*, the attorneys for both sides may challenge prospective jurors either for cause or peremptorily (for no cause).

attorney may follow the redirect examination with a *recross-examination*. When both attorneys have finished with the first witness, Kirby's attorney calls the succeeding witnesses in the plaintiff's case. Each witness is subject to examination by the attorneys in the manner just described.

**Expert Witnesses** As part of their cases, both the plaintiff and the defendant may present testimony from one or more expert witnesses, such as forensic scientists, physicians, and psychologists. An *expert witness* is a person who, by virtue of education, training, skill, or experience, has scientific, technical, or other specialized knowledge in a particular area beyond that of an average person. In Kirby's case, her attorney might hire an accident reconstruction specialist to establish Carvello's negligence or a physician to testify to the extent of Kirby's injuries.

Normally, witnesses can testify only about the facts of a case—that is, what they personally observed. When witnesses are qualified as experts in a particular field, however, they can offer their opinions and conclusions about the evidence in that field. Because numerous experts are available for hire and expert testimony is powerful and effective with juries, there is tremendous potential for abuse. Therefore, judges act as gatekeepers to ensure that the experts are qualified. If a party believes that the opponent's expert witness is not a qualified expert in the relevant field, that party can make a motion to prevent the witness from testifying.[9]

■ **CASE IN POINT 3.4** Yvette Downey bought a children's bedroom set from Bob's Discount Furniture Holdings, Inc. She later discovered that it was infested with bed bugs, which had spread throughout her home. Downey spoke with Edward Gordinier, a licensed and experienced exterminator, who identified the bedroom set as the source of the problem. Although Bob's retrieved the bedroom set and refunded the purchase price, it refused to pay for the costs of extermination or any other damages. Downey sued.

Before the trial, Downey's attorney named Gordinier as a witness but did not submit a written report describing his anticipated testimony or specifying his qualifications. The defendants filed a motion to prevent his testimony. The district court refused to allow Gordinier to testify, but that decision was reversed on appeal. The appellate court concluded that Gordinier was not the type of expert who regularly was hired by plaintiffs to testify in court, in which case a report would have been required. Gordinier was simply an expert on bugs, and he was allowed to give his opinion on the infestation.[10] ■

**Possible Motion and Judgment** At the conclusion of the plaintiff's case, the defendant's attorney may ask the judge to direct a verdict for the defendant on the ground that the plaintiff has presented no evidence to support her or his claim. This is called a **motion for a judgment as a matter of law** (or a **motion for a directed verdict** in state courts). In considering the motion, the judge looks at the evidence in the light most favorable to the plaintiff and grants the motion only if there is insufficient evidence to raise an issue of fact. (Motions for directed verdicts at this stage of a trial are seldom granted.)

**Defendant's Evidence** The defendant's attorney then presents the evidence and witnesses for the defendant's case. Witnesses are called and examined by the defendant's attorney. The plaintiff's attorney has the right to cross-examine them, and there may be a redirect examination and possibly a recross-examination.

At the end of the defendant's case, either attorney can move for a directed verdict. Again, the test is whether the jury can, through any reasonable interpretation of the evidence, find for the party against whom the motion has been made. After the defendant's attorney has finished introducing evidence, the plaintiff's attorney can present a **rebuttal** by offering additional evidence that refutes the defendant's case. The defendant's attorney can, in turn, refute that evidence in a **rejoinder.**

### 3–3d Closing Arguments, Jury Instructions, and Verdict

After both sides have rested their cases, each attorney presents a **closing argument.** In the closing argument, each attorney summarizes the facts and evidence presented during the trial and indicates why the facts and evidence support his or her client's claim. In addition to generally urging a verdict in favor of the client, the closing argument typically reveals the shortcomings of the points made by the opposing party during the trial.

**Jury Instructions** Attorneys usually present closing arguments whether or not the trial was heard by a jury. If it was a jury trial, the attorneys will have met with the judge before the closing arguments to determine how the jury will be instructed on the law. The attorneys can refer to these instructions in their closing arguments. After closing arguments are completed, the judge instructs the jury in the law that applies to the case (these instructions are often called *charges*). The jury then retires to the jury room to deliberate a verdict.

Juries are instructed on the standard of proof they must apply to the case. In most civil cases, the standard of proof is a *preponderance of the evidence.*[11] In other words, the plaintiff (Kirby in our hypothetical case) need only show that her factual claim is more likely to be true than the defendant's. (In a criminal trial, the prosecution has a higher standard of proof to meet—it must prove its case *beyond a reasonable doubt.*)

---

9. See Edward J. Imwinkelried, *The Methods of Attacking Scientific Evidence,* 5th ed. (2014).

10. *Downey v. Bob's Discount Furniture Holdings, Inc.*, 633 F.3d 1 (1st Cir. 2011).

11. Note that some civil claims must be proved by "clear and convincing evidence," meaning that the evidence must show that the truth of the party's claim is *highly* probable. This standard is often applied in situations that present a particular danger of deception, such as allegations of fraud.

**Verdict** Once the jury has reached a decision, it issues a **verdict** in favor of one party. The verdict specifies the jury's factual findings. In some cases, the jury also decides on the amount of the *award* (the compensation to be paid to the prevailing party). After the announcement of the verdict, which marks the end of the trial itself, the jurors are dismissed.

See Concept Summary 3.2 for a review of trial procedures.

# 3–4 Posttrial Motions

After the jury has rendered its verdict, either party may make a posttrial motion. The prevailing party usually requests that the court enter a judgment in accordance with the verdict. The nonprevailing party frequently files one of the motions discussed next.

## 3–4a Motion for a New Trial

At the end of the trial, the losing party may make a motion to set aside the adverse verdict and any judgment and to hold a new trial. After looking at all the evidence, the judge will grant the **motion for a new trial** only if she or he believes that the jury was in error and that it is not appropriate to grant judgment for the other side.

Usually, a new trial is granted only when the jury verdict is obviously the result of a misapplication of the law or a misunderstanding of the evidence presented at trial. A new trial can also be granted on the grounds of newly discovered evidence, misconduct by the participants during the trial (such as when a juror has made prejudicial and inflammatory remarks), or an error by the judge.

## 3–4b Motion for Judgment *N.O.V.*

If Kirby wins and if Carvello's attorney has previously moved for a judgment as a matter of law, then Carvello's

---

### Concept Summary 3.2

**Trial Procedure**

| | |
|---|---|
| **Opening Statements** | • Each party's attorney is allowed to present an opening statement indicating what the attorney will attempt to prove during the course of the trial. |
| **Examination of Witnesses** | • Plaintiff's introduction and direct examination of witnesses, cross-examination by defendant's attorney, possible redirect examination by plaintiff's attorney, and possible recross-examination by defendant's attorney. <br> • Both the plaintiff and the defendant may present testimony from one or more expert witnesses. <br> • At the close of the plaintiff's case, the defendant may make a motion for a directed verdict (or for judgment as a matter of law). If granted by the court, this motion will end the trial before the defendant presents witnesses. <br> • Defendant's introduction and direct examination of witnesses, cross-examination by plaintiff's attorney, possible redirect examination by defendant's attorney, and possible recross-examination by plaintiff's attorney. <br> • Possible rebuttal of defendant's argument by plaintiff's attorney, who presents more evidence. <br> • Possible rejoinder by defendant's attorney to meet that evidence. |
| **Closing Arguments, Jury Instructions, and Verdict** | • Each party's attorney argues in favor of a verdict for his or her client. <br> • The judge instructs (or charges) the jury as to how the law applies to the issue, and the jury retires to deliberate. <br> • When the jury renders its verdict, the trial comes to an end. |

attorney can make a second motion for a judgment as a matter of law (the terminology used in federal courts). State courts may use different terms for these motions.

In many state courts, if the defendant's attorney moved earlier for a directed verdict, he or she may now make a **motion for judgment** *n.o.v.*—from the Latin *non obstante veredicto*, meaning "notwithstanding the verdict." Such a motion will be granted only if the jury's verdict was unreasonable and erroneous.

If the judge grants the motion, then the jury's verdict will be set aside, and a judgment will be entered in favor of the opposing party (Carvello). If the motion is denied, Carvello may then appeal the case. (Kirby may also appeal the case, even though she won at trial. She might appeal, for example, if she received a smaller monetary award than she had sought.)

## 3–5 The Appeal

Either party may appeal not only the jury's verdict but also the judge's ruling on any pretrial or posttrial motion. Many of the appellate court cases that appear in this text involve appeals of motions for summary judgment or other motions that were denied by trial court judges.

Note that a party must have legitimate grounds to file an appeal (some legal error) and that few trial court decisions are reversed on appeal. Moreover, the expenses associated with an appeal can be considerable.

### 3–5a Filing the Appeal

If Carvello decides to appeal the verdict in Kirby's favor, then his attorney must file a *notice of appeal* with the clerk of the trial court within a prescribed period of time. Carvello then becomes the *appellant* or *petitioner*. The clerk of the trial court sends to the reviewing court (usually an intermediate court of appeals) the *record on appeal*. The record contains all the pleadings, motions, and other documents filed with the court and a complete written transcript of the proceedings, including testimony, arguments, jury instructions, and judicial rulings.

Carvello's attorney will file an appellate **brief** with the reviewing court. The brief is a formal legal document outlining the facts and issues of the case, the judge's rulings or jury's findings that should be reversed or modified, the applicable law, and arguments on Carvello's behalf (citing applicable statutes and relevant cases as precedents). The attorney for the *appellee* (Kirby, in our hypothetical case) usually files an answering brief. Carvello's attorney can file a reply, although it is not required. The reviewing court then considers the case.

### 3–5b Appellate Review

A court of appeals does not hear any evidence. Rather, it reviews the record for errors of law. Its decision concerning a case is based on the record on appeal and the briefs and arguments. The attorneys present oral arguments, after which the case is taken under advisement. The court then issues a written opinion. In general, appellate courts do not reverse findings of fact unless the findings are unsupported or contradicted by the evidence.

An appellate court has the following options after reviewing a case:

1. The court can *affirm* the trial court's decision. (Most decisions are affirmed.)
2. The court can *reverse* the trial court's judgment if it concludes that the trial court erred or that the jury did not receive proper instructions.
3. The appellate court can *remand* (send back) the case to the trial court for further proceedings consistent with its opinion on the matter.
4. The court might also affirm or reverse a decision *in part*. For example, the court might affirm the jury's finding that Carvello was negligent but remand the case for further proceedings on another issue (such as the extent of Kirby's damages).
5. An appellate court can also *modify* a lower court's decision. If the appellate court decides that the jury awarded an excessive amount in damages, for example, the court might reduce the award to a more appropriate, or fairer, amount.

### 3–5c Higher Appellate Courts

If the reviewing court is an intermediate appellate court, the losing party may decide to appeal the decision to the state's highest court, usually called its supreme court. Although the losing party has a right to ask (petition) a higher court to review the case, the party does not have a right to have the case heard by the higher appellate court. Appellate courts normally have discretionary power and can accept or reject an appeal. Like the United States Supreme Court, state supreme courts generally deny most petitions for appeal.

If the petition for review is granted, new briefs must be filed before the state supreme court, and the attorneys may be allowed or requested to present oral arguments. Like the intermediate appellate courts, the state supreme court can reverse or affirm the lower appellate court's decision or remand the case. At this point, the case typically has reached its end (unless a federal question is at issue and one of the parties has legitimate grounds to seek review by a federal appellate court).

Concept Summary 3.3 reviews the options that the parties may pursue after the trial.

## 3–6 Enforcing the Judgment

The uncertainties of the litigation process are compounded by the lack of guarantees that any judgment will be enforceable. Even if the jury awards Kirby the full amount of damages requested ($500,000), for example, Carvello's auto insurance coverage might have lapsed. If so, the company would not pay any of the damages. Alternatively, Carvello's insurance policy might be limited to $250,000, meaning that Carvello personally would have to pay the remaining $250,000.

### 3–6a Requesting Court Assistance in Collecting the Judgment

If the defendant does not have the funds available to pay the judgment, the plaintiff can go back to the court and request that the court issue a writ of execution. A **writ of execution** is an order directing the sheriff to seize and sell the defendant's nonexempt assets, or property (certain assets are exempted by law from creditors' actions). The proceeds of the sale are then used to pay the damages owed, and any excess proceeds are returned to the defendant. Alternatively, the nonexempt property itself could be transferred to the plaintiff in lieu of an outright payment. (Creditors' remedies, discussed elsewhere in this text, may also be available.)

### 3–6b Availability of Assets

The problem of collecting a judgment is less pronounced when a party is seeking to satisfy a judgment against a defendant with substantial assets that can be easily located, such as a major corporation. Usually, one of the factors considered by the plaintiff and his or her attorney before a lawsuit is initiated is whether the defendant has sufficient assets to cover the amount of damages sought. In addition, during the discovery process, attorneys routinely seek information about the location of the defendant's assets that might potentially be used to satisfy a judgment.

---

### Concept Summary 3.3

#### Posttrial Options

| Posttrial Motions | • *Motion for a new trial*—If the judge believes that the jury was in error but is not convinced that the losing party should have won, the motion normally is granted. It can also be granted on the basis of newly discovered evidence, misconduct by the participants during the trial, or error by the judge.<br>• *Motion for judgment n.o.v.* ("*notwithstanding the verdict*")—The party making the motion must have filed a motion for a directed verdict at the close of the presentation of evidence during the trial. The motion will be granted if the judge is convinced that the jury was in error. |
|---|---|
| The Appeal | Either party can appeal the trial court's judgment to an appropriate court of appeals.<br>• *Filing the appeal*—The appealing party must file a notice of appeal with the clerk of the trial court, who forwards the record on appeal to the appellate court. Attorneys file appellate briefs.<br>• *Appellate review*—The appellate court does not hear evidence but bases its opinion, which it issues in writing, on the record on appeal and the attorneys' briefs and oral arguments. The court may affirm or reverse all (or part) of the trial court's judgment and/or remand the case for further proceedings consistent with its opinion. Most decisions are affirmed on appeal.<br>• *Further review*—In some cases, further review may be sought from a higher appellate court, such as a state supreme court. If a federal question is involved, the case may ultimately be appealed to the United States Supreme Court. |

## Reviewing: Court Procedures

Ronald Metzgar placed his fifteen-month-old son, Matthew, awake and healthy, in his playpen. Ronald left the room for five minutes and on his return found Matthew lifeless. A toy block had lodged in the boy's throat, causing him to choke to death. Ronald called 911, but efforts to revive Matthew were to no avail. There was no warning of a choking hazard on the box containing the block. Matthew's parents hired an attorney and sued Playskool, Inc., the manufacturer of the block, alleging that the manufacturer had been negligent in failing to warn of the block's hazard. Playskool filed a motion for summary judgment, arguing that the danger of a young child's choking on a small block was obvious. Using the information presented in the chapter, answer the following questions.

1. Suppose that the attorney the Metzgars hired agreed to represent them on a contingency-fee basis. What does that mean?
2. How would the Metzgars' attorney likely have served process (the summons and complaint) on Playskool, Inc.?
3. Should Playskool's request for summary judgment be granted? Why or why not?
4. Suppose that the judge denied Playskool's motion and the case proceeded to trial. After hearing all the evidence, the jury found in favor of the defendant. What options do the plaintiffs have at this point if they are not satisfied with the verdict?

**Debate This ...** *Some consumer advocates argue that attorneys' high contingency fees—sometimes reaching 40 percent—unfairly deprive winning plaintiffs of too much of their awards. Should the government cap contingency fees at, say, 20 percent of the award? Why or why not?*

## Terms and Concepts

affidavit 56
affirmative defense 52
answer 51
brief 65
closing argument 63
complaint 50
counterclaim 52
cross-examination 61
default judgment 50
deposition 59
direct examination 61
discovery 57
e-evidence 60
Federal Rules of Civil Procedure (FRCP) 48

hearsay 61
impeach 59
interrogatories 59
metadata 60
motion 52
motion for a directed verdict 63
motion for a judgment as a matter of law 63
motion for a new trial 64
motion for judgment *n.o.v.* 65
motion for judgment on the pleadings 56
motion for summary judgment 56
motion to dismiss 53
opening statement 61

pleadings 50
pretrial conference 60
pretrial motion 53
rebuttal 63
rejoinder 63
relevant evidence 61
rules of evidence 61
service of process 50
summons 50
verdict 64
*voir dire* 61
writ of execution 66

## Issue Spotters

1. At the trial, after Sue calls her witnesses, offers her evidence, and otherwise presents her side of the case, Tom has at least two choices between courses of actions. Tom can call his first witness. What else might he do? (See *The Trial.*)

2. After the trial, the judge issues a judgment that includes a grant of relief for Sue, but the relief is less than Sue wanted. Neither Sue nor Tom is satisfied with this result. Who can appeal to a higher court? (See *The Appeal.*)

• **Check your answers to the Issue Spotters against the answers provided in Appendix D at the end of this text.**

## Business Scenarios

**3–1. Discovery Rules.** In the past, the rules of discovery were very restrictive, and trials often turned on elements of surprise. For example, a plaintiff would not necessarily know until the trial what the defendant's defense was going to be. In the last several decades, however, new rules of discovery have substantially changed this situation. Now each attorney can access practically all of the evidence that the other side intends to present at trial, with the exception of certain information—namely, the opposing attorney's work product. Work product is not a precise concept. Basically, it includes all of the attorney's thoughts on the case. Can you see any reason why such information should not be made available to the opposing attorney? Discuss fully. (See *Pretrial Procedures*.)

**3–2. Motions.** When and for what purpose is each of the following motions made? Which of them would be appropriate if a defendant claimed that the only issue between the parties was a question of law and that the law was favorable to the defendant's position? (See *Pretrial Procedures*.)

**(a)** A motion for judgment on the pleadings.

**(b)** A motion for a directed verdict.

**(c)** A motion for summary judgment.

**(d)** A motion for judgment *n.o.v.*

**3–3. Motion for a New Trial.** Washoe Medical Center, Inc., admitted Shirley Swisher for the treatment of a fractured pelvis. During her stay, Swisher suffered a fatal fall from her hospital bed. Gerald Parodi, the administrator of her estate, and others filed an action against Washoe seeking damages for the alleged lack of care in treating Swisher. During *voir dire*, when the plaintiffs' attorney returned a few minutes late from a break, the trial judge led the prospective jurors in a standing ovation. The judge joked with one of the prospective jurors, whom he had known in college, about his fitness to serve as a judge and personally endorsed another prospective juror's business. After the trial, the jury returned a verdict in favor of Washoe. The plaintiffs moved for a new trial, but the judge denied the motion. The plaintiffs then appealed, arguing that the tone set by the judge during *voir dire* prejudiced their right to a fair trial. Should the appellate court agree? Why or why not? (See *Posttrial Motions*.)

**3–4. Discovery.** Advance Technology Consultants, Inc. (ATC), contracted with RoadTrac, LLC, to provide software and client software systems for the products of global positioning satellite (GPS) technology being developed by RoadTrac. RoadTrac agreed to provide ATC with hardware with which ATC's software would interface. Problems soon arose, however. ATC claimed that RoadTrac's hardware was defective, making it difficult to develop the software. Road-Trac contended that its hardware was fully functional and that ATC had simply failed to provide supporting software.

ATC told RoadTrac that it considered their contract terminated. RoadTrac filed a suit in a Georgia state court against ATC alleging breach of contract. During discovery, RoadTrac requested ATC's customer lists and marketing procedures. ATC objected to providing this information because Road-Trac and ATC had become competitors in the GPS industry. Should a party to a lawsuit have to hand over its confidential business secrets as part of a discovery request? Why or why not? What limitations might a court consider imposing before requiring ATC to produce this material? (See *Pretrial Procedures*.)

## Business Case Problems

**3–5. Jury Misconduct.** Michelle Fleshner worked for Pepose Vision Institute (PVI), a surgical practice. She was fired after she provided information to the U.S. Department of Labor about PVI's overtime pay policy. She sued for wrongful termination, and the jury awarded her $125,000. After the trial, a juror told PVI's attorneys that another juror had made anti-Semitic statements during jury deliberations. The comments concerned a witness who testified on PVI's behalf. According to the juror, the other juror said, about the witness: "She is a Jewish witch." "She is a penny-pinching Jew." "She was such a cheap Jew that she did not want to pay Plaintiff unemployment compensation." Another juror confirmed the remarks. PVI filed a motion for a new trial on the basis of juror misconduct. The trial judge held that the comments had not prevented a fair trial from occurring. PVI appealed. Do you think such comments are sufficient to require a new trial, or must a juror's bias be discovered during *voir dire* for it to matter? Explain. [*Fleshner v. Pepose Vision Institute*, 304 S.W.3d 81 (Mo. 2010)] (See *The Trial*.)

**3–6. Service of Process.** Dr. Kevin Bardwell owns Northfield Urgent Care, LLC, a Minnesota medical clinic. Northfield ordered flu vaccine from Clint Pharmaceuticals, a licensed distributer of flu vaccine located in Tennessee. The parties signed a credit agreement that specified that any disputes would be litigated in the Tennessee state courts. When Northfield failed to pay what it owed for the vaccine, Clint Pharmaceuticals filed a lawsuit in Tennessee and served process on the clinic via registered mail to Dr. Bardwell, the registered agent of Northfield.

Bardwell's wife, who worked as a receptionist at the clinic and handled inquiries on the clinic's Facebook site, signed for the letter. Bardwell did not appear on the trial date, however, and the Tennessee court entered a default judgment against Northfield. When Clint Pharmaceuticals attempted to collect on the judgment in Minnesota, Bardwell claimed that the judgment was unenforceable. He asserted that he had not been properly served because his wife was not a registered agent. Should the Minnesota court invalidate the Tennessee judgment? Was service of process proper when it was mailed to the defendant medical clinic and the wife of the physician who owned the clinic opened the letter? Explain. [*Clint Pharmaceuticals v. Northfield Urgent Care, LLC*, 2012 WL 3792546 (Minn.App. 2012).] (See *Pretrial Procedures*.)

### 3–7. Business Case Problem with Sample Answer—Discovery.

 Jessica Lester died from injuries suffered in an auto accident caused by the driver of a truck owned by Allied Concrete Co. Jessica's widower, Isaiah, filed a suit against Allied for damages. The defendant requested copies of all of Isaiah's Facebook photos and other postings. Before responding, Isaiah "cleaned up" his Facebook page. Allied suspected that some items had been deleted, including a photo of Isaiah holding a beer can while wearing a T-shirt that declared "I [heart] hot-moms." Can this material be recovered? If so, how? What effect might Isaiah's "postings" have on the result in this case? Discuss. [*Allied Concrete Co. v. Lester*, 736 S.E.2d 699 (2013)] (See *Pretrial Procedures*.)

- For a sample answer to Problem 3–7, go to Appendix E at the end of this text.

### 3–8. Motion for Summary Judgment.

Rebecca Nichols drove a truck for Tri-National Logistics, Inc. (TNI). On a delivery trip, Nichols's fellow driver, James Paris, made unwelcome sexual advances. Paris continued to make advances during a subsequent mandatory layover. Nichols reported this behavior to their employer. TNI nevertheless left her with Paris in Pharr, Texas, for another seven days with no alternative form of transportation before sending a driver to pick her up. She filed a suit in a federal district court against TNI, alleging discrimination on the basis of sex in violation of Title VII of the Civil Rights Act. Disputed facts included whether Nichols subjectively felt abused by Paris and whether their employer was aware of his conduct and failed to take appropriate action.

Could TNI successfully file a motion for summary judgment at this point? Explain. [*Nichols v. Tri-National Logistics, Inc*, 809 F.3d 981 (8th Cir. 2016)] (See *Pretrial Procedures*.)

### 3–9. A Question of Ethics—Service of Process.

 *Narnia Investments, Ltd., filed a suit in a Texas state court against several defendants, including Harvestons Securities, Inc., a securities dealer. (Securities are investments that include stocks and bonds.) Harvestons is registered with the state of Texas. Thus, a party may serve a summons and a copy of a complaint on Harvestons by serving the Texas Securities Commissioner. In this case, the return of service indicated that process had been served on the commissioner "by delivering to JoAnn Kocerek defendant, in person, a true copy of this [summons] together with the accompanying copy(ies) of the [complaint]."*

*Harvestons did not file an answer, and Narnia obtained a default judgment against the defendant for $365,000, plus attorneys' fees and interest. Five months after this judgment, Harvestons filed a motion for a new trial, which the court denied. Harvestons appealed to a state intermediate appellate court, claiming that it had not been served in strict compliance with the rules governing service of process.* [Harvestons Securities, Inc. v. Narnia Investments, Ltd., *218 S.W.3d 126 (Tex.App.—Houston 2007)*] (See *Pretrial Procedures*.)

**(a)** Harvestons asserted that Narnia's service was invalid, in part, because "the return of service states that process was delivered to 'JoAnn Kocerek'" and did not show that she "had the authority to accept process on behalf of Harvestons or the Texas Securities Commissioner." Should such a detail, if it is required, be strictly construed and applied? Should it apply in this case? Explain.

**(b)** Who is responsible for ensuring that service of process is accomplished properly? Was it accomplished properly in this case? Why or why not?

## Legal Reasoning Group Activity

### 3–10. Court Procedures.

Bento Cuisine is a lunch-cart business. It occupies a street corner in Texarkana, a city that straddles the border of Arkansas and Texas. Across the street—and across the state line, which runs down the middle of the street—is Rico's Tacos. The two businesses compete for customers. Recently, Bento has begun to suspect that Rico's is engaging in competitive behavior that is illegal. Bento's manager overheard several of Rico's employees discussing these competitive tactics while on a break at a nearby Starbucks. Bento files a lawsuit against Rico's in a federal court based on diversity jurisdiction. (See *Pretrial Procedures*.)

**(a)** The first group will discuss whether Rico's could file a motion claiming that the federal court lacks jurisdiction over this dispute.

**(b)** The second group will assume that the case goes to trial. Bento's manager believes that Bento's has both the law and the facts on its side. Nevertheless, at the end of the trial, the jury decides against Bento, and the judge issues a ruling in favor of Rico's. If Bento is unwilling to accept this result, what are its options?

**(c)** As discussed in this chapter, hearsay is literally what a witness says he or she heard another person say. A third group will decide whether Bento's manager can testify about what he heard some of Rico's employees say to one another while at a coffee shop. This group will also discuss what makes the admissibility of hearsay evidence potentially unethical.

# Answers to the *Issue Spotters*

**1. *Tom can call his first witness. What else might he do?*** Tom could file a motion for a directed verdict. This motion asks the judge to direct a verdict for Tom on the ground that Sue presented no evidence that would justify granting Sue relief. The judge grants the motion if there is insufficient evidence to raise an issue of fact.

**2. *Who can appeal to a higher court?*** Either a plaintiff or a defendant, or both, can appeal a judgment to a higher court. An appellate court can affirm, reverse, or remand a case, or take any of these actions in combination. To appeal successfully, it is best to appeal on the basis of an error of law, because appellate courts do not usually reverse on findings of fact.

# Sample Answers for *Business Case Problems with Sample Answer*

**Problem 3–7. *Discovery.*** Yes. The items that were deleted from a Facebook page can be recovered. Normally, a party must hire an expert to recover material in an electronic format, and this can be time consuming and expensive.

Electronic evidence, or e-evidence, consists of all computer-generated or electronically recorded information, such as posts on Facebook and other social media sites. The effect that e-evidence can have in a case depends on its relevance and what it reveals. In the facts presented in this problem, Isaiah should be sanctioned—he should be required to cover Allied's cost to hire the recovery expert and attorney's fees to confront the misconduct. In a jury trial, the court might also instruct the jury to presume that any missing items are harmful to Isaiah's case. If all of the material is retrieved and presented at the trial, any prejudice to Allied's case might thereby be mitigated. If not, the court might go so far as to order a new trial.

In the actual case on which this problem is based, Allied hired an expert, who determined that Isaiah had in fact removed some photos and other items from his Facebook page. After the expert testified about the missing material, Isaiah provided Allied with all of it, including the photos that he had deleted. Allied sought a retrial, but the court instead reduced the amount of Isaiah's damages by the amount that it cost Allied to address his "misconduct."

# Chapter 3

# CHAPTER

# Courts and Alternative Dispute Resolution

The United States has fifty-two court systems—one for each of the fifty states, one for the District of Columbia, and a federal system. Keep in mind that the federal courts are not superior to the state courts. They are simply an independent system of courts, which derives its authority from Article III, Section 2, of the U.S. Constitution. By the power given to it under the U.S. Constitution, Congress has extended the federal court system to U.S. territories such as Guam, Puerto Rico, and the Virgin Islands.[1]

1. In Guam and the Virgin Islands, territorial courts serve as both federal courts and state courts. In Puerto Rico, they serve only as federal courts.

As we shall see, the United States Supreme Court is the final controlling voice over all of these fifty-two systems, at least when questions of federal law are involved. The Supreme Court's decisions—whether on free speech and social media, health-care subsidies, environmental regulation, or same-sex marriage—represent the last word in the most controversial legal debates in our society. Nevertheless, many of the legal issues that arise in our daily lives, such as the use of social media by courts, employers, and law enforcement, have not yet come before the nation's highest court. The lower courts usually resolve

such pressing matters, making these courts equally important in our legal system.

Although an understanding of our nation's court systems is beneficial for anyone, it is particularly crucial for businesspersons, who will likely face a lawsuit at some time during their careers. Anyone involved in business should be familiar with the basic requirements that must be met before a party can bring a lawsuit before a particular court.

## 2–1 The Judiciary's Role in American Government

The body of American law includes the federal and state constitutions, statutes passed by legislative bodies, administrative law, and the case decisions and legal principles that form the common law. These laws would be meaningless, however, without the courts to interpret and apply them. The essential role of the judiciary—the courts—in the American governmental system is to interpret the laws and apply them to specific situations.

### 2–1a Judicial Review

As the branch of government entrusted with interpreting the laws, the judiciary can decide, among other things, whether the laws or actions of the other two branches are constitutional. The process for making such a determination is known as **judicial review.** The power of judicial review enables the judicial branch to act as a check on the other two branches of government, in line with the

system of checks and balances established by the U.S. Constitution.[2]

### 2–1b The Origins of Judicial Review in the United States

The power of judicial review is not mentioned in the U.S. Constitution (although many constitutional scholars believe that the founders intended the judiciary to have this power). The United States Supreme Court explicitly established this power in 1803 in the case *Marbury v. Madison*.[3] In that decision, the Court stated, "It is emphatically the province [authority] and duty of the Judicial Department to say what the law is. . . . If two laws conflict with each other, the courts must decide

2. In a broad sense, judicial review occurs whenever a court "reviews" a case or legal proceeding—as when an appellate court reviews a lower court's decision. When discussing the judiciary's role in American government, however, the term *judicial review* refers to the power of the judiciary to decide whether the actions of the other two branches of government violate the U.S. Constitution.
3. 5 U.S. (1 Cranch) 137, 2 L.Ed. 60 (1803).

on the operation of each. . . . [I]f both [a] law and the Constitution apply to a particular case, . . . the Court must determine which of these conflicting rules governs the case. This is of the very essence of judicial duty." Since the *Marbury v. Madison* decision, the power of judicial review has remained unchallenged. Today, this power is exercised by both federal and state courts.

## 2–2 Basic Judicial Requirements

Before a lawsuit can be brought before a court, certain requirements must be met. These requirements relate to jurisdiction, venue, and standing to sue. We examine each of these important concepts here.

### 2–2a Jurisdiction

In Latin, *juris* means "law," and *diction* means "to speak." Thus, "the power to speak the law" is the literal meaning of the term **jurisdiction.** Before any court can hear a case, it must have jurisdiction over the person (or company) against whom the suit is brought (the defendant) or over the property involved in the suit. The court must also have jurisdiction over the subject matter of the dispute.

**Jurisdiction over Persons or Property** Generally, a particular court can exercise *in personam* **jurisdiction** (personal jurisdiction) over any person or business that resides in a certain geographic area. A state trial court, for instance, normally has jurisdictional authority over residents (including businesses) of a particular area of the state, such as a county or district. A state's highest court (often called the state supreme court[4]) has jurisdictional authority over all residents within the state.

A court can also exercise jurisdiction over property that is located within its boundaries. This kind of jurisdiction is known as *in rem* **jurisdiction**, or "jurisdiction over the thing." ■ **EXAMPLE 2.1** A dispute arises over the ownership of a boat in dry dock in Fort Lauderdale, Florida. The boat is owned by an Ohio resident, over whom a Florida court normally cannot exercise personal jurisdiction. The other party to the dispute is a resident of Nebraska. In this situation, a lawsuit concerning the boat could be brought in a Florida state court on the basis of the court's *in rem* jurisdiction. ■

**Long Arm Statutes and Minimum Contacts.** Under the authority of a state **long arm statute,** a court can exercise personal jurisdiction over certain out-of-state defendants based on activities that took place within the state. Before a court can exercise jurisdiction, though, it must be demonstrated that the defendant had sufficient contacts, or *minimum contacts*, with the state to justify the jurisdiction.[5]

Generally, the minimum-contacts requirement means that the defendant must have sufficient connection to the state for the judge to conclude that it is fair for the state to exercise power over the defendant. For instance, if an out-of-state defendant caused an automobile accident within the state or breached a contract formed there, a court will usually find that minimum contacts exist to exercise jurisdiction over that defendant. Similarly, a state may exercise personal jurisdiction over a nonresident defendant that is sued for selling defective goods within the state.

■ **CASE IN POINT 2.2** An Xbox game system caught fire in Bonnie Broquet's home in Texas and caused substantial personal injuries. Broquet filed a lawsuit in a Texas court against Ji-Haw Industrial Company, a nonresident company that made the Xbox components. Broquet alleged that Ji-Haw's components were defective and had caused the fire. Ji-Haw argued that the Texas court lacked jurisdiction over it, but a state appellate court held that the Texas long arm statute authorized the exercise of jurisdiction over the out-of-state defendant.[6] ■

**Corporate Contacts.** Because corporations are considered legal persons, courts use the same principles to determine whether it is fair to exercise jurisdiction over a corporation. A corporation normally is subject to personal jurisdiction in the state in which it is incorporated, has its principal office, and/or is doing business.

Courts apply the minimum-contacts test to determine if they can exercise jurisdiction over out-of-state corporations. The minimum-contacts requirement is usually met if the corporation advertises or sells its products within the state, or places its goods into the "stream of commerce" with the intent that the goods be sold in the state. ■ **EXAMPLE 2.3** A business is incorporated under the laws of Maine but has a branch office and manufacturing plant in Georgia. The corporation also advertises and sells its products in Georgia. These activities would likely constitute sufficient contacts with the state of

---

4. As will be discussed shortly, a state's highest court is often referred to as the state supreme court, but there are exceptions. For instance, in New York the supreme court is a trial court.

5. The minimum-contacts standard was first established in *International Shoe Co. v. State of Washington*, 326 U.S. 310, 66 S.Ct. 154, 90 L.Ed. 95 (1945).

6. *Ji-Haw Industrial Co. v. Broquet*, 2008 WL 441822 (Tex.App.—San Antonio 2008).

Georgia to allow a Georgia court to exercise jurisdiction over the corporation. ■

Some corporations do not sell or advertise their products in the general marketplace. Determining what constitutes minimum contacts in these situations can be more difficult. ■ **CASE IN POINT 2.4** Independence Plating Corporation is a New Jersey corporation that provides metal-coating services. Its only office and all of its personnel are located in New Jersey, and it does not advertise out of state. Independence had a long-standing business relationship with Southern Prestige Industries, Inc., a North Carolina company. Eventually, Southern Prestige filed suit in North Carolina against Independence for defective workmanship. Independence argued that North Carolina did not have jurisdiction over it, but the court held that Independence had sufficient minimum contacts with the state to justify jurisdiction. The two parties had exchanged thirty-two separate purchase orders in a period of less than twelve months.[7] ■

**Jurisdiction over Subject Matter** Subject-matter jurisdiction refers to the limitations on the types of cases a court can hear. Certain courts are empowered to hear certain kinds of disputes. In both the federal and the state court systems, there are courts of general (unlimited) jurisdiction and courts of limited jurisdiction.

A *court of general jurisdiction* can decide cases involving a broad array of issues. An example of a court of general jurisdiction is a state trial court or a federal district court.

In contrast, a *court of limited jurisdiction* can hear only specific types of cases. An example of a state court of limited jurisdiction is a probate court. **Probate courts** are state courts that handle only the disposition of a person's assets and obligations after that person's death, including issues relating to the custody and guardianship of children. An example of a federal court of limited subject-matter jurisdiction is a bankruptcy court. **Bankruptcy courts** handle only bankruptcy proceedings, which are governed by federal bankruptcy law.

A court's jurisdiction over subject matter is usually defined in the statute or constitution that created the court. In both the federal and the state court systems, a court's subject-matter jurisdiction can be limited by any of the following:

1. The subject of the lawsuit.
2. The sum in controversy.

3. Whether the case involves a felony (a serious type of crime) or a misdemeanor (a less serious type of crime).
4. Whether the proceeding is a trial or an appeal.

**Original and Appellate Jurisdiction** The distinction between courts of original jurisdiction and courts of appellate jurisdiction normally lies in whether the case is being heard for the first time. Courts having original jurisdiction are courts of the first instance, or trial courts. These are courts in which lawsuits begin, trials take place, and evidence is presented. In the federal court system, the *district courts* are trial courts. In the various state court systems, the trial courts are known by various names, as will be discussed shortly.

The key point here is that any court having original jurisdiction normally serves as a trial court. Courts having appellate jurisdiction act as reviewing, or appellate, courts. In general, cases can be brought before appellate courts only on appeal from an order or a judgment of a trial court or other lower courts.

**Jurisdiction of the Federal Courts** Because the federal government is a government of limited powers, the jurisdiction of the federal courts is limited. Federal courts have subject-matter jurisdiction in two situations: when a federal question is involved and when there is diversity of citizenship.

**Federal Questions.** Article III of the U.S. Constitution establishes the boundaries of federal judicial power. Section 2 of Article III states that "the judicial Power shall extend to all Cases, in Law and Equity, arising under this Constitution, the Laws of the United States, and Treaties made, or which shall be made, under their Authority."

In effect, this clause means that whenever a plaintiff's cause of action is based, at least in part, on the U.S. Constitution, a treaty, or a federal law, a **federal question** arises. Any lawsuit involving a federal question, such as a person's rights under the U.S. Constitution, can originate in a federal court. Note that in a case based on a federal question, a federal court will apply federal law.

**Diversity of Citizenship.** Federal district courts can also exercise original jurisdiction over cases involving **diversity of citizenship.** The most common type of diversity jurisdiction[8] requires *both* of the following:

---

7. *Southern Prestige Industries, Inc. v. Independence Plating Corp.*, 690 S.E.2d 768 (N.C. 2010).

8. Diversity jurisdiction also exists in cases between (1) a foreign country and citizens of a state or of different states and (2) citizens of a state and citizens or subjects of a foreign country. Cases based on these types of diversity jurisdiction occur infrequently.

1. The plaintiff and defendant must be residents of different states.
2. The dollar amount in controversy must exceed $75,000.

For purposes of diversity jurisdiction, a corporation is a citizen of both the state in which it is incorporated and the state in which its principal place of business is located.

A case involving diversity of citizenship can be filed in the appropriate federal district court. (If the case starts in a state court, it can sometimes be transferred, or "removed," to a federal court.) A large percentage of the cases filed in federal courts each year are based on diversity of citizenship. As noted before, a federal court will apply federal law in cases involving federal questions.

In a case based on diversity of citizenship, in contrast, a federal court will apply the relevant state law (which is often the law of the state in which the court sits).

The following case focused on whether diversity jurisdiction existed. A boat owner was severely burned when his boat exploded after being overfilled with fuel at a marina in the U.S. Virgin Islands. The owner filed a suit in a federal district court against the marina and sought a jury trial. The defendant argued that a plaintiff in an admiralty, or maritime, case (a case based on something that happened at sea) does not have a right to a jury trial unless the court has diversity jurisdiction. The defendant claimed that because both parties were citizens of the Virgin Islands, the court had no such jurisdiction.

**Case Analysis 2.1**

## Mala v. Crown Bay Marina, Inc.
United States Court of Appeals, Third Circuit, 704 F.3d 239 (2013).

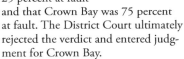

### In the Language of the Court
*SMITH*, Circuit Judge.
* * * *

Kelley Mala is a citizen of the United States Virgin Islands. * * * He went for a cruise in his powerboat near St. Thomas, Virgin Islands. When his boat ran low on gas, he entered Crown Bay Marina to refuel. Mala tied the boat to one of Crown Bay's eight fueling stations and began filling his tank with an automatic gas pump. Before walking to the cash register to buy oil, Mala asked a Crown Bay attendant to watch his boat.

By the time Mala returned, the boat's tank was overflowing and fuel was spilling into the boat and into the water. The attendant manually shut off the pump and acknowledged that the pump had been malfunctioning in recent days. Mala began cleaning up the fuel, and at some point, the attendant provided soap and water. Mala eventually departed the marina, but as he did so, the engine caught fire and exploded. Mala was thrown into the water and was severely burned. His boat was unsalvageable.

* * * Mala sued Crown Bay in the District Court of the Virgin Islands.

Mala's * * * complaint asserted * * * that Crown Bay negligently maintained its gas pump. [Negligence is the failure to exercise the standard of care that a reasonable person would exercise in similar circumstances. Negligence can form the basis for a legal claim.] The complaint also alleged that the District Court had admiralty and diversity jurisdiction over the case, and it requested a jury trial.
* * * *

* * * Crown Bay filed a motion to strike Mala's jury demand. Crown Bay argued that plaintiffs generally do not have a jury-trial right in admiralty cases—only when the court also has diversity jurisdiction. And Crown Bay asserted that the parties were not diverse in this case * * * . In response to this motion, the District Court ruled that both Mala and Crown Bay were citizens of the Virgin Islands. The court therefore struck Mala's jury demand, but nevertheless opted to empanel an advisory jury. [The court could accept or reject the advisory jury's verdict.]

* * * At the end of the trial, the advisory jury returned a verdict of $460,000 for Mala—$400,000 for pain and suffering and $60,000 in compensatory

damages. It concluded that Mala was 25 percent at fault and that Crown Bay was 75 percent at fault. The District Court ultimately rejected the verdict and entered judgment for Crown Bay.
* * * *

This appeal followed.
* * * *

Mala * * * argues that the District Court improperly refused to conduct a jury trial. This claim ultimately depends on whether the District Court had diversity jurisdiction.

The Seventh Amendment [to the U.S. Constitution] creates a right to civil jury trials in federal court: "In Suits at common law * * * the right of trial by jury shall be preserved." Admiralty suits are not "Suits at common law," which means that when a district court has only admiralty jurisdiction the plaintiff does not have a jury-trial right. But [a federal statute] allows plaintiffs to pursue state claims in admiralty cases as long as the district court also has diversity jurisdiction. In such cases [the statute] preserves whatever jury-trial right exists with respect to the underlying state claims.

*Case 2.1 Continues*

**Case 2.1 Continued**

Mala argues that the District Court had both admiralty and diversity jurisdiction. As a preliminary matter, the court certainly had admiralty jurisdiction. The alleged tort occurred on navigable water and bore a substantial connection to maritime activity.

The grounds for diversity jurisdiction are less certain. *District courts have jurisdiction only if the parties are completely diverse. This means that no plaintiff may have the same state or territorial citizenship as any defendant.* The parties agree that Mala was a citizen of the Virgin Islands. [Emphasis added.]

Unfortunately for Mala, the District Court concluded that Crown Bay also was a citizen of the Virgin Islands. Mala rejects this conclusion.

Mala bears the burden of proving that the District Court had diversity jurisdiction. Mala failed to meet that burden because he did not offer evidence that Crown Bay was anything other than a citizen of the Virgin Islands. Mala contends that Crown Bay admitted to being a citizen of Florida, but Crown Bay actually denied Mala's allegation.

Absent evidence that the parties were diverse, we are left with Mala's allegations. *Allegations are insufficient at trial. And they are especially insufficient on appeal*, where we review the District Court's underlying factual findings for clear error. Under this standard, we will not reverse unless we are left with the definite and firm conviction that Crown Bay was in fact a citizen of Florida. Mala has not presented any credible evidence that Crown Bay was a citizen of Florida—much less evidence that would leave us with the requisite firm conviction. [Emphasis added.]

* * * Accordingly, the parties were not diverse and Mala does not have a jury-trial right.

* * * *

* * * For these reasons we will affirm the District Court's judgment.

**Legal Reasoning Questions**

**1.** What is "diversity of citizenship"?

**2.** How does the presence—or lack—of diversity of citizenship affect a lawsuit?

**3.** What did the court conclude with respect to the parties' diversity of citizenship in this case?

---

**Exclusive versus Concurrent Jurisdiction** When both federal and state courts have the power to hear a case, as is true in lawsuits involving diversity of citizenship, **concurrent jurisdiction** exists. When cases can be tried only in federal courts or only in state courts, **exclusive jurisdiction** exists.

Federal courts have exclusive jurisdiction in cases involving federal crimes, bankruptcy, most patent and copyright claims, suits against the United States, and some areas of admiralty law. State courts also have exclusive jurisdiction over certain subjects—for instance, divorce and adoption.

When concurrent jurisdiction exists, a party may choose to bring a suit in either a federal court or a state court. Many factors can affect a party's decision to litigate in a federal versus a state court. Examples include the availability of different remedies, the distance to the respective courthouses, or the experience or reputation of a particular judge.

For instance, if the dispute involves a trade secret, a party might conclude that a federal court—which has exclusive jurisdiction over copyrights and patents—would have more expertise in the matter. In contrast, a plaintiff might choose to litigate in a state court if the court has a reputation for awarding substantial amounts of damages or if the judge is perceived as being pro-plaintiff. The concepts of exclusive and concurrent jurisdiction are illustrated in Exhibit 2–1.

**Jurisdiction in Cyberspace** The Internet's capacity to bypass political and geographic boundaries undercuts the traditional basis on which courts assert personal jurisdiction. As discussed, for a court to compel a defendant to come before it, the defendant must have a sufficient connection—that is, minimum contacts—with the state. When a defendant's only contacts with the state are through a Web site, however, it can be difficult to determine whether these contacts are sufficient for a court to exercise jurisdiction.

**The "Sliding-Scale" Standard.** The courts have developed a "sliding-scale" standard to determine when they can exercise personal jurisdiction over an out-of-state defendant based on the defendant's Web activities. The sliding-scale standard identifies three types of Internet business contacts and outlines the following rules for jurisdiction:

**1.** When the defendant conducts substantial business over the Internet (such as contracts and sales), jurisdiction is proper.

**2.** When there is some interactivity through a Web site, jurisdiction may be proper, depending on the

**EXHIBIT 2–1** Exclusive and Concurrent Jurisdiction

**Exclusive Federal Jurisdiction**
(cases involving federal crimes, federal antitrust law, bankruptcy, patents, copyrights, trademarks, suits against the United States, some areas of admiralty law, and certain other matters specified in federal statutes)

**Concurrent Jurisdiction**
(most cases involving federal questions, diversity-of-citizenship cases)

**Exclusive State Jurisdiction**
(cases involving all matters not subject to federal jurisdiction—for example, divorce and adoption cases)

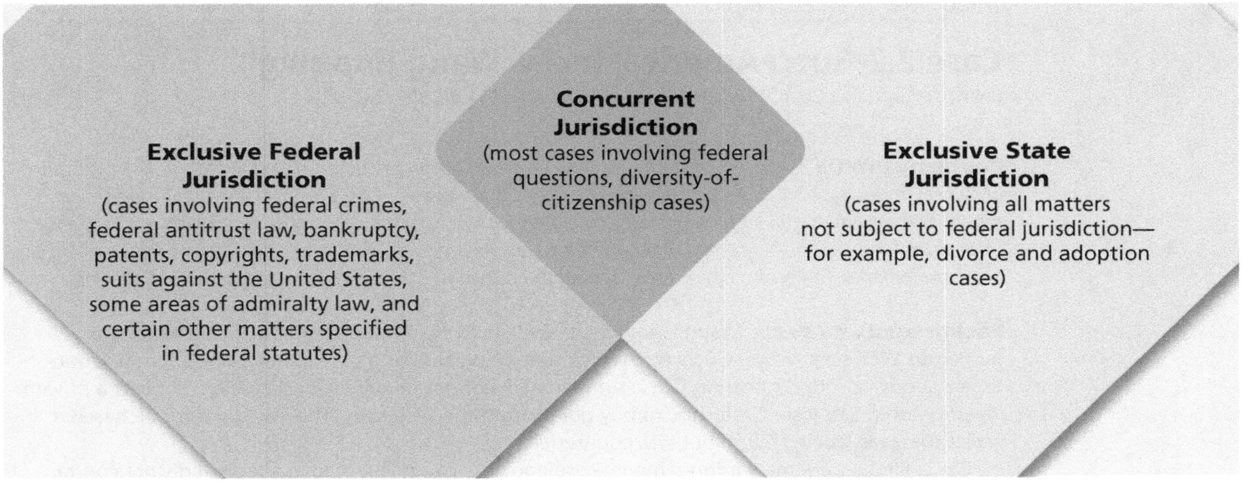

circumstances. Even a single contact can satisfy the minimum-contacts requirement in certain situations.

3. When a defendant merely engages in passive advertising on the Web, jurisdiction is never proper.[9] An Internet communication is typically considered passive if people have to voluntarily access it to read the message and active if it is sent to specific individuals.

■ **CASE IN POINT 2.5** Samantha Guffey lives in Oklahoma. She placed a winning bid on eBay for a used 2009 Volvo XC90 from Motorcars of Nashville, Inc. (MNI), a Tennessee corporation. Before she won the auction, she spoke with Otto Ostonakulov at the dealership. Later, Ostonakulov sent the necessary paperwork to Guffey in Oklahoma. She signed and returned it by mail, and he arranged for MNI to ship the Volvo to Oklahoma.

When the car was delivered to Guffey, she discovered it was not in the condition advertised. She filed a lawsuit in Oklahoma against MNI and Ostonakulov, alleging fraud and a violation of state consumer protection laws. Guffey's complaint alleged that the defendants were active "power sellers" on eBay, averaging twelve to twenty-five cars for sale every day. The sellers claimed that the Oklahoma court lacked jurisdiction over them, and a trial court dismissed the complaint. Guffey appealed. The reviewing court found that Oklahoma had jurisdiction because the sellers' "use of eBay to make multiple sales is systemic and appears to be a core part of their business." They had negotiated with Guffey directly to sell her a vehicle in Oklahoma and had regularly used eBay to sell vehicles to remote parties in the past.[10] ■

**International Jurisdictional Issues.** Because the Internet is international in scope, it obviously raises international jurisdictional issues. The world's courts seem to be developing a standard that echoes the requirement of minimum contacts applied by the U.S. courts.

Most courts are indicating that minimum contacts—doing business within the jurisdiction, for instance—are enough to compel a defendant to appear and that a physical presence in the country is not necessary. The effect of this standard is that a business firm has to comply with the laws in any jurisdiction in which it targets customers for its products. This situation is complicated by the fact that many countries' laws on particular issues—free speech, for instance—are very different from U.S. laws.

The following case illustrates how federal courts apply a sliding-scale standard to determine if they can exercise jurisdiction over a foreign defendant whose only contact with the United States is through a Web site.

---

9. For a leading case on this issue, see *Zippo Manufacturing Co. v. Zippo Dot Com, Inc.*, 952 F.Supp. 1119 (W.D.Pa. 1997).

10. *Guffey v. Ostonakulov*, 2014 OK 6, 321 P.3d 971 (Ok.Sup. 2014). Note that a single sale on eBay does not necessarily form the basis for jurisdiction. Jurisdiction depends on whether the seller regularly uses eBay as a means for doing business with remote buyers. See *Hinners v. Robey*, 336 S.W.3d 891 (Ky.Sup. 2008).

## Spotlight on Gucci

# Case 2.2 Gucci America, Inc. v. Wang Huoqing

United States District Court, Northern District of California, 2011 WL 30972 (2011).

**Company Profile** *Gucci America, Inc., a New York corporation headquartered in New York City, is part of Gucci Group, a global fashion firm with offices in China, France, Great Britain, Italy, and Japan. Gucci makes and sells high-quality luxury goods, including footwear, belts, sunglasses, handbags, wallets, jewelry, fragrances, and children's clothing. In connection with its products, Gucci uses twenty-one federally registered trademarks. Gucci also operates a number of boutiques, some of which are located in California.*

**Background and Facts** Wang Huoqing, a resident of the People's Republic of China, operates numerous Web sites. When Gucci discovered that Wang Huoqing's Web sites offered for sale counterfeit goods—products bearing Gucci's trademarks but not genuine Gucci articles—it hired a private investigator in San Jose, California, to buy goods from the Web sites. The investigator purchased a wallet that was labeled Gucci but was counterfeit.

Gucci filed a trademark infringement lawsuit against Wang Huoqing in a federal district court in California seeking damages and an injunction to prevent further infringement. Wang Huoqing was notified of the lawsuit via e-mail but did not appear in court. Gucci asked the court to enter a default judgment—that is, a judgment entered when the defendant fails to appear. First, however, the court had to determine whether it had personal jurisdiction over Wang Huoqing based on the Internet sales.

## In the Language of the Court

Joseph C. *SPERO*, United States Magistrate Judge.

\* \* \* \*

\* \* \* Under California's long-arm statute, federal courts in California may exercise jurisdiction to the extent permitted by the Due Process Clause of the Constitution. The Due Process Clause allows federal courts to exercise jurisdiction where \* \* \* the defendant has had sufficient minimum contacts with the forum to subject him or her to the specific jurisdiction of the court. The courts apply a three-part test to determine whether specific jurisdiction exists:

> (1) The nonresident defendant must do some act or consummate some transaction with the forum or perform some act by which he purposefully avails himself of the privilege of conducting activities in the forum, thereby invoking the benefits and protections of its laws; (2) the claim must be one which arises out of or results from the defendant's forum-related activities; and (3) exercise of jurisdiction must be reasonable.

\* \* \* \*

In order to satisfy the first prong of the test for specific jurisdiction, a defendant must have either purposefully availed itself of the privilege of conducting business activities within the forum or purposefully directed activities toward the forum. *Purposeful availment typically consists of action taking place in the forum that invokes the benefits and protections of the laws of the forum, such as executing or performing a contract within the forum.* To show purposeful availment, a plaintiff must show that the defendant "engage[d] in some form of affirmative conduct allowing or promoting the transaction of business within the forum state." [Emphasis added.]

"In the Internet context, the Ninth Circuit utilizes a sliding scale analysis under which 'passive' websites do not create sufficient contacts to establish purposeful availment, whereas interactive websites may create sufficient contacts, depending on how interactive the website is." \* \* \* *Personal jurisdiction is appropriate where an entity is conducting business over the Internet and has offered for sale and sold its products to forum [California] residents.* [Emphasis added.]

Here, the allegations and evidence presented by Plaintiffs in support of the Motion are sufficient to show purposeful availment on the part of Defendant Wang Huoqing. Plaintiffs have alleged that Defendant operates "fully interactive Internet websites operating under the Subject Domain Names" and have presented evidence in the form of copies of web pages showing that the websites are, in fact, interactive.

Case 2.2 Continued

*** Additionally, Plaintiffs allege Defendant is conducting counterfeiting and infringing activities within this Judicial District and has advertised and sold his counterfeit goods in the State of California. *** Plaintiffs have also presented evidence of one actual sale within this district, made by investigator Robert Holmes from the website bag2do.cn.*** Finally, Plaintiffs have presented evidence that Defendant Wang Huoqing owns or controls the twenty-eight websites listed in the Motion for Default Judgment. *** Such commercial activity in the forum amounts to purposeful availment of the privilege of conducting activities within the forum, thus invoking the benefits and protections of its laws. Accordingly, the Court concludes that Defendant's contacts with California are sufficient to show purposeful availment.

**Decision and Remedy** *The U.S. District Court for the Northern District of California held that it had personal jurisdiction over the foreign defendant, Wang Huoqing. The court entered a default judgment against Wang Huoqing and granted Gucci an injunction.*

**Critical Thinking**

- **What If the Facts Were Different?** *Suppose that Gucci had not presented evidence that Wang Huoqing had made one actual sale through his Web site to a resident of the court's district (the private investigator). Would the court still have found that it had personal jurisdiction over Wang Huoqing? Why or why not?*
- **Legal Environment** *Is it relevant to the analysis of jurisdiction that Gucci America's principal place of business is in New York rather than California? Explain.*

---

**Minimum Contacts and Smartphones.** The widespread use of cellular phones, particularly smartphones, also complicates the determination of personal jurisdiction. People use their smartphones while traveling to make purchases, negotiate business deals, enter contracts, and download applications (apps). If a person traveling in another state (or nation) uses a smartphone to form a contract, does that forum have jurisdiction over the person? Is the party that creates an app subject to jurisdiction anywhere the app is downloaded or used? Because an app differs from a Web page, what degree of interactivity is required for apps to confer jurisdiction in the sliding-scale analysis? The courts will be addressing these questions in coming years and adapting traditional notions of jurisdiction to ever-changing technology.

Concept Summary 2.1 reviews the various types of jurisdiction, including jurisdiction in cyberspace.

### 2–2b Venue

Jurisdiction has to do with whether a court has authority to hear a case involving specific persons, property, or subject matter. **Venue**[11] is concerned with the most appropriate location for a trial. For instance, two state courts (or two federal courts) may have the authority to exercise jurisdiction over a case. Nonetheless, it may be more appropriate or convenient to hear the case in one court than in the other.

The concept of venue reflects the policy that a court trying a case should be in the geographic neighborhood (usually the county) where the incident occurred or where the parties reside. Venue in a civil case typically is where the defendant resides or does business, whereas venue in a criminal case normally is where the crime occurred.

In some cases, pretrial publicity or other factors may require a change of venue to another community, especially in criminal cases in which the defendant's right to a fair and impartial jury has been impaired. Note, though, that venue has lost some significance in today's world because of the Internet and 24/7 news reporting. Courts now rarely grant requests for a change of venue. Because everyone has instant access to all information about a purported crime, courts reason that no community is more or less informed or prejudiced for or against a defendant.

### 2–2c Standing to Sue

Before a party can bring a lawsuit to court, that party must have **standing to sue,** or a sufficient stake in a matter to justify seeking relief through the court system. Standing means that the party that filed the action in court has a legally protected interest at stake in the litigation. At times, a person can have standing to sue on behalf of another person, such as a minor (child) or a mentally incompetent person.

---

11. Pronounced *ven-*yoo.

# Concept Summary 2.1

## Jurisdiction

**Personal**

Exists when a defendant:
- Is located in the court's territorial boundaries.
- Qualifies under state long arm statutes.
- Is a corporation doing business within the state.
- Advertises, sells, or places goods into commerce within the state.

**Property**

- Exists when the property that is subject to a lawsuit is located within the court's territorial boundaries.

**Subject Matter**

Limits the court's jurisdictional authority to particular types of cases.
- *General jurisdiction*—Exists when a court can hear cases involving a broad array of issues.
- *Limited jurisdiction*—Exists when a court is limited to a specific subject matter, such as probate or divorce.

**Original**

- Exists with courts that have the authority to hear a case for the first time (trial courts, district courts).

**Appellate**

- Exists with courts of appeal and review. Generally, appellate courts do not have original jurisdiction.

**Federal**

A federal court can exercise jurisdiction:
- When the plaintiff's cause of action involves a federal question (is based at least in part on the U.S. Constitution, a treaty, or a federal law).
- In cases between citizens of different states (or cases involving U.S. citizens and foreign countries or their citizens) when the amount in controversy exceeds $75,000 (diversity-of-citizenship jurisdiction).

**Concurrent**

- Exists when both federal and state courts have authority to hear the same case.

**Exclusive**

- Exists when only state courts or only federal courts have authority to hear a case.

**Cyberspace**

- The courts have developed a sliding-scale standard to use in determining when jurisdiction over a Web site owner or operator in another state is proper.

Standing can be broken down into three elements:

1. *Harm.* The party bringing the action must have suffered harm—an invasion of a legally protected interest—or must face imminent harm. The controversy must be real and substantial rather than hypothetical.
2. *Causation.* There must be a causal connection between the conduct complained of and the injury.
3. *Remedy.* It must be likely, as opposed to merely speculative, that a favorable court decision will remedy the injury suffered.

■ **CASE IN POINT 2.6** Harold Wagner obtained a loan through M.S.T. Mortgage Group to buy a house in Texas. After the sale, M.S.T. transferred its interest in the loan to another lender, which, in turn, assigned it to another lender (a common practice in the mortgage industry). Eventually, when Wagner failed to make the loan payments, CitiMortgage, Inc., notified him that it was going to foreclose on the property and sell the house.

Wagner filed a lawsuit, claiming that the lenders had improperly assigned the mortgage loan. In 2014, a federal district court ruled that Wagner lacked standing to contest the assignment. Under Texas law, only the parties directly involved in an assignment can challenge its validity. In this case, the assignment was between two lenders and did not directly involve Wagner.[12] ■

---

12. *Wagner v. CitiMortgage, Inc.*, 995 F.Supp.2d 621 (N.D.Tex. 2014).

# 2–3 The State and Federal Court Systems

Each state has its own court system. Additionally, there is a system of federal courts. The right-hand side of Exhibit 2–2 illustrates the basic organizational framework characteristic of the court systems in many states. The exhibit also shows how the federal court system is structured. We turn now to an examination of these court systems, beginning with the state courts.

## 2–3a The State Court Systems

No two state court systems are exactly the same. Typically, though, a state court system includes several levels, or tiers, of courts, as shown in Exhibit 2–2. State courts may include (1) trial courts of limited jurisdiction, (2) trial courts of general jurisdiction, (3) appellate courts (intermediate appellate courts), and (4) the state's highest court (often called the state supreme court).

Generally, any person who is a party to a lawsuit has the opportunity to plead the case before a trial court and then, if he or she loses, before at least one level of appellate court. If the case involves a federal statute or a federal constitutional issue, the decision of the state supreme court may be further appealed to the United States Supreme Court. Note that lawsuits can take years to resolve through the courts, especially since many states have experienced large cuts in court funding in recent years. In fact, the United States Supreme Court decided a

**EXHIBIT 2–2** The State and Federal Court Systems

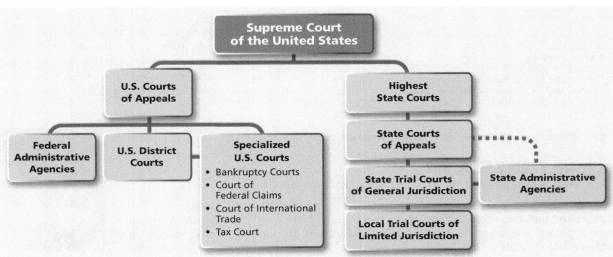

case in 2015 involving a trademark dispute that had been in the courts for more than sixteen years.[13]

The states use various methods to select judges for their courts. Usually, voters elect judges, but in some states judges are appointed. For instance, in Iowa, the governor appoints judges, and then the general population decides whether to confirm their appointment in the next general election. The states usually specify the number of years that judges will serve.

**Trial Courts** Trial courts are exactly what their name implies—courts in which trials are held and testimony is taken. State trial courts have either general or limited jurisdiction, as defined earlier.

**General Jurisdiction.** Trial courts that have general jurisdiction as to subject matter may be called county, district, superior, or circuit courts.[14] State trial courts of general jurisdiction have jurisdiction over a wide variety of subjects, including both civil disputes and criminal prosecutions. In some states, trial courts of general jurisdiction may hear appeals from courts of limited jurisdiction.

**Limited Jurisdiction.** Courts of limited jurisdiction as to subject matter are generally inferior trial courts or minor judiciary courts. Limited jurisdiction courts might include local municipal courts (which could include separate traffic courts and drug courts) and domestic relations courts (which handle divorce and child-custody disputes).

**Small claims courts** are inferior trial courts that hear only civil cases involving claims of less than a certain amount, such as $5,000 (the amount varies from state to state). Procedures in small claims courts are generally informal, and lawyers are not required (in a few states, lawyers are not even allowed). Decisions of small claims

---

13. *B&B Hardware, Inc. v. Hargis Industries, Inc.,* ___ U.S. ___, 135 S.Ct. 1293, 191 L.Ed.2d 222 (2015).
14. The name in Ohio and Pennsylvania is Court of Common Pleas. The name in New York is Supreme Court, Trial Division.

courts and municipal courts may sometimes be appealed to a state trial court of general jurisdiction.

A few states have also established Islamic law courts, which are courts of limited jurisdiction that serve the American Muslim community. These courts decide cases with reference to the *sharia,* a system of law used in most Islamic countries that is derived from the Qur'an and the sayings and doings of Muhammad and his followers.

**Appellate, or Reviewing, Courts** Every state has at least one court of appeals (appellate court, or reviewing court), which may be an intermediate appellate court or the state's highest court. About three-fourths of the states have intermediate appellate courts.

Generally, courts of appeals do not conduct new trials, in which evidence is submitted to the court and witnesses are examined. Rather, an appellate court panel of three or more judges reviews the record of the case on appeal, which includes a transcript of the trial proceedings. The appellate court hears arguments from attorneys and determines whether the trial court committed an error.

Reviewing courts focus on questions of law, not questions of fact. A **question of fact** deals with what really happened in regard to the dispute being tried—such as whether a party actually burned a flag. A **question of law** concerns the application or interpretation of the law—such as whether flag-burning is a form of speech protected by the First Amendment to the U.S. Constitution. Only a judge, not a jury, can rule on questions of law.

Appellate courts normally defer (give significant weight) to the trial court's findings on questions of fact because the trial court judge and jury were in a better position to evaluate testimony. The trial court judge and jury can directly observe witnesses' gestures, demeanor, and other nonverbal behavior during the trial. An appellate court cannot.

In the following case, neither the administrative agency that initially ruled on the dispute nor the trial court to which the agency's decision was appealed made a finding on a crucial question of fact. Faced with that circumstance, what should a state appellate court do?

---

**Case 2.3**

## Johnson v. Oxy USA, Inc.

Court of Appeals of Texas, Houston—14th District, __ S.W.3d __ , 2016 WL 93559 (2016).

**Background and Facts** Jennifer Johnson was working as a finance analyst for Oxy USA, Inc., when Oxy changed the job's requirements. To meet the new standards, Johnson took courses to become a certified public accountant. Oxy's "Educational Assistance Policy" was to reimburse employees for the

Case 2.3 Continued

cost of such courses. Johnson further agreed that Oxy could withhold the reimbursed amount from her final paycheck if she quit Oxy within a year. When she resigned less than a year later, Oxy withheld that amount from her last check. Johnson filed a claim for the amount with the Texas Workforce Commission (TWC). The TWC ruled that she was not entitled to the unpaid wages. She filed a suit in a Texas state court against Oxy, alleging breach of contract. The court affirmed the TWC's ruling. Johnson appealed.

## In the Language of the Court

Ken *WISE*, Justice

\* \* \* \*

\* \* \* The trial court \* \* \* held that Johnson's [claim for breach of contract was] barred by *res judicata* ["a matter judged"]. In a court of law, a claimant typically cannot pursue one remedy to an unfavorable outcome and then seek the same remedy in another proceeding before the same or a different tribunal. Res judicata *bars the relitigation of claims that have been finally adjudicated or that could have been litigated in the prior action.* [Emphasis added.]

Johnson argues that *res judicata* does not apply here because the TWC did not render a final judgment on the merits of her claim that Oxy misinterpreted its Educational Assistance Policy. Specifically, Johnson claims she was "denied the right of full adjudication of her claim because the TWC refused to consider her arguments at the administrative level as beyond its jurisdiction." To support this contention, Johnson points to the following excerpt from the \* \* \* decision:

> \* \* \* The TWC does not interpret contracts between employers and employee but only enforces the Texas Payday Law [the Texas state law that governs the timing of employees' paychecks]. \* \* \* The question of whether the employer properly interpreted their policy on reimbursed educational expenses versus a business expense is a question for a different forum.

According to Johnson, this language shows that the TWC refused to consider the merits of the issue she raised as "beyond its reach." In contrast, the defendants contend that Johnson's claims are barred by *res judicata* because they are based on claims previously decided by the TWC.

\* \* \* \*

*In Johnson's case, however, the TWC did not decide the key question of fact in dispute—whether Oxy violated its own Educational Assistance Policy when it withheld Johnson's final wages as reimbursement for the CPA courses.* In fact, the TWC explicitly refused to do so, stating that the agency "does not interpret contracts between employers and employee." \* \* \* Because this question goes to the heart of Johnson's breach of contract \* \* \* claim, we hold that *res judicata* does not bar [that] claim. [Emphasis added.]

The defendants argue that because Johnson seeks to recover the same wages in this suit as she did in her claim with the TWC, *res judicata* must bar her common law cause of action. However, \* \* \* *res judicata* would only bar a claim if TWC's order is considered final. \* \* \* Here, the order in Johnson's case made no such findings with regard to the Educational Assistance Policy. The order expressly declined to address that issue. Therefore, \* \* \* *res judicata* will not bar Johnson's breach of contract \* \* \* claim.

**Decision and Remedy** *A state intermediate appellate court reversed the lower court's decision. "The TWC did not decide the key question of fact in dispute—whether Oxy violated its own Educational Assistance Policy when it withheld Johnson's final wages. In fact, the TWC explicitly refused to do so, stating that the agency 'does not interpret contracts between employers and employee.'" The appellate court remanded the case for a trial on the merits.*

**Critical Thinking**
- **Legal Environment** *Who can decide questions of fact? Who can rule on questions of law? Why?*
- **Global** *In some cases, a court may be asked to determine and interpret the law of a foreign country. Some states consider the issue of what the law of a foreign country requires to be a question of fact. Federal rules of procedure provide that this issue is a question of law. Which position seems more appropriate? Why?*

**Highest State Courts** The highest appellate court in a state is usually called the supreme court but may be designated by some other name. For instance, in both New York and Maryland, the highest state court is called the Court of Appeals. The highest state court in Maine and Massachusetts is the Supreme Judicial Court. In West Virginia, it is the Supreme Court of Appeals.

The decisions of each state's highest court on all questions of state law are final. Only when issues of federal law are involved can the United States Supreme Court overrule a decision made by a state's highest court. ■ **EXAMPLE 2.7** A city enacts an ordinance that prohibits citizens from engaging in door-to-door advocacy without first registering with the mayor's office and receiving a permit. A religious group then sues the city, arguing that the law violates the freedoms of speech and religion guaranteed by the First Amendment. If the state supreme court upholds the law, the group could appeal the decision to the United States Supreme Court, because a constitutional (federal) issue is involved. ■

## 2–3b The Federal Court System

The federal court system is basically a three-tiered model consisting of (1) U.S. district courts (trial courts of general jurisdiction) and various courts of limited

---

### MANAGERIAL STRATEGY

### Should You Consent to Have Your Business Case Decided by a U.S. Magistrate Judge?

You have a strong case in a contract dispute with one of your business's suppliers. The supplier is located in another state. Your attorney did everything necessary to obtain your "day in court." The court in question is a federal district court. But you have just found out that your case may not be heard for several years—or even longer. Your attorney tells you that the case can be heard in just a few months if you consent to place it in the hands of a U.S. magistrate judge.[a] Should you consent?

#### A Short History of U.S. Magistrate Judges

Congress authorized the creation of a new federal judicial officer, the U.S. magistrate, in 1968 to help reduce delays in the U.S. district courts.[b] These junior federal officers were to conduct a wide range of judicial proceedings as set out by statute and as assigned by the district judges under whom they served. In 1979, Congress gave U.S. magistrates consent jurisdiction, which authorized them to conduct all civil trials as long as the parties consent.[c] Currently, magistrate judges dispose of over one million civil and criminal district court matters, which include motions and hearings.

#### The Selection and Quality of Magistrate Judges

As mentioned, federal district judges are nominated by the president, confirmed by the Senate, and appointed for life. In contrast, U.S. magistrate judges are selected by federal district court judges based on the recommendations of a merit screening committee. They serve an eight-year term (which can be renewed).

By statute, magistrate judges must be chosen through a merit selection process. Applicants are interviewed by a screening committee of lawyers and others from the district in which the position will be filled.[d] Political party affiliation plays no part in the process.

A variety of experienced attorneys, administrative law judges, state court judges, and others apply for magistrate judge positions. A typical opening receives about a hundred applicants. The merit selection panel selects the five most qualified, who are then voted on by federal district court judges.

Because the selection process for a magistrate judge is not the same as for a district judge, some critics have expressed concerns about the quality of magistrate judges. Some groups, such as People for the American Way, are not in favor of allowing magistrate judges the power to decide cases. These critics believe that because of their limited terms, they are not completely immune from outside pressure.

#### Business Questions

1. *If you were facing an especially complex legal dispute—one involving many facets and several different types of law—would you consent to allowing a U.S. magistrate judge to decide the case? Why or why not?*

2. *If you had to decide whether to allow a U.S. magistrate judge to hear your case, what information might you ask your attorney to provide concerning that individual?*

a. 28 U.S.C. Sec 636(c); *Roell v. Withrow*, 538 U.S. 580, 123 S.Ct. 1698, 155 L.Ed.2d 775 (2003).
b. Federal Magistrates Act, 82 Stat. 1107, October 17, 1968.
c. U.S.C. Section 636(c)(1).

d. 28 U.S.C. Section 631(b)(5).

jurisdiction, (2) U.S. courts of appeals (intermediate courts of appeals), and (3) the United States Supreme Court.

Unlike state court judges, who are usually elected, federal court judges—including the justices of the Supreme Court—are appointed by the president of the United States, subject to confirmation by the U.S. Senate. Federal judges receive lifetime appointments under Article III of the U.S. Constitution, which states that federal judges "hold their offices during good Behaviour." In the entire history of the United States, only seven federal judges have been removed from office through impeachment proceedings.

Certain federal court officers are not chosen in the way just described. This chapter's *Managerial Strategy* feature describes how U.S. magistrate judges are selected.

**U.S. District Courts** At the federal level, the equivalent of a state trial court of general jurisdiction is the district court. U.S. district courts have original jurisdiction in matters involving a federal question and concurrent jurisdiction with state courts when diversity jurisdiction exists. Federal cases typically originate in district courts. There are other federal courts with original, but special (or limited), jurisdiction, such as the federal bankruptcy courts and tax courts.

Every state has at least one federal district court. The number of judicial districts can vary over time, primarily owing to population changes and corresponding changes in caseloads. Today, there are ninety-four federal judicial districts. Exhibit 2–3 shows the boundaries of both the U.S. district courts and the U.S. courts of appeals.

**U.S. Courts of Appeals** In the federal court system, there are thirteen U.S. courts of appeals—referred to as U.S. circuit courts of appeals. Twelve of these courts (including the Court of Appeals for the D.C. Circuit) hear appeals from the federal district courts located within their respective judicial circuits (shown in Exhibit 2–3).[15]

---

15. Historically, judges were required to "ride the circuit" and hear appeals in different courts around the country, which is how the name "circuit court" came about.

**EXHIBIT 2–3** Geographic Boundaries of the U.S. Courts of Appeals and U.S. District Courts

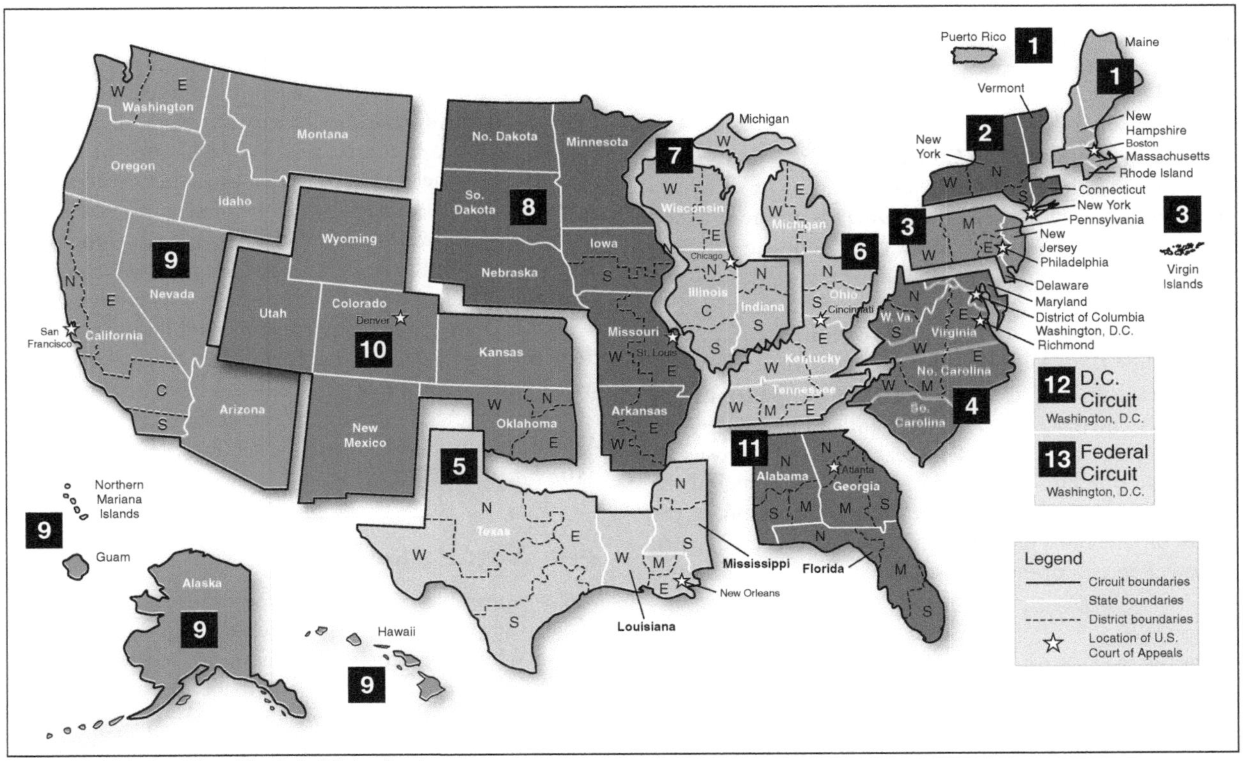

Source: Administrative Office of the United States Courts.

The Court of Appeals for the Thirteenth Circuit, called the Federal Circuit, has national appellate jurisdiction over certain types of cases, including those involving patent law and those in which the U.S. government is a defendant.

The decisions of a circuit court of appeals are binding on all courts within the circuit court's jurisdiction. These decisions are final in most cases, but appeal to the United States Supreme Court is possible.

**The United States Supreme Court** The highest level of the three-tiered federal court system is the United States Supreme Court. According to the U.S. Constitution, there is only one national Supreme Court. All other courts in the federal system are considered "inferior." Congress is empowered to create inferior courts as it deems necessary. The inferior courts that Congress has created include the second tier in our model—the U.S. circuit courts of appeals—as well as the district courts and the various federal courts of limited, or specialized, jurisdiction.

The United States Supreme Court consists of nine justices. Although the Supreme Court has original, or trial, jurisdiction in rare instances (set forth in Article III, Sections 1 and 2), most of its work is as an appeals court. The Supreme Court can review any case decided by any of the federal courts of appeals. It also has appellate authority over cases involving federal questions that have been decided in the state courts. The Supreme Court is the final authority on the Constitution and federal law.

**Appeals to the Supreme Court.** To bring a case before the Supreme Court, a party requests the Court to issue a writ of *certiorari*.[16] A **writ of *certiorari*** is an order issued by the Supreme Court to a lower court requiring the latter to send it the record of the case for review. The Court will not issue a writ unless at least four of the nine justices approve of it. This is called the **rule of four.**

Whether the Court will issue a writ of *certiorari* is entirely within its discretion, and most petitions for writs are denied. (Although thousands of cases are filed with the Supreme Court each year, it hears, on average, fewer than one hundred of these cases.)[17] A denial of the request to issue a writ of *certiorari* is not a decision on the merits of the case, nor does it indicate agreement with the lower court's opinion. Also, denial of the writ has no

value as a precedent. Denial simply means that the lower court's decision remains the law in that jurisdiction.

**Petitions Granted by the Court.** Typically, the Court grants petitions when cases raise important constitutional questions or when the lower courts have issued conflicting decisions on a significant issue. The justices, however, never explain their reasons for hearing certain cases and not others, so it is difficult to predict which type of case the Court might select.

Concept Summary 2.2 reviews the courts in the federal and state court systems.

# 2–4 Alternative Dispute Resolution

**Litigation**—the process of resolving a dispute through the court system—is expensive and time consuming. Litigating even the simplest complaint is costly, and because of the backlog of cases pending in many courts, several years may pass before a case is actually tried. For these and other reasons, more and more businesspersons are turning to **alternative dispute resolution (ADR)** as a means of settling their disputes.

The great advantage of ADR is its flexibility. Methods of ADR range from the parties sitting down together and attempting to work out their differences to multinational corporations agreeing to resolve a dispute through a formal hearing before a panel of experts. Normally, the parties themselves can control how they will attempt to settle their dispute. They can decide what procedures will be used, whether a neutral third party will be present or make a decision, and whether that decision will be legally binding or nonbinding. ADR also offers more privacy than court proceedings and allows disputes to be resolved relatively quickly.

Today, more than 90 percent of civil lawsuits are settled before trial using some form of ADR. Indeed, most states either require or encourage parties to undertake ADR prior to trial. Many federal courts have instituted ADR programs as well. In this section, we examine the basic forms of ADR.

## 2–4a Negotiation

The simplest form of ADR is **negotiation,** a process in which the parties attempt to settle their dispute informally, with or without attorneys to represent them. Attorneys frequently advise their clients to negotiate a settlement voluntarily before they proceed to trial. Parties may even try to negotiate a settlement during a trial or after the trial but before an appeal.

---

**16.** Pronounced sur-shee-uh-*rah*-ree.
**17.** From the mid-1950s through the early 1990s, the Supreme Court reviewed more cases per year than it has since then. In the Court's 1982–1983 term, for example, the Court issued written opinions in 151 cases. In contrast, during the Court's 2015–2016 term, the Court issued written opinions in only 81 cases.

## Concept Summary 2.2

### Types of Courts

| Trial Courts | Trial courts are courts of original jurisdiction in which actions are initiated. <br> • *State courts* —Courts of general jurisdiction can hear any case that has not been specifically designated for another court. Courts of limited jurisdiction include, among others, domestic relations courts, probate courts, municipal courts, and small claims courts. <br> • *Federal courts* —The federal district court is the equivalent of the state trial court. Federal courts of limited jurisdiction include the bankruptcy courts and others shown in Exhibit 2–2. |
|---|---|
| **Intermediate Appellate Courts** | Courts of appeals are reviewing courts. Generally, appellate courts do not have original jurisdiction. <br> • About three-fourths of the states have intermediate appellate courts. <br> • In the federal court system, the U.S. circuit courts of appeals are the intermediate appellate courts. |
| **Supreme Courts** | The highest state court is that state's supreme court, although it may be called by some other name. <br> • Appeal from state supreme courts to the United States Supreme Court is possible only if a federal question is involved. <br> • The United States Supreme Court is the highest court in the federal court system and the final authority on the Constitution and federal law. |

Negotiation traditionally involves just the parties themselves and (typically) their attorneys. The attorneys, though, are advocates—they are obligated to put their clients' interests first.

### 2–4b Mediation

In **mediation,** a neutral third party acts as a mediator and works with both sides in the dispute to facilitate a resolution. The mediator, who need not be a lawyer, usually charges a fee for his or her services (which can be split between the parties). States that require parties to undergo ADR before trial often offer mediation as one of the ADR options or (as in Florida) the only option.

During mediation, the mediator normally talks with the parties separately as well as jointly, emphasizes their points of agreement, and helps them to evaluate their options. Although the mediator may propose a solution (called a mediator's proposal), he or she does not make a decision resolving the matter.

One of the biggest advantages of mediation is that it is less adversarial than litigation. In mediation, the mediator takes an active role and attempts to bring the parties together so that they can come to a mutually satisfactory resolution. The mediation process tends to reduce the antagonism between the disputants, allowing them to resume their former relationship while minimizing hostility. For this reason, mediation is often the preferred form of ADR for disputes between business partners, employers and employees, or other parties involved in long-term relationships.

### 2–4c Arbitration

A more formal method of ADR is **arbitration,** in which an arbitrator (a neutral third party or a panel of experts) hears a dispute and imposes a resolution on the parties. Arbitration differs from other forms of ADR in that the third party hearing the dispute makes a decision for the parties. Exhibit 2–4 outlines the basic differences among the three traditional forms of ADR.

Usually, the parties in arbitration agree that the third party's decision will be *legally binding*, although the parties can also agree to *nonbinding* arbitration. In nonbinding arbitration, the parties can go forward with a lawsuit if they do not agree with the arbitrator's decision. Arbitration that is mandated by the courts often is not binding on the parties.

In some respects, formal arbitration resembles a trial, although usually the procedural rules are much less restrictive than those governing litigation. In a typical arbitration, the parties present opening arguments and ask for specific remedies. Both sides present evidence and may call and examine witnesses. The arbitrator then renders a decision.

**The Arbitrator's Decision** The arbitrator's decision is called an **award.** It is usually the final word on the matter. Although the parties may appeal an arbitrator's decision, a court's review of the decision will be much more restricted in scope than an appellate court's review of a trial court's decision. The general view is that because the parties were free to frame the issues and set the powers of the arbitrator at the outset, they cannot complain about the results. A court will set aside an award only in the event of one of the following:

1. The arbitrator's conduct or "bad faith" substantially prejudiced the rights of one of the parties.
2. The award violates an established public policy.
3. The arbitrator exceeded her or his powers—that is, arbitrated issues that the parties did not agree to submit to arbitration.

**Arbitration Clauses** Almost any commercial matter can be submitted to arbitration. Frequently, parties include an **arbitration clause** in a contract specifying that any dispute arising under the contract will be resolved through arbitration rather than through the court system. Parties can also agree to arbitrate a dispute *after* it arises.

**Arbitration Statutes** Most states have statutes (often based, in part, on the Uniform Arbitration Act) under which arbitration clauses will be enforced. Some state statutes compel arbitration of certain types of disputes, such as those involving public employees.

At the federal level, the Federal Arbitration Act (FAA), enacted in 1925, enforces arbitration clauses in contracts involving maritime activity and interstate commerce. As you will see in later chapters, the courts have defined *interstate commerce* broadly, and so arbitration

**EXHIBIT 2–4  Basic Differences in the Traditional Forms of ADR**

| | Type of ADR | | |
|---|---|---|---|
| | **Negotiation** | **Mediation** | **Arbitration** |
| **Description** | Parties meet informally with or without their attorneys and attempt to agree on a resolution. This is the simplest and least expensive method of ADR. | A neutral third party meets with the parties and emphasizes points of agreement to bring them toward resolution of their dispute, reducing hostility between the parties. | The parties present their arguments and evidence before an arbitrator at a formal hearing. The arbitrator renders a decision to resolve the parties' dispute. |
| **Neutral Third Party Present?** | No | Yes | Yes |
| **Who Decides the Resolution?** | The parties themselves reach a resolution. | The parties, but the mediator may suggest or propose a resolution. | The arbitrator imposes a resolution on the parties that may be either binding or nonbinding. |

agreements involving transactions only slightly connected to the flow of interstate commerce may fall under the FAA. The FAA established a national policy favoring arbitration that the United States Supreme Court has continued to reinforce.[18]

**CASE IN POINT 2.8** Cleveland Construction, Inc. (CCI), was the general contractor on a project to build a grocery store in Houston, Texas. CCI hired Levco Construction, Inc., as a subcontractor. Their contract included an arbitration provision stating that any disputes would be resolved by arbitration in Ohio. When a dispute arose between the parties, Levco filed a suit against CCI in a Texas state court. CCI sought to compel arbitration in Ohio under the Federal Arbitration Act (FAA), but a Texas statute allows a party to void a contractual provision that requires arbitration outside Texas. Ultimately, a Texas appellate court held that the FAA preempted (took priority over) the state law. CCI could compel arbitration in Ohio.[19]

**The Issue of Arbitrability** The terms of an arbitration agreement can limit the types of disputes that the parties agree to arbitrate. Disputes can arise, however, when the parties do not specify limits or when the parties disagree on whether a particular matter is covered by their arbitration agreement.

When one party files a lawsuit to compel arbitration, it is up to the court to resolve the issue of *arbitrability*. That is, the court must decide whether the matter is one that must be resolved through arbitration. If the court finds that the subject matter in controversy is covered by the agreement to arbitrate, then it may compel arbitration.

Usually, a court will allow a claim to be arbitrated if the court finds that the relevant statute (the state arbitration statute or the FAA) does not exclude such claims. No party, however, will be ordered to submit a particular dispute to arbitration unless the court is convinced that the party has consented to do so. Additionally, the courts will not compel arbitration if it is clear that the arbitration rules and procedures are inherently unfair to one of the parties.

**Mandatory Arbitration in the Employment Context** A significant question for businesspersons has concerned mandatory arbitration clauses in employment contracts. Many employees claim they are at a disadvantage when they are forced, as a condition of being hired,

to agree to arbitrate all disputes and thus waive their rights under statutes designed to protect employees.

The United States Supreme Court, however, has held that mandatory arbitration clauses in employment contracts are generally enforceable. **CASE IN POINT 2.9** In a landmark decision, *Gilmer v. Interstate Johnson Lane Corp.*,[20] the Supreme Court held that a claim brought under a federal statute prohibiting age discrimination could be subject to arbitration. The Court concluded that the employee had waived his right to sue when he agreed, as part of a required application to be a securities representative, to arbitrate "any dispute, claim, or controversy" relating to his employment.

Since the *Gilmer* decision, some courts have refused to enforce one-sided arbitration clauses.[21] Nevertheless, the policy favoring enforcement of mandatory arbitration agreements in employment contracts remains strong.

**CASE IN POINT 2.10** Stephanie Cruise was hired by Kroger Co. to work in its deli. Her job application had included a clause requiring arbitration of "employment-related disputes." When Cruise was fired four years later, she filed a lawsuit claiming that Kroger had violated a number of laws prohibiting employment discrimination. Kroger filed a motion to compel arbitration. A state appellate court concluded that the arbitration clause in the employment application established that the parties had agreed to arbitrate their "employment-related disputes." Cruise's claims fell within the meaning of that agreement, and therefore she was required to arbitrate.[22]

## 2–4d Other Types of ADR

The three forms of ADR just discussed are the oldest and traditionally the most commonly used forms. In addition, a variety of newer types of ADR have emerged, including those described here.

1. In **early neutral case evaluation,** the parties select a neutral third party (generally an expert in the subject matter of the dispute) and explain their respective positions to that person. The case evaluator assesses the strengths and weaknesses of each party's claims.
2. In a **mini-trial,** each party's attorney briefly argues the party's case before the other party and a panel of representatives from each side who have the authority to settle the dispute. Typically, a neutral third party (usually an expert in the area being disputed) acts as

18. See, for example, *AT&T Mobility LLC v. Concepcion*, 563 U.S. 333, 131 S.Ct. 1740, 179 L.Ed.2d 742 (2011).
19. *Cleveland Construction, Inc. v. Levco Construction, Inc.*, 359 S.W.3d 843 (Tex.App. 2012).
20. 500 U.S. 20, 111 S.Ct. 1647, 114 L.Ed.2d 26 (1991).
21. See, for example, *Mohamed v. Uber Technologies, Inc.*, 2015 WL 3749716 (N.D.Cal. 2015); *Macias v. Excel Building Services, LLC*, 767 F.Supp.2d 1002 (N.D.Cal. 2011).
22. *Cruise v. Kroger Co.*, 233 Cal.App.4th 390, 183 Cal.Rptr.3d 17 (2015).

an adviser. If the parties fail to reach an agreement, the adviser renders an opinion as to how a court would likely decide the issue.

3. Numerous federal courts hold **summary jury trials,** in which the parties present their arguments and evidence and the jury renders a verdict. The jury's verdict is not binding, but it does act as a guide to both sides in reaching an agreement during the mandatory negotiations that immediately follow the trial.

4. Other alternatives being employed by the courts include summary proceedings, which dispense with some formal court procedures, and the appointment of special masters to assist judges in deciding complex issues.

### 2–4e Providers of ADR Services

ADR services are provided by both government agencies and private organizations. A major provider of ADR services is the American Arbitration Association (AAA), which handles more than 200,000 claims a year in its numerous offices worldwide. Most of the largest U.S. law firms are members of this nonprofit association.

Cases brought before the AAA are heard by an expert or a panel of experts in the area relating to the dispute and are usually settled quickly. Generally, about half of the panel members are lawyers. To cover its costs, the AAA charges a fee, paid by the party filing the claim. In addition, each party to the dispute pays a specified amount for each hearing day, as well as a special additional fee in cases involving personal injuries or property loss.

Hundreds of for-profit firms around the country also provide dispute-resolution services. Typically, these firms hire retired judges to conduct arbitration hearings or otherwise assist parties in settling their disputes. The judges follow procedures similar to those of the federal courts and use similar rules. Usually, each party to the dispute pays a filing fee and a designated fee for a hearing session or conference.

### 2–4f Online Dispute Resolution

An increasing number of companies and organizations are offering dispute-resolution services using the Internet. The settlement of disputes in these forums is known as **online dispute resolution (ODR).** The disputes resolved have most commonly involved rights to domain names (Web site addresses) or the quality of goods sold via the Internet, including goods sold through Internet auction sites.

Rules being developed in online forums may ultimately become a code of conduct for everyone who does business in cyberspace. Most online forums do not automatically apply the law of any specific jurisdiction. Instead, results are often based on general, universal legal principles. As with most offline methods of dispute resolution, any party may appeal to a court at any time.

ODR may be best for resolving small- to medium-sized business liability claims, which may not be worth the expense of litigation or traditional ADR methods. In addition, some cities use ODR as a means of resolving claims against them. ■ **EXAMPLE 2.11** New York City uses Cybersettle.com to resolve auto accident, sidewalk, and other personal-injury claims made against the city. Parties with complaints submit their demands, and the city submits its offers confidentially online. If an offer exceeds a demand, the claimant keeps half the difference as a bonus, plus the original claim. ■

## 2–5 International Dispute Resolution

Businesspersons who engage in international business transactions normally take special precautions to protect themselves in the event that a party with whom they are dealing in another country breaches an agreement. Often, parties to international contracts include special clauses in their contracts providing for how disputes arising under the contracts will be resolved. Sometimes, international treaties (formal agreements among several nations) even require parties to arbitrate any disputes.

### 2–5a Forum-Selection and Choice-of-Law Clauses

Parties to international transactions often include forum-selection and choice-of-law clauses in their contracts. These clauses designate the jurisdiction (court or country) where any dispute arising under the contract will be litigated and which nation's law will be applied.

When an international contract does not include such clauses, any legal proceedings arising under the contract will be more complex and attended by much more uncertainty. For instance, litigation may take place in two or more countries, with each country applying its own national law to the particular transactions.

Furthermore, even if a plaintiff wins a favorable judgment in a lawsuit litigated in the plaintiff's country, the defendant's country could refuse to enforce the court's judgment. The judgment may be enforced in the defendant's country for reasons of courtesy. The United States, for instance, will generally enforce a foreign court's decision if it is consistent with U.S. national law and policy. Other nations, however, may not be as accommodating as the United States, and the plaintiff may be left empty-handed.

### 2–5b Arbitration Clauses

International contracts also often include arbitration clauses that require a neutral third party to decide any contract disputes. Many of the institutions that offer arbitration, such as the International Chamber of Commerce or the Hong Kong International Arbitration Centre, have formulated model clauses for parties to use. In international arbitration proceedings, the third party may be a neutral entity, a panel of individuals representing both parties' interests, or some other group or organization.

The United Nations Convention on the Recognition and Enforcement of Foreign Arbitral Awards[23] has been implemented in more than 145 countries, including the United States. This convention assists in the enforcement of arbitration clauses, as do provisions in specific treaties among nations. The American Arbitration Association provides arbitration services for international as well as domestic disputes.

---

23. June 10, 1958, 21 U.S.T. 2517, T.I.A.S. No. 6997 (the "New York Convention").

## Reviewing: Courts and Alternative Dispute Resolution

Stan Garner resides in Illinois and promotes boxing matches for SuperSports, Inc., an Illinois corporation. Garner created the concept of "Ages" promotion—a three-fight series of boxing matches pitting an older fighter (George Foreman) against a younger fighter. The concept had titles for each of the three fights, including "Battle of the Ages." Garner contacted Foreman and his manager, who both reside in Texas, to sell the idea, and they arranged a meeting in Las Vegas, Nevada. During negotiations, Foreman's manager signed a nondisclosure agreement prohibiting him from disclosing Garner's promotional concepts unless the parties signed a contract. Nevertheless, after negotiations fell through, Foreman used Garner's "Battle of the Ages" concept to promote a subsequent fight. Garner filed a suit against Foreman and his manager in a federal district court located in Illinois, alleging breach of contract. Using the information presented in the chapter, answer the following questions.

1. On what basis might the federal district court in Illinois exercise jurisdiction in this case?
2. Does the federal district court have original or appellate jurisdiction?
3. Suppose that Garner had filed his action in an Illinois state court. Could an Illinois state court have exercised personal jurisdiction over Foreman or his manager? Why or why not?
4. Now suppose that Garner had filed his action in a Nevada state court. Would that court have had personal jurisdiction over Foreman or his manager? Explain.

**Debate This ...** *In this age of the Internet, when people communicate via e-mail, texts, tweets, Facebook, and Skype, is the concept of jurisdiction losing its meaning?*

## Terms and Concepts

alternative dispute resolution (ADR) 40
arbitration 41
arbitration clause 42
award 42
bankruptcy court 28
concurrent jurisdiction 30
diversity of citizenship 28
early neutral case evaluation 43
exclusive jurisdiction 30

federal question 28
*in personam* jurisdiction 27
*in rem* jurisdiction 27
judicial review 26
jurisdiction 27
litigation 40
long arm statute 27
mediation 41
mini-trial 43
negotiation 40

online dispute resolution (ODR) 44
probate court 28
question of fact 36
question of law 36
rule of four 40
small claims court 36
standing to sue 33
summary jury trial 44
venue 33
writ of *certiorari* 40

# Issue Spotters

1. Sue uses her smartphone to purchase a video security system for her architectural firm from Tipton, Inc., a company located in a different state. The system arrives a month after the projected delivery date, is of poor quality, and does not function as advertised. Sue files a suit against Tipton in a state court. Does the court in Sue's state have jurisdiction over Tipton? What factors will the court consider in determining jurisdiction? (See *Basic Judicial Requirements*.)

2. The state in which Sue resides requires that her dispute with Tipton be submitted to mediation or nonbinding arbitration. If the dispute is not resolved, or if either party disagrees with the decision of the mediator or arbitrator, will a court hear the case? Explain. (See *Alternative Dispute Resolution*.)

• **Check your answers to the Issue Spotters against the answers provided in Appendix D at the end of this text.**

# Business Scenarios

**2–1. Standing.** Jack and Maggie Turton bought a house in Jefferson County, Idaho, located directly across the street from a gravel pit. A few years later, the county converted the pit to a landfill. The landfill accepted many kinds of trash that cause harm to the environment, including major appliances, animal carcasses, containers with hazardous content warnings, leaking car batteries, and waste oil. The Turtons complained to the county, but the county did nothing. The Turtons then filed a lawsuit against the county alleging violations of federal environmental laws pertaining to groundwater contamination and other pollution. Do the Turtons have standing to sue? Why or why not? (See *Basic Judicial Requirements*.)

# Business Case Problems

**2–2. Venue.** Brandy Austin used powdered infant formula manufactured by Nestlé USA, Inc., to feed her infant daughter. Austin claimed that a can of the formula was contaminated with *Enterobacter sakazakii* bacteria, causing severe injury to the infant. The bacteria can cause infections of the bloodstream and central nervous system—in particular, meningitis (inflammation of the tissue surrounding the brain or spinal cord). Austin filed an action against Nestlé in Hennepin County District Court in Minnesota. Nestlé argued for a change of venue because the alleged harm had occurred in South Carolina. Austin is a South Carolina resident and had given birth to her daughter in that state. Should the case be transferred to a South Carolina venue? Why or why not? [*Austin v. Nestlé USA, Inc.*, 677 F.Supp.2d 1134 (D.Minn. 2009)] (See *Basic Judicial Requirements*.)

**2–3. Arbitration.** PRM Energy Systems owned patents licensed to Primenergy to use in the United States. Their contract stated that "all disputes" would be settled by arbitration. Kobe Steel of Japan was interested in using the technology represented by PRM's patents. Primenergy agreed to let Kobe use the technology in Japan without telling PRM. When PRM learned about the secret deal, the firm filed a suit against Primenergy for fraud and theft. Does this dispute go to arbitration or to trial? Why? [*PRM Energy Systems v. Primenergy*, 592 F.3d 830 (8th Cir. 2010)] (See *Alternative Dispute Resolution*.)

**2–4. Spotlight on the National Football League— Arbitration.** Bruce Matthews played football for the Tennessee Titans. As part of his contract, he agreed to submit any dispute to arbitration. He also agreed that Tennessee law would determine all matters related to workers' compensation. After Matthews retired, he filed a workers' compensation claim in California. The arbitrator ruled that Matthews could pursue his claim in California but only under Tennessee law. Should this award be set aside? Explain. [*National Football League Players Association v. National Football League Management Council*, 2011 WL 1137334 (S.D.Cal. 2011)] (See *Alternative Dispute Resolution*.)

**2–5. Minimum Contacts.** Seal Polymer Industries sold two freight containers of latex gloves to Med-Express, Inc., a company based in North Carolina. When Med-Express failed to pay the $104,000 owed for the gloves, Seal Polymer sued in an Illinois court and obtained a judgment against Med-Express. Med-Express argued that it did not have minimum contacts with Illinois because it was incorporated under North Carolina law and had its principal place of business in North Carolina. Therefore, the Illinois judgment based on personal jurisdiction was invalid. Was this argument alone sufficient to prevent the Illinois judgment from being collected against Med-Express in North Carolina? Why or why not? [*Seal Polymer Industries v. Med-Express, Inc.*, 725 S.E.2d 5 (N.C.App. 2012)] (See *Basic Judicial Requirements*.)

**2–6. Arbitration.** Horton Automatics and the Industrial Division of the Communications Workers of America, the union that represented Horton's workers, negotiated a collective bargaining agreement. If an employee's discharge for a workplace-rule violation was submitted to arbitration, the agreement limited the arbitrator to determining whether the rule was reasonable and whether the employee had violated it. When Horton discharged employee Ruben de la Garza, the union appealed to arbitration. The arbitrator found that de la Garza had violated a reasonable safety rule, but "was not totally convinced" that Horton should have treated the violation more seriously than other rule violations. The arbitrator ordered de la Garza reinstated. Can a court set aside this order? Explain. [*Horton Automatics v. The Industrial Division of the Communications Workers of America, AFL-CIO*, 2013 WL 59204 (5th Cir. 2013)] (See *Alternative Dispute Resolution*.)

**2–7. Business Case Problem with Sample Answer— Corporate Contacts.** LG Electronics, Inc., a South Korean

company, and nineteen other foreign companies participated in the global market for cathode ray tube (CRT) products. CRTs were integrated as components in consumer goods, including television sets, and were sold for many years in high volume in the United States, including the state of Washington. The state filed a suit in a Washington state court against LG and the others, alleging a conspiracy to raise prices and set production levels in the market for CRTs in violation of a state consumer protection statute. The defendants filed a motion to dismiss the suit for lack of personal jurisdiction. Should this motion be granted? Explain. [*State of Washington v. LG Electronics, Inc.*, 341 P.3d 346 (Wash.App., Div. 1 2015)] (See *Basic Judicial Requirements*.)

• For a sample answer to Problem 2–7, go to Appendix E at the end of this text.

**2–8. Appellate, or Reviewing, Courts.** Angelica Westbrook was employed as a collector for Franklin Collection Service, Inc. During a collection call, Westbrook told a debtor that a $15 processing fee was an "interest" charge. This violated company policy. Westbrook was fired. She filed a claim for unemployment benefits, which the Mississippi Department of Employment Security (MDES) approved. Franklin objected. At an MDES hearing, a Franklin supervisor testified that she had heard Westbrook make the false statement, although she admitted that there had been no similar incidents

with Westbrook. Westbrook denied making the statement, but added that if she had said it, she did not remember it. The agency found that Franklin's reason for terminating Westbrook did not amount to the misconduct required to disqualify her for benefits and upheld the approval. Franklin appealed to a state intermediate appellate court. Is the court likely to uphold the agency's findings of fact? Explain. [*Franklin Collection Service, Inc. v. Mississippi Department of Employment Security*, 184 So.3d 330 (Miss.App. 2016)] (See *The State and Federal Court Systems*.)

**2–9. A Question of Ethics—Agreement to Arbitrate.**

*Nellie Lumpkin, who suffered from various illnesses, including dementia, was admitted to the Picayune Convalescent Center, a nursing home. Because of her mental condition, her daughter, Beverly McDaniel, filled out the admissions paperwork and signed the admissions agreement. It included a clause requiring parties to submit to arbitration any disputes that arose. After Lumpkin left the center two years later, she sued, through her husband, for negligent treatment and malpractice during her stay. The center moved to force the matter to arbitration. The trial court held that the arbitration agreement was not enforceable. The center appealed. [Covenant Health & Rehabilitation of Picayune, LP v. Lumpkin, 23 So.3d 1092 (Miss.App. 2009)] (See Alternative Dispute Resolution.)*

**(a)** Should a dispute involving medical malpractice be forced into arbitration? This is a claim of negligent care, not a breach of a commercial contract. Is it ethical for medical facilities to impose such a requirement? Is there really any bargaining over such terms? Discuss fully.

**(b)** Should a person with limited mental capacity be held to an arbitration clause agreed to by the next of kin who signed on behalf of that person? Why or why not?

## Legal Reasoning Group Activity

**2–10. Access to Courts.** Assume that a statute in your state requires that all civil lawsuits involving damages of less than $50,000 be arbitrated. Such a case can be tried in court only if a party is dissatisfied with the arbitrator's decision. The statute also provides that if a trial does not result in an improvement of more than 10 percent in the position of the party who demanded the trial, that party must pay the entire cost of the arbitration proceeding. (See *Alternative Dispute Resolution*.)

**(a)** One group will argue that the state statute violates litigants' rights of access to the courts and trial by jury.

**(b)** Another group will argue that the statute does not violate litigants' right of access to the courts.

**(c)** A third group will evaluate how the determination on right of access would be changed if the statute was part of a pilot program that affected only a few judicial districts in the state.

# Answers to the *Issue Spotters*

**1.** *Does the court in Sue's state have jurisdiction over Tipton? What factors will the court consider in determining jurisdiction?* Yes, the court in Sue's state has jurisdiction over Tipton on the basis of the company's minimum contacts with the state.

Courts look at the following factors in determining whether minimum contacts exist: the quantity of the contacts, the nature and quality of the contacts, the source and connection of the cause of action to the contacts, the interest of the forum state, and the convenience of the parties. Attempting to exercise jurisdiction without sufficient minimum contacts would violate the due process clause. Generally, courts have found that jurisdiction is proper when there is substantial business conducted online (with contracts, sales, and so on). Even when there is only some interactivity through a Web site, courts have sometimes held that jurisdiction is proper. Jurisdiction is not proper when there is merely passive advertising.

Here, all of these factors suggest that the defendant had sufficient minimum contacts with the state to justify the exercise of jurisdiction over the defendant. Two especially important factors were that the plaintiff sold the security system to a resident of the state and that litigating in the defendant's state would be relatively inconvenient for the plaintiff.

**2.** *If the dispute is not resolved, or if either party disagrees with the decision of the mediator or arbitrator, will a court hear the case? Explain.* Yes, if the dispute is not resolved, or if either party disagrees with the decision of the mediator or arbitrator, a court will hear the case. It is required that the dispute be submitted to mediation or arbitration, but this outcome is not binding.

# Sample Answers for *Business Case Problems with Sample Answer*

**Problem 2–7.** *Corporate Contacts.* No, the defendants' motion to dismiss the suit for lack of personal jurisdiction should not be granted. A corporation normally is subject to jurisdiction in a state in which it is doing business. A court applies the minimum-contacts test to determine whether it can exercise jurisdiction over an out-of-state corporation. This requirement is met if the corporation sells its products within the state or places its goods in the "stream of commerce" with the intent that the goods be sold in the state.

In this problem, the state of Washington filed a suit in a Washington state court against LG Electronics, Inc., and nineteen other foreign companies that participated in the global market for cathode ray tube (CRT) products. The state alleged a conspiracy to raise prices and set production levels in the market for CRTs in violation of a state consumer protection statute. The defendants filed a motion to dismiss the suit for lack of personal jurisdiction. These goods were sold for many years in high volume in the United States, including the state of Washington. In other words, the corporations purposefully established minimum contacts in the state of Washington. This is a sufficient basis for a Washington state court to assert personal jurisdiction over the defendants.

In the actual case on which this problem is based, the court dismissed the suit for lack of personal jurisdiction. On appeal, a state intermediate appellate court reversed on the reasoning stated above.

# Chapter 4

# CHAPTER

# Business and the Constitution

Laws that govern business have their origin in the lawmaking authority granted by the U.S. Constitution, which is the supreme law in this country.[1] Neither Congress nor any state may pass a law that is in conflict with the Constitution.

Constitutional disputes frequently come before the courts. For instance, numerous states challenged the Obama administration's Affordable Care Act on constitutional grounds. The United States Supreme Court decided in 2012 that the provisions of this law, which required most Americans to have health insurance by 2014, did not exceed the constitutional authority of the federal government. The Court's decision in the matter continues to have a significant impact on the business environment.

---

1. See Appendix B for the full text of the U.S. Constitution.

## 4-1 The Constitutional Powers of Government

Following the Revolutionary War, the states adopted the Articles of Confederation. The Articles created a *confederal form of government* in which the states had the authority to govern themselves and the national government could exercise only limited powers. Problems soon arose because the nation was facing an economic crisis and state laws interfered with the free flow of commerce. A national convention was called, and the delegates drafted the U.S. Constitution. This document, after its ratification by the states in 1789, became the basis for an entirely new form of government.

### 4-1a A Federal Form of Government

The new government created by the U.S. Constitution reflected a series of compromises made by the convention delegates on various issues. Some delegates wanted sovereign power to remain with the states. Others wanted the national government alone to exercise sovereign power. The end result was a compromise—a **federal form of government** in which the national government and the states *share* sovereign power.

**Federal Powers** The Constitution sets forth specific powers that can be exercised by the national (federal) government. It further provides that the national government has the implied power to undertake actions necessary to carry out its expressly designated powers (or *enumerated powers*). All other powers are expressly "reserved" to the states under the Tenth Amendment to the U.S. Constitution.

**Regulatory Powers of the States** As part of their inherent **sovereignty** (power to govern themselves), state governments have the authority to regulate certain affairs within their borders. As mentioned, this authority stems, in part, from the Tenth Amendment, which reserves all powers not delegated to the national government to the states or to the people.

State regulatory powers are often referred to as **police powers.** The term encompasses more than just the enforcement of criminal laws. Police powers also give state governments broad rights to regulate private activities to protect or promote the public order, health, safety, morals, and general welfare. Fire and building codes, antidiscrimination laws, parking regulations, zoning restrictions, licensing requirements, and thousands of other state statutes have been enacted pursuant to states' police powers. Local governments, such as cities, also exercise police powers.[2] Generally, state laws enacted pur-

---

2. Local governments derive their authority to regulate their communities from the state, because they are creatures of the state. In other words, they cannot come into existence unless authorized by the state to do so.

suant to a state's police powers carry a strong presumption of validity.

## 4–1b Relations among the States

The U.S. Constitution also includes provisions concerning relations among the states in our federal system. Particularly important are the *privileges and immunities clause* and the *full faith and credit clause.*

**The Privileges and Immunities Clause** Article IV, Section 2, of the Constitution provides that the "Citizens of each State shall be entitled to all Privileges and Immunities of Citizens in the several States." This clause is often referred to as the interstate **privileges and immunities clause.**[3] It prevents a state from imposing unreasonable burdens on citizens of another state—particularly with regard to means of livelihood or doing business.

When a citizen of one state engages in basic and essential activities in another state (the "foreign state"), the foreign state must have a *substantial reason* for treating the nonresident differently than its own residents. Basic activities include transferring property, seeking employment, and accessing the court system. The foreign state must also establish that its reason for the discrimination is *substantially related* to the state's ultimate purpose in adopting the legislation or regulating the activity.[4]

**The Full Faith and Credit Clause** Article IV, Section 1, of the U.S. Constitution provides that "Full Faith and Credit shall be given in each State to the public Acts, Records, and judicial Proceedings of every other State." This clause, which is referred to as the **full faith and credit clause,** applies only to civil matters. It ensures that rights established under deeds, wills, contracts, and similar instruments in one state will be honored by other states. It also ensures that any judicial decision with respect to such property rights will be honored and enforced in all states.

The legal issues raised by same-sex marriage involve, among other things, the full faith and credit clause, because that clause requires each state to honor marriage decrees issued by another state. See this chapter's *Managerial Strategy* feature for a discussion of marriage equality laws.

The full faith and credit clause has contributed to the unity of American citizens because it protects their legal rights as they move about from state to state. It also protects the rights of those to whom they owe obligations, such as persons who have been awarded monetary damages by courts. The ability to enforce such rights is extremely important for the conduct of business in a country with a very mobile citizenry.

## 4–1c The Separation of Powers

To make it more difficult for the national government to use its power arbitrarily, the Constitution provided for three branches of government. The legislative branch makes the laws, the executive branch enforces the laws, and the judicial branch interprets the laws. Each branch performs a separate function, and no branch may exercise the authority of another branch.

Additionally, a system of **checks and balances** allows each branch to limit the actions of the other two branches, thus preventing any one branch from exercising too much power. Some examples of these checks and balances include the following:

1. The legislative branch (Congress) can enact a law, but the executive branch (the president) has the constitutional authority to veto that law.
2. The executive branch is responsible for foreign affairs, but treaties with foreign governments require the advice and consent of the Senate.
3. Congress determines the jurisdiction of the federal courts, and the president appoints federal judges, with the advice and consent of the Senate. The judicial branch has the power to hold actions of the other two branches unconstitutional.[5]

## 4–1d The Commerce Clause

To prevent states from establishing laws and regulations that would interfere with trade and commerce among the states, the Constitution expressly delegated to the national government the power to regulate interstate commerce. Article I, Section 8, of the U.S. Constitution explicitly permits Congress "[t]o regulate Commerce with foreign Nations, and among the several States, and with the Indian Tribes." This clause, referred to as the **commerce clause,** has had a greater impact on business than any other provision in the Constitution. The commerce clause provides the basis for the national government's extensive regulation of state and even local affairs.

---

3. Interpretations of this clause commonly use the terms *privilege* and *immunity* synonymously. Generally, the terms refer to certain rights, benefits, or advantages enjoyed by individuals.
4. This test was first announced in *Supreme Court of New Hampshire v. Piper,* 470 U.S. 274, 105 S.Ct. 1272, 84 L.Ed.2d 205 (1985). For another example, see *Lee v. Miner,* 369 F.Supp.2d 527 (D.Del. 2005).

5. The power of judicial review was established by the United States Supreme Court in *Marbury v. Madison,* 5 U.S. (1 Cranch) 137, 2 L.Ed. 60 (1803).

## MANAGERIAL STRATEGY — Marriage Equality and the Constitution

The debate over same-sex marriage has been raging across the country for years. The legal issues raised by marriage equality involve privacy rights and equal protection. Although marriage equality may not appear at first glance to be business related, it is an important legal issue for managers. Companies like Barilla Pasta, Chick-fil-A, Exxon Mobil, and Target Corporation have lost significant business for purportedly supporting anti-gay organizations and legislation.

### The Definition of Marriage

Before 1996, federal law did not define marriage, and the U.S. government recognized any marriage that was recognized by a state. Then Congress passed the Defense of Marriage Act (DOMA), which explicitly defined marriage as a union of one man and one woman. DOMA was later challenged, and a number of federal courts found it to be unconstitutional in the context of bankruptcy, public employee benefits, and estate taxes. In 2013, the United States Supreme Court struck down part of DOMA as unconstitutional.[a] Today, once again, no federal law defines marriage.

### Bans on Same-Sex Marriage Eliminated by the Supreme Court

During this period, federal courts became increasingly likely to invalidate state bans on same-sex marriage. In 2013, a federal district court held that Utah's same-sex marriage ban was unconstitutional.[b] In 2014, federal district courts in Arkansas, Mississippi, and Oklahoma struck down state same-sex marriage bans.[c] Moreover, public sentiment on the issue had shifted, and more states recognized the rights of same-sex couples. By 2015, thirty-seven states, as well as the District of Columbia, had legalized same-sex marriage.

In 2015, the United States Supreme Court determined that the remaining state-level prohibitions on same-sex marriage were unconstitutional. In a landmark decision, the Court ruled that the Fourteenth Amendment requires individual states to (1) issue marriage licenses to same-sex couples and (2) recognize same-sex marriages performed in other states.[d]

The landmark Supreme Court decision requiring all states to recognize same-sex marriage means that businesses must make adjustments. Company policies need to be revised to specify how same-sex partners will be treated in terms of family and medical leave, health-insurance coverage, pensions, and other benefits.

#### Business Questions

1. *Can a business manager's religious beliefs legally factor into the business's hiring and treatment of same-sex partners? Why or why not?*

2. *Must business owners in all states provide the same benefits to employees in a same-sex union as they do to heterosexual couples?*

a. *Windsor v. United States*, ___ U.S. ___, 133 S.Ct. 2675, 186 L.Ed.2d 808 (2013).
b. *Kitchen v. Herbert*, 961 F.Supp.2d 1181 (D.Utah 2013).
c. *Campaign for Southern Equality v. Bryant*, 64 F.Supp.3d 906 (S.D. Miss. 2014); *Jernigan v. Crane*, 64 F.Supp.3d 1260 (E.D.Ark. 2014); and *Bishop v. U.S. ex rel. Holder*, 962 F.Supp.2d 1252 (N.D. Okla. 2014).
d. *Obergefell v. Hodges*, ___ U.S. ___, 135 S.Ct. 2584, 192 L.Ed.2d 609 (2015).

---

Initially, the courts interpreted the commerce clause to apply only to commerce between the states (*interstate* commerce) and not commerce within the states (*intrastate* commerce). That changed in 1824, however, when the United States Supreme Court decided the landmark case of *Gibbons v. Ogden*.[6] The Court held that commerce within the states could also be regulated by the national government as long as the commerce *substantially affected* commerce involving more than one state.

**The Expansion of National Powers under the Commerce Clause** As the nation grew and faced new kinds of problems, the commerce clause became a vehicle for the additional expansion of the national government's regulatory powers. Even activities that seemed purely local in nature came under the regulatory reach of the national government if those activities were deemed to substantially affect interstate commerce. In 1942, the Supreme Court held that wheat production by an individual farmer intended wholly for consumption on his own farm was subject to federal regulation.[7]

The following *Classic Case* involved a challenge to the scope of the national government's constitutional authority to regulate local activities.

6. 22 U.S. (9 Wheat.) 1, 6 L.Ed. 23 (1824).

7. *Wickard v. Filburn*, 317 U.S. 111, 63 S.Ct. 82, 87 L.Ed. 122 (1942).

## Classic Case 4.1

# Heart of Atlanta Motel v. United States

Supreme Court of the United States, 379 U.S. 241, 85 S.Ct. 348, 13 L.Ed.2d 258 (1964).

**Background and Facts** In the 1950s, the United States Supreme Court ruled that racial segregation imposed by the states in school systems and other public facilities violated the Constitution. Privately owned facilities were not affected until Congress passed the Civil Rights Act of 1964, which prohibited racial discrimination in "establishments affecting interstate commerce."

The owner of the Heart of Atlanta Motel, in violation of the Civil Rights Act of 1964, refused to rent rooms to African Americans. The motel owner brought an action in a federal district court to have the Civil Rights Act declared unconstitutional on the ground that Congress had exceeded its constitutional authority to regulate commerce by enacting the statute.

The owner argued that his motel was not engaged in interstate commerce but was "of a purely local character." The motel, however, was accessible to state and interstate highways. The owner advertised nationally, maintained billboards throughout the state, and accepted convention trade from outside the state (75 percent of the guests were residents of other states).

The district court ruled that the act did not violate the Constitution and enjoined (prohibited) the owner from discriminating on the basis of race. The motel owner appealed. The case ultimately went to the United States Supreme Court.

### In the Language of the Court

Mr. Justice *CLARKE* delivered the opinion of the Court.

* * * *

While the Act as adopted carried no congressional findings, the record of its passage through each house is replete with evidence of the burdens that discrimination by race or color places upon interstate commerce * * * . This testimony included the fact that our people have become increasingly mobile with millions of all races traveling from State to State; that Negroes in particular have been the subject of discrimination in transient accommodations, having to travel great distances to secure the same; that often they have been unable to obtain accommodations and have had to call upon friends to put them up overnight. * * * These exclusionary practices were found to be nationwide, the Under Secretary of Commerce testifying that there is "no question that this discrimination in the North still exists to a large degree" and in the West and Midwest as well * * * . This testimony indicated a qualitative as well as quantitative effect on interstate travel by Negroes. The former was the obvious impairment of the Negro traveler's pleasure and convenience that resulted when he continually was uncertain of finding lodging. As for the latter, there was evidence that this uncertainty stemming from racial discrimination had the effect of discouraging travel on the part of a substantial portion of the Negro community * * * . We shall not burden this opinion with further details since the voluminous testimony presents overwhelming evidence that discrimination by hotels and motels impedes interstate travel.

* * * *

It is said that the operation of the motel here is of a purely local character. But, assuming this to be true, "if it is interstate commerce that feels the pinch, it does not matter how local the operation that applies the squeeze." * * * *Thus the power of Congress to promote interstate commerce also includes the power to regulate the local incidents thereof, including local activities in both the States of origin and destination, which might have a substantial and harmful effect upon that commerce.* [Emphasis added.]

**Decision and Remedy** *The United States Supreme Court upheld the constitutionality of the Civil Rights Act of 1964. The power of Congress to regulate interstate commerce permitted the enactment of legislation that could halt local discriminatory practices.*

**Impact of This Case on Today's Law** *If the United States Supreme Court had invalidated the Civil Rights Act of 1964, the legal landscape of the United States would be much different today. The act prohibits discrimination based on race, color, national origin, religion, or gender in all "public accommodations," including hotels and restaurants.*

Case 4.1 Continues

*The act also prohibits discrimination in employment based on these criteria. Although state laws now prohibit many of these forms of discrimination as well, the protections available vary from state to state—and it is not certain whether such laws would have been passed had the outcome in this case been different.*

**Critical Thinking**
- **What If the Facts Were Different?** *If this case had involved a small, private retail business that did not advertise nationally, would the result have been the same? Why or why not?*

---

**The Commerce Clause Today** Today, at least theoretically, the power over commerce authorizes the national government to regulate almost every commercial enterprise in the United States. The breadth of the commerce clause permits the national government to legislate in areas in which Congress has not explicitly been granted power. Only occasionally has the Supreme Court curbed the national government's regulatory authority under the commerce clause.[8]

The Supreme Court has, for instance, allowed the federal government to regulate noncommercial activities relating to medical marijuana that take place wholly within a state's borders. ■ **CASE IN POINT 4.1** More than half the states, including California, have adopted laws that legalize marijuana for medical purposes (and a handful of states now permit the recreational use of marijuana). Marijuana possession, however, is illegal under the federal Controlled Substances Act (CSA).[9] After the federal government seized the marijuana that two seriously ill California women were using on the advice of their physicians, the women filed a lawsuit. They argued that it was unconstitutional for the federal statute to prohibit them from using marijuana for medical purposes that were legal within the state.

The Supreme Court, though, held that Congress has the authority to prohibit the *intrastate* possession and noncommercial cultivation of marijuana as part of a larger regulatory scheme (the CSA).[10] In other words, the federal government may still prosecute individuals for possession of marijuana regardless of whether they reside in a state that allows the medical or recreational use of marijuana. ■

**The "Dormant" Commerce Clause** The Supreme Court has interpreted the commerce clause to mean that the national government has the *exclusive* authority to regulate commerce that substantially affects trade and commerce among the states. This express grant of authority to the national government is often referred to as the "positive" aspect of the commerce clause. But this positive aspect also implies a negative aspect—that the states do *not* have the authority to regulate interstate commerce. This negative aspect of the commerce clause is often referred to as the "dormant" (implied) commerce clause.

The dormant commerce clause comes into play when state regulations affect interstate commerce. In this situation, the courts weigh the state's interest in regulating a certain matter against the burden that the state's regulation places on interstate commerce. Because courts balance the interests involved, it is difficult to predict the outcome in a particular case. State laws that alter conditions of competition to favor in-state interests over out-of-state competitors in a market (such as wineries or construction workers) are usually invalidated, however.[11]

■ **CASE IN POINT 4.2** Maryland imposed personal income taxes on its residents at the state level and the county level. Maryland residents who paid income tax in another state were allowed a credit against the *state* portion of their Maryland taxes, but not the *county* portion. Several Maryland residents who had earned profits in and paid taxes to other states but had not received a credit against their county tax liability sued. They claimed that Maryland's system discriminated against intrastate commerce because those who earned income in other states paid more taxes than residents whose only income came from within Maryland. When the case reached the United States Supreme Court in 2015, the

---

8. See, for example, *United States v. Morrison*, 529 U.S. 598, 120 S.Ct. 1740, 146 L.Ed.2d 658 (2000), holding that the federal Violence Against Women Act violated Congress's commerce clause authority.
9. 21 U.S.C. Sections 801 *et seq.*
10. *Gonzales v. Raich*, 545 U.S. 1, 125 S.Ct. 2195, 162 L.Ed.2d 1 (2005).

11. See *Family Winemakers of California v. Jenkins*, 592 F.3d 1 (1st Cir. 2010); and *Tri-M Group, LLC v. Sharp*, 638 F.3d 406 (3d Cir. 2011).

Court held that Maryland's personal income tax scheme violated the dormant commerce clause.[12] ■

### 4–1e The Supremacy Clause and Federal Preemption

Article VI of the U.S. Constitution, commonly referred to as the **supremacy clause,** provides that the Constitution, laws, and treaties of the United States are "the supreme Law of the Land." When there is a direct conflict between a federal law and a state law, the state law is rendered invalid. Because some powers are *concurrent* (shared by the federal government and the states), however, it is necessary to determine which law governs in a particular circumstance.

**Preemption** When Congress chooses to act exclusively in a concurrent area, **preemption** occurs. In this circumstance, a valid federal statute or regulation will take precedence over a conflicting state or local law or regulation on the same general subject.

**Congressional Intent** Often, it is not clear whether Congress, in passing a law, intended to preempt an entire subject area. In these situations, the courts determine whether Congress intended to exercise exclusive power.

No single factor is decisive as to whether a court will find preemption. Generally, though, congressional intent to preempt will be found if a federal law regulating an activity is so pervasive, comprehensive, or detailed that the states have little or no room to regulate in that area. Also, when a federal statute creates an agency to enforce the law, matters that may come within the agency's jurisdiction will likely preempt state laws.

■ **CASE IN POINT 4.3** A man who alleged that he had been injured by a faulty medical device (a balloon catheter that was inserted into his artery following a heart attack) sued the manufacturer. The case ultimately came before the United States Supreme Court. The Court noted that the relevant federal law (the Medical Device Amendments of 1976) had included a preemption provision. Furthermore, the device had passed the U.S. Food and Drug Administration's rigorous premarket approval process. Therefore, the Court ruled that the federal regulation of medical devices preempted the man's state law claims.[13] ■

### 4–1f The Taxing and Spending Powers

Article I, Section 8, of the U.S. Constitution provides that Congress has the "Power to lay and collect Taxes, Duties, Imposts, and Excises." Section 8 further requires uniformity in taxation among the states, and thus Congress may not tax some states while exempting others.

In the distant past, if Congress attempted to regulate indirectly, by taxation, an area over which it had no authority, the courts would invalidate the tax. Today, however, if a tax measure is reasonable, it generally is held to be within the national taxing power. Moreover, the expansive interpretation of the commerce clause almost always provides a basis for sustaining a federal tax.

Article I, Section 8, also gives Congress its spending power—the power "to pay the Debts and provide for the common Defence and general Welfare of the United States." Congress can spend revenues not only to carry out its expressed powers but also to promote any objective it deems worthwhile, so long as it does not violate the Bill of Rights. The spending power necessarily involves policy choices, with which taxpayers (and politicians) may disagree.

## 4–2 Business and the Bill of Rights

The importance of a written declaration of the rights of individuals caused the first Congress of the United States to submit twelve amendments to the U.S. Constitution to the states for approval. Ten of these amendments, known as the **Bill of Rights,** were adopted in 1791 and embody a series of protections for the individual against various types of interference by the federal government.[14]

The protections guaranteed by these ten amendments are summarized in Exhibit 4–1.[15] Some of these constitutional protections apply to business entities as well as individuals. For example, corporations exist as separate legal entities, or *legal persons,* and enjoy many of the same rights and privileges as *natural persons* do.

---

12. *Comptroller of Treasury of Maryland v. Wynne,* ___ U.S. ___, 135 S.Ct. 1787, 191 L.Ed.2d 813 (2015).
13. *Riegel v. Medtronic, Inc.,* 552 U.S. 312, 128 S.Ct. 999, 169 L.Ed.2d 892 (2008).

14. Another of these proposed amendments was ratified more than two hundred years later (in 1992) and became the Twenty-seventh Amendment to the Constitution. See Appendix B.
15. See the Constitution in Appendix B for the complete text of each amendment.

**EXHIBIT 4–1 Protections Guaranteed by the Bill of Rights**

| | |
|---|---|
| **First Amendment:** | Guarantees the freedoms of religion, speech, and the press and the rights to assemble peaceably and to petition the government. |
| **Second Amendment:** | States that the right of the people to keep and bear arms shall not be infringed. |
| **Third Amendment:** | Prohibits, in peacetime, the lodging of soldiers in any house without the owner's consent. |
| **Fourth Amendment:** | Prohibits unreasonable searches and seizures of persons or property. |
| **Fifth Amendment:** | Guarantees the rights to *indictment* (formal accusation) by a grand jury, to due process of law, and to fair payment when private property is taken for public use. The Fifth Amendment also prohibits compulsory self-incrimination and double jeopardy (trial for the same crime twice). |
| **Sixth Amendment:** | Guarantees the accused in a criminal case the right to a speedy and public trial by an impartial jury and with counsel. The accused has the right to cross-examine witnesses against him or her and to solicit testimony from witnesses in his or her favor. |
| **Seventh Amendment:** | Guarantees the right to a trial by jury in a civil case involving at least twenty dollars. |
| **Eighth Amendment:** | Prohibits excessive bail and fines, as well as cruel and unusual punishment. |
| **Ninth Amendment:** | Establishes that the people have rights in addition to those specified in the Constitution. |
| **Tenth Amendment:** | Establishes that those powers neither delegated to the federal government nor denied to the states are reserved to the states and to the people. |

## 4–2a Limits on Federal and State Governmental Actions

As originally intended, the Bill of Rights limited only the powers of the national government. Over time, however, the United States Supreme Court "incorporated" most of these rights into the protections against state actions afforded by the Fourteenth Amendment to the Constitution.

**The Fourteenth Amendment** The Fourteenth Amendment, passed in 1868 after the Civil War, provides, in part, that "[n]o State shall . . . deprive any person of life, liberty, or property, without due process of law." Starting in 1925, the Supreme Court began to define various rights and liberties guaranteed in the U.S. Constitution as constituting "due process of law," which was required of state governments under that amendment.

Today, most of the rights and liberties set forth in the Bill of Rights apply to state governments as well as the national government. In other words, neither the federal government nor state governments can deprive persons of those rights and liberties.

**Judicial Interpretation** The rights secured by the Bill of Rights are not absolute. Many of the rights guaranteed by the first ten amendments are set forth in very general terms. The Second Amendment states that people have a right to keep and bear arms, but it does not describe the extent of this right. As the Supreme Court has noted, this right does not mean that people can "keep and carry any weapon whatsoever in any manner whatsoever and for whatever purpose."[16] Legislatures can prohibit the carrying of concealed weapons or certain types of weapons, such as machine guns.

Ultimately, the United States Supreme Court, as the final interpreter of the Constitution, gives meaning to these rights and determines their boundaries. Changing public views on controversial topics, such as privacy in an era of terrorist threats or the rights of gay men and lesbians, can affect the way the Supreme Court decides a case.

## 4–2b Freedom of Speech

A democratic form of government cannot survive unless people can freely voice their political opinions and criticize government actions or policies. Freedom of speech,

---

**16.** *District of Columbia v. Heller*, 554 U.S. 570, 128 S.Ct. 2783, 171 L.Ed.2d 637 (2008).

particularly political speech, is thus a prized right, and traditionally the courts have protected this right to the fullest extent possible.

**Symbolic speech**—gestures, movements, articles of clothing, and other forms of expressive conduct—is also given substantial protection by the courts. The Supreme Court has held that the burning of the American flag as part of a peaceful protest is a constitutionally protected form of expression.[17] Similarly, wearing a T-shirt with a photo of a presidential candidate is a constitutionally protected form of expression. ■ **EXAMPLE 4.4** As a form of expression, Nate has gang signs tattooed on his torso, arms, neck, and legs. If a reasonable person would interpret this conduct as conveying a message, then it might be a protected form of symbolic speech. ■

**Reasonable Restrictions** A balance must be struck between a government's obligation to protect its citizens and those citizens' exercise of their rights. Expression—oral, written, or symbolized by conduct—is therefore subject to reasonable restrictions. Reasonableness is analyzed on a case-by-case basis.

**Content-Neutral Laws.** Laws that regulate the time, manner, and place, but not the content, of speech receive less scrutiny by the courts than do laws that restrict the content of expression. If a restriction imposed by the government is content neutral, then a court may allow it. To be content neutral, the restriction must be aimed at combatting some societal problem, such as crime or drug abuse, and not be aimed at suppressing the expressive conduct or its message.

Courts have often protected nude dancing as a form of symbolic expression but typically allow content-neutral laws that ban all public nudity. ■ **CASE IN POINT 4.5** Ria Ora was charged with dancing nude at an annual "anti-Christmas" protest in Harvard Square in Cambridge, Massachusetts, under a statute banning public displays of open and gross lewdness. Ora argued that the statute was overbroad and unconstitutional, and a trial court agreed. On appeal, however, a state appellate court upheld the statute as constitutional in situations in which there was an unsuspecting or unwilling audience.[18] ■

**Laws That Restrict the Content of Speech.** Any law that regulates the content of expression must serve a compelling state interest and must be narrowly written to achieve that interest. Under the **compelling government**

**interest** test, the government's interest is balanced against the individual's constitutional right to free expression. For the statute to be valid, there must be a compelling government interest that can be furthered only by the law in question.

The United States Supreme Court has held that schools may restrict students' speech at school events. ■ **CASE IN POINT 4.6** Some high school students held up a banner saying "Bong Hits 4 Jesus" at an off-campus but school-sanctioned event. The Supreme Court ruled that the school did not violate the students' free speech rights when school officials confiscated the banner and suspended the students for ten days. Because the banner could reasonably be interpreted as promoting drugs, the Court concluded that the school's actions were justified. Several justices disagreed, however, noting that the majority's holding creates an exception that will allow schools to censor any student speech that mentions drugs.[19] ■

**Corporate Political Speech** Political speech by corporations also falls within the protection of the First Amendment. Many years ago, the United States Supreme Court struck down as unconstitutional a Massachusetts statute that prohibited corporations from making political contributions or expenditures that individuals were permitted to make.[20] The Court has also held that a law forbidding a corporation from including inserts with its bills to express its views on controversial issues violates the First Amendment.[21]

Corporate political speech continues to be given significant protection under the First Amendment. ■ **CASE IN POINT 4.7** In *Citizens United v. Federal Election Commission,*[22] the Supreme Court issued a landmark decision that overturned a twenty-year-old precedent on campaign financing. The case involved Citizens United, a nonprofit corporation that runs a *political action committee* (an organization that registers with the government and campaigns for or against political candidates).

Citizens United had produced a film called *Hillary: The Movie* that was critical of Hillary Clinton, who was seeking the Democratic nomination for presidential candidate. Campaign-finance law restricted Citizens United from broadcasting the movie. The Court ruled that these

---

**17.** *Texas v. Johnson,* 491 U.S. 397, 109 S.Ct. 2533, 105 L.Ed.2d 342 (1989).

**18.** *Commonwealth v. Ora,* 451 Mass. 125, 883 N.E.2d 1217 (2008).

**19.** *Morse v. Frederick,* 551 U.S. 393, 127 S.Ct. 2618, 168 L.Ed.2d 290 (2007).

**20.** *First National Bank of Boston v. Bellotti,* 435 U.S. 765, 98 S.Ct. 1407, 55 L.Ed.2d 707 (1978).

**21.** *Consolidated Edison Co. v. Public Service Commission,* 447 U.S. 530, 100 S.Ct. 2326, 65 L.Ed.2d 319 (1980).

**22.** 558 U.S. 310, 130 S.Ct. 876, 175 L.Ed.2d 753 (2010).

restrictions were unconstitutional and that the First Amendment prevents limits from being placed on independent political expenditures by corporations. ■

**Commercial Speech** The courts also give substantial protection to *commercial speech,* which consists of communications—primarily advertising and marketing—made by business firms that involve only their commercial interests. The protection given to commercial speech under the First Amendment is less extensive than that afforded to noncommercial speech, however.

A state may restrict certain kinds of advertising, for instance, in the interest of preventing consumers from being misled. States also have a legitimate interest in roadside beautification and therefore may impose restraints on billboard advertising. ■ **EXAMPLE 4.8** Café Erotica, a nude dancing establishment, sues the state after being denied a permit to erect a billboard along an interstate highway in Florida. Because the law directly advances a substantial government interest in highway beautification and safety, a court will likely find that it is not an unconstitutional restraint on commercial speech. ■

Generally, a restriction on commercial speech will be considered valid as long as it meets three criteria:

1. It must seek to implement a substantial government interest.
2. It must directly advance that interest.
3. It must go no further than necessary to accomplish its objective.

At issue in the following case was whether a government agency had unconstitutionally restricted commercial speech when it prohibited the inclusion of a certain illustration on beer labels.

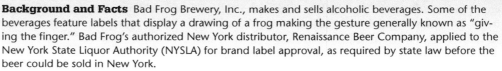

## Spotlight on Beer Labels

## Case 4.2 Bad Frog Brewery, Inc. v. New York State Liquor Authority
United States Court of Appeals, Second Circuit, 134 F.3d 87 (1998).

**Background and Facts** Bad Frog Brewery, Inc., makes and sells alcoholic beverages. Some of the beverages feature labels that display a drawing of a frog making the gesture generally known as "giving the finger." Bad Frog's authorized New York distributor, Renaissance Beer Company, applied to the New York State Liquor Authority (NYSLA) for brand label approval, as required by state law before the beer could be sold in New York.

The NYSLA denied the application, in part, because "the label could appear in grocery and convenience stores, with obvious exposure on the shelf to children of tender age." Bad Frog filed a suit in a federal district court against the NYSLA, asking for, among other things, an injunction against the denial of the application. The court granted summary judgment in favor of the NYSLA. Bad Frog appealed to the U.S. Court of Appeals for the Second Circuit.

### In the Language of the Court
Jon O. NEWMAN, Circuit Judge:
* * * *

* * * To support its asserted power to ban Bad Frog's labels [NYSLA advances] * * * the State's interest in "protecting children from vulgar and profane advertising" * * * .

[This interest is] substantial * * * . *States have a compelling interest in protecting the physical and psychological wellbeing of minors* * * * . [Emphasis added.]
* * * *

* * * NYSLA endeavors to advance the state interest in preventing exposure of children to vulgar displays by taking only the limited step of barring such displays from the labels of alcoholic beverages. *In view of the wide currency of vulgar displays throughout contemporary society, including comic books targeted directly at children, barring such displays from labels for alcoholic beverages cannot realistically be expected to reduce children's exposure to such displays to any significant degree.* [Emphasis added.]

* * * If New York decides to make a substantial effort to insulate children from vulgar displays in some significant sphere of activity, at least with respect to materials likely to be seen by children, NYSLA's label prohibition might well be found to make a justifiable contribution to the material

Case 4.2 Continued

advancement of such an effort, but its currently isolated response to the perceived problem, applicable only to labels on a product that children cannot purchase, does not suffice. * * * A state must demonstrate that its commercial speech limitation is part of a substantial effort to advance a valid state interest, not merely the removal of a few grains of offensive sand from a beach of vulgarity.

* * * *

* * * Even if we were to assume that the state materially advances its asserted interest by shielding children from viewing the Bad Frog labels, it is plainly excessive to prohibit the labels from all use, including placement on bottles displayed in bars and taverns where parental supervision of children is to be expected. Moreover, to whatever extent NYSLA is concerned that children will be harmfully exposed to the Bad Frog labels when wandering without parental supervision around grocery and convenience stores where beer is sold, that concern could be less intrusively dealt with by placing restrictions on the permissible locations where the appellant's products may be displayed within such stores.

**Decision and Remedy** *The U.S. Court of Appeals for the Second Circuit reversed the judgment of the district court and remanded the case for the entry of a judgment in favor of Bad Frog. The NYSLA's ban on the use of the labels lacked a "reasonable fit" with the state's interest in shielding minors from vulgarity. In addition, the NYSLA had not adequately considered alternatives to the ban.*

**Critical Thinking**
- **What If the Facts Were Different?** *If Bad Frog had sought to use the offensive label to market toys instead of beer, would the court's ruling likely have been the same? Why or why not?*
- **Legal Environment** *Whose interests are advanced by the banning of certain types of advertising?*

---

**Unprotected Speech** The United States Supreme Court has made it clear that certain types of speech will not be protected under the First Amendment. Unprotected speech includes fighting words, or words that are likely to incite others to respond violently. It also includes speech that harms the good reputation of another, or defamatory speech. In addition, speech that violates criminal laws (threatening speech or possession of child pornography, for instance) is not constitutionally protected.

**Threatening Speech.** Note that in the case of threatening speech, the speaker must have posed a "true threat"—that is, must have meant to communicate a serious intent to commit an unlawful, violent act against a particular person or group. ■ **CASE IN POINT 4.9** After Anthony Elonis's wife, Tara, left him and took their two children, Elonis was upset and experienced problems at work. A coworker filed five sexual harassment reports against him. When Elonis posted a photograph of himself in a Halloween costume holding a toy knife to the coworker's neck, he was fired from his job. Elonis then began posting violent statements on his Facebook page, mostly focusing on his former wife and talking about killing her.

Elonis continued to post statements about killing his wife and eventually was arrested and prosecuted for his online posts. Elonis was convicted by a jury of violating a statute and ordered to serve time in prison. He appealed

to the United States Supreme Court, which held that it is not enough that a reasonable person might view the defendant's Facebook posts as threats. Elonis must have intended to issue threats or known that his statements would be viewed as threats to be convicted of a crime. The Court reversed Elonis's conviction and remanded the case back to the lower court to determine if there was sufficient evidence of intent.[23] ■

**Obscene Speech.** The First Amendment, as interpreted by the Supreme Court, also does not protect obscene speech. Numerous state and federal statutes make it a crime to disseminate and possess obscene materials, including child pornography. Objectively defining obscene speech has proved difficult, however. It is even more difficult to prohibit the dissemination of obscenity and pornography online.

Most of Congress's attempts to pass legislation protecting minors from pornographic materials on the Internet have been struck down on First Amendment grounds when challenged in court. One exception is a law that requires public schools and libraries to install **filtering software** on computers to keep children from accessing adult content.[24] Such software is designed to

---

23. *Elonis v. United States*, ___ U.S. ___, 135 S.Ct. 2001, 192 L.Ed.2d 1 (2015).
24. Children's Internet Protection Act (CIPA), 17 U.S.C. Sections 1701–1741.

prevent persons from viewing certain Web sites based on a site's Internet address or its **meta tags,** or key words. The Supreme Court held that the act does not unconstitutionally burden free speech because it is flexible and libraries can disable the filters for any patrons who ask.[25]

Another exception is a law that makes it a crime to intentionally distribute *virtual child pornography*—which uses computer-generated images, not actual people—without indicating that it is computer-generated.[26] In a case challenging the law's constitutionality, the Supreme Court held that the statute is valid because it does not prohibit a substantial amount of protected speech.[27] Nevertheless, because of the difficulties of policing the Internet, as well as the constitutional complexities of prohibiting obscenity through legislation, online obscenity remains a legal issue.

## 4–2c Freedom of Religion

The First Amendment states that the government may neither establish any religion nor prohibit the free exercise of religious practices. The first part of this constitutional provision is referred to as the **establishment clause,** and the second part is known as the **free exercise clause**. Government action, both federal and state, must be consistent with this constitutional mandate.

**The Establishment Clause** The establishment clause prohibits the government from establishing a state-sponsored religion, as well as from passing laws that promote (aid or endorse) religion or show a preference for one religion over another. Although the establishment clause involves the separation of church and state, it does not require a complete separation.

**Applicable Standard.** Establishment clause cases often involve such issues as the legality of allowing or requiring school prayers, using state-issued vouchers to pay tuition at religious schools, and teaching creation theories versus evolution. Federal or state laws that do not promote or place a significant burden on religion are constitutional even if they have some impact on religion. For a government law or policy to be constitutional, it must not have the primary effect of promoting or inhibiting religion.

**Religious Displays.** Religious displays on public property have often been challenged as violating the establishment clause, and the United States Supreme Court has

ruled on a number of such cases. Generally, the Court has focused on the proximity of the religious display (such as a Christian Christmas symbol) to nonreligious symbols (such as reindeer and candy canes) or symbols from different religions (such as a menorah, a nine-branched candelabrum used in celebrating Hanukkah).

The Supreme Court took a slightly different approach when it held that public displays having historical, as well as religious, significance do not necessarily violate the establishment clause.[28] Still, historical significance must be carefully weighed against religious elements in establishment clause cases.

■ **CASE IN POINT 4.10** Mount Soledad is a prominent hill near San Diego. There has been a forty-foot cross on top of Mount Soledad since 1913. In the 1990s, a war memorial with six walls listing the names of veterans was constructed next to the cross. The site was privately owned until 2006, when Congress authorized the property's transfer to the federal government "to preserve a historically significant war memorial."

Steve Trunk and the Jewish War Veterans filed lawsuits claiming that the cross violated the establishment clause because it endorsed the Christian religion. A federal appellate court agreed, finding that the primary effect of the memorial as a whole sent a strong message of endorsement of Christianity and exclusion of non-Christian veterans. The court noted that although not all cross displays at war memorials violate the establishment clause, the cross in this case physically dominated the site. Additionally, it was originally dedicated to religious purposes, had a long history of religious use, and was the only portion visible to drivers on the freeway below.[29] ■

**The Free Exercise Clause** The free exercise clause guarantees that people can hold any religious beliefs they want or can hold no religious beliefs. The constitutional guarantee of personal freedom restricts only the actions of the government, however, and not those of individuals or private businesses.

**Restrictions Must Be Necessary.** The government must have a compelling state interest for restricting the free exercise of religion, and the restriction must be the only way to further that interest. ■ **CASE IN POINT 4.11** Gregory Holt, an inmate in an Arkansas state prison, was a devout Muslim who wished to grow a beard in accord with his religious beliefs. The Arkansas Department of

**25.** *United States v. American Library Association*, 539 U.S. 194, 123 S.Ct. 2297, 156 L.Ed.2d 221 (2003).

**26.** The Prosecutorial Remedies and Other Tools to End the Exploitation of Children Today Act (Protect Act), 18 U.S.C. Section 2252A(a)(5)(B).

**27.** *United States v. Williams*, 553 U.S. 285, 128 S.Ct. 1830, 170 L.Ed.2d 650 (2008).

**28.** *Van Orden v. Perry*, 545 U.S. 677, 125 S.Ct. 2854, 162 L.Ed.2d 607 (2005). The Court held that a six-foot-tall monument of the Ten Commandments on the Texas state capitol grounds did not violate the establishment clause because the Ten Commandments have historical significance.

**29.** *Trunk v. City of San Diego*, 629 F.3d 1099 (9th Cir. 2011).

Correction prohibited inmates from growing beards (except for medical reasons). Holt asked for an exemption to grow a half-inch beard on religious grounds, and prison officials denied his request. Holt filed a suit in a federal district court against Ray Hobbs, the director of the department, and others.

A federal statute prohibits the government from taking any action that substantially burdens the religious exercise of an institutionalized person unless the action constitutes the least restrictive means of furthering a compelling governmental interest. The defendants argued that beards compromise prison safety—a compelling government interest—because contraband can be hidden in them and because an inmate can quickly shave his beard to disguise his identity.

The district court dismissed Holt's suit, and the dismissal was affirmed on appeal. Holt then appealed to the United States Supreme Court. The Court noted that "an item of contraband would have to be very small indeed to be concealed by a 1/2–inch beard." Moreover, the Court reasoned that the department could satisfy its security concerns by simply searching the beard, the way it already searches prisoners' hair and clothing. The Court concluded that the department's grooming policy, which prevented Holt from growing a half-inch beard, violated his right to exercise his religious beliefs.[30] ■

**Restrictions Must Not Be a Substantial Burden.** To comply with the free exercise clause, a government action must not place a substantial burden on religious practices. A burden is substantial if it pressures an individual to modify his or her behavior and to violate his or her beliefs.

At issue in the following case was whether forcing a state prison inmate to choose between daily nutrition and a religious practice is a substantial burden.

---

30. *Holt v. Hobbs*, ___ U.S. ___, 135 S.Ct. 853, 190 L.Ed.2d 747 (2015).

---

**Case Analysis 4.3**

## Thompson v. Holm
United States Court of Appeals, Seventh Circuit, 809 F.3d 376 (2016).

### In the Language of the Court
*ROVNER*, Circuit Judge.

Michael Thompson, a Muslim inmate incarcerated at Waupun Correctional Institution in Wisconsin, sued members of the prison staff for violating his right under the First Amendment to exercise his religion freely. The violation occurred, Thompson says, when for two days prison staff prevented him from fasting properly during Ramadan.

* * * A central religious practice of the Islamic faith is a sunrise-to-sunset fast during the month of Ramadan. The prison normally accommodates this practice by providing Ramadan "meal bags" at sunset to each Muslim prisoner listed as eligible. The prison's chaplain determines eligibility. Each Ramadan meal bag contains two meals: the post-sunset dinner and the next morning's pre-sunrise breakfast. A prisoner who eats at the prison cafeteria during Ramadan forfeits his right to the meal bags for the rest of the month-long fast. Thompson, a practicing Muslim, began fasting for Ramadan after sunrise on August 11—the first day of Ramadan. He received his daily meal bags until August 21, about one-third into the month.

* * * Thompson says that shortly before August 21, as he was on his way back to his cell, Randall Lashock, a prison guard, handed him a meal bag. When Thompson arrived at his cell, he found that a guard had already left a meal bag for him there. Thompson could not leave his cell to return the extra bag without risking a conduct violation, so he left one of the two bags unopened for Lashock to retrieve. Lashock asserts that when he later retrieved that extra meal bag from Thompson's cell, he found Thompson eating from both bags.

Thompson received no meal bags on August 21 and 22. Lashock was supposed to deliver the Ramadan meal bags to every prisoner on the eligibility list. But on those two days, Lashock brought Thompson nothing, even though * * * he remained on the list. Receiving no meals, and learning from [prison guards] Bruce Bleich and Matthew Larson when he complained to them that he would have to go to the cafeteria if he wanted to eat, Thompson felt pressure to break his fast by going to the cafeteria. But he knew that under the prison's policy he could not do that without forfeiting meal bags for the rest of the month-long fast. He also had hunger pangs and felt tired and unwell. Because of his hunger, exhaustion, and anxiety, he missed one of his morning prayers and did not properly experience Ramadan, which is meant to be a time of peace and focus.

* * * *

While he was receiving no meal bags, Thompson asked other prison officials to explain why Lashock was not bringing him food * * * . Bleich and Larson told him that Captain William Holm had ordered his name removed from the list because he had stolen a meal bag; they too refused to bring him any meals. But Holm * * * did not remove Thompson from the list and had no authority to do so; only the chaplain could do that.

* * * On August 23, Thompson received a Ramadan meal bag at sunset

**Case 4.3 Continues**

**Case 4.3 Continued**

and continued to receive a bag each day until the end of Ramadan.

Thompson [filed a suit in a federal district court against] Lashock, Holm, Bleich, and Larson * * * for violating his First Amendment rights, and the defendants moved for summary judgment. * * * They argued the lack of meal bags for two days did not substantially burden Thompson's free-exercise rights.

Thompson responded that the defendants unlawfully withheld his meal bags. * * * By forcing him to choose between adequate nutrition and a central tenet of his religion, the defendants substantially burdened his free-exercise rights.

[The court] granted the defendants' motion for summary judgment. The judge ruled that receiving no meal bags for just two days was not a substantial burden on Thompson's free-exercise rights because he kept fasting, praying, and reading the Koran.

On appeal Thompson challenges the entry of summary judgment.

We begin our analysis by asking whether the denial of meal bags substantially burdened Thompson's free exercise rights. The answer is yes. *Without the meal bags, Thompson was forced to choose between foregoing adequate nutrition or violating a central tenet of his religion. Facing that choice for "only" two days was not, as defendants argue, a "de minimis" [minimal] burden.* Not only did Thompson receive no proper meal for 55 hours, leaving him weak and tired, he did not know if he would ever be put back on the Ramadan list and get regular food. This uncertainty put pressure on him to resign himself to the cafeteria; the anxiety left him unable to practice Ramadan properly. [Emphasis added.]
* * * *

We next consider whether Thompson produced sufficient evidence that all the defendants were personally involved in imposing this burden. Once again, the answer is yes. We consider the defendants individually, beginning with

Lashock. He was responsible for delivering the meal bags to all inmates on the eligibility list. Yet he personally denied them to Thompson for two days even though * * * Thompson remained on the list. As to Holm, * * * Holm lied about whether he had removed Thompson from the meal list. Finally, as to Bleich and Larson, they also bear responsibility for depriving Thompson of his food. By (falsely) telling Thompson that Holm had removed him from the religious meal list, refusing to bring him any meals, and warning him to go to the cafeteria if he wanted to eat, * * * they were involved in a joint effort to pressure Thompson to break his fast.
* * * *

Accordingly, we VACATE the judgment. This case is REMANDED for further proceedings consistent with this order.

**Legal Reasoning Questions**

**1.** What is the standard for determining whether a restriction on a religious practice is constitutional under the First Amendment?

**2.** How did that standard apply to the prison guards' conduct in this case?

**3.** Were all of the guards personally involved in the alleged violation of the First Amendment? Explain.

---

**Public Welfare Exception.** When religious *practices* work against public policy and the public welfare, the government can act. For instance, the government can require that a child receive certain types of vaccinations or medical treatment if his or her life is in danger—regardless of the child's or parent's religious beliefs. When public safety is an issue, an individual's religious beliefs often have to give way to the government's interest in protecting the public.

■ **EXAMPLE 4.12** A woman of the Muslim faith may choose not to appear in public without a scarf, known as a *hijab*, over her head. Nevertheless, due to public safety concerns, many courts today do not allow the wearing of any headgear (hats or scarves) in courtrooms. ■

## 4–2d Searches and Seizures

The Fourth Amendment protects the "right of the people to be secure in their persons, houses, papers, and effects."

Before searching or seizing private property, law enforcement officers must usually obtain a **search warrant**—an order from a judge or other public official authorizing the search or seizure. Because of the strong government interest in protecting the public, however, a warrant normally is not required for seizures of spoiled or contaminated food. Nor are warrants required for searches of businesses in such highly regulated industries as liquor, guns, and strip mining.

To obtain a search warrant, law enforcement officers must convince a judge that they have reasonable grounds, or **probable cause,** to believe a search will reveal evidence of a specific illegality. To establish probable cause, the officers must have trustworthy evidence that would convince a reasonable person that the proposed search or seizure is more likely justified than not.

■ **CASE IN POINT 4.13** Citlalli Flores was driving across the border into the United States from Tijuana, Mexico, when a border protection officer became suspicious because she was acting nervous and looking around inside her car.

On further inspection, the officer found thirty-six pounds of marijuana hidden in the car's quarter panels. Flores claimed that she had not known about the marijuana.

Flores was arrested for importing marijuana into the United States. She then made two jail-recorded phone calls in which she asked her cousin to delete whatever he felt needed to be removed from Flores's Facebook page. The government got a warrant to search Flores's Facebook messages, where they found references to her "carrying" or "bringing" marijuana into the United States that day. Flores's Facebook posts were later used as evidence against her at trial, and she was convicted.

On appeal, the court held that the phone calls had given the officers probable cause to support a warrant to search Flores's social networking site for incriminating statements. Her conviction was affirmed.[31] ■

### 4–2e Self-Incrimination

The Fifth Amendment guarantees that no person "shall be compelled in any criminal case to be a witness against himself." Thus, in any court proceeding, an accused person cannot be forced to give testimony that might subject him or her to any criminal prosecution. The guarantee applies to both federal and state proceedings because the due process clause of the Fourteenth Amendment (discussed shortly) extends the protection to state courts.

The Fifth Amendment's guarantee against self-incrimination extends only to natural persons. Neither corporations nor partnerships receive Fifth Amendment protection. When a partnership is required to produce business records, it must therefore do so even if the information provided incriminates the individual partners of the firm. In contrast, sole proprietors and sole practitioners (those who individually own their businesses) cannot be compelled to produce their business records. These individuals have full protection against self-incrimination because they function in only one capacity, and there is no separate business entity.

---

## 4–3 Due Process and Equal Protection

Other constitutional guarantees of great significance to Americans are mandated by the *due process clauses* of the Fifth and Fourteenth Amendments and the *equal protection clause* of the Fourteenth Amendment.

### 4–3a Due Process

Both the Fifth and Fourteenth Amendments provide that no person shall be deprived "of life, liberty, or property, without due process of law." The **due process clause** of these constitutional amendments has two aspects—procedural and substantive. Note that the due process clause applies to "legal persons" (that is, corporations), as well as to individuals.

**Procedural Due Process** *Procedural* due process requires that any government decision to take life, liberty, or property must be made equitably. In other words, the government must give a person proper notice and an opportunity to be heard. Fair procedures must be used in determining whether a person will be subjected to punishment or have some burden imposed on her or him.

Fair procedure has been interpreted as requiring that the person have at least an opportunity to object to a proposed action before an impartial, neutral decision maker (who need not be a judge). ■ **EXAMPLE 4.14** Doyle Burns, a nursing student in Kansas, poses for a photograph standing next to a placenta used as a lab specimen. Although she quickly deletes the photo from her library, it ends up on Facebook. When the director of nursing sees the photo, Burns is expelled. She sues for reinstatement and wins. The school violated Burns's due process rights by expelling her from the nursing program for taking a photo without giving her an opportunity to present her side to school authorities. ■

**Substantive Due Process** *Substantive* due process focuses on the content of legislation rather than the fairness of procedures. Substantive due process limits what the government may do in its legislative and executive capacities. Legislation must be fair and reasonable in content and must further a legitimate governmental objective.

If a law or other governmental action limits a fundamental right, the state must have a legitimate and compelling interest to justify its action. Fundamental rights include interstate travel, privacy, voting, marriage and family, and all First Amendment rights. Thus, for instance, a state must have a substantial reason for taking any action that infringes on a person's free speech rights.

In situations not involving fundamental rights, a law or action does not violate substantive due process if it rationally relates to any legitimate government purpose. It is almost impossible for a law or action to fail the "rationality" test. Under this test, almost any business regulation will be upheld as reasonable.

---

31. *United States v. Flores*, 830 F.3d 1028 (9th Cir. 2015).

## 4–3b Equal Protection

Under the Fourteenth Amendment, a state may not "deny to any person within its jurisdiction the equal protection of the laws." The United States Supreme Court has interpreted the due process clause of the Fifth Amendment to make the **equal protection clause** applicable to the federal government as well. Equal protection means that the government cannot enact laws that treat similarly situated individuals differently.

Equal protection, like substantive due process, relates to the substance of a law or other governmental action. When a law or action limits the liberty of *all* persons, it may violate substantive due process. When a law or action limits the liberty of *some* persons but not others, it may violate the equal protection clause. ■ **EXAMPLE 4.15** If a law prohibits all advertising on the sides of trucks, it raises a substantive due process question. If the law makes an exception to allow truck owners to advertise their own businesses, it raises an equal protection issue. ■

In an equal protection inquiry, when a law or action distinguishes between or among individuals, the basis for the distinction—that is, the classification—is examined. Depending on the classification, the courts apply different levels of scrutiny, or "tests," to determine whether the law or action violates the equal protection clause. The courts use one of three standards: strict scrutiny, intermediate scrutiny, or the "rational basis" test.

**Strict Scrutiny** If a law or action prohibits or inhibits some persons from exercising a fundamental right, the law or action will be subject to "strict scrutiny" by the courts. Under this standard, the classification must be necessary to promote a *compelling state interest.*

Compelling state interests include remedying past unconstitutional or illegal discrimination but do not include correcting the general effects of "society's discrimination." ■ **EXAMPLE 4.16** For a city to give preference to minority applicants in awarding construction contracts, it normally must identify past unconstitutional or illegal discrimination against minority construction firms. Because the policy is based on suspect traits (race and national origin), it will violate the equal protection clause *unless* it is necessary to promote a compelling state interest. ■ Generally, few laws or actions survive strict-scrutiny analysis by the courts.

**Intermediate Scrutiny** Another standard, that of *intermediate scrutiny,* is applied in cases involving discrimination based on gender or legitimacy (children born out of wedlock). Laws using these classifications must be *substantially related to important government*

*objectives.* ■ **EXAMPLE 4.17** An important government objective is preventing illegitimate teenage pregnancies. Males and females are not similarly situated in this regard because only females can become pregnant. Therefore, a law that punishes men but not women for statutory rape will be upheld even though it treats men and women unequally. ■

The state also has an important objective in establishing time limits (called *statutes of limitation*) for how long after an event a particular type of action can be brought. Nevertheless, the limitation period must be substantially related to the important objective of preventing fraudulent or outdated claims. ■ **EXAMPLE 4.18** A state law requires illegitimate children to bring paternity suits within six years of their births in order to seek support from their fathers. A court will strike down this law if legitimate children are allowed to seek support from their parents at any time. Distinguishing between support claims on the basis of legitimacy is not related to the important government objective of preventing fraudulent or outdated claims. ■

**The "Rational Basis" Test** In matters of economic or social welfare, a classification will be considered valid if there is any conceivable *rational basis* on which the classification might relate to a legitimate government interest. It is almost impossible for a law or action to fail the rational basis test.

■ **CASE IN POINT 4.19** A Kentucky statute prohibits businesses that sell substantial amounts of staple groceries or gasoline from applying for a license to sell wine and liquor. A local grocer (Maxwell's Pic-Pac) filed a lawsuit against the state, alleging that the statute and the regulation were unconstitutional under the equal protection clause. The court applied the rational basis test and ruled that the statute and regulation were rationally related to a legitimate government interest in reducing access to products with high alcohol content.

The court cited the problems caused by alcohol, including drunk driving, and noted that the state's interest in limiting access to such products extends to the general public. Grocery stores and gas stations pose a greater risk of exposing members of the public to alcohol. For these and other reasons, the state can restrict these places from selling wine and liquor.[32] ■

# 4-4 Privacy Rights

The U.S. Constitution does not explicitly mention a general right to privacy. In a 1928 Supreme Court case,

---

32. *Maxwell's Pic-Pac, Inc. v. Dehner,* 739 F.3d 936 (6th Cir. 2014).

*Olmstead v. United States,*[33] Justice Louis Brandeis stated in his dissent that the right to privacy is "the most comprehensive of rights and the right most valued by civilized men." The majority of the justices at that time, however, did not agree with Brandeis.

It was not until the 1960s that the Supreme Court endorsed the view that the Constitution protects individual privacy rights. In a landmark 1965 case, *Griswold v. Connecticut,*[34] the Supreme Court held that a constitutional right to privacy was implied by the First, Third, Fourth, Fifth, and Ninth Amendments.

Today, privacy rights receive protection under various federal statutes as well the U.S. Constitution. State constitutions and statutes also secure individuals' privacy rights, often to a significant degree. Privacy rights are also protected to an extent under tort law, consumer law, and employment law.

### 4–4a Federal Privacy Legislation

In the last several decades, Congress has enacted a number of statutes that protect the privacy of individuals in various areas of concern. Most of these statutes deal with personal information collected by governments or private businesses.

In the 1960s, Americans were sufficiently alarmed by the accumulation of personal information in government files that they pressured Congress to pass laws permitting individuals to access their files. Congress responded by passing the Freedom of Information Act, which allows any person to request copies of any information on her or him contained in federal government files. Congress later enacted the Privacy Act, which also gives persons the right to access such information.

In the 1990s, responding to the growing need to protect the privacy of individuals' health records—particularly computerized records—Congress passed the Health Insurance Portability and Accountability Act (HIPAA).[35] This act defines and limits the circumstances in which an individual's "protected health information" may be used or disclosed by health-care providers, health-care plans, and others. These and other major federal laws protecting privacy rights are listed and briefly described in Exhibit 4–2.

---

33. 277 U.S. 438, 48 S.Ct. 564, 72 L.Ed. 944 (1928).
34. 381 U.S. 479, 85 S.Ct. 1678, 14 L.Ed.2d 510 (1965).

35. HIPAA was enacted as Pub. L. No. 104-191 (1996) and is codified in 29 U.S.C.A. Sections 1181 *et seq.*

**EXHIBIT 4–2  Federal Legislation Relating to Privacy**

| Freedom of Information Act (1966) | Provides that individuals have a right to obtain access to information about them collected in government files. |
|---|---|
| Privacy Act (1974) | Protects the privacy of individuals about whom the federal government has information. Regulates agencies' use and disclosure of data, and gives individuals access to and a means to correct inaccuracies. |
| Electronic Communications Privacy Act (1986) | Prohibits the interception of information communicated by electronic means. |
| Health Insurance Portability and Accountability Act (1996) | Requires health-care providers and health-care plans to inform patients of their privacy rights and of how their personal medical information may be used. States that medical records may not be used for purposes unrelated to health care or disclosed without permission. |
| Financial Services Modernization Act (Gramm-Leach-Bliley Act) (1999) | Prohibits the disclosure of nonpublic personal information about a consumer to an unaffiliated third party unless strict disclosure and opt-out requirements are met. |

## 4–4b The USA Patriot Act and the USA Freedom Act

The USA Patriot Act was passed by Congress in the wake of the terrorist attacks of September 11, 2001.[36] The Patriot Act has given government officials increased authority to monitor Internet activities (such as e-mail and Web site visits) and to gain access to personal financial information and student information. Law enforcement officials can track the telephone and e-mail communications of one party to find out the identity of the other party or parties. Privacy advocates argue that this law adversely affects the constitutional rights of all Americans, and it has been widely criticized in the media.

While the bulk of the Patriot Act is permanent law, its most controversial surveillance provisions had to be reauthorized every four years and expired in June 2015. Most of the expired provisions were restored by the USA Freedom Act, which extends surveillance authority through 2019.[37] The Freedom Act did amend a portion of the Patriot Act in an attempt to stop the National Security Agency (NSA) from collecting mass phone data. (Note, however, that the act still allows the data to be collected by private phone companies, and the NSA can obtain data about targeted individuals through these companies.)

36. The Uniting and Strengthening America by Providing Appropriate Tools Required to Intercept and Obstruct Terrorism Act of 2001, also known as the USA Patriot Act, was enacted as Pub. L. No. 107-56 (2001) and last reauthorized by Pub. L. No. 112-114 (2011).

37. The full title of this statute is Uniting and Strengthening America by Fulfilling Rights and Ending Eavesdropping, Dragnet-collection and Online Monitoring, H.R. 3361.

## Reviewing: Business and the Constitution

A state legislature enacted a statute that required any motorcycle operator or passenger on the state's highways to wear a protective helmet. Jim Alderman, a licensed motorcycle operator, sued the state to block enforcement of the law. Alderman asserted that the statute violated the equal protection clause because it placed requirements on motorcyclists that were not imposed on other motorists. Using the information presented in the chapter, answer the following questions.

1. Why does this statute raise equal protection issues instead of substantive due process concerns?
2. What are the three levels of scrutiny that the courts use in determining whether a law violates the equal protection clause?
3. Which standard of scrutiny, or test, would apply to this situation? Why?
4. Applying this standard, is the helmet statute constitutional? Why or why not?

**Debate This** . . . *Legislation aimed at "protecting people from themselves" concerns the individual as well as the public in general. Protective helmet laws are just one example of such legislation. Should individuals be allowed to engage in unsafe activities if they choose to do so?*

## Terms and Concepts

| | | |
|---|---|---|
| Bill of Rights 75 | federal form of government 70 | privileges and immunities clause 71 |
| checks and balances 71 | filtering software 79 | probable cause 82 |
| commerce clause 71 | free exercise clause 80 | search warrant 82 |
| compelling government interest 77 | full faith and credit clause 71 | sovereignty 70 |
| due process clause 83 | meta tag 80 | supremacy clause 75 |
| equal protection clause 84 | police powers 70 | symbolic speech 77 |
| establishment clause 80 | preemption 75 | |

## Issue Spotters

1. Can a state, in the interest of energy conservation, ban all advertising by power utilities if conservation could be accomplished by less restrictive means? Why or why not? (See *Business and the Bill of Rights*.)

2. Suppose that a state imposes a higher tax on out-of-state companies doing business in the state than it imposes on in-state companies. Is this a violation of equal protection if the only reason for the tax is to protect the local firms from out-of-state competition? Explain. (See *The Constitutional Powers of Government*.)

• **Check your answers to the Issue Spotters against the answers provided in Appendix D at the end of this text.**

## Business Scenarios

**4–1. Commerce Clause.** A Georgia state law requires the use of contoured rear-fender mudguards on trucks and trailers operating within Georgia state lines. The statute further makes it illegal for trucks and trailers to use straight mudguards. In approximately thirty-five other states, straight mudguards are legal. Moreover, in Florida, straight mudguards are explicitly required by law. There is some evidence suggesting that contoured mudguards might be a little safer than straight mudguards. Discuss whether this Georgia statute violates any constitutional provisions. (See *The Constitutional Powers of Government*.)

**4–2. Equal Protection.** With the objectives of preventing crime, maintaining property values, and preserving the quality of urban life, New York City enacted an ordinance to regulate the locations of adult entertainment establishments. The ordinance expressly applied to female, but not male, topless entertainment. Adele Buzzetti owned the Cozy Cabin, a New York City cabaret that featured female topless dancers. Buzzetti and an anonymous dancer filed a suit in a federal district court against the city, asking the court to block the enforcement of the ordinance. The plaintiffs argued, in part, that the ordinance violated the equal protection clause. Under the equal protection clause, what standard applies to the court's consideration of this ordinance? Under this test, how should the court rule? Why? (See *Due Process and Equal Protection*.)

## Business Case Problems

**4–3. Spotlight on Plagiarism—Due Process.**  The Russ College of Engineering and Technology of Ohio University announced in a press conference that it had found "rampant and flagrant plagiarism" in the theses of mechanical engineering graduate students. Faculty singled out for "ignoring their ethical responsibilities" included Jay Gunasekera, chair of the department. Gunasekera was prohibited from advising students. He filed a suit against Dennis Irwin, the dean of Russ College, for violating his due process rights. What does due process require in these circumstances? Why? [*Gunasekera v. Irwin,* 551 F.3d 461 (6th Cir. 2009)] (See *Due Process and Equal Protection.*)

**4–4. Business Case Problem with Sample Answer— The Dormant Commerce Clause.**  In 2001, Puerto Rico enacted a law that requires specific labels on cement sold in Puerto Rico and imposes fines for any violations of these requirements. The law prohibits the sale or distribution of cement manufactured outside Puerto Rico that does not carry a required label warning that the cement may not be used in government-financed construction projects. Antilles Cement Corp., a Puerto Rican firm that imports foreign cement, filed a complaint in federal court, claiming that this law violated the dormant commerce clause. (The dormant commerce clause doctrine applies not only to commerce among the states and U.S. territories, but also to international commerce.) Did the 2001 Puerto Rican law violate the dormant commerce clause? Why or why not? [*Antilles Cement Corp. v. Fortuno,* 670 F.3d 310 (1st Cir. 2012)] (See *The Constitutional Powers of Government.*)

• **For a sample answer to Problem 4–4, go to Appendix E at the end of this text.**

**4–5. Freedom of Speech.** Mark Wooden sent an e-mail to an alderwoman for the city of St. Louis. Attached was a nineteen-minute audio file that compared her to the biblical character Jezebel. The audio said she was a "bitch in the Sixth Ward," spending too much time with the rich and powerful and too little time with the poor. In a menacing, maniacal tone, Wooden said that he was "dusting off a sawed-off shotgun," called himself a "domestic terrorist," and referred to the assassination of President John Kennedy, the murder of federal judge John Roll, and the shooting of Representative Gabrielle Giffords. Feeling threatened, the alderwoman called the police. Wooden was convicted of harassment under a state criminal statute. Was this conviction unconstitutional under the First Amendment? Discuss. [*State of Missouri v. Wooden,* 388 S.W.3d 522 (Mo. 2013)] (See *Business and the Bill of Rights.*)

**4–6. Equal Protection.** Abbott Laboratories licensed SmithKline Beecham Corp. to market an Abbott human immunodeficiency virus (HIV) drug in conjunction with one of SmithKline's drugs. Abbott then increased the price of its drug fourfold, forcing SmithKline to increase its prices and thereby driving business to Abbott's own combination drug. SmithKline filed a suit in a federal district court against Abbott. During jury selection, Abbott struck the only self-identified gay person among the potential jurors. (The pricing of HIV drugs is of considerable concern in the gay community.) Could the equal protection clause be applied to prohibit discrimination based on sexual orientation in jury selection? Discuss. [*SmithKline Beecham Corp. v. Abbott Laboratories,* 740 F.3d 471 (9th Cir. 2014)] (See *Due Process and Equal Protection.*)

**4–7. Procedural Due Process.** Robert Brown applied for admission to the University of Kansas School of Law. Brown answered "no" to questions on the application asking if he had a criminal history and acknowledged that a false answer constituted "cause for . . . dismissal." In fact, Brown had criminal convictions for domestic battery and driving under the influence. He was accepted for admission to the school. When school officials discovered his history, however, he was notified of their intent to dismiss him and given an opportunity to respond in writing. He demanded a hearing. The officials refused to grant Brown a hearing and then expelled him. Did the school's actions deny Brown due process? Discuss. [*Brown v. University of Kansas,* 599 Fed.Appx. 833 (10th Cir. 2015)] (See *Due Process and Equal Protection.*)

**4–8. The Commerce Clause.** Regency Transportation, Inc., operates a freight business throughout the eastern United States. Regency maintains its corporate headquarters, four warehouses, and a maintenance facility and terminal location for repairing and storing vehicles in Massachusetts. All of the vehicles in Regency's fleet were bought in other states. Massachusetts imposes a use tax on all taxpayers subject to its jurisdiction, including those that do business in interstate commerce, as Regency does. When Massachusetts imposed the tax on the purchase price of each tractor and trailer in Regency's fleet, the trucking firm challenged the assessment as discriminatory under the commerce clause. What is the chief consideration under the commerce clause when a state law affects interstate commerce?

Is Massachusetts's use tax valid? Explain. [*Regency Transportation, Inc. v. Commissioner of Revenue,* 473 Mass. 459, 42 N.E.3d 1133 (2016)] (See *The Constitutional Powers of Government.*)

**4–9. A Question of Ethics—Defamation.** *Aric Toll owns and manages the Balboa Island Village Inn, a restaurant and bar in Newport Beach, California. Anne Lemen lives across from the inn. Lemen complained to the authorities about the inn's customers, whom she called "drunks" and "whores." She referred to Aric's wife as "Madam Whore" and told neighbors that the owners were involved in illegal drugs and prostitution. Lemen told Ewa Cook, a bartender at the Inn, that Cook "worked for Satan." She repeated her statements to potential customers, and the inn's sales dropped more than 20 percent. The inn filed a suit against Lemen. [Balboa Island Village Inn, Inc. v. Lemen, 40 Cal.4th 1141, 156 P.3d 339 (2007)] (See Business and the Bill of Rights.)*

**(a)** Are Lemen's statements about the inn's owners, customers, and activities protected by the U.S. Constitution? Should such statements be protected? In whose favor should the court rule? Why?

**(b)** Did Lemen behave unethically in the circumstances of this case? Explain.

**4–10. Special Case Analysis—Freedom of Religion.** Go to Case Analysis 4.3, *Thompson v. Holm.* Read the excerpt, and answer the following questions.

**(a) Issue:** The focus in this case was on an allegation of the violation of which clause of the U.S. Constitution, and by what means?

**(b) Rule of Law:** What is required to establish that this clause has been violated?

**(c) Applying the Rule of Law:** How did the court determine whether the claim of a violation was supported in this case?

**(d) Conclusion:** What did the federal appellate court conclude with respect to the plaintiff's claim, and what did the court order as the next step in the case?

# Legal Reasoning Group Activity

**4–11. Free Speech and Equal Protection.** For many years, New York City has had to deal with the vandalism and defacement of public property caused by unauthorized graffiti. In an effort to stop the damage, the city banned the sale of aerosol spray-paint cans and broad-tipped indelible markers to persons under twenty-one years of age. The new rules also prohibited people from possessing these items on property other than their own. Within a year, five people under age twenty-one were cited for violations of these regulations, and 871 individuals were arrested for actually making graffiti.

Lindsey Vincenty and other artists wished to create graffiti on legal surfaces, such as canvas, wood, and clothing. Unable to buy supplies in the city or to carry them into the city from elsewhere, Vincenty and others filed a lawsuit on behalf of themselves and other young artists against Michael

Bloomberg, the city's mayor, and others. The plaintiffs claimed that, among other things, the new rules violated their right to freedom of speech.

**(a)** One group will argue in favor of the plaintiffs and provide several reasons why the court should hold that the city's new rules violate the plaintiffs' freedom of speech. (See *Business and the Bill of Rights.*)

**(b)** Another group will develop a counterargument that outlines the reasons why the new rules do not violate free speech rights. (See *Business and the Bill of Rights.*)

**(c)** A third group will argue that the city's ban violates the equal protection clause because it applies only to persons under age twenty-one. (See *Due Process and Equal Protection.*)

# Answers to the *Issue Spotters*

**1.** *Can a state, in the interest of energy conservation, ban all advertising by power utilities if conservation could be accomplished by less restrictive means? Why or why not?* No. Even if commercial speech is neither related to illegal activities nor misleading, it may be restricted if a state has a substantial interest that cannot be achieved by less restrictive means. In this case, the interest in energy conservation is substantial, but it could be achieved by less restrictive means. That would be the utilities' defense against the enforcement of this state law.

**2.** *Is this a violation of equal protection if the only reason for the tax is to protect the local firms from out-of-state competition? Explain.* Yes. The tax would limit the liberty of some persons (out-of-state businesses), so it is subject to a review under the equal protection clause. Protecting local businesses from out-of-state competition is not a legitimate government objective. Thus, such a tax would violate the equal protection clause.

# Sample Answers for *Business Case Problems with Sample Answer*

**Problem 4–4.** *The Dormant Commerce Clause.* The court ruled that, like a state, Puerto Rico generally may not enact policies that discriminate against out-of-state commerce. The law requiring companies that sell cement in Puerto Rico to place certain labels on their products is clearly an attempt to regulate the cement market. The law imposed labeling regulations that affect transactions between the citizens of Puerto Rico and private companies. State laws that on their face discriminate against foreign commerce are almost always invalid, and this Puerto Rican law is such a law. The discriminatory labeling requirement placed sellers of cement manufactured outside Puerto Rico at a competitive disadvantage. This law therefore contravenes the dormant commerce clause.

# Chapter 5

# CHAPTER

# Criminal Law and Cyber Crime

riminal law is an important part of the legal environment of business. Society imposes a variety of sanctions to protect businesses from harm so that they can compete and flourish. These sanctions include damages for various types of tortious conduct, damages for breach of contract, and various equitable remedies. Additional sanctions are imposed under criminal law.

Many statutes regulating business provide for criminal as well as civil penalties.

In this chapter, after explaining some essential differences between criminal law and civil law, we look at how crimes are classified and at the elements that must be present for criminal liability to exist. We then examine the various categories of crimes, the defenses that can be raised to avoid criminal liability, and the rules of criminal procedure.

We conclude the chapter with a discussion of crimes that occur in cyberspace, which are often called *cyber crimes.* Cyber attacks are becoming all too common—even e-mail and data of government agencies and of former U.S. presidents have been hacked.

## 10–1 Civil Law and Criminal Law

*Civil law* pertains to the duties that exist between persons or between persons and their governments. Criminal law, in contrast, has to do with crime. A **crime** can be defined as a wrong against society set forth in a statute and punishable by a fine and/or imprisonment—or, in some cases, death.

Because crimes are *offenses against society as a whole,* they are prosecuted by a public official, such as a district attorney (D.A.) or an attorney general (A.G.), not by the victims. Once a crime has been reported, the D.A.'s office decides whether to file criminal charges and to what extent to pursue the prosecution or carry out additional investigation.

### 10–1a Key Differences between Civil Law and Criminal Law

Because the state has extensive resources at its disposal when prosecuting criminal cases, there are numerous procedural safeguards to protect the rights of defendants. We look here at one of these safeguards—the higher burden of proof that applies in a criminal case—as well as the harsher sanctions for criminal acts compared with those for civil wrongs. Exhibit 10–1

summarizes these and other key differences between civil law and criminal law.

**Burden of Proof** In a civil case, the plaintiff usually must prove his or her case by a *preponderance of the evidence.* Under this standard, the plaintiff must convince the court that based on the evidence presented by both parties, it is more likely than not that the plaintiff's allegation is true.

In a criminal case, in contrast, the government must prove its case **beyond a reasonable doubt.** If the jury views the evidence in the case as reasonably permitting either a guilty or a not guilty verdict, then the jury's verdict must be not guilty. In other words, the government (prosecutor) must prove beyond a reasonable doubt that the defendant has committed every essential element of the offense with which she or he is charged.

Note also that in a criminal case, the jury's verdict normally must be unanimous—agreed to by all members of the jury—to convict the defendant.[1] (In a civil trial by jury, in contrast, typically only three-fourths of the jurors need to agree.)

---

1. A few states allow jury verdicts that are not unanimous. Arizona, for example, allows six of eight jurors to reach a verdict in criminal cases. Louisiana and Oregon have also relaxed the requirement of unanimous jury verdicts.

**EXHIBIT 10–1  Key Differences between Civil Law and Criminal Law**

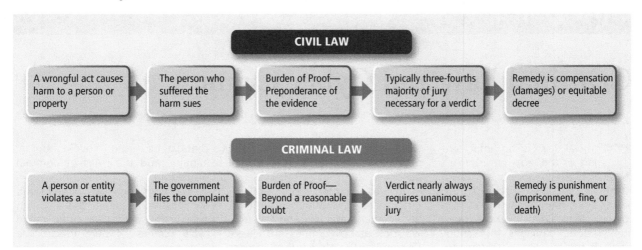

## Criminal Sanctions

The sanctions imposed on criminal wrongdoers are normally harsher than those applied in civil cases. Remember that the purpose of tort law is to enable a person harmed by a wrongful act to obtain compensation from the wrongdoer, rather than to punish the wrongdoer. In contrast, criminal sanctions are designed to punish those who commit crimes and to deter others from committing similar acts in the future.

Criminal sanctions include fines as well as the much stiffer penalty of the loss of one's liberty by incarceration in a jail or prison. Most criminal sanctions also involve probation and sometimes require performance of community service, completion of an educational or treatment program, or payment of restitution. The harshest criminal sanction is, of course, the death penalty.

## 10–1b  Civil Liability for Criminal Acts

Some torts, such as assault and battery, provide a basis for a criminal prosecution as well as a civil action in tort. ■ **EXAMPLE 10.1** Jonas is walking down the street, minding his own business, when a person attacks him. In the ensuing struggle, the attacker stabs Jonas several times, seriously injuring him. A police officer restrains and arrests the assailant. In this situation, the attacker may be subject both to criminal prosecution by the state and to a tort lawsuit brought by Jonas to obtain compensation for his injuries. ■

Exhibit 10–2 illustrates how the same wrongful act can result in both a civil (tort) action and a criminal action against the wrongdoer.

## 10–1c  Classification of Crimes

Depending on their degree of seriousness, crimes are classified as felonies or misdemeanors. **Felonies** are serious crimes punishable by death or by imprisonment for more than one year.[2] Many states also define different degrees of felony offenses and vary the punishment according to the degree.[3] For instance, most jurisdictions punish a burglary that involves forced entry into a home at night more harshly than a burglary that involves breaking into a nonresidential building during the day.

**Misdemeanors** are less serious crimes, punishable by a fine or by confinement for up to a year. **Petty offenses** are minor violations, such as jaywalking or violations of building codes, considered to be a subset of misdemeanors. Even for petty offenses, however, a guilty party can be put in jail for a few days, fined, or both, depending on state or local law. Whether a crime is a felony or a misdemeanor can determine in which court the case is tried and, in some states, whether the defendant has a right to a jury trial.

---

2. Federal law and most state laws use this definition, but there is some variation among states as to the length of imprisonment associated with a felony conviction.

3. Note that the Model Penal Code is not a uniform code and each state has developed its own set of laws governing criminal acts. Thus, types of crimes and prescribed punishments may differ from one jurisdiction to another.

**EXHIBIT 10–2** Civil (Tort) Lawsuit and Criminal Prosecution for the Same Act

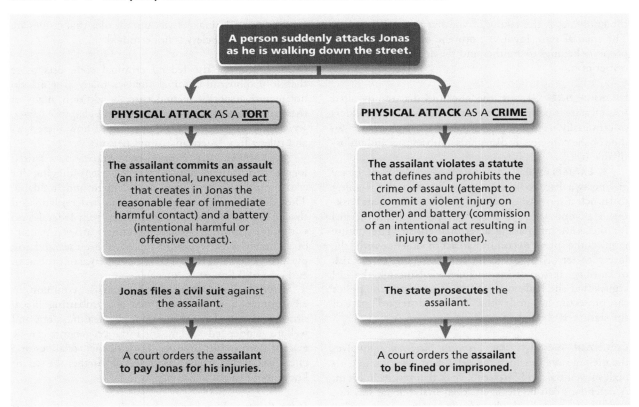

## 10–2 Criminal Liability

The following two elements normally must exist *simultaneously* for a person to be convicted of a crime:

1. The performance of a prohibited act *(actus reus)*.
2. A specified state of mind, or intent, on the part of the actor *(mens rea)*.

### 10–2a The Criminal Act

Every criminal statute prohibits certain behavior. Most crimes require an act of *commission*—that is, a person must *do* something in order to be accused of a crime. In criminal law, a prohibited act is referred to as the **actus reus**,[4] or guilty act. In some instances, an act of omission can be a crime, but only when a person has a legal duty to perform the omitted act, such as filing a tax return.

The guilty act requirement is based on one of the premises of criminal law—that a person should be punished for harm done to society. For a crime to exist, the guilty act must thus cause some harm to a person or to property. Thinking about killing someone or about stealing a car may be morally wrong, but the thoughts do no harm until they are translated into action.

Of course, a person can be punished for *attempting* murder or robbery, but normally only if he or she has taken substantial steps toward the criminal objective. Additionally, the person must have specifically intended to commit the crime to be convicted of an attempt.

### 10–2b State of Mind

*Mens rea*,[5] or wrongful mental state, also is typically required to establish criminal liability. The required mental state, or intent, is indicated in the applicable statute or law. Murder, for instance, involves the guilty act of

---

4. Pronounced *ak*-tuhs *ray*-uhs.

5. Pronounced *mehns ray*-uh.

killing another human being, and the guilty mental state is the desire, or intent, to take another's life. For theft, the guilty act is the taking of another person's property. The mental state involves both the awareness that the property belongs to another and the desire to deprive the owner of it.

**Recklessness** A court can also find that the required mental state is present when a defendant's acts are reckless or criminally negligent. A defendant is *criminally reckless* if he or she consciously disregards a substantial and unjustifiable risk.

■ **EXAMPLE 10.2** A fourteen-year-old New Jersey girl posts a Facebook message saying that she is going to launch a terrorist attack on her high school and asking if anyone wants to help. The police arrest the girl for the crime of making a terrorist threat. The statute requires the intent to commit an act of violence with "the intent to terrorize" or "in reckless disregard of the risk of causing" terror or inconvenience. Although the girl argues that she had no intent to cause harm, the police can prosecute her under the "reckless disregard" part of the statute. ■

**Criminal Negligence** *Criminal negligence* involves the mental state in which the defendant takes an unjustified, substantial, and foreseeable risk that results in harm. A defendant can be negligent even if she or he was not actually aware of the risk but *should have been aware* of it.[6]

A homicide is classified as *involuntary manslaughter* when it results from an act of criminal negligence and there is no intent to kill. ■ **EXAMPLE 10.3** Dr. Conrad Murray, the personal physician of pop star Michael Jackson, was convicted of involuntary manslaughter for prescribing the drug that led to Jackson's sudden death. Murray had given Jackson propofol, a powerful anesthetic normally used in surgery, as a sleep aid on the night of his death, even though he knew that Jackson had already taken other sedatives. ■

**Strict Liability and Overcriminalization** An increasing number of laws and regulations impose criminal sanctions for strict liability crimes. Strict liability crimes are offenses that do not require a wrongful mental state to establish criminal liability.

Proponents of strict liability criminal laws argue that they are necessary to protect the public and the environment. Critics say laws that criminalize conduct without requiring intent have led to *overcriminalization*. They argue that when the requirement of intent is removed,

_____
6. Model Penal Code Section 2.02(2)(d).

people are more likely to commit crimes unknowingly—and perhaps even innocently. When an honest mistake can lead to a criminal conviction, the idea that crimes are a wrong against society is undermined.

**Federal Crimes.** The federal criminal code lists more than four thousand criminal offenses, many of which do not require a specific mental state. In addition, many of these rules do not require intent. See this chapter's *Managerial Strategy* feature for a discussion of how these laws and rules affect American businesspersons.

■ **EXAMPLE 10.4** Eddie Leroy Anderson, a retired logger and former science teacher, went digging for arrowheads with his son near a campground in Idaho. They did not realize that they were on federal land and that it is a felony to remove artifacts from federal land without a permit. Although the crime carries a penalty of as much as two years in prison, the father and son pleaded guilty, and each received a sentence of probation and a $1,500 fine. ■

Strict liability crimes are particularly common in environmental laws, laws aimed at combatting illegal drugs, and other laws affecting public health, safety, and welfare. Under federal law, for instance, tenants can be evicted from public housing if one of their relatives or a guest used illegal drugs—regardless of whether the tenant knew about the drug activity.

**State Crimes.** Many states have also enacted laws that punish behavior as criminal without the need to show criminal intent. ■ **EXAMPLE 10.5** In Arizona, a hunter who shoots an elk outside the area specified by the hunting permit has committed a crime. The hunter can be convicted of the crime regardless of her or his intent or knowledge of the law. ■

## 10–2c Corporate Criminal Liability

A corporation is a legal entity created under the laws of a state. At one time, it was thought that a corporation could not incur criminal liability because, although a corporation is a legal person, it can act only through its agents (corporate directors, officers, and employees). Therefore, the corporate entity itself could not "intend" to commit a crime. Over time, this view has changed. Obviously, corporations cannot be imprisoned, but they can be fined or denied certain legal privileges (such as necessary licenses).

**Liability of the Corporate Entity** Today, corporations normally are liable for the crimes committed by their agents and employees within the course and scope of

**The Criminalization of American Business**

What do Bank of America, Citigroup, JPMorgan Chase, and Goldman Sachs have in common? All paid hefty fines for purportedly misleading investors about mortgage-backed securities. In fact, these companies paid the government a total of $50 billion in fines. The payments were made in lieu of criminal prosecutions.

Today, several hundred thousand federal rules that apply to businesses carry some form of criminal penalty. That is in addition to more than four thousand federal laws, many of which carry criminal sanctions for their violation. From 2000 to the beginning of 2017, about 2,200 corporations either were convicted or pleaded guilty to violating federal statutes or rules.

### Criminal Convictions

The first successful criminal conviction in a federal court against a company—the New York Central and Hudson River Railroad—was upheld by the Supreme Court in 1909 (the violation: cutting prices).[a] Many other successful convictions followed.

One landmark case developed the *aggregation test,* now called the Doctrine of Collective Knowledge.[b] This test aggregates the omissions and acts of two or more persons in a corporation, thereby constructing an *actus reus* and a *mens rea* out of the conduct and knowledge of several individuals.

Not all government attempts at applying criminal law to corporations survive. In 2013, for example, Sentinel Offender Services, LLC, prevailed on appeal. There was no actual evidence to show that the company had acted with specific intent to commit theft by deception.[c]

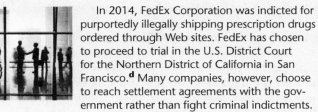

In 2014, FedEx Corporation was indicted for purportedly illegally shipping prescription drugs ordered through Web sites. FedEx has chosen to proceed to trial in the U.S. District Court for the Northern District of California in San Francisco.[d] Many companies, however, choose to reach settlement agreements with the government rather than fight criminal indictments.

**Many Pay Substantial
Fines in Lieu of Prosecution**

More than three hundred corporations reached so-called non-prosecution agreements with the government from 2000 to the beginning of 2017. These agreements typically involve multimillion- or multibillion-dollar fines. This number does not include fines paid to the Environmental Protection Agency or to the Fish and Wildlife Service.

According to law professors Margaret Lemos and Max Minzner, "Public enforcers often seek large monetary awards for self-interested reasons divorced from the public interest and deterrents. The incentives are strongest when enforcement agencies are permitted to retain all or some of the proceeds of enforcement."[e]

**Business Questions**

1. *Why might a corporation's managers agree to pay a large fine rather than to be indicted and proceed to trial?*

2. *How does a manager determine the optimal amount of legal research to undertake to prevent her or his company from violating the many thousands of federal regulations?*

---

a. *New York Central and Hudson River Railroad v. United States,* 212 U.S. 481, 29 S.Ct. 304, 53 L.Ed 613 (1909).
b. *United States v. Bank of New England,* 821 F.2d 844 (1st Cir. 1987).
c. *McGee v. Sentinel Offender Services, LLC,* 719 F.3d 1236 (11th Cir. 2013).

d. *United States v. FedEx Corp.,* Case No. CR14-380 Northern District, California, July 17, 2014.
e. Margaret Lemos and Max Minzner, "For-Profit Public Enforcement," *Harvard Law Review 127,* January 17, 2014.

---

their employment.[7] For liability to be imposed, the prosecutor generally must show that the corporation could have prevented the act or that a supervisor authorized or had knowledge of the act. In addition, corporations can be criminally liable for failing to perform specific duties imposed by law (such as duties under environmental laws or securities laws).

■ **CASE IN POINT 10.6** A prostitution ring, the Gold Club, was operating out of some motels in West Virginia. A motel manager, who was also a corporate officer, gave discounted rates to Gold Club prostitutes, and they paid him in cash. The corporation received a portion of the

---

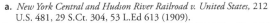

7. See Model Penal Code Section 2.07.

funds generated by the Gold Club's illegal operations. A jury found that the corporation was criminally liable because a supervisor within the corporation—the motel manager—had knowledge of the prostitution activities and the corporation had allowed it to continue.[8] ■

**Liability of Corporate Officers and Directors** Corporate directors and officers are personally liable for the crimes they commit, regardless of whether the crimes were committed for their private benefit or on the corporation's behalf. Additionally, corporate directors and officers may be held liable for the actions of employees under their supervision. Under the *responsible corporate officer* doctrine, a court may impose criminal liability on a corporate officer who participated in, directed, or merely knew about a given criminal violation.

■ **CASE IN POINT 10.7** Austin DeCoster owned and controlled Quality Egg, LLC, an egg production and processing company with facilities across Iowa. His son Peter DeCoster was the chief operating officer. Due to unsanitary conditions in some of its facilities, Quality shipped and sold eggs that contained salmonella bacteria, which sickened thousands of people across the United States.

The federal government prosecuted the DeCosters under the responsible corporate officer doctrine, in part, for Quality's failure to comply with regulations on egg production facilities. The DeCosters ultimately pleaded guilty to violating three criminal statutes. But when they were ordered to serve three months in jail, the DeCosters challenged the sentence as unconstitutional. The court held that the sentence of incarceration was appropriate because the evidence suggested that the defendants knew about the unsanitary conditions in their processing plants.[9] ■

# 10–3 Types of Crimes

Federal, state, and local laws provide for the classification and punishment of hundreds of thousands of different criminal acts. Generally, though, criminal acts fall into five broad categories: violent crime (crimes against persons), property crime, public order crime, white-collar crime, and organized crime. In addition, when crimes are committed in cyberspace rather the physical world, we often refer to them as cyber crimes.

## 10–3a Violent Crime

Certain crimes are called *violent crimes,* or crimes against persons, because they cause others to suffer harm or death. Murder is a violent crime. So is sexual assault, or rape. **Robbery**—defined as the taking of money, personal property, or any other article of value from a person by means of force or fear—is also a violent crime. Typically, states have more severe penalties for *aggravated robbery*—robbery with the use of a deadly weapon.

Assault and battery, which were discussed in the context of tort law, are also classified as violent crimes. ■ **EXAMPLE 10.8** Former rap star Flavor Flav (whose real name is William Drayton) was arrested in Las Vegas on assault and battery charges. During an argument with his fiancée, Drayton allegedly threw her to the ground and then grabbed two kitchen knives and chased her son. ■

Each violent crime is further classified by degree, depending on the circumstances surrounding the criminal act. These circumstances include the intent of the person committing the crime and whether a weapon was used. For crimes other than murder, the level of pain and suffering experienced by the victim is also a factor.

## 10–3b Property Crime

The most common type of criminal activity is property crime, in which the goal of the offender is some form of economic gain or the damaging of property. Robbery is a form of property crime, as well as a violent crime, because the offender seeks to gain the property of another.

**Burglary** Traditionally, **burglary** was defined as breaking and entering the dwelling of another at night with the intent to commit a felony. This definition was aimed at protecting an individual's home and its occupants.

Most state statutes have eliminated some of the requirements found in the common law definition. The time of day at which the breaking and entering occurs, for instance, is usually immaterial. State statutes frequently omit the element of breaking, and some states do not require that the building be a dwelling. When a deadly weapon is used in a burglary, the perpetrator can be charged with *aggravated burglary* and punished more severely.

The defendant in the following case challenged whether the evidence presented by the state was sufficient to support his conviction for burglary.

---

8. As a result of the convictions, the motel manager was sentenced to fifteen months in prison, and the corporation was ordered to forfeit the motel property. *United States v. Singh*, 518 F.3d 236 (4th Cir. 2008).
9. *United States v. Quality Egg, LLC*, 99 F.Supp.3d 920 (N.D. Iowa 2015).

# State of Minnesota v. Smith

Court of Appeals of Minnesota, 2015 WL 303643 (2015).

**Background and Facts** Over a Labor Day weekend in Rochester, Minnesota, two homes and the Rochester Tennis Center, a business, were burglarized. One day later, at the nearby Bell Tower Inn, cleaning personnel found a garbage bag in the room of Albert Smith. The bag contained a passport that belonged to the owner of one of the burglarized homes and documents that belonged to the business.

Police officers arrested Smith. They found a Sentry safe stolen in one of the burglaries in Smith's room. A search of a bag in his possession revealed other stolen items, as well as burglary tools. Smith claimed that he had bought some of the items from a man named Mali and had bought other items on Craigslist. He said that he had found the documents from the tennis center in a dumpster. Convicted of burglary in a Minnesota state court, Smith appealed.

## In the Language of the Court

CHUTICH, Judge.

\* \* \* \*

\* \* \* Both burglarized homes and the burglarized business were within a few blocks of the hotel where Smith stayed over the Labor Day weekend, and each burglary occurred during the holiday weekend. In fact, two of the burglaries occurred in the morning and early evening of September 3. On the morning of September 4, only hours after two of the burglaries occurred, Smith possessed property stolen in each of the three burglaries. Some of the items found in Smith's possession were worthless to anyone but their owners, including a passport, a birth certificate, and property documents. In addition, the hotel manager saw Smith carrying the stolen Sentry safe into the hotel during the relevant time frame and identified the safe found in Smith's room as the Sentry safe. When the police confronted Smith in the hotel, he was carrying a bag that contained numerous stolen electronics and burglary tools, including a flashlight and gloves.

\* \* \* Smith possessed property reported as stolen from both homes and the business, and the nature of several of the items he possessed suggested that they came directly from the burglaries. \* \* \* The assortment of items found in Smith's possession, from the electronics to the financially worthless documents, as well as gloves and a flashlight, illustrate Smith's guilt of each of the burglaries. The mishmash of items found in defendant's possession looks like the raw loot that a thief quickly grabbed and made off with. Moreover, *the brief time that passed between the burglaries and the discovery of the stolen items in Smith's possession, along with the close proximity of the hotel to the burglarized homes and tennis center, are consistent with the findings that Smith was the thief.* [Emphasis added.]

Smith contends that a reasonable inference can be drawn from his alternate explanation of the events that is inconsistent with finding him guilty of the burglaries, namely that he obtained the valuable stolen items from Mali or from Craigslist, while he found the tennis club's records in a dumpster. The [trial] court, however, did not find Smith's testimony credible, determining that Smith "demonstrated a flexible approach to the truth—a looseness with the facts, in which the incriminatory truth is conceded only when and to the extent it is inescapable." Further, we consider it improbable, considering the timing and locations of the break-ins, that Smith came into possession of stolen items from a September 3 burglary by way of Mali, while finding additional stolen items from another September 3 burglary that same evening by fortuitously finding them in a dumpster. \* \* \* The only rational hypothesis that can be drawn from the proved circumstances is that Smith committed the burglaries.

**Decision and Remedy** *A state intermediate appellate court affirmed Smith's conviction for burglary. The appellate court concluded that the circumstances "are consistent with guilt and inconsistent with any rational hypothesis except that of guilt."*

## Critical Thinking

• **Social** *Who is in the best position to evaluate the credibility of the evidence and the witnesses in a case? Why?*

**Larceny** Under the common law, the crime of **larceny** involved the unlawful taking and carrying away of someone else's personal property with the intent to permanently deprive the owner of possession. Put simply, larceny is stealing, or theft. Whereas robbery involves force or fear, larceny does not. Therefore, picking pockets is larceny, not robbery. Similarly, an employee taking company products and supplies home for personal use without permission is committing larceny.

Most states have expanded the definition of property that is subject to larceny statutes. Stealing computer programs may constitute larceny even though the "property" is not physical (see the discussion of computer crime later in this chapter). The theft of natural gas, Internet access, or television cable service can also constitute larceny.

**Obtaining Goods by False Pretenses** Obtaining goods by means of false pretenses is a form of theft that involves trickery or fraud, such as using someone else's credit-card number without permission to purchase an iPad. Statutes dealing with such illegal activities vary widely from state to state. They often apply not only to property, but also to services and cash.

■ **CASE IN POINT 10.9** While Matthew Steffes was incarcerated, he started a scheme to make free collect calls from prison. (A *collect call* is a telephone call in which the calling party places a call at the called party's expense.) Steffes had his friends and family members set up new phone number accounts by giving false information to AT&T. This information included fictitious business names, as well as personal identifying information stolen from a health-care clinic. Once a new phone number was working, Steffes made unlimited collect calls to it without paying the bill until AT&T eventually shut down the account. For nearly two years, Steffes used sixty fraudulently obtained phone numbers to make hundreds of collect calls. The loss to AT&T was more than $28,000.

Steffes was convicted in a state court of theft by fraud of property in excess of $10,000. He appealed, arguing that he had not made false representations to AT&T. The Wisconsin Supreme Court affirmed his conviction. The court held that Steffes had made false representations to AT&T by providing fictitious business names and stolen personal identifying information to the phone company. He made these false representations so that he could make phone calls without paying for them, which deprived the company of its "property"—meaning its electricity.[10] ■

10. *State of Wisconsin v. Steffes,* 347 Wis.2d 683, 832 N.W.2d 101 (2013).

**Theft** Sometimes, state statutes consolidate the crime of obtaining goods by false pretenses with other property offenses, such as larceny and embezzlement (discussed shortly), into a single crime called simply "theft." Under such a statute, it is not necessary for a defendant to be charged specifically with larceny or obtaining goods by false pretenses. *Petty theft* is the theft of a small quantity of cash or low-value goods. *Grand theft* is the theft of a larger amount of cash or higher-value property.

**Receiving Stolen Goods** It is a crime to receive goods that a person knows or should have known were stolen or illegally obtained. To be convicted, the recipient of such goods need not know the true identity of the owner or the thief, and need not have paid for the goods. All that is necessary is that the recipient knows or should know that the goods are stolen, which implies an intent to deprive the true owner of those goods.

**Arson** The willful and malicious burning of a building (or, in some states, a vehicle or other item of personal property) is the crime of **arson.** At common law, arson applied only to burning down another person's house. The law was designed to protect human life. Today, arson statutes have been extended to cover the destruction of any building, regardless of ownership, by fire or explosion.

Every state has a special statute that covers the act of burning a building for the purpose of collecting insurance. (Of course, the insurer need not pay the claim when insurance fraud is proved.)

**Forgery** The fraudulent making or altering of any writing (including an electronic record) in a way that changes the legal rights and liabilities of another is **forgery.** ■ **EXAMPLE 10.10** Without authorization, Severson signs Bennett's name to the back of a check made out to Bennett and attempts to cash it. Severson is committing forgery. ■ Forgery also includes changing trademarks, falsifying public records, counterfeiting, and altering a legal document.

## 10–3c Public Order Crime

Historically, societies have always outlawed activities that are considered contrary to public values and morals. Today, the most common public order crimes include public drunkenness, prostitution, gambling, and illegal drug use. These crimes are sometimes referred to as *victimless crimes* because they normally harm only the offender. From a broader perspective, however, they are deemed detrimental to society as a whole because they may create an environment that gives rise to property and violent crimes.

■ **EXAMPLE 10.11** A flight attendant observes a man and woman engaging in sex acts while on a flight to Las Vegas. A criminal complaint is filed, and the two defendants plead guilty in federal court to misdemeanor disorderly conduct. ■

### 10–3d White-Collar Crime

Crimes occurring in the business context are popularly referred to as *white-collar crimes,* although this is not an official legal term. Ordinarily, **white-collar crime** involves an illegal act or series of acts committed by an individual or business entity using some nonviolent means to obtain a personal or business advantage.

Usually, this kind of crime takes place in the course of a legitimate business occupation. Corporate crimes fall into this category. Certain property crimes, such as larceny and forgery, may also be white-collar crimes if they occur within the business context. The crimes discussed next normally occur only in the business context.

**Embezzlement** When a person who is entrusted with another person's property fraudulently appropriates it, **embezzlement** occurs. Embezzlement is not larceny, because the wrongdoer does not *physically* take the property from another's possession, and it is not robbery, because no force or fear is used.

Typically, embezzlement is carried out by an employee who steals funds a small amount at a time over a long period. Banks are particularly prone to this problem, but embezzlement can occur in any firm. In a number of businesses, corporate officers or accountants have fraudulently converted funds for their own benefit and then "fixed" the books to cover up their crimes.

Embezzlement occurs whether the embezzler takes the funds directly from the victim or from a third person. If the financial officer of a large corporation pockets checks from third parties that were given to her to deposit into the corporate account, she is embezzling.

The intent to return embezzled property—or its actual return—is not a defense to the crime of embezzlement, as the following *Spotlight Case* illustrates.

## Spotlight on White-Collar Crime

### Case 10.2 People v. Sisuphan

Court of Appeal of California, First District, 181 Cal.App.4th 800, 104 Cal.Rptr.3d 654 (2010).

**Background and Facts** Lou Sisuphan was the director of finance at a Toyota dealership. His responsibilities included managing the financing contracts for vehicle sales and working with lenders to obtain payments. Sisuphan complained repeatedly to management about the performance and attitude of one of the finance managers, Ian McClelland. The general manager, Michael Christian, would not terminate McClelland "because he brought a lot of money into the dealership."

One day, McClelland accepted $22,600 in cash and two checks totaling $7,275.51 from a customer in payment for a car. McClelland placed the cash, the checks, and a copy of the receipt in a large envelope. As he tried to drop the envelope into the safe through a mechanism at its top, the envelope became stuck. While McClelland went for assistance, Sisuphan wiggled the envelope free and kept it. On McClelland's return, Sisuphan told him that the envelope had dropped into the safe. When the payment turned up missing, Christian told all the managers he would not bring criminal charges if the payment was returned within twenty-four hours.

After the twenty-four-hour period had lapsed, Sisuphan told Christian that he had taken the envelope, and he returned the cash and checks to Christian. Sisuphan claimed that he had no intention of stealing the payment but had taken it to get McClelland fired. Christian fired Sisuphan the next day, and the district attorney later charged Sisuphan with embezzlement.

After a jury trial, Sisuphan was found guilty. Sisuphan appealed, arguing that the trial court had erred by excluding evidence that he had returned the payment. The trial court had concluded that the evidence was not relevant because return of the property is not a defense to embezzlement.

*Case 10.2 Continues*

**Case 10.2 Continued**

## In the Language of the Court
*JENKINS,* J. [Judge]
* * * *

*Fraudulent intent is an essential element of embezzlement. Although restoration of the property is not a defense, evidence of repayment may be relevant to the extent it shows that a defendant's intent at the time of the taking was not fraudulent.* Such evidence is admissible "only when [a] defendant shows a relevant and probative [confirming] link in his subsequent actions from which it might be inferred his original intent was innocent." The question before us, therefore, is whether evidence that Sisuphan returned the money reasonably tends to prove he lacked the requisite intent at the time of the taking. [Emphasis added.]

Section 508 [of the California Penal Code], which sets out the offense of which Sisuphan was convicted, provides: "Every clerk, agent, or servant of any person who fraudulently appropriates to his own use, or secretes with a fraudulent intent to appropriate to his own use, any property of another which has come into his control or care by virtue of his employment * * * is guilty of embezzlement." Sisuphan denies he ever intended "to use the [money] to financially better himself, even temporarily" and contends the evidence he sought to introduce showed "he returned the [money] without having appropriated it to his own use in any way." He argues that this evidence negates fraudulent intent because it supports his claim that he took the money to get McClelland fired and acted "to help his company by drawing attention to the inadequacy and incompetency of an employee." We reject these contentions.

In determining whether Sisuphan's intent was fraudulent at the time of the taking, the issue is not whether he intended to spend the money, but whether he intended to use it for a purpose other than that for which the dealership entrusted it to him. *The offense of embezzlement contemplates a principal's entrustment of property to an agent for certain purposes and the agent's breach of that trust by acting outside his authority in his use of the property.* * * * Sisuphan's undisputed purpose—to get McClelland fired—was beyond the scope of his responsibility and therefore outside the trust afforded him by the dealership. Accordingly, even if the proffered [submitted] evidence shows he took the money for this purpose, it does not tend to prove he lacked fraudulent intent, and the trial court properly excluded this evidence. [Emphasis added.]

**Decision and Remedy** *The California appellate court affirmed the trial court's decision. The fact that Sisuphan had returned the payment was irrelevant. He was guilty of embezzlement.*

**Critical Thinking**
- **Legal Environment** *Why was Sisuphan convicted of embezzlement instead of larceny? What is the difference between these two crimes?*
- **Ethical** *Given that Sisuphan returned the cash, was it fair of the dealership's general manager to terminate Sisuphan's employment? Why or why not?*

---

**Mail and Wire Fraud** Among the most potent weapons against white-collar criminals are the federal laws that prohibit mail fraud[11] and wire fraud.[12] These laws make it a federal crime to devise any scheme that uses U.S. mail, commercial carriers (FedEx, UPS), or wire (telegraph, telephone, television, the Internet, e-mail) with the intent to defraud the public. These laws are often applied when persons send out advertisements or e-mails with the intent to fraudulently obtain cash or property by false pretenses.

■ **CASE IN POINT 10.12** Cisco Systems, Inc., offers a warranty program to authorized resellers of Cisco parts.

Iheanyi Frank Chinasa and Robert Kendrick Chambliss devised a scheme to intentionally defraud Cisco with respect to this program and to obtain replacement parts to which they were not entitled. The two men planned and used specific language in numerous e-mails and Internet service requests that they sent to Cisco to convince Cisco to ship them new parts via commercial carriers. Ultimately, Chinasa and Chambliss were convicted of mail and wire fraud and of conspiracy to commit mail and wire fraud.[13] ■

---

11. The Mail Fraud Act, 18 U.S.C. Sections 1341–1342.
12. 18 U.S.C. Section 1343.

13. *United States v. Chinasa,* 789 F.Supp.2d 691 (E.D.Va. 2011). See also *United States v. Lyons,* 569 F.3d 995 (9th Cir. 2009).

The maximum penalty under these statutes is substantial. Persons convicted of mail, wire, and Internet fraud may be imprisoned for up to twenty years and/or fined. If the violation affects a financial institution or involves fraud in connection with emergency disaster-relief funds, the violator may be fined up to $1 million, imprisoned for up to thirty years, or both.

**Bribery** The crime of bribery involves offering to give something of value to a person in an attempt to influence that person in a way that serves a private interest. Three types of bribery are considered crimes: bribery of public officials, commercial bribery, and bribery of foreign officials.

The bribe itself can be anything the recipient considers to be valuable, but the defendant must have intended it as a bribe. Realize that the *crime of bribery occurs when the bribe is offered*—it is not required that the bribe be accepted. *Accepting a bribe* is a separate crime.

Commercial bribery involves corrupt dealings between private persons or businesses. Typically, people make commercial bribes to obtain proprietary information, cover up an inferior product, or secure new business. Industrial espionage sometimes involves commercial bribes. ■ **EXAMPLE 10.13** Kent Peterson works at the firm of Jacoby & Meyers. He offers to pay Laurel, an employee in a competing firm, to give him that firm's trade secrets and pricing schedules. Peterson has committed commercial bribery. ■ So-called kickbacks, or payoffs for special favors or services, are a form of commercial bribery in some situations.

**Bankruptcy Fraud** Federal bankruptcy law allows individuals and businesses to be relieved of oppressive debt through bankruptcy proceedings. Numerous white-collar crimes may be committed during the many phases of a bankruptcy action. A creditor may file a false claim against the debtor, which is a crime. Also, a debtor may fraudulently transfer assets to favored parties before or after the bankruptcy is filed. For instance, a company-owned automobile may be "sold" at a bargain price to a trusted friend or relative. Closely related to the crime of fraudulent transfer of property is the crime of fraudulent concealment of property, such as the hiding of gold coins.

**Insider Trading** An individual who obtains "inside information" about the plans of a publicly listed corporation can often make stock-trading profits by purchasing or selling corporate securities based on this information. *Insider trading* is a violation of securities law. Basically, a person who possesses inside information and has a duty not to disclose it to outsiders may not trade on that information. A person may not profit from the purchase or sale of securities based on inside information until the information is made available to the public.

**Theft of Trade Secrets and Other Intellectual Property** The Economic Espionage Act[14] makes the theft of trade secrets a federal crime. The act also makes it a federal crime to buy or possess another person's trade secrets, knowing that the trade secrets were stolen or otherwise acquired without the owner's authorization.

Violations of the Economic Espionage Act can result in steep penalties: imprisonment for up to ten years and a fine of up to $500,000. A corporation or other organization can be fined up to $5 million. Additionally, any property acquired as a result of the violation, such as airplanes and automobiles, is subject to criminal forfeiture, or seizure by the government. Similarly, any property used in the commission of the violation is subject to forfeiture.

## 10–3e Organized Crime

White-collar crime takes place within the confines of the legitimate business world. *Organized crime,* in contrast, operates *illegitimately* by, among other things, providing illegal goods and services. Traditionally, organized crime has been involved in gambling, prostitution, illegal narcotics, counterfeiting, and loan sharking (lending funds at higher-than-legal interest rates), along with more recent ventures into credit-card scams and cyber crime.

**Money Laundering** The profits from organized crime and illegal activities amount to billions of dollars a year. These profits come from illegal drug transactions and, to a lesser extent, from racketeering, prostitution, and gambling. Under federal law, banks, savings and loan associations, and other financial institutions are required to report currency transactions involving more than $10,000. Consequently, those who engage in illegal activities face difficulties in depositing their cash profits from illegal transactions.

As an alternative to storing the cash from illegal transactions in a safe-deposit box, wrongdoers and racketeers often launder "dirty" money through legitimate businesses to make it "clean." **Money laundering** is engaging in financial transactions to conceal the identity, source, or destination of illegally gained funds.

■ **EXAMPLE 10.14** Leo Harris, a successful drug dealer, becomes a partner with a restaurateur. Little by little, the restaurant shows increasing profits. As a partner

---

14. 18 U.S.C. Sections 1831–1839.

in the restaurant, Harris is able to report the "profits" of the restaurant as legitimate income on which he pays federal and state taxes. He can then spend those funds without worrying that his lifestyle may exceed the level possible with his reported income. ■

**Racketeering** To curb the entry of organized crime into the legitimate business world, Congress enacted the Racketeer Influenced and Corrupt Organizations Act (RICO).[15] The statute makes it a federal crime to:

1. Use income obtained from racketeering activity to purchase any interest in an enterprise.
2. Acquire or maintain an interest in an enterprise through racketeering activity.
3. Conduct or participate in the affairs of an enterprise through racketeering activity.
4. Conspire to do any of the preceding activities.

**Broad Application of RICO.** The broad language of RICO has allowed it to be applied in cases that have little or nothing to do with organized crime. RICO incorporates by reference twenty-six separate types of federal crimes and nine types of state felonies.[16] If a person commits two of these offenses, he or she is guilty of "racketeering activity."

Under the criminal provisions of RICO, any individual found guilty is subject to a fine of up to $25,000 per violation, imprisonment for up to twenty years, or both. Additionally, any assets (property or cash) that were acquired as a result of the illegal activity or that were "involved in" or an "instrumentality of" the activity are subject to government forfeiture.

**Civil Liability.** In the event of a RICO violation, the government can seek not only criminal penalties but also civil penalties. The government can, for instance, seek the divestiture of a defendant's interest in a business or the dissolution of the business. (Divestiture refers to the taking of possession—or forfeiture—of the defendant's interest and its subsequent sale.)

Moreover, in some cases, the statute allows private individuals to sue violators and potentially recover three times their actual losses (treble damages), plus attorneys' fees, for business injuries caused by a RICO violation. This is perhaps the most controversial aspect of RICO and one that continues to cause debate in the nation's federal courts. The prospect of receiving treble damages in

civil RICO lawsuits has given plaintiffs a financial incentive to pursue businesses and employers for violations.

See Concept Summary 10.1 for a review of the different types of crimes.

# 10-4 Defenses to Criminal Liability

Persons charged with crimes may be relieved of criminal liability if they can show that their criminal actions were justified under the circumstances. In certain situations, the law may also allow a person to be excused from criminal liability because she or he lacks the required mental state. We look at several defenses to criminal liability here.

Note that procedural violations (such as obtaining evidence without a valid search warrant) may also operate as defenses. Evidence obtained in violation of a defendant's constitutional rights may not be admitted in court. If the evidence is suppressed, then there may be no basis for prosecuting the defendant.

## 10-4a Justifiable Use of Force

Probably the best-known defense to criminal liability is **self-defense.** Other situations, however, also justify the use of force: the defense of one's dwelling, the defense of other property, and the prevention of a crime. In all of these situations, it is important to distinguish between deadly and nondeadly force. *Deadly force* is likely to result in death or serious bodily harm. *Nondeadly force* is force that reasonably appears necessary to prevent the imminent use of criminal force.

Generally speaking, people can use the amount of nondeadly force that seems necessary to protect themselves, their dwellings, or other property, or to prevent the commission of a crime. Deadly force can be used in self-defense only when the defender *reasonably believes* that imminent death or grievous bodily harm will otherwise result. In addition, normally the attacker must be using unlawful force, and the defender must not have initiated or provoked the attack.

Many states are expanding the situations in which the use of deadly force can be justified. Florida, for instance, allows the use of deadly force to prevent the commission of a "forcible felony," including robbery, carjacking, and sexual battery.

## 10-4b Necessity

Sometimes, criminal defendants can be relieved of liability by showing **necessity**—that a criminal act was

---

**15.** 18 U.S.C. Sections 1961–1968.
**16.** See 18 U.S.C. Section 1961(1)(A). The crimes listed in this section include murder, kidnapping, gambling, arson, robbery, bribery, extortion, money laundering, securities fraud, counterfeiting, dealing in obscene matter, dealing in controlled substances (illegal drugs), and a number of others.

## Concept Summary 10.1

### Types of Crimes

| | |
|---|---|
| **Violent Crime** | Crimes that cause others to suffer harm or death, such as murder, assault and battery, and robbery. |
| **Property Crime** | Crimes in which the goal of the offender is some form of economic gain or the damaging of property. Property crime includes theft-related offenses such as burglary, larceny, and forgery. |
| **Public Order Crime** | Crimes that are contrary to public values and morals, such as public drunkenness and prostitution. |
| **White-Collar Crime** | An illegal act or series of acts committed by an individual or business entity using some nonviolent means to obtain a personal or business advantage. These crimes are usually committed in the course of a legitimate occupation. Examples include embezzlement, bribery, and fraud. |
| **Organized Crime** | Crime conducted by groups operating illegitimately to provide illegal goods and services, such as narcotics. Organized crime may also include money laundering and racketeering. |

necessary to prevent an even greater harm. ■ **EXAMPLE 10.15** Jake Trevor is a convicted felon and, as such, is legally prohibited from possessing a firearm. While he and his wife are in a convenience store, a man draws a gun, points it at the cashier, and demands all the cash in the register. Afraid that the man will start shooting, Trevor grabs the gun and holds onto it until police arrive. In this situation, if Trevor is charged with possession of a firearm, he can assert the defense of necessity. ■

### 10–4c Insanity

A person who suffers from a mental illness may be incapable of the state of mind required to commit a crime. Thus, insanity may be a defense to a criminal charge. Note that an insanity defense does not enable a person to avoid imprisonment. It simply means that if the defendant successfully proves insanity, she or he will be placed in a mental institution.

■ **EXAMPLE 10.16** James Holmes opened fire with an automatic weapon in a crowded Colorado movie theater during a screening of *The Dark Knight Rises*, killing twelve people and injuring seventy. Holmes had been a graduate student but had suffered from mental health problems and had left school. Before the incident, he had no criminal history. Holmes's attorneys asserted the defense of insanity to try to avoid a possible death sentence. Although a jury ultimately rejected the defense and convicted Holmes of multiple counts of murder in 2015, he was sentenced to life in prison rather than death. If the insanity defense had been successful, Holmes would have been confined to a mental institution, not a prison. ■

**Model Penal Code** The courts have had difficulty deciding what the test for legal insanity should be. Federal courts and some states use the substantial-capacity test set forth in the Model Penal Code:

> A person is not responsible for criminal conduct if at the time of such conduct as a result of mental disease or defect he or she lacks substantial capacity either to appreciate the wrongfulness of his [or her] conduct or to conform his [or her] conduct to the requirements of the law.

**M'Naghten and Other Tests** Some states use the *M'Naghten* test.[17] Under this test, a person is not responsible if, at the time of the offense, he or she did not know the nature and quality of the act or did not know that the act was wrong. Other states use the irresistible-impulse test. A person operating under an irresistible impulse may know an act is wrong but cannot refrain from doing it.

Under any of these tests, proving insanity is extremely difficult. For this reason, the insanity defense is rarely used and usually is not successful. Four states have abolished the insanity defense.

### 10–4d Mistake

Everyone has heard the saying "Ignorance of the law is no excuse." Ordinarily, ignorance of the law or a mistaken idea about what the law requires is not a valid defense. A *mistake of fact,* however, as opposed to a *mistake of law,* can normally excuse criminal responsibility if it negates the mental state necessary to commit a crime.

■ **EXAMPLE 10.17** Oliver Wheaton mistakenly walks off with Julie Tyson's briefcase. If Wheaton genuinely thought that the case was his, there is no theft. Theft requires knowledge that the property belongs to another. (If Wheaton's act causes Tyson to incur damages, however, she may sue him in a civil tort action for trespass to personal property or conversion.) ■

### 10–4e Duress

**Duress** exists when the *wrongful threat* of one person induces another person to perform an act that he or she would not otherwise have performed. In such a situation, duress is said to negate the mental state necessary to commit a crime because the defendant was forced or compelled to commit the act.

Duress can be used as a defense to most crimes except murder. Both the definition of duress and the types of crimes that it can excuse vary among the states, however. Generally, to successfully assert duress as a defense, the defendant must reasonably have believed that he or she was in immediate danger, and the jury (or judge) must conclude that the defendant's belief was reasonable.

### 10–4f Entrapment

**Entrapment** is a defense designed to prevent police officers or other government agents from enticing persons

to commit crimes in order to later prosecute them for those crimes. In the typical entrapment case, an undercover agent *suggests* that a crime be committed and somehow pressures or induces an individual to commit it. The agent then arrests the individual for the crime.

For entrapment to be considered a defense, both the suggestion and the inducement must take place. The defense is not intended to prevent law enforcement agents from setting a trap for an unwary criminal. Rather, its purpose is to prevent them from pushing the individual into a criminal act. The crucial issue is whether the person who committed a crime was predisposed to commit the illegal act or did so only because the agent induced it.

### 10–4g Statute of Limitations

With some exceptions, such as the crime of murder, statutes of limitations apply to crimes just as they do to civil wrongs. In other words, the government must initiate criminal prosecution within a certain number of years. If a criminal action is brought after the statutory time period has expired, the accused person can raise the statute of limitations as a defense.

The running of the time period in a statute of limitations may be *tolled*—that is, suspended or stopped temporarily—if the defendant is a minor or is not in the jurisdiction. When the defendant reaches the age of majority or returns to the jurisdiction, the statutory time period begins to run again.

### 10–4h Immunity

Accused persons are understandably reluctant to give information if it will be used to prosecute them, and they cannot be forced to do so. The privilege against **self-incrimination** is guaranteed by a clause in the Fifth Amendment to the U.S. Constitution. The clause reads "nor shall [any person] be compelled in any criminal case to be a witness against himself."

When the state wishes to obtain information from a person accused of a crime, the state can grant *immunity* from prosecution. Alternatively, the state can agree to prosecute the accused for a less serious offense in exchange for the information. Once immunity is given, the person has an absolute privilege against self-incrimination and therefore can no longer refuse to testify on Fifth Amendment grounds.

Often, a grant of immunity from prosecution for a serious crime is part of the **plea bargaining** between the defending and prosecuting attorneys. The defendant

---

17. A rule derived from *M'Naghten's* Case, 8 Eng.Rep. 718 (1843).

may be convicted of a lesser offense, while the state uses the defendant's testimony to prosecute accomplices for serious crimes carrying heavy penalties.

## 10–5 Criminal Procedures

Criminal law brings the force of the state, with all of its resources, to bear against the individual. Criminal procedures are designed to protect the constitutional rights of individuals and to prevent the arbitrary use of power on the part of the government.

The U.S. Constitution provides specific safeguards for those accused of crimes. The United States Supreme Court has ruled that most of these safeguards apply not only in federal court but also in state courts by virtue of the due process clause of the Fourteenth Amendment. These protections include the following:

1. The Fourth Amendment protection from unreasonable searches and seizures.
2. The Fourth Amendment requirement that no warrant for a search or an arrest be issued without probable cause.
3. The Fifth Amendment requirement that no one be deprived of "life, liberty, or property without due process of law."
4. The Fifth Amendment prohibition against **double jeopardy** (trying someone twice for the same criminal offense).[18]
5. The Fifth Amendment requirement that no person be required to be a witness against (incriminate) himself or herself.
6. The Sixth Amendment guarantees of a speedy trial, a trial by jury, a public trial, the right to confront witnesses, and the right to a lawyer at various stages in some proceedings.
7. The Eighth Amendment prohibitions against excessive bail and fines and against cruel and unusual punishment.

### 10–5a Fourth Amendment Protections

The Fourth Amendment protects the "right of the people to be secure in their persons, houses, papers, and effects." Before searching or seizing private property, normally law enforcement officers must obtain a **search warrant**—an order from a judge or other public official authorizing the search or seizure.

Advances in technology allow the authorities to track phone calls and vehicle movements with greater ease and precision. The use of such technology can constitute a search within the meaning of the Fourth Amendment. ■ **CASE IN POINT 10.18** Antoine Jones owned and operated a nightclub in the District of Columbia. Government agents suspected that he was also trafficking in narcotics. As part of their investigation, agents obtained a warrant to attach a global positioning system (GPS) device to Jones's wife's car, which Jones regularly used. The warrant authorized installation in the District of Columbia within ten days, but agents installed the device on the eleventh day in Maryland.

The agents then tracked the vehicle's movement for about a month, eventually arresting Jones for possession and intent to distribute cocaine. Jones was convicted. He appealed, arguing that the government did not have a valid warrant for the GPS tracking. The United States Supreme Court held that the attachment of a GPS tracking device to a suspect's vehicle does constitute a Fourth Amendment search. The Court did not rule on whether the search in this case was unreasonable, however, and allowed Jones's conviction to stand.[19] ■

**Probable Cause** To obtain a search warrant, law enforcement officers must convince a judge that they have reasonable grounds, or **probable cause,** to believe a search will reveal a specific illegality. Probable cause requires the officers to have trustworthy evidence that would convince a reasonable person that the proposed search or seizure is more likely justified than not.

■ **CASE IN POINT 10.19** Based on a tip that Oscar Gutierrez was involved in drug trafficking, law enforcement officers went to his home with a drug-sniffing dog. The dog alerted officers to the scent of narcotics at the home's front door. Officers knocked for fifteen minutes, but no one answered. Eventually, they entered and secured the men inside the home. They then obtained a search warrant based on the dog's positive alert. Officers found eleven pounds of methamphetamine in the search, and Gutierrez was convicted.

On appeal, a court held that the search was permissible because the evidence of the drug-sniffing dog's positive alert for the presence of drugs established probable cause for the warrant.[20] The court noted that a recent

---

18. The prohibition against double jeopardy does not preclude the crime victim from bringing a *civil* suit against that same person to recover damages, however. Additionally, a state's prosecution of a crime will not prevent a separate federal prosecution of the same crime, and vice versa.

19. *United States v. Jones*, __ U.S. __, 132 S.Ct. 945, 181 L.Ed.2d 911 (2012).
20. *United States v. Gutierrez*, 760 F.3d 750 (7th Cir. 2014).

United States Supreme Court decision would have prohibited the search. In that decision, the Court held that police officers cannot bring drug-sniffing dogs onto the front porch of a person's home without a warrant.[21] But the officers' conduct in this case had occurred before the Supreme Court's decision, so the officers could reasonably rely on the sniff evidence. ■

**Scope of Warrant** The Fourth Amendment prohibits general warrants. It requires a specific description of what is to be searched or seized. General searches through a person's belongings are impermissible. The search cannot extend beyond what is described in the warrant. Nevertheless, if a warrant is issued for a person's residence, items in that residence may be searched even if they do not belong to that individual.

**Reasonable Expectation of Privacy** The Fourth Amendment protects only against searches that violate a person's *reasonable expectation of privacy*. A reasonable expectation of privacy exists if (1) the individual actually expects privacy and (2) the person's expectation is one that society as a whole would consider legitimate.

■ **CASE IN POINT 10.20** Angela Marcum was the drug court coordinator responsible for collecting money for the District Court of Pittsburg County, Oklahoma. She was romantically involved with James Miller, an assistant district attorney. The state charged Marcum with obstructing an investigation of suspected embezzlement and offered in evidence text messages sent and received by her and Miller. The state had obtained a search warrant and collected the records of the messages from U.S. Cellular, Miller's phone company.

Marcum filed a motion to suppress the messages, which the court granted. The state appealed. A state intermediate appellate court reversed the lower court's judgment. Marcum had no reasonable expectation of privacy in U.S. Cellular's records of her text messages in Miller's account. "Once the messages were both transmitted and received, the expectation of privacy was lost."[22] ■

## 10–5b The Exclusionary Rule

Under what is known as the **exclusionary rule,** any evidence obtained in violation of the constitutional rights spelled out in the Fourth, Fifth, and Sixth Amendments generally is not admissible at trial. All evidence derived from the illegally obtained evidence is known as the "fruit of the poisonous tree," and it normally must also be excluded from the trial proceedings. For instance, if a confession is obtained after an illegal arrest, the arrest is the "poisonous tree," and the confession, if "tainted" by the arrest, is the "fruit."

The purpose of the exclusionary rule is to deter police from conducting warrantless searches and engaging in other misconduct. The rule can sometimes lead to injustice, however. If evidence of a defendant's guilt was obtained improperly (without a valid search warrant, for instance), it normally cannot be used against the defendant in court.

## 10–5c The *Miranda* Rule

In *Miranda v. Arizona,*[23] a landmark case decided in 1966, the United States Supreme Court established the rule that individuals who are arrested must be informed of certain constitutional rights. Suspects must be informed of their Fifth Amendment right to remain silent and their Sixth Amendment right to counsel. If the arresting officers fail to inform a criminal suspect of these constitutional rights, any statements the suspect makes normally will not be admissible in court.

Although the Supreme Court's decision in the *Miranda* case was controversial, it has survived several attempts by Congress to overrule it. Over time, however, the Supreme Court has made a number of exceptions to the *Miranda* ruling.

For instance, the Court has recognized a "public safety" exception that allows certain statements to be admitted even if the defendant was not given *Miranda* warnings. A defendant's statements that reveal the location of a weapon would be admissible under this exception.

Additionally, a suspect must unequivocally and assertively ask to exercise her or his right to counsel in order to stop police questioning. Saying "Maybe I should talk to a lawyer" during an interrogation after being taken into custody is not enough.

## 10–5d Criminal Process

A criminal prosecution differs significantly from a civil case in several respects. These differences reflect the desire to safeguard the rights of the individual against the state. Exhibit 10–3 summarizes the major steps in processing a criminal case, several of which we discuss here.

---

21. *Florida v. Jardines,* 569 U.S. 1, 133 S.Ct. 1409, 185 L.Ed.2d 495 (2013).
22. *State of Oklahoma v. Marcum,* 319 P.3d 681 (2014).

23. 384 U.S. 436, 86 S.Ct. 1602, 16 L.Ed.2d 694 (1966).

**EXHIBIT 10–3** Major Procedural Steps in a Criminal Case

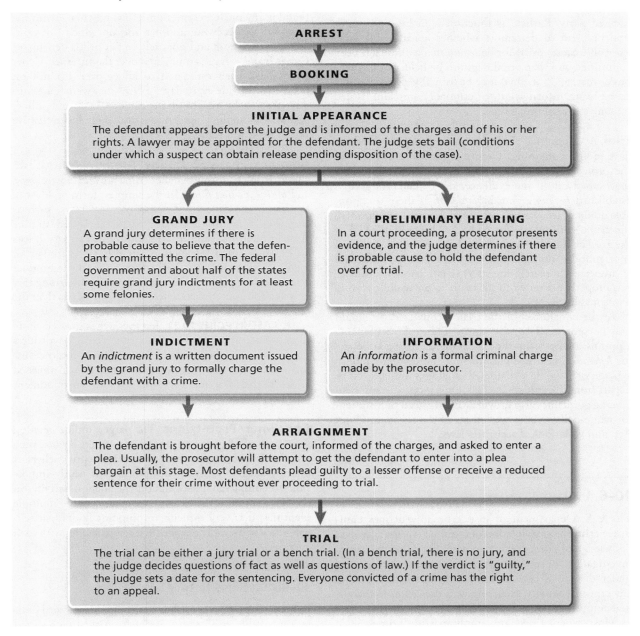

**Arrest** Before a warrant for arrest can be issued, there must be probable cause to believe that the individual in question has committed a crime. Note that probable cause involves a substantial likelihood that the person has committed a crime, not just a possibility. Arrests can be made without a warrant if there is no time to obtain one, but the action of the arresting officer is still judged by the standard of probable cause.

**Indictment or Information** Individuals must be formally charged with having committed specific crimes before they can be brought to trial. If issued by a grand jury, such a charge is called an **indictment.**[24] A **grand jury** does not determine the guilt or innocence of an accused party. Rather, its function is to hear the state's evidence and to determine whether a reasonable basis (probable cause) exists for believing that a crime has been committed and that a trial ought to be held. For less serious crimes, an individual may be formally charged with a crime by an **information,** or criminal complaint, issued by a government prosecutor.

**Trial** At a criminal trial, the accused person does not have to prove anything. The entire burden of proof is on the prosecutor (the state). The prosecution must show that, based on all the evidence, the defendant's guilt is established *beyond a reasonable doubt.* If there is reasonable doubt as to whether a criminal defendant committed the crime with which she or he has been charged, then the verdict must be "not guilty." Returning a verdict of "not guilty" is not the same as stating that the defendant is innocent. It merely means that not enough evidence was properly presented to the court to prove guilt beyond a reasonable doubt.

At the conclusion of the trial, a convicted defendant will be sentenced by the court. The U.S. Sentencing Commission performs the task of standardizing sentences for *federal* crimes. The commission's guidelines establish a range of possible penalties, but judges are allowed to depart from the guidelines if circumstances warrant. Sentencing guidelines also provide for enhanced punishment for white-collar crimes, violations of the Sarbanes-Oxley Act, and violations of securities laws.[25]

# 10–6 Cyber Crime

The U.S. Department of Justice broadly defines **computer crime** as any violation of criminal law that involves knowledge of computer technology for its perpetration, investigation, or prosecution. Many computer crimes fall under the broad label of **cyber crime,** which describes any criminal activity occurring via a computer in the virtual community of the Internet.

Most cyber crimes are simply existing crimes, such as fraud and theft, in which the Internet is the instrument of wrongdoing. Here, we look at several types of activities that constitute cyber crimes against persons or property.

## 10–6a Cyber Fraud

Fraud is any misrepresentation knowingly made with the intention of deceiving another and on which a reasonable person would and does rely to her or his detriment. **Cyber fraud** is fraud committed over the Internet. Cyber scams have been estimated to affect over 1.5 million people worldwide every day.[26] Scams that were once conducted solely by mail or phone can now be found online, and new technology has led to increasingly more creative ways to commit fraud.

**Advance Fee and Online Auction Fraud** Two widely reported forms of cyber crime are *advance fee fraud* and *online auction fraud.* In the simplest form of advance fee fraud, consumers order and pay for items, such as automobiles or antiques, that are never delivered. Online auction fraud is also fairly straightforward. A person lists an expensive item for auction, on either a legitimate or a fake auction site, and then refuses to send the product after receiving payment. Or, as a variation, the wrongdoer may send the purchaser an item that is worth less than the one offered in the auction.

■ **CASE IN POINT 10.21** Jeremy Jaynes grossed more than $750,000 per week selling nonexistent or worthless products such as "penny stock pickers" and "Internet history erasers." By the time he was arrested, he had amassed an estimated $24 million from his various fraudulent schemes.[27] ■

**Consumer Protections** The larger online auction sites, such as eBay, try to protect consumers against such schemes by providing warnings about deceptive sellers or offering various forms of insurance. It is nearly impossible to completely block fraudulent auction activity on the Internet, however. Because users can assume multiple identities, it is very difficult to pinpoint fraudulent sellers—they will simply change their screen names with each auction.

## 10–6b Cyber Theft

In cyberspace, thieves are not subject to the physical limitations of the "real" world. A thief can steal data stored in a networked computer with Internet access from anywhere on the globe. Only the speed of the connection and the thief's computer equipment limit the quantity of data that can be stolen.

---

24. Pronounced in-*dyte*-ment.
25. The sentencing guidelines were amended in 2003, as required under the Sarbanes-Oxley Act of 2002, to impose stiffer penalties for corporate securities fraud.

26. *2013 Norton Report* (Mountain View, Calif.: Symantec, 2014), pg. 8.
27. *Jaynes v. Commonwealth of Virginia,* 276 Va. 443, 666 S.E.2d 303 (2008).

**Identity Theft** Not surprisingly, there has been a marked increase in identity theft in recent years. **Identity theft** occurs when the wrongdoer steals a form of identification—such as a name, date of birth, or Social Security number—and uses the information to access the victim's financial resources. According to the federal government, about 7 percent of Americans have been victims of identity theft.

More than half of identity thefts involve the misappropriation of an existing credit-card account. In most situations, the legitimate holders of credit cards are not held responsible for the costs of purchases made with a stolen number. The loss is born by the businesses and banks.

The Internet has provided relatively easy access to private data that includes credit-card numbers and more. Frequent Web surfers surrender a wealth of information about themselves. Web sites use "cookies" to collect data on those who visit their sites and make purchases. Often, sites store information such as the consumer's name, e-mail address, and credit-card number. Identity thieves may be able to steal this information by fooling a Web site into thinking that they are the true account holders.

In addition, people often enter important personal information, such as their birthdays, hometowns, or employers, on social media sites. Identity thieves can use such information to convince a third party to reveal someone's Social Security or bank account number.

Identity theft can be committed in the course of pursuing other criminal objectives. In the following case, for example, the defendant was charged with identity theft in connection with the filing of five thousand false income tax returns to obtain refunds. He challenged his conviction on these charges and sought a new trial.

---

**Case Analysis 10.3**

# United States v. Warner

United States Court of Appeals, Eleventh Circuit, 2016 WL 403166 (2016).

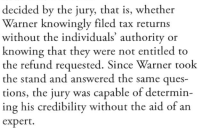

### In the Language of the Court

*PER CURIAM* [By the Whole Court]:

\* \* \* \*

A [federal district court] jury convicted Mauricio Warner on all 50 counts of an indictment that charged him with obtaining individuals' identities and using such identities to file over 5,000 false income tax returns resulting in millions of dollars in refunds that were deposited in bank accounts Warner controlled. [The court sentenced Warner to prison for a total of 240 months.] He now appeals his convictions. He seeks the vacation of his convictions and a new trial on the grounds that the District Court abused its discretion (1) in refusing to permit a polygraph examiner to testify to the results of a polygraph examination he administered to Warner; (2) admitting into evidence government Exhibits 500 and 500A, spreadsheets of fraudulently submitted tax returns, as business records; and (3) permitting each juror to have a copy of the indictment throughout trial.

\* \* \* \*

A district court's decision to admit or exclude expert testimony under Federal Rule of Evidence 702 is reviewed for abuse of discretion, which is the standard we apply in reviewing evidentiary rulings in general. *A district court abuses its discretion when it applies the wrong law, follows the wrong procedure, bases its decision on clearly erroneous facts, or commits a clear error in judgment.* [Emphasis added.]

Federal Rule of Evidence 702 provides that an expert witness may testify in the form of an opinion if the expert's specialized knowledge will assist the trier of fact to understand the evidence or to determine a fact at issue.

The results of a polygraph examination are not inadmissible *per se*. The trial judge in the exercise of discretion may admit the results of such examination to impeach or corroborate witness testimony.

The District Court did not abuse its discretion in concluding that the polygraph examination was inadmissible under Rule 702. The question

posed by the examiner addressed an issue that was to be decided by the jury, that is, whether Warner knowingly filed tax returns without the individuals' authority or knowing that they were not entitled to the refund requested. Since Warner took the stand and answered the same questions, the jury was capable of determining his credibility without the aid of an expert.

\* \* \* \*

Federal Rule of Evidence 1006 authorizes the admission into evidence of a summary of voluminous business records but only where the originals or duplicates of those originals are available for examination or copying by the other party.

The business record exception to the hearsay rule under Federal Rule of Evidence 803(6) states, in relevant part, that a record will be admitted if:

(A) the record was made at or near the time by—or from information transmitted by—someone with knowledge;

**Case 10.3 Continues**

**Case 10.3 Continued**

(B) the record was kept in the course of a regularly conducted activity of a business, organization, occupation, or calling, whether or not for profit;

(C) making the record was a regular practice of that activity;

(D) all these conditions are shown by the testimony of the custodian or another qualified witness * * *;

(E) the opponent does not show that the source of information or the method of circumstances of preparation indicate a lack of trustworthiness.

Rule 803(6) requires that both the underlying records and the report summarizing those records be prepared and maintained for business purposes in the ordinary course of business and not for purposes of litigation. * * * *The touchstone of admissibility under Rule 803(6) is reliability, and a trial judge has broad discretion to determine the admissibility of such evidence.* [Emphasis added.]

Computer-generated business records are admissible under the following circumstances: (1) the records must be kept pursuant to some routine procedure designed to assure their accuracy, (2) they must be created for motives that would tend to assure accuracy (preparation for litigation, for example, is not such a motive), and (3) they must not themselves be mere accumulations of hearsay or uninformed opinion.

* * * A typed summary of handwritten business records created solely for litigation [is] inadmissible hearsay evidence. [This is] distinguishable from * * * records [that consist of] electronically stored information and the summary [is] simply a printout of that information.

* * * *

* * * Airline check-in and reservation records and flight manifests that [are] kept in the ordinary course of business and printed at the government's request [for a trial are admissible]. Computer data compiled and presented in computer printouts prepared specifically for trial is admissible under Rule 803(6), even though the printouts themselves are not kept in the ordinary course of business.

We find no abuse of discretion in admitting government Exhibits 500 and 500A under Rule 803(6). Although the spreadsheets were formatted to be easier to understand and printed for litigation, the underlying records were kept in the ordinary course of business and the data was not modified or combined when entered into the spreadsheet.

* * * *

The decision to provide the jury with a copy of an indictment is committed to the district court's sound discretion.

As a general rule, a trial court may, in the exercise of discretion, allow the indictment to be taken into the jury room. Likewise, a court may provide the jury copies of the indictment before trial, provided that the court gives specific instructions that the indictment is not evidence.

There was no abuse of discretion here. The court specifically instructed the jurors on two separate occasions that the indictment was not evidence or proof of any guilt. Even if the court's lack of contemporaneous instructions was error, it was harmless.

For the foregoing reasons, Warner's convictions are
AFFIRMED.

**Legal Reasoning Questions**

**1.** What three reasons did the defendant assert to support a request for a new trial?

**2.** What standard applies to an appellate court's consideration of a contention that a trial court's evidentiary ruling was in error?

**3.** What were the appellate court's conclusions with respect to the trial court's rulings in this case? What reasons support these conclusions?

---

**Password Theft** The more personal information a cyber criminal obtains, the easier it is for him or her to find a victim's online user name at a particular Web site. Once the online user name has been compromised, it is easier to steal the victim's password, which is often the last line of defense to financial information.

Numerous software programs aid identity thieves in illegally obtaining passwords. A technique called *keystroke logging*, for instance, relies on software that embeds itself in a victim's computer and records every keystroke made on that computer. User names and passwords are then recorded and sold to the highest bidder. Internet users should also be wary of any links contained within e-mails sent from unknown sources. These links can sometimes be used to illegally obtain personal information.

**Phishing** A form of identity theft known as **phishing** has added a different wrinkle to the practice. In a phishing attack, the perpetrator "fishes" for financial data and passwords from consumers by posing as a legitimate business, such as a bank or credit-card company. The "phisher" sends an e-mail asking the recipient to update or confirm vital information. Often, the e-mail includes a threat that an account or some other service will be discontinued if the information is not provided. Once the unsuspecting individual enters the information, the phisher can sell it or use it to masquerade as that person or to drain his or her bank or credit account.

■ **EXAMPLE 10.22** Customers of Wells Fargo Bank received official-looking e-mails telling them to type in personal information in an online form to complete a mandatory installation of a new Internet security certificate. But the Web site was bogus. When people filled out the forms, their computers were infected and funneled their data to a computer server. The cyber criminals then sold the data. ■ Phishing scams have also spread to text messaging and social networking sites.

## 10–6c Hacking

A **hacker** is someone who uses one computer to break into another. The danger posed by hackers has increased significantly because of **botnets,** or networks of computers that have been appropriated by hackers without the knowledge of their owners. A hacker may secretly install a program on thousands, even millions, of personal computer "robots," or "bots." The program, in turn, allows the hacker to forward transmissions to an even larger number of systems.

■ **EXAMPLE 10.23** Almost as soon as Apple, Inc., introduced a new mobile-payment system in late 2014, cyber thieves began hacking into the company's smartphones and tablets to make purchases with stolen credit-card numbers. At about the same time, cyber criminals were stealing the credit-card data of at least 60 million Home Depot customers and illegally accessing the financial information of 76 million JPMorgan Chase clients. In 2015, hackers stole the personal information of 19.7 million individuals from the U.S. Office of Personnel Management's background-investigation databases.

It has also been demonstrated that hackers can take over the dashboard computer systems that control cars—General Motors' OnStar system, for example. This risk of takeover extends to numerous wireless-enabled medical devices in use today, such as pacemakers, insulin pumps, and neurostimulators. A criminal could hack someone's car or pacemaker with the intent of causing the person harm. ■

**Malware** Botnets are one of the latest forms of **malware,** a term that refers to any program that is harmful to a computer or, by extension, a computer user. Malware can be programmed to perform a number of functions, such as prompting host computers to continually "crash" and reboot or otherwise infecting the systems.

One type of malware is a **worm**—a software program that is capable of reproducing itself as it spreads from one computer to the next. The Conficker worm, for instance, spread to more than a million personal computers around the world within a three-week period. It was transmitted to some computers through the use of Facebook and Twitter.

A **virus,** another form of malware, is also able to reproduce itself, but must be attached to an "infested" host file to travel from one computer network to another. For instance, hackers are now capable of corrupting banner ads that use Adobe's Flash Player. When an Internet user clicks on the banner ad, a virus is installed.

■ **EXAMPLE 10.24** During the 2013 holiday season, a group of Eastern European hackers managed to gain access to Target's computer system. Once "inside," these hackers infected the in-store devices that Target customers use to swipe their credit and debit cards with "memory scraper" malware nicknamed Kaptoxa. Over the course of several weeks, the malware was used to steal the credit- and debit-card data of as many as 40 million Target customers. Personal data such as passwords, phone numbers, and addresses were stolen from at least 70 million more customers. Some experts estimate that the incident resulted in billions of dollars in losses to consumers, their banks, and others. ■

**Service-Based Hacking** Today, many companies offer "software as a service." Instead of buying software to install on a computer, the user connects to Web-based software. The user can then write e-mails, edit spreadsheets, or perform other tasks using his or her Web browser.

Cyber criminals have adapted this distribution method to provide "crimeware as a service." A would-be thief no longer has to be a computer hacker to create a botnet or steal banking information and credit-card numbers. He or she can rent the online services of cyber criminals to do the work for a small price. Fake security software (also known as scareware) is a common example. The thief can even target individual groups, such as U.S. physicians or British attorneys.

**Cyberterrorism** Cyberterrorists, as well as hackers, may target businesses. The goals of a hacking operation might include a wholesale theft of data, such as a merchant's customer files, or the monitoring of a computer to discover a business firm's plans and transactions. A cyberterrorist might also want to insert false codes or data. For instance, the processing control system of a food manufacturer could be changed to alter the levels of ingredients so that consumers of the food would become ill.

A cyberterrorist attack on a major financial institution, such as the New York Stock Exchange or a large bank, could leave securities or money markets in flux. Such an attack could seriously affect U.S. citizens, business operations, and national security.

## 10–6d Prosecuting Cyber Crime

Cyber crime has raised new issues in the investigation of crimes and the prosecution of offenders. Determining the "location" of a cyber crime and identifying a criminal in cyberspace present significant challenges for law enforcement.

**Jurisdiction and Identification Challenges** A threshold issue is, of course, jurisdiction. Each state and nation has jurisdiction, or authority, over crimes committed within its boundaries. But geographic boundaries simply do not apply in cyberspace. A person who commits an act against a business in California, where the act is a cyber crime, might never have set foot in California. Instead, the perpetrator might reside in another state, or even another nation, where the act may not be a crime. Indeed, many cyber crimes emanate from Russia and China.

Identifying the wrongdoer can also be difficult. Cyber criminals do not leave physical traces, such as fingerprints or DNA samples, as evidence of their crimes. Even electronic "footprints" can be hard to find and follow. For instance, cyber criminals may employ software such as Tor to mask their IP addresses (codes that identify individual computers) and the IP addresses of those with whom they communicate. Law enforcement has to hire computer forensic experts to bypass the software and track down the criminal. For these reasons, laws written to protect physical property are often difficult to apply in cyberspace.

**The Computer Fraud and Abuse Act** Perhaps the most significant federal statute specifically addressing cyber crime is the Counterfeit Access Device and Computer Fraud and Abuse Act.[28] This act is commonly known as the Computer Fraud and Abuse Act (CFAA).

Among other things, the CFAA provides that a person who accesses a computer online, without authority, to obtain classified, restricted, or protected data (or attempts to do so) is subject to criminal prosecution. Such data could include financial and credit records, medical records, legal files, military and national security files, and other confidential information. The data can be located in government or private computers. The crime has two elements: accessing a computer without authority and taking data.

The theft is a felony if it is committed for a commercial purpose or for private financial gain, or if the value of the stolen data (or computer time) exceeds $5,000. Penalties include fines and imprisonment for up to twenty years. A person who violates the CFAA can also be sued in a civil action for damages.

---

28. 18 U.S.C. Section 1030.

## Reviewing: Criminal Law and Cyber Crime

Edward Hanousek worked for Pacific & Arctic Railway and Navigation Company (P&A) as a roadmaster of the White Pass & Yukon Railroad in Alaska. Hanousek was responsible "for every detail of the safe and efficient maintenance and construction of track, structures and marine facilities of the entire railroad," including special projects. One project was a rock quarry, known as "6-mile," above the Skagway River. Next to the quarry, and just beneath the surface, ran a high-pressure oil pipeline owned by Pacific & Arctic Pipeline, Inc., P&A's sister company. When the quarry's backhoe operator punctured the pipeline, an estimated 1,000 to 5,000 gallons of oil were discharged into the river. Hanousek was charged with negligently discharging a harmful quantity of oil into a navigable water of the United States in violation of the criminal provisions of the Clean Water Act (CWA). Using the information presented in the chapter, answer the following questions.

1. Did Hanousek have the required mental state *(mens rea)* to be convicted of a crime? Why or why not?
2. Which theory discussed in the chapter would enable a court to hold Hanousek criminally liable for violating the statute if he participated in, directed, or merely knew about the specific violation?
3. Could the backhoe operator who punctured the pipeline also be charged with a crime in this situation? Explain.
4. Suppose that at trial, Hanousek argued that he should not be convicted because he was not aware of the requirements of the CWA. Would this defense be successful? Why or why not?

**Debate This** . . . *Because of overcriminalization, particularly by the federal government, Americans may be breaking the law regularly without knowing it. Should Congress rescind many of the more than four thousand federal crimes now on the books?*

## Terms and Concepts

| | | |
|---|---|---|
| *actus reus* 189 | beyond a reasonable doubt 187 | burglary 192 |
| arson 194 | botnet 207 | computer crime 204 |

## Issue Spotters

**1.** Dana takes her roommate's credit card without permission, intending to charge expenses that she incurs on a vacation. Her first stop is a gas station, where she uses the card to pay for gas. With respect to the gas station, has she committed a crime? If so, what is it? (See *Types of Crimes.*)

**2.** Without permission, Ben downloads consumer credit files from a computer belonging to Consumer Credit Agency. He then sells the data to Dawn. Has Ben committed a crime? If so, what is it? (See *Cyber Crime.*)

• **Check your answers to the Issue Spotters against the answers provided in Appendix D at the end of this text.**

## Business Scenarios

**10–1. Types of Cyber Crimes.** The following situations are similar, but each represents a variation of a particular crime. Identify the crime and point out the differences in the variations. (See *Cyber Crime.*)

**(a)** Chen, posing fraudulently as Diamond Credit Card Co., sends an e-mail to Emily, stating that the company has observed suspicious activity in her account and has frozen the account. The e-mail asks her to reregister her credit-card number and password to reopen the account.

**(b)** Claiming falsely to be Big Buy Retail Finance Co., Conner sends an e-mail to Dino, asking him to confirm or update his personal security information to prevent his Big Buy account from being discontinued.

**(c)** Felicia posts her résumé on GotWork.com, an online job-posting site, seeking a position in business and managerial finance and accounting. Hayden, who misrepresents himself as an employment officer with International Bank & Commerce Corp., sends her an e-mail asking for more personal information.

**10–2. Cyber Scam.** Kayla, a student at Learnwell University, owes $20,000 in unpaid tuition. If Kayla does not pay the tuition, Learnwell will not allow her to graduate. To obtain the funds to pay the debt, she sends e-mails to people that she does not personally know asking for financial help to send Milo, her disabled child, to a special school. In reality, Kayla has no children. Is this a crime? If so, which one? (See *Cyber Crime.*)

## Business Case Problems

**10–3. Credit-Card Theft.** Jacqueline Barden was shopping for school clothes with her children when her purse and automobile were taken. In Barden's purse were her car keys, credit and debit cards, and the children's Social Security cards and birth certificates, which were needed for enrollment at school. Immediately after the purse and car were stolen, Rebecca Mary Turner attempted to use Barden's credit card at a local Exxon gas station, but the card was declined. The gas station attendant recognized Turner because she had previously written bad checks and used credit cards that did not belong to her.

Turner was later arrested while attempting to use one of Barden's checks to pay for merchandise at a Wal-Mart—where the clerk also recognized Turner from prior criminal activity. Turner claimed that she had not stolen Barden's purse or car. Instead, she said that a friend had told her he had some checks and credit cards and asked her to try using them at Wal-Mart. Turner was convicted at trial. She appealed, claiming that there was insufficient evidence that she committed credit- and debit-card theft. Was the evidence sufficient to uphold her conviction? Why or why not? [*Turner v. State of Arkansas*, 2012 Ark.App. 150 (2012)] (See *Types of Crimes.*)

**10–4. Business Case Problem with Sample Answer—Criminal Liability.**  During the morning rush hour, David Green threw bottles and plates from a twenty-sixth-floor hotel balcony overlooking Seventh Avenue in New York City. A video of the incident also showed him doing cartwheels while holding a beer bottle and sprinting toward the balcony while holding a glass steadily in his hand. When he saw police on the street below and on the roof of the building across the street, he suspended his antics but resumed tossing objects off the balcony after the police left. He later admitted that he could recall what he had done, but claimed to have been intoxicated and said his only purpose was to amuse himself and his friends. Did Green have the mental state required to establish criminal liability? Discuss. [*State of New York v. Green*, 104 A.D.3d 126, 958 N.Y.S.2d 138 (1 Dept. 2013)] (See *Criminal Liability.*)

- **For a sample answer to Problem 10–4, go to Appendix E at the end of this text.**

**10–5. White-Collar Crime.** Matthew Simpson and others created and operated a series of corporate entities to defraud telecommunications companies, creditors, credit reporting agencies, and others. Through these entities, Simpson and his confederates used routing codes and spoofing services to make long-distance calls appear to be local. They stole other firms' network capacity and diverted payments to themselves. They leased goods and services without paying for them. To hide their association with their corporate entities and with each other, they used false identities, addresses, and credit histories, and issued false bills, invoices, financial statements, and credit references. Did these acts constitute mail and wire fraud? Discuss. [*United States v. Simpson*, 741 F.3d 539 (5th Cir. 2014)] (See *Types of Crimes.*)

**10–6. Defenses to Criminal Liability.** George Castro told Ambrosio Medrano that a bribe to a certain corrupt Los Angeles County official would buy a contract with the county hospitals. To share in the deal, Medrano recruited Gustavo Buenrostro. In turn, Buenrostro contacted his friend James Barta, the owner of Sav–Rx, which provides prescription benefit management services. Barta was asked to pay a "finder's fee" to Castro. He did not pay, even after frequent e-mails and calls with deadlines and ultimatums delivered over a period of months. Eventually, Barta wrote Castro a Sav–Rx check for $6,500, saying that it was to help his friend Buenrostro. Castro was an FBI agent, and the county official and contract were fictional. Barta was charged with conspiracy to commit bribery. At trial, the government conceded that Barta was not predisposed to commit the crime.

Could he be absolved of the charge on a defense of entrapment? Explain. [*United States v. Barta*, 776 F.3d 931 (7th Cir. 2015)] (See *Defenses to Criminal Liability.*)

**10–7. Criminal Procedures.** Federal officers obtained a warrant to arrest Kateena Norman on charges of credit-card fraud and identity theft. Evidence of the crime included videos, photos, and a fingerprint on a fraudulent check. A previous search of Norman's house had uncovered credit cards, new merchandise, and identifying information for other persons. An Internet account registered to the address had been used to apply for fraudulent credit cards, and a fraudulently obtained rental car was parked on the property. As the officers arrested Norman outside her house, they saw another woman and a caged pit bull inside. They further believed that Norman's boyfriend, who had a criminal record and was also suspected of identify theft, could be there. In less than a minute, the officers searched only those areas within the house in which a person could hide. Would it be reasonable to admit evidence revealed in this "protective sweep" during Norman's trial on the arrest charges? Discuss. [*United States v. Norman*, __ F.3d __, 2016 WL 324949 (11th Cir. 2016)] (See *Criminal Procedures.*)

**10–8. A Question of Ethics—Criminal Process.**  *Gary Peters fraudulently told an undocumented immigrant that Peters could help him obtain lawful status. Peters said that he knew immigration officials and asked for money to aid in the process. The victim paid Peters at least $25,000 in wire transfers and checks. Peters had others call the victim, falsely represent that they were agents with the U.S. Department of Homeland Security, and induce continued payments. He threatened to contact authorities to detain or deport the victim and his wife. Peters was convicted of wire fraud in a federal district court.* [United States v. Peters, 597 Fed.Appx. 1033 (11th Cir. 2015)] (See *Criminal Procedures.*)

**(a)** Peters had previously committed theft and fraud. The court stated, "This is the person he is. He steals from his relatives. He steals from his business partner. He steals from immigrants. He steals from anybody he comes into contact with." What does Peters's conduct indicate about his ethics?

**(b)** Peters's attorney argued that his client's criminal history was partially due to "difficult personal times" caused by divorce, illness, and job loss. Despite this claim, Peters was sentenced to forty-eight months imprisonment, which exceeded the federal sentencing guidelines but was less than the statutory maximum of twenty years. Was this sentence too harsh? Was it too lenient? Discuss.

# Legal Reasoning Group Activity

**10–9. Cyber Crime.** Cyber crime costs consumers millions of dollars per year, and it costs businesses, including banks and other credit-card issuers, even more. Nonetheless, when cyber criminals are caught and convicted, they are rarely ordered to pay restitution or sentenced to long prison terms. (See *Cyber Crime.*)

**(a)** One group should argue that stiffer sentences would reduce the amount of cyber crime.

**(b)** A second group should determine how businesspersons can best protect themselves from cyber crime and avoid the associated costs.

# Answers to the *Issue Spotters*

**1.** *With respect to the gas station, has she committed a crime? If so, what is it?* Yes. With respect to the gas station, she has obtained goods by false pretenses. She might also be charged with larceny and forgery, and most states have special statutes covering illegal use of credit cards.

**2.** *Has Ben committed a crime? If so, what is it?* Yes. The Counterfeit Access Device and Computer Fraud and Abuse Act provides that a person who accesses a computer online, without permission, to obtain classified data—such as consumer credit files in a credit agency's database—is subject to criminal prosecution. The crime has two elements: accessing the computer without permission and taking data. It is a felony if done for private financial gain. Penalties include fines and imprisonment for up to twenty years. The victim of the theft can also bring a civil suit against the criminal to obtain damages and other relief.

# Sample Answers for *Business Case Problems with Sample Answer*

**Problem 10–4.** *Criminal Liability.* Yes, Green exhibited the required mental state to establish criminal liability. A wrongful mental state (*mens rea*) is one of the elements typically required to establish criminal liability. The required mental state, or intent, is indicated in an applicable statute or law. For example, for murder, the required mental state is the intent to take another's life. A court can also find that the required mental state is present when a defendant's acts are reckless or criminally negligent. A defendant is criminally reckless if he or she consciously disregards a substantial and unjustifiable risk.

In this problem, Green was clearly aware of the danger to which he was exposing people on the street below. Although he did not indicate that he specifically intended to harm anyone, the risk of death created by his conduct was obvious. He must have known what was likely to happen if a bottle or plate thrown from the height of twenty-six stories hit a pedestrian or the windshield of an occupied motor vehicle on the street below. Despite his claim that he was intoxicated, he was sufficiently aware to stop throwing things from the balcony when he saw police in the area, and he later recalled what he had done and what had happened.

In the actual case on which this problem is based, after a jury trial, Green was convicted of reckless endangerment. On appeal, a state intermediate appellate court affirmed the conviction, based in part on the reasoning stated above.

# Chapter 6

# CHAPTER

# Formation of Traditional and E-Contracts

No aspect of modern life is entirely free of contractual relationships. You acquire rights and obligations, for instance, when you borrow funds, buy or lease a house, obtain insurance, and purchase goods or services. Contract law is designed to provide stability and predictability, as well as certainty, in the marketplace.

Contract law deals with, among other things, the formation and keeping of promises. A **promise** is a declaration by a person (the *promisor*) to do or not to do a certain act. As a result, the person to whom the promise is made (the *promisee*) has a right to expect or demand that something either will or will not happen in the future.

Like other types of law, contract law reflects our social values, interests, and expectations at a given point in time. It shows, for instance, to what extent our society allows people to make promises or commitments that are legally binding. It distinguishes between promises that create only *moral* obligations (such as a promise to take a friend to lunch) and promises that are legally binding (such as a promise to pay for items ordered online).

Contract law also demonstrates which excuses our society accepts for breaking certain types of promises. In addition, it indicates which promises are considered to be contrary to public policy—against the interests of society as a whole—and therefore legally invalid. When the person making a promise is a child or is mentally incompetent, for instance, a question will arise as to whether the promise should be enforced. Resolving such questions is the essence of contract law.

## 12–1 An Overview of Contract Law

Before we look at the numerous rules that courts use to determine whether a particular promise will be enforced, it is necessary to understand some fundamental concepts of contract law. In this section, we describe the sources and general function of contract law and introduce the objective theory of contracts.

### 12–1a Sources of Contract Law

The common law governs all contracts except when it has been modified or replaced by statutory law, such as the Uniform Commercial Code (UCC), or by administrative agency regulations. Contracts relating to services, real estate, employment, and insurance, for instance, generally are governed by the common law of contracts.

Contracts for the sale and lease of goods, however, are governed by the UCC—to the extent that the UCC has modified general contract law. In the discussion of general contract law that follows, we indicate in footnotes the areas in which the UCC has significantly altered common law contract principles.

### 12–1b The Definition of a Contract

A **contract** is "a promise or a set of promises for the breach of which the law gives a remedy, or the performance of which the law in some way recognizes as a duty."[1] Put simply, a contract is an agreement that can be enforced in court. It is formed by two or more parties who agree to perform or to refrain from performing some act now or in the future.

Generally, contract disputes arise when there is a promise of future performance. If the contractual promise is not fulfilled, the party who made it is subject to the sanctions of a court. That party may be required to pay damages for failing to perform the contractual promise. In a few instances, the party may be required to perform the promised act.

---

1. *Restatement (Second) of Contracts*, Section 1. *Restatements of the Law* are scholarly books that restate the existing common law principles distilled from court opinions as sets of rules on particular topics. Courts often refer to the *Restatements* for guidance. The *Restatement* dealing with contracts will be referred to throughout the material on contract law. *Second* in the title indicates that this *Restatement* is in its second edition. A third edition is being drafted.

## 12–1c The Objective Theory of Contracts

In determining whether a contract has been formed, the element of intent is of prime importance. In contract law, intent is determined by what is called the **objective theory of contracts,** not by the personal or subjective intent, or belief, of a party.

The theory is that a party's intention to enter into a legally binding agreement, or contract, is judged by outward, objective facts. The facts are as interpreted by a *reasonable* person, rather than by the party's own secret, subjective intentions. Objective facts may include:

1. What the party said when entering into the contract.
2. How the party acted or appeared (intent may be manifested by conduct as well as by oral or written words).
3. The circumstances surrounding the transaction.

■ **CASE IN POINT 12.1** Cornell University in New York offered Leslie Weston an associate professorship for an initial term of five years. The offer letter described the position as being "with tenure," but it stated that the offer of tenure would have to be confirmed by the university's review process after she was hired. For a variety of reasons, Weston delayed her tenure submission for five years and, when she finally submitted it, she was not awarded tenure.

Cornell gave Weston a two-year extension, this time as an "associate professor without tenure," to allow her an opportunity to improve and resubmit her tenure package. Although she resubmitted her tenure request, it was again denied, resulting in her eventual termination. Weston sued Cornell for breach of contract, and lost. The court held that Cornell's two-year extension of Weston's position had clearly modified the original contract by stating that she was working as an associate professor "without tenure." Weston's subjective beliefs and unsupported arguments regarding the modification of her employment agreement were irrelevant.[2] ■

## 12–1d Requirements of a Valid Contract

The following list briefly describes the four requirements that must be met before a valid contract exists. If any of these elements is lacking, no contract will have been formed. (Each requirement will be explained more fully later in this chapter.)

1. *Agreement.* An agreement to form a contract includes an *offer* and an *acceptance.* One party must offer to enter into a legal agreement, and another party must accept the terms of the offer.

2. *Consideration.* Any promises made by the parties to the contract must be supported by legally sufficient and bargained-for *consideration* (something of value received or promised, such as money, to convince a person to make a deal).
3. *Contractual capacity.* Both parties entering into the contract must have the contractual *capacity* to do so. The law must recognize them as possessing characteristics that qualify them as competent parties.
4. *Legality.* The contract's purpose must be to accomplish some goal that is legal and not against public policy.

## 12–1e Defenses to the Enforceability of a Contract

Even if all of the requirements listed above are satisfied, a contract may be unenforceable if the following requirements are not met. These requirements typically are raised as *defenses* to the enforceability of an otherwise valid contract.

1. *Voluntary consent.* The consent of both parties must be voluntary. For instance, if a contract was formed as a result of fraud, undue influence, mistake, or duress, the contract may not be enforceable.
2. *Form.* The contract must be in whatever form the law requires. Some contracts must be in writing to be enforceable.

## 12–1f Types of Contracts

There are many types of contracts. They are categorized based on legal distinctions as to their formation, performance, and enforceability.

**Bilateral versus Unilateral Contracts** Every contract involves at least two parties. The **offeror** is the party making the offer. The **offeree** is the party to whom the offer is made. Whether the contract is classified as *bilateral* or *unilateral* depends on what the offeree must do to accept the offer and bind the offeror to a contract.

If the offeree can accept simply by promising to perform, the contract is a **bilateral contract.** Hence, a bilateral contract is a "promise for a promise." No performance, such as payment of funds or delivery of goods, need take place for a bilateral contract to be formed. The contract comes into existence at the moment the promises are exchanged.

If the offer is phrased so that the offeree can accept the offer only by completing the contract performance, the contract is a **unilateral contract.** Hence, a unilateral

---

2. *Weston v. Cornell University*, 136 A.D.3d 1094, 24 N.Y.S.3d 448 (N.Y.A.D. 2016).

contract is a "promise for an act." In other words, a unilateral contract is formed not at the moment when promises are exchanged but at the moment when the contract is *performed*.

■ **EXAMPLE 12.2** Reese says to Celia, "If you drive my car from New York to Los Angeles, I'll give you $1,000." Only on Celia's completion of the act—bringing the car to Los Angeles—does she fully accept Reese's offer to pay $1,000. If she chooses not to accept the offer to drive the car to Los Angeles, there are no legal consequences. ■

### Formal versus Informal Contracts

**Formal contracts** are contracts that require a special form or method of creation (formation) to be enforceable.[3] One example is *negotiable instruments,* which include checks, drafts, promissory notes, bills of exchange, and certificates of deposit. Negotiable instruments are formal contracts because the Uniform Commercial Code (UCC) requires a special language to create them. *Letters of credit,* which are frequently used in international sales contracts, are another type of formal contract.

**Informal contracts** (also called *simple contracts*) include all other contracts. No special form is required (except for certain types of contracts that must be in writing), as the contracts are usually based on their substance rather than their form. Typically, businesspersons put their contracts in writing (including electronic records) to establish proof of a contract's existence should disputes arise.

### Express versus Implied Contracts

Contracts may also be categorized as *express* or *implied*. In an **express contract,** the terms of the agreement are fully and explicitly stated in words, oral or written. A signed lease for an apartment or a house is an express written contract. If one classmate calls another on the phone and agrees to buy her textbooks from last semester for $200, an express oral contract has been made.

A contract that is implied from the conduct of the parties is called an **implied contract** (or sometimes an *implied-in-fact contract*). This type of contract differs from an express contract in that the conduct of the parties, rather than their words, creates and defines the terms of the contract.

**Requirements for Implied Contracts.** For an implied contract to arise, certain requirements must be met. Normally, if the following conditions exist, a court will hold that an implied contract was formed:

1. The plaintiff furnished some service or property.
2. The plaintiff expected to be paid for that service or property, and the defendant knew or should have known that payment was expected.
3. The defendant had a chance to reject the services or property and did not.

■ **EXAMPLE 12.3** Alex, a small-business owner, needs an accountant to complete his tax return. He drops by a local accountant's office, explains his situation to the accountant, and learns what fees she charges. The next day, he returns and gives the receptionist all of the necessary documents to complete his return. Then he walks out without saying anything further to the accountant. In this situation, Alex has entered into an implied contract to pay the accountant the usual fees for her services. The contract is implied because of Alex's conduct and hers. She expects to be paid for completing the tax return, and by bringing in the records she will need to do the job, Alex has implied an intent to pay her. ■

**Mixed Contracts with Express and Implied Terms.** Note that a contract may be a mixture of an express contract and an implied contract. In other words, a contract may contain some express terms and some implied terms. During the construction of a home, for instance, the homeowner often asks the builder to make changes in the original specifications.

■ **CASE IN POINT 12.4** Lamar Hopkins hired Uhrhahn Construction & Design, Inc., for several projects in building his home. For each project, the parties signed a written contract that was based on a cost estimate and specifications and that required changes to the agreement to be in writing. While the work was in progress, however, Hopkins repeatedly asked Uhrhahn to deviate from the contract specifications, which Uhrhahn did. None of these requests was made in writing.

One day, Hopkins asked Uhrhahn to use Durisol blocks instead of the cinder blocks specified in the original contract, indicating that the cost would be the same. Uhrhahn used the Durisol blocks but demanded extra payment when it became clear that the Durisol blocks were more complicated to install. Although Hopkins had paid for the other deviations from the contract that he had orally requested, he refused to pay Uhrhahn for the substitution of the Durisol blocks. Uhrhahn sued for breach of contract. The court found that Hopkins, through his conduct, had waived the provision requiring written contract modification and created an implied contract to pay the extra cost of installing the Durisol blocks.[4] ■

---

3. See *Restatement (Second) of Contracts*, Section 6, which explains that formal contracts include (1) contracts under seal, (2) recognizances, (3) negotiable instruments, and (4) letters of credit.

4. *Uhrhahn Construction & Design, Inc. v. Hopkins*, 179 P.3d 808 (Utah App. 2008).

**Executed versus Executory Contracts** Contracts are also classified according to the degree to which they have been performed. A contract that has been fully performed on both sides is called an **executed contract.** A contract that has not been fully performed by the parties is called an **executory contract.** If one party has fully performed but the other has not, the contract is said to be executed on the one side and executory on the other, but the contract is still classified as executory.

■ **EXAMPLE 12.5** Jackson, Inc., agreed to buy ten tons of coal from the Northern Coal Company. Northern delivered the coal to Jackson's steel mill, where it is being burned. At this point, the contract is executed on the part of Northern and executory on Jackson's part. After Jackson pays Northern, the contract will be executed on both sides. ■

**Enforceable versus Unenforceable Contracts**
A **valid contract** has the necessary elements to entitle at least one of the parties to enforce it in court. Those elements, as mentioned earlier, consist of (1) an agreement (offer and acceptance), (2) supported by legally sufficient consideration, (3) made by parties who have the legal capacity to enter into the contract, and (4) a legal purpose.

Valid contracts may be enforceable or unenforceable. An **unenforceable contract** is one that cannot be enforced because of certain legal defenses against it. It is not unenforceable because a party failed to satisfy a legal requirement of the contract. Rather, it is a valid contract rendered unenforceable by some statute or law. For instance, certain contracts must be in writing, and if they are not, they will not be enforceable except in certain exceptional circumstances.

**Voidable Contracts.** A **voidable contract** is a valid contract but one that can be avoided at the option of one or both of the parties. The party having the option can elect either to avoid any duty to perform or to *ratify* (make valid) the contract. If the contract is avoided, both parties are released from it. If it is ratified, both parties must fully perform their respective legal obligations. For instance, contracts made by minors generally are voidable at the option of the minor (with certain exceptions). Contracts made by mentally incompetent persons and intoxicated persons may also be voidable.

**Void Contracts.** A **void contract** is no contract at all. None of the parties have any legal obligations if a contract is void. A contract can be void because one of the parties was determined by a court to be mentally incompetent, for instance, or because the purpose of the contract was illegal.

To review the various types of contracts, see Concept Summary 12.1.

---

## Concept Summary 12.1

### Types of Contracts

| Formation | • *Bilateral*—A promise for a promise.<br>• *Unilateral*—A promise for an act—that is, acceptance is the completed performance of the act.<br>• *Formal*—Requires a special form for creation.<br>• *Informal*—Requires no special form for creation.<br>• *Express*—Formed by words, such as oral, written, or a combination.<br>• *Implied*—Formed by the conduct of the parties. |
|---|---|
| **Performance** | • *Executed*—A fully performed contract.<br>• *Executory*—A contract not fully performed. |
| **Enforceability** | • *Valid*—The contract has the necessary contractual elements: agreement (offer and acceptance), consideration, legal capacity of the parties, and legal purpose.<br>• *Voidable*—One party has the option of avoiding or enforcing the contractual obligation.<br>• *Unenforceable*—A contract exists, but it cannot be enforced because of a legal defense.<br>• *Void*—No contract exists, or there is a contract without legal obligations. |

## 12–2 Agreement

An essential element for contract formation is **agreement**—the parties must agree on the terms of the contract and manifest to each other their *mutual assent* (agreement) to the same bargain. Ordinarily, agreement is evidenced by two events: an *offer* and an *acceptance*. One party offers a certain bargain to another party, who then accepts that bargain. Once an agreement is reached, if the other elements of a contract (consideration, capacity, and legality) are present, a valid contract is formed.

### 12–2a Requirements of the Offer

An **offer** is a promise or commitment to do or refrain from doing some specified action in the future. The party making an offer is called the *offeror*, and the party to whom the offer is made is called the *offeree*. Under the common law, three elements are necessary for an offer to be effective:

1. The offeror must have a serious intention to become bound by the offer.

2. The terms of the offer must be reasonably certain, or definite, so that the parties and the court can ascertain the terms of the contract.

3. The offer must be communicated to the offeree.

Once an effective offer has been made, the offeree's acceptance of that offer creates a legally binding contract (providing the other essential elements for a valid and enforceable contract are present).

**Intention** The first requirement for an effective offer is a serious intent on the part of the offeror. Serious intent is not determined by the subjective intentions, beliefs, and assumptions of the offeror. Rather, it is determined by what a reasonable person in the offeree's position would conclude that the offeror's words and actions meant.

Offers made in obvious anger, jest, or undue excitement do not meet the serious-and-objective-intent test. A reasonable person would realize that such offers were not made seriously. Because these offers are not effective, an offeree's acceptance does not create an agreement.

In the classic case presented next, the court considered whether an offer made "after a few drinks" met the serious-and-objective-intent requirement.

**Classic Case 12.1**

# Lucy v. Zehmer

Supreme Court of Appeals of Virginia, 196 Va. 493, 84 S.E.2d 516 (1954).

**Background and Facts** W. O. Lucy, the plaintiff, filed a suit against A. H. and Ida Zehmer, the defendants, to compel the Zehmers to transfer title of their property, known as the Ferguson Farm, to the Lucys (W. O. and his wife) for $50,000, as the Zehmers had allegedly agreed to do. Lucy had known A. H. Zehmer for fifteen or twenty years and for the last eight years or so had been anxious to buy the Ferguson Farm from him. One night, Lucy stopped to visit the Zehmers in the combination restaurant, filling station, and motor court they operated. While there, Lucy tried to buy the Ferguson Farm once again. This time he tried a new approach. According to the trial court transcript, Lucy said to Zehmer, "I bet you wouldn't take $50,000 for that place." Zehmer replied, "Yes, I would too; you wouldn't give fifty." Throughout the evening, the conversation returned to the sale of the Ferguson Farm for $50,000. All the while, the men continued to drink whiskey and engage in light conversation.

Eventually, Lucy enticed Zehmer to write up an agreement to the effect that the Zehmers would sell the Ferguson Farm to Lucy for $50,000 complete. Later, Lucy sued Zehmer to compel him to go through with the sale. Zehmer argued that he had been drunk and that the offer had been made in jest and hence was unenforceable. The trial court agreed with Zehmer, and Lucy appealed.

### In the Language of the Court
*BUCHANAN, J. [Justice] delivered the opinion of the court.*
* * * *

In his testimony, Zehmer claimed that he "was high as a Georgia pine," and that the transaction "was just a bunch of two doggoned drunks bluffing to see who could talk the biggest and say the most." That claim is inconsistent with his attempt to testify in great detail as to what was said and what was done.

**Case 12.1 Continues**

**Case 12.1 Continued**

* * * *

The appearance of the contract, the fact that it was under discussion for forty minutes or more before it was signed; Lucy's objection to the first draft because it was written in the singular, and he wanted Mrs. Zehmer to sign it also; the rewriting to meet that objection and the signing by Mrs. Zehmer; the discussion of what was to be included in the sale, the provision for the examination of the title, the completeness of the instrument that was executed, the taking possession of it by Lucy with no request or suggestion by either of the defendants that he give it back, are facts which furnish persuasive evidence that the execution of the contract was a serious business transaction rather than a casual, jesting matter as defendants now contend.

* * * *

In the field of contracts, as generally elsewhere, *we must look to the outward expression of a person as manifesting his intention rather than to his secret and unexpressed intention.* The law imputes to a person an intention corresponding to the reasonable meaning of his words and acts. [Emphasis added.]

* * * *

Whether the writing signed by the defendants and now sought to be enforced by the complainants was the result of a serious offer by Lucy and a serious acceptance by the defendants, or was a serious offer by Lucy and an acceptance in secret jest by the defendants, in either event it constituted a binding contract of sale between the parties.

**Decision and Remedy** *The Supreme Court of Appeals of Virginia determined that the writing was an enforceable contract and reversed the ruling of the lower court. The Zehmers were required by court order to follow through with the sale of the Ferguson Farm to the Lucys.*

**Impact of This Case on Today's Law** *This is a classic case in contract law because it illustrates so clearly the objective theory of contracts with respect to determining whether a serious offer was intended. Today, the courts continue to apply the objective theory of contracts and routinely cite* Lucy v. Zehmer *as a significant precedent in this area.*

**Critical Thinking**
- **What If the Facts Were Different?** *Suppose that the day after Lucy signed the purchase agreement, he decided that he did not want the farm after all, and Zehmer sued Lucy to perform the contract. Would this change in the facts alter the court's decision that Lucy and Zehmer had created an enforceable contract? Why or why not?*

## Situations in Which Intent May Be Lacking

The concept of intention can be further clarified by looking at statements that are *not* offers and situations in which the parties' intent to be bound might be questionable.

1. *Expressions of opinion.* An expression of opinion is not an offer. It does not indicate an intention to enter into a binding agreement.
2. *Statements of future intent.* A statement of an intention to do something in the future (such as "I plan to sell my Verizon stock") is not an offer.
3. *Preliminary negotiations.* A request or invitation to negotiate is not an offer. It only expresses a willingness to discuss the possibility of entering into a contract. Statements such as "Will you sell your farm?" or "I wouldn't sell my car for less than $8,000" are examples.
4. *Invitations to bid.* When a government entity or private firm needs to have construction work done, contractors are invited to submit bids. The invitation to submit bids is not an offer. The bids that contractors submit are offers, however, and the government entity or private firm can bind the contractor by accepting the bid.
5. *Advertisements and price lists.* In general, representations made in advertisements and price lists are treated not as offers to contract but as invitations to negotiate.[5]
6. *Live and online auctions.* In a live auction, a seller "offers" goods for sale through an auctioneer, but this is not an offer to form a contract. Rather, it is an invitation asking bidders to submit offers. In the context of an auction, a bidder is the offeror, and the auctioneer is the offeree. The offer is accepted when the auctioneer strikes the hammer.

---

5. *Restatement (Second) of Contracts*, Section 26, Comment b.

The most familiar type of auction today takes place online through Web sites like eBay and eBid. "Offers" to sell an item on these sites generally are treated as invitations to negotiate.

**Agreements to Agree.** Traditionally, agreements to agree—that is, agreements to agree to the material terms of a contract at some future date—were not considered to be binding contracts. The modern view, however, is that agreements to agree may be enforceable agreements (contracts) if it is clear that the parties intended to be bound by the agreements. In other words, under the modern view the emphasis is on the parties' intent rather than on form.

**Preliminary Agreements.** A preliminary agreement can constitute a binding contract if the parties have agreed on all essential terms and no disputed issues remain to be resolved. ■ **CASE IN POINT 12.6** Basis Technology Corporation created software and provided technical services for a Japanese-language Web site belonging to Amazon.com, Inc. The agreement between the two companies allowed for separately negotiated contracts for additional services that Basis might provide to Amazon. Later, a dispute arose and Basis sued Amazon for various claims involving these contracts and for failure to pay for services performed by Basis. During the trial, the two parties appeared to reach an agreement to settle out of court via a series of e-mail exchanges outlining the settlement. When Amazon reneged, Basis served a motion to enforce the proposed settlement. The trial judge entered a judgment against Amazon, which appealed. The Appeals Court of Massachusetts affirmed the trial court's finding that Amazon intended to be bound by the terms of the e-mail exchange, which contained a complete and unambiguous statement of the parties' settlement terms.[6] ■

In contrast, if the parties agree on certain major terms but leave other terms open for further negotiation, a preliminary agreement is not binding. The parties are bound only in the sense that they have committed themselves to negotiate the undecided terms in good faith in an effort to reach a final agreement.

**Definiteness of Terms** The second requirement for an effective offer involves the definiteness of its terms. An offer must have reasonably definite terms so that a court can determine if a breach has occurred and give an appropriate remedy.[7] The specific terms required depend, of course, on the type of contract. Generally, a contract must include the following terms, either expressed in the contract or capable of being reasonably inferred from it:

1. The identification of the parties.
2. The identification of the object or subject matter of the contract (also the quantity, when appropriate), including the work to be performed, with specific identification of such items as goods, services, and land.
3. The consideration to be paid.
4. The time of payment, delivery, or performance.

An offer may invite an acceptance to be worded in such specific terms that the contract is made definite. ■ **EXAMPLE 12.7** Nintendo of America, Inc., contacts your Play 2 Win Games store and offers to sell "from one to twenty-five Nintendo 3DS.XL gaming systems for $75 each. State number desired in acceptance." You agree to buy twenty systems. Because the quantity is specified in the acceptance, the terms are definite, and the contract is enforceable. ■

When the parties have clearly manifested their intent to form a contract, courts sometimes are willing to supply a missing term in a contract, especially a sales contract.[8] But a court will not rewrite a contract if the parties' expression of intent is too vague or uncertain to be given any precise meaning.

**Communication** The third requirement for an effective offer is communication—the offer must be communicated to the offeree. Ordinarily, one cannot agree to a bargain without knowing that it exists. ■ **CASE IN POINT 12.8** Adwoa Gyabaah was hit by a bus owned by Rivlab Transportation Corporation. Gyabaah filed a suit in a New York state court against the bus company. Rivlab's insurer offered to tender the company's policy limit of $1 million in full settlement of Gyabaah's claims. On the advice of her attorney, Jeffrey Aronsky, Gyabaah signed a release (a contract forfeiting the right to pursue a legal claim) to obtain the settlement funds.

The release, however, was not sent to Rivlab or its insurer, National Casualty. Moreover, Gyabaah claimed that she had not decided whether to settle. Two months later, Gyabaah changed lawyers and changed her mind about signing the release. Her former attorney, Aronsky, filed a motion to enforce the release so that he could obtain his fees from the settlement funds. The court denied the motion, and Aronsky appealed. The reviewing court held that there was no binding settlement agreement. The release was never delivered to Rivlab

---

6. *Basis Technology Corp. v. Amazon.com, Inc.*, 71 Mass.App.Ct. 29, 878 N.E.2d 952 (2008).
7. *Restatement (Second) of Contracts*, Section 33.

8. See UCC 2–204. Article 2 of the UCC modifies general contract law by requiring *less* specificity, or definiteness of terms, in sales and lease contracts.

or its insurer nor was acceptance of the settlement offer otherwise communicated to them.[9] ■

### 12–2b Termination of the Offer

The communication of an effective offer to an offeree gives the offeree the power to transform the offer into a binding, legal obligation (a contract) by an acceptance. This power of acceptance does not continue forever, though. It can be terminated either by action of the parties or by operation of law.

**Termination by Action of the Offeror** The offeror's act of revoking, or withdrawing, an offer is known as **revocation.** Unless an offer is irrevocable, the offeror usually can revoke the offer, as long as the revocation is communicated to the offeree before the offeree accepts. Revocation may be accomplished by either of the following:

1.  Express repudiation of the offer (such as "I withdraw my previous offer of October 17").
2.  Performance of acts that are inconsistent with the existence of the offer and are made known to the offeree (for instance, selling the offered property to another person in the offeree's presence).

In most states, a revocation becomes effective when the offeree or the offeree's *agent* (a person acting on behalf of the offeree) actually receives it. Therefore, a revocation sent via FedEx on April 1 and delivered at the offeree's residence or place of business on April 3 becomes effective on April 3.

Although most offers are revocable, some can be made irrevocable—that is, they cannot be revoked. One form of irrevocable offer is an **option contract.** An option contract is created when an offeror promises to hold an offer open for a specified period of time in return for a payment (consideration) given by the offeree. An option contract takes away the offeror's power to revoke the offer for the period of time specified in the option.

Option contracts are frequently used in conjunction with the sale or lease of real estate. ■ **EXAMPLE 12.9** Tyler agrees to lease a house from Jackson, the property owner. The lease contract includes a clause stating that Tyler is paying an additional $15,000 for an option to purchase the property within a specified period of time. If Tyler decides not to purchase the house after the specified period has lapsed, he loses the $15,000, and Jackson is free to sell the property to another buyer. ■

**Termination by Action of the Offeree** If the offeree rejects the offer—by words or by conduct—the offer is terminated. Any subsequent attempt by the offeree to accept will be construed as a new offer, giving the original offeror (now the offeree) the power of acceptance.

Like a revocation, a rejection of an offer is effective only when it is actually received by the offeror or the offeror's agent. ■ **EXAMPLE 12.10** Goldfinch Farms offers to sell specialty Maitake mushrooms to a Japanese buyer, Kinoko Foods. If Kinoko rejects the offer by sending a letter via U.S. mail, the rejection will not be effective (and the offer will not be terminated) until Goldfinch receives the letter. ■

**Inquiries about an Offer.** Merely inquiring about the "firmness" of an offer does not constitute rejection. ■ **EXAMPLE 12.11** Raymond offers to buy Francie's digital pen for $100. She responds, "Is that your best offer?" A reasonable person would conclude that Francie has not rejected the offer but has merely made an inquiry. Francie could still accept and bind Raymond to the $100 price. ■

**Counteroffer.** A **counteroffer** is a rejection of the original offer and the simultaneous making of a new offer. ■ **EXAMPLE 12.12** Burke offers to sell his home to Lang for $270,000. Lang responds, "Your price is too high. I'll offer to purchase your house for $250,000." Lang's response is a counteroffer because it rejects Burke's offer to sell at $270,000 and creates a new offer by Lang to purchase the home for $250,000. ■

At common law, the **mirror image rule** requires the offeree's acceptance to match the offeror's offer exactly—to mirror the offer. Any change in, or addition to, the terms of the original offer automatically terminates that offer and substitutes the counteroffer. The counteroffer, of course, need not be accepted, but if the original offeror does accept the terms of the counteroffer, a valid contract is created.[10]

**Termination by Operation of Law** The power of the offeree to transform the offer into a binding, legal obligation can be terminated by operation of law through the occurrence of any of the following events:

1.  Lapse of time.
2.  Destruction of the specific subject matter of the offer.
3.  Death or incompetence of the offeror or the offeree.
4.  Supervening illegality of the proposed contract.

---

9. *Gyabaah v. Rivlab Transportation Corp.*, 102 A.D.3d 451, 958 N.Y.S.2d 109 (N.Y.A.D. 2013).

10. The mirror image rule has been greatly modified in regard to sales contracts. Section 2–207 of the UCC provides that a contract is formed if the offeree makes a definite expression of acceptance (such as signing a form in the appropriate location), even though the terms of the acceptance modify or add to the terms of the original offer.

**Lapse of Time.** An offer terminates automatically by law when the period of time *specified in the offer* has passed. If the offer states that it will be left open until a particular date, then the offer will terminate at midnight on that day. If the offer states that it will be open for a number of days, this time period normally begins to run when the offeree *receives* the offer (not when it is formed or sent).

If the offer does not specify a time for acceptance, the offer terminates at the end of a *reasonable* period of time. What constitutes a reasonable period of time depends on the subject matter of the contract, business and market conditions, and other relevant circumstances. An offer to sell farm produce, for instance, will terminate sooner than an offer to sell farm equipment. Farm produce is perishable and is also subject to greater fluctuations in market value.

**Destruction, Death, or Incompetence.** An offer is automatically terminated if the specific subject matter of the offer (such as a smartphone or a house) is destroyed before the offer is accepted.[11] Notice of the destruction is not required for the offer to terminate. An offeree's power of acceptance is also terminated when the offeror or offeree dies or is legally incapacitated—*unless the offer is irrevocable.*

**Supervening Illegality.** A statute or court decision that makes an offer illegal automatically terminates the offer. ■ **EXAMPLE 12.13** Lee offers to lend Kim $10,000 at an annual interest rate of 15 percent. Before Kim can accept the offer, a law is enacted that prohibits interest rates higher than 8 percent. Lee's offer is automatically terminated. (If the statute is enacted after Kim accepts the

---

11. *Restatement (Second) of Contracts*, Section 36.

offer, a valid contract is formed, but the contract may still be unenforceable.) ■

Concept Summary 12.2 reviews the ways in which an offer can be terminated.

### 12–2c Acceptance

**Acceptance** is a voluntary act by the offeree that shows assent (agreement) to the terms of an offer. The offeree's act may consist of words or conduct. The acceptance must be unequivocal and must be communicated to the offeror. Generally, only the person to whom the offer is made or that person's agent can accept the offer and create a binding contract.

**Unequivocal Acceptance** To exercise the power of acceptance effectively, the offeree must accept unequivocally. This is the *mirror image rule* previously discussed. An acceptance may be unequivocal even though the offeree expresses dissatisfaction with the contract. For instance, "I accept the offer, but can you give me a better price?" is an effective acceptance.

An acceptance cannot impose new conditions or change the terms of the original offer. If it does, the acceptance may be considered a counteroffer, which is a rejection of the original offer. For instance, the statement "I accept the offer but only if I can pay on ninety days' credit" is a counteroffer and not an unequivocal acceptance.

Note that even when the additional terms are construed as a counteroffer, the other party can accept the terms by words or by conduct. ■ **CASE IN POINT 12.14** Lagrange Development is a nonprofit corporation in Ohio that acquires and rehabilitates real property. Sonja Brown presented Lagrange with a written offer to buy a

---

### Concept Summary 12.2

#### Methods by Which an Offer Can Be Terminated

| By Action of the Parties | • Revocation<br>• Rejection<br>• Counteroffer |
|---|---|
| By Operation of Law | • Lapse of time<br>• Destruction of the subject matter<br>• Death or incompetence of the offeror or offeree<br>• Supervening illegality |

particular house for $79,900. Lagrange's executive director, Terry Glazer, penciled in modifications to the offer—an increased purchase price of $84,200 and a later date for acceptance. Glazer initialed the changes and signed the document.

Brown initialed the date change but not the price increase, and did not sign the revised document. Nevertheless, Brown went through with the sale and received ownership of the property. When a dispute later arose as to the purchase price, a court found that Glazer's modification of the terms had constituted a counteroffer, which Brown had accepted by performance. Therefore, the contract was enforceable for the modified price of $84,200.[12] ■

**Silence as Acceptance** Ordinarily, silence cannot constitute acceptance, even if the offeror states, "By your silence and inaction, you will be deemed to have accepted this offer." An offeree should not be obligated to act affirmatively to reject an offer when no consideration (nothing of value) has passed to the offeree to impose such a duty.

In some instances, however, the offeree does have a duty to speak, and her or his silence or inaction

will operate as an acceptance. Silence can constitute an acceptance when the offeree has had prior dealings with the offeror. ■ **EXAMPLE 12.15** Marabel's restaurant routinely receives shipments of produce from a certain supplier. That supplier notifies Marabel's that it is raising its prices because its crops were damaged by a late freeze. If the restaurant does not respond in any way, the silence may operate as an acceptance, and the supplier will be justified in continuing regular shipments. ■

**Communication of Acceptance** Whether the offeror must be notified of the acceptance depends on the nature of the contract. In a unilateral contract, the full performance of some act is called for. Acceptance is usually evident, and notification is therefore unnecessary (unless the law requires it or the offeror asks for it). In a bilateral contract, in contrast, communication of acceptance is necessary, because acceptance is in the form of a promise. The bilateral contract is formed when the promise is made rather than when the act is performed.

At issue in the following case was the validity and enforceability of a waiver of liability on the back page of a gym's membership agreement. In this case, the court had to determine whether the circumstances indicated that the offeree's acceptance of the agreement was unequivocal and clearly communicated.

---

12. *Brown v. Lagrange Development Corp.*, 2015 WL 223877 (Ohio App. 2015).

---

**Case Analysis 12.2**

# Hinkal v. Pardoe

Superior Court of Pennsylvania, 2016 PA Super 11, 133 A.3d 738 (2016).

### In the Language of the Court
Opinion by STABILE, J. [Judge]

* * * *

[Melinda Hinkal filed a suit in a Pennsylvania state court against personal trainer Gavin Pardoe and Gold's Gym, Inc., alleging that] she sustained a serious neck injury while using a piece of exercise equipment under * * * Pardoe's direction [at Gold's Gym. Hinkal] alleges that she suffered a rupture of the C5 disc in her neck requiring two separate surgeries. [Gold's and Pardoe] filed a Motion for Summary Judgment [asserting] that as a member of Gold's Gym [Hinkal] signed * * * a Membership Agreement [that] contains legally valid "waiver of liability" provisions, which in turn, bar [her] claims.

The trial court concluded that the waiver language set forth in Gold's Membership Agreement was valid and enforceable.

[Hinkal] filed a timely appeal to this [state intermediate appellate] Court.

* * * *

* * * Appellant [Hinkal] questions whether the waiver on the back page of her membership agreement is valid and enforceable. The language on the back page of the agreement reads in pertinent part as follows:

WAIVER OF LIABILITY; ASSUMPTION OF RISK: Member acknowledges that the use of Gold's Gym's facilities, equipment, services and programs involves an inherent risk of personal injury to Member. * * *

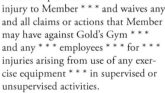

Member voluntarily agrees to assume all risks of personal injury to Member * * * and waives any and all claims or actions that Member may have against Gold's Gym * * * and any * * * employees * * * for * * * injuries arising from use of any exercise equipment * * * in supervised or unsupervised activities.

The Gold's Gym Membership Agreement signed by Appellant further instructs:

Do not sign this Agreement until you have read both sides. The terms on each side of this form are a part of this Agreement. * * * By signing this Agreement, Member acknowledges that This Agreement is a contract that will become legally binding upon its acceptance.

*Case 12.2 Continues*

**Case 12.2 Continued**

The signature line follows immediately and the words "Notice: See other side for important information" appear in bold typeface below the signature line.

* * * *

* * * Appellant * * * asserts that her claim is not barred by the "exclusion clause" on the back of the membership agreement. * * * Appellant contends the waiver is invalid because the waiver language appeared on the back of the agreement, she never read or was told to read the back of the agreement, and the clause was not "brought home" to her in a way that could suggest she was aware of the clause and its contents. However, * * * Appellant admitted she did not read the agreement prior to signing it. * * * Her failure to read her agreement does not render it either invalid or unenforceable. *The law of Pennsylvania is clear. One who is about to sign a contract has a duty to read that contract first.* * * * It is well established that, in the absence of fraud, the failure

to read a contract before signing it is an unavailing excuse or defense and cannot justify an avoidance, modification or nullification of the contract. [Emphasis added.]

[To support her claim, Appellant cites *Beck-Hummel v. Ski Shawnee, Inc.,* a previous case before this court, but] the signed Gold's Gym membership agreement cannot be compared in any way to the unread and unsigned disclaimer on a ski facility ticket in [*Beck-Hummel.*]

* * * *

* * * In [*Beck-Hummel,*] the release provision was contained on the face of an entry ticket purchased for use of a ski facility. The ticket did not require a signature or an express acknowledgment that its terms were read and accepted before using the facility. Nothing about the ticket ensured that a purchaser would be aware of its release provision. The purchasers were mere recipients of the document. In short, there was not sufficient evidence to find conclusively

that there was a meeting of the minds that part of the consideration for use of the facility was acceptance of a release provision. In stark contrast, here there is a written, signed and acknowledged agreement between the parties.

* * * *

Here, without reading it, Appellant signed the membership agreement, which included an unambiguous directive not to sign before reading both sides, a clear pronouncement that the terms on both sides of the form are part of the agreement, and a straightforward statement that the agreement constitutes the entire agreement between the parties. * * * We find no genuine issue as to any material fact or any error in the lower court's determination that the waiver was valid and enforceable. Appellant is not entitled to relief based on [this] issue.

* * * *

Order affirmed.

## Legal Reasoning Questions

1. What indicated that the terms in the agreement at issue in this case were accepted?

2. What were the appellant's arguments in support of her claim? Which of those contentions did the court imply was irrelevant? Why?

3. How did the court distinguish its conclusion in this case from its decision in *Beck-Hummel*?

---

**Mode and Timeliness of Acceptance** In bilateral contracts, acceptance must be timely. The general rule is that acceptance in a bilateral contract is timely if it is made before the offer is terminated. Problems may arise, though, when the parties involved are not dealing face to face. In such situations, the offeree should use an authorized mode of communication.

**The Mailbox Rule.** Acceptance takes effect, thus completing formation of the contract, at the time the offeree sends or delivers the communication via the mode expressly or impliedly authorized by the offeror. This is the so-called **mailbox rule,** also called the *deposited acceptance rule,* which the majority of courts follow. Under this rule, if the authorized mode of communication is the mail, then an acceptance becomes valid when it is dispatched (placed in the control of the U.S. Postal Service)—*not* when it is received by the offeror. (Note, however, that if the offer

stipulates when acceptance will be effective, then the offer will not be effective until the time specified.)

The mailbox rule does not apply to instantaneous forms of communication, such as when the parties are dealing face to face, by telephone, by fax, and (usually) by e-mail. Under the Uniform Electronic Transactions Act, e-mail is considered sent when it either leaves the control of the sender or is received by the recipient. This rule takes the place of the mailbox rule when the parties have agreed to conduct transactions electronically and allows an e-mail acceptance to become effective when sent.

**Authorized Means of Acceptance.** A means of communicating acceptance can be expressly authorized by the offeror or impliedly authorized by the facts and circumstances of the situation. An acceptance sent by means not expressly or impliedly authorized normally is not effective until it is received by the offeror.

When an offeror specifies how acceptance should be made (for instance, by overnight delivery), *express authorization* is said to exist. The contract is not formed unless the offeree uses that specified mode of acceptance. Moreover, both offeror and offeree are bound in contract the moment this means of acceptance is employed.

If the offeror does not expressly authorize a certain mode of acceptance, then acceptance can be made by *any reasonable means*. Courts look at the prevailing business usages and the surrounding circumstances to determine whether the mode of acceptance used was reasonable. Usually, the offeror's choice of a particular means in making the offer implies that the offeree can use the *same or a faster means* for acceptance.

**Substitute Method of Acceptance.** Sometimes, the offeror authorizes a particular method of acceptance, but the offeree accepts by a different means. In that situation, the acceptance may still be effective if the substituted method serves the same purpose as the authorized means.

Acceptance by a substitute method is not effective on dispatch, however. No contract will be formed until the acceptance is received by the offeror. ■ **EXAMPLE 12.16** Bennion's offer specifies acceptance via FedEx overnight delivery, but the offeree accepts instead by overnight delivery from UPS. The substitute method of acceptance will still be effective, but not until the offeror (Bennion) receives it from UPS. ■

## 12–3 E-Contracts

Numerous contracts are formed online. Electronic contracts, or **e-contracts,** must meet the same basic requirements (agreement, consideration, contractual capacity, and legality) as paper contracts. Disputes concerning e-contracts, however, tend to center on contract terms and whether the parties voluntarily agreed to those terms.

Online contracts may be formed not only for the sale of goods and services but also for *licensing*. The "sale" of software generally involves a license, or a right to use the software, rather than the passage of title (ownership rights) from the seller to the buyer. When you download a software application (app) on your smartphone, for instance, you typically must agree to the terms of use in a licensing agreement.

Although we typically refer to the offeror and the offeree as a *seller* and a *buyer*, in many online transactions these parties would be more accurately described as a *licensor* and a *licensee*.

### 12–3a Online Offers

Sellers doing business via the Internet can protect themselves against contract disputes and legal liability by creating offers that clearly spell out the terms that will govern their transactions if the offers are accepted. All important terms should be conspicuous and easy to view.

The seller's Web site should include a hypertext link to a page containing the full contract so that potential buyers are made aware of the terms to which they are assenting. The contract generally must be displayed online in a readable format, such as a twelve-point typeface. All provisions should be reasonably clear.

**Provisions to Include** An important point to keep in mind is that the offeror (the seller) controls the offer and thus the resulting contract. The seller should therefore anticipate the terms he or she wants to include in a contract and provide for them in the offer. In some instances, a standardized contract form may suffice.

At a minimum, an online offer should include the following provisions:

1. *Acceptance of terms.* A clause that clearly indicates what constitutes the buyer's agreement to the terms of the offer, such as a box containing the words "I accept" that the buyer can click.
2. *Payment.* A provision specifying how payment for the goods (including any applicable taxes) must be made.
3. *Return policy.* A statement of the seller's refund and return policies.
4. *Disclaimer.* Disclaimers of liability for certain uses of the goods. For instance, an online seller of business forms may add a disclaimer that the seller does not accept responsibility for the buyer's reliance on the forms rather than on an attorney's advice.
5. *Limitation on remedies.* A provision specifying the remedies available to the buyer if the goods are found to be defective or if the contract is otherwise breached. Any limitation of remedies should be clearly spelled out.
6. *Privacy policy.* A statement indicating how the seller will use the information gathered about the buyer.
7. *Dispute resolution.* Provisions relating to dispute settlement, which we examine more closely in the following section.

**Dispute-Settlement Provisions** Online offers frequently include provisions relating to dispute settlement. For instance, an offer might include an arbitration clause specifying that any dispute arising under the contract will be arbitrated in a designated forum. The parties might also select the forum and the law that will govern any disputes.

**Forum-Selection Clause.** Many online contracts contain a **forum-selection clause** indicating the forum, or location (such as a court or jurisdiction), in which contract disputes will be resolved. Significant jurisdictional issues may arise when parties are at a great distance, as they often are when they form contracts via the Internet. A forum-selection clause will help to avert future jurisdictional problems and also help to ensure that the seller will not be required to appear in court in a distant state.

■ **CASE IN POINT 12.17** Scott Rosendahl enrolled in an online college, Ashford University. He claimed that the school's adviser had told him that Ashford offered one of the cheapest undergraduate degree programs in the country. In fact, it did not. Rosendahl later sued the school, claiming that it had violated unfair competition laws and false advertising laws and had engaged in fraud and negligent misrepresentation.

The university argued that its enrollment agreement clearly contained a requirement that all disputes be arbitrated. Rosendahl, like other students, had electronically assented to this agreement when he enrolled. Ashford presented the online application forms to the court, and the court dismissed Rosendahl's lawsuit. Rosendahl had agreed to arbitrate any disputes he had with Ashford.[13] ■

**Choice-of-Law Clause.** Some online contracts may also include a *choice-of-law clause,* specifying that any contract dispute will be settled according to the law of a particular jurisdiction, such as a state or country. Choice-of-law clauses are particularly common in international contracts, but they may also appear in e-contracts to specify which state's laws will govern in the United States.

## 12–3b Online Acceptances

The *Restatement (Second) of Contracts,* which is a compilation of common law contract principles, states that parties may agree to a contract "by written or spoken words or by other action or by failure to act."[14] The Uniform Commercial Code (UCC), which governs sales contracts, has a similar provision. Section 2–204 of the UCC states that any contract for the sale of goods "may be made in any manner sufficient to show agreement, including conduct by both parties which recognizes the existence of such a contract." The courts have used these provisions in determining what constitutes an online acceptance.

**Click-On Agreements** The courts have concluded that the act of clicking on a box labeled "I accept" or "I agree" can indicate acceptance of an online offer. The agreement resulting from such an acceptance is often called a **click-on agreement** (sometimes referred to as a *click-on license* or *click-wrap agreement*).

Generally, the law does not require that the parties have read all of the terms in a contract for it to be effective. Therefore, clicking on a box that states "I agree" to certain terms can be enough. The terms may be contained on a Web site through which the buyer is obtaining goods or services. They may also appear on a screen when software is downloaded from the Internet.

■ **CASE IN POINT 12.18** The "Terms of Use" that govern Facebook users' accounts include a forum-selection clause that provides for the resolution of all disputes in a court in Santa Clara County, California. To sign up for a Facebook account, a person must click on a box indicating that he or she has agreed to this term.

Mustafa Fteja was an active user of facebook.com when his account was disabled. He sued Facebook in a federal court in New York, claiming that it had disabled his Facebook page without justification and for discriminatory reasons. Facebook filed a motion to transfer the case to California under the forum-selection clause. The court found that the clause in Facebook's online contract was binding and transferred the case. When Fteja clicked on the button to accept the contract terms, he agreed to resolve all disputes with Facebook in Santa Clara County, California.[15] ■

**Shrink-Wrap Agreements** With a **shrink-wrap agreement** (or *shrink-wrap license*), the terms are expressed inside the box in which the goods are packaged. (The term *shrink-wrap* refers to the plastic that covers the box.) Usually, the party who opens the box is told that she or he agrees to the terms by keeping whatever is in the box. Similarly, when a purchaser opens a software package, he or she agrees to abide by the terms of the limited license agreement.

In most instances, a shrink-wrap agreement is not between a retailer and a buyer, but is between the manufacturer of the hardware or software and the ultimate buyer-user of the product. The terms generally concern warranties, remedies, and other issues associated with the use of the product.

**Shrink-Wrap Agreements and Enforceable Contract Terms.** In some cases, the courts have enforced the terms of shrink-wrap agreements in the same way as the terms

---

**13.** *Rosendahl v. Bridgepoint Education, Inc.,* 2012 WL 667049 (S.D.Cal. 2012).

**14.** *Restatement (Second) of Contracts,* Section 19.

**15.** *Fteja v. Facebook, Inc.,* 841 F.Supp.2d 829 (S.D.N.Y. 2012).

of other contracts. These courts have reasoned that by including the terms with the product, the seller proposed a contract. The buyer could accept this contract by using the product after having an opportunity to read the terms. Thus, a buyer's failure to object to terms contained within a shrink-wrapped software package may constitute an acceptance of the terms by conduct.

**Shrink-Wrap Terms That May Not Be Enforced.** Sometimes, however, the courts have refused to enforce certain terms included in shrink-wrap agreements because the buyer did not expressly consent to them. An important factor is when the parties formed their contract.

If a buyer orders a product over the telephone, for instance, and is not informed of an arbitration clause or a forum-selection clause at that time, the buyer clearly has not expressly agreed to these terms. If the buyer discovers the clauses *after* the parties have entered into a contract, a court may conclude that those terms were proposals for additional terms and were not part of the contract.

**Browse-Wrap Terms** Like the terms of click-on agreements, **browse-wrap terms** can occur in transactions conducted over the Internet. Unlike click-on agreements, however, browse-wrap terms do not require Internet users to assent to the terms before downloading or using certain software. In other words, a person can install the software without clicking "I agree" to the terms of a license. Browse-wrap terms are often unenforceable because they do not satisfy the agreement requirement of contract formation.

## 12–3c Federal Law on E-Signatures and E-Documents

An **e-signature** has been defined as "an electronic sound, symbol, or process attached to or logically associated with a record and executed or adopted by a person with the intent to sign the record."[16] In 2000, Congress enacted the Electronic Signatures in Global and National Commerce Act (E-SIGN Act).[17]

The E-SIGN Act provides that no contract, record, or signature may be "denied legal effect" solely because it is in electronic form. In other words, under this law, an electronic signature is as valid as a signature on paper, and an e-document can be as enforceable as a paper one. For an e-signature to be enforceable, however, the contracting parties must have agreed to use electronic signatures.

For an electronic document to be valid, it must be in a form that can be retained and accurately reproduced.

**E-Signature Technologies** Electronic documents can be signed in a number of ways. E-signature technologies include encrypted digital signatures, names intended as signatures at the end of e-mail messages, and clicks on a Web page if the clicks include some means of identification.

Note that although courts do not question that documents can be signed electronically under the E-SIGN Act, some courts will question the validity of the signatures themselves. For instance, a court might find that a typed name at the bottom of e-mail is not admissible as the person's signature. For this reason, many businesses use special software, such as DocuSign or EchoSign, that is designed to create an e-signature that looks similar to a person's handwritten signature.

**Exclusions** The E-SIGN Act does not apply to all types of documents. Documents that are exempt include court papers, divorce decrees, evictions, foreclosures, health-insurance terminations, prenuptial agreements, and wills. Also, the only agreements governed by the UCC that fall under this law are those covered by Articles 2 and 2A (sales and lease contracts) and UCC 1–107 and 1–206. Despite these limitations, the E-SIGN Act has significantly expanded online contracting.

## 12–3d The Uniform Electronic Transactions Act

The National Conference of Commissioners on Uniform State Laws and the American Law Institute promulgated the Uniform Electronic Transactions Act (UETA) in 1999. The UETA has been adopted, at least in part, by forty-eight states, resulting in more uniformity among state laws governing electronic transactions. Among other things, the UETA declares that a signature may not be denied legal effect or enforceability solely because it is in electronic form.

The primary purpose of the UETA is to remove barriers to e-commerce by giving the same legal effect to electronic records and signatures as is given to paper documents and signatures. As mentioned, the UETA broadly defines an *e-signature* as "an electronic sound, symbol, or process attached to or logically associated with a record and executed or adopted by a person with the intent to sign the record."[18] A **record** is "information

---

16. This definition is from the Uniform Electronic Transactions Act, discussed next.
17. 15 U.S.C. Sections 7001 *et seq.*

18. UETA 102(8).

that is inscribed on a tangible medium or that is stored in an electronic or other medium and is retrievable in perceivable [visual] form."[19]

**The Scope and Applicability of the UETA** The UETA does not create new rules for electronic contracts. Rather, it establishes that records, signatures, and contracts may not be denied enforceability solely due to their electronic form.

The UETA does not apply to all writings and signatures. It covers only electronic records and electronic signatures *relating to a transaction*. A *transaction* is defined as an interaction between two or more people relating to business, commercial, or governmental activities.[20] The act specifically does not apply to wills or testamentary trusts or to transactions governed by the UCC (other than those covered by Articles 2 and 2A). In addition, the provisions of the UETA allow the states to exclude its application to other areas of law.

The UETA does not apply to a transaction unless each of the parties has previously agreed to conduct transactions by electronic means. The agreement may be explicit, or it may be implied by the conduct of the parties and the surrounding circumstances. It may sometimes be reasonable to infer that a person who gives out a business card with an e-mail address on it has consented to transact business electronically, for instance. Agreement may also be inferred from an e-mail or even a verbal communication between the parties.

**The Federal E-SIGN Act and the UETA** The E-SIGN Act, discussed earlier, explicitly provides that if a state has enacted the uniform version of the UETA, that law is not preempted by the E-SIGN Act. In other words, if the state has enacted the UETA without modification, state law will govern. But many states have enacted non-uniform (modified) versions of the UETA, usually to exclude other areas of state law from the UETA's terms. The E-SIGN Act specifies that those exclusions will be preempted to the extent that they are inconsistent with the E-SIGN Act's provisions.

The E-SIGN Act also allows the states to enact alternative requirements for the use of electronic records or electronic signatures. Generally, however, the requirements must be consistent with the provisions of the E-SIGN Act and must specifically refer to the E-SIGN Act.

---

**19.** UETA 102(15).
**20.** UETA 2(12) and 3.

## 12–4 Consideration

The fact that a promise has been made does not mean the promise can or will be enforced. Under the common law, a primary basis for the enforcement of promises is consideration. **Consideration** usually is defined as the value given in return for a promise (in a bilateral contract) or in return for a performance (in a unilateral contract). It is the inducement, price, or motive that causes a party to enter into an agreement. As long as consideration is present, the courts generally do not interfere with contracts based on the amount of consideration paid.

Often, consideration is broken down into two parts: (1) something of *legally sufficient value* must be given in exchange for the promise, and (2) there must be a *bargained-for* exchange.

### 12–4a Legally Sufficient Value

To be legally sufficient, consideration must be something of value in the eyes of the law and may consist of the following:

1. A promise to do something that one has no prior legal duty to do.
2. The performance of an action that one is otherwise not obligated to undertake.
3. The refraining from an action that one has a legal right to undertake (called a **forbearance**).

Consideration in bilateral contracts normally consists of a promise in return for a promise. In a contract for the sale of goods, for instance, the seller promises to ship specific goods to the buyer, and the buyer promises to pay for those goods. Each of these promises constitutes consideration for the contract.

In contrast, unilateral contracts involve a promise in return for a performance (an action). ■ **EXAMPLE 12.19** Anita says to her neighbor, "When you finish painting the garage, I will pay you $800." Anita's neighbor paints the garage. The act of painting the garage is the consideration that creates Anita's contractual obligation to pay her neighbor $800. ■

### 12–4b Bargained-for Exchange

The second element of consideration is that it must provide the basis for the bargain struck between the contracting parties. That is, the item of value must be given or promised by the promisor (offeror) in return for the promisee's promise, performance, or promise of performance. This element of bargained-for exchange distinguishes contracts from gifts. ■ **CASE IN POINT 12.20** USS–POSCO Industries (UPI) hired Floyd Case as an entry-level laborer and side trim operator. Because UPI faced a shortage of skilled maintenance technical electrical (MTE) workers, it decided to implement an educational program for its existing employees. UPI would cover the costs ($46,000) of a program that required 135 weeks of instruction, 90 weeks of on-the-job training, and 45 weeks of classroom work.

Case applied for and was accepted into the program. UPI paid his wages, benefits, and training expenses, but it did not guarantee him a position as an MTE worker. Case signed a reimbursement agreement to participate stating that if he voluntarily left UPI within 30 months after completing the program, he would (absent a compelling hardship) refund $30,000 to UPI. Two months after completing the program and starting work as an MTE worker, Case left UPI for a position with another employer as an electrician. He refused to refund $30,000 to UPI and UPI sued for breach.

Case argued that the reimbursement agreement lacked consideration because UPI had no obligation to keep Case employed, and thus there was no bargained-for exchange. The court disagreed. "The exchange, frankly, is obvious: Case got continued wages and fronted education costs, and UPI got Case's agreement to repay those costs if he both completed the training and left the company before it could benefit from the investment." The court enforced the agreement and ordered Case to refund $30,000 to UPI.[21] ■

## 12–4c Agreements That Lack Consideration

Sometimes, one of the parties (or both parties) to an agreement may think that consideration has been exchanged when in fact it has not. Here, we look at some situations in which the parties' promises or actions do not qualify as contractual consideration.

**Preexisting Duty** Under most circumstances, a promise to do what one already has a legal duty to do does not constitute legally sufficient consideration. The preexisting legal duty may be imposed by law or may arise out of a previous contract.

If a party is already bound by contract to perform a certain duty, that duty cannot serve as consideration for a second contract. ■ **EXAMPLE 12.21** Ajax Contractors begins construction on a seven-story office building and after three months demands an extra $75,000 on its contract. If the extra $75,000 is not paid, the contractor will stop working. The owner of the land, finding no one else to complete the construction, agrees to pay the extra $75,000. The agreement is unenforceable because it is not supported by legally sufficient consideration. Ajax Contractors had a preexisting contractual duty to complete the building. ■

**Unforeseen Difficulties.** The rule regarding preexisting duty is meant to prevent extortion and the so-called holdup game. Nonetheless, if, during performance of a contract, extraordinary difficulties arise that were totally unforeseen at the time the contract was formed, a court may allow an exception to the rule. The key is whether the court finds that the modification is fair and equitable in view of circumstances not anticipated by the parties when the contract was made.

Suppose that in *Example 12.21*, Ajax Contractors had asked for the extra $75,000 because it encountered a rock formation that no one knew existed. If the landowner agrees to pay the extra $75,000 to excavate the rock and the court finds that it is fair to do so, Ajax Contractors can enforce the agreement. If rock formations are common in the area, however, the court may determine that the contractor should have known of the risk. In that situation, the court may choose to apply the preexisting duty rule and prevent Ajax Contractors from obtaining the extra $75,000.

**Rescission and New Contract.** The law recognizes that two parties can mutually agree to rescind, or cancel, their contract, at least to the extent that it is *executory* (still to be carried out). **Rescission**[22] is the unmaking of a contract so as to return the parties to the positions they occupied before the contract was made.

Sometimes, parties rescind a contract and make a new contract at the same time. When this occurs, it is often difficult to determine whether there was consideration for the new contract, or whether the parties had a preexisting duty under the previous contract. If a court finds there was a preexisting duty, then the new contract will be invalid because there was no consideration.

**Past Consideration** Promises made in return for actions or events that have already taken place are unenforceable. These promises lack consideration in that the element of bargained-for exchange is missing. In short, you can bargain for something to take place now or in

---

21. *USS–POSCO Industries v. Case*, 244 Cal.App.4th 197, 197 Cal.Rptr.3d 791 (Div. 1 2016).

22. Pronounced reh-*sih*-zhen.

the future but not for something that has already taken place. Therefore, **past consideration** is no consideration.

■ **CASE IN POINT 12.22** Jamil Blackmon became friends with Allen Iverson when Iverson was a high school student who showed tremendous promise as an athlete. One evening, Blackmon suggested that Iverson use "The Answer" as a nickname in the summer league basketball tournaments. Blackmon said that Iverson would be "The Answer" to all of the National Basketball Association's woes. Later that night, Iverson said that he would give Blackmon 25 percent of any proceeds from the merchandising of products that used "The Answer" as a logo or a slogan. Because Iverson's promise was made in return for past consideration, it was unenforceable. In effect, Iverson stated his intention to give Blackmon a gift.[23] ■

In a variety of situations, an employer will often ask a new employee to sign a *noncompete agreement,* also called a *covenant not to compete.* Under such an agreement, the employee agrees not to compete with the employer for a certain period of time after the employment relationship ends. When a current employee is required to sign a noncompete agreement, his or her employment is not sufficient consideration for the agreement, because the individual is already employed. To be valid, the agreement requires new consideration.

**Illusory Promises** If the terms of the contract express such uncertainty of performance that the promisor has not definitely promised to do anything, the promise is said to be *illusory*—without consideration and unenforceable. A promise is illusory when it fails to bind the promisor.

---
23. *Blackmon v. Iverson,* 324 F.Supp.2d 602 (E.D.Pa. 2003).

■ **EXAMPLE 12.23** The president of Tuscan Corporation says to her employees, "If profits continue to be high, everyone will get a 10 percent bonus at the end of the year—if management agrees." This is an *illusory promise,* or no promise at all, because performance depends solely on the discretion of management. There is no bargained-for consideration. The statement indicates only that management may or may not do something in the future. Therefore, even though the employees work hard and profits remain high, the company is not obligated to pay the bonus now or later. ■

Exhibit 12–1 illustrates some common situations in which promises or actions do not constitute contractual consideration.

### 12–4d Settlement of Claims

Businesspersons and others often enter into contracts to settle legal claims. It is important to understand the nature of consideration given in these kinds of settlement agreements, or contracts. A claim may be settled through an *accord and satisfaction*, a *release*, or a *covenant not to sue.*

**Accord and Satisfaction** In an **accord and satisfaction,** a debtor offers to pay, and a creditor accepts, a lesser amount than the creditor originally claimed was owed. The *accord* is the agreement. In the accord, one party undertakes to give or perform, and the other to accept, in satisfaction of a claim, something other than that on which the parties originally agreed. *Satisfaction* is the performance (usually payment) that takes place after the accord is executed.

**EXHIBIT 12–1 Examples of Agreements That Lack Consideration**

| PREEXISTING DUTY | PAST CONSIDERATION | ILLUSORY PROMISES |
|---|---|---|
| When a person already has a legal duty to perform an action, there is no legally sufficient consideration. | When a person makes a promise in return for actions or events that have already taken place, there is no consideration. | When a person expresses contract terms with such uncertainty that the terms are not definite, the promise is illusory. |
| *Example:* A firefighter cannot receive a cash reward from a business owner for putting out a fire in a downtown commercial district. As a city employee, the firefighter had a duty to extinguish the fire. | *Example:* A real estate agent sold a friend's house without charging a commission, and in return, the friend promises to give the agent $1,000. The friend's promise is simply an intention to give a gift. | *Example:* A storeowner promises a $500 bonus to each employee who works Christmas Day, as long as the owner feels that they did their jobs well. The owner's promise is just a statement of something she may or may not do in the future. |

A basic rule is that there can be no satisfaction unless there is first an accord. In addition, for accord and satisfaction to occur, the amount of the debt *must be in dispute.*

**Liquidated Debts.** If a debt is *liquidated,* accord and satisfaction cannot take place. A **liquidated debt** is one whose amount has been ascertained, fixed, agreed on, settled, or exactly determined.

In most states, a creditor's acceptance of a lesser sum than the entire amount of a liquidated debt is *not* satisfaction, and the balance of the debt is still legally owed. The reason for this rule is that the debtor has given no consideration to satisfy the obligation of paying the balance to the creditor. The debtor had a preexisting legal obligation to pay the entire debt.

**Unliquidated Debts.** An **unliquidated debt** is the opposite of a liquidated debt. The amount of the debt is *not* settled, fixed, agreed on, ascertained, or determined, and reasonable persons may differ over the amount owed. In these circumstances, acceptance of a lesser sum operates as satisfaction, or discharge, of the debt because there is valid consideration. The parties give up a legal right to contest the amount in dispute.

**Release** A **release** is a contract in which one party forfeits the right to pursue a legal claim against the other party. It bars any further recovery beyond the terms stated in the release.

A release will generally be binding if it meets the following requirements:

1. The agreement is made in good faith (honestly).
2. The release contract is in a signed writing (required in many states).
3. The contract is accompanied by consideration.

Clearly, an individual is better off knowing the extent of his or her injuries or damages before signing a release. ■ **EXAMPLE 12.24** Lupe's car is damaged in an automobile accident caused by Dexter's negligence. Dexter offers to give her $3,000 if she will release him from further liability resulting from the accident. Lupe agrees and signs the release. If Lupe later discovers that it will cost $4,200 to repair her car, she normally cannot recover the additional amount from Dexter. ■

**Covenant Not to Sue** Unlike a release, a **covenant not to sue** does not always bar further recovery. The parties simply substitute a contractual obligation for some other type of legal action based on a valid claim. Suppose that, in *Example 12.24,* Lupe agrees with Dexter not to sue for damages in a tort action if he will pay for the damage to her car. If Dexter fails to pay for the repairs, Lupe can bring an action against him for breach of contract.

As the following case illustrates, a covenant not to sue can form the basis for a dismissal of the claims of either party to the covenant.

## Spotlight on Nike

### Case 12.3 Already, LLC v. Nike, Inc.

Supreme Court of the United States, __ U.S. __, 133 S.Ct. 721, 184 L.Ed.2d 553 (2013).

**Background and Facts** Nike, Inc., designs, makes, and sells athletic footwear, including a line of shoes known as "Air Force 1." Already, LLC, also designs and markets athletic footwear, including the "Sugar" and "Soulja Boy" lines. Nike filed a suit in a federal district court against Already, alleging that Soulja Boys and Sugars infringed the Air Force 1 trademark. Already filed a counterclaim, contending that the Air Force 1 trademark was invalid. While the suit was pending, Nike issued a covenant not to sue. Nike promised not to raise any trademark claims against Already or any affiliated entity based on Already's existing footwear designs or any future Already designs that constituted a "colorable imitation" of Already's current products. Nike then filed a motion to dismiss its own claims and to dismiss Already's counterclaim. Already opposed the dismissal of its counterclaim, but the court granted Nike's motion. The U.S. Court of Appeals for the Second Circuit affirmed. Already appealed to the United States Supreme Court.

*Case 12.3 Continues*

Case 12.3 Continued

## In the Language of the Court

Chief Justice *ROBERTS* delivered the opinion of the Court.

* * * *

* * * A defendant cannot automatically moot a case simply by ending its unlawful conduct once sued. [A matter is *moot* if it involves no actual controversy for the court to decide, and federal courts will dismiss moot cases.] Otherwise, a defendant could engage in unlawful conduct, stop when sued to have the case declared moot, then pick up where he left off, repeating this cycle until he achieves all his unlawful ends. Given this concern, * * * *a defendant claiming that its voluntary compliance moots a case bears the formidable burden of showing that it is absolutely clear the allegedly wrongful behavior could not reasonably be expected to recur.* [This is the voluntary cessation test. Emphasis added.]

* * * *

We begin our analysis with the terms of the covenant:

[Nike] unconditionally and irrevocably covenants to refrain from making *any* claim(s) or demand(s) * * * against Already or *any* of its * * * related business entities * * * [including] distributors * * * and employees of such entities and *all* customers * * * on account of any *possible* cause of action based on or involving trademark infringement * * * relating to the NIKE Mark based on the appearance of *any* of Already's current and/or previous footwear product designs, and *any* colorable imitations thereof, regardless of whether that footwear is produced * * * or otherwise used in commerce.

The breadth of this covenant suffices to meet the burden imposed by the voluntary cessation test.

In addition, Nike originally argued that the Sugars and Soulja Boys infringed its trademark; in other words, Nike believed those shoes were "colorable imitations" of the Air Force 1s. Nike's covenant now allows Already to produce all of its existing footwear designs—including the Sugar and Soulja Boy—and any "colorable imitation" of those designs. * * * It is hard to imagine a scenario that would potentially infringe Nike's trademark and yet not fall under the covenant. Nike, having taken the position in court that there is no prospect of such a shoe, would be hard pressed to assert the contrary down the road. If such a shoe exists, the parties have not pointed to it, there is no evidence that Already has dreamt of it, and we cannot conceive of it. It sits, as far as we can tell, on a shelf between Dorothy's ruby slippers and Perseus's winged sandals.

* * * *

* * * Given the covenant's broad language, and given that Already has asserted no concrete plans to engage in conduct not covered by the covenant, we can conclude the case is moot because the challenged conduct cannot reasonably be expected to recur.

**Decision and Remedy** *The United States Supreme Court affirmed the judgment of the lower court. Under the covenant not to sue, Nike could not file a claim for trademark infringement against Already, and Already could not assert that Nike's trademark was invalid.*

### Critical Thinking

- **Economic** *Why would any party agree to a covenant not to sue?*
- **Legal Environment** *Which types of contracts are similar to covenants not to sue? Explain.*

---

## 12–4e Promissory Estoppel

Sometimes, individuals rely on promises to their detriment, and their reliance may form a basis for a court to infer contract rights and duties. Under the doctrine of **promissory estoppel** (also called *detrimental reliance*), a person who has reasonably and substantially relied on the promise of another may be able to obtain some measure of recovery.

Promissory estoppel is applied in a wide variety of contexts in which a promise is otherwise unenforceable, such as when a promise is made *without consideration*. Under this doctrine, a court may enforce an otherwise unenforceable promise to avoid the injustice that would otherwise result. For the promissory estoppel doctrine to be applied, the following elements are required:

1. There must be a clear and definite promise.
2. The promisor should have expected that the promisee would rely on the promise.
3. The promisee reasonably relied on the promise by acting or refraining from some act.
4. The promisee's reliance was definite and resulted in substantial detriment.
5. Enforcement of the promise is necessary to avoid injustice.

If these requirements are met, a promise may be enforced even though it is not supported by consideration.[24] In essence, the promisor will be **estopped** (prevented) from asserting the lack of consideration as a defense.

## 12–5 Contractual Capacity

In addition to agreement and consideration, for a contract to be deemed valid, the parties to the contract must have **contractual capacity**—the legal ability to enter into a contractual relationship. Courts generally presume the existence of contractual capacity, but in some situations, as when a person is young or mentally incompetent, capacity may be lacking or questionable.

### 12–5a Minors

Today, in almost all states, the *age of majority* (when a person is no longer a minor) for contractual purposes is eighteen years.[25] In addition, some states provide for the termination of minority on marriage. Minority status may also be terminated by a minor's *emancipation,* which occurs when a child's parent or legal guardian relinquishes the legal right to exercise control over the child. Normally, minors who leave home to support themselves are considered emancipated.

The general rule is that a minor can enter into any contract that an adult can, except contracts prohibited by law for minors (for instance, the purchase of tobacco or alcoholic beverages). A contract entered into by a minor, however, is voidable at the option of that minor, subject to certain exceptions.

The legal avoidance, or setting aside, of a contractual obligation is referred to as **disaffirmance.** To disaffirm, a minor must express his or her intent, through words or conduct, not to be bound to the contract.

■ **CASE IN POINT 12.25** S.L. was a female sixteen-year-old minor who worked at a KFC Restaurant operated by PAK Foods Houston, LLC. PAK Foods' policy was to resolve any dispute with an employee through arbitration. At the employer's request, S.L. signed an acknowledgment of this policy. S.L. was injured on the job and subsequently terminated her employment. S.L.'s mother, Marissa Garcia, filed a suit on S.L.'s behalf in a Texas state court against PAK Foods to recover the medical expenses for the injury. PAK Foods filed a motion to compel arbitration. The court denied the motion, and PAK Foods appealed. A state intermediate appellate court affirmed the decision. A minor may disaffirm a contract at his or her option. The court concluded that S.L. opted to disaffirm the agreement to arbitrate by terminating her employment and filing the lawsuit.[26] ■

Note that an adult who enters into a contract with a minor cannot avoid his or her contractual duties on the ground that the minor can do so. Unless the minor exercises the option to disaffirm the contract, the adult party normally is bound by it.

### 12–5b Intoxication

Intoxication is a condition in which a person's normal capacity to act or think is inhibited by alcohol or some other drug. A contract entered into by an intoxicated person can be either voidable or valid (and thus enforceable).

If the person was sufficiently intoxicated to lack mental capacity, then the agreement may be voidable even if the intoxication was purely voluntary. If a contract is voidable because one party was intoxicated, that person has the option of disaffirming it while intoxicated and for a reasonable time after becoming sober. If, despite intoxication, the person understood the legal consequences of the agreement, the contract will be enforceable.

Courts look at objective indications of the intoxicated person's condition to determine if he or she possessed or lacked the required capacity. It is difficult to prove that a person's judgment was so severely impaired that he or she could not comprehend the legal consequences of entering into a contract. Therefore, courts rarely permit contracts to be avoided due to intoxication.

### 12–5c Mental Incompetence

Contracts made by mentally incompetent persons can be void, voidable, or valid. If a court has previously determined that a person is mentally incompetent, any

---

24. *Restatement (Second) of Contracts*, Section 90.
25. The age of majority may still be twenty-one for other purposes, such as the purchase and consumption of alcohol.

26. *PAK Foods Houston, LLC v. Garcia*, 433 S.W.3d 171 (Tex.App.—Houston 2014).

contract made by that person is *void*—no contract exists. Only a guardian appointed by the court to represent a mentally incompetent person can enter into binding legal obligations on that person's behalf.

If a court has not previously judged a person to be mentally incompetent but the person was incompetent at the time the contract was formed, the contract may be voidable.[27] A contract is *voidable* if the person did not know he or she was entering into the contract or lacked the mental capacity to comprehend its nature, purpose, and consequences.

A contract entered into by a mentally incompetent person (not previously declared incompetent) may also be *valid* if the person had capacity *at the time the contract was formed.* Some people who are incompetent due to age or illness have *lucid intervals*—temporary periods of sufficient intelligence, judgment, and will. During such intervals, they will be considered to have legal capacity to enter into contracts.

## 12–6 Legality

For a contract to be valid and enforceable, it must be formed for a legal purpose. A contract to do something that is prohibited by federal or state statutory law is illegal and, as such, void from the outset and thus unenforceable. Additionally, a contract to commit a tortious act (such as an agreement to engage in fraud) is contrary to public policy and therefore illegal and unenforceable.

### 12–6a Contracts Contrary to Statute

Statutes often set forth rules specifying which terms and clauses may be included in contracts and which are prohibited. We now examine several ways in which contracts may be contrary to statute and thus illegal.

**Contracts to Commit a Crime** Any contract to commit a crime is in violation of a statute. Thus, a contract to sell illegal drugs in violation of criminal laws is unenforceable, as is a contract to cover up a corporation's violation of an environmental or other law.

Sometimes, the object or performance of a contract is rendered illegal by a statute *after* the parties entered into the contract. In that situation, the contract is considered to be discharged by law.

**Usury** Almost every state has a statute that sets the maximum rate of interest that can be charged for different types of transactions, including ordinary loans. A lender who makes a loan at an interest rate above the lawful maximum commits **usury.**

Although usurious contracts are illegal, most states simply limit the interest that the lender may collect on the contract to the lawful maximum interest rate in that state. In a few states, the lender can recover the principal amount of the loan but no interest. In addition, states can make exceptions to facilitate business transactions. For instance, nearly all states allow higher-interest-rate loans for borrowers who could not otherwise obtain funds.

**Gambling** Gambling is the creation of risk for the purpose of assuming it. Any scheme that involves the distribution of property by chance among persons who have paid valuable consideration for the opportunity (chance) to receive the property is gambling.

Traditionally, the states deemed gambling contracts illegal and thus void. Today, many states allow (and regulate) certain forms of gambling, such as horse racing, video poker machines, and charity-sponsored bingo. In addition, nearly all states allow state-operated lotteries and gambling on Native American reservations. Even in states that permit certain types of gambling, though, courts often find that gambling contracts are illegal.

**Licensing Statutes** All states require members of certain professions—including physicians, lawyers, real estate brokers, accountants, architects, electricians, and stockbrokers—to have licenses. Some licenses are obtained only after extensive schooling and examinations, which indicate to the public that a special skill has been acquired. Others require only that the applicant be of good moral character and pay a fee.

Whether a contract with an unlicensed person is legal and enforceable depends on the purpose of the licensing statute. If the statute's purpose is to protect the public from unauthorized practitioners (such as unlicensed attorneys and electricians), then a contract involving an unlicensed practitioner is generally illegal and unenforceable. If the statute's purpose is merely to raise government revenues, however, a court may enforce the contract and fine the unlicensed person.

### 14–6b Contracts Contrary to Public Policy

Although contracts involve private parties, some are not enforceable because of the negative impact they would have on society. These contracts are said to be *contrary*

---

27. This is the rule in the majority of states. See, for example, *Hernandez v. Banks*, 65 A.3d 59 (D.C. 2013).

*to public policy.* Examples include a contract to commit an immoral act, such as selling a child, and a contract that prohibits marriage. Business contracts that may be against public policy include contracts in restraint of trade and unconscionable contracts or clauses.

**Contracts in Restraint of Trade** The United States has a strong public policy favoring competition in the economy. Thus, contracts in restraint of trade (anticompetitive agreements) generally are unenforceable because they are contrary to public policy. Typically, such contracts also violate one or more federal or state antitrust statutes.

An exception is recognized when the restraint is reasonable and is contained in an ancillary (secondary or subordinate) clause in a contract. Such restraints often are included in contracts for the sale of an ongoing business and in employment contracts.

**Covenants Not to Compete and the Sale of an Ongoing Business.** Many contracts involve a type of restraint called a **covenant not to compete,** or a restrictive covenant (promise). A covenant not to compete may be created when a merchant who sells a store agrees not to open a new store in a certain geographic area surrounding the old business. Such an agreement enables the seller to sell, and the purchaser to buy, the goodwill and reputation of an ongoing business without having to worry that the seller will open a competing business a block away. Provided the restrictive covenant is reasonable and is an ancillary part of the sale of an ongoing business, it is enforceable.

**Covenants Not to Compete in Employment Contracts.** Sometimes, agreements not to compete (also referred to as *noncompete agreements*) are included in employment contracts. People in middle- or upper-level management positions commonly agree not to work for competitors or not to start competing businesses for a specified period of time after termination of employment.

Noncompete agreements are legal in most states so long as the specified period of time (of restraint) is not excessive in duration and the geographic restriction is reasonable. What constitutes a reasonable time period may be shorter in the online environment than in conventional employment contracts. Because the geographical restrictions apply worldwide, the time restrictions may be shorter.

A restraint that is found to be overly broad will not be enforced. ■ **CASE IN POINT 12.26** An insurance firm in New York City, Brown & Brown, Inc., hired Theresa Johnson to perform actuarial analysis. On her first day of work, Johnson was asked to sign a nonsolicitation covenant. The covenant prohibited her from soliciting or servicing any of Brown's clients for two years after the termination of her employment.

Less than five years later, when Johnson's employment with Brown was terminated, she went to work for Lawley Benefits Group, LLC. Brown sued to enforce the covenant. A state appellate court ruled that the covenant was overly broad and unenforceable. It attempted to restrict Johnson from working for any of Brown's clients, without regard to whether she had had a relationship with those clients.[28] ■

**Enforcement Issues.** The laws governing the enforceability of covenants not to compete vary significantly from state to state. California prohibits the enforcement of covenants not to compete altogether. In some states, including Texas, such a covenant will not be enforced unless the employee has received some benefit in return for signing the noncompete agreement. This is true even if the covenant is reasonable as to time and area. If the employee receives no benefit, the covenant will be deemed void.

Occasionally, depending on the jurisdiction, courts will *reform* covenants not to compete. If a covenant is found to be unreasonable in time or geographic area, the court may convert the terms into reasonable ones and then enforce the reformed covenant. Such court actions present a problem, though, in that the judge implicitly becomes a party to the contract. Consequently, courts usually resort to contract **reformation** only when necessary to prevent undue burdens or hardships.

**Unconscionable Contracts or Clauses** A court ordinarily does not look at the fairness or equity of a contract (or inquire into the adequacy of consideration). Persons are assumed to be reasonably intelligent, and the courts will not come to their aid just because they have made unwise or foolish bargains.

In certain circumstances, however, bargains are so oppressive that the courts relieve innocent parties of part or all of their duties. Such bargains are deemed **unconscionable**[29] because they are so unscrupulous or grossly unfair as to be "void of conscience." The Uniform Commercial Code (UCC) incorporates the concept of unconscionability in its provisions regarding the sale and lease of goods.[30]

A contract can be unconscionable on either procedural or substantive grounds. *Procedural* unconscionability often involves inconspicuous print, unintelligible language ("legalese"), or the lack of an opportunity to read the contract or ask questions about its meaning. This

---

28. *Brown & Brown, Inc. v. Johnson,* 115 A.D.3d 52, 980 N.Y.S.2d 631 (2014).
29. Pronounced un-*kon*-shun-uh-bul.
30. See UCC 2–302 and 2A–719.

type of unconscionability typically arises when a party's lack of knowledge or understanding of the contract terms deprived him or her of any meaningful choice. *Substantive* unconscionability occurs when contracts, or portions of contracts, are oppressive or overly harsh. Courts generally focus on provisions that deprive one party of the benefits of the agreement or leave that party without a remedy for nonperformance by the other.

**Exculpatory Clauses** Often closely related to the concept of unconscionability are **exculpatory clauses,** which release a party from liability in the event of monetary or physical injury *no matter who is at fault.* Indeed, courts sometimes refuse to enforce such clauses on the ground that they are unconscionable.

**Often Violate Public Policy.** Most courts view exculpatory clauses with disfavor. Exculpatory clauses found in rental agreements for commercial property are frequently held to be contrary to public policy, and such clauses are almost always unenforceable in residential property leases. Courts also usually hold that exculpatory clauses are against public policy in the employment context.

**When Courts Will Enforce Exculpatory Clauses.** Courts do enforce exculpatory clauses if they are reasonable, do not violate public policy, and do not protect parties from liability for intentional misconduct. The language used must not be ambiguous, and the parties must have been in relatively equal bargaining positions.

Businesses such as health clubs, racetracks, amusement parks, skiing facilities, horse-rental operations, golf-cart concessions, and skydiving organizations frequently use exculpatory clauses to limit their liability for patrons' injuries. ■ **CASE IN POINT 12.27** Colleen Holmes participated in the Susan G. Komen Race for the Cure in St. Louis, Missouri. Her signed entry form included an exculpatory clause under which Holmes agreed to release the event sponsors from liability "for any injury or damages I might suffer in connection with my participation in this Event."

During the race, Holmes sustained injuries when she tripped and fell over an audiovisual box left on the ground by one of the sponsors. She filed a negligence suit against the sponsor whose employees had placed the box on the ground without barricades or warnings of its presence. The court held that the language used in the exculpatory clause clearly released all sponsors and their agents and employees from liability for future negligence. Holmes could not sue for the injuries she sustained during the race.[31] ■

31. *Holmes v. Multimedia KSDK, Inc.,* 395 S.W.3d 557, (Mo.App. 2013).

Courts also may enforce reasonable exculpatory clauses in loan documents, real estate contracts, and trust agreements. See this chapter's *Managerial Strategy* feature for more about exculpatory clauses that will not be considered unconscionable.

## 12–7 Form

A contract that is otherwise valid may still be unenforceable if it is not in the proper form. Certain types of contracts are required to be in writing or evidenced by a memorandum or electronic record. The writing requirement does not mean that an agreement must be a formal written contract. An exchange of e-mails that evidences the parties' agreement usually is sufficient, provided that they are "signed," or agreed to, by the party against whom enforcement is sought.

Every state has a statute that stipulates what types of contracts must be in writing, often referred to as the **Statute of Frauds.** The actual name of the Statute of Frauds is misleading because the statute does not apply to fraud. Rather, it denies enforceability to certain contracts that do not comply with its writing requirements.

The following types of contracts are generally required to be in writing or evidenced by a written memorandum or electronic record:

1. Contracts involving interests in land.
2. Contracts that cannot *by their terms* be performed within *one year from the day after* the date of formation.
3. Collateral, or secondary, contracts, such as promises to answer for the debt or duty of another and promises by the administrator or executor of an estate to pay a debt of the estate personally—that is, out of her or his own pocket.
4. Promises made in consideration of marriage.
5. Under the Uniform Commercial Code, contracts for the sale of goods priced at $500 or more.

A contract that is oral when it is required to be evidenced by a writing or an electronic record is voidable by a party who does not wish to follow through with the agreement.

## 12–8 Third Party Rights

Once it has been determined that a valid and legally enforceable contract exists, attention can turn to the rights and duties of the parties to the contract. A contract

## Creating Liability Waivers That Are Not Unconscionable

Blanket liability waivers that absolve a business from virtually every event, even those caused by the business's own negligence, are usually unenforceable because they are unconscionable. Exculpatory waivers are common, nonetheless. We observe such waivers in gym memberships, on ski lift tickets, on admissions tickets to sporting events, and in simple contracts for the use of campgrounds.

Typically, courts view liability waivers as voluntarily bargained for whether or not they have been read. Thus, a waiver included in the fine print on the back of an admission ticket or on an entry sign to a stadium may be upheld. In general, if such waivers are unambiguous and conspicuous, the assumption is that patrons have had a chance to read them and have accepted their terms.

### Activities with Inherent Risks

Cases challenging liability waivers have been brought against skydiving operations, skiing operations, bobsledding operations, white-water rafting companies, and health clubs. For example, in *Bergin v. Wild Mountain, Inc.,*[a] an appellate court in Minnesota upheld a ski resort's liability waiver.

In that case, the plaintiff hit a snowmaking mound, which was "an inherent risk of skiing." Before the accident, the plaintiff had stated that he knew "that an inherent risk of serious injury in downhill skiing was hitting snowmaking mounds." Furthermore, he had not rejected the season pass that contained the

resort's exculpatory clause. Thus, the ski resort prevailed.

### Overly Broad Waivers

While most liability waivers have survived legal challenges, some have not. In *Bagley v. Mt. Bachelor, Inc.,*[b] the Supreme Court of Oregon ruled against a ski resort's "very broad" liability waiver. The case involved an eighteen-year-old, Myles Bagley, who was paralyzed from the waist down after a snowboarding accident at Mt. Bachelor ski resort. The season pass that Bagley signed included a liability waiver. The waiver stated that the signer agreed not to sue the resort for injury even if "caused by negligence."

Bagley argued that the resort had created a dangerous condition because of the way it had set up a particular ski jump. He sued for $21.5 million and eventually won the right to go forward with his lawsuit. The Oregon Supreme Court found that, for various reasons, enforcement of the release would have been unconscionable. "Because the release is unenforceable, genuine issues of fact exist that preclude summary judgment in defendant's favor."

### Business Questions

1. *If you are running a business, why would you opt to include overly broad waivers in your contracts with customers?*

2. *Under what circumstances would you, as a business owner, choose to aggressively defend your business against a customer's liability lawsuit?*

a. 2014 WL 996788 (Minn.App. 2014).

b. 356 Or. 543, 340 P.3d 27 (2014).

---

is a private agreement between the parties who have entered into it, and traditionally these parties alone have rights and liabilities under the contract. This principle is referred to as **privity of contract.** A *third party*—one who is not a direct party to a particular contract—normally does not have rights under that contract.

There are exceptions to the rule of privity of contract. One exception allows a party to a contract to transfer the rights or duties arising from the contract to another person through an *assignment* (of rights) or a *delegation* (of duties). Another exception involves a *third party beneficiary contract*—a contract in which the parties to the contract intend that the contract benefit a third party.

In a bilateral contract, one party has a *right* to require the other to perform some task, and the other has a *duty*

to perform it. The transfer of contractual *rights* to a third party is known as an **assignment.** The transfer of contractual *duties* to a third party is known as a **delegation.** An assignment or a delegation occurs *after* the original contract was made.

## 12–8a Assignments

In an assignment, the party assigning the rights to a third party is known as the *assignor,*[32] and the party receiving the rights is the *assignee.*[33] When rights under a contract are assigned unconditionally, the rights of the assignor

---

32. Pronounced uh-*sye*-nore.
33. Pronounced uh-*sye*-nee.

are extinguished. The third party (the assignee) has a right to demand performance from the other original party to the contract. The assignee takes only those rights that the assignor originally had, however.

Assignments are important because they are used in many types of business financing. Banks, for instance, frequently assign their rights to receive payments under their loan contracts to other firms, which pay for those rights.

As a general rule, all rights can be assigned. Exceptions are made, however, under certain circumstances, including the following:

1. The assignment is prohibited by statute.
2. The contract is personal.
3. The assignment significantly changes the risk or duties of the *obligor* (the person contractually obligated to perform).
4. The contract prohibits assignment.

## 12–8b Delegations

Just as a party can transfer rights through an assignment, a party can also transfer duties. Duties are not assigned, however, they are *delegated*. The party delegating the duties is the *delegator*, and the party to whom the duties are delegated is the *delegatee*. Normally, a delegation of duties does not relieve the delegator of the obligation to perform in the event that the delegatee fails to do so.

No special form is required to create a valid delegation of duties. As long as the delegator expresses an intention to make the delegation, it is effective. The delegator need not even use the word *delegate*.

As a general rule, any duty can be delegated. There are, however, some circumstances in which delegation is prohibited:

1. When special trust has been placed in the *obligor*.
2. When performance depends on the personal skill or talents of the obligor.
3. When performance by a third party will vary materially from that expected by the *obligee* (the person to whom an obligation is owed) under the contract.
4. When the contract expressly prohibits delegation by including an *antidelegation clause*.

If a delegation of duties is enforceable, the obligee must accept performance from the delegatee. As noted, a valid delegation of duties does not relieve the delegator of obligations under the contract. Although there are many exceptions, the general rule today is that the obligee can sue both the delegatee and the delegator if the duties are not performed.

## 12–8c Third Party Beneficiaries

Another exception to the doctrine of privity of contract arises when the contract is intended to benefit a third party. When the original parties to the contract agree that the contract performance should be rendered to or directly benefit a third person, the third person becomes an *intended* **third party beneficiary** of the contract. As the **intended beneficiary** of the contract, the third party has legal rights and can sue the promisor directly for breach of the contract.

■ **CASE IN POINT 12.28** The classic case that gave third party beneficiaries the right to bring a suit directly against a promisor was decided in 1859. The case involved three parties—Holly, Lawrence, and Fox. Holly had borrowed $300 from Lawrence. Shortly thereafter, Holly loaned $300 to Fox, who in return promised Holly that he would pay Holly's debt to Lawrence on the following day. When Lawrence failed to obtain the $300 from Fox, he sued Fox to recover the funds. The court had to decide whether Lawrence could sue Fox directly (rather than suing Holly). The court held that when "a promise [is] made for the benefit of another, he for whose benefit it is made may bring an action for its breach."[34] ■

The law distinguishes between *intended* beneficiaries and *incidental* beneficiaries. An incidental beneficiary is a third person who receives a benefit from a contract even though that person's benefit is not the reason the contract was made. Because the benefit is unintentional, an incidental beneficiary cannot sue to enforce the contract. Only intended beneficiaries acquire legal rights in a contract.

---

34. *Lawrence v. Fox*, 20 N.Y. 268 (1859).

## Reviewing: Formation of Traditional and E-Contracts

Shane Durbin wanted to have a recording studio custom-built in his home. He sent invitations to a number of local contractors to submit bids on the project. Rory Amstel submitted the lowest bid, which was $20,000 less than any of the other bids Durbin received. Durbin called Amstel to ascertain the type and quality of the materials that were included in the bid and to find out if he could substitute a superior brand of acoustic tiles for the same bid price. Amstel said he would have to check into the price difference. The parties also discussed a possible start date for construction. Two weeks later, Durbin changed his mind and decided not to go forward with his plan to build a recording studio. Amstel filed a suit against Durbin for breach of contract. Using the information presented in the chapter, answer the following questions.

1. Did Amstel's bid meet the requirements of an offer? Explain.
2. Was there an acceptance of the offer? Why or why not?
3. How is an offer terminated? Assuming that Durbin did not inform Amstel that he was rejecting the offer, was the offer terminated at any time described here? Explain.

**Debate This** . . . *The terms and conditions in click-on agreements are so long and detailed that no one ever reads the agreements. Therefore, the act of clicking on "I agree" is not really an acceptance.*

## Terms and Concepts

acceptance 242
accord and satisfaction 250
agreement 238
assignment 257
bilateral contract 235
browse-wrap terms 247
click-on agreement 246
consideration 248
contract 234
contractual capacity 253
counteroffer 241
covenant not to compete 255
covenant not to sue 251
delegation 257
disaffirmance 253
e-contract 245
e-signature 247
estopped 253
exculpatory clause 256

executed contract 237
executory contract 237
express contract 236
forbearance 248
formal contract 236
forum-selection clause 246
implied contract 236
informal contract 236
intended beneficiary 258
liquidated debt 251
mailbox rule 244
mirror image rule 241
objective theory of contracts 235
offer 238
offeror 235
offeree 235
option contract 241
past consideration 250
privity of contract 257

promise 234
promissory estoppel 252
record 247
reformation 255
release 251
rescission 249
revocation 241
shrink-wrap agreement 246
Statute of Frauds 256
third party beneficiary 258
unconscionable 255
unenforceable contract 237
unilateral contract 235
unliquidated debt 251
usury 254
valid contract 237
void contract 237
voidable contract 237

## Issue Spotters

1. Applied Products, Inc., does business with Beltway Distributors, Inc., online. Under the Uniform Electronic Transactions Act, what determines the effect of the electronic documents evidencing the parties' deal? Is a party's "signature" necessary? Explain. (See *E-Contracts.*)

2. Joan, who is sixteen years old, moves out of her parents' home and signs a one-year lease for an apartment at Kenwood Apartments. Joan's parents tell her that she can return to live with them at any time. Unable to pay the rent, Joan moves back to her parents' home two months later. Can Kenwood enforce the lease against Joan? Why or why not? (See *Contractual Capacity.*)

• **Check your answers to the Issue Spotters against the answers provided in Appendix D at the end of this text.**

## Business Scenarios

**12–1. Unilateral Contract.** Rocky Mountain Races, Inc., sponsors the "Pioneer Trail Ultramarathon," with an advertised first prize of $10,000. The rules require the competitors to run 100 miles from the floor of Blackwater Canyon to the top of Pinnacle Mountain. The rules also provide that Rocky reserves the right to change the terms of the race at any time. Monica enters the race and is declared the winner. Rocky offers her a prize of $1,000 instead of $10,000. Did Rocky and Monica have a contract? Explain. (See *An Overview of Contract Law.*)

**12–2. Preexisting Duty.** Tabor is a buyer of file cabinets manufactured by Martin. Martin's contract with Tabor calls for delivery of fifty file cabinets at $40 per cabinet in five equal installments. After delivery of two installments (twenty cabinets), Martin informs Tabor that because of inflation, Martin is losing money. Martin will promise to deliver the remaining thirty cabinets only if Tabor will pay $50 per cabinet. Tabor agrees in writing to do so. Discuss whether Martin can legally collect the additional $100 on delivery to Tabor of the next installment of ten cabinets. (See *Consideration.*)

## Business Case Problems

**12–3. Business Case Problem with Sample Answer—Online Acceptances.**  Heather Reasonover opted to try Internet service from Clearwire Corp. Clearwire sent her a confirmation e-mail and a modem. When Reasonover plugged in the modem, an "I accept terms" box appeared. Without clicking on the box, Reasonover quit the page. She had not seen Clearwire's "Terms of Service," accessible only through its Web site. Although the e-mail she received and the printed materials included with the model included URLs to the company's Web site, neither URL gave direct access to the "Terms of Service." A clause in the "Terms of Service" required subscribers to submit any dispute to arbitration. Is Reasonover bound to this clause? Why or why not? [*Kwan v. Clearwire Corp.,* 2012 WL 32380 (W.D.Wash. 2012)] (See *E-Contracts.*)

• For a sample answer to Problem 12–3, go to Appendix E at the end of this text.

**12–4. Spotlight on Kansas City Chiefs—Consideration.**  On Brenda Sniezek's first day of work for the Kansas City Chiefs Football Club, she signed a document that purported to compel arbitration of any disputes that she might have with the Chiefs. In the document, Sniezek agreed to comply at all times with and be bound by the constitution and bylaws of the National Football League (NFL). She agreed to refer all disputes to the NFL Commissioner for a binding decision. On the Commissioner's decision, she agreed to release the Chiefs and others from any related claims. Nowhere in the document did the Chiefs agree to do anything. Was there consideration for the arbitration provision? Explain. [*Sniezek v. Kansas City Chiefs Football Club,* 402 S.W.3d 580 (Mo.App. W.D. 2013)] (See *Consideration.*)

**12–5. Requirements of the Offer.** Technical Consumer Products, Inc. (TCP), makes and distributes energy-efficient lighting products. Emily Bahr was TCP's district sales manager in Minnesota, North Dakota, and South Dakota when the company announced the details of a bonus plan. A district sales manager who achieved 100 percent year-over-year sales growth and a 42 percent gross margin would earn 200 percent of his or her base salary as a bonus. TCP retained absolute discretion to modify the plan. Bahr's base salary was $42,500. Her final sales results for the year showed 113 percent year-over-year sales growth and a 42 percent gross margin. She anticipated a bonus of $85,945, but TCP could not afford to pay the bonuses as planned, and Bahr received only $34,229. In response to Bahr's claim for breach of contract, TCP argued that the bonus plan was too indefinite to be an offer. Is TCP correct? Explain. [*Bahr v. Technical Consumer Products, Inc.,* 601 Fed.Appx. 359 (6th Cir. 2015)] (See *Agreement.*)

**12–6. Acceptance.** Altisource Portfolio Solutions, Inc., is a global corporation that provides real property owners with a variety of services, including property preservation—repairs, debris removal, and so on. Lucas Contracting, Inc., is a small trade contractor in Carrollton, Ohio. On behalf of Altisource, Berghorst Enterprises, LLC, hired Lucas to perform preservation work on certain foreclosed properties in eastern Ohio. When Berghorst did not pay for the work, Lucas filed a suit in an Ohio state court against Altisource. Before the trial, Lucas e-mailed the terms of a settlement. The same day, Altisource e-mailed a response that did not challenge or contradict Lucas's proposal and indicated agreement to it. Two days later, however, Altisource forwarded a settlement document that contained additional terms. Which proposal most likely satisfies the element of agreement to establish a contract? Explain. [*Lucas Contracting, Inc. v. Altisource Portfolio Solutions, Inc.,* __ Ohio App.3d __, 2016-Ohio-474, __ N.E.2d __ (2016)] (See *Agreement.*)

**12–7. Agreements That Lack Consideration.** Arkansas-Missouri Forest Products, LLC (Ark-Mo), sells supplies to make wood pallets. Blue Chip Manufacturing (BCM) makes pallets. Mark Garnett, an owner of Ark-Mo, and Stuart Lerner, an owner of BCM, went into business together. Garnett and Lerner agreed that Ark-Mo would have a 30-percent ownership interest in their future projects. When Lerner formed Blue Chip Recycling, LLC (BCR), to manage a pallet repair facility in California, however, he allocated only a 5-percent interest to Ark-Mo. Garnett objected. In a "Telephone Deal," Lerner then promised Garnett that Ark-Mo would receive a

30-percent interest in their future projects in the Midwest, and Garnett agreed to forgo an ownership interest in BCR. But when Blue Chip III, LLC (BC III), was formed to operate a repair facility in the Midwest, Lerner told Garnett that he "was not getting anything." Ark-Mo filed a suit in a Missouri state court against Lerner, alleging breach of contract. Was there consideration to support the Telephone Deal? Explain. [*Arkansas-Missouri Forest Products, LLC v. Lerner*, 486 S.W.3d 438 (Mo.App.E.D. 2016)] (See *Consideration*.)

**12–8. Legality.** Sue Ann Apolinar hired a guide through Arkansas Valley Adventures, LLC, for a rafting excursion on the Arkansas River. At the outfitter's office, Apolinar signed a release that detailed potential hazards and risks, including "overturning," "unpredictable currents," "obstacles" in the water, and "drowning." The release clearly stated that her signature discharged Arkansas Valley from liability for all claims arising in connection with the trip. On the river, while attempting to maneuver around a rapid, the raft capsized. The current swept Apolinar into a logjam where, despite efforts to save her, she drowned. Her son, Jesus Espinoza, Jr., filed a suit in a federal district court against the rafting company, alleging negligence. What are the arguments for and against enforcing the release that Apolinar signed? Discuss. [*Espinoza v. Arkansas Valley Adventures, LLC,* 809 F.3d 1150 (10th Cir. 2016)] (See *Legality*.)

**12–9. A Question of Ethics—Promissory Estoppel.**

 *Claudia Aceves borrowed from U.S. Bank to buy a home. Two years later, she could no longer afford the monthly payments. The bank notified her that it planned to foreclose on her home. (Foreclosure is a process that allows a lender to repossess and sell the property that secures a loan.) Aceves filed for bankruptcy. The bank offered to modify Aceves's mortgage if she would forgo bankruptcy. She agreed. Once she withdrew the filing, however, the bank foreclosed. [Aceves v. U.S. Bank, N.A., 192 Cal.App.4th 218, 120 Cal.Rptr.3d 507 (2 Dist. 2011)] (See Consideration.)*

**(a)** Could Aceves succeed on a claim of promissory estoppel? Why or why not?

**(b)** Did Aceves or U.S. Bank behave unethically? Discuss.

## Legal Reasoning Group Activity

**12–10. Covenants Not to Compete.** Assume that you are part of a group of executives at a large software corporation. The company is considering whether to incorporate covenants not to compete into its employment contracts. You know that there are some issues with the enforceability of these covenants, and you want to make an informed decision. (See *Legality*.)

**(a)** One group should make a list of what interests are served by enforcing covenants not to compete.

**(b)** A second group should create a list of what interests are served by refusing to enforce covenants not to compete.

**(c)** A third group is to consider whether a court should reform (and then enforce) a covenant not to compete that it determines is illegal. The group should create an argument for and an argument against reformation.

# Answers to the *Issue Spotters*

**1.** *Under the Uniform Electronic Transactions Act, what determines the effect of the electronic documents evidencing the parties' deal? Is a party's "signature" necessary? Explain.* First, it might be noted that the UETA does not apply unless the parties to a contract agree to use e-commerce in their transaction. In this deal, of course, the parties used e-commerce. The UETA removes barriers to e-commerce by giving the same legal effect to e-records and e-signatures as to paper documents and signatures. The UETA does not include rules for those transactions, however.

**2.** *Can Kenwood enforce the lease against Joan? Why or why not?* No. Joan is a minor and may disaffirm this contract. Because the apartment was a necessary, however, she remains liable for the reasonable value of her occupancy of the apartment.

# Sample Answers for *Business Case Problems with Sample Answer*

**Problem 12–3.** *Online Acceptances.* No. A shrink-wrap agreement is an agreement whose terms are expressed inside the box in which the goods are packaged. The party who opens the box may be informed that he or she agrees to the terms by keeping whatever is in the box. In many cases, the courts have enforced the terms of shrink-wrap agreements just as they enforce the terms of other contracts. But not all of the terms presented in shrink-wrap agreements have been enforced by the courts. One important consideration is whether the buyer had adequate notice of the terms.

A click-on agreement is formed when a buyer, completing a transaction on a computer, is required to indicate his or her assent to be bound by the terms of an offer by clicking on a button that says, for example, "I agree." In Reasonover's situation, no such agreement was formed with respect to Clearwire's "Terms of Service" (TOS). The e-mail did not give adequate notice of the TOS. It did not contain a direct link to the terms—accessing them required clicks on further links through the firm's homepage. The written, shrink-wrap materials accompanying the modem did not provide adequate notice of the TOS. There was only a reference to Clearwire's Web site in small print at the bottom of one page. Similarly, Reasonover's access to an "I accept terms" box did not establish notice of the terms. She did not click on the box but quit the page. Even if any of these references was sufficient notice, Reasonover kept the modem only because Clearwire told her that she could not return it.

In the actual case on which this problem is based, the court refused to compel arbitration on the basis of the clause in Clearwire's TOS.

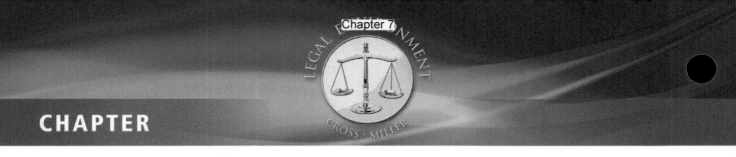

# Chapter 7

# CHAPTER

# Contract Performance, Breach, and Remedies

In a perfect world, every party who signed a contract would perform his or her duties completely and in a timely fashion, thereby discharging the contract. The real world is more complicated. Events often occur that affect our performance or our ability to perform contractual duties.

In addition, the duty to perform under a contract is not always absolute. It may instead be *conditioned* on the occurrence or nonoccurrence of a certain event. The legal environment of business requires the identification of some point at which the parties can reasonably know that their duties have ended.

Normally, people enter into contracts to secure some advantage. When it is no longer advantageous for a party to fulfill her or his contractual obligations, that party may breach, or fail to perform, the contract. Once one party breaches the contract, the nonbreaching party can choose one or more of several remedies.

A *remedy* is the relief provided to an innocent party when the other party has breached the contract. It is the means employed to enforce a right or to redress an injury. Remedies may include monetary damages, rescission and restitution, specific performance, and reformation.

## 13–1 Voluntary Consent

An otherwise valid contract may still be unenforceable if the parties have not genuinely agreed to its terms. A lack of *voluntary consent* (assent) can be used as a defense to the contract's enforceability.

**Voluntary consent** may be lacking because of a mistake, misrepresentation, undue influence, or duress—in other words, because there is no true "meeting of the minds." Generally, a party who demonstrates that he or she did not truly agree to the terms of a contract has a choice. That party can choose either to carry out the contract or to rescind (cancel) it and thus avoid the entire transaction.

### 13–1a Mistakes

We all make mistakes, so it is not surprising that mistakes are made when contracts are formed. In certain circumstances, contract law allows a contract to be avoided on the basis of mistake.

It is important to distinguish between *mistakes of fact* and *mistakes of value or quality*. Only a mistake of fact makes a contract voidable. Also, the mistake must involve some *material fact*—a fact that a reasonable person would consider important when determining his or her course of action.

Mistakes of fact occur in two forms—*bilateral* and *unilateral*. A unilateral mistake is made by only *one* of the parties. A bilateral, or mutual, mistake is made by *both* of the contracting parties. We look next at these two types of mistakes and illustrate them graphically in Exhibit 13–1.

**Unilateral Mistakes of Fact** A **unilateral mistake** is made by only one of the parties. In general, a unilateral mistake does not give the mistaken party any right to relief from the contract. Normally, the contract is enforceable.

■ **EXAMPLE 13.1** Elena intends to sell her jet ski for $2,500. When she learns that Chin is interested in buying a used jet ski, she sends him an e-mail offering to sell the jet ski to him. When typing the e-mail, however, she mistakenly keys in the price of $1,500. Chin immediately sends Elena an e-mail reply accepting her offer. Even though Elena intended to sell her personal jet ski for $2,500, she has made a unilateral mistake and is bound by the contract to sell it to Chin for $1,500. ■

This general rule has at least two exceptions.[1] The contract may not be enforceable if:

---

1. The *Restatement (Second) of Contracts*, Section 153, liberalizes the general rule to take into account the modern trend of allowing avoidance even though only one party has been mistaken.

**EXHIBIT 13–1  Mistakes of Fact**

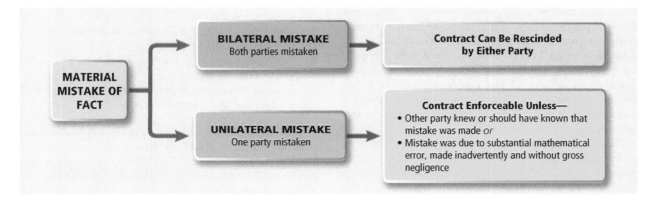

1. The *other* party to the contract knows or should have known that a mistake of fact was made.
2. The error was due to a *substantial* mathematical mistake in addition, subtraction, division, or multiplication and was made inadvertently and without gross (extreme) negligence. If, for instance, a contractor's bid was significantly low because he or she made a mistake in addition when totaling the estimated costs, any contract resulting from the bid normally may be rescinded.

Of course, in both situations, the mistake must still involve some material fact.

**Bilateral (Mutual) Mistakes of Fact** A **bilateral mistake** is a "mutual misunderstanding concerning a basic assumption on which the contract was made."[2] Note that, as with unilateral mistakes, the mistake must be about a material fact.

When both parties are mistaken about the same material fact, the contract can be rescinded by either party. ■ **CASE IN POINT 13.2** Coleman Holdings LP bought a parcel of real estate subject to setback restrictions imposed in a document entitled "Partial Release of Restrictions" that effectively precluded building a structure on the property. Lance and Joanne Eklund offered to buy the parcel from Coleman, intending to combine it with an adjacent parcel and build a home. Coleman gave the Eklunds a title report that referred to the "Partial Release of Restrictions," but they were not given a copy of the release.

Mistakenly believing that the document released restrictions on the property, the Eklunds did not investigate further. Meanwhile, Coleman also mistakenly believed that the setback restrictions had been removed. After buying the property and discovering the restrictions, the Eklunds filed a suit in a Nevada state court against Coleman, seeking rescission of the sale. The court ordered the deal rescinded. The Nevada Supreme Court affirmed the order. "The parties made a mutual mistake in their mutual belief that the parcel had no setback restrictions."[3] ■

A word or term in a contract may be subject to more than one reasonable interpretation. If the parties to the contract attach materially different meanings to the term, a court may allow the contract to be rescinded because there has been no true "meeting of the minds."

**Mistakes of Value** If a mistake concerns the future market value or quality of the object of the contract, the mistake is one of *value,* and the contract normally is enforceable. ■ **EXAMPLE 13.3** Sung buys a violin from Bev for $250. Although the violin is very old, neither party believes that it is valuable. Later, however, an antiques dealer informs the parties that the violin is rare and worth thousands of dollars. Here, both parties were mistaken, but the mistake is a mistake of *value* rather than a mistake of *fact.* Because mistakes of value do not warrant contract rescission, Bev cannot rescind the contract. ■

The reason that mistakes of value do not affect the enforceability of contracts is that value is variable. Depending on the time, place, and other circumstances, the same item may be worth considerably different amounts. When parties form a contract, their agreement establishes the value of the object of their transaction—for the moment. Each party is considered to have assumed the risk that the value will change in the future or prove to be different from what he or she thought. Without this rule, almost any party who did not receive what she or he considered a fair bargain could argue mistake.

---

2. *Restatement (Second) of Contracts,* Section 152.

3. *Coleman Holdings Limited Partnership v. Eklund,* 2015 WL 428567 (Nev. Sup.Ct. 2015).

## 13–1b Fraudulent Misrepresentation

Although fraud is a tort, the presence of fraud also affects the authenticity of the innocent party's consent to the contract. When an innocent party is fraudulently induced to enter into a contract, the contract usually can be avoided, because that party has not *voluntarily* consented to its terms.[4] The innocent party can either rescind the contract and be restored to her or his original position or enforce the contract and seek damages for any harms resulting from the fraud.

Generally, fraudulent misrepresentation refers only to misrepresentation that is consciously false and is intended to mislead another. The person making the fraudulent misrepresentation knows or believes that the assertion is false or knows that she or he does not have a basis (stated or implied) for the assertion.[5] Typically,

fraudulent misrepresentation consists of the following elements:

1. A misrepresentation of a material fact must occur.
2. There must be an intent to deceive.
3. The innocent party must justifiably rely on the misrepresentation.
4. To collect damages, a party must have been harmed as a result of the misrepresentation.

Like other actions based in the common law, a cause of action based on fraud can be subject to a statute of limitations. Of course, a cause based on a statute can also be subject to a statute of limitations. The limitations periods governing these actions may be different. In the following case, the issue was which limit to apply to a specific fraud claim—the three-year limit that applied to certain statute-based actions or the six-year limit that applied to common law actions.

---

4. *Restatement (Second) of Contracts,* Sections 163 and 164.
5. *Restatement (Second) of Contracts,* Section 162.

---

### Case 13.1

# Schneiderman v. Trump Entrepreneur Initiative, LLC

New York Supreme Court, Appellate Division, First Department, 137 A.D.3d 409, 26 N.Y.S.3d 66 (2016).

**Background and Facts** Donald Trump and Michael Sexton formed Trump University, LLC—later known as Trump Entrepreneur Initiative, LLC (TEI)—to sell courses in real estate investing. To attract students, Trump made a promotional video. In it, he said, "We're going to have professors that are absolutely terrific—terrific people, terrific brains, successful, the best. . . . All people that are hand-picked by me."

New York Attorney General Eric Schneiderman brought a proceeding in a New York state court against TEI, Trump, and Sexton, alleging that they had operated an illegal educational institution between 2005 and 2011. The attorney general sought an injunction, damages, penalties, and restitution under a state statute that provided for these remedies in cases of "persistent fraud." TEI was charged with intentionally misleading more than 5,000 students, including over 600 New York residents, into paying as much as $35,000 each to participate in its programs. Among other things, according to the attorney general, Trump did not handpick the instructors as he claimed.

The court dismissed the claim on the ground that it exceeded a three-year limit imposed on all statutory causes of action. The court also held that the specific statute did not provide the state with an independent cause of action for fraud. The attorney general appealed.

### In the Language of the Court
*MAZZARELLI, J.P. [Justice Presiding], RENWICK, SAXE, MOSKOWITZ, J.J. [Justices]*
* * * *

* * * [New York] Executive Law Section 63(12) states, in relevant part:

> Whenever any person shall engage in repeated fraudulent or illegal acts or otherwise demonstrate persistent fraud or illegality in the carrying on, conducting or transaction of business, the attorney general may apply * * * to the supreme court of the state of New York * * * for an order enjoining the continuance of such business activity or of any fraudulent or illegal acts and directing restitution and damages * * * and the court may award [such] relief * * * as it may deem proper.

Case 13.1 Continues

* * * *

[In its ruling, the lower court cited *People v. Charles Schwab & Co., Inc.,* 109 A.D.3d 445, 971 N.Y.S.2d 267 (1 Dept. 2013).] In *Charles Schwab,* the Attorney General had brought an enforcement action asserting claims under Section 63(12) * * * . The court dismissed the Section 63(12) claim.

On appeal to this Court, * * * we found that the court had properly dismissed that claim, stating that the section does not create independent claims, but merely authorizes the Attorney General to seek injunctive and other relief * * * in cases involving persistent fraud.

Although the holding of *Charles Schwab* purported to be based on the [New York] Court of Appeals' ruling in *State v. Cortelle Corp.,* 38 N.Y.2d 83, 378 N.Y.S.2d 654, 341 N.E.2d 223 (1975), *Cortelle* does not, in fact, hold that the Attorney General cannot bring a standalone cause of action for fraud under Executive Law Section 63(12).

* * * *

In *Cortelle,* the Court of Appeals [found] that * * * causes of action [under Section 63(12)] address-ing * * * allegedly fraudulent practices did not rely on liabilities, penalties, or forfeitures created or imposed by statute. *Specifically, Section 63(12) did not make unlawful the alleged fraudulent practices, but only provided standing in the Attorney General to seek redress and additional remedies for recognized wrongs which pre-existed the statute.* [Emphasis added.]

* * * *

* * * Other New York courts addressing that issue * * * have generally allowed for independent causes of action for fraud under Section 63(12).

* * * *

Thus, *Charles Schwab* does not comport with prevailing authority.

* * * Hence, we hold that the Attorney General is, in fact, authorized to bring a cause of action for fraud under Section 63(12).

**Decision and Remedy** *A state intermediate appellate court reversed the lower court's dismissal of the fraud claim, holding that the three-year limit on statutory causes of action did not apply. Because material issues of fact still existed as to that claim, however, the court remanded the case for further proceedings.*

**Critical Thinking**

- **Legal Environment** *The statute at the center of this case provides for remedies that may not be available at common law. Why would those additional remedies be sought, and when would they most likely be awarded?*
- **What If the Facts Were Different?** *Suppose that Trump University, or Trump Entrepreneur Initiative, had offered courses in real estate investing only online. Would the result in this case have been different? Explain.*

---

**Misrepresentation by Words or Conduct** The first element of proving fraud is to show that misrepresentation of a material fact has occurred. This misrepresentation can occur by words or actions. For instance, the statement "This sculpture was created by Michelangelo" is a misrepresentation of fact if another artist sculpted the statue. Similarly, if a customer asks to see only paintings by Jasper Johns and the gallery owner immediately leads the customer to paintings that were not done by Johns, the owner's actions can be a misrepresentation.

Misrepresentation also occurs when a party takes specific action to conceal a fact that is material to the contract. Therefore, if a seller, by her or his actions, prevents a buyer from learning of some fact that is material to the contract, such behavior constitutes misrepresentation by conduct.

**■ CASE IN POINT 13.4** Actor Tom Selleck contracted to purchase a horse named Zorro for his daughter from Dolores Cuenca. Cuenca acted as though Zorro were fit to ride in competitions, when in reality the horse was unfit for this use because of a medical condition. Selleck filed a lawsuit against Cuenca for wrongfully concealing the horse's condition and won. A jury awarded Selleck more than $187,000 for Cuenca's misrepresentation by conduct.[6] ■

Note that statements of opinion and representations of future facts (predictions) generally are not subject to claims of fraud. For instance, the statement "This land will be worth twice as much next year" is a statement

---

6. *Selleck v. Cuenca,* Case No. GIN056909, North County of San Diego, California, decided September 9, 2009.

of opinion, not fact. A fact is objective and verifiable, whereas an opinion is usually subject to debate. Contracting parties should know the difference and should not rely on statements of opinion. Nevertheless, in certain situations, such as when a naïve purchaser relies on an opinion from an expert, the innocent party may be entitled to rescission.

**Injury to the Innocent Party** Most courts do not require a showing of injury when the action is to rescind the contract. These courts hold that because rescission returns the parties to the positions they held before the contract was made, a showing of injury to the innocent party is unnecessary.

In contrast, to recover damages caused by fraud, proof of harm is universally required. The measure of damages is ordinarily equal to the property's value had it been delivered as represented, less the actual price paid for the property. (Additionally, because fraud actions necessarily involve wrongful conduct, courts may also sometimes award punitive damages, which are not ordinarily available in contract actions.)

## 13–1c Undue Influence

**Undue influence** arises from relationships in which one party can greatly influence another party, thus overcoming that party's free will. A contract entered into under excessive or undue influence lacks voluntary consent and is therefore voidable.[7]

**One Party Dominates the Other** In various types of relationships, one party may have the opportunity to dominate and unfairly influence another party. Minors and elderly people, for instance, are often under the influence of guardians (persons who are legally responsible for them). If a guardian induces a young or elderly ward (a person whom the guardian looks after) to enter into a contract that benefits the guardian, the guardian may have exerted undue influence. Undue influence can arise from a number of fiduciary relationships, such as physician-patient, parent-child, husband-wife, or guardian-ward situations.

The essential feature of undue influence is that the party being taken advantage of does not, in reality, exercise free will in entering into a contract. It is not enough that a person is elderly or suffers from some physical or mental impairment. There must be clear and convincing

evidence that the person did not act out of her or his free will.[8] Similarly, the existence of a fiduciary relationship alone is insufficient to prove undue influence.

**Presumption of Undue Influence in Certain Situations** When the dominant party in a fiduciary relationship benefits from that relationship, a presumption of undue influence arises. The dominant party must exercise the utmost good faith in dealing with the other party. When a contract enriches the dominant party, the court will often *presume* that the contract was made under undue influence.

■ **EXAMPLE 13.5** Erik is the guardian for Kinsley, his ward. Erik is the dominant party in this relationship. On Kinsley's behalf, he enters into a contract from which he benefits financially. If Kinsley challenges the contract, the court will likely presume that the guardian has taken advantage of his ward. To rebut (refute) this presumption, Erik has to show that he made full disclosure to Kinsley and that consideration was present. He must also show that Kinsley received, if available, independent and competent advice before completing the transaction. Unless the presumption can be rebutted, the contract will be rescinded. ■

## 13–1d Duress

Agreement to the terms of a contract is not voluntary if one of the parties is *forced* into the agreement. The use of threats to force a party to enter into a contract constitutes **duress.** Similarly, the use of blackmail or extortion to induce consent to a contract is duress. Duress is both a defense to the enforcement of a contract and a ground for the rescission of a contract.

To establish duress, there must be proof of a threat to do something that the threatening party has no right to do. Generally, for duress to occur, the threatened act must be wrongful or illegal. It also must render the person who is threatened incapable of exercising free will. A threat to exercise a legal right, such as the right to sue someone, ordinarily does not constitute duress.

## 13–1e Adhesion Contracts and Unconscionability

Sometimes, the terms of a contract are dictated by a party with overwhelming bargaining power. The signer must agree to those terms or go without the commodity or service in question. In these situations, questions

---

7. *Restatement (Second) of Contracts*, Section 177.

8. See, for example, *Ayers v. Shaffer*, 286 Va. 212, 748 S.E.2d 83 (2013).

Knowingly or not, many consumers sign contracts that include arbitration clauses. Such clauses require that dissatisfied consumers submit to arbitration, rather than pursue litigation through the court system. Not surprisingly, there is a growing movement in protest of arbitration clauses of this kind, which some believe are unfair to consumers.

### Governing Arbitration Law

For the most part, federal law encourages arbitration through the Federal Arbitration Act (FAA).[a] Generally, federal courts have ruled in favor of contracts with arbitration clauses if those clauses provide a meaningful way for consumers to seek redress for alleged harms.

Over the past few years, the United States Supreme Court has held that the FAA preempts state courts' interpretations of arbitration clauses. For instance, in *AT&T Mobility, LLC v. Concepcion*,[b] the Court ruled that federal law preempts state laws that bar enforcement of arbitration clauses prohibiting class-action suits. Later, in *DIRECTV, Inc. v. Imburgia*,[c] the Court again upheld an arbitration clause, citing the *Concepcion* case. The Court stated that the FAA "is the law of the United States, and [the] *Concepcion* [case] is an authoritative interpretation of the act." The Court stated that "the judges of every

State must follow it" because of the supremacy clause of the U.S. Constitution.

### Federal Attempts to Circumvent the Supreme Court's Decisions

Even within the federal government, certain entities wish to reduce the use of arbitration clauses in consumer contracts. In the fall of 2015, the Consumer Financial Protection Bureau announced that it would seek to implement new rules barring contracts from substituting private arbitration for class-action litigation. Such rules would apply to checking accounts, credit cards, and other financial products. If that federal agency is successful, it will undoubtedly face litigation that will go to the Supreme Court.

### Why Arbitration Is So Prevalent

Many corporations favor arbitration clauses in consumer contracts because arbitration is less expensive than litigation. Arbitration is certainly the preferred remedy for disputes involving relatively small sums— disputes over cell phone contracts, for instance. While individuals may feel that they are at a disadvantage if they are forced to go to arbitration, for the economy as a whole, there are benefits. In particular, according to some estimates, the rate of growth in liability costs has fallen relative to the growth in the economy since 2003. Ultimately, consumers on average pay lower costs for products and services when corporations spend less on litigation.

**Critical Thinking** *What might happen if arbitration clauses were prohibited in all consumer contracts?*

**a.** 9 U.S.C. Sections 1 *et seq.*

**b.** 563 U.S. 333, 131 S.Ct. 1740, 179 L.Ed.2d 742 (2011). See also *American Express Co. v. Italian Colors Restaurant*, ___ U.S. ___, 133 S.Ct. 2304, 186 L.Ed.2d 417 (2013).

**c.** ___ U.S. ___, 135 S.Ct. 1547, 191 L.Ed.2d 636 (2015).

concerning voluntary consent may arise. (Many such contracts include arbitration provisions, as discussed in this chapter's *Ethics Today* feature.)

**Adhesion contracts** are written *exclusively* by one party and presented to the other party on a take-it-or-leave-it basis. These contracts often use standard forms, which give the adhering party no opportunity to negotiate the contract terms.

Standard-form contracts often contain fine-print provisions that shift a risk ordinarily borne by one party to the other. A variety of businesses use such contracts. To avoid enforcement of the contract or of a particular clause, the plaintiff normally must show that the contract or particular term is unconscionable.

## 13–2 Performance and Discharge

The most common way to **discharge,** or terminate, contractual duties is by the **performance** of those duties. For instance, a buyer and seller enter into an agreement via e-mail for the sale of a 2018 Lexus RX for $44,000. This contract will be discharged by performance when the buyer pays $44,000 to the seller and the seller transfers possession of the Lexus to the buyer.

Sometimes, of course, promises are not completely performed as stated in the contract, or one party refuses to perform. In addition, a party's obligation to perform can be discharged in other ways, such as by agreement or by an event that makes performance impossible.

### 13–2a Conditions

In most contracts, promises of performance are not expressly conditioned or qualified. Instead, they are *absolute promises.* They must be performed, or the parties promising the acts will be in breach of contract.

In some situations, however, performance is *conditioned.* A **condition** is a qualification in a contract based on a possible future event. The occurrence or nonoccurrence of the event will trigger the performance of a legal obligation or terminate an existing obligation under a contract.[9] If the condition is not satisfied, the obligations of the parties are discharged. A condition that must be fulfilled before a party's performance can be required is called a **condition precedent.** The condition precedes the absolute duty to perform.

A contract to lease university housing, for instance, may be conditioned on the person's being a student at the university. ■ **CASE IN POINT 13.6**  James Maciel leased an apartment in a university-owned housing facility for Regent University (RU) students in Virginia. The lease ran until the end of the fall semester. Maciel had an option to renew the lease semester by semester as long as he maintained his status as an RU student.

When Maciel told RU that he intended to withdraw, the university told him that he had to move out of the apartment by May 31, the final day of the semester. Maciel asked for two additional weeks, but the university denied the request. On June 1, RU changed the locks on the apartment. Maciel entered through a window and e-mailed the university that he planned to stay "for another one or two weeks." He was convicted of trespassing. He appealed, arguing that he had "legal authority" to occupy the apartment. The reviewing court affirmed his conviction. "Regent's deadline was consistent with the lease agreement, and Maciel's eligibility to reside in student housing was *conditioned* upon his status as a Regent student." In other words, being enrolled as a student in RU was a condition precedent to living in its student housing.[10] ■

### 13–2b Discharge by Performance

The great majority of contracts, as noted earlier, are discharged by performance. The contract comes to an end when both parties fulfill their respective duties by performing the acts they have promised.

Performance can also be accomplished by *tender.* **Tender** is an unconditional offer to perform by a person who is ready, willing, and able to do so. Therefore, a seller who places goods at the disposal of a buyer has tendered delivery and can demand payment. A buyer who offers to pay for goods has tendered payment and can demand delivery of the goods.

Once performance has been tendered, the party making the tender has done everything possible to carry out the terms of the contract. If the other party then refuses to perform, the party making the tender can sue for breach of contract. There are two basic types of performance— *complete performance* and *substantial performance.*

**Complete Performance**  When a party performs exactly as agreed, there is no question as to whether the contract has been performed. When a party's performance is perfect, it is said to be complete. Normally, conditions expressly stated in a contract must fully occur in all respects for complete performance (strict performance) of the contract to take place. Any deviation breaches the contract and discharges the other party's obligation to perform.

Most construction contracts, for instance, require the builder to meet certain specifications. If the specifications are conditions, complete performance is required to avoid material breach (*material breach* will be discussed shortly). If the conditions are met, the other party to the contract must then fulfill her or his obligation to pay the builder.

If the parties to the contract did not expressly make the specifications a condition, however, and the builder fails to meet the specifications, performance is not complete. What effect does such a failure have on the other party's obligation to pay? The answer is part of the doctrine of *substantial performance.*

**Substantial Performance**  A party who in good faith performs substantially all of the terms of a contract can enforce the contract against the other party under the doctrine of substantial performance. The basic requirements for performance to qualify as substantial performance are as follows:

1. The party must have performed in good faith. Intentional failure to comply with the contract terms is a breach of the contract.

2. The performance must not vary greatly from the performance promised in the contract. An omission, variance, or defect in performance is considered minor if it can easily be remedied by compensation (monetary damages).

3. The performance must create substantially the same benefits as those promised in the contract.

---

9. The *Restatement (Second) of Contracts,* Section 224, defines a condition as "an event, not certain to occur, which must occur, unless its nonoccurrence is excused, before performance under a contract becomes due."

10. *Maciel v. Commonwealth,* 2011 WL 65942 (Va.App. 2011).

**Courts Must Decide.** Courts decide whether the performance was substantial on a case-by-case basis, examining all of the facts of the particular situation. ■ **CASE IN POINT 13.7** Eugene Pegg had been an electrician in North Dakota for thirty years and had brought a large customer, Sungold, with him through several employers. When an acquaintance, Kelly Kohn, started Kohn Electric, LLC, Pegg approached him to become partners.

Kohn and Pegg orally agreed that Pegg could become a partner in Kohn Electric if he contributed $10,000 in capital and the Sungold account. In return, Pegg was to receive 10 percent of the gross revenue generated by the Sungold account, among other things. Pegg paid $9,152.49 for a pickup truck titled in Kohn Electric's name and paid for tools and equipment for the business. Later, the relationship soured, and Pegg quit. Pegg sued in a state court to recover the proceeds due under the agreement. Kohn denied that they were partners, but he paid Pegg $9,152.49 for the truck.

The state court found that there was an oral partnership agreement and that Pegg had substantially performed by contributing the pickup and bringing in the Sungold account. Therefore, he was entitled to damages in an amount equal to 10 percent of the gross revenue generated from the Sungold account. The court's decision was affirmed on appeal.[11] ■

**Effect on Duty to Perform.** If one party's performance is substantial, the other party's duty to perform remains absolute. In other words, the parties must continue performing under the contract. For instance, the party who substantially performed is entitled to payment. If performance is not substantial, there is a material breach (to be discussed shortly), and the nonbreaching party is excused from further performance.

**Measure of Damages.** Because substantial performance is not perfect, the other party is entitled to damages to compensate for the failure to comply with the contract. The measure of the damages is the cost to bring the object of the contract into compliance with its terms, if that cost is reasonable under the circumstances.

What if the cost is unreasonable? Then the measure of damages is the difference in value between the performance rendered and the performance that would have been rendered if the contract had been performed completely.

■ **CASE IN POINT 13.8** In a classic case, the plaintiff, Jacob & Youngs, Inc., was a builder that had contracted with George Kent to construct a country residence for him. A specification in the building contract required that "all wrought-iron pipe must be well galvanized, lap welded pipe of the grade known as 'standard pipe' of Reading manufacture." Jacob & Youngs installed substantially similar pipe that was not of Reading manufacture. When Kent became aware of the difference, he ordered the builder to remove all of the plumbing and replace it with the Reading type. To do so would have required removing finished walls that encased the plumbing—an expensive and difficult task.

The builder explained that the plumbing was of the same quality, appearance, value, and cost as Reading pipe. When Kent nevertheless refused to pay the $3,483.46 still owed for the work, Jacob & Youngs sued to compel payment. The dispute ended up before the Court of Appeals of New York, the state's highest court, which concluded that "the measure of the allowance is not the cost of replacement, which would be great, but the difference in value, which would be either nominal or nothing." Therefore, New York's highest court held that Jacob & Youngs had substantially performed the contract.[12] ■

### Performance to the Satisfaction of Another

Contracts often state that completed work must personally satisfy one of the parties or a third person. When the subject matter of the contract is *personal,* the obligation is conditional, and performance must actually satisfy the party specified in the contract. For instance, contracts for portraits, works of art, and tailoring are considered personal because they involve matters of personal taste. Therefore, only the personal satisfaction of the party fulfills the condition. (An exception exists, of course, if a court finds that the party is expressing dissatisfaction simply to avoid payment or otherwise is not acting in good faith.)

Most other contracts need to be performed only to the satisfaction of a reasonable person unless they *expressly state otherwise.* When the subject matter of the contract is mechanical, courts are more likely to find that the performing party has performed satisfactorily if a reasonable person would be satisfied with what was done. ■ **EXAMPLE 13.9** Mason signs a contract with Jen to mount a new heat pump on a concrete platform to her satisfaction. Such a contract normally need only be performed to the satisfaction of a reasonable person. ■

### Material Breach of Contract

A **breach of contract** is the nonperformance of a contractual duty. The breach is *material* when performance is not at least substantial.[13]

---

11. *Pegg v. Kohn,* 861 N.W.2d 764, 2015 ND 79 (2015).

12. *Jacob & Youngs v. Kent,* 230 N.Y. 239, 129 N.E. 889 (1921).

13. *Restatement (Second) of Contracts,* Section 241.

As mentioned earlier, when there is a material breach, the nonbreaching party is excused from the performance of contractual duties. That party can also sue the breaching party for damages resulting from the breach.

■ **EXAMPLE 13.10**  When country singer Garth Brooks's mother died, he donated $500,000 to a hospital in his hometown in Oklahoma to build a new women's health center named after his mother. After several years passed and the health center was not built, Brooks demanded a refund. The hospital refused, claiming that while it had promised to honor his mother in some way, it had not promised to build a women's health center. Brooks sued for breach of contract. A jury determined that the hospital's failure to build a women's health center and name it after Brooks's mother was a material breach of the contract. The jury awarded Brooks $1 million in damages. ■

**Material versus Minor Breach.** If the breach is *minor* (not material), the nonbreaching party's duty to perform is not entirely excused, but it can sometimes be suspended until the breach has been remedied. Once the minor breach has been cured, the nonbreaching party must resume performance of the contractual obligations.

Both parties in the following case were arguably in breach of their contract. Which party's breach was material?

**Case Analysis 13.2**

# Kohel v. Bergen Auto Enterprises, L.L.C.
Superior Court of New Jersey, Appellate Division, ___ A.3d___, 2013 WL 439970 (2013).

### In the Language of the Court
*PER CURIAM.* [By the Whole Court]
* * * *

On May 24, 2010, plaintiffs Marc and Bree Kohel entered into a sales contract with defendant Bergen Auto Enterprises, L.L.C. d/b/a Wayne Mazda Inc. (Wayne Mazda), for the purchase of a used 2009 Mazda. Plaintiffs agreed to pay $26,430.22 for the Mazda and were credited $7,000 as a trade-in, for their 2005 Nissan Altima. As plaintiffs still owed $8,118.28 on the Nissan, Wayne Mazda assessed plaintiffs a net pay-off of this amount and agreed to remit the balance due to satisfy the outstanding lien.

Plaintiffs took possession of the Mazda with temporary plates and left the Nissan with defendant. A few days later, a representative of defendant advised plaintiffs that the Nissan's vehicle identification tag (VIN tag) was missing. The representative claimed it was unable to sell the car and offered to rescind the transaction. Plaintiffs refused.

When the temporary plates on the Mazda expired on June 24, 2010, defendant refused to provide plaintiffs with the permanent plates they had paid for. In addition, defendant refused to pay off plaintiffs' outstanding loan on the Nissan, as they had agreed. As a result,

plaintiffs were required to continue to make monthly payments on both the Nissan and the Mazda.

On July 28, 2010, plaintiffs filed a complaint in [a New Jersey state court] against Wayne Mazda * * * . Plaintiffs alleged breach of contract.
* * * *

On February 2, 2012, the court rendered an oral decision finding that there was a breach of contract by Wayne Mazda * * * . On February 17, 2012, the court entered judgment in the amount of $5,405.17 in favor of plaintiffs against Wayne Mazda. [The defendant appealed to a state intermediate appellate court.]
* * * *

Defendant argues that plaintiffs' delivery of the Nissan without a VIN tag was, itself, a breach of the contract of sale and precludes a finding that defendant breached the contract. However, the trial court found that plaintiffs were not aware that the Nissan lacked a VIN tag when they offered it in trade. Moreover, defendant's representatives examined the car twice before accepting it in trade and did not notice the missing VIN until they took the car to an auction where they tried to sell it. *There is a material distinction in plaintiffs' conduct, which the court found*

*unintentional, and defendant's refusal to release the permanent plates for which the plaintiffs had paid, an action the court concluded was done to maintain "leverage."* [Emphasis added.]

* * * The evidence * * * indicated that * * * the problem with the missing VIN tag could be rectified. Marc Kohel applied and paid for a replacement VIN tag at Meadowlands [Nissan for $35.31]. While he initially made some calls to Meadowlands, he did not follow up in obtaining the VIN tag after the personnel at Wayne Mazda began refusing to take his calls.

* * * The court concluded that "Wayne Mazda didn't handle this as— as adroitly [skillfully] as they could * * * ." Kevin DiPiano, identified in the complaint as the owner and/or CEO of Wayne Mazda, would not even take [the plaintiffs'] calls to discuss this matter. The court found:

> Mr. DiPiano could have been a better businessman, could have been a little bit more compassionate or at least responsive, you know? He was not. He acted like he didn't care. That obviously went a long way to infuriate the plaintiffs. I don't blame them for being infuriated.

**Case 13.2 Continues**

**Case 13.2 Continued**

* * * *

* * * Here, plaintiffs attempted to remedy the VIN tag issue but this resolution was frustrated by defendant's unreasonable conduct. We thus reject defendant's argument that plaintiffs' failure to obtain the replacement VIN tag amounted to a repudiation of the contract.

* * * *

Affirmed.

### Legal Reasoning Questions

**1.** What is a material breach of contract? When a material breach occurs, what are the nonbreaching party's options?

**2.** What is a minor breach of contract? When a minor breach occurs, is the nonbreaching party excused from performance? Explain.

**3.** In this case, the defendant—Wayne Mazda—argued that the plaintiffs should not be granted relief for the defendant's breach. What were the defendant's main arguments in support of this position?

---

**Underlying Policy.** Note that any breach entitles the nonbreaching party to sue for damages, but only a material breach discharges the nonbreaching party from the contract. The policy underlying these rules allows a contract to go forward when only minor problems occur but allows it to be terminated if major difficulties arise. Exhibit 13–2 reviews how performance can discharge a contract.

**Anticipatory Repudiation** Before either party to a contract has a duty to perform, one of the parties may refuse to carry out his or her contractual obligations. This is called **anticipatory repudiation**[14] of the contract.

When an anticipatory repudiation occurs, it is treated as a material breach of the contract, and the nonbreaching party is permitted to bring an action for damages immediately. The nonbreaching party can file suit even though the scheduled time for performance under the contract may still be in the future. Until the nonbreaching party treats an early repudiation as a breach, however, the repudiating party can retract the anticipatory repudiation by proper notice and restore the parties to their original obligations.[15]

An anticipatory repudiation is treated as a present, material breach for two reasons. First, the nonbreaching

---

**14.** *Restatement (Second) of Contracts*, Section 253; Section 2–610 of the Uniform Commercial Code (UCC).

**15.** See UCC 2–611.

## EXHIBIT 13–2 Discharge by Performance

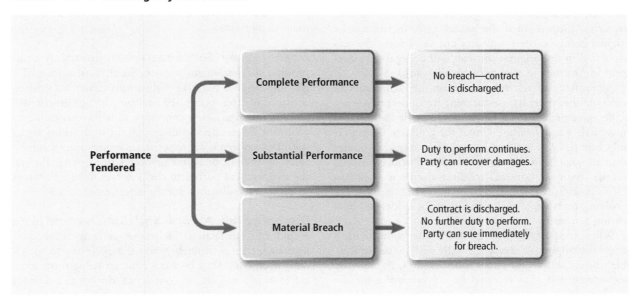

party should not be required to remain ready and willing to perform when the other party has already repudiated the contract. Second, the nonbreaching party should have the opportunity to seek a similar contract elsewhere and may have a duty to do so to minimize his or her loss.

**Time for Performance** If no time for performance is stated in a contract, a *reasonable time* is implied. If a specific time is stated, the parties must usually perform by that time. Unless time is expressly stated to be vital, though, a delay in performance will not destroy the performing party's right to payment.

When time is expressly stated to be "of the essence" or vital, the parties normally must perform within the stated time period because the time element becomes a condition. Nevertheless, a court may find that a party who fails to complain about the other party's delay has waived the breach of the time provision.

## 13–2c Discharge by Agreement

Any contract can be discharged by agreement of the parties. The agreement can be contained in the original contract, or the parties can form a new contract for the express purpose of discharging the original contract.

**Discharge by Mutual Rescission** As mentioned previously, *rescission* is the process by which a contract is canceled or terminated and the parties are returned to the positions they occupied prior to forming it. For **mutual rescission** to take place, the parties must make another agreement that also satisfies the legal requirements for a contract. There must be an *offer,* an *acceptance,* and *consideration.* Ordinarily, if the parties agree to rescind the original contract, their promises not to perform the acts stipulated in the original contract will be legal consideration for the second contract (the rescission).

Agreements to rescind most executory contracts (in which neither party has performed) are enforceable, even if the agreement is made orally and even if the original agreement was in writing. Under the Uniform Commercial Code (UCC), however, agreements to rescind a sales contract must be in writing (or contained in an electronic record) when the contract requires a written rescission [UCC 2–209(2), (4)]. Agreements to rescind contracts involving transfers of realty also must be evidenced by a writing or record.

When one party has fully performed, an agreement to cancel the original contract normally will *not* be enforceable unless there is additional consideration. Because the performing party has received no consideration for the

promise to call off the original bargain, additional consideration is necessary to support a rescission contract.

**Discharge by Novation** A contractual obligation may also be discharged through novation. A **novation** occurs when both of the parties to a contract agree to substitute a third party for one of the original parties. The requirements of a novation are as follows:

1. A previous valid obligation.
2. An agreement by all parties to a new contract.
3. The extinguishing of the old obligation (discharge of the prior party).
4. A new contract that is valid.

■ **EXAMPLE 13.11** Union Corporation contracts to sell its pharmaceutical division to British Pharmaceuticals, Ltd. Before the transfer is completed, Union, British Pharmaceuticals, and a third company, Otis Chemicals, execute a new agreement to transfer all of British Pharmaceuticals' rights and duties in the transaction to Otis Chemicals. As long as the new contract is supported by consideration, the novation will discharge the original contract (between Union and British Pharmaceuticals) and replace it with the new contract (between Union and Otis Chemicals). ■

A novation expressly or impliedly revokes and discharges a prior contract. The parties involved may expressly state in the new contract that the old contract is now discharged. If the parties do not expressly discharge the old contract, it will be impliedly discharged if the new contract's terms are inconsistent with the old contract's terms. It is this immediate discharge of the prior contract that distinguishes a novation from both an accord and satisfaction, discussed shortly, and an assignment of all rights.

**Discharge by Settlement Agreement** A compromise, or settlement agreement, that arises out of a genuine dispute over the obligations under an existing contract will be recognized at law. The agreement will be substituted as a new contract and will either expressly or impliedly revoke and discharge the obligations under the prior contract. In contrast to a novation, a substituted agreement does not involve a third party. Rather, the two original parties to the contract form a different agreement to substitute for the original one.

**Discharge by Accord and Satisfaction** In an accord and satisfaction, the parties agree to accept performance that is different from the performance originally promised. An *accord* is a contract to perform some act to satisfy an existing contractual duty that is not yet discharged. A *satisfaction* is the performance of the accord agreement. An accord and its satisfaction discharge the original contractual obligation.

Once the accord has been made, the original obligation is merely suspended until the accord agreement is fully performed. If it is not performed, the obligee (the one to whom performance is owed) can file a lawsuit based on either the original obligation or the accord.

■ **EXAMPLE 13.12** Fahreed has a judgment against Ling for $8,000. Later, both parties agree that the judgment can be satisfied by Ling's transfer of his automobile to Fahreed. This agreement to accept the auto in lieu of $8,000 in cash is the accord. If Ling transfers the car to Fahreed, the accord is fully performed, and the debt is discharged. If Ling refuses to transfer the car, the accord is breached. Because the original obligation was merely suspended, Fahreed can sue Ling to enforce the original judgment for $8,000 in cash or bring an action for breach of the accord. ■

### 13–2d Discharge by Operation of Law

Under specified circumstances, contractual duties may be discharged by operation of law. These circumstances include material alteration of the contract, the running of the statute of limitations, bankruptcy, and the impossibility or impracticability of performance.

**Material Alteration of the Contract** To discourage parties from altering written contracts, the law allows an innocent party to be discharged when the other party has materially altered a written contract without consent. For instance, suppose that a party alters a material term of a contract, such as the stated quantity or price, without the knowledge or consent of the other party. In this situation, the party who was unaware of the alteration can treat the contract as discharged.

**Statutes of Limitations** Statutes of limitations restrict the period during which a party can sue on a particular cause of action. After the applicable limitations period has passed, a suit can no longer be brought. The limitations period for bringing suits for breach of oral contracts usually is two to three years, and for written contracts, four to five years. Parties generally have ten to twenty years to file for recovery of amounts awarded in judgments, depending on state law.

Lawsuits for breach of a contract for the sale of goods usually must be brought within four years after the cause of action has accrued [UCC 2–725]. A cause of action for a sales contract generally accrues when the breach occurs, even if the aggrieved party is not aware of the

breach. A breach of warranty normally occurs when the seller delivers the goods to the buyer. By their original agreement, the parties can reduce this four-year period to not less than one year, but they cannot agree to extend it.

**Bankruptcy** A proceeding in bankruptcy attempts to allocate the debtor's assets to the creditors in a fair and equitable fashion. Once the assets have been allocated, the debtor receives a **discharge in bankruptcy.** A discharge in bankruptcy ordinarily prevents the creditors from enforcing most of the debtor's contracts. Partial payment of a debt *after* discharge in bankruptcy will not revive the debt.

**Impossibility of Performance** After a contract has been made, supervening events (such as a fire) may make performance impossible in an objective sense. This is known as **impossibility of performance** and can discharge a contract. The doctrine of impossibility of performance applies only when the parties could not have reasonably foreseen, at the time the contract was formed, the event that rendered performance impossible. Performance may also become so difficult or costly due to some unforeseen event that a court will consider it commercially unfeasible, or impracticable, as will be discussed shortly.

*Objective impossibility* ("It can't be done") must be distinguished from *subjective impossibility* ("I'm sorry, I simply can't do it"). An example of subjective impossibility occurs when a party cannot deliver goods on time because of freight car shortages or cannot make payment on time because the bank is closed. In effect, in each of these situations the party is saying, "It is impossible for *me* to perform," not "It is impossible for *anyone* to perform." Accordingly, such excuses do not discharge a contract, and the nonperforming party is normally held in breach of contract.

**When Performance Is Impossible.** Three basic types of situations may qualify as grounds for the discharge of contractual obligations based on impossibility of performance:[16]

1. *When one of the parties to a personal contract dies or becomes incapacitated prior to performance.* ■ **EXAMPLE 13.13** Frederic, a famous dancer, contracts with Ethereal Dancing Guild to play a leading role in its new ballet. Before the ballet can be performed, Frederic becomes ill and dies. His personal performance was essential to the completion of the contract. Thus, his death discharges the contract and his estate's liability for his nonperformance. ■

---

16. *Restatement (Second) of Contracts*, Sections 262–266; UCC 2–615.

2. *When the specific subject matter of the contract is destroyed.* ■ **EXAMPLE 13.14** A-1 Farm Equipment agrees to sell Gunther the green tractor on its lot and promises to have the tractor ready for Gunther to pick up on Saturday. On Friday night, however, a truck veers off the nearby highway and smashes into the tractor, destroying it beyond repair. Because the contract was for this specific tractor, A-1's performance is rendered impossible owing to the accident. ■

3. *When a change in law renders performance illegal.* ■ **CASE IN POINT 13.15** Scott Harvard was a senior executive officer of Hampton Roads Bankshares (HRB) in Virginia. Harvard's employment contract included a "golden parachute"—a payment of approximately three times his average annual compensation if he quit. During the 2008 recession, Congress enacted the Emergency Economic Stabilization Act (EESA) to stabilize the financial system.[17] The EESA included the Troubled Assets Relief Program (TARP), which allowed the government to buy "troubled assets" from financial institutions to promote market stability. HRB participated in TARP.

Later, when Harvard quit the firm, HRB refused to pay him the golden parachute amount because it believed that the EESA had made it illegal for them to do so. Harvard sued HRB to obtain payment. Ultimately, the Virginia Supreme Court ruled that payment of the golden parachute would violate the EESA, and therefore HRB's obligation to pay it was discharged. Because the purpose of the contractual obligation (providing a golden parachute) had been rendered illegal, performance was objectively impossible.[18] ■

**Temporary Impossibility.** An occurrence or event that makes performance temporarily impossible operates to suspend performance until the impossibility ceases. Once the temporary event ends, the parties ordinarily must perform the contract as originally planned. ■ **EXAMPLE 13.16** Mindy and Lyn Carr contract to rent a sailboat from Key West Rentals for a month-long trip. The day before their trip is scheduled to begin, a hurricane hits the coast where the boat is docked, causing damage. The hurricane makes performance temporarily impossible, and the Carrs postpone their trip. Once the repairs are made to the dock and the boat, however, Key West Rentals would be required to perform the contract as

originally planned. The Carrs have a right to rent the boat for a month for the previously agreed-on price. ■

Sometimes, the lapse of time and the change in circumstances surrounding the contract make it substantially more burdensome for the parties to perform the promised acts. In that situation, a court might hold that the contract is discharged.

**Commercial Impracticability** Courts may also excuse parties from their performance when it becomes much more difficult or expensive than the parties originally contemplated at the time the contract was formed. For instance, a contract could be discharged because a party would otherwise have had to pay ten times more than the original estimate to perform the contract.

For someone to invoke the doctrine of **commercial impracticability** successfully, however, the anticipated performance must become *significantly* more difficult or costly.[19] In addition, the added burden of performing *must not have been foreseeable by the parties when the contract was made.*

**Frustration of Purpose** Closely allied with the doctrine of commercial impracticability is the doctrine of **frustration of purpose.** In principle, a contract will be discharged if supervening circumstances make it impossible to attain the purpose both parties had in mind when they made the contract. As with commercial impracticability and impossibility, the supervening event must not have been reasonably foreseeable at the time the contract was formed.

There are some differences between these doctrines, however. Commercial impracticability usually involves an event that increases the cost or difficulty of performance. In contrast, frustration of purpose typically involves an event that decreases the value of what a party receives under the contract.

## 13–3 Damages

A breach of contract entitles the nonbreaching party to sue for monetary damages. In contract law, damages compensate the nonbreaching party for the loss of the bargain (whereas tort law damages compensate for harm suffered as a result of another's wrongful act). Often, courts say that innocent parties are to be placed in the position they would have occupied had the contract been fully performed.

17. 12 U.S.C. Section 5201.
18. *Hampton Roads Bankshares, Inc. v. Harvard*, 291 Va. 42, 781 S.E.2d 172 (2016).
19. *Restatement (Second) of Contracts*, Section 264.

Collecting damages through a court judgment requires litigation, however, which can be expensive and time consuming. In addition, court judgments are often difficult to enforce, particularly if the breaching party does not have sufficient assets to pay the damages awarded. For these reasons, most parties settle their lawsuits for damages (or other remedies) prior to trial.

### 13–3a Types of Damages

There are four broad categories of damages:

1. Compensatory (to cover direct losses and costs).
2. Consequential (to cover indirect and foreseeable losses).
3. Punitive (to punish and deter wrongdoing).
4. Nominal (to recognize wrongdoing when no monetary loss is shown).

Compensatory and punitive damages were discussed in the context of tort law. Here, we look at these types of damages, as well as consequential and nominal damages, in the context of contract law.

**Compensatory Damages** Damages that compensate the nonbreaching party for the *loss of the bargain* are known as *compensatory damages*. These damages compensate the injured party only for damages actually sustained and proved to have arisen directly from the loss of the bargain caused by the breach of contract. They simply replace what was lost because of the wrong or damage and, for this reason, are often said to "make the person whole."

■ **CASE IN POINT 13.17** Janet Murley was the vice president of marketing at Hallmark Cards, Inc., until Hallmark eliminated her position as part of a corporate restructuring. Murley and Hallmark entered into a separation agreement under which she agreed not to work in the greeting card industry for eighteen months and not to disclose or use any of Hallmark's confidential information. In exchange, Hallmark gave Murley a $735,000 severance payment.

After eighteen months, Murley took a job with Recycled Paper Greetings (RPG) for $125,000 and disclosed confidential Hallmark information to RPG. Hallmark sued for breach of contract and won. The jury awarded $860,000 in damages (the $735,000 severance payment and $125,000 that Murley received from RPG). Murley appealed. The appellate court held that Hallmark was entitled only to the return of the $735,000 severance payment. Hallmark was not entitled to the other $125,000 because that additional award would have left Hallmark better off than if Murley had not breached the contract.[20] ■

**Standard Measure.** The standard measure of compensatory damages is the difference between the value of the breaching party's promised performance under the contract and the value of her or his actual performance. This amount is reduced by any loss that the injured party has avoided.

■ **EXAMPLE 13.18** Randall contracts to perform certain services exclusively for Hernandez during the month of March for $4,000. Hernandez cancels the contract and is in breach. Randall is able to find another job during March but can earn only $3,000. He can sue Hernandez for breach and recover $1,000 as compensatory damages. Randall can also recover from Hernandez the amount that he spent to find the other job. ■ Expenses that are caused directly by a breach of contract—such as those incurred to obtain performance from another source—are known as **incidental damages.**

Note that the measure of compensatory damages often varies by type of contract. Certain types of contracts deserve special mention.

**Sale of Goods.** In a contract for the sale of goods, the usual measure of compensatory damages is an amount equal to the difference between the contract price and the market price [UCC 2–708, 2–713]. ■ **EXAMPLE 13.19** Medik Laboratories contracts to buy ten model UTS network servers from Cal Industries for $4,000 each. Cal Industries, however, fails to deliver the ten servers to Medik. The market price of the servers at the time Medik learns of the breach is $4,500. Therefore, Medik's measure of damages is $5,000 (10 × $500), plus any incidental damages (expenses) caused by the breach. ■

Sometimes, the buyer breaches when the seller has not yet produced the goods. In that situation, compensatory damages normally equal lost profits on the sale, not the difference between the contract price and the market price.

**Sale of Land.** Ordinarily, because each parcel of land is unique, the remedy for a seller's breach of a contract for a sale of real estate is specific performance. That is, the buyer is awarded the parcel of property for which she or he bargained. (*Specific performance* will be discussed more fully later in this chapter.) The majority of states follow this rule.

When the *buyer* is the party in breach, the measure of damages is typically the difference between the contract price and the market price of the land. The same measure is used when specific performance is not available (because the seller has sold the property to someone else, for instance).

---

20. *Hallmark Cards, Inc. v. Murley,* 703 F.3d 456 (8th Cir. 2013).

**Construction Contracts.** The measure of damages in a building or construction contract varies depending on which party breaches and when the breach occurs.

1. *Breach by owner.* The owner may breach at three different stages—before, during, or after performance. If the owner breaches *before performance has begun,* the contractor can recover only the profits that would have been made on the contract. (Profits equal the total contract price less the cost of materials and labor.) If the owner breaches *during performance,* the contractor can recover the profits plus the costs incurred in partially constructing the building. If the owner breaches *after the construction has been completed,* the contractor can recover the entire contract price, plus interest.

2. *Breach by contractor.* When the construction contractor breaches the contract—either by failing to begin construction or by stopping work partway through the project—the measure of damages is the cost of completion. The cost of completion includes reasonable compensation for any delay in performance. If the contractor finishes late, the measure of damages is the loss of use.

3. *Breach by both owner and contractor.* When the performance of both parties—the construction contractor and the owner—falls short of what their contract required, the courts attempt to strike a fair balance in awarding damages.

**Consequential Damages** Foreseeable damages that result from a party's breach of contract are called **consequential damages,** or *special damages.* They differ from compensatory damages in that they are caused by special circumstances beyond the contract itself. They flow from the consequences, or results, of a breach. When a seller fails to deliver goods, knowing that the buyer is planning to use or resell those goods immediately, a court may award consequential damages for the loss of profits from the planned resale.

■ **EXAMPLE 13.20** Marty contracts to buy a certain quantity of Quench, a specialty sports drink, from Nathan. Nathan knows that Marty has contracted with Ruthie to resell and ship the Quench within hours of its receipt. The beverage will then be sold to fans attending the Super Bowl. Nathan fails to deliver the Quench on time. Marty can recover the consequential damages—the loss of profits from the planned resale to Ruthie—caused by the nondelivery. (If Marty purchases Quench from another vender, he can also recover compensatory damages for any difference between the contract price and the market price.) ■

For the nonbreaching party to recover consequential damages, the breaching party must have known (or had reason to know) that special circumstances would cause the nonbreaching party to suffer an additional loss.

**Punitive Damages** Punitive damages are very seldom awarded in lawsuits for breach of contract. Because punitive damages are designed to punish a wrongdoer and set an example to deter similar conduct in the future, they have no legitimate place in contract law. A contract is simply a civil relationship between the parties. The law may compensate one party for the loss of the bargain—no more and no less. When a person's actions cause both a breach of contract and a tort (such as fraud), however, punitive damages may be available.

**Nominal Damages** When no actual damage or financial loss results from a breach of contract and only a technical injury is involved, the court may award **nominal damages** to the innocent party. Awards of nominal damages are often small, such as one dollar, but they do establish that the defendant acted wrongfully. Most lawsuits for nominal damages are brought as a matter of principle under the theory that a breach has occurred and some damages must be imposed regardless of actual loss.

## 13–3b Mitigation of Damages

In most situations, when a breach of contract occurs, the innocent injured party is held to a duty to mitigate, or reduce, the damages that he or she suffers. Under this doctrine of **mitigation of damages,** the duty owed depends on the nature of the contract.

For instance, some states require a landlord to use reasonable means to find a new tenant if a tenant abandons the premises and fails to pay rent. If an acceptable tenant is found, the landlord is required to lease the premises to this tenant to mitigate the damages recoverable from the former tenant.

The former tenant is still liable for the difference between the amount of the rent under the original lease and the rent received from the new tenant. If the landlord has not taken reasonable steps to find a new tenant, a court will likely reduce any award made by the amount of rent the landlord could have received had he or she done so.

## 13–3c Liquidated Damages versus Penalties

A **liquidated damages** provision in a contract specifies that a certain dollar amount is to be paid in the event of a *future* default or breach of contract. (*Liquidated* means determined, settled, or fixed.)

Liquidated damages differ from penalties. Like liquidated damages, a **penalty** specifies a certain amount to be paid in the event of a default or breach of contract. Unlike liquidated damages, it is designed to penalize the breaching party, not to make the innocent party whole.

Liquidated damages provisions usually are enforceable. In contrast, if a court finds that a provision calls for a penalty, the agreement as to the amount will not be enforced. Recovery will be limited to actual damages.

**Enforceability** To determine if a particular provision is for liquidated damages or for a penalty, a court must answer two questions:

1. When the contract was entered into, was it apparent that damages would be difficult to estimate in the event of a breach?
2. Was the amount set as damages a reasonable estimate and not excessive?

If the answers to both questions are yes, the provision normally will be enforced. If either answer is no, the provision usually will not be enforced.

In the following *Spotlight Case,* the court had to decide whether a clause in a contract was an enforceable liquidated damages provision or an unenforceable penalty.

## Spotlight on Liquidated Damages

# Case 13.3 Kent State University v. Ford

Court of Appeals of Ohio, Eleventh District, Portage County, 26 N.E.3d 868, 2015-Ohio-41 (2015).

**Background and Facts** Gene Ford signed a five-year contract with Kent State University in Ohio to work as the head coach for the men's basketball team. The contract provided that if Ford quit before the end of the term, he would pay liquidated damages to the school. The amount was to equal his salary ($300,000) multiplied by the number of years remaining on the contract. Laing Kennedy, Kent State's athletic director, told Ford that the contract would be renegotiated within a few years. Four years before the contract expired, however, Ford left Kent State and began to coach for Bradley University at an annual salary of $700,000. Kent State filed a suit in an Ohio state court against Ford, alleging breach of contract. The court enforced the liquidated damages clause and awarded the university $1.2 million. Ford appealed, arguing that the liquidated damages clause in his employment contract was an unenforceable penalty.

### In the Language of the Court
Diane V. *GRENDELL,* J. [Judge]
* * * *

* * * The parties agreed on an amount of damages, stated in clear terms in Ford's * * * employment contract. * * * *It is apparent that such damages were difficult, if not impossible, to determine.* * * * The departure of a university's head basketball coach may result in a decrease in ticket sales, impact the ability to successfully recruit players and community support for the team, and require a search for both a new coach and additional coaching staff. Many of these damages cannot be easily measured or proven. This is especially true given the nature of how such factors may change over the course of different coaches' tenures with a sports program or team. [Emphasis added.]
* * * *

* * * Kennedy's statements to Ford that the contract would be renegotiated within a few years made it clear that Kent State desired Ford to have long-term employment, which was necessary to establish the stability in the program that would benefit recruitment, retention of assistant coaching staff, and community participation and involvement. The breach of the contract impacted all of these areas.
* * * *

Regarding the alleged unreasonableness of the damages, * * * based on the record, we find that the damages were reasonable. * * * Finding a coach of a similar skill and experience level as Ford, which was gained based partially on the investment of Kent State in his development, would have an increased cost. This is evident from the fact that Ford was able to more than double his yearly salary when hired by Bradley University. The salary Ford earned at Bradley shows the loss of market value in coaching

**Case 13.3 Continues**

**Case 13.3 Continued**

experienced by Kent State, $400,000 per year, for four years. Although this may not have been known at the time the contract was executed, it could have been anticipated, and was presumably why Kent State wanted to renegotiate the contract * * * . There was also an asserted decrease in ticket sales, costs associated with the trips for the coaching search, and additional potential sums that may be expended.

* * * *

*As discussed extensively above, there was justification for seeking liquidated damages to compensate for Kent State's losses, and, thus, there was a valid compensatory purpose for including the clause.* * * * Given all of the circumstances and facts in this case, and the consideration of the factors above, we cannot find that the liquidated damages clause was a penalty. [Emphasis added.]

**Decision and Remedy** *A state intermediate appellate court affirmed the lower court's award. At the time Ford's contract was entered into, ascertaining the damages resulting from a breach was "difficult, if not impossible." The court found, "based on the record, . . . that the damages were reasonable." Thus, the clause was not a penalty—it had "a valid compensatory purpose."*

**Critical Thinking**

- **Cultural** *How does a college basketball team's record of wins and losses, and its ranking in its conference, support the court's decision in this case?*

---

**Liquidated Damages Common in Certain Contracts** Liquidated damages provisions are frequently used in construction contracts. For instance, a provision requiring a construction contractor to pay $300 for every day he or she is late in completing the project is a liquidated damages provision. Such provisions are also common in contracts for the sale of goods [UCC 2–718(1)]. In addition, contracts with entertainers and professional athletes often include liquidated damages provisions.

## 13-4 Equitable Remedies

Sometimes, damages are an inadequate remedy for a breach of contract. In these situations, the nonbreaching party may ask the court for an equitable remedy. Equitable remedies include rescission and restitution, specific performance, and reformation.

### 13-4a Rescission and Restitution

*Rescission* is essentially an action to undo, or terminate, a contract—to return the contracting parties to the positions they occupied prior to the transaction.[21] When

---

21. The rescission discussed here is unilateral rescission, in which only one party wants to undo the contract. In mutual rescission, both parties agree to undo the contract. Mutual rescission discharges the contract. Unilateral rescission generally is available as a remedy for breach of contract.

---

fraud, a mistake, duress, undue influence, misrepresentation, or lack of capacity to contract is present, unilateral rescission is available. Rescission may also be available by statute. The failure of one party to perform entitles the other party to rescind the contract. The rescinding party must give prompt notice to the breaching party.

Generally, to rescind a contract, both parties must make **restitution** to each other by returning goods, property, or funds previously conveyed. If the property or goods can be returned, they must be. If the goods or property have been consumed, restitution must be made in an equivalent dollar amount.

Essentially, restitution involves the plaintiff's recapture of a benefit conferred on the defendant that has unjustly enriched her or him. ■ **EXAMPLE 13.21** Katie contracts with Mikhail to design a house for her. Katie pays Mikhail $9,000 and agrees to make two more payments of $9,000 (for a total of $27,000) as the design progresses. The next day, Mikhail calls Katie and tells her that he has taken a position with a large architectural firm in another state and cannot design the house. Katie decides to hire another architect that afternoon. Katie can obtain restitution of the $9,000. ■

Restitution may be appropriate when a contract is rescinded, but the right to restitution is not limited to rescission cases. Because an award of restitution basically returns something to its rightful owner, a party can seek restitution in actions for breach of contract, tort actions, and other types of actions.

## 13–4b Specific Performance

The equitable remedy of **specific performance** calls for the performance of the act promised in the contract. This remedy is attractive to a nonbreaching party because it provides the exact bargain promised in the contract. It also avoids some of the problems inherent in a suit for damages, such as collecting a judgment and arranging another contract. In addition, the actual performance may be more valuable than the monetary damages.

Normally, however, specific performance will not be granted unless the party's legal remedy (monetary damages) is inadequate. For this reason, contracts for the sale of goods rarely qualify for specific performance. The legal remedy—monetary damages—is ordinarily adequate in such situations because substantially identical goods can be bought or sold in the market. Only if the goods are unique will a court grant specific performance. For instance, paintings, sculptures, or rare books or coins are so unique that monetary damages will not enable a buyer to obtain substantially identical substitutes in the market.

**Sale of Land** A court may grant specific performance to a buyer in an action for a breach of contract involving the sale of land. In this situation, the legal remedy of monetary damages may not compensate the buyer adequately. After all, every parcel of land is unique: the same land in the same location obviously cannot be obtained elsewhere. Only when specific performance is unavailable (such as when the seller has sold the property to someone else) will monetary damages be awarded instead.

A seller of land can also seek specific performance of the contract. ■ **CASE IN POINT 13.22** Developer Charles Ghidorzi formed Crabtree Ridge, LLC, for the sole purpose of purchasing twenty-three acres of vacant land from Cohan Lipp, LLC. Crabtree signed a contract agreeing to pay $3.1 million for the land, which would be developed and paid for in three phases. When an environmental survey showed that the land might contain some wetlands that could not be developed, Crabtree backed out of the deal. Lipp sued Crabtree for breach of contract, seeking specific performance. The court held that Lipp was entitled to specific performance of the land-sale contract.[22] ■

**Contracts for Personal Services** Contracts for personal services require one party to work personally for another party. Courts generally refuse to grant specific performance of personal-service contracts. One reason is that to order a party to perform personal services against

his or her will amounts to a type of involuntary servitude (slavery) forbidden by the U.S. Constitution.

Moreover, the courts do not want to monitor contracts for personal services, which usually require the exercise of personal judgment or talent. ■ **EXAMPLE 13.23** Nicole contracts with a surgeon to perform surgery to remove a tumor on her brain. If he refuses, the court would not compel (nor would Nicole want) the surgeon to perform under those circumstances. A court cannot ensure meaningful performance in such a situation. ■

## 13–4c Reformation

**Reformation** is an equitable remedy used when the parties have *imperfectly* expressed their agreement in writing. Reformation allows a court to rewrite the contract to reflect the parties' true intentions.

Exhibit 13–3 graphically summarizes the remedies, including reformation, that are available to the nonbreaching party.

**Fraud or Mutual Mistake Is Present** Courts order reformation most often when fraud or mutual mistake (such as a clerical error) is present. Typically, a party seeks reformation so that some other remedy may then be pursued.

■ **EXAMPLE 13.24** If Carson contracts to buy a forklift from Yoshie but their contract mistakenly refers to a crane, a mutual mistake has occurred. Accordingly, a court can reform the contract so that it conforms to the parties' intentions and accurately refers to the forklift being sold. ■

**Written Contract Incorrectly States the Parties' Oral Agreement** A court will also reform a contract when two parties enter into a binding oral contract but later make an error when they attempt to put the terms into writing. Normally, a court will allow into evidence the correct terms of the oral contract, thereby reforming the written contract.

**Covenants Not to Compete** Courts also may reform contracts that contain a written covenant not to compete. Such covenants are often included in contracts for the sale of ongoing businesses and in employment contracts. The agreements restrict the area and time in which one party can directly compete with the other party.

A covenant not to compete may be for a valid and legitimate purpose, but may impose unreasonable area or time restraints. In such instances, some courts will reform the restraints by making them reasonable and will then enforce

---

22. *Cohan Lipp, LLC v. Crabtree Ridge, LLC*, 358 Wis.2d 711, 856 N.W.2d 346 (2014).

custom page
169

**EXHIBIT 13-3** Remedies for Breach of Contract

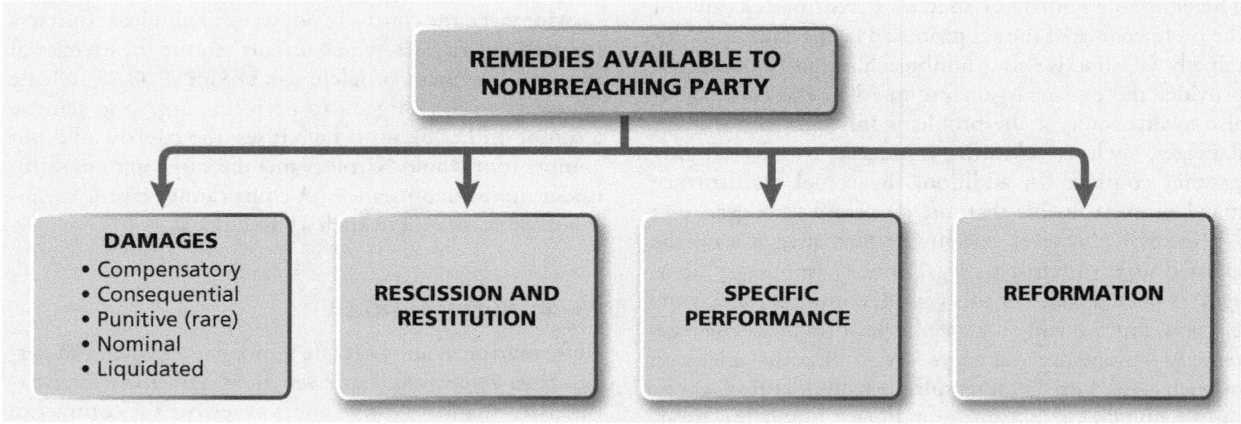

the entire contract as reformed. Other courts will throw out the entire restrictive covenant as illegal. Thus, when businesspersons create restrictive covenants, they must make sure that the restrictions imposed are reasonable.

■ **CASE IN POINT 13.25** Cardiac Study Center, Inc., a medical practice group, hired Dr. Robert Emerick. Later, Emerick became a shareholder of Cardiac and signed an agreement that included a covenant not to compete. The covenant stated that a physician who left the group promised not to practice competitively in the surrounding area for a period of five years.

After Cardiac began receiving complaints from patients and other physicians about Emerick, it terminated his employment. Emerick sued Cardiac, claiming that the covenant not to compete that he had signed was unreasonable and should be declared illegal. Ultimately, a state appellate court held that the covenant was both reasonable and enforceable. Cardiac had a legitimate interest in protecting its existing client base and prohibiting Emerick from taking its clients.[23] ■

## 13-5 Waiver of Breach

Under certain circumstances, a nonbreaching party may be willing to accept a defective performance of the contract. This knowing relinquishment of a legal right (that is, the right to require satisfactory and full performance) is called a **waiver.**

23. *Emerick v. Cardiac Study Center, Inc.*, 166 Wash.App. 1039 (2012).

### 13-5a Consequences of a Waiver of Breach

When a waiver of a breach of contract occurs, the party waiving the breach cannot take any later action on it. In effect, the waiver erases the past breach, and the contract continues as if the breach had never occurred. Of course, the waiver of breach of contract extends only to the matter waived and not to the whole contract.

### 13-5b Reasons for Waiving a Breach

Businesspersons often waive breaches of contract to obtain whatever benefit is still possible out of the contract. ■ **EXAMPLE 13.26** A seller, Purdue Resources, contracts with a buyer, Bladco Enterprises, to deliver ten thousand tons of coal on or before November 1. The contract calls for Bladco to pay by November 10 for coal delivered. Because of a coal miners' strike, coal is hard to find. Purdue breaches the contract by not tendering delivery until November 5. Bladco will likely choose to waive the seller's breach, accept delivery of the coal, and pay as contracted. ■

### 13-5c Waiver of Breach and Subsequent Breaches

Ordinarily, a waiver by a contracting party will not operate to waive subsequent, additional, or future breaches of contract. This is always true when the subsequent breaches are unrelated to the first breach. ■ **EXAMPLE 13.27** Ashton owns a multimillion-dollar apartment complex that is under construction. Ashton allows the contractor to complete a stage of construction late. By doing so, Ashton waives his right to sue for the delay. Ashton does not, however, waive the right to sue for failure to comply with engineering specifications on the same job. ■

**Pattern-of-Conduct Exception** A waiver can extend to subsequent defective performance if a reasonable person would conclude that similar defective performance in the future will be acceptable. Therefore, a *pattern of conduct* that waives a number of successive breaches will operate as a continued waiver. To change this result, the nonbreaching party should give notice to the breaching party that full performance will be required in the future.

**Effect on the Contract** The party who has rendered defective or less-than-full performance remains liable for the damages caused by the breach of contract. In effect, the waiver operates to keep the contract going. The waiver prevents the nonbreaching party from declaring the contract at an end or rescinding the contract. The contract continues, but the nonbreaching party can recover damages caused by the defective or less-than-full performance.

## 13–6 Contract Provisions Limiting Remedies

A contract may include provisions stating that no damages can be recovered for certain types of breaches or that damages will be limited to a maximum amount. A contract may also provide that the only remedy for breach is replacement, repair, or refund of the purchase price. Finally, a contract may provide that one party can seek injunctive relief if the other party breaches the contract.

Provisions stating that no damages can be recovered are called *exculpatory clauses*. Provisions that affect the availability of certain remedies are called *limitation-of-liability clauses*. The Uniform Commercial Code (UCC) provides that in a contract for the sale of goods, remedies can be limited [UCC 2–719(1)].

Whether a limitation-of-liability clause in a contract will be enforced depends on the type of breach that is excused by the provision. Normally, a provision excluding liability for fraudulent or intentional injury will not be enforced. Likewise, a clause excluding liability for illegal acts, acts that are contrary to public policy, or violations of law will not be enforced. A clause that excludes liability for negligence may be enforced in some situations when the parties have roughly equal bargaining positions.

## Reviewing: Contract Performance, Breach, and Remedies

Val's Foods signs a contract to buy 1,500 pounds of basil from Sun Farms, a small organic herb grower, as long as an independent organization inspects the crop and certifies that it contains no pesticide or herbicide residue. Val's has a contract with several restaurant chains to supply pesto and intends to use Sun Farms' basil in the pesto to fulfill these contracts. While Sun Farms is preparing to harvest the basil, an unexpected hailstorm destroys half the crop. Sun Farms attempts to purchase additional basil from other farms, but it is late in the season, and the price is twice the normal market price. Sun Farms is too small to absorb this cost and immediately notifies Val's that it will not fulfill the contract. Using the information presented in the chapter, answer the following questions.

1. Suppose that the basil does not pass the chemical-residue inspection. Which concept discussed in the chapter might allow Val's to refuse to perform the contract in this situation?
2. Under which legal theory or theories might Sun Farms claim that its obligation under the contract has been discharged by operation of law? Discuss fully.
3. Suppose that Sun Farms contacts every basil grower in the country and buys the last remaining chemical-free basil anywhere. Nevertheless, Sun Farms is able to ship only 1,475 pounds to Val's. Would this fulfill Sun Farms' obligations to Val's? Why or why not?
4. Now suppose that Sun Farms sells its operations to Happy Valley Farms. As a part of the sale, all three parties agree that Happy Valley will provide the basil as stated under the original contract. What is this type of agreement called?

**Debate This** . . . *Courts should always uphold limitation-of-liability clauses, whether or not the two parties to the contract had equal bargaining power.*

## Terms and Concepts

## Issue Spotters

**1.** Ready Foods contracts to buy two hundred carloads of frozen pizzas from Stealth Distributors. Before Ready or Stealth starts performing, can the parties call off the deal? What if Stealth has already shipped the pizzas? Explain your answers. (See *Performance and Discharge*.)

**2.** Greg contracts to build a storage shed for Haney, who pays Greg in advance, but Greg completes only half the work. Haney pays Ipswich $500 to finish the shed. If Haney sues Greg, what will be the measure of recovery? (See *Damages*.)

• **Check your answers to the Issue Spotters against the answers provided in Appendix D at the end of this text.**

## Business Scenarios

**13–1. Undue Influence.** Juan is an elderly man who lives with his nephew, Samuel. Juan is totally dependent on Samuel's support. Samuel tells Juan that unless he transfers a tract of land he owns to Samuel for a price 35 percent below its market value, Samuel will no longer support and take care of him. Juan enters into the contract. Discuss fully whether Juan can set aside this contract. (See *Voluntary Consent*.)

**13–2. Conditions of Performance.** The Caplans contract with Faithful Construction, Inc., to build a house for them for $360,000. The specifications state "all plumbing bowls and fixtures . . . to be Crane brand." The Caplans leave on vacation, and during their absence, Faithful is unable to buy and install Crane plumbing fixtures. Instead, Faithful installs Kohler brand fixtures, an equivalent in the industry. On completion of the building contract, the Caplans inspect the work, discover the substitution, and refuse to accept the house, claiming Faithful has breached the conditions set forth in the specifications. Discuss fully the Caplans' claim. (See *Performance and Discharge*.)

## Business Case Problems

**13–3. Limitation-of-Liability Clauses.** Mia Eriksson was a seventeen-year-old competitor in horseback-riding events. Her riding coach was Kristi Nunnink. Eriksson signed an agreement that released Nunnink from all liability except for damages caused by Nunnink's "direct, willful and wanton negligence." During an event at Galway Downs in Temecula, California, Eriksson's horse struck a hurdle. She fell from the horse and the horse fell on her, causing her death. Her parents, Karan and Stan Eriksson, filed a suit in a California state court against Nunnink for wrongful death. Is the limitation-of-liability agreement that Eriksson signed likely to be enforced in her parents' case? If so, how will it affect their claim? Explain. [*Eriksson v. Nunnink*, 233 Cal.App.4th 708, 183 Cal.Rptr.3d 234 (4 Dist. 2015)] (See *Contract Provisions Limiting Remedies*.)

**13–4. Business Case Problem with Sample Answer— Discharge by Operation of Law.**  Dr. Jake Lambert signed an employment agreement with Baptist Health Services, Inc., to provide cardiothoracic surgery services to Baptist Memorial Hospital–North Mississippi, Inc., in Oxford, Mississippi. Complaints about Lambert's behavior arose almost immediately. He was evaluated by a team of doctors and psychologists, who diagnosed him as suffering from obsessive-compulsive personality disorder and concluded that he was unfit to practice medicine. Based on this conclusion, the hospital suspended his staff privileges. Citing the suspension, Baptist Health Services claimed that Lambert had breached his employment contract. What is Lambert's best defense to this claim? Explain. [*Baptist Memorial Hospital–North Mississippi, Inc. v. Lambert,*

157 So.3d 109 (Miss.App. 2015)] (See *Performance and Discharge.*)

- **For a sample answer to Problem 13–4, go to Appendix E at the end of this text.**

**13–5. Fraudulent Misrepresentation.** Vianna Stibal owns and operates the ThetaHealing Institute of Knowledge (THInK) in Idaho Falls, Idaho. ThetaHealing is Stibal's "self-discovered" healing method. In her book *Go Up and Seek God,* Stibal stated that she had been diagnosed with cancer and had cured herself using ThetaHealing. But Stibal's representation that she cured herself of cancer was false, and she knew it—her medical records did not confirm a cancer diagnosis. Believing Stibal's claim, Kara Alexander traveled from New York to Idaho to pay for, and attend, classes in ThetaHealing from Stibal. Later, Alexander began to question the validity of her THinK degree. What are the elements of a cause of action for fraudulent misrepresentation? Do the facts in this situation meet these requirements? Discuss. [*Alexander v. Stibal,* 160 Idaho 10, 368 P.3d 630 (2016)] (See *Voluntary Consent.*)

**13–6. Damages.** Robert Morris was a licensed insurance agent working for his father's independent insurance agency when he contacted Farmers Insurance Exchange in Alabama about becoming a Farmers agent. According to Farmers' company policy, Morris was an unsuitable candidate due to his relationship with his father's agency. But no Farmers representative told Morris of this policy, and none of the documents that he signed expressed it. Farmers trained Morris and appointed him its agent. About three years later, however, Farmers terminated the appointment for "a conflict of interest because his father was in the insurance business." Morris filed a suit in an Alabama state court against Farmers, claiming that he had been fraudulently induced to leave his father's agency to work for Farmers. If Morris was successful, what type of damages was he most likely awarded? What was the measure of damages? Discuss. [*Farmers Insurance Exchange v. Morris,* __ So.3d __, 2016 WL 661671 (Ala. 2016)] (See *Damages.*)

**13–7. Conditions.** H&J Ditching & Excavating, Inc., was hired by JRSF, LLC, to perform excavating and grading work on Terra Firma, a residential construction project in West Knox County, Tennessee. Cornerstone Community Bank financed the project with a loan to JRSF. As the work progressed, H&J received payments totaling 90 percent of the price on its contract. JRSF then defaulted on the loan from Cornerstone, and Cornerstone foreclosed and took possession of the property. H&J filed a suit in a Tennessee state court against the bank to recover the final payment on its contract. The bank responded that H&J had not received its payment because it had failed to obtain an engineer's certificate of final completion, a condition under its contract with JRSF. H&J responded that it had completed all the work it had contracted to do. What type of contract condition does obtaining the engineer's certificate represent? Is H&J entitled to the final payment? Discuss. [*H&J Ditching & Excavating, Inc. v. Cornerstone Community Bank,* __ S.W.3d __, 2016 WL 675554 (Tenn.App. 2016)] (See *Performance and Discharge.*)

**13–8. A Question of Ethics—Remedies.** *On a weekday, Tamara Cohen, a real estate broker, showed a townhouse owned by Ray and Harriet Mayer to Jessica Seinfeld, the wife of comedian Jerry Seinfeld. On the weekend, when Cohen was unavailable because her religious beliefs prevented her from working, the Seinfelds revisited the townhouse on their own and agreed to buy it. The contract stated that the "buyers will pay buyer's real estate broker's fees." [Cohen v. Seinfeld, 15 Misc.3d 1118(A), 839 N.Y.S.2d 432 (Sup. 2007)] (See Equitable Remedies.)*

(a) Is Cohen entitled to payment even though she was not available to show the townhouse to the Seinfelds on the weekend? Explain.

(b) What obligation do parties involved in business deals owe to each other with respect to their religious beliefs? How might the situation in this case have been avoided?

**13–9. Special Case Analysis—Material Breach.** Go to Case Analysis 13.2, *Kohel v. Bergen Auto Enterprises, L.L.C.* Read the excerpt, and answer the following questions.

(a) **Issue:** This case involved allegations of breach of contract involving which parties and for what actions?

(b) **Rule of Law:** What is the difference between a *material* breach and a *minor* breach of contract?

(c) **Applying the Rule of Law:** How did the court determine which party was in material breach of the contract in this case?

(d) **Conclusion:** Was the defendant liable for breach? Why or why not?

# Legal Reasoning Group Activity

**13–10. Anticipatory Repudiation.** ABC Clothiers, Inc., has a contract with Taylor & Sons, a retailer, to deliver one thousand summer suits to Taylor's place of business on or before May 1. On April 1, Taylor receives a letter from ABC informing him that ABC will not be able to make the delivery as scheduled. Taylor is very upset, as he had planned a big ad campaign and wants to sue ABC right away. (See *Performance and Discharge.*)

(a) The first group will discuss whether Taylor can immediately sue ABC for breach of contract (on April 2).

(b) Now suppose that Taylor's son, Tom, tells his father that they cannot file a lawsuit until ABC actually fails to deliver the suits on May 1. The second group will decide who is correct, Taylor senior or Tom.

(c) Assume that Taylor & Sons can either file immediately or wait until ABC fails to deliver the goods. The third group will evaluate which course of action is better, given the circumstances.

# Answers to the *Issue Spotters*

1. *Before Ready or Stealth starts performing, can the parties call off the deal? What if Stealth has already shipped the pizzas? Explain your answers.* Contracts that are executory on both sides—contracts on which neither party has performed—can be rescinded solely by agreement. Contracts that are executed on one side—contracts on which one party has performed—can be rescinded only if the party who has performed receives consideration for the promise to call off the deal.

2. *If Haney sues Greg, what will be the measure of recovery?* A nonbreaching party is entitled to his or her benefit of the bargain under the contract. Here, the innocent party is entitled to be put in the position she would have been in if the contract had been fully performed. The measure of the benefit is the cost to complete the work ($500). These are compensatory damages.

# Sample Answers for *Business Case Problems with Sample Answer*

**Problem 13–4.** *Discharge by Operation of Law.* Lambert's best defense to Baptist's allegation of breach of contract is the doctrine of impossibility. Under this doctrine, if, after a contract has been made, a supervening event makes performance impossible in an objective sense, the contract is discharged. The doctrine applies only when the parties could not have reasonably foreseen the event that renders the performance impossible. One of the situations in which this doctrine applies occurs when a party whose personal performance is essential to the completion of the contract becomes incapacitated prior to performance.

In the facts of this problem, Baptist hired Lambert to provide certain surgical services to Baptist Memorial Hospital–North Mississippi. When complaints about his behavior arose, a team of doctors and psychologists conducted an evaluation, diagnosed him as suffering from obsessive-compulsive personality disorder, and concluded that he was unfit to practice medicine. The hospital suspended his staff privileges. Baptist terminated his employment and filed a suit against him for breach. The doctrine of impossibility discharges Lambert from the performance of his contract—his performance was made impossible through no fault of his own.

In the actual case on which this problem is based, in Baptist's suit against Lambert, the court issued a judgment in the defendant's favor. A state intermediate appellate court applied the doctrine of impossibility to affirm this judgment.

# Chapter 8

# CHAPTER

# Tort Law

Part of doing business today—and, indeed, part of everyday life—is the risk of being involved in a lawsuit. The list of circumstances in which businesspersons can be sued is long and varied. A customer who is injured by a security guard at a business establishment, for instance, may sue the business owner, claiming that the security guard's conduct was intentionally wrongful. A person who slips and falls at a retail store may sue the company for negligence.

Any time that one party's allegedly wrongful conduct causes injury to another, an action may arise under the law of *torts* (the word *tort* is French for "wrong"). Through tort law, society compensates those who have suffered injuries as a result of the wrongful conduct of others. Many of the lawsuits brought by or against business firms are based on various tort theories.

## 6–1 The Basis of Tort Law

Two notions serve as the basis of all **torts:** wrongs and compensation. Tort law is designed to compensate those who have suffered a loss or injury due to another person's wrongful act. In a tort action, one person or group brings a lawsuit against another person or group to obtain compensation (monetary damages) or other relief for the harm suffered.

### 6–1a The Purpose of Tort Law

Generally, the purpose of tort law is to provide remedies for the violation of various *protected interests*. Society recognizes an interest in personal physical safety. Thus, tort law provides remedies for acts that cause physical injury or that interfere with physical security and freedom of movement. Society also recognizes an interest in protecting property, and tort law provides remedies for acts that cause destruction of or damage to property.

### 6–1b Damages Available in Tort Actions

Because the purpose of tort law is to compensate the injured party for the damage suffered, you need to have an understanding of the types of damages that plaintiffs seek in tort actions. Note that legal usage distinguishes between the terms *damage* and *damages. Damage* refers to harm or injury to persons or property, while **damages** refers to monetary compensation for such harm or injury.

**Compensatory Damages** A plaintiff is awarded **compensatory damages** to compensate or reimburse the plaintiff for actual losses. Thus, the goal is to make the plaintiff whole and put her or him in the same position that she or he would have been in had the tort not occurred. Compensatory damages awards are often broken down into *special damages* and *general damages.*

**Special damages** compensate the plaintiff for quantifiable monetary losses, such as medical expenses and lost wages and benefits (now and in the future). Special damages might also be awarded to compensate for extra costs, the loss of irreplaceable items, and the costs of repairing or replacing damaged property.

■ **CASE IN POINT 6.1** Seaway Marine Transport operates the *Enterprise,* a large cargo ship, which has twenty-two hatches for storing coal. When the *Enterprise* positioned itself to receive a load of coal on the shores of Lake Erie, in Ohio, it struck a land-based coal-loading machine operated by Bessemer & Lake Erie Railroad Company. A federal court found Seaway liable and awarded $522,000 in special damages to compensate Bessemer for the cost of repairing the damage to the loading boom.[1] ■

**General damages** compensate individuals (not companies) for the nonmonetary aspects of the harm suffered, such as pain and suffering. A court might award general damages for physical or emotional pain and suffering, loss of companionship, loss of consortium (losing

---

1. *Bessemer & Lake Erie Railroad Co. v. Seaway Marine Transport,* 357 F.3d 596 (6th Cir. 2010).

the emotional and physical benefits of a spousal relationship), disfigurement, loss of reputation, or loss or impairment of mental or physical capacity.

**Punitive Damages** Occasionally, the courts also award **punitive damages** in tort cases to punish the wrongdoer and deter others from similar wrongdoing. Punitive damages are appropriate only when the defendant's conduct was particularly egregious (flagrant) or reprehensible (blameworthy).

Usually, this means that punitive damages are available in *intentional* tort actions and only rarely in negligence lawsuits (negligence actions will be discussed later in this chapter). They may be awarded, however, in suits involving *gross negligence*. Gross negligence can be defined as an intentional failure to perform a manifest duty in reckless disregard of the consequences of such a failure for the life or property of another.

Courts exercise great restraint in granting punitive damages to plaintiffs in tort actions because punitive damages are subject to limitations under the due process clause of the U.S. Constitution. The United States Supreme Court has held that to the extent that an award of punitive damages is grossly excessive, it furthers no legitimate purpose and violates due process requirements.[2] Consequently, an appellate court will sometimes reduce the amount of punitive damages awarded to a plaintiff on the ground that it is excessive and thereby violates the due process clause.

**Legislative Caps on Damages** State laws may limit the amount of damages—both punitive and general—that can be awarded to the plaintiff. More than half of the states have placed caps ranging from $250,000 to $750,000 on noneconomic general damages (such as for pain and suffering), especially in medical malpractice suits. More than thirty states have limited punitive damages, with some imposing outright bans.

### 6–1c Classification of Torts

There are two broad classifications of torts: *intentional torts* and *unintentional torts* (torts involving negligence). The classification of a particular tort depends largely on how the tort occurs (intentionally or negligently) and the surrounding circumstances. Intentional torts result from the intentional violation of person or property (fault plus intent). Negligence results from the breach of a duty to act reasonably (fault without intent).

2. *State Farm Mutual Automobile Insurance Co. v. Campbell*, 538 U.S. 408, 123 S.Ct. 1513, 155 L.Ed.2d 585 (2003).

### 6–1d Defenses

Even if a plaintiff proves all the elements of a tort, the defendant can raise a number of legally recognized *defenses* (reasons why the plaintiff should not obtain damages). A successful defense releases the defendant from partial or full liability for the tortious act.

The defenses available may vary depending on the specific tort involved. A common defense to intentional torts against persons, for instance, is *consent*. When a person consents to the act that damages her or him, there is generally no liability. The most widely used defense in negligence actions is *comparative negligence*.

In addition, most states have a *statute of limitations* that establishes the time limit (often two years from the date of discovering the harm) within which a particular type of lawsuit can be filed. After that time period has run, the plaintiff can no longer file a claim.

## 6–2 Intentional Torts against Persons

An **intentional tort,** as the term implies, requires intent. The **tortfeasor** (the one committing the tort) must intend to commit an act, the consequences of which interfere with another's personal or business interests in a way not permitted by law. An evil or harmful motive is not required—in fact, the person committing the action may even have a beneficial motive for doing what turns out to be a tortious act.

In tort law, *intent* means only that the person intended the consequences of his or her act or knew with substantial certainty that specific consequences would result from the act. The law generally assumes that individuals intend the *normal* consequences of their actions. Thus, forcefully pushing another—even if done in jest—is an intentional tort (if injury results), because the object of a strong push can ordinarily be expected to fall down.

In addition, intent can be transferred when a defendant intends to harm one individual, but unintentionally harms a second person. This is called **transferred intent.** ■ **EXAMPLE 6.2** Alex swings a bat intending to hit Blake but misses and hits Carson instead. Carson can sue Alex for the tort of battery (discussed shortly) because Alex's intent to harm Blake can be transferred to Carson. ■

### 6–2a Assault

An **assault** is any intentional and unexcused threat of immediate harmful or offensive contact—words or acts that create a reasonably believable threat. An assault can occur even if there is no actual contact with the plaintiff, provided that the defendant's conduct creates a reasonable apprehension of imminent harm in the plaintiff. Tort law aims to protect individuals from having to expect harmful or offensive contact.

## 6–2b Battery

If the act that created the apprehension is *completed* and results in harm to the plaintiff, it is a **battery**—an unexcused and harmful or offensive physical contact *intentionally* performed. ■ **EXAMPLE 6.3** Ivan threatens Jean with a gun and then shoots her. The pointing of the gun at Jean is an assault. The firing of the gun (if the bullet hits Jean) is a battery. ■

The contact can be harmful, or it can be merely offensive (such as an unwelcome kiss). Physical injury need not occur. The contact can involve any part of the body or anything attached to it—for instance, a hat, a purse, or a jacket. The contact can be made by the defendant or by some force set in motion by the defendant, such as a rock thrown by the defendant. Whether the contact is offensive is determined by the *reasonable person standard*.[3]

If the plaintiff shows that there was contact, and the jury (or judge, if there is no jury) agrees that the contact was offensive, then the plaintiff has a right to compensation. A plaintiff may be compensated for the emotional harm or loss of reputation resulting from a battery, as well as for physical harm. A defendant may assert self-defense or defense of others in an attempt to justify his or her conduct.

## 6–2c False Imprisonment

*False imprisonment* is the intentional confinement or restraint of another person's activities without justification. False imprisonment interferes with the freedom to move without restraint. The confinement can be accomplished through the use of physical barriers, physical restraint, or threats of physical force. Moral pressure does not constitute false imprisonment. It is essential that the person being restrained does not wish to be restrained. (The plaintiff's consent to the restraint bars any liability.)

Businesspersons often face suits for false imprisonment after they have attempted to confine a suspected shoplifter for questioning. Under the "privilege to detain" granted to merchants in most states, a merchant can use *reasonable force* to detain or delay persons suspected of shoplifting and hold them for the police. Although laws pertaining to this privilege vary from state to state, generally any detention must be conducted in a *reasonable* manner and for only a *reasonable* length of time. Undue force or unreasonable detention can lead to liability for the business.

Cities and counties may also face lawsuits for false imprisonment if they detain individuals without reason. ■ **CASE IN POINT 6.4** Police arrested Adetokunbo Shoyoye for riding the subway without a ticket and for a theft that had been committed by someone who had stolen his identity. A court ordered him to be released, but a county employee mistakenly confused Shoyoye's paperwork with that of another person who was scheduled to be sent to state prison. As a result, instead of being released, Shoyoye was held in county jail for more than two weeks. Shoyoye later sued the county for false imprisonment and won.[4] ■

## 6–2d Intentional Infliction of Emotional Distress

The tort of *intentional infliction of emotional distress* involves an intentional act that amounts to extreme and outrageous conduct resulting in severe emotional distress to another. To be **actionable** (capable of serving as the ground for a lawsuit), the act must be extreme and outrageous to the point that it exceeds the bounds of decency accepted by society.

**Outrageous Conduct** Courts in most jurisdictions are wary of emotional distress claims and confine them to situations involving truly outrageous behavior. Generally, repeated annoyances (such as those experienced by a person who is being stalked), coupled with threats, are enough. Acts that cause indignity or annoyance alone usually are not sufficient.

■ **EXAMPLE 6.5** A father attacks a man who has had consensual sexual relations with the father's nineteen-year-old daughter. The father handcuffs the man to a steel pole and threatens to kill him unless he leaves town immediately. The father's conduct may be sufficiently extreme and outrageous to be actionable as an intentional infliction of emotional distress. ■

**Limited by the First Amendment** When the outrageous conduct consists of speech about a public figure,

---

3. The *reasonable person standard* is an "objective" test of how a reasonable person would have acted under the same circumstances. See "The Duty of Care and Its Breach" later in this chapter.

4. *Shoyoye v. County of Los Angeles*, 203 Cal.App.4th 947, 137 Cal.Rptr.3d 839 (2012).

the First Amendment's guarantee of freedom of speech also limits emotional distress claims.

■ **CASE IN POINT 6.6** *Hustler* magazine once printed a false advertisement that showed a picture of the late Reverend Jerry Falwell and described him as having lost his virginity to his mother in an outhouse while he was drunk. Falwell sued the magazine for intentional infliction of emotional distress and won, but the United States Supreme Court overturned the decision. The Court held that parodies of public figures are protected under the First Amendment from intentional infliction of emotional distress claims. (The Court uses the same standards that apply to public figures in defamation lawsuits, discussed next.)[5] ■

## 6–2e Defamation

The freedom of speech guaranteed by the First Amendment is not absolute. The courts are required to balance the vital guarantee of free speech against other pervasive

---

5. *Hustler Magazine, Inc. v. Falwell*, 485 U.S. 46, 108 S.Ct. 876, 99 L.Ed.2d 41 (1988). For another example of how the courts protect parody, see *Busch v. Viacom International, Inc.*, 477 F.Supp.2d 764 (N.D.Tex. 2007), involving a false endorsement of televangelist Pat Robertson's diet shake.

and strong social interests, including society's interest in preventing and redressing attacks on reputation.

**Defamation** of character involves wrongfully hurting a person's good reputation. The law imposes a general duty on all persons to refrain from making false, defamatory *statements of fact* about others. Breaching this duty in writing or other permanent form (such as a digital recording) involves the tort of **libel.** Breaching this duty orally involves the tort of **slander.** The tort of defamation also arises when a false statement of fact is made about a person's product, business, or legal ownership rights to property.

Establishing defamation involves proving the following elements:

1. The defendant made a false statement of fact.
2. The statement was understood as being about the plaintiff and tended to harm the plaintiff's reputation.
3. The statement was published to at least one person other than the plaintiff.
4. If the plaintiff is a public figure, she or he must also prove *actual malice,* discussed later in the chapter.

The following case involved the application of free speech guarantees to online reviews of professional services.

---

## Case Analysis 6.1

# Blake v. Giustibelli

District Court of Appeal of Florida, Fourth District, 182 So.3d 881, 41 Fla.L.Weekly D122 (2016).

### In the Language of the Court

*CIKLIN*, C.J. [Chief Judge]

\* \* \* \*

[Ann-Marie] Giustibelli represented Copia Blake in a dissolution of marriage proceeding brought against Peter Birzon. After a breakdown in the attorney-client relationship between Giustibelli and her client[,] Blake, and oddly, Birzon as well, took to the Internet to post defamatory reviews of Giustibelli. In response, Giustibelli brought suit [in a Florida state court against Blake and Birzon], pleading a count for libel.

Blake's and Birzon's posted Internet reviews contained the following statements:

> This lawyer represented me in my divorce. She was combative and

explosive and took my divorce to a level of anger which caused major suffering of my minor children. She insisted I was an emotionally abused wife who couldn't make rational decisions which caused my case to drag on in the system for a year and a half so her FEES would continue to multiply!! She misrepresented her fees with regards to the contract I initially signed. The contract she submitted to the courts for her fees were 4 times her original quote and pages of the original had been exchanged to support her claims, only the signature page was the same. Shame on me that I did not have an original copy, but like an idiot \* \* \* I trusted my lawyer. Don't mistake sincerity for honesty because I assure you, that in this attorney's case, they are NOT the same thing. She absolutely perpetuates

the horrible image of attorneys who are only out for the money and themselves. Although I know this isn't the case and there are some very good honest lawyers out there, Mrs. Giustibelli is simply not one of the "good ones." Horrible horrible experience. Use anyone else, it would have to be a better result.

\* \* \* \*

No integrity. Will say one thing and do another. Her fees outweigh the truth. Altered her charges to 4 times the original quote with no explanation. Do not use her. Don't mistake sincerity for honesty. In her case, they're not at all the same. Will literally lie to your face if it means more money for her. Get someone else.

**Case 6.1 Continues**

**Case 6.1 Continued**

\* \* \* Anyone else would do a superior effort for you.

\* \* \* \*

I accepted an initial VERY fair offer from my ex. Mrs. Giustibelli convinced me to "crush" him and that I could have permanent etc. Spent over a year (and 4 times her original estimate) to arrive at the same place we started at. Caused unnecessary chaos and fear with my kids, convinced me that my ex cheated (which he didn't), that he was hiding money (which he wasn't), and was mad at ME when I realized her fee circus had gone on long enough and finally said "stop." Altered her fee structures, actually replaced original documents with others to support her charges and generally gave the kind of poor service you only hear about. I'm not a disgruntled

ex-wife. I'm just the foolish person who believes that a person's word should be backed by integrity. Not even remotely true in this case. I've had 2 prior attorneys and never ever have I seen ego and monies be so blatantly out of control.

Both Blake and Birzon admitted to posting the reviews on various Internet sites. The evidence showed that Blake had agreed to pay her attorney the amount reflected on the written retainer agreement—$300 an hour. Blake and Birzon both admitted at trial that Giustibelli had not charged Blake four times more than what was quoted in the agreement. The court entered judgment in favor of Giustibelli and awarded punitive damages of $350,000.

On appeal, Blake and Birzon argue that their Internet reviews constituted

statements of opinion and thus were protected by the First Amendment and not actionable as defamation. We disagree. *An action for libel will lie for a false and unprivileged publication by letter, or otherwise, which exposes a person to distrust, hatred, contempt, ridicule or obloquy [censure or disgrace] or which causes such person to be avoided, or which has a tendency to injure such person in their office, occupation, business or employment.* [Emphasis added.]

Here, all the reviews contained allegations that Giustibelli lied to Blake regarding the attorney's fee. Two of the reviews contained the allegation that Giustibelli falsified a contract. These are factual allegations, and the evidence showed they were false.

\* \* \* \*

*Affirmed.*

### Legal Reasoning Questions

**1.** What is the standard for the protection of free speech guaranteed by the First Amendment?

**2.** How did this standard apply to the statements posted online by Blake and Birzon?

**3.** The First Amendment normally protects statements of opinion, and this can be an effective defense against a charge of defamation. Does it seem reasonable to disregard this defense, however, if *any* assertion of fact within a statement of opinion is false? Explain.

---

**Statement-of-Fact Requirement** Often at issue in defamation lawsuits (including online defamation) is whether the defendant made a statement of fact or a *statement of opinion.* Statements of opinion normally are not actionable, because they are protected under the First Amendment.

In other words, making a negative statement about another person is not defamation unless the statement is false and represents something as a fact rather than a personal opinion. ■ **EXAMPLE 6.7** The statement "Lane cheats on his taxes," if false, can lead to liability for defamation. The statement "Lane is a jerk" cannot constitute defamation because it is clearly an opinion. ■

**The Publication Requirement** The basis of the tort of defamation is the publication of a statement or statements that hold an individual up to contempt, ridicule, or

hatred. *Publication* here means that the defamatory statements are communicated (either intentionally or accidentally) to persons other than the defamed party.

The courts have generally held that even dictating a letter to a secretary constitutes publication, although the publication may be privileged (a concept that will be explained shortly). Moreover, if a third party merely overhears defamatory statements by chance, the courts usually hold that this also constitutes publication. Defamatory statements made via the Internet are actionable as well. Note also that any individual who repeats or republishes defamatory statements normally is liable even if that person reveals the source of the statements. ■ **CASE IN POINT 6.8** Eddy Ramirez, a meat cutter at Costco Wholesale Corporation, was involved in a workplace incident with a coworker, and Costco gave him a notice of suspension. After an investigation in which coworkers were interviewed, Costco fired Ramirez. Ramirez sued, claiming that the suspension notice was defamatory. The court ruled in Costco's favor. Ramirez could not establish defamation, because he had not shown that the suspension notice was published to any third parties. Costco did nothing beyond what was necessary to investigate the events that led to Ramirez's termination.[6] ∎

**Damages for Libel** Once a defendant's liability for libel is established, general damages are presumed as a matter of law. General damages are designed to compensate the plaintiff for nonspecific harms such as disgrace or dishonor in the eyes of the community, humiliation, injured reputation, and emotional distress—harms that are difficult to measure. In other words, to recover damages, the plaintiff need not prove that he or she was actually harmed in any specific way as a result of the libelous statement.

**Damages for Slander** In contrast to cases alleging libel, in a case alleging slander, the plaintiff must prove *special damages* to establish the defendant's liability. The plaintiff must show that the slanderous statement caused her or him to suffer actual economic or monetary losses.

Unless this initial hurdle of proving special damages is overcome, a plaintiff alleging slander normally cannot go forward with the suit and recover any damages. This requirement is imposed in slander cases because oral statements have a temporary quality. In contrast, a libelous (written) statement has the quality of permanence and can be circulated widely, especially through tweets and blogs. Also, libel usually results from some degree of deliberation by the author.

**Slander *Per Se*** Exceptions to the burden of proving special damages in cases alleging slander are made for certain types of slanderous statements. If a false statement constitutes "slander *per se*," it is actionable with no proof of special damages required. In most states, the following four types of declarations are considered to be slander *per se*:

1. A statement that another has a "loathsome" disease (such as a sexually transmitted disease).
2. A statement that another has committed improprieties while engaging in a profession or trade.
3. A statement that another has committed or has been imprisoned for a serious crime.

4. A statement that a person is unchaste or has engaged in serious sexual misconduct. (This usually applies only to unmarried persons and sometimes only to women.)

**Defenses to Defamation** Truth is normally an absolute defense against a defamation charge. In other words, if a defendant in a defamation case can prove that the allegedly defamatory statements of fact were true, normally no tort has been committed.

∎ **CASE IN POINT 6.9** David McKee, a neurologist, went to examine a patient who had been transferred from the intensive care unit (ICU) to a private room. In the room were family members of the patient, including his son. The patient's son later made the following post on a "rate your doctor" Web site: "[Dr. McKee] seemed upset that my father had been moved [into a private room]. Never having met my father or his family, Dr. McKee said 'When you weren't in ICU, I had to spend time finding out if you transferred or died.' When we gaped at him, he said 'Well, 44 percent of hemorrhagic strokes die within 30 days. I guess this is the better option.'"

McKee filed suit for defamation but lost. The court found that all the statements made by the son were essentially true, and truth is a complete defense to a defamation action.[7] ∎ In other words, true statements are not actionable no matter how disparaging. Even the presence of minor inaccuracies of expression or detail does not render basically true statements false.

Other defenses to defamation may exist if the speech is privileged or if it concerns a public figure. We discuss these defenses next. Note that the majority of defamation actions are filed in state courts, and state laws differ somewhat in the defenses they allow.

**Privileged Communications.** In some circumstances, a person will not be liable for defamatory statements because she or he enjoys a **privilege,** or immunity. Privileged communications are of two types: absolute and qualified.[8] Only in judicial proceedings and certain government proceedings is an *absolute privilege* granted. Thus, statements made by attorneys and judges in the courtroom during a trial are absolutely privileged, as are statements made by government officials during legislative debate.

---

6. *Ramirez v. Costco Wholesale Corp.,* 2014 WL 2696737 (Ct.Sup.Ct. 2014).

7. *McKee v. Laurion,* 825 N.W.2d 725 (Minn.Sup. 2013).
8. Note that the term *privileged communication* in this context is not the same as privileged communication between a professional, such as an attorney, and his or her client.

In other situations, a person will not be liable for defamatory statements because he or she has a *qualified,* or *conditional, privilege.* An employer's statements in written evaluations of employees, for instance, are protected by a qualified privilege. Generally, if the statements are made in good faith and the publication is limited to those who have a legitimate interest in the communication, the statements fall within the area of qualified privilege.

■ **EXAMPLE 6.10** Jorge has worked at Google for five years and is being considered for a management position. His supervisor, Lydia, writes a memo about Jorge's performance to those evaluating him for the position. The memo contains certain negative statements, which Lydia honestly believes are true. If Lydia limits the disclosure of the memo to company representatives, her statements will likely be protected by a qualified privilege. ■

**Public Figures.** Politicians, entertainers, professional athletes, and others in the public eye are considered **public figures.** Public figures are regarded as "fair game." False and defamatory statements about public figures that are published in the media will not constitute defamation unless the statements are made with **actual malice.**[9] To be made with actual malice, a statement must be made *with either knowledge of its falsity or a reckless disregard of the truth.*

Statements made about public figures, especially when they are communicated via a public medium, usually relate to matters of general interest. They are made about people who substantially affect all of us. Furthermore, public figures generally have some access to a public medium for answering belittling falsehoods about themselves. For these reasons, public figures have a greater burden of proof in defamation cases—to show actual malice—than do private individuals.

■ **CASE IN POINT 6.11** *In Touch* magazine published a story about a former call girl who claimed to have slept with legendary soccer player David Beckham more than once. Beckham sued *In Touch* magazine for libel, seeking $25 million in damages. He said that he had never met the woman, had not cheated on his wife with her, and had not paid her for sex. After months of litigation, a federal district court dismissed the case because Beckham could not show that the magazine had acted with actual malice. Whether or not the statements in the article were accurate, there was no evidence that the defendants had made the statements with knowledge of their falsity or reckless disregard for the truth.[10] ■

---

9. *New York Times Co. v. Sullivan,* 376 U.S. 254, 84 S.Ct. 710, 11 L.Ed.2d 686 (1964).
10. *Beckham v. Bauer Pub. Co., L.P.,* 2011 WL 977570 (2011).

## 6–2f Invasion of Privacy

A person has a right to solitude and freedom from prying public eyes—in other words, to privacy. The courts have held that certain amendments to the U.S. Constitution imply a right to privacy. Some state constitutions explicitly provide for privacy rights, as do a number of federal and state statutes.

Tort law also safeguards these rights through the tort of *invasion of privacy.* Generally, to sue successfully for an invasion of privacy, a person must have a reasonable expectation of privacy, and the invasion must be highly offensive. (See this chapter's *Digital Update* feature for a discussion of how invasion of privacy claims can arise when someone posts pictures or videos taken with digital devices.)

**Invasion of Privacy under the Common Law**
The following four acts qualify as an invasion of privacy under the common law:

1. *Intrusion into an individual's affairs or seclusion.* Invading someone's home or searching someone's briefcase or laptop without authorization is an invasion of privacy. This tort has been held to extend to eavesdropping by wiretap, unauthorized scanning of a bank account, compulsory blood testing, and window peeping. ■ **EXAMPLE 6.12** A female sports reporter for ESPN is digitally videoed while naked through the peephole in the door of her hotel room. She will probably win a lawsuit against the man who took the video and posted it on the Internet. ■

2. *False light.* Publication of information that places a person in a false light is also an invasion of privacy. For instance, writing a story that attributes to a person ideas and opinions not held by that person is an invasion of privacy. (Publishing such a story could involve the tort of defamation as well.) ■ **EXAMPLE 6.13** An Iowa newspaper prints an article saying that nineteen-year-old Yassine Alam is part of the terrorist organization Islamic State of Iraq (ISIL). Next to the article is a photo of Yassine's brother, Salaheddin. Salaheddin can sue the paper for putting him in a false light by using his photo. If the report is not true, and Yassine is not involved with ISIL, Yassine can sue the paper for defamation. ■

3. *Public disclosure of private facts.* This type of invasion of privacy occurs when a person publicly discloses private facts about an individual that an ordinary person would find objectionable or embarrassing. A newspaper account of a private citizen's sex life or financial affairs could be an actionable invasion of

## DIGITAL UPDATE    Revenge Porn and Invasion of Privacy

Nearly every digital device today takes photos and videos at virtually no cost. Software allows the recording of conversations via Skype. Many couples immortalize their "private moments" using such digital devices. One partner may take a racy selfie and send it as an attachment to a text message to the other partner, for example.

Occasionally, after a couple breaks off their relationship, one of them seeks a type of digital revenge. The result, called revenge porn, has been defined in the Cyber Civil Rights Initiative as "the online distribution of sexually explicit images of a non-consenting individual with the intent to humiliate that person."

Until relatively recently, few states had criminal statutes that covered revenge porn. Therefore, victims have sued on the basis of (1) invasion of privacy, (2) public disclosure of private facts, and (3) intentional infliction of emotional distress.

### It Is More Than Just Pictures and Videos

Perhaps the worst form of revenge porn occurs when the perpetrator provides detailed information about the victim. Such information may include the victim's name, Facebook page, address, and phone number, as well as the victim's workplace and children's names. This information, along with the sexually explicit photos and videos, are posted on hosting Web sites. Many such Web sites have been shut down, as was the case with IsAnybodyDown? and Texxxan.com. But others are still active, usually with offshore servers and foreign domain name owners.

### The Injurious Results of Revenge Porn

Of course, victims of revenge porn suffer extreme embarrassment. They may also have their reputations ruined. Some have lost their jobs. Others have been unable to obtain jobs because employers have seen their pictures online. A number of victims have been stalked in the physical world and harassed online and offline. When attempts to have offending photos removed from Web sites have failed, victims have changed their phone numbers and sometimes their names.

### A Class-Action Lawsuit

Hollie Toups, along with twenty-two other female plaintiffs, sued the domain name registrar and Web hosting company GoDaddy in a Texas court. Although GoDaddy did not create the defamatory and offensive material at issue, GoDaddy knew of the content and did not remove it. The plaintiffs asserted causes of action "for intentional infliction of emotional distress," among other claims.

Additionally, the plaintiffs argued that "by its knowing participation in these unlawful activities, GoDaddy has also committed the intentional Texas tort of invasion of privacy . . . as well as intrusion on Plaintiffs' right to seclusion, the public disclosure of their private facts, [and] the wrongful appropriation of their names and likenesses. . . ." GoDaddy sought to dismiss the case, and an appeals court eventually granted the motion to dismiss.[a]

Another Texas woman had better luck. The woman's ex-boyfriend had uploaded videos of her to YouTube and other sites. At the time she made the complaint, revenge porn was not a crime in Texas. Nevertheless, in a jury trial in 2014, she won a $500,000 award. Since then, a handful of states have made revenge porn a crime. In 2015, a California man, Kevin Bollaert, was convicted for creating a revenge porn Web site and sentenced to serve eighteen years in prison.

**Critical Thinking** *Should domain name hosting companies be liable for revenge porn?*

a. *GoDaddy.com, LLC. v. Toups*, 429 S.W.3d 752 (Tex.App.—Beaumont 2014).

---

privacy. This is so even if the information revealed is true, because it should not be a matter of public concern.

4. *Appropriation of identity.* Using a person's name, picture, likeness, or other identifiable characteristic for commercial purposes without permission is also an invasion of privacy. An individual's right to privacy normally includes the right to the exclusive use of her or his identity. ■ **EXAMPLE 6.14** An advertising agency asks a singer with a distinctive voice and stage presence to take part in a marketing campaign for a new automobile. The singer rejects the offer. If the

agency then uses someone who imitates the singer's voice and dance moves in the ad, it will be actionable as an appropriation of identity. ■

**Appropriation Statutes** Most states today have codified the common law tort of appropriation of identity in statutes that establish the distinct tort of appropriation, or right of publicity. States differ as to the degree of likeness that is required to impose liability for appropriation, however.

Some courts have held that even when an animated character in a video or a video game is made to look like an actual person, there are not enough similarities to constitute appropriation. ■ **CASE IN POINT 6.15** Robert Burck is a street entertainer in New York City who has become famous as "The Naked Cowboy." Burck performs wearing only a white cowboy hat, white cowboy boots, and white underwear. He carries a guitar strategically placed to give the illusion of nudity. Burck sued Mars, Inc., the maker of M&Ms candy, over a video it showed on billboards in Times Square that depicted a blue M&M dressed exactly like The Naked Cowboy. The court, however, held that the use of Burck's signature costume did not amount to appropriation.[11] ■

_____

11. _Burck v. Mars, Inc._, 571 F.Supp.2d 446 (S.D.N.Y. 2008).

## 6–2g Fraudulent Misrepresentation

A misrepresentation leads another to believe in a condition that is different from the condition that actually exists. Although persons sometimes make misrepresentations accidentally because they are unaware of the existing facts, the tort of **fraudulent misrepresentation (fraud),** involves _intentional_ deceit for personal gain. The tort includes several elements:

1. A misrepresentation of material facts or conditions with knowledge that they are false or with reckless disregard for the truth.
2. An intent to induce another party to rely on the misrepresentation.
3. A justifiable reliance on the misrepresentation by the deceived party.
4. Damages suffered as a result of that reliance.
5. A causal connection between the misrepresentation and the injury suffered.

For fraud to occur, more than mere **puffery,** or _seller's talk,_ must be involved. Fraud exists only when a person represents as a fact something he or she knows is untrue. For instance, it is fraud to claim that the roof of a building does not leak when one knows that it does. Facts are objectively ascertainable, whereas seller's talk (such as "I am the best accountant in town") is not, because the use of the word _best_ is subjective.

In the following case, the court considered each of the elements of fraud.

**Case 6.2**

# Revell v. Guido

New York Supreme Court, Appellate Division, Third Department, 124 A.D.3d 1006, 2 N.Y.S.3d 252 (2015).

**Background and Facts** Joseph Guido bought a parcel of land in Stillwater, New York, that contained nine rental houses. The houses shared a waste disposal system that was defective. Guido had a new septic system installed. When town officials discovered sewage on the property, Guido had the system partially replaced. Prospective buyers, including Danny Revell, were given a property information sheet that stated, "Septic system totally new—each field totally replaced." In response to a questionnaire from the buyers' bank, Guido denied any knowledge of environmental problems.

A month after the buyers bought the houses, the septic system failed and required substantial repairs. The lender foreclosed on the property. The buyers filed a suit in a New York state court against Guido and his firm, Real Property Solutions, LLC, alleging fraud. A jury found fraud and awarded damages. The court issued a judgment in the plaintiffs' favor. The defendants appealed.

## In the Language of the Court

_EGAN, Jr.,_ J: [Judge:]
    * * * *

    _To prevail upon their cause of action for fraud, plaintiffs were required to establish that defendants, with the intent to deceive, misrepresented or omitted a material fact that they knew to be false and that plaintiffs,_

Case 6.2 Continued

*in turn, justifiably relied upon such misrepresentation or omission, thereby incurring damages.* As to the misrepresentation element, plaintiffs point to the statement made on the property information sheet * * * , as well as Guido's responses to certain of the inquiries contained on the environmental questionnaire. In this regard, the record reflects that the [replacement] septic system * * * was not "totally new," as it retained the original pump house structure and, more to the point, utilized the holding tanks that originally were part of the system * * * . There also is no question that Guido provided false answers to various inquiries posed on the environmental questionnaire. For example, Guido disavowed any knowledge of "governmental notification relating to past or recurrent violations of environmental laws with respect to the property * * * "—despite having been advised by the Town of Stillwater * * * that partially treated sewage was discovered on the property. [Emphasis added.]

As to the intent element, * * * given the arguably cavalier [offhand] manner in which Guido completed the environmental questionnaire, as well as his extensive knowledge regarding the * * * problems with the original septic system * * * , the jury could properly find that Guido made the cited misrepresentations with the intent to deceive plaintiffs.

With respect to the issue of justifiable reliance, Revell * * * conducted a visual inspection of the property prior to making an offer and did not observe any conditions indicative of a problem with the septic system. * * * If a septic system was represented to be "totally new" and a visual inspection of the property did not reveal any red flags, [that is,] boggy areas, odors or liquids bubbling up to the surface, one would assume that the system was working properly. * * * The jury [could] find that plaintiffs' reliance upon the representation contained in the property information sheet was reasonable.
* * * *

Nor are we persuaded that plaintiffs failed to tender sufficient admissible proof to substantiate the damages awarded by the jury. During the trial, the parties stipulated to the admission into evidence of a binder containing, among other things, an abundance of receipts, invoices, billing statements and canceled checks detailing plaintiffs' expenditures related to the subject property—and plaintiffs' forensic accountant, in turn, utilized such documents to arrive at a damages figure. * * * We are satisfied that plaintiffs tendered sufficient admissible proof to sustain the damages awarded by the jury.

**Decision and Remedy** *The state intermediate appellate court affirmed the lower court's judgment in the plaintiffs' favor. The facts of the case and the plaintiffs' proof met all of the requirements for establishing fraud.*

**Critical Thinking**
- **Legal Environment** *Financing for the purchase of the property was conditioned on the bank's review of Guido's answers to the environmental questionnaire. How could the court conclude that the plaintiffs justifiably relied on misrepresentations made to the bank? Explain.*
- **What If the Facts Were Different?** *If a visual inspection of the property had revealed "boggy areas, odors or liquids bubbling up to the surface" indicating that the septic system was not working properly, would the outcome of this case have been different?*

---

**Statement of Fact versus Opinion** Normally, the tort of fraudulent misrepresentation occurs only when there is reliance on a *statement of fact*. Sometimes, however, reliance on a *statement of opinion* may involve the tort of fraudulent misrepresentation if the individual making the statement of opinion has superior knowledge of the subject matter. For instance, when a lawyer makes a statement of opinion about the law in a state in which the lawyer is licensed to practice, a court might treat it as a statement of fact.

**Negligent Misrepresentation** Sometimes, a tort action can arise from misrepresentations that are made negligently rather than intentionally. The key difference between intentional and negligent misrepresentation is whether the person making the misrepresentation had actual knowledge of its falsity. Negligent misrepresentation requires only that the person making the statement or omission did not have a reasonable basis for believing its truthfulness.

Liability for negligent misrepresentation usually arises when the defendant who made the misrepresentation owed a duty of care to the plaintiff to supply correct information. (We discuss the duty of care in more detail later in the chapter.) Statements or omissions made by attorneys and accountants to their clients, for instance, can lead to liability for negligent misrepresentation.

## 6–2h Abusive or Frivolous Litigation

Tort law recognizes that people have a right not to be sued without a legally just and proper reason, and therefore it protects individuals from the misuse of litigation. Torts related to abusive litigation include malicious prosecution and abuse of process. If a party initiates a lawsuit out of malice and without a legitimate legal reason, and ends up losing the suit, that party can be sued for *malicious prosecution*. *Abuse of process* can apply to any person using a legal process against another in an improper manner or to accomplish a purpose for which the process was not designed.

The key difference between the torts of abuse of process and malicious prosecution is the level of proof. Unlike malicious prosecution, abuse of process is not limited to prior litigation and does not require the plaintiff to prove malice. It can be based on the wrongful use of subpoenas, court orders to attach or seize real property, or other types of formal legal process.

Concept Summary 6.1 reviews intentional torts against persons.

## Concept Summary 6.1

### Intentional Torts against Persons

| | |
|---|---|
| **Assault and Battery** | Any unexcused and intentional act that causes another person to be apprehensive of immediate harm is an assault. An assault resulting in physical contact is a battery. |
| **False Imprisonment** | An intentional confinement or restraint of another person's movement without justification. |
| **Intentional Infliction of Emotional Distress** | An intentional act that amounts to extreme and outrageous conduct resulting in severe emotional distress to another. |
| **Defamation (Libel or Slander)** | A false statement of fact, not made under privilege, that is communicated to a third person and that causes damage to a person's reputation. For public figures, the plaintiff must also prove that the statement was made with actual malice. |
| **Invasion of Privacy** | Publishing or otherwise making known or using information relating to a person's private life and affairs, with which the public has no legitimate concern, without that person's permission or approval. |
| **Fraudulent Misrepresentation (Fraud)** | A false representation made by one party, through misstatement of facts or through conduct, with the intention of deceiving another and on which the other reasonably relies to his or her detriment. |
| **Abusive or Frivolous Litigation** | The filing of a lawsuit without legitimate grounds and with malice. Alternatively, the use of a legal process in an improper manner. |

### 6-2i Wrongful Interference

The torts known as *business torts* generally involve wrongful interference with another's business rights. Public policy favors free competition, and these torts protect against tortious interference with legitimate business. Business torts involving wrongful interference generally fall into two categories: interference with a contractual relationship and interference with a business relationship.

**Wrongful Interference with a Contractual Relationship** Three elements are necessary for wrongful interference with a contractual relationship to occur:

1. A valid, enforceable contract must exist between two parties.
2. A third party must know that this contract exists.
3. This third party must *intentionally induce* a party to the contract to breach the contract.

■ **CASE IN POINT 6.16** A landmark case in this area involved an opera singer, Joanna Wagner, who was under contract to sing for a man named Lumley for a specified period of years. A man named Gye, who knew of this contract, nonetheless "enticed" Wagner to refuse to carry out the agreement, and Wagner began to sing for Gye. Gye's action constituted a tort because it interfered with the contractual relationship between Wagner and Lumley. (Wagner's refusal to carry out the agreement also entitled Lumley to sue Wagner for breach of contract.)[12] ■

The body of tort law relating to wrongful interference with a contractual relationship has increased greatly in recent years. In principle, any lawful contract can be the basis for an action of this type. The contract could be between a firm and its employees or a firm and its customers. Sometimes, a competitor of a firm lures away one of the firm's key employees. In this situation, the original employer can recover damages from the competitor only if it can be shown that the competitor knew of the contract's existence and intentionally induced the breach.

**Wrongful Interference with a Business Relationship** Businesspersons devise countless schemes to attract customers. They are prohibited, however, from unreasonably interfering with another's business in their attempts to gain a greater share of the market.

There is a difference between *competitive practices* and *predatory behavior*—actions undertaken with the intention of unlawfully driving competitors completely out of the market. Attempting to attract customers in general is a legitimate business practice, whereas specifically targeting the customers of a competitor is more likely to be predatory. A plaintiff claiming predatory behavior must show that the defendant used predatory methods to intentionally harm an established business relationship or gain a prospective economic advantage.

■ **EXAMPLE 6.17** A shopping mall contains two athletic shoe stores: Joe's and Ultimate Sport. Joe's cannot station an employee at the entrance of Ultimate Sport's to divert customers to Joe's by telling them that Joe's will beat Ultimate Sport's prices. This type of activity constitutes the tort of wrongful interference with a business relationship, which is commonly considered to be an unfair trade practice. If this activity were permitted, Joe's would reap the benefits of Ultimate Sport's advertising. ■

**Defenses to Wrongful Interference** A person will not be liable for the tort of wrongful interference with a contractual or business relationship if it can be shown that the interference was justified or permissible. Bona fide competitive behavior—such as marketing and advertising strategies—is a permissible interference even if it results in the breaking of a contract.

■ **EXAMPLE 6.18** Taylor Meats advertises so effectively that it induces Sam's Restaurant to break its contract with Burke's Meat Company. In that situation, Burke's Meat Company will be unable to recover against Taylor Meats on a wrongful interference theory. The public policy that favors free competition through advertising outweighs any possible instability that such competitive activity might cause in contractual relations. ■

---

# 6–3 Intentional Torts against Property

Intentional torts against property include trespass to land, trespass to personal property, conversion, and disparagement of property. These torts are wrongful actions that interfere with individuals' legally recognized rights with regard to their land or personal property.

The law distinguishes real property from personal property. *Real property* is land and things permanently attached to the land, such as a house. *Personal property* consists of all other items, including cash and securities (such as stocks and bonds).

### 6–3a Trespass to Land

A **trespass to land** occurs when a person, without permission, does any of the following:

---

12. *Lumley v. Gye*, 118 Eng.Rep. 749 (1853).

1. Enters onto, above, or below the surface of land that is owned by another.
2. Causes anything to enter onto land owned by another.
3. Remains on land owned by another or permits anything to remain on it.

Actual harm to the land is not an essential element of this tort, because the tort is designed to protect the right of an owner to exclusive possession.

Common types of trespass to land include walking or driving on another's land, shooting a gun over another's land, and throwing rocks at a building that belongs to someone else. Another common form of trespass involves constructing a building so that part of it extends onto an adjoining landowner's property.

**Establishing Trespass** Before a person can be a trespasser, the real property owner (or another person in actual and exclusive possession of the property, such as a renter) must establish that person as a trespasser. For instance, "posted" trespass signs expressly establish as a trespasser a person who ignores these signs and enters onto the property. A guest in your home is not a trespasser, unless he or she has been asked to leave and refuses. Any person who enters onto another's property to commit an illegal act (such as a thief entering a lumberyard at night to steal lumber) is impliedly a trespasser, with or without posted signs.

**Liability for Harm** At common law, a trespasser is liable for any damage caused to the property and generally cannot hold the owner liable for injuries that the trespasser sustains on the premises. This common law rule is being modified in many jurisdictions, however, in favor of a *reasonable duty of care* rule that varies depending on the status of the parties.

For instance, a landowner may have a duty to post a notice that guard dogs patrol the property. Also, if young children are attracted to the property by some object, such a swimming pool or a sand pile, and are injured, the landowner may be held liable (under the *attractive nuisance doctrine*). Still, an owner can normally use reasonable force to remove a trespasser from the premises or detain the trespasser for a reasonable time without liability for damages.

**Defenses against Trespass to Land** One defense to a claim of trespass is to show that the trespass was warranted, such as when a trespasser enters a building to assist someone in danger. Another defense exists when the trespasser can show that she or he had a *license* to come onto the land.

A **licensee** is one who is invited (or allowed to enter) onto the property of another for the licensee's benefit. A person who enters another's property to read an electric meter, for example, is a licensee. When you purchase a ticket to attend a movie or sporting event, you are licensed to go onto the property of another to view that movie or event.

Note that licenses to enter onto another's property are *revocable* by the property owner. If a property owner asks an electric meter reader to leave and she or he refuses to do so, the meter reader at that point becomes a trespasser.

## 6–3b Trespass to Personal Property

Whenever any individual wrongfully takes or harms the personal property of another or otherwise interferes with the lawful owner's possession and enjoyment of personal property, **trespass to personal property** occurs. This tort may also be called *trespass to chattels* or *trespass to personalty*.[13] In this context, harm means not only destruction of the property, but also anything that diminishes its value, condition, or quality.

Trespass to personal property involves intentional meddling with a possessory interest (one arising from possession), including barring an owner's access to personal property. ■ **EXAMPLE 6.19** Kelly takes Ryan's business law book as a practical joke and hides it so that Ryan is unable to find it for several days before the final examination. Here, Kelly has engaged in a trespass to personal property (and also *conversion,* the tort discussed next). ■

If it can be shown that trespass to personal property was warranted, then a complete defense exists. Most states, for instance, allow automobile repair shops to hold a customer's car (under what is called an *artisan's lien*) when the customer refuses to pay for repairs already completed.

## 6–3c Conversion

Any act that deprives an owner of personal property or of the use of that property without the owner's permission and without just cause can constitute **conversion.** Even the taking of electronic records and data may form the basis of a conversion claim. Often, when conversion occurs, a trespass to personal property also occurs. The original taking of the personal property from the owner was a trespass. Wrongfully retaining the property is conversion.

---

13. Pronounced *per*-sun-ul-tee.

**Failure to Return Goods** Conversion is the civil side of crimes related to theft, but it is not limited to theft. Even when the rightful owner consented to the initial taking of the property, so no theft or trespass occurred, a failure to return the property may still be conversion. ■ **EXAMPLE 6.20** Chen borrows Mark's iPad mini to use while traveling home from school for the holidays. When Chen returns to school, Mark asks for his iPad back, but Chen says that he gave it to his little brother for Christmas. In this situation, Mark can sue Chen for conversion, and Chen will have to either return the iPad or pay damages equal to its replacement value. ■

**Intention** Conversion can occur even when a person mistakenly believed that she or he was entitled to the goods. In other words, good intentions are not a defense against conversion. Someone who buys stolen goods, for instance, may be sued for conversion even if he or she did not know the goods were stolen. If the true owner of the goods sues the buyer, the buyer must either return the property to the owner or pay the owner the full value of the property.

Conversion can also occur from an employee's unauthorized use of a credit card. ■ **CASE IN POINT 6.21** Nicholas Mora worked for Welco Electronics, Inc., but had also established his own company, AQM Supplies. Mora used Welco's credit card without permission and deposited more than $375,000 into AQM's account, which he then transferred to his personal account. Welco sued. A California court held that Mora was liable for conversion. The court reasoned that when Mora misappropriated Welco's credit card and used it, he took part of Welco's credit balance with the credit-card company.[14] ■

### 6-3d Disparagement of Property

**Disparagement of property** occurs when economically injurious falsehoods are made about another's product or property rather than about another's reputation (as in the tort of defamation). *Disparagement of property* is a general term for torts that can be more specifically referred to as *slander of quality* or *slander of title.*

**Slander of Quality** The publication of false information about another's product, alleging that it is not what its seller claims, constitutes the tort of **slander of quality,** or **trade libel.** To establish trade libel, the plaintiff must prove that the improper publication caused a third person to refrain from dealing with the plaintiff and that the plaintiff sustained economic damages (such as lost profits) as a result.

An improper publication may be both a slander of quality and a defamation of character. For instance, a statement that disparages the quality of a product may also, by implication, disparage the character of a person who would sell such a product.

**Slander of Title** When a publication falsely denies or casts doubt on another's legal ownership of property, resulting in financial loss to the property's owner, the tort of **slander of title** occurs. Usually, this is an intentional tort in which someone knowingly publishes an untrue statement about another's ownership of certain property with the intent of discouraging a third person from dealing with the person slandered. For instance, it would be difficult for a car dealer to attract customers after competitors published a notice that the dealer's stock consisted of stolen automobiles.

See Concept Summary 6.2 for a review of intentional torts against property.

## 6-4 Unintentional Torts—Negligence

The tort of **negligence** occurs when someone suffers injury because of another's failure to live up to a required *duty of care.* In contrast to intentional torts, in torts involving negligence, the tortfeasor neither wishes to bring about the consequences of the act nor believes that they will occur. The person's conduct merely creates a risk of such consequences. If no risk is created, there is no negligence.

Moreover, the risk must be foreseeable. In other words, it must be such that a reasonable person engaging in the same activity would anticipate the risk and guard against it. In determining what is reasonable conduct, courts consider the nature of the possible harm.

Many of the actions giving rise to the intentional torts discussed earlier in the chapter constitute negligence if the element of intent is missing (or cannot be proved). ■ **EXAMPLE 6.22** Juan walks up to Maya and intentionally shoves her. Maya falls and breaks her arm as a result. In this situation, Juan is liable for the intentional tort of battery. If Juan carelessly bumps into Maya, however, and she falls and breaks her arm as a result, Juan's action constitutes negligence. In either situation, Juan has committed a tort. ■

---

**14.** *Welco Electronics, Inc. v. Mora,* 223 Cal.App.4th 202, 166 Cal.Rptr.3d 877 (2014).

## Concept Summary 6.2

### Intentional Torts against Property

| | |
|---|---|
| **Trespass to Land** | The invasion of another's real property without consent or privilege. Once a person is expressly or impliedly established as a trespasser, the property owner has specific rights, which may include the right to detain or remove the trespasser. |
| **Trespass to Personal Property** | The intentional interference with an owner's right to use, possess, or enjoy his or her personal property without the owner's consent. |
| **Conversion** | The wrongful possession or use of another person's personal property without just cause. |
| **Disparagement of Property** | Any economically injurious falsehood that is made about another's product or property; an inclusive term for the torts of *slander of quality* and *slander of title*. |

To succeed in a negligence action, the plaintiff must prove each of the following:

1. *Duty.* The defendant owed a duty of care to the plaintiff.
2. *Breach.* The defendant breached that duty.
3. *Causation.* The defendant's breach caused the plaintiff's injury.
4. *Damages.* The plaintiff suffered a legally recognizable injury.

### 6–4a The Duty of Care and Its Breach

Central to the tort of negligence is the concept of a **duty of care.** The basic principle underlying the duty of care is that people are free to act as they please so long as their actions do not infringe on the interests of others. When someone fails to comply with the duty to exercise reasonable care, a potentially tortious act may have been committed.

Failure to live up to a standard of care may be an act (accidentally setting fire to a building) or an omission (neglecting to put out a campfire). It may be a careless act or a carefully performed but nevertheless dangerous act that results in injury. In determining whether the duty of care has been breached, courts consider several factors:

1. The nature of the act (whether it is outrageous or commonplace).
2. The manner in which the act was performed (cautiously versus heedlessly).
3. The nature of the injury (whether it is serious or slight).

Creating even a very slight risk of a dangerous explosion might be unreasonable, whereas creating a distinct possibility of someone's burning his or her fingers on a stove might be reasonable.

**The Reasonable Person Standard** Tort law measures duty by the **reasonable person standard.** In determining whether a duty of care has been breached, the courts ask how a reasonable person would have acted in the same circumstances. The reasonable person standard is said to be objective. It is not necessarily how a particular person *would* act. It is society's judgment of how an ordinarily prudent person *should* act. If the so-called reasonable person existed, he or she would be careful, conscientious, even tempered, and honest.

The degree of care to be exercised varies, depending on the defendant's occupation or profession, her or his relationship with the plaintiff, and other factors. Generally, whether an action constitutes a breach of the duty of care is determined on a case-by-case basis. The outcome depends on how the judge (or jury) decides that a reasonable person in the position of the defendant would have acted in the particular circumstances of the case.

Note that the courts frequently use the reasonable person standard in other areas of law as well as in negligence cases. Indeed, the principle that individuals are required to exercise a reasonable standard of care in their activities is a pervasive concept in business law.

**The Duty of Landowners** Landowners are expected to exercise reasonable care to protect individuals coming onto their property from harm. In some jurisdictions, landowners may even have a duty to protect trespassers against certain risks. Landowners who rent or lease premises to tenants are expected to exercise reasonable care to ensure that the tenants and their guests are not harmed in common areas, such as stairways, entryways, and laundry rooms.

**The Duty to Warn Business Invitees of Risks.** Retailers and other business operators who explicitly or implicitly invite persons to come onto their premises have a duty to exercise reasonable care to protect these **business invitees.** The duty normally requires storeowners to warn business invitees of foreseeable risks, such as construction zones or wet floors, about which the owners knew or *should have known.*

■ **EXAMPLE 6.23** Liz enters Kwan's neighborhood market, slips on a wet floor, and sustains injuries as a result. If there was no sign or other warning that the floor was wet at the time Liz slipped, the owner, Kwan, would be liable for damages. A court would hold that Kwan was negligent because he failed to exercise a reasonable degree of care to protect customers against foreseeable risks about which he knew or should have known. That a patron might slip on the wet floor and be injured was a foreseeable risk, and Kwan should have taken care to avoid this risk or warn the customer of it. ■

A business owner also has a duty to discover and remove any hidden dangers that might injure a customer or other invitee. Hidden dangers might include uneven surfaces or defects in the pavement of a parking lot or a walkway, or merchandise that has fallen off shelves in a store.

**Obvious Risks Provide an Exception.** Some risks are so obvious that an owner need not warn of them. For instance, a business owner does not need to warn customers to open a door before attempting to walk through it. Other risks, however, even though they may seem obvious

to a business owner, may not be so in the eyes of another, such as a child. In addition, even if a risk is obvious, a business owner is not necessarily excused from the duty to protect customers from foreseeable harm from that risk.

■ **CASE IN POINT 6.24** Giorgio's Grill is a restaurant in Florida that becomes a nightclub after hours. At those times, traditionally, as the manager of Giorgio's knew, the staff and customers throw paper napkins into the air as the music plays. The napkins land on the floor, but no one picks them up. One night, Jane Izquierdo went to Giorgio's. Although she had been to the club on prior occasions and knew about the napkin-throwing tradition, she slipped and fell, breaking her leg. She sued Giorgio's for negligence, but lost at trial because a jury found that the risk of slipping on the napkins was obvious. A state appellate court reversed, however, holding that the obviousness of a risk does not discharge a business owner's duty to its invitees to maintain the premises in a safe condition.[15] ■

**The Duty of Professionals** Persons who possess superior knowledge, skill, or training are held to a higher standard of care than others. Professionals—including physicians, dentists, architects, engineers, accountants, and lawyers, among others—are required to have a standard minimum level of special knowledge and ability. In determining what constitutes reasonable care in the case of professionals, the law takes their training and expertise into account. Thus, an accountant's conduct is judged not by the reasonable person standard, but by the reasonable accountant standard.

If a professional violates his or her duty of care toward a client, the client may bring a suit against the professional, alleging **malpractice,** which is essentially professional negligence. For instance, a patient might sue a physician for *medical malpractice.* A client might sue an attorney for *legal malpractice.*

## 6–4b Causation

Another element necessary to a negligence action is *causation.* If a person breaches a duty of care and someone suffers injury, the person's act must have caused the harm for it to constitute the tort of negligence.

**Courts Ask Two Questions** In deciding whether the requirement of causation is met, the court must address two questions:

---

15. *Izquierdo v. Gyroscope, Inc.*, 946 So.2d 115 (Fla.App. 2007).

1. *Is there causation in fact?* Did the injury occur because of the defendant's act, or would it have occurred anyway? If the injury would not have occurred without the defendant's act, then there is causation in fact.

   **Causation in fact** usually can be determined by use of the *but for* test: "but for" the wrongful act, the injury would not have occurred. This test seeks to determine whether there was a cause-and-effect relationship between the act and the injury suffered. In theory, causation in fact is limitless. One could claim, for example, that "but for" the creation of the world, a particular injury would not have occurred. Thus, as a practical matter, the law has to establish limits, and it does so through the concept of proximate cause.

2. *Was the act the proximate, or legal, cause of the injury?* **Proximate cause,** or *legal cause*, exists when the connection between an act and an injury is strong enough to justify imposing liability. Proximate cause asks whether the injuries sustained were foreseeable or were too remotely connected to the incident to trigger liability. Judges use proximate cause to limit the scope of the defendant's liability to a subset of the total number of potential plaintiffs that might have been harmed by the defendant's actions.

   ■ **EXAMPLE 6.25** Ackerman carelessly leaves a campfire burning. The fire not only burns down the forest but also sets off an explosion in a nearby chemical plant that spills chemicals into a river, killing all the fish for twenty miles downstream and ruining the economy of a tourist resort. Should Ackerman be liable to the resort owners? To the tourists whose vacations were ruined? These are questions of proximate cause that a court must decide. ■

Both of these causation questions must be answered in the affirmative for liability in tort to arise. If there is causation in fact but a court decides that the defendant's action is not the proximate cause of the plaintiff's injury, the causation requirement has not been met. Therefore, the defendant normally will not be liable to the plaintiff.

**Foreseeability** Questions of proximate cause are linked to the concept of foreseeability because it would be unfair to impose liability on a defendant unless the defendant's actions created a foreseeable risk of injury. Generally, if the victim or the consequences of a harm done were unforeseeable, there is no proximate cause.

Probably the most cited case on the concept of foreseeability and proximate cause is the *Palsgraf* case, which established foreseeability as the test for proximate cause. ■ **CASE IN POINT 6.26** Helen Palsgraf was waiting for a train on a station platform. A man carrying a package was rushing to catch a train that was moving away from a platform across

the tracks from Palsgraf. As the man attempted to jump aboard the moving train, he seemed unsteady and about to fall. A railroad guard on the car reached forward to grab him, and another guard on the platform pushed him from behind to help him board the train.

In the process, the man's package, which (unknown to the railroad guards) contained fireworks, fell on the railroad tracks and exploded. There was nothing about the package to indicate its contents. The repercussions of the explosion caused weighing scales at the other end of the train platform to fall on Palsgraf, causing injuries for which she sued the railroad company. At the trial, the jury found that the railroad guards had been negligent in their conduct. The railroad company appealed. New York's highest state court held that the railroad company was not liable to Palsgraf. The railroad had not been negligent toward her, because injury to her was not foreseeable.[16] ■

## 6–4c The Injury Requirement and Damages

For tort liability to arise, the plaintiff must have suffered a *legally recognizable* injury. To recover damages, the plaintiff must have suffered some loss, harm, wrong, or invasion of a protected interest. Essentially, the purpose of tort law is to compensate for legally recognized harms and injuries resulting from wrongful acts. If no harm or injury results from a given negligent action, there is nothing to compensate, and no tort exists.

For instance, if you carelessly bump into a passerby, who stumbles and falls as a result, you may be liable in tort if the passerby is injured in the fall. If the person is unharmed, however, there normally can be no lawsuit for damages, because no injury was suffered.

Compensatory damages are the norm in negligence cases. A court will award punitive damages only if the defendant's conduct was grossly negligent, reflecting an intentional failure to perform a duty with reckless disregard of the consequences to others.

## 6–4d Good Samaritan Statutes

Most states now have what are called **Good Samaritan statutes.**[17] Under these statutes, someone who is aided voluntarily by another cannot turn around and sue the "Good Samaritan" for negligence. These laws were passed largely to protect physicians and medical personnel who

---

16. *Palsgraf v. Long Island Railroad Co.,* 248 N.Y. 339, 162 N.E. 99 (1928).
17. These laws derive their name from the Good Samaritan story in the Bible. In the story, a traveler who had been robbed and beaten lay along the roadside, ignored by those passing by. Eventually, a man from the region of Samaria (the "Good Samaritan") stopped to render assistance to the injured person.

volunteer their services in emergency situations to those in need, such as individuals hurt in car accidents.

### 6–4e Dram Shop Acts

Many states have also passed **dram shop acts,**[18] under which a bar's owner or bartender may be held liable for injuries caused by a person who became intoxicated while drinking at the bar. The owner or bartender may also be held responsible for continuing to serve a person who was already intoxicated.

Some states' statutes also impose liability on *social hosts* (persons hosting parties) for injuries caused by guests who became intoxicated at the hosts' homes. Under these statutes, it is unnecessary to prove that the bar owner, bartender, or social host was negligent. ■ **EXAMPLE 6.27** Jane hosts a Super Bowl party at which Brett, a minor, sneaks alcoholic drinks. Jane is potentially liable for damages resulting from Brett's drunk driving after the party. ■

---

## 6–5 Defenses to Negligence

Defendants often defend against negligence claims by asserting that the plaintiffs have failed to prove

---

18. Historically, a dram was a small unit of liquid, and distilled spirits (strong alcoholic liquor) were sold in drams. Thus, a dram shop was a place where liquor was sold in drams.

the existence of one or more of the required elements for negligence. Additionally, there are three basic *affirmative* defenses in negligence cases (defenses that a defendant can use to avoid liability even if the facts are as the plaintiff states): *assumption of risk, superseding cause,* and *contributory and comparative negligence.*

### 6–5a Assumption of Risk

A plaintiff who voluntarily enters into a risky situation, knowing the risk involved, will not be allowed to recover. This is the defense of **assumption of risk,** which requires two elements:

1. Knowledge of the risk.
2. Voluntary assumption of the risk.

The defense of assumption of risk is frequently asserted when the plaintiff was injured during a recreational activity that involves known risk, such as skiing or skydiving. (Courts do not apply the assumption of risk doctrine in emergency situations.)

Assumption of risk can apply not only to participants in sporting events, but also to spectators and bystanders who are injured while attending those events. In the following *Spotlight Case,* the issue was whether a spectator at a baseball game voluntarily assumed the risk of being hit by an errant ball thrown while the players were warming up before the game.

---

### Spotlight on the Seattle Mariners

## Case 6.3 Taylor v. Baseball Club of Seattle, LP

Court of Appeals of Washington, 132 Wash.App. 32, 130 P.3d 835 (2006).

**Background and Facts** Delinda Taylor went to a Seattle Mariners baseball game at Safeco Field with her boyfriend and her two minor sons. Their seats were four rows up from the field along the right field foul line. They arrived more than an hour before the game so that they could see the players warm up and get their autographs. When she walked in, Taylor saw that a Mariners pitcher, Freddy Garcia, was throwing a ball back and forth with José Mesa right in front of their seats.

As Taylor stood in front of her seat, she looked away from the field, and a ball thrown by Mesa got past Garcia and struck her in the face, causing serious injuries. Taylor sued the Mariners for the allegedly negligent warm-up throw. The Mariners filed a motion for summary judgment in which they argued that Taylor, a longtime Mariners fan, was familiar with baseball and the inherent risk of balls entering the stands. Thus, the motion asserted, Taylor had assumed the risk of her injury. The trial court granted the motion and dismissed Taylor's case. Taylor appealed.

**In the Language of the Court**
*DWYER,* J. [Judge]
* * * *

* * * For many decades, courts have required baseball stadiums to screen some seats—generally those behind home plate—to provide protection to spectators who choose it.

*Case 6.3 Continues*

**Case 6.3 Continued**

A sport spectator's assumption of risk and a defendant sports team's duty of care are accordingly discerned under the doctrine of primary assumption of risk. * * * "Implied *primary* assumption of risk arises where a plaintiff has impliedly consented (often in advance of any negligence by defendant) to relieve defendant of a duty to plaintiff regarding specific *known* and appreciated risks."

* * * *

Under this implied primary assumption of risk, defendant must show that plaintiff had full subjective understanding of the specific risk, both its nature and presence, and that he or she voluntarily chose to encounter the risk.

* * * It is undisputed that the warm-up is part of the sport, that spectators such as Taylor purposely attend that portion of the event, and that the Mariners permit ticket-holders to view the warm-up.

* * * We find the fact that Taylor was injured during warm-up is not legally significant because that portion of the event is necessarily incident to the game.

* * * *

Here, there is no evidence that the circumstances leading to Taylor's injury constituted an unusual danger. It is undisputed that it is the normal, every-day practice at all levels of baseball for pitchers to warm up in the manner that led to this incident. *The risk of injuries such as Taylor's are within the normal comprehension of a spectator who is familiar with the game.* Indeed, the possibility of an errant ball entering the stands is part of the game's attraction for many spectators. [Emphasis added.]

* * * The record contains substantial evidence regarding Taylor's familiarity with the game. She attended many of her sons' baseball games, she witnessed balls entering the stands, she had watched Mariners' games both at the Kingdome and on television, and she knew that there was no screen protecting her seats, which were close to the field. In fact, as she walked to her seat she saw the players warming up and was excited about being in an unscreened area where her party might get autographs from the players and catch balls.

**Decision and Remedy** *The state intermediate appellate court affirmed the lower court's judgment. As a spectator who chose to sit in an unprotected area of seats, Taylor voluntarily undertook the risk associated with being hit by an errant baseball thrown during the warm-up before the game.*

**Critical Thinking**
- **What If the Facts Were Different?** *Would the result in this case have been different if it had been Taylor's minor son, rather than Taylor herself, who had been struck by the ball? Should courts apply the doctrine of assumption of risk to children? Discuss.*
- **Legal Environment** *What is the basis underlying the defense of assumption of risk? How does that basis support the court's decision in this case?*

---

## 6–5b Superseding Cause

An unforeseeable intervening event may break the causal connection between a wrongful act and an injury to another. If so, the intervening event acts as a **superseding cause**—that is, it relieves the defendant of liability for injuries caused by the intervening event.

■ **EXAMPLE 6.28** While riding his bicycle, Derrick negligently runs into Julie, who is walking on the sidewalk. As a result of the impact, Julie falls and fractures her hip. While she is waiting for help to arrive, a small aircraft crashes nearby and explodes, and some of the fiery debris hits her, causing her to sustain severe burns. Derrick will be liable for the damages related to Julie's fractured hip, because the risk of injuring her with his bicycle was foreseeable. Normally, though, Derrick will not be liable for the burns caused by the plane crash, because he could not have foreseen the risk that a plane would crash nearby and injure Julie. ■

## 6–5c Contributory Negligence

All individuals are expected to exercise a reasonable degree of care in looking out for themselves. In the past, under the common law doctrine of **contributory negligence,** a plaintiff who was also negligent (who failed to exercise a reasonable degree of care) could not recover anything from the defendant. Under this rule, no matter how insignificant the plaintiff's negligence was relative to the defendant's negligence, the plaintiff would be precluded from recovering any damages. Today, only a few jurisdictions still follow this doctrine.

## 6–5d Comparative Negligence

In most states, the doctrine of contributory negligence has been replaced by a **comparative negligence** standard. Under this standard, both the plaintiff's and the defendant's negligence are computed, and the liability for damages is distributed accordingly.

Some jurisdictions have adopted a "pure" form of comparative negligence that allows the plaintiff to recover, even if the extent of his or her fault is greater than that of the defendant. Under pure comparative negligence, if the plaintiff was 80 percent at fault and the defendant 20 percent at fault, the plaintiff can recover 20 percent of his or her damages.

Many states' comparative negligence statutes, however, contain a "50 percent" rule that prevents the plaintiff from recovering any damages if she or he was more than 50 percent at fault. Under this rule, a plaintiff who was 35 percent at fault can recover 65 percent of his or her damages, but a plaintiff who was 65 percent (more than 50 percent) at fault can recover nothing.

## Reviewing: Tort Law

Elaine Sweeney went to Ragged Mountain Ski Resort in New Hampshire with a friend. Elaine went snow tubing down a run designed exclusively for snow tubers. There were no Ragged Mountain employees present in the snow-tube area to instruct Elaine on the proper use of a snow tube. On her fourth run down the trail, Elaine crossed over the center line between snow-tube lanes, collided with another snow tuber, and was injured. Elaine filed a negligence action against Ragged Mountain seeking compensation for the injuries that she sustained. Two years earlier, the New Hampshire state legislature had enacted a statute that prohibited a person who participates in the sport of skiing from suing a ski-area operator for injuries caused by the risks inherent in skiing. Using the information presented in the chapter, answer the following questions.

1. What defense will Ragged Mountain probably assert?
2. The central question in this case is whether the state statute establishing that skiers assume the risks inherent in the sport bars Elaine's suit. What would your decision be on this issue? Why?
3. Suppose that the court concludes that the statute applies only to skiing and not to snow tubing. Will Elaine's lawsuit be successful? Explain.
4. Now suppose that the jury concludes that Elaine was partly at fault for the accident. Under what theory might her damages be reduced in proportion to the degree to which her actions contributed to the accident and her resulting injuries?

**Debate This . . .**  *Each time a state legislature enacts a law that applies the assumption of risk doctrine to a particular sport, participants in that sport suffer.*

## Terms and Concepts

| | | |
|---|---|---|
| actionable 114 | contributory negligence 130 | general damages 112 |
| actual malice 118 | conversion 124 | Good Samaritan statute 128 |
| assault 113 | damages 112 | intentional tort 113 |
| assumption of risk 129 | defamation 115 | libel 115 |
| battery 114 | disparagement of property 125 | licensee 124 |
| business invitee 127 | dram shop act 129 | malpractice 127 |
| causation in fact 128 | duty of care 126 | negligence 125 |
| comparative negligence 131 | fraudulent misrepresentation | privilege 117 |
| compensatory damages 112 | (fraud) 120 | proximate cause 128 |

## Issue Spotters

1. Jana leaves her truck's motor running while she enters a Kwik-Pik Store. The truck's transmission engages, and the vehicle crashes into a gas pump, starting a fire that spreads to a warehouse on the next block. The warehouse collapses, causing its billboard to fall and injure Lou, a bystander. Can Lou recover from Jana? Why or why not? (See *Unintentional Torts—Negligence*.)

2. A water pipe bursts, flooding a Metal Fabrication Company utility room and tripping the circuit breakers on a panel in the room. Metal Fabrication contacts Nouri, a licensed electrician with five years' experience, to check the damage and turn the breakers back on. Without testing for short circuits, which Nouri knows that he should do, he tries to switch on a breaker. He is electrocuted, and his wife sues Metal Fabrication for damages, alleging negligence. What might the firm successfully claim in defense? (See *Defenses to Negligence*.)

• **Check your answers to the Issue Spotters against the answers provided in Appendix D at the end of this text.**

## Business Scenarios

**6–1. Defamation.** Richard is an employee of the Dun Construction Corp. While delivering materials to a construction site, he carelessly backs Dun's truck into a passenger vehicle driven by Green. This is Richard's second accident in six months. When the company owner, Dun, learns of this latest accident, a heated discussion ensues, and Dun fires Richard. Dun is so angry that he immediately writes a letter to the union of which Richard is a member and to all other construction companies in the community, stating that Richard is the "worst driver in the city" and that "anyone who hires him is asking for legal liability." Richard files a suit against Dun, alleging libel on the basis of the statements made in the letters. Discuss the results. (See *Intentional Torts against Persons*.)

**6–2. Liability to Business Invitees.** Kim went to Ling's Market to pick up a few items for dinner. It was a stormy day, and the wind had blown water through the market's door each time it opened. As Kim entered through the door, she slipped and fell in the rainwater that had accumulated on the floor. The manager knew of the weather conditions but had not posted any sign to warn customers of the water hazard. Kim injured her back as a result of the fall and sued Ling's for damages. Can Ling's be held liable for negligence? Discuss. (See *Unintentional Torts—Negligence*.)

## Business Case Problems

**6–3. Spotlight on Intentional Torts—Defamation.**

Sharon Yeagle was an assistant to the vice president of student affairs at Virginia Polytechnic Institute and State University (Virginia Tech). As part of her duties, Yeagle helped students participate in the Governor's Fellows Program. The *Collegiate Times*, Virginia Tech's student newspaper, published an article about the university's success in placing students in the program. The article's text surrounded a block quotation attributed to Yeagle with the phrase "Director of Butt Licking" under her name. Yeagle sued the *Collegiate Times* for defamation. She argued that the phrase implied the commission of sodomy and was therefore actionable. What is *Collegiate Times* defense to this claim? [*Yeagle v. Collegiate Times*, 497 S.E.2d 136 (Va. 1998)] (See *Intentional Torts against Persons*.)

**6–4. Intentional Infliction of Emotional Distress.** While living in her home country of Tanzania, Sophia Kiwanuka signed an employment contract with Anne Margareth Bakilana, a Tanzanian living in Washington, D.C. Kiwanuka traveled to the United States to work as a babysitter and maid in Bakilana's house. When Kiwanuka arrived, Bakilana confiscated her passport, held her in isolation, and forced her to work long hours under threat of having her deported. Kiwanuka worked seven days a week without breaks and was subjected to regular verbal and psychological abuse by Bakilana. Kiwanuka filed a complaint against Bakilana for intentional infliction of emotional distress, among other claims. Bakilana argued that Kiwanuka's complaint should be dismissed because the allegations were insufficient to show outrageous intentional conduct that resulted in severe emotional distress.

If you were the judge, in whose favor would you rule? Why? [*Kiwanuka v. Bakilana*, 844 F.Supp.2d 107 (D.D.C. 2012)] (See *Intentional Torts against Persons*.)

**6–5. Business Case Problem with Sample Answer—Negligence.** At the Weatherford Hotel in Flagstaff, Arizona,

in Room 59, a balcony extends across thirty inches of the room's only window, leaving a twelve-inch gap with a three-story drop to the concrete below. A sign prohibits smoking in the room but invites guests to "step out onto the balcony" to smoke. Toni Lucario was a guest in Room 59 when she climbed out of the window and fell to her death. Patrick McMurtry, her estate's personal representative, filed a suit against the Weatherford. Did the hotel breach a duty of care to Locario? What might the Weatherford assert in its defense? Explain. [*McMurtry v. Weatherford Hotel, Inc.*, 231 Ariz. 244, 293 P.3d 520 (2013)] (See *Unintentional Torts—Negligence*.)

- **For a sample answer to Problem 6–5, go to Appendix E at the end of this text.**

**6–6. Negligence.** Ronald Rawls and Zabian Bailey were in an auto accident in Bridgeport, Connecticut. Bailey rear-ended Rawls at a stoplight. Evidence showed it was more likely than not that Bailey failed to apply his brakes in time to avoid the collision, failed to turn his vehicle to avoid the collision, failed to keep his vehicle under control, and was inattentive to his surroundings. Rawls filed a suit in a Connecticut state court against his insurance company, Progressive Northern Insurance Co., to obtain benefits under an underinsured motorist clause, alleging that Bailey had been negligent. Could Rawls collect? Discuss. [*Rawls v. Progressive Northern Insurance Co.*, 310 Conn. 768, 83 A.3d 576 (2014)] (See *Unintentional Torts—Negligence*.)

**6–7. Negligence.** Charles Robison, an employee of West Star Transportation, Inc., was ordered to cover an unevenly loaded flatbed trailer with a 150-pound tarpaulin (a waterproof cloth). The load included uncrated equipment and pallet crates of different heights, about thirteen feet off the ground at its highest point. While standing on the load, manipulating the tarpaulin without safety equipment or assistance, Robison fell and sustained a traumatic head injury. He filed a suit against West Star to recover for his injury. Was West Star "negligent in failing to provide a reasonably safe place to work," as Robison claimed? Explain. [*West Star Transportation, Inc. v. Robison*, 457 S.W.3d 178 (Tex.App.—Amarillo 2015)] (See *Unintentional Torts—Negligence*.)

**6–8. Negligence.** DSC Industrial Supply and Road Rider Supply are located in North Kitsap Business Park in Seattle, Washington. Both firms are owned by Paul and Suzanne Marshall. The Marshalls had outstanding commercial loans from Frontier Bank. The bank dispatched one of its employees, Suzette Gould, to North Kitsap to "spread Christmas cheer" to the Marshalls as an expression of appreciation for their business. Approaching the entry to Road Rider, Gould tripped over a concrete "wheel stop" and fell, suffering a broken arm and a dislocated elbow. The stop was not clearly visible, it had not been painted a contrasting color, and it was not marked with a sign. Gould had not been aware of the stop before she tripped over it. Is North Kitsap liable to Gould for negligence? Explain. [*Gould v. North Kitsap Business Park Management, LLC*, 2016 WL 236455 (2016)] (See *Unintentional Torts—Negligence*.)

**6–9. A Question of Ethics—Wrongful Interference.**

*White Plains Coat & Apron Co. is a New York–based linen rental business. Cintas Corp. is a competitor. White Plains had five-year exclusive contracts with some of its customers. As a result of Cintas's soliciting of business, dozens of White Plains' customers breached their contracts and entered into rental agreements with Cintas. White Plains filed a suit against Cintas, alleging wrongful interference.* [*White Plains Coat & Apron Co. v. Cintas Corp.*, 8 N.Y.3d 422, 867 N.E.2d 381 (2007)] (See *Intentional Torts against Persons*.)

**(a)** What are the two important policy interests at odds in wrongful interference cases? Which of these interests should be accorded priority?

**(b)** The U.S. Court of Appeals for the Second Circuit asked the New York Court of Appeals to answer a question: Is a general interest in soliciting business for profit a sufficient defense to a claim of wrongful interference with a contractual relationship? What do you think? Why?

## Legal Reasoning Group Activity

**6–10. Negligence.** Donald and Gloria Bowden hosted a cookout at their home in South Carolina, inviting mostly business acquaintances. Justin Parks, who was nineteen years old, attended the party. Alcoholic beverages were available to all of the guests, even those who, like Parks, were between the ages of eighteen and twenty-one. Parks consumed alcohol at the party and left with other guests. One of these guests detained Parks at the guest's home to give Parks time to "sober up." Parks then drove himself from this guest's home and was killed in a one-car accident. At the time of death, he had a blood alcohol content of 0.291 percent, which exceeded the state's limit for driving a motor vehicle. Linda Marcum, Parks's mother, filed a suit in a South Carolina state court against the Bowdens and others, alleging that they were negligent. (See *Unintentional Torts—Negligence*.)

**(a)** The first group will present arguments in favor of holding the social hosts liable in this situation.

**(b)** The second group will formulate arguments against holding the social hosts liable based on principles in this chapter.

**(c)** The third group will determine the reasons why some courts do not treat social hosts the same as parents who serve alcoholic beverages to their underage children.

# Answers to the *Issue Spotters*

**1. *Can Lou recover from Jana? Why or why not?*** Probably. To recover on the basis of negligence, the injured party as a plaintiff must show that the truck's owner owed the plaintiff a duty of care, that the owner breached that duty, that the plaintiff was injured, and that the breach caused the injury.

In this situation, the owner's actions breached the duty of reasonable care. The billboard falling on the plaintiff was the direct cause of the injury, not the plaintiff's own negligence. Thus, liability turns on whether the plaintiff can connect the breach of duty to the injury. This involves the test of proximate cause—the question of foreseeability. The consequences to the injured party must have been a foreseeable result of the owner's carelessness.

**2. *What might the firm successfully claim in defense?*** The company might defend against this electrician's claim by asserting that the electrician should have known of the risk and, therefore, the company had no duty to warn. According to the problem, the danger is common knowledge in the electrician's field and should have been apparent to this electrician, given his years of training and experience. In other words, the company most likely had no need to warn the electrician of the risk.

The firm could also raise comparative negligence. Both parties' negligence, if any, could be weighed and the liability distributed proportionately. The defendant could also assert assumption of risk, claiming that the electrician voluntarily entered into a dangerous situation, knowing the risk involved.

# Sample Answers for *Business Case Problems with Sample Answer*

**Problem 6–5. *Negligence.*** Negligence requires proof that (1) the defendant owed a duty of care to the plaintiff, (2) the defendant breached that duty, (3) the defendant's breach caused the plaintiff's injury, and (4) the plaintiff suffered a legally recognizable injury. With respect to the duty of care, a business owner has a duty to use reasonable care to protect business invitees. This duty includes an obligation to discover and correct or warn of unreasonably dangerous conditions that the owner of the premises should reasonably foresee might endanger an invitee. Some risks are so obvious that an owner need not warn of them. But even if a risk is obvious, a business owner may not be excused from the duty to protect its customers from foreseeable harm.

Because Lucario was the Weatherford's business invitee, the hotel owed her a duty of reasonable care to make its premises safe for her use. The balcony ran nearly the entire width of the window in Lucario's room. She could have reasonably believed that the window was a means of access to the balcony. The window/balcony configuration was dangerous, however, because the window opened wide enough for an adult to climb out, but the twelve-inch gap between one side of the window and the balcony was unprotected. This unprotected gap opened to a drop of more than three stories to a concrete surface below.

Should the hotel have anticipated the potential harm to a guest who opened the window in Room 59 and attempted to access the balcony? The hotel encouraged guests to "step out onto the balcony" to smoke. The dangerous condition of the window/balcony configuration could have been remedied at a minimal cost. These circumstances could be perceived as creating an "unreasonably dangerous" condition. And it could be concluded that the hotel created or knew of the condition and failed to take reasonable steps to warn of it or correct it. Of course, the Weatherford might argue that the window/ balcony configuration was so obvious that the hotel was not liable for Lucario's fall.

In the actual case on which this problem is based, the court concluded that the Weatherford did not breach its duty of care to Lucario. On McMurtry's appeal, a state intermediate appellate court held that this conclusion was in error, vacated the lower court's judgment in favor of the hotel on this issue, and remanded the case.

# Chapter 9

# CHAPTER

# Strict Liability and Product Liability

In this chapter, we look at a category of tort called **strict liability,** or *liability without fault.* Under the doctrine of strict liability, a person who engages in certain activities can be held responsible for any harm that results to others, even if the person used the utmost care.

We then look at an area of tort law of particular importance to businesspersons—product liability. The manufacturers and sellers of products may incur **product liability** when product defects cause injury or property damage to consumers, users, or bystanders.

Although multimillion-dollar product liability claims often involve big automakers, pharmaceutical companies, or tobacco companies, many businesses face potential liability. For instance, a number of product liability lawsuits have been filed claiming that energy drinks like Monster, Red Bull, and Rockstar have serious adverse effects—especially on young people. A man who swallowed a bone fragment while eating sued McDonald's in 2015 for allegedly defective chicken McNuggets.

Product liability lawsuits also reach across international borders. Takata Corporation, a global company that supplies seat belts, airbags, and other automobile safety systems, is being sued by hundreds of plaintiffs in the United States. Takata manufactured allegedly defective airbags, which violently exploded and ejected metal debris, resulting in injuries and deaths.[1] Takata has already paid a $70 million penalty to the National Highway Safety Administration for failing to promptly disclose defects in its airbags, millions of which have now been recalled.

---

1. *In re Takata Airbag Products Liability Litigation,* 84 F.Supp.3d 1371 (2015).

## 7–1 Strict Liability

The modern concept of strict liability traces its origins, in part, to an English case decided in 1868. ■ **CASE IN POINT 7.1** In the coal-mining area of Lancashire, England, the Rylands, who were mill owners, had constructed a reservoir on their land. Water from the reservoir broke through a filled-in shaft of an abandoned coal mine nearby and flooded the connecting passageways in an active coal mine owned by Fletcher.

Fletcher sued the Rylands, and the court held that the defendants (the Rylands) were liable, even though the circumstances did not fit within existing tort liability theories. The court held that a "person who for his own purposes brings on his land and collects and keeps there anything likely to do mischief if it escapes . . . is *prima facie*[2] answerable for all the damage which is the natural consequence of its escape."[3] ■

---

2. *Prima facie* is Latin for "at first sight." Legally, it refers to a fact that is presumed to be true unless contradicted by evidence.
3. *Rylands v. Fletcher,* 3 L.R.–E & I App. [Law Reports, English & Irish Appeal Cases] (H.L. [House of Lords] 1868).

British courts liberally applied the doctrine that emerged from the case. Initially, though, few U.S. courts accepted the doctrine, presumably because the courts were worried about its effect on the expansion of American business. Today, however, the doctrine of strict liability is the norm rather than the exception.

### 7–1a Abnormally Dangerous Activities

Strict liability for damages proximately caused by an abnormally dangerous, or ultrahazardous, activity is one application of strict liability. Courts apply the doctrine of strict liability in these situations because of the extreme risk of the activity. Abnormally dangerous activities are those that involve a high risk of serious harm to persons or property that cannot be completely guarded against by the exercise of reasonable care.

Activities such as blasting or storing explosives qualify as abnormally dangerous, for instance. Even if blasting with dynamite is performed with all reasonable care, there is still a risk of injury. Considering the potential for harm, it seems reasonable to ask the person engaged in the activity to pay for injuries caused by that activity. Although there is no fault, there is still responsibility because of the dangerous nature of the undertaking.

Similarly, persons who keep wild animals are strictly liable for any harm inflicted by the animals. The basis for applying strict liability is that wild animals, should they escape from confinement, pose a serious risk of harm to people in the vicinity. Even an owner of domestic animals (such as dogs or horses) may be strictly liable for harm caused by those animals if the owner knew, or should have known, that the animals were dangerous or had a propensity to harm others.

### 7–1b Application of Strict Liability to Product Liability

A significant application of strict liability is in the area of product liability—liability of manufacturers and sellers for harmful or defective products. Liability here is a matter of social policy and is based on two factors:

1. The manufacturer can better bear the cost of injury because it can spread the cost throughout society by increasing the prices of its goods.
2. The manufacturer is making a profit from its activities and therefore should bear the cost of injury as an operating expense.

We discuss product liability in detail next. Strict liability is also applied in certain types of *bailments* (a bailment exists when goods are transferred temporarily into the care of another).

## 7–2 Product Liability

Those who make, sell, or lease goods can be held liable for physical harm or property damage caused by those goods to a consumer, user, or bystander. This is called *product liability*. Product liability may be based on the theories of negligence, misrepresentation, strict liability, and warranties. Multiple theories of liability can be, and often are, asserted in the same case. We look here at product liability based on negligence and on misrepresentation.

### 7–2a Based on Negligence

*Negligence* is the failure to exercise the degree of care that a reasonable, prudent person would have exercised under the circumstances. If a manufacturer fails to exercise "due care" to make a product safe, a person who is injured by the product may sue the manufacturer for negligence.

**Due Care Must Be Exercised** Manufacturers must use due care in all of the following areas:

1. Designing the product.
2. Selecting the materials.
3. Using the appropriate production process.
4. Assembling and testing the product.
5. Placing adequate warnings on the label to inform the user of dangers of which an ordinary person might not be aware.
6. Inspecting and testing any purchased components used in the product.

**Privity of Contract Not Required** A product liability action based on negligence does not require *privity of contract* between the injured plaintiff and the defendant-manufacturer. **Privity of contract** refers to the relationship that exists between the parties to a contract. Privity is the reason that normally only the parties to a contract can enforce that contract.

In the context of product liability law, though, privity is not required. A person who is injured by a defective product may bring a negligence suit even though he or she was not the one who actually purchased the product—and thus is not in privity. A manufacturer, seller, or lessor is liable for failure to exercise due care to *any person* who sustains an injury proximately caused by a negligently made (defective) product.

A 1916 landmark decision established this exception to the privity requirement. ■ **CASE IN POINT 7.2** Donald MacPherson suffered injuries while riding in a Buick automobile that suddenly collapsed because one of the wheels was made of defective wood. The spokes crumbled into fragments, throwing MacPherson out of the vehicle and injuring him.

MacPherson had purchased the car from a Buick dealer, but he brought a lawsuit against the manufacturer, Buick Motor Company, alleging negligence. Buick itself had not made the wheel but had bought it from another manufacturer. There was evidence, though, that the defects could have been discovered by a reasonable inspection by Buick and that no such inspection had taken place. The primary issue was whether Buick owed a duty of care to anyone except the immediate purchaser of the car—that is, the Buick dealer. Although Buick itself had not manufactured the wheel, New York's highest state court held that Buick had a duty to inspect the wheels and that Buick "was responsible for the finished product." Therefore, Buick was liable to MacPherson for the injuries he sustained.[4] ■

---

4. *MacPherson v. Buick Motor Co.,* 217 N.Y. 382, 111 N.E. 1050 (1916).

**"Cause in Fact" and Proximate Cause** In a product liability suit based on negligence, as in any action alleging that the defendant was negligent, the plaintiff must show that the defendant's conduct was the "cause in fact" of an injury. "Cause in fact" requires showing that "but for" the defendant's action, the injury would not have occurred.

It must also be determined that the defendant's act was the *proximate cause* of the injury. This determination focuses on the foreseeability of the consequences of the act and whether the defendant should be held legally responsible. For proximate cause to become a relevant issue, however, a plaintiff first must establish cause in fact. The cause of a serious accident was at issue in the following case.

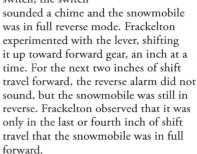

### Case Analysis 7.1

# Schwarck v. Arctic Cat, Inc.
Court of Appeals of Michigan, 2016 WL 191992 (2016).

## In the Language of the Court
*PER CURIAM.* [By the Whole Court]
* * * *

* * * Karen Schwarck * * * was operating an Arctic Cat [660 snowmobile] near Mackinac Island's Grand Hotel [in Michigan] with her sister, Edith Bonno, as passenger. The sisters met their demise when the Arctic Cat went, in reverse, backward through a wooden fence and over the West Bluff of the Island.

[Donald Schwarck and Joshua Bonno] the spouses of decedents, as their personal representatives, filed this action [in a Michigan state court] against defendant Arctic Cat [the manufacturer of the 660]. Plaintiffs alleged that the Arctic Cat 660 was negligently designed * * * without a backup alarm that operated throughout all the reverse travel positions and as a result proximately caused decedents' injuries.

Defendant filed a motion for summary [judgment]. Defendant denied the existence of a "silent reverse zone," but argued that even if such a zone existed, it was not a cause of the accident because the alarm was intended as a warning to bystanders and not as an indicator of shift position for operators.
* * * *

* * * The court issued its decision and order in favor of defendant. [The plaintiffs appealed.]
* * * *

There is no dispute that on the day of the accident decedent Schwarck was driving the Arctic Cat 660 * * * and that she attempted to execute a three-point

or K-turn * * * . To make the turn decedent Schwarck had to turn left to face north, stop, reverse south, stop, and then complete the turn to drive east. * * * Plaintiffs argue that after decedent Schwarck reversed, she stopped a second time and shifted forward, and not hearing the reverse alarm, believed she was in forward, and accelerated. As a result, the craft went in reverse through the fence and off the bluff.

The trial court determined that there were no material questions of fact on * * * the operability of the reverse alarm. * * * It was undisputed that an inspection of the Arctic Cat post-accident showed the reverse alarm to be operable.
* * * *

* * * [But] the court's conclusion that the reverse alarm was working at the time of the accident does not determine whether its operational process constituted a product defect. Plaintiffs' claim was that the reverse alarm was defective because it did not sound during the entire time the vehicle was in reverse. Plaintiffs' causation theory was that the Arctic Cat's reverse alarm caused decedent Schwarck to be confused about whether she was in forward or reverse gear and that the confusion led to the accident that caused decedents' deaths.

[Plaintiffs' expert John Frackelton, an accident reconstructionist and snowmobile mechanic,] observed that the shift lever traveled from full reverse to full forward in a distance of four inches. Frackelton's testing revealed that when the lever was shifted all the way down

and pressed against the reverse buffer switch, the switch sounded a chime and the snowmobile was in full reverse mode. Frackelton experimented with the lever, shifting it up toward forward gear, an inch at a time. For the next two inches of shift travel forward, the reverse alarm did not sound, but the snowmobile was still in reverse. Frackelton observed that it was only in the last or fourth inch of shift travel that the snowmobile was in full forward.

* * * Frackelton observed that the transition from full reverse to full forward was smooth and accomplished with little pressure. He opined that an operator could "become accustomed to the highly repeatable return performance." On two occasions, however, Frackelton pushed the gearshift forward and the Arctic Cat did not return to forward gear as expected.

* * * Frackelton's opinion * * * creates a material question of fact as to whether the alarm failed to sound at all times when the gear was in reverse. Defendant argues that the alarm served its intended purpose which is to notify bystanders and not operators that the snowmobile is in reverse and that it was unreasonable for decedent Schwarck to rely on the alarm to determine the gear of the snowmobile. *The fact that the manufacturer's intended purpose for the alarm was to warn third-parties is not dispositive of the issue of whether decedent Schwarck relied on the alarm to*

**Case 7.1 Continued**

*determine her gear or whether that reliance was reasonable or a foreseeable misuse of the alarm and snowmobile.* Decedent Schwarck is assumed to have acted with due care for her own safety. Her widower averred that, based upon his observations, decedent Schwarck had a practice and routine of relying upon the sounding of the alarm as a signal that she was in reverse. Evidence from Frackelton's test runs also demonstrate that despite manual control of the shift lever, the lever could stop just short of the forward position and prevent the snowmobile from going into drive. [Emphasis added.]

Reasonable minds could differ as to whether a reverse alarm that does not sound throughout the reverse trajectory or only operates in a partial manner is defective.

* * * *

Legal cause becomes a relevant issue after cause in fact has been established. * * * *To establish legal cause, the plaintiff* *must show that it was foreseeable that the defendant's conduct may create a risk of harm to the victim, and * * * that the result of that conduct and intervening causes were foreseeable. * * * It is foreseeable that an operator of the Arctic Cat* may rely on the sound of the reverse alarm to indicate when the snowmobile is no longer in reverse and experience unexpected travel backward because the alarm does not sound during the entire reverse gear. It is further foreseeable that unanticipated reverse travel may cause a risk of harm to the operator. * * * Frackelton's tests regarding speed velocity without aggressive throttle demonstrate how the Arctic Cat can travel almost thirty feet in just 5.4 seconds. Not only can an operator of the Arctic Cat find him or herself unexpectedly travelling in reverse, but also doing so quickly. Plaintiffs' other expert [Lila Laux, a psychologist and engineer] testified * * * that time is * * * required for the operator to determine how to respond to the unexpected stimuli, to engage the brake, and for the brake to activate. [Emphasis added.]

A jury could infer that traveling backward when one thought he or she would go forward is an unexpected stimulus. It is also a reasonable inference, from the opinions of both plaintiffs' experts, that it was foreseeable that the operator would be surprised by the rearward motion. Given the evidence, reasonable minds may differ as to whether decedent Schwarck did not or could not correct the snowmobile's rearward direction in the time allotted.

Based on the whole record, there is evidence that warrants submission of this case to a jury to determine whether the reverse alarm was defective and whether that defect caused decedent Schwarck and Bonno's deaths.

* * * *

[The trial court's judgment is] vacated and remanded for proceedings consistent with this opinion.

**Legal Reasoning Questions**

1. According to the plaintiffs, what was the product defect at the center of this case? According to the defendant, why was this not a defect?

2. How did the plaintiffs use evidence to support their claim?

3. Why did the court conclude that this case should be submitted to a jury? Explain.

## 7–2b Misrepresentation

When a user or consumer is injured as a result of a manufacturer's or seller's fraudulent misrepresentation, the basis of liability may be the tort of fraud. In this situation, the misrepresentation must have been made knowingly or with reckless disregard for the facts. The intentional mislabeling of packaged cosmetics, for instance, or the intentional concealment of a product's defects would constitute fraudulent misrepresentation.

In addition, the misrepresentation must be of a material fact, and the seller must have intended to induce the buyer's reliance on the misrepresentation. Misrepresentation on a label or advertisement is enough to show an intent to induce the reliance of anyone who may use the product. In addition, the buyer must have relied on the misrepresentation.

## 7–3 Strict Product Liability

As mentioned earlier, under the doctrine of strict liability, people may be liable for the results of their acts regardless of their intentions or their exercise of reasonable care. In addition, liability does not depend on privity of contract. Thus, the injured party does not have to be the buyer, as required under contract warranty theories. In the 1960s, courts applied the doctrine of strict liability in several landmark cases involving manufactured goods, and it has since become a common method of holding manufacturers liable.

## 7–3a Strict Product Liability and Public Policy

The law imposes strict product liability as a matter of public policy. This public policy rests on a threefold assumption:

1. Consumers should be protected against unsafe products.
2. Manufacturers and distributors should not escape liability for faulty products simply because they are not in privity of contract with the ultimate user of those products.
3. Manufacturers and distributors can better bear the costs associated with injuries caused by their products, because they can ultimately pass the costs on to all consumers in the form of higher prices.

**Development of the Doctrine** California was the first state to impose strict product liability in tort on manufacturers. ■ **CASE IN POINT 7.3** William Greenman was injured when his Shopsmith combination power tool threw off a piece of wood that struck him in the head. He sued the manufacturer, claiming that he had followed the product's instructions and the product must be defective. In a landmark decision, *Greenman v. Yuba Power Products, Inc.,*[5] the California Supreme Court set out the reason for applying tort law rather than contract law (including laws governing warranties) in cases involving consumers who were injured by defective products.

According to the *Greenman* court, the "purpose of such liability is to [e]nsure that the costs of injuries resulting from defective products are borne by the manufacturers . . . rather than by the injured persons who are powerless to protect themselves." ■ Today, the majority of states recognize strict product liability, although some state courts limit its application to situations involving personal injuries (rather than property damage).

**Stated Public Policy** Public policy may be expressed in a statute or in the common law. Sometimes, public policy may be revealed in a court's interpretation of a statute, as in the following case.

---

5. 59 Cal.2d 57, 377 P.2d 897, 27 Cal.Rptr. 697 (1962).

## Spotlight on Injuries from Vaccines

### Case 7.2 Bruesewitz v. Wyeth, LLC

Supreme Court of the United States, 562 U.S. 223, 131 S.Ct. 1068, 179 L.Ed.2d 1 (2011).

**Company Profile** *Wyeth, LLC—a subsidiary of Pfizer, Inc.—is an international pharmaceutical and health-care company with its corporate headquarters in Madison, New Jersey. Wyeth develops, makes, and markets medical therapies, clinical programs, nutritional supplements, prescription drugs, and other health-care products, including over-the-counter medications. Wyeth was incorporated in 1926. In 1994, the company bought Lederle Laboratories. Since 1948, Lederle had been making the diphtheria, tetanus, and pertussis (DTP) vaccine for children.*

**Background and Facts** When Hannah Bruesewitz was six months old, her pediatrician administered a dose of the DTP vaccine according to the Centers for Disease Control's recommended childhood immunization schedule. Within twenty-four hours, Hannah began to experience seizures. She suffered more than one hundred seizures during the next month. Her doctors diagnosed her with "residual seizure disorder" and "developmental delay."

Hannah's parents, Russell and Robalee Bruesewitz, filed a claim for relief in the U.S. Court of Federal Claims under the National Childhood Vaccine Injury Act (NCVIA). The NCVIA had set up a no-fault compensation program for persons injured by vaccines. The claim was denied. The Bruesewitzes then filed a suit in a state court against Wyeth, LLC, the maker of the vaccine, alleging strict product liability. The suit was moved to a federal district court. The court held that the claim was preempted by the NCVIA, which includes provisions protecting manufacturers from liability for "a vaccine's unavoidable, adverse side effects." The U.S. Court of Appeals for the Third Circuit affirmed the district court's judgment. The Bruesewitzes appealed to the United States Supreme Court.

**Case 7.2 Continued**

## In the Language of the Court

Justice *SCALIA* delivered the opinion of the Court.

\* \* \* \*

In the 1970's and 1980's vaccines became, one might say, victims of their own success. They had been so effective in preventing infectious diseases that the public became much less alarmed at the threat of those diseases, and much more concerned with the risk of injury from the vaccines themselves.

Much of the concern centered around vaccines against \* \* \* DTP, which were blamed for children's disabilities \* \* \* . This led to a massive increase in vaccine-related tort litigation. \* \* \* This destabilized the DTP vaccine market, causing two of the three domestic manufacturers to withdraw.

\* \* \* \*

To stabilize the vaccine market and facilitate compensation, Congress enacted the NCVIA in 1986. The Act establishes a no-fault compensation program designed to work faster and with greater ease than the civil tort system. A person injured by a vaccine, or his legal guardian, may file a petition for compensation in the United States Court of Federal Claims.

\* \* \* \*

Successful claimants receive compensation for medical, rehabilitation, counseling, special education, and vocational training expenses; diminished earning capacity; pain and suffering; and $250,000 for vaccine-related deaths. Attorney's fees are provided \* \* \* . These awards are paid out of a fund created by a \* \* \* tax on each vaccine dose.

The *quid pro quo* [something done in exchange] for this, designed to stabilize the vaccine market, was the provision of significant tort-liability protections for vaccine manufacturers. \* \* \* *Manufacturers are generally immunized from liability* \* \* \* *if they have complied with all regulatory requirements* \* \* \* . \* \* \* *And most relevant to the present case, the Act expressly eliminates liability for a vaccine's unavoidable, adverse side effects.* [Emphasis added.]

\* \* \* \*

The Act's structural *quid pro quo* leads to the \* \* \* conclusion: The vaccine manufacturers fund from their sales an informal, efficient compensation program for vaccine injuries; in exchange they avoid costly tort litigation.

**Decision and Remedy** *The United States Supreme Court affirmed the lower court's judgment. The NCVIA preempted the Bruesewitzes' claim against Wyeth for compensation for the injury to their daughter caused by the DTP vaccine's side effects. The Court found that the NCVIA's compensation program strikes a balance between paying victims harmed by vaccines and protecting the vaccine industry from collapsing under the costs of tort liability.*

**Critical Thinking**
- **Economic** *What is the public policy expressed by the provisions of the NCVIA?*
- **Political** *If the public wants to change the policy outlined in this case, which branch of the government—and at what level—should be lobbied to make the change? Explain.*

---

## 7–3b The Requirements for Strict Product Liability

After the *Restatement (Second) of Torts* was issued in 1964, Section 402A became a widely accepted statement of how the doctrine of strict liability should be applied to sellers of goods (including manufacturers, processors, assemblers, packagers, bottlers, wholesalers, distributors, retailers, and lessors). The bases for an action in strict liability that are set forth in Section 402A can be summarized as a set of six requirements.

1. The product must be in a *defective condition* when the defendant sells it.

2. The defendant must normally be engaged in the *business of selling* (or otherwise distributing) that product.

3. The product must be *unreasonably dangerous* to the user or consumer because of its defective condition (in most states).

4. The plaintiff must incur *physical harm* to self or property by use or consumption of the product.

5. The defective condition must be the *proximate cause* of the injury or damage.
6. The *goods must not have been substantially changed* from the time the product was sold to the time the injury was sustained.

Depending on the jurisdiction, if these requirements are met, a manufacturer's liability to an injured party can be almost unlimited.

**Proving a Defective Condition**  Under these requirements, in any action against a manufacturer, seller, or lessor, the plaintiff need not show why or in what manner the product became defective. The plaintiff does, however, have to prove that the product was defective at the time it left the hands of the seller or lessor. The plaintiff must also show that this defective condition made the product "unreasonably dangerous" to the user or consumer.

Unless evidence can be presented to support the conclusion that the product was defective when it was sold or leased, the plaintiff will not succeed. If the product was delivered in a safe condition and subsequent mishandling made it harmful to the user, the seller or lessor normally is not strictly liable.

**Unreasonably Dangerous Products**  The *Restatement* recognizes that many products cannot be made entirely safe for all uses. Thus, sellers or lessors are liable only for products that are *unreasonably* dangerous. A court could consider a product so defective as to be an **unreasonably dangerous product** in either of the following situations:

1. The product was dangerous beyond the expectation of the ordinary consumer.
2. A less dangerous alternative was *economically* feasible for the manufacturer, but the manufacturer failed to produce it.

As will be discussed next, a product may be unreasonably dangerous due to the manufacturing process, the design, or the warning.

## 7–3c Product Defects

The *Restatement (Third) of Torts: Products Liability* defines the three types of product defects that have traditionally been recognized in product liability law—manufacturing defects, design defects, and inadequate warnings.

**Manufacturing Defects**  According to Section 2(a) of the *Restatement (Third) of Torts,* a product "contains a manufacturing defect when the product departs from its intended design even though all possible care was exercised in the preparation and marketing of the product." Basically, a manufacturing defect is a departure from a product unit's design specifications that results in products that are physically flawed, damaged, or incorrectly assembled. A glass bottle that is made too thin and explodes in a consumer's face is an example of a product with a manufacturing defect.

**Quality Control.**  Usually, manufacturing defects occur when a manufacturer fails to assemble, test, or check the quality of a product adequately. Liability is imposed on the manufacturer (and on the wholesaler and retailer) regardless of whether the manufacturer's quality control efforts were "reasonable." The idea behind holding defendants strictly liable for manufacturing defects is to encourage greater investment in product safety and stringent quality control standards.

**Expert Testimony.**  Cases involving allegations of a manufacturing defect are often decided based on the opinions and testimony of experts. ■ **CASE IN POINT 7.4**  Kevin Schmude purchased an eight-foot stepladder and used it to install radio-frequency shielding in a hospital room. While Schmude was standing on the ladder, it collapsed, and he was seriously injured. He filed a lawsuit against the ladder's maker, Tricam Industries, Inc., based on a manufacturing defect.

Experts testified that the preexisting holes in the ladder's top cap did not properly line up with the holes in the rear right rail and backing plate. As a result of the misalignment, the rear legs of the ladder were not securely fastened in place, causing the ladder to fail. A jury concluded that this manufacturing defect made the ladder unreasonably dangerous and awarded Schmude more than $677,000 in damages.[6] ■

**Design Defects**  Unlike a product with a manufacturing defect, a product with a design defect is made in conformity with the manufacturer's design specifications. Nevertheless, the product results in injury to the user because the design itself was faulty. A product "is defective in design when the foreseeable risks of harm posed by the product could have been reduced or avoided by the adoption of a reasonable alternative design by the seller or other distributor, or a predecessor in the commercial chain of distribution, and the omission of the alternative design renders the product not reasonably safe."[7]

---

6. *Schmude v. Tricam Industries, Inc.*, 550 F.Supp.2d 846 (E.D.Wis. 2008).
7. *Restatement (Third) of Torts: Products Liability*, Section 2(b).

**Test for Design Defects.** To successfully assert a design defect, a plaintiff has to show that:

1. A reasonable alternative design was available.
2. As a result of the defendant's failure to adopt the alternative design, the product was not reasonably safe.

In other words, a manufacturer or other defendant is liable only when the harm was reasonably preventable.

**Factors to Be Considered.** According to the *Restatement,* a court can consider a broad range of factors in deciding claims of design defects. These include the magnitude and probability of the foreseeable risks, as well as the relative advantages and disadvantages of the product as it was designed and as it could have been designed.

**Risk-Utility Analysis.** Most courts engage in a risk-utility analysis to determine whether the risk of harm from the product as designed outweighs its utility to the user and to the public. ■ **CASE IN POINT 7.5** Benjamin Riley, the county sheriff, was driving his Ford F-150 pickup truck near Ehrhardt, South Carolina, when it collided with another vehicle. The impact caused Riley's truck to leave the road and roll over. The driver's door of the truck opened in the collision, and Riley was ejected and killed.

Riley's widow, Laura, as the representative of his estate, filed a product liability suit against Ford Motor Company. She alleged that the design of the door-latch system of the truck allowed the door to open in the collision. A state court awarded the estate $900,000 in damages "because of the stature of Riley and what he's done in life, what he's contributed to his family."

Ford appealed, but the court found that a reasonable alternative design was available for the door-latch system. Evidence showed that Ford was aware of the safety problems presented by the current system (a rod-linkage system). After conducting a risk-utility analysis of a different system (a cable-linkage system), Ford had concluded that the alternative system was feasible and perhaps superior. The state's highest court affirmed the damages award.[8] ■

**Consumer-Expectation Test.** Other courts apply the consumer-expectation test to determine whether a product's design was defective. Under this test, a product is unreasonably dangerous when it fails to perform in the manner that would reasonably be expected by an ordinary consumer.

■ **CASE IN POINT 7.6** A representative from Wilson Sporting Goods Company gave Edwin Hickox an umpire's mask that was designed to be safer than other such masks. The mask had a newly designed throat guard that angled forward instead of extending straight down. Hickox was wearing the mask while working as an umpire at a game when he was struck by a ball and injured. He suffered a concussion and damage to his inner ear, which caused permanent hearing loss.

Hickox and his wife sued Wilson for product liability based on a defective design and won. Wilson appealed. The reviewing court affirmed the jury's verdict. The design was defective because "an ordinary consumer would have expected the mask to perform more safely than it did." The evidence presented to the jury had shown that Wilson's mask was more dangerous than comparable masks sold at the time.[9] ■

**Inadequate Warnings** A product may also be deemed defective because of inadequate instructions or warnings. A product will be considered defective "when the foreseeable risks of harm posed by the product could have been reduced or avoided by the provision of reasonable instructions or warnings by the seller or other distributor . . . and the omission of the instructions or warnings renders the product not reasonably safe."[10] Generally, a seller must also warn consumers of the harm that can result from the *foreseeable misuse* of its product.

**Content of Warnings.** Important factors for a court to consider include the risks of a product, the "content and comprehensibility" and "intensity of expression" of warnings and instructions, and the "characteristics of expected user groups."[11] Courts apply a "reasonableness" test to determine if the warnings adequately alert consumers to the product's risks. For instance, children will likely respond readily to bright, bold, simple warning labels, whereas educated adults might need more detailed information. For more on tips on making sure a product's warnings are adequate, see this chapter's *Managerial Strategy* feature.

■ **CASE IN POINT 7.7** Jeffrey Johnson went to an emergency room for an episode of atrial fibrillation, a heart rhythm disorder. Dr. David Hahn used a defibrillator manufactured by Medtronic, Inc., to deliver electric shocks to Johnson's heart. The defibrillator had synchronous and asynchronous modes, and it reverted to the

---

8. *Riley v. Ford Motor Co.,* 414 S.C. 185, 777 S.E.2d 824 (2015).

9. *Wilson Sporting Goods Co. v. Hickox,* 59 A.3d 1267 (D.C.App. 2013).
10. *Restatement (Third) of Torts: Products Liability,* Section 2(c).
11. *Restatement (Third) of Torts: Products Liability,* Section 2, Comment h.

## MANAGERIAL STRATEGY

# When Is a Warning Legally Bulletproof?

A company can sell a perfectly manufactured and designed product, yet still face product liability lawsuits for failure to provide appropriate warnings. According to the *Restatement (Third) of Torts,* a product may be deemed defective because of inadequate instructions or warnings when the foreseeable risks of harm posed by the product could have been reduced by reasonable warnings offered by the seller or other distributor.

Manufacturers and distributors have a duty to warn users of any hidden dangers of their products. Additionally, they have a duty to instruct users in how to use the product to avoid any dangers. Warnings generally must be clear and specific. They must also be conspicuous.

### When No Warning Is Required

Not all products have to provide warnings. People are expected to know that knives can cut fingers, for example, so a seller need not place a bright orange label on each knife sold reminding consumers of this danger. Most household products are generally safe when used as intended.

In a New Jersey case, an appeals court reviewed a product liability case against the manufacturer of a Razor A–type kick scooter. A ten-year-old boy was injured when he fell and struck his face on the scooter's handlebars. The padded end caps on the handlebars had deteriorated, and the boy's mother had thrown them away, exposing the metal ends.

The boy and his mother sued, claiming that the manufacturer was required to provide a warning to prevent injuries of this type. The appellate court noted, however, that the plaintiffs were not able to claim that the Razor A was defective. "Lacking evidence that Razor A's end-cap design was defective, plaintiffs cannot show that Razor A had a duty to warn of such a defect, and therefore cannot make out their failure to warn claim."[a]

### Warnings on Medications

In a case involving a prescription medication, a woman suffered neurological disorders after taking a generic drug to treat her gastroesophageal reflux disease. Part of her complaint asserted strict liability for failure to warn. The plaintiff claimed that the manufacturer had not updated its label to indicate that usage should not exceed twelve weeks. The reviewing court reasoned that "The adequacy of the instructions . . . made no difference to the outcome . . . because [the plaintiff alleges that her prescribing physician] did not read those materials."[b]

In contrast, in a 2014 Pennsylvania case, a family was awarded over $10 million in a lawsuit against Johnson & Johnson for defective warnings on bottles of children's Motrin. A three-year-old girl suffered burns over 84 percent of her skin, experienced brain damage, and went blind after suffering a reaction to the drug. The drug did have a specific warning label that instructed consumers to stop taking the medication and contact a physician in the event of an allergic reaction. Nonetheless, Johnson & Johnson was found liable for failing to warn about the known risk of severe side effects.[c]

### Business Questions

1. *To protect themselves, manufacturers have been forced to include lengthy safety warnings for their products. What might be the downside of such warnings?*

2. *Does a manufacturer have to create safety warnings for every product? Why or why not?*

---

**a.** *Vann v. Toys R Us,* 2014 WL3537937 (N.J.Sup. A.D. 2014).

**b.** *Brinkley v. Pfizer, Inc.,* 772 F.3d 1133 (8th Cir. 2014).

**c.** *Maya v. Johnson and Johnson,* 97 A.3d 1203, 2014 PA Super. 152 (2014).

---

asynchronous mode after each use. Hahn intended to deliver synchronized shocks, which would have required him to select the synchronous mode for each shock. But Hahn did not read the device's instructions, which Medtronic had provided both in a manual and on the device itself. As a result, the physician delivered one synchronized shock, followed by twelve asynchronous shocks that endangered Johnson's life.

Johnson and his wife filed a product liability suit against Medtronic, asserting that Medtronic had provided inadequate warnings about the defibrillator and that the device had a design defect. A Missouri appellate court held that the Johnsons could not pursue a claim based on the inadequacy of Medtronic's warnings, but they could pursue a claim alleging a design defect. The court reasoned that, in some cases, "a manufacturer may be held liable where it chooses to warn of the danger . . . rather than preclude the danger by design."[12] ∎

---

12. *Johnson v. Medtronic, Inc.,* 365 S.W.3d 226 (Mo.App. 2012).

**Obvious Risks.** There is no duty to warn about risks that are obvious or commonly known. Warnings about such risks do not add to the safety of a product and could even detract from it by making other warnings seem less significant. As will be discussed later in the chapter, the obviousness of a risk and a user's decision to proceed in the face of that risk may be a defense in a product liability suit based on an inadequate warning.

■ **EXAMPLE 7.8** Sixteen-year-old Lana White attempts to do a back flip on a trampoline and fails. She is paralyzed as a result. There are nine warning labels affixed to the trampoline, an instruction manual with safety warnings, and a placard at the entrance advising users not to do flips. If White sues the manufacturer for inadequate warnings in this situation, she is likely to lose. The warning labels are probably sufficient to make the risks obvious and insulate the manufacturer from liability for her injuries. ■

Risks that may seem obvious to some users, though, will not be obvious to all users, especially when the users are likely to be children. A young child may not be able to read or understand warning labels or comprehend the risk of certain activities. To avoid liability, the manufacturer would have to prove that the warnings it provided were adequate to make the risk of injury obvious to a young child.[13]

**State Laws and Constitutionality.** An action alleging that a product is defective due to an inadequate label can be based on state law, but that law must not violate the U.S. Constitution. ■ **CASE IN POINT 7.9** California once enacted a law imposing restrictions and a labeling requirement on the sale or rental of "violent video games" to minors. Although the video game industry had adopted a voluntary rating system for games, the legislators deemed those labels inadequate.

The Video Software Dealers Association and the Entertainment Software Association immediately filed a suit in federal court to invalidate the law, and the law was struck down. The state appealed to the United States Supreme Court. The Court found that the definition of a violent video game in California's law was unconstitutionally vague and violated the First Amendment's guarantee of freedom of speech.[14] ■

### 7–3d Market-Share Liability

Ordinarily, in all product liability claims, a plaintiff must prove that the defective product that caused his or her injury was the product of a specific defendant. In a few situations, however, courts have dropped this requirement when plaintiffs could not prove which of many distributors of a harmful product supplied the particular product that caused the injuries. Under a theory of **market-share liability,** a court can hold each manufacturer responsible for a percentage of the plaintiff's damages that is equal to the percentage of its market share.

■ **CASE IN POINT 7.10** Suffolk County Water Authority (SCWA) is a municipal water supplier in New York. SCWA discovered the presence of a toxic chemical—perchlorethylene (PCE), which is used by dry cleaners and others—in its local water. SCWA filed a product liability lawsuit against Dow Chemical Corporation and other companies that manufactured and distributed PCE. Dow filed a motion to dismiss the case for failure to state a claim, since SCWA could not identify each defendant whose allegedly defective product caused the water contamination.

A state trial court refused to dismiss the action, holding that SCWA's allegations were sufficient to invoke market-share liability. Under market-share liability, the burden of identification shifts to defendants if the plaintiff establishes a *prima facie* case on every element of the claim except identification of the specific defendant. (A *prima facie* case is one in which the plaintiff has presented sufficient evidence for the claim to go forward.)[15] ■

Many jurisdictions do not recognize the market-share theory of liability because they believe that it deviates too significantly from traditional legal principles. Jurisdictions that do recognize market-share liability apply it only when it is difficult to determine which company made a particular product.

### 7–3e Other Applications of Strict Product Liability

Almost all courts extend the strict liability of manufacturers and other sellers to injured bystanders. Thus, if a defective forklift that will not go into reverse injures a passerby, that individual can sue the manufacturer for product liability (and possibly also sue the forklift operator for negligence).

Strict product liability also applies to suppliers of component parts. ■ **EXAMPLE 7.11** Toyota buys brake pads from a subcontractor and puts them in Corollas without changing their composition. If those pads are defective, both the supplier of the brake pads and Toyota will be held strictly liable for the injuries caused by the defects. ■

---

13. See, for example, *Bunch v. Hoffinger Industries, Inc.*,123 Cal.App.4th 1278, 20 Cal.Rptr.3d 780 (2004).

14. *Video Software Dealers Association v. Schwarzenegger*, 556 F.3d 950 (9th Cir. 2009); *Brown v. Entertainment Merchants Association*, ___ U.S. ___, 131 S.Ct. 2729, 180 L.Ed.2d 708 (2011).

15. *Suffolk County Water Authority v. Dow Chemical Co.*, 44 Misc.3d 569, 987 N.Y.S.2d 819 (N.Y.Sup. 2014).

## 7-4 Defenses to Product Liability

Defendants in product liability suits can raise a number of defenses. One defense, of course, is to show that there is no basis for the plaintiff's claim. Thus, for instance, in an action based on negligence, If a defendant can show that the plaintiff has *not* met the requirements for such an action (such as causation), then generally the defendant will not be liable.

Similarly, in a case involving strict product liability, a defendant can claim that the plaintiff failed to meet one of the requirements. For instance, if the defendant shows that the goods were altered after they were sold, normally the defendant will not be held liable.

In the following case, a product's safety switch had been disabled before the plaintiff used the product.

**Case 7.3**

## VeRost v. Mitsubishi Caterpillar Forklift America, Inc.

New York Supreme Court, Appellate Division, Fourth Department, 124 A.D.3d 1219, 1 N.Y.S.3d 589 (2015).

**Background and Facts** Drew VeRost was employed at a manufacturing facility in Buffalo, New York, owned by Nuttall Gear, LLC. While operating a forklift at Nuttall's facility, VeRost climbed out of the seat and attempted to engage a lever on the vehicle. As he stood on the front of the forklift and reached for the lever with his hand, he inadvertently stepped on the vehicle's gearshift. The activated gears caused part of the forklift to move backward, injuring him. He filed a suit in a New York state court against the forklift's maker, Mitsubishi Caterpillar Forklift America, Inc., and others, asserting claims in product liability.

The defendants established that the vehicle had been manufactured with a safety switch that would have prevented the accident had it not been disabled after delivery to Nuttall. The court issued a summary judgment in the defendants' favor. VeRost appealed.

### In the Language of the Court
*MEMORANDUM:*
    * * * *

The forklift in question was manufactured by defendant Mitsubishi Caterpillar Forklift America, Inc. (MCFA), and sold new to Nuttall Gear by defendants Buffalo Lift Trucks, Inc. (Buffalo Lift) and Mullen Industrial Handling Corp. (Mullen). The forklift as manufactured was equipped with a seat safety switch that would render the forklift inoperable if the operator was not in the driver's seat. At the time of the accident, however, someone had intentionally disabled the safety switch by installing a "jumper wire" under the seat of the forklift. As a result, the forklift still had power when the operator was not in the driver's seat. Of the 10 forklifts owned by Nuttall Gear, seven had "jumper wires" installed that disabled the safety switches.

The complaint asserts causes of action against MCFA, Buffalo Lift and Mullen sounding in strict products liability, alleging, *inter alia* ["among other things"], that the forklift was defectively designed and that those defendants failed to provide adequate "warnings for the safe operation, maintenance repair and servicing of the forklift." * * * Following discovery, the * * * defendants * * * each moved for summary judgment dismissing the complaint against them, contending that the forklift was safe when it was manufactured and delivered to Nuttall Gear, and that it was thereafter rendered unsafe by a third party who deactivated the safety switch. * * * [The] Supreme Court [of New York] granted the motions and dismissed the complaint in its entirety, and this appeal ensued.

We conclude that the court properly granted the motions of the * * * defendants. * * * *A manufacturer, who has designed and produced a safe product, will not be liable for injuries resulting from substantial alterations or modifications of the product by a third party which render the product defective or otherwise unsafe.* Here, the * * * defendants established as a matter of law that the forklift was not defectively designed by establishing that, when it was manufactured and delivered to Nuttall Gear, it had a safety switch that would have prevented plaintiff's accident, and a third party thereafter made a substantial modification to the forklift by disabling the safety switch. [Emphasis added.]

**Case 7.3 Continued**

**Decision and Remedy** *The state intermediate appellate court affirmed the lower court's judgment in Mitsubishi's favor. To succeed in an action based on product liability, the goods at issue must not have been substantially changed from the time the product was sold to the time the injury was sustained. VeRost could not meet this requirement.*

**Critical Thinking**

- **Legal Environment** *Could VeRost succeed in an action against Nuttall, alleging that the company's failure to maintain the forklift in a safe condition constituted negligence? Discuss.*

---

## 7–4a Preemption

A defense that has been successfully raised by defendants in recent years is preemption—that government regulations preempt claims for product liability (see *Spotlight Case* 7.2). An injured party may not be able to sue the manufacturer of defective products that are subject to comprehensive federal regulatory schemes.

■ **CASE IN POINT 7.12** Medical devices are subject to extensive government regulation and undergo a rigorous premarket approval process. The United States Supreme Court decided in *Riegel v. Medtronic, Inc.,* that a man who was injured by an approved medical device (a balloon catheter) could not sue its maker for product liability. The Court reasoned that Congress had created a comprehensive scheme of federal safety oversight for medical devices. The U.S. Food and Drug Administration is required to review the design, labeling, and manufacturing of medical devices before they are marketed to make sure that they are safe and effective. Because premarket approval is a "rigorous process," it preempts all common law claims challenging the safety or effectiveness of a medical device that has been approved.[16] ■

Since the *Medtronic* decision, some courts have extended the preemption defense to other product liability actions. Other courts have been unwilling to deny an injured party relief simply because the federal government was supposed to ensure a product's safety.[17] Even the United States Supreme Court refused to extend the preemption defense to preclude a drug maker's liability in one subsequent case.[18]

## 7–4b Assumption of Risk

Assumption of risk can sometimes be used as a defense in a product liability action. To establish assumption of risk, the defendant must show the following:

1. The plaintiff knew and appreciated the risk created by the product defect.
2. The plaintiff voluntarily assumed the risk—by express agreement or by words or conduct—even though it was unreasonable to do so.

Some states do not allow the defense of assumption of risk in strict product liability claims, however. ■ **CASE IN POINT 7.13** When Savannah Boles became a customer of Executive Tans, she signed a contract. One part of the contract stated that signers used the company's tanning booths at their own risk. It also released the manufacturer and others from liability for any injuries.

Later, Boles's fingers were partially amputated when they came into contact with a tanning booth's fan. Boles sued the manufacturer for strict product liability. The Colorado Supreme Court held that assumption of risk was not applicable because strict product liability is driven by public-policy considerations. The theory focuses on the nature of the product rather than the conduct of either the manufacturer or the person injured.[19] ■

## 7–4c Product Misuse

Similar to the defense of voluntary assumption of risk is that of **product misuse,** which occurs when a product is used for a purpose for which it was not intended. The courts have severely limited this defense, however, and it is now recognized as a defense *only when the particular use was not foreseeable.* If the misuse is reasonably foreseeable, the seller must take measures to guard against it.

---

**16.** *Riegel v. Medtronic, Inc.,* 552 U.S. 312, 128 S.Ct. 999, 169 L.Ed.2d 892 (2008).

**17.** See, for example, *McGuan v. Endovascular Technologies, Inc.,* 182 Cal. App.4th 974, 106 Cal.Rptr.3d 277 (2010), and *Paduano v. American Honda Motor Co.,* 169 Cal.App.4th 1453, 88 Cal.Rptr.3d 90 (2009).

**18.** *Wyeth v. Levine,* 555 U.S. 555, 129 S.Ct. 1187, 173 L.Ed.2d 51 (2009).

**19.** *Boles v. Sun Ergoline, Inc.,* 223 P.3d 724 (Col.Sup.Ct. 2010).

■ **CASE IN POINT 7.14** David Stults developed bronchiolitis obliterans ("popcorn lung") from consuming multiple bags of microwave popcorn daily for several years. When Stults filed a lawsuit against the popcorn manufacturers, they asked the court for a summary judgment in their favor. The court denied the defendants' motion and found that a manufacturer has a duty to warn of dangers associated with reasonably foreseeable misuses of a product. If it is foreseeable that a person might consume several bags of microwave popcorn a day, then the manufacturer might have to warn users about the potential health risks associated with doing so.[20] ■

## 7–4d Comparative Negligence (Fault)

Comparative negligence, or fault, can also affect strict liability claims. Today, courts in many jurisdictions consider the negligent or intentional actions of both the plaintiff and the defendant when apportioning liability and damages. A defendant may be able to limit some of its liability if it can show that the plaintiff's misuse of the product contributed to his or her injuries.

When proved, comparative negligence differs from other defenses in that it does not completely absolve the defendant of liability. It can, however, reduce the total amount of damages that will be awarded to the plaintiff. Note that some jurisdictions allow only intentional conduct to affect a plaintiff's recovery, whereas other states allow ordinary negligence to be used as a defense to product liability.

## 7–4e Commonly Known Dangers

The dangers associated with certain products (such as matches and sharp knives) are so commonly known that, as mentioned, manufacturers need not warn users of those dangers. If a defendant succeeds in convincing the court that a plaintiff's injury resulted from a *commonly known danger,* the defendant will not be liable.

■ **CASE IN POINT 7.15** In a classic example from 1957, Marguerite Jamieson was injured when an elastic exercise rope slipped off her foot and struck her in the eye, causing a detachment of the retina. Jamieson claimed that the manufacturer should be liable because it had failed to warn users that the exerciser might slip off a foot in such a manner.

The court stated that to hold the manufacturer liable in these circumstances "would go beyond the reasonable dictates of justice in fixing the liabilities of manufacturers." After all, stated the court, "almost every physical object can be inherently dangerous or potentially dangerous in a sense. . . . A manufacturer cannot manufacture a knife that will not cut or a hammer that will not mash a thumb or a stove that will not burn a finger. The law does not require [manufacturers] to warn of such common dangers."[21] ■

## 7–4f Knowledgeable User

A related defense is the *knowledgeable user* defense. If a particular danger (such as electrical shock) is or should be commonly known by particular users of a product (such as electricians), the manufacturer need not warn these users of the danger.

■ **CASE IN POINT 7.16** The parents of teenagers who had become overweight and developed health problems filed a product liability suit against McDonald's. The plaintiffs claimed that the fast-food chain had failed to warn customers of the adverse health effects of eating its food. The court rejected this claim, however, based on the knowledgeable user defense.

The court found that it is well known that the food at McDonald's contains high levels of cholesterol, fat, salt, and sugar and is therefore unhealthful. The court stated: "If consumers know (or reasonably should know) the potential ill health effects of eating at McDonald's, they cannot blame McDonald's if they, nonetheless, choose to satiate their appetite with a surfeit [excess] of supersized McDonald's products."[22] ■

## 7–4g Statutes of Limitations and Repose

Statutes of limitations restrict the time within which an action may be brought. The statute of limitations for product liability cases varies according to state law. Usually, the injured party must bring a product liability claim within two to four years. Often, the running of the prescribed period is **tolled** (that is, suspended) until the party suffering an injury has discovered it or should have discovered it.

To ensure that sellers and manufacturers will not be left vulnerable to lawsuits indefinitely, many states have passed **statutes of repose,** which place *outer* time limits on product liability actions. For instance, a statute of repose may require that claims be brought within twelve years from the date of sale or manufacture of the defective product. If the plaintiff does not bring an action before the prescribed period expires, the seller cannot be held liable.

Concept Summary 7.1 reviews the possible defenses in product liability actions.

20. *Stults v. International Flavors and Fragrances, Inc.,* 31 F.Supp.3d 1015 (N.D. Iowa 2014).

21. *Jamieson v. Woodward & Lothrop,* 247 F.2d 23 (D.C.Cir. 1957).
22. *Pelman v. McDonald's Corp.,* 237 F.Supp.2d 512 (S.D.N.Y. 2003).

## Concept Summary 7.1

### Defenses to Product Liability

| | |
|---|---|
| **Preemption** | If the product is subject to comprehensive federal safety regulations |
| **Assumption of Risk** | When the user or consumer knew the risk and voluntarily assumed it |
| **Product Misuse** | If the consumer misused the product in an unforeseeable way |
| **Comparative Negligence** | Apportions liability if the defendant was also negligent |
| **Commonly Known Dangers** | If the product was commonly known to be dangerous |
| **Knowledgeable User** | If the particular danger is commonly known by particular users of the product |
| **Statutory Time Periods** | If the statute of limitations or statute of repose period has expired |

## Reviewing: Strict Liability and Product Liability

Shalene Kolchek bought a Great Lakes Spa from Val Porter, a dealer who was selling spas at the state fair. Kolchek signed an installment contract. Porter then handed her the manufacturer's paperwork and arranged for the spa to be delivered and installed for her. Three months later, Kolchek left her six-year-old daughter, Litisha, alone in the spa. While exploring the spa's hydromassage jets, Litisha stuck her index finger into one of the jet holes and was unable to remove her finger from the jet.

Litisha yanked hard, injuring her finger, then panicked and screamed for help. Kolchek was unable to remove Litisha's finger, and the local police and rescue team were called to assist. After a three-hour operation that included draining the spa, sawing out a section of the spa's plastic molding, and slicing the jet casing, Litisha's finger was freed. Following this procedure, the spa was no longer functional. Litisha was taken to the local emergency room, where she was told that a bone in her finger was broken in two places. Using the information presented in the chapter, answer the following questions.

1. Under which theories of product liability can Kolchek sue Porter to recover for Litisha's injuries?
2. Would privity of contract be required for Kolchek to succeed in a product liability action against Great Lakes? Explain.
3. For an action in strict product liability against Great Lakes, what six requirements must Kolchek meet?
4. What defenses to product liability might Porter or Great Lakes be able to assert?

**Debate This** . . . *All liability suits against tobacco companies for lung cancer should be thrown out of court now and forever.*

## Terms and Concepts

## Issue Spotters

1. Rim Corporation makes tire rims that it sells to Superior Vehicles, Inc., which installs them on cars. One set of rims is defective, which an inspection would reveal. Superior does not inspect the rims. The car with the defective rims is sold to Town Auto Sales, which sells the car to Uri. Soon, the car is in an accident caused by the defective rims, and Uri is injured. Is Superior Vehicles liable? Explain your answer. (See *Strict Product Liability*.)

2. Bensing Company manufactures generic drugs for the treatment of heart disease. A federal law requires generic drug makers to use labels that are identical to the labels on brand-name versions of the drugs. Hunter Rothfus purchased Bensing's generic drugs in Ohio and wants to sue Bensing for defective labeling based on its failure to comply with Ohio state common law (rather than the federal labeling requirements). What defense might Bensing assert to avoid liability under state law? (See *Defenses to Product Liability*.)

- **Check your answers to the Issue Spotters against the answers provided in Appendix D at the end of this text.**

## Business Scenarios

**7–1. Strict Liability.** Danny and Marion Klein were injured when part of a fireworks display went astray and exploded near them. They sued Pyrodyne Corp., the pyrotechnic company that was hired to set up and discharge the fireworks. The Kleins alleged, among other things, that the company should be strictly liable for damages caused by the fireworks display. Will the court agree with the Kleins? What factors will the court consider in making its decision? Discuss fully. (See *Strict Liability*.)

**7–2. Product Liability.** Jason Clark, an experienced hunter, bought a paintball gun. Clark practiced with the gun and knew how to screw in the carbon dioxide cartridge, pump the gun, and use its safety and trigger. Although Clark was aware that he could purchase protective eyewear, he chose not to buy it.

Clark had taken gun safety courses and understood that it was "common sense" not to shoot anyone in the face. Clark's friend, Chris Wright, also owned a paintball gun and was similarly familiar with the gun's use and its risks.

Clark, Wright, and their friends played a game that involved shooting paintballs at cars whose occupants also had the guns. One night, while Clark and Wright were cruising with their guns, Wright shot at Clark's car, but hit Clark in the eye. Clark filed a product liability lawsuit against the manufacturer of Wright's paintball gun to recover for the injury. Clark claimed that the gun was defectively designed. During the trial, Wright testified that his gun "never malfunctioned." In whose favor should the court rule? Why? (See *Product Liability*.)

## Business Case Problems

**7–3. Design Defects.** Yun Tung Chow tried to unclog a floor drain in the kitchen of the restaurant where he worked. He used a drain cleaner called Lewis Red Devil Lye that contained crystalline sodium hydroxide. The product label said to wear eye protection, to put one tablespoon of lye directly into the drain, and to keep one's face away from the drain because there could be dangerous backsplash.

Without eye protection, Chow mixed three tablespoons of lye in a can and poured that mixture down the drain while bending over it. Liquid splashed back into his face, causing injury. He brought a product liability suit based on inadequate warnings and design defect. The trial court granted summary judgment to the manufacturer, and Chow appealed. An expert for Chow stated that the product was defective because it had a tendency to backsplash. Is that a convincing argument? Why or why not? [*Yun Tung Chow v. Reckitt & Coleman, Inc.,* 69 A.D.3d 413, 891 N.Y.S.2d 402 (N.Y.A.D. 1 Dept. 2010)] (See *Strict Product Liability*.)

**7–4. Strict Product Liability.** David Dobrovolny bought a new Ford F-350 pickup truck. A year later, the truck spontaneously caught fire in Dobrovolny's driveway. The truck was destroyed, but no other property was damaged, and no one was injured. Dobrovolny filed a suit in a Nebraska state court against Ford Motor Co. on a theory of strict product liability to recover the cost of the truck. Nebraska limits the application of strict product liability to situations involving personal injuries. Is Dobrovolny's claim likely to succeed? Why or why not? Is there another basis for liability on which he might recover? Explain. [*Dobrovolny v. Ford Motor Co.,* 281 Neb. 86, 793 N.W.2d 445 (2011)] (See *Strict Product Liability*.)

**7–5. Product Misuse.** Five-year-old Cheyenne Stark was riding in the backseat of her parents' Ford Taurus. Cheyenne was not sitting in a booster seat. Instead, she was using a seatbelt designed by Ford, but was wearing the shoulder belt behind her back. The car was involved in a collision. As a result, Cheyenne suffered a spinal cord injury and was paralyzed from the waist down. The family filed a suit against Ford Motor Co., alleging that the seatbelt was defectively designed. Could Ford successfully claim that Cheyenne had misused the seatbelt? Why or why not? [*Stark v. Ford Motor Co.*, 365 N.C. 468, 723 S.E.2d 753 (2012)] (See *Defenses to Product Liability*.)

**7–6. Business Case Problem with Sample Answer— Product Liability.** While driving on Interstate 40 in North  Carolina, Carroll Jett became distracted by a texting system in the cab of his tractor-trailer truck. He smashed into several vehicles that were slowed or stopped in front of him, injuring Barbara and Michael Durkee and others. The injured motorists filed a suit in a federal district court against Geologic Solutions, Inc., the maker of the texting system, alleging product liability. Was the accident caused by Jett's inattention or the texting device? Should a manufacturer be required to design a product that is incapable of distracting a driver? Discuss. [*Durkee v. Geologic Solutions, Inc.*, 2013 WL 14717 (4th Cir. 2013)] (See *Product Liability*.)

- **For a sample answer to Problem 7–6, go to Appendix E at the end of this text.**

**7–7. Strict Product Liability.** Medicis Pharmaceutical Corp. makes Solodyn, a prescription oral antibiotic. Medicis warns physicians that "autoimmune syndromes, including drug-induced lupus-like syndrome," may be associated with use of the drug. Amanda Watts had chronic acne. Her physician prescribed Solodyn. Information included with the drug did not mention the risk of autoimmune disorders, and Watts was not otherwise advised of it. She was prescribed the drug twice, each time for twenty weeks. Later, she experienced debilitating joint pain and, after being hospitalized, was diagnosed with lupus. On what basis could Watts recover from Medicis in an action grounded in product liability? Explain. [*Watts v. Medicis Pharmaceutical Corp.*, 236 Ariz. 511, 342 P.3d 847 (2015)] (See *Strict Product Liability*.)

**7–8. Strict Product Liability.** Duval Ford, LLC, sold a new Ford F-250 pick-up truck to David Sweat. Before taking delivery, Sweat ordered a lift kit to be installed on the truck by a Duval subcontractor. Sweat also replaced the tires and modified the suspension system to increase the towing capacity. Later, through Burkins Chevrolet, Sweat sold the truck to

Shaun Lesnick. Sweat had had no problems with the truck's steering or suspension, but Lesnick did. He had the steering repaired and made additional changes, including installing a steering stabilizer and replacing the tires. Two months later, Lesnick was driving the truck when the steering and suspension suddenly failed, and the truck flipped over, causing Lesnick severe injuries. Could Lesnick successfully claim that Duval and Burkins had failed to warn him of the risk of a lifted truck? Explain. [*Lesnick v. Duval Ford, LLC*, 41 Fla.L.Weekly D281, __ So.3d __ (1 Dist. 2016)] (See *Strict Product Liability*.)

**7–9. A Question of Ethics—Dangerous Products.** *Susan*  *Calles lived with her four daughters—Amanda, age eleven; Victoria, age five; and Jenna and Jillian, age three. In March 1998, Calles bought an Aim N Flame utility lighter, which she stored on the top shelf of her kitchen cabinet. A trigger can ignite the Aim N Flame after an "ON/OFF" switch is slid to the "on" position. On the night of March 31, Calles and Victoria left to get videos. Jenna and Jillian were in bed, and Amanda was watching television. Calles returned to find fire trucks and emergency vehicles around her home. Robert Finn, a fire investigator, determined that Jenna had started a fire using the lighter. Jillian suffered smoke inhalation, was hospitalized, and died on April 21. Calles filed a suit in an Illinois state court against Scripto-Tokai Corp., which distributed the Aim N Flame, and others. In her suit, which was grounded, in part, in strict liability claims, Calles alleged that the lighter was an "unreasonably dangerous product." Scripto filed a motion for summary judgment. [Calles v. Scripto-Tokai Corp., 224 Ill.2d 247, 864 N.E.2d 249, 309 Ill. Dec. 383 (2007)] (See Strict Product Liability.)*

**(a)** A product is "unreasonably dangerous" when it is dangerous beyond the expectation of the ordinary consumer. Whose expectation—Calles's or Jenna's—applies? Does the lighter pass this test? Explain.

**(b)** Calles presented evidence as to the likelihood and seriousness of injury from lighters that do not have child-safety devices. Scripto argued that the Aim N Flame is an alternative source of fire and is safer than a match. Calles admitted that she knew the dangers presented by lighters in the hands of children. Scripto admitted that it had been a defendant in several suits for injuries under similar circumstances. How should the court rule? Why?

## Legal Reasoning Group Activity

**7–10. Product Liability.** Bret D'Auguste was an experienced skier when he rented equipment to ski at Hunter Mountain Ski Bowl in New York. When D'Auguste entered an extremely difficult trail, he noticed immediately that the surface consisted of ice with almost no snow. He tried to exit the steeply declining trail by making a sharp right turn, but in the attempt, his left ski snapped off. D'Auguste lost his balance, fell, and slid down the mountain, striking his face and head against a fence along the trail. According to a report by a rental shop employee, one of the bindings on D'Auguste's skis had a "cracked heel housing." D'Auguste filed a lawsuit

against the bindings' manufacturer on a theory of strict product liability. The manufacturer filed a motion for summary judgment. (See *Product Liability*.)

**(a)** The first group will take the position of the manufacturer and develop an argument for why the court should *grant* the summary judgment motion and dismiss the strict product liability claim.

**(b)** The second group will take the position of D'Auguste and formulate a basis for why the court should *deny* the motion and allow the strict product liability claim.

# Answers to the *Issue Spotters*

**1.** *Is Superior Vehicles liable? Explain your answer.* Yes. The manufacturer is liable for the injuries to the user of the product. A manufacturer is liable for its failure to exercise due care to any person who sustains an injury proximately caused by a negligently made (defective) product.

**2.** *What defense might Bensing assert to avoid liability under state law?* Bensing can assert the defense of preemption. An injured party may not be able to sue the manufacturer of defective products that are subject to comprehensive federal regulatory schemes. If the federal government has a comprehensive regulatory scheme (such as it does with medical devices and vaccines), then it is assumed that the rules were designed to ensure a product's safety, and the federal rules will preempt any state regulations. Therefore, Bensing could not be held liable under state law if it complied with the federal drug-labeling requirements.

# Sample Answers for *Business Case Problems with Sample Answer*

**Problem 7–6.** *Product Liability.* Here, the accident was caused by Jett's inattention, not by the texting device in the cab of his truck. In a product liability case based on a design defect, the plaintiff has to prove that the product was defective at the time it left the hands of the seller or lessor. The plaintiff must also show that this defective condition made it "unreasonably dangerous" to the user or consumer. If the product was delivered in a safe condition and subsequent mishandling made it harmful to the user, the seller or lessor normally is not liable. To successfully assert a design defect, a plaintiff has to show that a reasonable alternative design was available and that the defendant failed to use it.

The plaintiffs could contend that the defendant manufacturer of the texting device owed them a duty of care because injuries to vehicle drivers and passengers, and others on the roads, were reasonably foreseeable due to the product's design, which (1) required the driver to divert his eyes from the road to view an incoming text from the dispatcher, and (2) permitted the receipt of texts while the vehicle was moving. But manufacturers are not required to design a product incapable of distracting a driver. The duty owed by a manufacturer to the user or consumer of a product does not require guarding against hazards that are commonly known or obvious or protecting against injuries that result from a user's careless conduct. That is what happened here.

In the actual case on which this problem is based, the court reached the same conclusion, based on the reasoning stated above, and an intermediate appellate court affirmed the judgment.

# Chapter 10

# CHAPTER

# Creditor-Debtor Relations and Bankruptcy

Many people in today's economy are struggling to pay their debts. Although in the old days, debtors were punished and sometimes even sent to prison for failing to pay what they owed, debtors today rarely go to jail. They have many other options, including bankruptcy—the last resort in resolving debtor-creditor problems.

Bankruptcy relief is provided under federal law. Although state laws may play a role in bankruptcy proceedings, particularly state laws governing property, the governing law is based on federal legislation.

The right to petition for bankruptcy relief under federal law is an essential aspect of our capitalistic society, in which we have great opportunities for financial success but may also encounter financial difficulties. Therefore, every businessperson should have some understanding of this topic.

## 15–1 Laws Assisting Creditors

Normally, creditors have no problem collecting the debts owed to them. When disputes arise over the amount owed, however, or when the debtor simply cannot or will not pay, what happens? What remedies are available to creditors when a debtor **defaults** (fails to pay as promised)? Here, we discuss some basic laws that assist the debtor and creditor in resolving their dispute.

The remedies we discuss next are available regardless of whether a creditor is secured or unsecured. *Secured creditors* are those whose loans are backed by *collateral,* which is specific property (such as a car or a house) pledged by a borrower to ensure repayment. The loans made by *unsecured creditors,* such as companies that provide credit cards, are not backed by collateral.

### 15–1a Liens

A **lien** is an encumbrance on (claim against) property to satisfy a debt or protect a claim for the payment of a debt. Liens may arise under the common law (usually by possession of the property) or under statutory law. *Mechanic's liens* are statutory liens, whereas *artisan's liens* were recognized at common law. *Judicial liens* may be used by a creditor to collect on a debt before or after a judgment is entered by a court. Liens are a very important tool for creditors because they generally take priority over other claims against the same property.

**Mechanic's Liens** Sometimes, a person who has contracted for labor, services, or materials to be furnished for making improvements on real property does not immediately pay for the improvements. When that happens, the creditor can place a **mechanic's lien** on the property.

A mechanic's lien creates a special type of debtor-creditor relationship in which the real estate itself becomes security for the debt. If the property owner fails to pay the debt, the lienholder is technically entitled to foreclose on the real estate and sell it. (*Foreclosure* is the process by which a creditor legally takes a debtor's property to satisfy a debt.) The sale proceeds are then used to pay the debt and the costs of the legal proceedings. The surplus, if any, is paid to the former owner.

In the real world, however, small-amount mechanic's liens are rarely the basis of foreclosure. Rather, these liens simply remain on the books of the state until the house is sold. At closing (when the sale is finalized), the seller agrees to pay any mechanic's liens out of the proceeds of the sale before the seller receives any of the funds.

State law governs the procedures that must be followed to create a mechanic's (or other statutory) lien. Generally, the lienholder must file a written notice of lien within a specific time period (usually within 60 to 120 days) from the last date that material or labor was provided.

In the following case, the state mechanic's lien statute required the lien to be filed no more than 90 days after "the completion of the work." The contractor that filed the lien and the owner of the project against which the lien was filed disputed the meaning of the term "completion."

# Picerne Construction Corp. v. Villas

California Court of Appeal, Third District, 244 Cal.App.4th 1201, 199 Cal.Rptr.3d 257 (2016).

## In the Language of the Court

MAURO, J. [Judge]

* * * *

Castellino [Villas, LLC] and Picerne [Construction Corporation] entered into an agreement in which Picerne would build an apartment complex called Castellino Villas at Laguna West (project or property) in the City of Elk Grove [California] (the City). The project consisted of 11 apartment buildings, separate garages, a clubhouse, and other facilities.

* * * *

The City issued certificates of occupancy for the 11 buildings within the project * * * after a city inspector conducted a final inspection of each building. The first certificates of occupancy were issued on May 3, 2006. The final certificate of occupancy was issued on July 25, 2006.

Picerne employees and subcontractors continued to perform work at the project after July 25, 2006.

* * * *

[John] Olsen [Castellino's representative for the project] signed a document titled "Owner's Acceptance of Site" for Castellino on September 8, 2006.

* * * *

Castellino began renting apartments at the property in October 2006.

Picerne recorded a claim of mechanic's lien on November 28, 2006.

Picerne filed a complaint [in a California state court] to foreclose its mechanic's lien on December 29, 2006.

* * * *

* * * The trial court * * * determined * * * Picerne is entitled to foreclose its lien.

* * * *

[On appeal to this court] Castellino * * * contends Picerne does not have a valid mechanic's lien because Picerne did not record a claim of mechanic's lien within 90 days after substantial completion of the project.

* * * *

*In order to have a valid mechanic's lien, a claimant must record a claim of lien within a prescribed period of time after completion of the work of improvement * * *. The failure of a claimant to timely record a claim of lien precludes the enforcement of a mechanic's lien.* [Emphasis added.]

[When Picerne filed its lien, mechanic's liens were governed by California Civil Code Section 3115, which] provided, "Each original contractor [a contractor who has a direct contractual relationship with the owner for the work], in order to enforce a lien, must record his claim of lien after he completes his contract and before the expiration of 90 days after the completion of the work of improvement." [According to Section 3116, the term "work of improvement" means the entire structure or scheme of improvement as a whole.]

* * * The [California State] Legislature defined the term completion as "actual completion of the work of improvement." In addition, * * * deemed to be equivalent to a completion [was] the acceptance by the owner or his agent of the work of improvement.

Substantial evidence supports the trial court's finding that the owner accepted the project as of September 8, 2006. * * * Picerne timely recorded its claim of mechanic's lien within 90 days after September 8, 2006.

* * * *

Castellino * * * nevertheless claims that the time for Picerne to record its claim of mechanic's lien began to run before September 8, 2006. [Castellino] asserts the phrase "completion of the work of improvement" in Section 3115 means substantial completion of the work of improvement, and the project was substantially completed by July 25, 2006, when the City issued the final certificate of occupancy.

There are cases construing the * * * mechanic's lien statute which interpreted "completion" as substantial completion.

* * * *

[But these cases were decided before the Legislature amended Section 3115 to define] completion of the work of improvement as actual completion of the work of improvement * * *. The Legislature did not define "completion of the work of improvement" as substantial completion. Courts have looked at whether the work at issue was required under the claimant's contract in determining whether a work of improvement was completed.

Castellino argues that interpreting the term "completion" * * * to mean substantial completion would be sound public policy because it would ensure transparency, visibility, objectivity, and certainty in the relationship between the contractor and the owner in the filing of mechanic's liens. However, following the language of the statute by construing "completion" as "actual completion" does not create uncertainty when reference can be made to the parties' agreement and the labor and materials furnished. Moreover, * * * deemed equivalent to completion [is] acceptance of the work of improvement.

In addition, contrary to Castellino's argument, public policy supports the interpretation of completion as actual completion in this specific context. *The mechanic's lien statute is intended [primarily to benefit] persons who perform labor or furnish materials for works of improvement, and it is to be liberally construed for the protection of laborers and material suppliers, with doubts concerning the meaning of the statute generally resolved in favor of the lien claimant.* Interpreting

**Case 15.1 Continues**

**Case 15.1 Continued**

completion as actual completion gives lien claimants the maximum amount of time to assert their rights before such rights are cut off, whereas interpreting completion as substantial completion could cut off mechanic's lien rights much earlier. The interpretation espoused by Castellino would contravene the purpose of California's mechanic's lien law to protect the right to payment of those who have furnished labor or materials to works of improvement. Our construction of the term "completion" * * * effectuates the intent of the mechanic's lien law. [Emphasis added.]

Substantial evidence supports the trial court's findings that even though the City had issued certificates of occupancy for the 11 buildings within the project, roof and stairway work required under the general contract continued between July 25, 2006 and September 19, 2006. Elizar Ortiz [an installer employed by Picerne's stairway subcontractor] testified he worked 22½ hours on September 15, 18, and 19, 2006, installing grip tape on all of the stairs at the project. The general contract called for the installation of anti-slip grip tape on all concrete stair treads. Ortiz's testimony established the work he performed on September 15, 18, and 19, 2006 was not corrective or repair work.

The president of Picerne's roofing subcontractor testified his company performed roofing work at the project after July 25, 2006. He said such work included straightening out some of the valleys in the roofs, installing nailers and hips on the roof ridges, and nailing trim. * * * The roof and stairway work performed after July 25, 2006, is not comparable to adding a few strokes of paint or turning a screw.

Picerne recorded a claim of mechanic's lien * * * within 90 days of the date Castellino accepted the project and when the stairway and roofing subcontractors performed work required under their contracts. Accordingly, the trial court did not err in concluding Picerne timely recorded its claim of mechanic's lien.

* * * *

* * * The judgment is affirmed.

### Legal Reasoning Questions

**1.** How did the California legislature define the term "completion"? Was this definition clear? Discuss.

**2.** How did the owner of the project at the center of this case want the court to interpret "completion"? What arguments support this contention?

**3.** Ultimately, how did the court define "completion"? Why?

---

**Artisan's Liens** When a debtor fails to pay for labor and materials furnished for the repair or improvement of *personal* property, a creditor can recover payment through an **artisan's lien.** As mentioned, artisan's liens usually take priority over other creditors' claims to the same property.[1]

**Lienholder Must Retain Possession.** In contrast to a mechanic's lien, an artisan's lien is *possessory.* That is, the lienholder ordinarily must have retained possession of the property and have expressly or impliedly agreed to provide the services on a cash, not a credit, basis. The lien remains in existence as long as the lienholder maintains possession, and the lien is terminated once possession is *voluntarily* surrendered, unless the surrender is only temporary.[2]

■ **CASE IN POINT 15.1** Carrollton Exempted Village School District (in Ohio) hired Clean Vehicle Solutions America, LLC (CVSA, based in New York), to convert ten school buses from diesel to compressed natural gas.

The contract price was $660,000. The district paid a $400,000 deposit and agreed to pay installments of $26,000 to CVSA after the delivery of each converted bus. After the first two buses were delivered, the district refused to continue the contract, claiming that the conversion made the two buses unsafe to drive.

Both parties filed breach of contract lawsuits. CVSA also asserted an artisan's lien over two other buses that it still had in its possession because it had started converting them to natural gas and spent $65,000 doing so. Regardless of the outcome in the parties' lawsuits, CVSA has an artisan's lien that gives it a priority claim to those two buses so long as they remain in its possession. The buses will act as security for the district's payment of at least the amount CVSA has spent converting them to natural gas.[3] ■

**Foreclosure on Personal Property.** Modern statutes permit the holder of an artisan's lien to foreclose and sell the property subject to the lien to satisfy the debt. As with

---

1. An artisan's lien has priority over a filed statutory lien (such as a title lien on an automobile or a lien filed under Article 9 of the UCC) and a bailee's lien (such as a storage lien).

2. Involuntary surrender of possession by a lienholder, such as when a police officer seizes goods from a lienholder, does not terminate the lien.

3. *Clean Vehicle Solutions America, LLC v. Carrollton Exempted Village School District Board of Education*, 2015 WL 5459852 (S.D.N.Y. 2015).

a mechanic's lien, the lienholder is required to give notice to the owner of the property before the foreclosure and sale. The sale proceeds are used to pay the debt and the costs of the legal proceedings, and the surplus, if any, is paid to the former owner.

**Judicial Liens** When a debt is past due, a creditor can bring a legal action against the debtor to collect the debt. If the action is successful, the court awards the creditor a judgment against the debtor (usually for the amount of the debt plus any interest and legal costs incurred). Frequently, however, the creditor is unable to collect the awarded amount.

To ensure that a judgment in the creditor's favor will be collectible, the creditor may request that certain property of the debtor be seized to satisfy the debt. (As will be discussed, under state or federal statutes, some kinds of property are exempt from attachment by creditors.) A court's order to seize the debtor's property is known as a *writ of attachment* if it is issued before a judgment. If the order is issued after a judgment, it is referred to as a *writ of execution.*

**Writ of Attachment.** In the context of judicial liens, **attachment** refers to a court-ordered seizure and taking into custody of property before a judgment is obtained on a past-due debt. Because attachment is a *prejudgment* remedy, it occurs either at the time a lawsuit is filed or immediately afterward.

A creditor must comply with the specific state's statutory restrictions and requirements. The due process clause of the Fourteenth Amendment to the U.S. Constitution requires that the debtor be given notice and an opportunity to be heard. The creditor must have an enforceable right to payment of the debt under law and must follow certain procedures. Otherwise, the creditor can be liable for damages for wrongful attachment.

The typical procedure for attachment is as follows:

1. The creditor files with the court an *affidavit* (a written statement, made under oath). The affidavit states that the debtor has failed to pay and indicates the statutory grounds under which attachment is sought.
2. The creditor must post a bond to cover at least the court costs, the value of the property attached, and the value of the loss of use of that property suffered by the debtor.
3. When the court is satisfied that all the requirements have been met, it issues a **writ of attachment.** The writ directs the sheriff or other officer to seize the debtor's nonexempt property. If the creditor prevails at trial, the seized property can be sold to satisfy the judgment.

**Writ of Execution.** If a creditor wins a judgment against a debtor and the debtor will not or cannot pay the amount due, the creditor can request a **writ of execution** from the court. A writ of execution is an order that directs the sheriff to seize (levy) and sell any of the debtor's nonexempt real or personal property. The writ applies only to property that is within the court's geographic jurisdiction (usually the county in which the courthouse is located).

The proceeds of the sale are used to pay the judgment, accrued interest, and costs of the sale. Any excess is paid to the debtor. The debtor can pay the judgment and redeem the nonexempt property at any time before the sale takes place. (Because of exemption laws and bankruptcy laws, however, many judgments are practically uncollectible.)

## 15–1b Garnishment

An order for **garnishment** permits a creditor to collect a debt by seizing property of the debtor that is being held by a third party. As a result of a garnishment proceeding, for instance, the debtor's employer may be ordered by the court to turn over a portion of the debtor's wages to pay the debt. Many other types of property can be garnished as well, including funds in a bank account, tax refunds, pensions, and trust funds. It is only necessary that the property is not exempt from garnishment and is in the possession of a third party.

■ **CASE IN POINT 15.2** When Edward G. Tinsley divorced Michelle Townsend, they entered into a marital settlement contract. They agreed to sell the marital home and split the proceeds evenly. But Tinsley refused to cooperate with the sale. A court therefore appointed a trustee to sell the house for them and ordered the sheriff to evict Tinsley. Tinsley then conveyed the house to a trust established in his name. Even after the sheriff evicted Tinsley from the house and changed the locks, Tinsley managed to move back in and change the locks again.

Tinsley was arrested for trespassing and charged with contempt of court (for disobeying court orders). In the meantime, Tinsley secretly sold the home for $150,000 and deposited the proceeds into a bank account held in the name of Edward G. Tinsley Living Trust at SunTrust Bank. After learning of the sale, the court-appointed trustee obtained a writ of garnishment on all of Tinsley's and his trust's bank accounts at SunTrust Bank. Despite numerous objections from Tinsley (and a trial and appeal), Sun Trust eventually complied with the garnishment order and sent all the funds to the trustee.[4] ■

---

4. *Tinsley v. SunTrust Bank*, 2016 WL 687545 (Md.App. 2016).

**Procedures** Garnishment can be a prejudgment remedy, requiring a hearing before a court, but it is most often a postjudgment remedy. State law governs garnishment actions, so the specific procedures vary from state to state.

In some states, the judgment creditor needs to obtain only one order of garnishment, which will then apply continuously to the judgment debtor's wages until the entire debt is paid. In other states, the judgment creditor must go back to court for a separate order of garnishment for each pay period.

**Laws Limiting the Amount of Wages Subject to Garnishment** Both federal and state laws limit the amount that can be taken from a debtor's weekly take-home pay through garnishment proceedings.[5] Federal law provides a minimal framework to protect debtors from losing all their income to pay judgment debts.[6] State laws also provide dollar exemptions, and these amounts are often larger than those provided by federal law.

Under federal law, an employer cannot dismiss an employee because his or her wages are being garnished.

### 15–1c Creditors' Composition Agreements

Creditors may contract with the debtor for discharge of the debtor's liquidated debts (debts that are definite, or fixed, in amount) on payment of a sum less than that owed. These agreements are referred to as **creditors' composition agreements** (or *composition agreements*) and usually are held to be enforceable unless they are formed under duress.

### 15–1d Suretyship and Guaranty

When a third person promises to pay a debt owed by another in the event that the debtor does not pay, either a *suretyship* or a *guaranty* relationship is created. Exhibit 15–1 illustrates these relationships. The third person's creditworthiness becomes the security for the debt owed.

Suretyship and guaranty provide creditors with the right to seek payment from the third party if the primary debtor, or *principal,* defaults on her or his obligations. Normally a guaranty must be in writing to

be enforceable under the Statute of Frauds, unless its main purpose is to benefit the guarantor. Traditionally, a suretyship agreement did not require a writing to be enforceable, and oral surety agreements were sufficient. Today, however, some states require a writing to enforce a suretyship.

At common law, there were significant differences in the liability of a surety and a guarantor. Today, however, the distinctions outlined here have been abolished in some states.

**Suretyship** A contract of strict **suretyship** is a promise made by a third person to be responsible for the debtor's obligation. It is an express contract between the **surety** (the third party) and the creditor.

In the strictest sense, the surety is primarily liable for the debt of the principal. The creditor can demand payment from the surety from the moment the debt is due. The creditor need not exhaust all legal remedies against the principal debtor before holding the surety responsible for payment.

■ **EXAMPLE 15.3** Roberto Delmar wants to borrow from the bank to buy a used car. Because Roberto is still in college, the bank will not lend him the funds without a cosigner. Roberto's father, José Delmar, who has dealt with the bank before, agrees to cosign the note, thereby becoming a surety who is jointly liable for payment of the debt. When José Delmar cosigns the note, he becomes primarily liable to the bank. On the note's due date, the bank can seek payment from either Roberto or José Delmar, or both jointly. ■

**Guaranty** With a suretyship arrangement, the surety is *primarily* liable for the debtor's obligation. With a

### EXHIBIT 15–1 Suretyship and Guaranty Parties

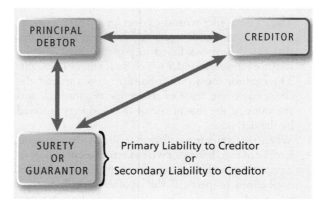

---

5. A few states (such as Texas) do not permit garnishment of wages by private parties except under a child-support order.
6. For instance, the federal Consumer Credit Protection Act, 15 U.S.C. Sections 1601–1693r, provides that a debtor can retain either 75 percent of his or her disposable earnings per week or an amount equivalent to thirty hours of work paid at federal minimum wage rates, whichever is greater.

guaranty arrangement, the **guarantor**—the third person making the guaranty—is *secondarily* liable.

The guarantor can be required to pay the obligation *only after the principal debtor defaults,* and usually only after the creditor has made an attempt to collect from the debtor. The guaranty contract terms determine the extent and time of the guarantor's liability.

■ **CASE IN POINT 15.4** To finance a development project in Delaware, Brandywine Partners, LLC, borrowed $15.9 million from HSBC Realty Credit Corp. (USA). As part of the deal, Brian O'Neill, principal for Brandywine, signed a guaranty that designated him the "primary obligor" for $8.1 million of the loan. Brandywine defaulted, and HSBC filed a suit in a federal district court against O'Neill to recover on the guaranty. O'Neill filed a counterclaim, alleging that HSBC had fraudulently induced him to sign the guaranty.

O'Neill argued that the loan agreement valued the property at $26.5 million and that HSBC knew this was not the property's real value. O'Neill also claimed that the parties had agreed that if Brandywine defaulted, HSBC could recover its loan by selling the property—before trying to collect from the guaranty.

The court ruled in favor of HSBC and dismissed O'Neill's counterclaim. A federal appellate court affirmed. The guaranty stated that O'Neill was familiar with the value of the property, that he was not relying on it as an inducement to sign the guaranty, and that HSBC made no representations to induce him to sign. The guaranty also provided that HSBC could enforce its rights against him without trying to recover on the property first.[7] ■

**Actions That Release the Surety and the Guarantor** Basically, the same actions will release either a surety or a guarantor from an obligation. For simplicity, this subsection and the following subsections will refer just to sureties, but remember that the same rules generally apply to guarantors.

1. *Material modification.* Making any material modification to the terms of the original contract without the surety's consent will discharge the surety's obligation. (The extent to which the surety is discharged depends on whether he or she was compensated and the amount of loss suffered from the modification. For instance, a father who receives no consideration for acting as a surety on his daughter's loan will be completely discharged if the loan contract is modified without his consent.)

2. *Surrender of property.* If a creditor surrenders the collateral to the debtor or impairs the collateral without the surety's consent, these acts can reduce the obligation of the surety. If the creditor's actions reduce the value of the property used as collateral, the surety is released to the extent of any loss suffered.

3. *Payment or tender of payment.* Naturally, any payment of the principal obligation by the debtor or by another person on the debtor's behalf will discharge the surety from the obligation. Even if the creditor refused to accept the payment when it was tendered, if the creditor knew about the suretyship, the obligation of the surety can be discharged.

**Defenses of the Surety and the Guarantor** Generally, the surety or guarantor can also assert any of the defenses available to the principal debtor to avoid liability on the obligation to the creditor. A few exceptions do exist, however. They apply to both sureties and guarantors, but again, for simplicity, we refer just to sureties.

1. *Incapacity and bankruptcy.* Incapacity and bankruptcy are personal defenses, which can be asserted only by the person who is affected. Therefore, the surety cannot assert the principal debtor's incapacity or bankruptcy as a defense. (A surety may assert his or her own incapacity or bankruptcy as a defense, of course.)

2. *Statute of limitations.* The surety cannot assert the statute of limitations as a defense. (In contrast, the principal debtor can claim the statute of limitations as a defense to payment.)

3. *Fraud.* If the creditor fraudulently induced the person to act as a surety on the debt, the surety or guarantor can assert fraud as a defense. In most states, the creditor must inform the surety, before the formation of the suretyship contract, of material facts known by the creditor that would substantially increase the surety's risk. Failure to so inform may constitute fraud and render the suretyship obligation voidable.

**Rights of the Surety and the Guarantor** When the surety or guarantor pays the debt owed to the creditor, he or she acquires certain rights, as discussed next. Again, for simplicity, the discussion refers just to sureties.

**The Right of Subrogation.** The surety has the legal **right of subrogation.** Simply stated, this means that any right that the creditor had against the debtor now becomes the right of the surety. Included are creditor rights in bankruptcy, rights to collateral possessed by the creditor, and rights to judgments obtained by the creditor. In short, the

---

7. *HSBC Realty Credit Corp. (USA) v. O'Neill,* 745 F.3d 564 (1st Cir. 2014).

surety now stands in the shoes of the creditor and may pursue any remedies that were available to the creditor against the debtor.

**The Right of Reimbursement.** The surety has a **right of reimbursement** from the debtor. Basically, the surety is entitled to receive from the debtor all outlays made on behalf of the suretyship arrangement. Such outlays can include expenses incurred as well as the actual amount of the debt paid to the creditor.

**The Right of Contribution.** Two or more sureties are called **co-sureties.** When a co-surety pays more than her or his proportionate share on a debtor's default, she or he has a **right of contribution.** That means the co-surety is entitled to recover from the other co-sureties the amount paid above the surety's obligation. Generally, a co-surety's liability either is determined by agreement or, in the absence of agreement, is set at the maximum liability under the suretyship contract.

■ **EXAMPLE 15.5** Yasser and Itzhak, two co-sureties, are obligated under a suretyship contract to guarantee Jules's debt. Itzhak's maximum liability is $15,000, and Yasser's is $10,000. Jules owes $10,000 and is in default. Itzhak pays the creditor the entire $10,000.

In the absence of an agreement to the contrary, Itzhak can recover $4,000 from Yasser. The amount of the debt that Yasser agreed to cover ($10,000) is divided by the total amount that he and Itzhak together agreed to cover ($25,000). The result is multiplied by the amount of the default, yielding the amount that Yasser owes—($10,000 ÷ $25,000) × $10,000 = $4,000. ■

# 15–2 Mortgages

When individuals purchase real property, they typically make a **down payment** in cash and borrow the remaining funds from a financial institution. The borrowed funds are secured by a **mortgage**—a written instrument that gives the creditor a lien on the debtor's real property as security for payment of a debt. The creditor is the *mortgagee,* and the debtor is the *mortgagor.*

## 15–2a Fixed-Rate versus Adjustable-Rate Mortgages

Lenders offer various types of mortgages to meet the needs of different borrowers, but a basic distinction is whether the interest rate is fixed or variable. A *fixed-rate mortgage* has a fixed, or unchanging, rate of interest, so the payments remain the same for the duration of the loan. Lenders determine the interest rate for a standard fixed-rate mortgage loan based on a variety of factors, including the borrower's credit history, credit score, income, and debts.

With an *adjustable-rate mortgage (ARM),* the rate of interest paid by the borrower changes periodically. Typically, the initial interest rate for an ARM is set at a relatively low fixed rate for a specified period, such as a year or three years. After that time, the interest rate adjusts annually or by some other period, such as biannually or monthly. The interest rate adjustment is calculated by adding a certain number of percentage points (called the margin) to an index rate (one of various government interest rates).

ARMs contractually shift the risk that the interest rate will change from the lender to the borrower. Borrowers will have lower initial payments if they are willing to assume the risk of interest rate increases.

## 15–2b Mortgage Provisions

Because a mortgage involves a transfer of real property, it must be in writing to comply with the Statute of Frauds. Mortgages normally are lengthy and formal documents containing many provisions, including the following:

1. *The terms of the underlying loan.* These include the loan amount, the interest rate, the period of repayment, and other important financial terms, such as the margin and index rate for an ARM.

2. *A prepayment penalty clause.* A **prepayment penalty clause** requires the borrower to pay a penalty if the mortgage is repaid in full within a certain period. A prepayment penalty helps to protect the lender should the borrower refinance within a short time after obtaining a mortgage.

3. *Provisions relating to the maintenance of the property.* Because the mortgage conveys an interest in the property to the lender, the lender often requires the borrower to maintain the property to protect the lender's investment.

4. *A statement obligating the borrower to maintain homeowner's insurance on the property.* **Homeowner's insurance** protects the lender's interest in the event of a loss due to certain hazards, such as fire or storm damage.

5. *A list of the non-loan financial obligations to be borne by the borrower.* For instance, the borrower typically is required to pay all property taxes, assessments, and other claims against the property.

6. *Creditor protections.* When creditors extend mortgages, they are advancing a significant amount of funds for a number of years. Consequently, creditors

usually require debtors to obtain **mortgage insurance** if they do not make a down payment of at least 20 percent of the purchase price.

Creditors record the mortgage with the appropriate office in the county where the property is located, so that their interest in the property is officially on record.

### 15–2c Mortgage Foreclosure

If the homeowner *defaults,* or fails to make the mortgage payments, the lender has the right to foreclose on the mortgaged property. **Foreclosure** is the legal process by which the lender repossesses and auctions off the property that has secured the loan. The lender must strictly comply with the state statute governing foreclosures.

Foreclosure is expensive and time consuming. It generally benefits neither the borrowers, who lose their homes, nor the lenders, which face the prospect of losses on their loans. Therefore, both lenders and borrowers are motivated to avoid foreclosure proceedings if possible. Methods of avoiding foreclosure include forbearance, workout agreements, and short sales. (In addition, a defaulting borrower can redeem the property before a foreclosure sale by paying the full amount of the debt, plus any interest and costs that have accrued.)

A **forbearance** is a postponement of part or all of the payments on a loan for a limited time. This option works well when the debtor can solve the problem by securing a new job, selling the property, or finding another acceptable solution.

A **workout agreement** is a contract that describes the respective rights and responsibilities of the borrower and the lender as they try to resolve the default. Usually, the lender agrees to delay seeking foreclosure. In exchange, the borrower provides additional financial information that might be used to modify the mortgage.

A lender may sometimes agree to a **short sale,** which is a sale of the property for less than the balance due on the mortgage loan. Typically, the borrower has to show some hardship, such as the loss of a job, a decline in the value of the home, a divorce, or a death in the household. The lender often has approval rights in a short sale, so the sale process may take much longer than an ordinary real estate transaction.

## 15–3 Protection for Debtors

The law protects debtors as well as creditors. Consumer protection statutes protect debtors' rights, for instance, and bankruptcy laws are designed specifically to assist debtors in need of help. In addition, in most states, certain types of real and personal property are exempt from execution or attachment. State exemption statutes usually include both real and personal property.

### 15–3a Exempted Real Property

Probably the most familiar exemption is the **homestead exemption.** The purpose of the homestead exemption is to ensure that the debtor will retain some form of shelter.

**The General Rule** Each state permits the debtor to retain the family home, either in its entirety or up to a specified dollar amount, free from the claims of unsecured creditors or trustees in bankruptcy. (Note that federal bankruptcy law places a cap on the amount that debtors filing bankruptcy can claim is exempt under their states' homestead exemption.)

■ **EXAMPLE 15.6** Vince Beere owes Chris Veltman $40,000. The debt is the subject of a lawsuit, and the court awards Veltman a judgment of $40,000 against Beere. Beere's homestead is valued at $50,000, and the homestead exemption is $25,000. There are no outstanding mortgages or other liens on his homestead. To satisfy the judgment debt, Beere's family home is sold at public auction for $45,000. The proceeds of the sale are distributed as follows:

1. Beere is given $25,000 as his homestead exemption.
2. Veltman is paid $20,000 toward the judgment debt, leaving a $20,000 deficiency judgment (that is, "leftover debt"). The deficiency judgment can be satisfied from any other nonexempt property (personal or real) that Beere may own, if permitted by state law. ■

**Limitations** In a few states, statutes allow the homestead exemption only if the judgment debtor has a family. If a judgment debtor does not have a family, a creditor may be entitled to collect the full amount realized from the sale of the debtor's home. In addition, the homestead exemption interacts with other areas of law and can sometimes operate to cancel out a portion of a lien on a debtor's real property.

### 15–3b Exempted Personal Property

Personal property that is most often exempt from satisfaction of judgment debts includes the following:

1. Household furniture up to a specified dollar amount.
2. Clothing and certain personal possessions, such as family pictures or a Bible.

3. A vehicle (or vehicles) for transportation (at least up to a specified dollar amount).
4. Certain classified animals, usually livestock but including pets.
5. Equipment that the debtor uses in a business or trade, such as tools or professional instruments, up to a specified dollar amount.

# 15–4 Bankruptcy Law

Article I, Section 8, of the U.S. Constitution gave Congress the power to establish "uniform laws on the subject of bankruptcies throughout the United States." Federal bankruptcy legislation was first enacted in 1898 and since then has undergone several modifications, most recently in the 2005 Bankruptcy Reform Act.[8] Federal bankruptcy laws (as amended) are called the Bankruptcy Code or, more simply, the Code.

Bankruptcy law in the United States has two main goals:

1. To protect a debtor by giving him or her a fresh start without creditors' claims.
2. To ensure equitable treatment of creditors who are competing for a debtor's assets.

Thus, the law attempts to balance the rights of the debtor and of the creditors.

Although the twin goals of bankruptcy remain the same, the balance between them shifted somewhat after the 2005 reform legislation. That law was enacted, in part, because of the growing concern that the law allowed too many debtors to avoid paying their debts. Thus, a major goal of the reforms was to require more consumers to pay as many of their debts as possible instead of having those debts fully extinguished in bankruptcy.

## 15–4a Bankruptcy Courts

Bankruptcy proceedings are held in federal bankruptcy courts, which are under the authority of U.S. district courts. Rulings from bankruptcy courts can be appealed to the district courts.

A bankruptcy court can conduct a jury trial if the appropriate district court has authorized it and the parties to the bankruptcy consent. Bankruptcy courts follow the Federal Rules of Bankruptcy Procedure rather than the Federal Rules of Civil Procedure. Bankruptcy court judges are appointed for terms of fourteen years.

## 15–4b Types of Bankruptcy Relief

The Bankruptcy Code is contained in Title 11 of the *United States Code* and has eight chapters. Chapters 1, 3, and 5 of the Code contain general definitional provisions, as well as provisions governing case administration, creditors, the debtor, and the estate. These three chapters normally apply to all kinds of bankruptcies.

Four chapters of the Code set forth the most important types of relief that debtors can seek:

1. Chapter 7 provides for **liquidation** proceedings (the selling of all nonexempt assets and the distribution of the proceeds to the debtor's creditors).
2. Chapter 11 governs reorganizations.
3. Chapter 12 (for family farmers and family fishermen) and 13 (for individuals) provide for the adjustment of debts by persons with regular incomes.[9]

Note that a debtor (except for a municipality) need not be insolvent[10] to file for bankruptcy relief under the Bankruptcy Code. Anyone obligated to a creditor can declare bankruptcy.

## 15–4c Special Requirements for Consumer-Debtors

A **consumer-debtor** is a debtor whose debts result primarily from the purchase of goods for personal, family, or household use. The Bankruptcy Code requires that the clerk of the court give all consumer-debtors written notice of the general purpose, benefits, and costs of each chapter under which they might proceed. In addition, the clerk must provide consumer-debtors with information on the types of services available from credit counseling agencies.

# 15–5 Liquidation Proceedings

Liquidation under Chapter 7 of the Bankruptcy Code is probably the most familiar type of bankruptcy proceeding and is often referred to as an *ordinary,* or

---

8. The full title of the act was the Bankruptcy Abuse Prevention and Consumer Protection Act, Pub. L. No. 109-8, 119 Stat. 23 (April 20, 2005).

9. There are no Chapters 2, 4, 6, 8, or 10 in Title 11. Such "gaps" are not uncommon in the *United States Code.* They occur because chapter numbers (or other subdivisional unit numbers) are sometimes reserved for future use when a statute is enacted. (A gap may also appear if a law has been repealed.)

10. The inability to pay debts as they become due is known as *equitable* insolvency. *Balance sheet* insolvency, which exists when a debtor's liabilities exceed assets, is not the test. Thus, debtors whose cash-flow problems become severe may petition for bankruptcy voluntarily or be forced into involuntary bankruptcy even though their assets far exceed their liabilities.

*straight, bankruptcy.* Put simply, a debtor in a liquidation bankruptcy turns all assets over to a **bankruptcy trustee,** a person appointed by the court to manage the debtor's funds. The trustee sells the nonexempt assets and distributes the proceeds to creditors. With certain exceptions, the remaining debts are then **discharged** (extinguished), and the debtor is relieved of the obligation to pay the debts.

Any "person"—defined as including individuals, partnerships, corporations, labor unions, and unincorporated organizations—may be a debtor in a liquidation proceeding. A husband and wife may file jointly for bankruptcy under a single petition. Railroads, insurance companies, banks, savings and loan associations, investment companies licensed by the Small Business Administration, and credit unions *cannot* be debtors in a liquidation bankruptcy, however. Other chapters of the Bankruptcy Code or other federal or state statutes apply to them.

A straight bankruptcy can be commenced by the filing of either a voluntary or an involuntary **petition in bankruptcy**—the document that is filed with a bankruptcy court to initiate bankruptcy proceedings. If a debtor files the petition, the bankruptcy is voluntary. If one or more creditors file a petition to force the debtor into bankruptcy, the bankruptcy is involuntary.

## 15–5a Voluntary Bankruptcy

To bring a voluntary petition in bankruptcy, the debtor files official forms designated for that purpose in the bankruptcy court. The law now requires that *before* debtors can file a petition, they must receive credit counseling from an approved nonprofit agency within the 180-day period preceding the date of filing. Debtors filing a Chapter 7 petition must include a certificate proving that they have received individual or group counseling from an approved agency within the last 180 days.

A consumer-debtor who is filing for liquidation bankruptcy must confirm the accuracy of the petition's contents. The debtor must also state in the petition, at the time of filing, that he or she understands the relief available under other chapters of the Code and has chosen to proceed under Chapter 7.

Attorneys representing the consumer-debtors must file an affidavit stating that they have informed the debtors of the relief available under each chapter of the Bankruptcy Code. In addition, the attorneys must reasonably attempt to verify the accuracy of the consumer-debtors' petitions and schedules (described next). Failure to do so is considered perjury.

**Chapter 7 Schedules** The voluntary petition must contain the following schedules:

1. A list of both secured and unsecured creditors, their addresses, and the amount of debt owed to each.
2. A statement of the financial affairs of the debtor.
3. A list of all property owned by the debtor, including property that the debtor claims is exempt.
4. A list of current income and expenses.
5. A certificate of credit counseling (as mentioned previously).
6. Proof of payments received from employers within sixty days prior to the filing of the petition.
7. A statement of the amount of monthly income, itemized to show how the amount is calculated.
8. A copy of the debtor's federal income tax return for the most recent year ending immediately before the filing of the petition.

The official forms must be completed accurately, sworn to under oath, and signed by the debtor. To conceal assets or knowingly supply false information on these schedules is a crime under the bankruptcy laws.

With the exception of tax returns, failure to file the required schedules within forty-five days after the filing of the petition will result in an automatic dismissal of the petition. (An extension may be granted, however.) The debtor has up to seven days before the date of the first creditors' meeting to provide a copy of the most recent tax returns to the trustee. In addition, a debtor may be required to file a tax return at the end of each tax year while the case is pending and to provide a copy to the court. This may be done at the request of the court or the **U.S. trustee**—a government official who performs administrative tasks that a bankruptcy judge would otherwise have to perform. (Debtors may also be required to file tax returns during Chapter 11 and 13 bankruptcies.)

**Substantial Abuse—Means Test** In the past, a bankruptcy court could dismiss a Chapter 7 petition if the use of Chapter 7 would constitute a "substantial abuse" of bankruptcy law. Today, the law provides a *means test* to determine a debtor's eligibility for Chapter 7.

The purpose of the test is to keep upper-income people from abusing the bankruptcy process by filing for Chapter 7, as was thought to have happened in the past. The test forces more people to file for Chapter 13 bankruptcy rather than have their debts discharged under Chapter 7.

**The Basic Formula.** A debtor wishing to file for bankruptcy must complete the means test to determine whether she or he qualifies for Chapter 7. The debtor's average monthly income in recent months is compared with the median income in the geographic area in which the person lives. (The U.S. Trustee Program provides these data at its Web site.) If the debtor's income is below the median income, the debtor usually is allowed to file for Chapter 7 bankruptcy, as there is no presumption of bankruptcy abuse.

### Applying the Means Test to Future Disposable Income.

If the debtor's income is above the median income, then further calculations must be made. The calculations are meant to determine whether the person will have sufficient disposable income in the future to repay at least some of his or her unsecured debts.

As a basis for the calculations, it is presumed that the debtor's recent monthly income will continue for the next sixty months. *Disposable income* is then calculated by subtracting living expenses and secured debt payments, such as mortgage payments, from monthly income.

Living expenses are amounts allowed under formulas used by the Internal Revenue Service (IRS). The IRS allowances include modest allocations for food, clothing, housing, utilities, transportation (including a car payment), health care, and other necessities. (The U.S. Trustee Program's Web site also provides these amounts.) The allowances do not include expenditures for items such as cell phones and cable television service.

### Can the Debtor Afford to Pay Unsecured Debts?

Once future disposable income has been estimated, that amount is used to determine whether the debtor will have income that could be applied to unsecured debts. The courts may also consider the debtor's bad faith or other circumstances indicating abuse.

■ **CASE IN POINT 15.7** Christopher Dean Ng and his wife filed for Chapter 7 bankruptcy, hoping primarily to discharge their mortgage debt of $464,830. At the time the petition was filed, Ng was forty-three years old and worked as an electronic technician. He earned a monthly salary of $7,439.47, as well as a military pension of $1,439.88 a month. His wife was not employed. From Ng's monthly salary, he made a voluntary contribution of $520 to an employer 401(k) plan and a $343 payment on a pension loan. In calculating his disposable income, Ng excluded these amounts.

The U.S. trustee filed a motion to dismiss Ng's petition due to substantial abuse. The trustee claimed that the retirement contributions should be disallowed. The court agreed and dismissed the Chapter 7 petition. The Ngs appealed, and the appellate court affirmed. Ng's retirement contributions were not reasonably necessary based on his age, his financial circumstances, and his testimony

that he was not planning to retire for at least twenty years. The Ngs could afford to repay some of their debts before they made monthly contributions toward retirement.[11] ■

**Additional Grounds for Dismissal** As already noted, a court can dismiss a debtor's voluntary petition for Chapter 7 relief for substantial abuse or for failure to provide the necessary documents within the specified time.

In addition, a court might dismiss a Chapter 7 in two other situations. First, if the debtor has been convicted of a violent crime or a drug-trafficking offense, the victim can file a motion to dismiss the voluntary petition.[12] Second, if the debtor fails to pay postpetition domestic-support obligations (which include child and spousal support), the court may dismiss the debtor's petition.

**Order for Relief** If the voluntary petition for bankruptcy is found to be proper, the filing of the petition will itself constitute an **order for relief.** (An order for relief is a court's grant of assistance to a petitioner.) Once a consumer-debtor's voluntary petition has been filed, the trustee and creditors must be given notice of the order for relief by mail not more than twenty days after entry of the order.

### 15–5b Involuntary Bankruptcy

An involuntary bankruptcy occurs when the debtor's creditors force the debtor into bankruptcy proceedings. An involuntary case cannot be filed against a charitable institution or a farmer (an individual or business that receives more than 50 percent of gross income from farming operations).

An involuntary petition should not be used as an everyday debt-collection device, and the Code provides penalties for the filing of frivolous petitions against debtors. If the court dismisses an involuntary petition, the petitioning creditors may be required to pay the costs and attorneys' fees incurred by the debtor in defending against the petition. If the petition was filed in bad faith, damages can be awarded for injury to the debtor's reputation. Punitive damages may also be awarded.

**Requirements** For an involuntary action to be filed, the following requirements must be met:

1. If the debtor has twelve or more creditors, three or more of these creditors having unsecured claims totaling at least $15,325 must join in the petition.

---

11. *In re Ng*, 422 Bankr. 118 (9th Cir. 2012).
12. Note that the court may not dismiss a case on this ground if the debtor's bankruptcy is necessary to satisfy a claim for a domestic-support obligation.

**2.** If a debtor has fewer than twelve creditors, one or more creditors having a claim totaling $15,325 or more may file.[13]

**Order for Relief** If the debtor challenges the involuntary petition, a hearing will be held, and the bankruptcy court will enter an order for relief if it finds either of the following:

**1.** The debtor is not paying debts as they come due.
**2.** A general receiver, assignee, or custodian took possession of, or was appointed to take charge of, substantially all of the debtor's property within 120 days before the filing of the petition.

If the court grants an order for relief, the debtor will be required to supply the same information in the bankruptcy schedules as in a voluntary bankruptcy.

### 15–5c Automatic Stay

The moment a petition, either voluntary or involuntary, is filed, an **automatic stay,** or suspension, of all actions by creditors against the debtor or the debtor's property normally goes into effect. The automatic stay prohibits creditors from taking any act to collect, assess, or recover a claim against the debtor that arose before the filing of the petition. The stay normally continues until the bankruptcy proceeding is closed or dismissed. (In some circumstances, it is possible to petition the bankruptcy court for relief from the automatic stay, as will be discussed shortly.)

If a creditor *knowingly* violates the automatic stay (a willful violation), any injured party, including the debtor, is entitled to recover actual damages, costs, and attorneys' fees. Punitive damages may be awarded as well.

■ **CASE IN POINT 15.8** Stefanie Kuehn filed for bankruptcy. When she requested a transcript from the university at which she had obtained her master's degree, the university refused because she owed more than $6,000 in tuition. Kuehn complained to the court. The court ruled that the university had violated the automatic stay by refusing to provide a transcript because it was attempting to collect an unpaid tuition debt.[14] ■

**The Adequate Protection Doctrine** Underlying the Code's automatic-stay provision for a secured creditor is a concept known as *adequate protection.* The **adequate protection doctrine,** among other things, protects secured creditors from losing their security as a result of the automatic stay.

The bankruptcy court can provide adequate protection by requiring the debtor or trustee to make periodic cash payments or a one-time cash payment. The court can also require the debtor or trustee to provide additional collateral or replacement liens to the extent that the stay may actually cause the value of the property to decrease.

**Exceptions to the Automatic Stay** The Code provides the following exceptions to the automatic stay:

**1.** Collection efforts can continue for domestic-support obligations. These obligations include any debt owed to or recoverable by a spouse, a former spouse, a child of the debtor, that child's parent or guardian, or a governmental unit.
**2.** Proceedings against the debtor related to divorce, child custody or visitation, domestic violence, and support enforcement are not stayed.
**3.** Investigations by a securities regulatory agency (such as an investigation into insider trading) can continue.
**4.** Certain statutory liens for property taxes are not stayed.

**Requests for Relief from the Automatic Stay** A secured creditor or other party in interest can petition the bankruptcy court for relief from the automatic stay. If a creditor or other party requests relief from the stay, the stay will automatically terminate sixty days after the request, unless the court grants an extension or the parties agree otherwise.

**Secured Property** The automatic stay on secured property terminates forty-five days after the creditors' meeting unless the debtor redeems or reaffirms certain debts. (Creditors' meetings and reaffirmation will be discussed later in this chapter.) In other words, the debtor cannot keep the secured property (such as a financed automobile), even if she or he continues to make payments on it, without reinstating the rights of the secured party to collect on the debt.

**Bad Faith** If the debtor had two or more bankruptcy petitions dismissed during the prior year, the Code presumes bad faith. In such a situation, the automatic stay does *not* go into effect until the court determines that the petition was filed in good faith.

In addition, the automatic stay on secured debts will terminate thirty days after the petition is filed if the debtor filed a bankruptcy petition that was dismissed within the prior year. Any party in interest can request that the court extend the stay by showing that the filing is in good faith.

---

**13.** 11 U.S.C. Section 303. The amounts stated in this chapter are in accordance with those computed on April 1, 2016.
**14.** *In re Kuehn*, 563 F.3d 289 (7th Cir. 2009).

## 15–5d Estate in Bankruptcy

On the commencement of a liquidation proceeding under Chapter 7, an *estate in bankruptcy* (sometimes called an *estate in property*) is created. The estate consists of all the debtor's interests in property currently held, wherever located. The estate in bankruptcy includes all of the following:

1. *Community property* (property jointly owned by married persons in certain states).
2. Property transferred in a transaction voidable by the trustee.
3. Proceeds and profits from the property of the estate.

Certain after-acquired property to which the debtor becomes entitled *within 180 days after filing* may also become part of the estate. Such after-acquired property includes gifts, inheritances, property settlements (from divorce), and life insurance death proceeds.

Generally, though, the filing of a bankruptcy petition fixes a dividing line. Property acquired prior to the filing of the petition becomes property of the estate, and property acquired after the filing of the petition, except as just noted, remains the debtor's.

## 15–5e The Bankruptcy Trustee

Promptly after the order for relief in the liquidation proceeding has been entered, a trustee is appointed. The basic duty of the trustee is to collect the debtor's available estate and reduce it to cash for distribution, preserving the interests of both the debtor and the unsecured creditors. The trustee is held accountable for administering the debtor's estate.

To enable the trustee to accomplish this duty, the Code gives the trustee certain powers, stated in both general and specific terms. These powers must be exercised within two years of the order for relief.

**Duties for Means Testing** The trustee is required to promptly review all materials filed by the debtor to determine if there is substantial abuse. Within ten days after the first meeting of the creditors (discussed shortly), the trustee must file a statement indicating whether the case is presumed to be an abuse under the means test. The trustee must provide a copy of this statement to all creditors within five days.

When there is a presumption of abuse, the trustee must either file a motion to dismiss the petition (or convert it to a Chapter 13 petition) or file a statement explaining why a motion would not be appropriate. If the debtor owes a domestic-support obligation (such as child support), the trustee must provide written notice of the bankruptcy to the claim holder (a former spouse, for instance).

**The Trustee's Powers** The trustee has the power to require persons holding the debtor's property at the time the petition is filed to deliver the property to the trustee.[15] To enable the trustee to implement this power, the Code provides that the trustee has rights *equivalent* to those of certain other parties, such as a creditor who has a judicial lien. This power of a trustee, which is equivalent to that of a lien creditor, is known as *strong-arm power*.

In addition, the trustee has specific *powers of avoidance*. They enable the trustee to set aside (avoid) a sale or other transfer of the debtor's property and take the property back for the debtor's estate. These powers apply to voidable rights available to the debtor, preferences, and fraudulent transfers by the debtor. Each power is discussed in more detail next. In addition, a trustee can avoid certain statutory liens (creditors' claims against the debtor's property).

The debtor shares most of the trustee's avoidance powers. Thus, if the trustee does not take action to enforce one of the rights just mentioned, the debtor in a liquidation bankruptcy can enforce that right.[16]

**Voidable Rights** A trustee steps into the shoes of the debtor. Thus, any reason that a debtor can use to obtain the return of her or his property can be used by the trustee as well. These grounds include fraud, duress, incapacity, and mutual mistake.

■ **EXAMPLE 15.9** Ben sells his boat to Tara. Tara gives Ben a check, knowing that she has insufficient funds in her bank account to cover the check. Tara has committed fraud. Ben has the right to avoid that transfer and recover the boat from Tara. If Ben files for bankruptcy relief under Chapter 7, the trustee can exercise the same right to recover the boat from Tara, and the boat becomes a part of the debtor's estate. ■

**Preferences** A debtor is not permitted to transfer property or to make a payment that favors—or gives a **preference** to—one creditor over others. The trustee is allowed to recover payments made both voluntarily and involuntarily to one creditor in preference over another.

---

15. Usually, though, the trustee takes constructive, rather than actual, possession of the debtor's property. For instance, to obtain control of a debtor's business inventory, a trustee might change the locks on the doors to the business and hire a security guard.
16. Under a Chapter 11 bankruptcy, for which no trustee other than the debtor generally exists, the debtor has the same avoidance powers as a trustee under Chapter 7. Under Chapters 12 and 13, a trustee must be appointed.

To have made a recoverable preferential payment, an *insolvent* debtor must have transferred property, for a *preexisting* debt, within *ninety days* before the filing of the bankruptcy petition. The transfer must have given the creditor more than the creditor would have received as a result of the bankruptcy proceedings. The Code presumes that a debtor is insolvent during the ninety-day period before filing a petition.

If a **preferred creditor** (one who has received a preferential transfer) has sold the property to an innocent third party, the trustee cannot recover the property from the innocent party. The preferred creditor, however, generally can be held liable for the value of the property.

**Preferences to Insiders.** Sometimes, the creditor receiving the preference is an insider. An **insider** is an individual, partner, partnership, corporation, or officer or director of a corporation (or a relative of one of these) who has a close relationship with the debtor. In this situation, the avoidance power of the trustee extends to transfers made within *one year* before filing. (If the transfer was fraudulent, as will be discussed shortly, the trustee can avoid transfers made within *two years* before filing.) The trustee must, however, prove that the debtor was insolvent when the transfer occurred and that it was made to or for the benefit of an insider.

**Transfers That Do Not Constitute Preferences.** Not all transfers are preferences. Most courts generally assume that payment for services rendered *within fifteen days* before the payment is not a preference. If a creditor receives payment in the ordinary course of business from a debtor, such as payment of last month's cell phone bill, the bankruptcy trustee cannot recover the payment.

To be recoverable, a preference must be a transfer for an antecedent (preexisting) debt, such as a year-old landscaping bill. In addition, the Code permits a consumer-debtor to transfer any property to a creditor up to a total value of $6,225 without the transfer's constituting a preference. Payment of domestic-support debts does not constitute a preference.

**Fraudulent Transfers** The trustee may avoid fraudulent transfers or obligations if they (1) were made within two years prior to the filing of the petition or (2) were made with actual intent to hinder, delay, or defraud a creditor. ■ **EXAMPLE 15.10** Amy is planning to petition for bankruptcy, so she sells her gold jewelry, worth $10,000, to a friend for $500. The friend agrees that in the future he will "sell" the jewelry back to Amy for the same amount. This is a fraudulent transfer that the trustee can undo. ■

Transfers made for less than reasonably equivalent consideration are also vulnerable if the debtor thereby became insolvent or was left engaged in business with an unreasonably small amount of capital. When a fraudulent transfer is made outside the Code's two-year limit, creditors may seek alternative relief under state laws. Some state laws may allow creditors to recover transfers made up to three years before the filing of a petition.

### 15–5f Exemptions

As just described, the trustee takes control of the debtor's property in a Chapter 7 bankruptcy, but an individual debtor is entitled to exempt (exclude) certain property from the bankruptcy.

**Federal Exemptions** The Bankruptcy Code exempts the following property, up to a specified dollar amount that changes every three years:[17]

1. A portion of equity in the debtor's home (the homestead exemption).
2. Motor vehicles, up to a certain value (usually just one vehicle).
3. Reasonably necessary clothing, household goods and furnishings, and household appliances (the aggregate value not to exceed a certain amount).
4. Jewelry, up to a certain value.
5. Tools of the debtor's trade or profession, up to a certain value.
6. A portion of unpaid but earned wages.
7. Pensions.
8. Public benefits, including public assistance (welfare), Social Security, and unemployment compensation, accumulated in a bank account.
9. Damages awarded for personal injury up to a certain amount.

Property that is *not* exempt under federal law includes bank accounts, cash, family heirlooms, collections of stamps and coins, second cars, and vacation homes.

**State Exemptions** Individual states have the power to pass legislation precluding debtors from using the federal exemptions within the state. A majority of the states have done this. In those states, debtors may use only state, not federal, exemptions. In the rest of the states, debtors may choose either the exemptions provided under state law or the federal exemptions.

---

17. The dollar amounts stated in the Bankruptcy Code are adjusted automatically every three years on April 1 based on changes in the Consumer Price Index. The adjusted amounts are rounded to the nearest $25.

**Limitations on the Homestead Exemption** The Bankruptcy Code limits the amount of equity that can be claimed under the homestead exemption. In general, if the debtor acquired the homestead within three and a half years preceding the date of filing, the maximum equity exempted is $155,675, even if state law would permit a higher amount.

In addition, the state homestead exemption is available only if the debtor has lived in a state for two years before filing the bankruptcy petition. Furthermore, a debtor who has violated securities laws, been convicted of a felony, or engaged in certain other intentional misconduct may not be permitted to claim the homestead exemption.

### 15–5g Creditors' Meeting

Within a reasonable time after the order for relief has been granted (not more than forty days), the trustee must call a meeting of the creditors listed in the schedules filed by the debtor. The bankruptcy judge does not attend this meeting. The debtor is required to attend (unless excused by the court) and to submit to examination under oath by the creditors and the trustee. At the meeting, the trustee ensures that the debtor is aware of the potential consequences of bankruptcy and of the possibility of filing under a different chapter of the Code.

### 15–5h Creditors' Claims

To be entitled to receive a portion of the debtor's estate, each creditor normally files a *proof of claim* with the bankruptcy court within ninety days of the creditors' meeting. A proof of claim is necessary if there is any dispute concerning the claim. The proof of claim lists the creditor's name and address, as well as the amount that the creditor asserts is owed to the creditor by the debtor.

When the debtor has no assets—called a "no-asset case"—creditors are notified of the debtor's petition for bankruptcy but are instructed not to file a claim. In no-asset cases, the unsecured creditors will receive no payment, and most, if not all, of these debts will be discharged.

### 15–5i Distribution of Property

The Code provides specific rules for the distribution of the debtor's property to secured and unsecured creditors. If any amount remains after the priority classes of creditors have been satisfied, it is turned over to the debtor.

**Distribution to Secured Creditors** The Code requires that consumer-debtors file a statement of intention with respect to secured collateral. They can choose to pay off the debt and redeem the collateral, claim it is exempt, reaffirm the debt and continue making payments, or surrender the property to the secured party.

If the collateral is surrendered to the secured party, the secured creditor can enforce the security interest. The secured party can either (1) accept the property in full satisfaction of the debt or (2) sell the collateral and use the proceeds to pay off the debt. Thus, the secured party has priority over unsecured parties as to the proceeds from the disposition of the collateral. Should the collateral be insufficient to cover the secured debt owed, the secured creditor becomes an unsecured creditor for the difference (deficiency).

There are limited exceptions to these rules. For instance, certain unsecured creditors can sometimes step into the shoes of secured tax creditors in Chapter 7 liquidation proceedings. In such situations, when the collateral securing the tax claims is sold, the unsecured creditors are paid first. This exception does not include holders of unsecured claims for administrative expenses incurred in Chapter 11 cases that are converted to Chapter 7 liquidations. In the following case, the plaintiff argued that it should.

**Case 15.2**

## *In re* Anderson
United States Court of Appeals, Fourth Circuit, 811 F.3d 166 (2016).

**Background and Facts** Henry Anderson filed a voluntary petition in a federal bankruptcy court for relief under Chapter 11 of the Bankruptcy Code. The U.S. Department of the Treasury, through the Internal Revenue Service (IRS), filed a proof of claim against the bankruptcy estate for $997,551.80, of which $987,082.88 was secured by the debtor's property. Stubbs & Perdue, P.A., served as Anderson's

Case 15.2 Continued

counsel. During the proceedings, the court approved compensation of $200,000 to Stubbs for its services. These fees constituted an unsecured claim against the estate for administrative expenses. Later, Anderson's case was converted to a Chapter 7 liquidation. The trustee accumulated $702,630.25 for distribution to the estate's creditors—not enough to pay the claims of both the IRS and Stubbs. The trustee excluded Stubbs's claim. Stubbs objected. The court dismissed Stubbs's objection. A federal district court upheld the dismissal. Stubbs appealed, arguing that the IRS's claim should be subordinated to Stubbs's claim for fees.

## In the Language of the Court

Pamela *HARRIS,* Circuit Judge:

\* \* \* \*

\* \* \* Before any of the events at issue here, Section 724(b)(2) \* \* \* provided all holders of administrative expense claims, like Stubbs, with the right to subordinate secured tax creditors in Chapter 7 liquidations. But that statutory scheme was criticized on the ground that it created perverse incentives, encouraging Chapter 11 debtors and their representatives to incur administrative expenses even where there was no real hope for a successful reorganization, to the detriment of secured tax creditors when Chapter 7 liquidation ultimately proved necessary.

\* \* \* Congress responded with a fix \* \* \* to limit the class of administrative expenses covered by Section 724(b)(2) \* \* \*. *In order to provide greater protection for holders of tax liens* \* \* \* *, unsecured Chapter 11 administrative expense claims would no longer take priority over secured tax claims in Chapter 7 liquidations.* [Emphasis added.]

\* \* \* \*

\* \* \* The Bankruptcy Technical Corrections Act [BTCA] \* \* \* clarified that Chapter 11 administrative expense claimants do not hold subordination rights under Section 724(b)(2).

\* \* \* Eleven months later, the Debtor's bankruptcy case converted from Chapter 11 to Chapter 7, implicating Section 724(b)(2) for the first time.

\* \* \* \*

\* \* \* *As a general rule, a court is to apply the law in effect at the time it renders its decision.* [Emphasis added.]

\* \* \* \*

Stubbs argues, however, that it would be unjust to apply the BTCA version of Section 724(b)(2) \* \* \* to disallow payment on its unsecured claim for Chapter 11 fees. Prior to the BTCA, Stubbs contends, it was entitled to subordinate the IRS's secured claim.

The problem with Stubbs's argument is its premise: that Stubbs held subordination rights under Section 724(b)(2) before the BTCA was enacted \* \* \* . Before the BTCA was enacted, Section 724(b)(2) had no application to the Debtor's case at all. It afforded Stubbs no entitlement to subordinate the IRS's secured tax claim for the threshold reason that it simply did not apply in the Chapter 11 proceedings that began in this case \* \* \* and did not end until \* \* \* eleven months *after* the BTCA's passage. The pre-BTCA version of Section 724(b)(2) that Stubbs invokes, in other words, never controlled this case.

**Decision and Remedy** *The U.S. Court of Appeals for the Fourth Circuit affirmed the dismissal of Stubbs's claim. Under Section 724(b)(2), "it is clear that Stubbs is not entitled to subordinate the IRS's secured tax claim in favor of its unsecured claim to Chapter 11 administrative expenses."*

### Critical Thinking

- **Legal Environment** *Why, as a general rule, should a court apply the law that is in effect at the time the court renders its decision?*
- **What If the Facts Were Different?** *Suppose that Anderson had filed his initial bankruptcy petition under Chapter 7, not under Chapter 11. Would the result have been different? Discuss.*

**Distribution to Unsecured Creditors** Bankruptcy law establishes an order of priority for debts owed to *unsecured* creditors, and they are paid in the order of their priority. Claims for domestic-support obligations, such as child support and alimony, have the highest priority among unsecured creditors, so these claims must be paid first. Each class, or group, must be fully paid before the next class is entitled to any of the remaining proceeds.

If there are insufficient proceeds to fully pay all the creditors in a class, the proceeds are distributed *proportionately* to the creditors in that class. Classes lower in priority receive nothing. In almost all Chapter 7 bankruptcies, the funds will be insufficient to pay all creditors.

Exhibit 15–2 illustrates the collection and distribution of property in most voluntary bankruptcies. The exhibit includes a listing of the classes of unsecured creditors.

## 15–5j Discharge

From the debtor's point of view, the primary purpose of liquidation is to obtain a fresh start through a discharge of debts. A discharge voids, or sets aside, any judgment on a discharged debt and prevents any action to collect it. Certain debts, however, are not dischargeable in bankruptcy. Also, certain debtors may not qualify to have all debts discharged in bankruptcy. These situations are discussed next.

**Exceptions to Discharge** Claims that are not dischargeable in bankruptcy include the following:

1. Claims for back taxes accruing within two years prior to bankruptcy.
2. Claims for amounts borrowed by the debtor to pay federal taxes or any nondischargeable taxes.[18]
3. Claims against property or funds obtained by the debtor under false pretenses or by false representations.
4. Claims by creditors who were not notified of the bankruptcy. These claims did not appear on the schedules the debtor was required to file.
5. Claims based on fraud or misuse of funds by the debtor while acting in a fiduciary capacity or claims involving the debtor's embezzlement or larceny.
6. Domestic-support obligations and property settlements as provided for in a separation agreement or divorce decree.
7. Claims for amounts due on a retirement account loan.
8. Claims based on willful or malicious conduct by the debtor toward another or the property of another. ■ **CASE IN POINT 15.11** Anthony Mickletz owned a pizza restaurant that employed John

---

18. Taxes accruing within three years prior to bankruptcy are nondischargeable, including federal and state income taxes, employment taxes, taxes on gross receipts, property taxes, excise taxes, customs duties, and any other taxes for which the government claims the debtor is liable in some capacity. See 11 U.S.C. Sections 507(a)(8) and 523(a)(1).

---

**EXHIBIT 15–2 Collection and Distribution of Property in Most Voluntary Bankruptcies**

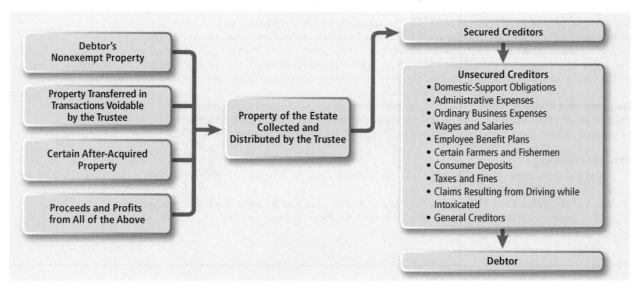

Carmello. One night after Carmello had finished his shift, Mickletz called him back into the restaurant and accused him of stealing. An argument ensued, and Mickletz shoved Carmello, causing him to fall and injure his back. Because Mickletz did not provide workers' compensation coverage as required by law, the state prosecuted him criminally. He was ordered to pay more than $45,000 in restitution to Carmello for his injuries. Carmello also filed a civil suit against Mickletz, which the parties agreed to settle for $175,000. Later, Mickletz filed a petition for bankruptcy. Carmello argued that these debts were nondischargeable, and the court agreed. The exception from discharge includes any debts for willful (deliberate or intentional) injury, and Mickletz's actions were deliberate.[19] ■

9. Certain government fines and penalties.
10. Student loans, unless payment of the loans imposes an undue hardship on the debtor and the debtor's dependents. (For an example of what constitutes undue hardship, see *Case in Point 15.12,* which follows this list.)
11. Consumer debts of more than $650 for luxury goods or services owed to a single creditor incurred within ninety days of the order for relief.
12. Cash advances totaling more than $925 that are extensions of open-end consumer credit obtained by the debtor within seventy days of the order for relief.
13. Judgments against a debtor as a result of the debtor's operation of a motor vehicle while intoxicated.
14. Fees or assessments arising from property in a homeowners' association, as long as the debtor retained an interest in the property.
15. Taxes with respect to which the debtor failed to provide required or requested tax documents.

■ **CASE IN POINT 15.12** At the time he filed for Chapter 7 bankruptcy, Terence Wolfe had not been consistently employed for twenty years. He had been fired from numerous positions for behavioral issues and had difficulty finding and holding a job. Wolfe had been diagnosed with personality disorders and ultimately was granted disability status by the U.S. government. He was living on disability payments of $1,126 per month at the time he filed for Chapter 7 bankruptcy.

Among Wolfe's debts were more than $131,000 in student loan debts. Wolfe sought to have these debts discharged because repaying them would constitute undue hardship. The court agreed and granted a discharge. According to the court, although Wolfe is intelligent, "he has been unable, for more than two decades, to maintain

full-time employment for any meaningful length of time. He is living at a minimal standard of living and it is unlikely that he will ever be able to repay these loans."[20] ■

Today, the federal government guarantees many student loans (similar to the way the government backs certain mortgages). When student loans are guaranteed, the lenders are not affected by default in the same way and have no reason to refuse to finance education. This bolsters the argument that student loan debts should be dischargeable in the same way as other types of debts. See this chapter's *Ethics Today* feature for a discussion of whether the law should make it easier to obtain a discharge of student loan debts.

**Objections to Discharge** In addition to the exceptions to discharge previously discussed, a bankruptcy court may also deny discharge based on the debtor's *conduct.* Grounds for denial of discharge of the debtor include the following:

1. The debtor's concealment or destruction of property with the intent to hinder, delay, or defraud a creditor.
2. The debtor's fraudulent concealment or destruction of financial records.
3. The grant of a discharge to the debtor within eight years before the petition was filed.
4. The debtor's failure to complete the required consumer education course.
5. The debtor's involvement in proceedings in which the debtor could be found guilty of a felony. (Basically, a court may not discharge any debt until the completion of felony proceedings against the debtor.)

When a discharge is denied under any of these circumstances, the debtor's assets are still distributed to the creditors. After the bankruptcy proceeding, however, the debtor remains liable for the unpaid portion of all claims.

In addition, a discharge may be revoked (taken back) within one year if it is discovered that the debtor acted fraudulently or dishonestly during the bankruptcy proceeding. If that occurs, a creditor whose claim was not satisfied in the distribution of the debtor's property can proceed with his or her claim against the debtor.

Whether a bankruptcy court properly denied a discharge based on the debtors' conduct was the issue in the following case.

---

19. *In re Mickletz,* 544 Bankr. 804 (E.D. Pa. 2016).

20. *In re Wolfe,* 501 Bankr. 426, 24 Fla.L.WeeklyFed. B235 (M.D.Fla. 2011).

## Case 15.3

# *In re* Cummings

United States Court of Appeals, Ninth Circuit, 595 Fed.Appx. 707 (2015).

**Background and Facts** Clarence and Pamela Cummings filed a petition for a Chapter 7 bankruptcy in a federal bankruptcy court. After the debtors filed two amended versions of the required schedules, the trustee asked for additional time to investigate. The court granted the request. The debtors then filed a third amended schedule. In it, they disclosed for the first time the existence of First Beacon Management Company, a corporation that they planned to use as part of their postbankruptcy "fresh start."

The trustee claimed that the Cummingses' failure to disclose their interest in First Beacon was a "false oath relating to a material fact made knowingly and fraudulently" in violation of the Bankruptcy Code. The court agreed and denied the debtors a discharge. The Bankruptcy Appellate Panel (BAP) affirmed the court's decision. The Cummingses appealed.

### In the Language of the Court
*MEMORANDUM.*
* * * *

Chapter 7 debtors Clarence Thomas Cummings and Pamela K. Cummings appeal the judgment of the Bankruptcy Appellate Panel ("BAP") affirming * * * the bankruptcy court's order denying discharge on the ground that the debtors made false oaths * * * . The bankruptcy court rejected the explanatory testimony of Mr. Cummings as "not credible" and "beyond not credible" and the BAP found that "there is ample evidence to support the bankruptcy court's findings.

* * * *

* * * Debtors claim that the bankruptcy court failed to consider other "voluminous independent and undisputed documentary evidence" introduced at trial that, they assert, "completely obliterated any suggestion of fraudulent intent."

* * * These materials do not advance debtors' claim of inadvertence [lack of intent] or otherwise suggest bankruptcy court error. To the contrary, *the documents corroborate the obviousness of debtors' fraud and the objective it advanced, [namely], to insulate First Beacon Management Co., * * * the new corporate anchor of their post-petition fresh start, from the stigma of bankruptcy.* [Emphasis added.]

Debtors' eventual disclosure of their interest in First Beacon on their third amended Schedule * * * does not negate their initial fraud. To the contrary, the sequence of debtors' filings substantiates the presence of fraud: they elected, twice, to amend their Schedule * * * without adding First Beacon, and disclosed First Beacon only after the issuance of an order granting the Trustee additional time to investigate.

* * * *

The Trustee fully carried its burden of proving by a preponderance of the evidence * * * that under the circumstances, debtors' failure to disclose their interest in First Beacon as debtor property was a "false oath" relating to a material fact made knowingly and fraudulently.

**Decision and Remedy** *The U.S. Court of Appeals for the Ninth Circuit affirmed the ruling of the Bankruptcy Appellate Panel. The Cummingses' bankruptcy filings revealed the presence of fraud. Thus, their Chapter 7 petition for discharge of their debts was denied.*

### Critical Thinking
- **Economic** *Why would a debtor risk the denial of a discharge to conceal assets? Discuss.*

---

## 15-5k Reaffirmation of Debt

An agreement to pay a debt dischargeable in bankruptcy is called a **reaffirmation agreement.** A debtor may wish to pay a debt—such as a debt owed to a family member, physician, bank, or some other creditor—even though the debt could be discharged in bankruptcy. Also, as

noted previously, a debtor cannot retain secured property while continuing to pay without entering into a reaffirmation agreement.

**Procedures** To be enforceable, reaffirmation agreements must be made before the debtor is granted a discharge. The agreement must be signed and filed with the court.

## ETHICS TODAY

### Should There Be More Relief for Student Loan Defaults?

According to many observers, student loan debt has reached crisis levels in the United States. Outstanding student loan balances total $1.2 *trillion* nationally and are growing by around $3,000 *per second*. About 20 percent are ninety or more days' delinquent or are in default. That is the highest delinquency rate among all forms of debt, including credit cards, automobile loans, and mortgages. The average student loan debt is more than $30,000.

#### Consequences of Default

Any student borrower who has not made regular payments for nine months is in default. If you are in default on a student loan, the U.S. Department of Education can do any of the following to collect:

1. Keep your tax refund if you were supposed to receive one.
2. Garnish your paycheck without obtaining a court judgment.
3. Take your federal benefits, such as Social Security retirement payments or disability payments.

In addition, in some states any professional license that you have can be revoked. The Department of Education can also bring a lawsuit against you. If it wins, it can collect the judgment from your bank accounts or place a lien on any real property that you own.

#### Caps on Interest Rates, Forgiveness, and Income-Based Plans

Recently, Congress attempted to ease the burden on student loan debtors by reducing the interest rates they can be charged. In addition, President Barack Obama signed an executive order putting into place an income-based repayment plan. This plan caps payments at no more than 10 percent of disposable income. Any balance not paid off after twenty years will be forgiven.

Should the federal government go further? Yes, at least according to President Obama. In 2015, Obama signed a presidential memorandum titled "Student Aid Bill of Rights." The memorandum directs the Department of Education to implement actions to ensure that the debt collection process for defaulted student loans "is fair, transparent, [and] charges reasonable fees to defaulted borrowers."

Critics point out that such student loan debt forgiveness could have a cost. They claim that colleges and universities might "hint" to potential students that they need not worry about taking on higher student loans because some portion will be forgiven by the federal government.

#### Political Impetus

Politicians are increasingly discussing student loan debt and the costs of higher education. Some are asking Congress to allow federal student loans to be discharged in most bankruptcy proceedings. Others advocate making college education free or at least reducing the costs charged to certain students. One plan calls for allowing students to refinance their loans at very low interest rates. Another proposal is to prohibit the federal government from profiting from student loan debt (the government brings in more than $41 billion a year from student loans).

**Critical Thinking** *Why does the Bankruptcy Code provide that student loans should not be dischargeable unless there is undue hardship? What argument can be made in favor of allowing student loans to be dischargeable?*

---

Court approval is required unless the debtor is represented by an attorney during the negotiation of the reaffirmation and submits the proper documents and certifications. Even when the debtor is represented by an attorney, court approval may be required if it appears that the reaffirmation will result in undue hardship to the debtor.

When court approval is required, a separate hearing will take place. The court will approve the reaffirmation only if it finds that the agreement will not result in undue hardship to the debtor and that the reaffirmation is consistent with the debtor's best interests.

**Required Disclosures** To discourage creditors from engaging in abusive reaffirmation practices, the law provides specific language for disclosures that must be given to debtors entering into reaffirmation agreements. Among other things, these disclosures explain that the debtor is not required to reaffirm any debt. They also inform the debtor that liens on secured property, such as mortgages and cars, will remain in effect even if the debt is not reaffirmed.

The reaffirmation agreement must disclose the amount of the debt reaffirmed, the rate of interest, the date payments begin, and the right to rescind. The disclosures also caution the debtor: "Only agree to reaffirm a debt if it is in your best interest. Be sure you can afford the payments you agree to make."

The original disclosure documents must be signed by the debtor, certified by the debtor's attorney, and filed with the court at the same time as the reaffirmation agreement. A reaffirmation agreement that is not accompanied by the original signed disclosures will not be effective.

■ **CASE IN POINT 15.13** Howard Lapides, who owned a seafood import business, signed a secured promissory note for $400,000 with Venture Bank for a revolving line-of-credit loan. Part of the collateral for that loan was a third mortgage on the Lapideses' home (two other banks held prior mortgages). Eventually, Howard and his wife filed for Chapter 7 bankruptcy protection, and their personal debts were discharged. Afterward, Venture Bank convinced the Lapideses to sign a reaffirmation agreement by telling them that it would refinance all three mortgages so that they could keep their house.

The Lapideses made twelve $3,500 payments to Venture Bank, but when the bank did not refinance the other mortgages, they stopped making payments. Venture Bank filed suit, but a court refused to enforce the reaffirmation agreement because it violated the Bankruptcy Code. The agreement had never been signed by Lapideses' attorney or filed with the bankruptcy court.[21] ■

# 15-6 Reorganizations

The type of bankruptcy proceeding most commonly used by corporate debtors is the Chapter 11 *reorganization.* In a reorganization, the creditors and the debtor formulate a plan under which the debtor pays a portion of the debts and is discharged of the remainder. The debtor is allowed to continue in business.

As noted, this type of bankruptcy generally involves a corporate reorganization. Nevertheless, any debtor (except a stockbroker or a commodities broker) who is eligible for Chapter 7 relief is eligible for relief under Chapter 11. Railroads are also eligible.

Congress has established a "fast-track" Chapter 11 procedure for small-business debtors whose liabilities do not exceed $2.49 million and who do not own or manage real estate. The fast track enables a debtor to avoid the appointment of a creditors' committee and also shortens the filing periods and relaxes certain other requirements. Because the process is shorter and simpler, it is less costly.

The same principles that govern the filing of a liquidation (Chapter 7) petition apply to reorganization (Chapter 11) proceedings. The case may be brought either voluntarily or involuntarily. The automatic-stay provision and its exceptions (such as substantial abuse), as well as the adequate protection doctrine, apply in reorganizations.

## 15-6a Workouts

In some instances, to avoid bankruptcy proceedings, creditors may prefer private, negotiated adjustments of creditor-debtor relations, also known as **workouts.** Often, these out-of-court workouts are much more flexible and thus more conducive to a speedy settlement. Speed is critical because delay is one of the most costly elements in any bankruptcy proceeding. Another advantage of workouts is that they avoid the various administrative costs of bankruptcy proceedings.

## 15-6b Best Interests of the Creditors

Once a Chapter 11 petition has been filed, a bankruptcy court can dismiss or suspend proceedings at any time if dismissal or suspension would better serve the interests of the creditors. Before taking such an action, the court must give notice and conduct a hearing. The Code also allows a court, after notice and a hearing, to dismiss a case under reorganization "for cause" when there is no reasonable likelihood of rehabilitation. Similarly, a court can dismiss when there is an inability to effect a plan or an unreasonable delay by the debtor that may harm the interests of creditors. A debtor whose petition is dismissed for these reasons can file a subsequent Chapter 11 petition in the future.

## 15-6c Debtor in Possession

On entry of the order for relief, the debtor generally continues to operate the business as a **debtor in possession (DIP).** The court, however, may appoint a trustee (often referred to as a *receiver*) to operate the debtor's business. The court will choose this action if gross mismanagement of the business is shown or if appointing a trustee is in the best interests of the estate.

The DIP's role is similar to that of a trustee in a liquidation bankruptcy. The DIP is entitled to avoid preferential payments and fraudulent transfers. The DIP can also exercise a trustee's strong-arm powers. The DIP has the power to decide whether to cancel or assume prepetition executory contracts (contracts that are not yet performed) or unexpired leases.

---

21. *Venture Bank v. Lapides,* 800 F.3d 442 (8th Cir. 2015).

### 15–6d Creditors' Committees

As soon as practicable after the entry of the order for relief, a creditors' committee of unsecured creditors is appointed.[22] The business's suppliers may serve on the committee. The committee can consult with the trustee or the DIP concerning the administration of the case or the formulation of the plan. Additional creditors' committees may be appointed to represent special interest creditors.

Generally, no orders affecting the estate will be entered without the consent of the committee or after a hearing in which the judge is informed of the committee's position. As mentioned earlier, businesses with debts of less than $2.49 million that do not own or manage real estate can avoid creditors' committees. In these fast-track proceedings, orders can be entered without a committee's consent.

### 15–6e The Reorganization Plan

A reorganization plan to rehabilitate the debtor is a plan to conserve and administer the debtor's assets in the hope of an eventual return to successful operation and solvency. The plan must be fair and equitable and must do the following:

1. Designate classes of claims and interests.
2. Specify the treatment to be afforded to the classes of creditors. (The plan must provide the same treatment for all claims in a particular class.)
3. Provide an adequate means for the plan's execution. (Individual debtors are required to utilize postpetition assets as necessary to execute the plan.)
4. Provide for payment of tax claims over a five-year period.

The plan need not provide for full repayment to unsecured creditors. Instead, creditors receive a percentage of each dollar owed to them by the debtor.

**Filing the Plan** Only the debtor may file a plan within the first 120 days after the date of the order for relief. This period may be extended, but not beyond eighteen months from the date of the order for relief. If the debtor does not meet the 120-day deadline or obtain an extension, any party may propose a plan. If a small-business debtor chooses to avoid a creditors' committee, the time for the debtor's filing is 180 days.

**Acceptance of the Plan** Once the plan has been developed, it is submitted to each class of creditors for acceptance. For the plan to be adopted, each class must accept it. A class has accepted the plan when a majority of the creditors in the class, representing two-thirds of the amount of the total claim, vote to approve it. If the debtor fails to procure creditor consent of the plan within 180 days, any party may propose a plan.

**Confirmation of the Plan** Confirmation is conditioned on the debtor's certifying that all postpetition domestic-support obligations have been paid in full. In addition, even when all classes of creditors accept the plan, the court may refuse to confirm it if it is not "in the best interests of the creditors." For small-business debtors, if the plan meets the listed requirements, the court must confirm the plan within forty-five days (unless this period is extended).

The plan can be modified on the request of the debtor, the DIP, the trustee, the U.S. trustee, or a holder of an unsecured claim. If an unsecured creditor objects to the plan, specific rules apply to the value of property to be distributed under the plan. Tax claims must be paid over a five-year period.

Even if only one class of creditors has accepted the plan, the court may still confirm the plan under the Code's so-called **cram-down provision.** In other words, the court may confirm the plan over the objections of a class of creditors. Before the court can exercise the right of cram-down confirmation, it must be demonstrated that the plan does not discriminate unfairly against any creditors and is fair and equitable.

**Discharge** The plan is binding on confirmation. Nevertheless, the law provides that confirmation of a plan does not discharge an individual debtor. *For individual debtors, the plan must be completed before discharge will be granted,* unless the court orders otherwise. For all other debtors, the court may order discharge at any time after the plan is confirmed.

On discharge, the debtor is given a reorganization discharge from all claims not protected under the plan. This discharge does not apply to any claims that would be denied discharge under liquidation.

## 15–7 Bankruptcy Relief under Chapter 12 and Chapter 13

In addition to bankruptcy relief through liquidation and reorganization, the Code also provides for family-farmer and family-fisherman debt adjustments (Chapter 12) and

---

22. If the debtor has filed a reorganization plan accepted by the creditors, the trustee may decide not to call a meeting of the creditors.

individuals' repayment plans (Chapter 13). The procedures for filing Chapter 12 and Chapter 13 plans are very similar. Because Chapter 13 plans are the more commonly used of the two types, we discuss Chapter 13 first.

## 15–7a Individuals' Repayment Plans—Chapter 13

Chapter 13 of the Bankruptcy Code provides for "Adjustment of Debts of an Individual with Regular Income." Individuals with regular income who owe fixed (liquidated) unsecured debts of less than $383,175 or fixed secured debts of less than $1,149,525 may take advantage of bankruptcy repayment plans. Partnerships and corporations are excluded.

Among those eligible are salaried employees and sole proprietors, as well as individuals who live on welfare, Social Security, fixed pensions, or investment income. Many small-business debtors have a choice of filing under either Chapter 11 or Chapter 13. Repayment plans offer some advantages because they are less expensive and less complicated than reorganization or liquidation proceedings.

**Filing the Petition** A Chapter 13 repayment plan case can be initiated only by the debtor's filing of a voluntary petition or by court conversion of a Chapter 7 petition. Recall that a court may convert a Chapter 7 petition because of a finding of substantial abuse under the means test. In addition, certain liquidation and reorganization cases may be converted to repayment plan cases with the consent of the debtor.[23]

A trustee, who will make payments under the plan, must be appointed. On the filing of a repayment plan petition, the automatic stay previously discussed takes effect. Although the stay applies to all or part of the debtor's consumer debt, it does not apply to any business debt incurred by the debtor or to any domestic-support obligations.

**Good Faith Requirement** The Bankruptcy Code imposes the requirement of good faith on a debtor at both the time of the filing of the petition and the time of the filing of the plan. The Code does not define good faith, but if the circumstances on the whole indicate bad faith, a court can dismiss a debtor's Chapter 13 petition.

**The Repayment Plan** A plan of rehabilitation by repayment must provide for the following:

1. The turning over to the trustee of such future earnings or income of the debtor as is necessary for execution of the plan.
2. Full payment through deferred cash payments of all claims entitled to priority, such as taxes.[24]
3. Identical treatment of all claims within a particular class. (The Code permits the debtor to list co-debtors, such as guarantors or sureties, as a separate class.)

The repayment plan may provide either for payment of all obligations in full or for payment of a lesser amount. The debtor must begin making payments under the proposed plan within thirty days after the plan has been filed and must continue to make "timely" payments.[25] If the debtor fails to make timely payments or to commence payments within the thirty-day period, the court can convert the case to a Chapter 7 bankruptcy or dismiss the petition.

**Allowable Expenses.** In putting together a repayment plan, a debtor must apply the means test to identify the amount of disposable income that will be available to repay creditors. The debtor is allowed to deduct certain expenses from monthly income to arrive at this amount, but only if they are appropriate.

■ **CASE IN POINT 15.14** Jason Ransom filed a Chapter 13 bankruptcy petition. Among his assets, he listed a Toyota Camry that he owned free of any debt. In his monthly expenses, he claimed a car-ownership deduction of $471 and a separate $388 deduction for costs to operate the car. He proposed a five-year plan that would repay about 25 percent of his unsecured debt.

FIA Card Services, N.A., an unsecured creditor, objected to the plan. FIA argued that Ransom was not entitled to the car-ownership allowance because he did not owe money on the car. Ultimately, the United States Supreme Court ruled in FIA's favor. A deduction is appropriate only if the debtor will incur that expense during the life of the Chapter 13 plan. A debtor who does not make loan or lease payments may not take a car-ownership deduction.[26] ■

---

23. A Chapter 13 repayment plan may be converted to a Chapter 7 liquidation at the request of the debtor or, under certain circumstances, by a creditor "for cause." A Chapter 13 case may be converted to a Chapter 11 case after a hearing.

24. As with a Chapter 11 reorganization plan, full repayment of all claims is not always required.
25. The bankruptcy trustee holds on to these payments until the court either confirms or denies the debtor's plan. If the court confirms the plan, the trustee distributes the funds to creditors as stated in the plan. If the court denies the debtor's plan, the trustee returns the funds, minus administrative expenses, to the debtor.
26. *Ransom v. FIA Card Services, N.A.,* 562 U.S. 61, 131 S.Ct. 716, 178 L.Ed.2d 603 (2011).

**Length of the Plan.** The length of the payment plan can be three or five years, depending on the debtor's family income. If the family income is greater than the median family income in the relevant geographic area under the means test, the term of the proposed plan must be three years.[27] The term may not exceed five years.

**Confirmation of the Plan.** After the plan is filed, the court holds a confirmation hearing, at which interested parties (such as creditors) may object to the plan. The hearing must be held at least twenty days, but no more than forty-five days, after the meeting of the creditors. The debtor must have filed all prepetition tax returns and paid all postpetition domestic-support obligations before a court will confirm any plan.

The court will confirm a plan with respect to each claim of a secured creditor under any of the following circumstances:

1. If the secured creditors have accepted the plan.
2. If the plan provides that secured creditors retain their liens until there is payment in full or until the debtor receives a discharge.
3. If the debtor surrenders the property securing the claims to the creditors.

In addition, for a motor vehicle purchased within 910 days before the petition is filed, the plan must provide that a creditor with a purchase-money security interest (PMSI) retains its lien until the entire debt is paid. For PMSIs on other personal property, the payment plan must cover debts incurred within a one-year period preceding the filing.

**Discharge** After the debtor has completed all payments, the court grants a discharge of all debts provided for by the repayment plan. Generally, all debts are dischargeable except the following:

1. Allowed claims not provided for by the plan.
2. Certain long-term debts provided for by the plan.
3. Certain tax claims and payments on retirement accounts.
4. Claims for domestic-support obligations.
5. Debts related to injury or property damage caused while driving under the influence of alcohol or drugs.

An order granting discharge is final as to the debts listed in the repayment plan. ■ **CASE IN POINT 15.15** Francisco Espinosa filed a petition for an individual repayment plan under Chapter 13 of the Bankruptcy Code. His plan proposed to pay only the principal on his

student loan and to discharge the interest. United Student Aid Funds, Inc. (the creditor), had notice of the plan and did not object. The court confirmed the plan without finding that payment of the student loan interest would cause undue hardship (as required under the Code).

Years later, United filed a motion asking the bankruptcy court to rule that its order confirming the plan was void because it was in violation of the rules governing bankruptcy. The court denied United's petition and ordered the creditor to cease its collection efforts. The case ultimately reached the United States Supreme Court, which affirmed the lower court's holding that the student loan debt was discharged.[28] ■

### 15–7b Family Farmers and Fishermen—Chapter 12

Congress created Chapter 12 of the Bankruptcy Code to help relieve economic pressure on small farmers. In 2005, Congress extended this protection to family fishermen, modified its provisions somewhat, and made it a permanent chapter in the Bankruptcy Code. (Previously, the statutes authorizing Chapter 12 had to be periodically renewed by Congress.)

Concept Summary 15.1 compares bankruptcy procedures under Chapters 7, 11, 12, and 13.

**Definitions** For purposes of Chapter 12, a *family farmer* is one whose gross income is at least 50 percent farm dependent and whose debts are at least 50 percent farm related. The total debt for a family farmer must not exceed $4,031,575. A partnership or close corporation that is at least 50 percent owned by the farm family can also qualify as a family farmer.[29]

A *family fisherman* is one whose gross income is at least 50 percent dependent on commercial fishing operations and whose debts are at least 80 percent related to commercial fishing. The total debt for a family fisherman must not exceed $1,868,200. As with family farmers, a partnership or close corporation can also qualify.

**Filing the Petition** The procedure for filing a family-farmer or family-fisherman bankruptcy plan is similar to the procedure for filing a repayment plan under Chapter 13. The debtor must file a plan not later than ninety days

---

**27.** See 11 U.S.C. Section 1322(d) for details on when the court will find that the Chapter 13 plan should extend to a five-year period.

**28.** *United Student Aid Funds, Inc. v. Espinosa*, 559 U.S. 260, 130 S.Ct. 1367, 176 L.Ed.2d 158 (2010).

**29.** Note that for a corporation or partnership to qualify under Chapter 12, at least 80 percent of the value of the firm's assets must consist of assets related to the farming operation.

# Concept Summary 15.1

## Forms of Bankruptcy Relief Compared

| FORM | CHAPTER 7 | CHAPTER 11 | CHAPTERS 12 AND 13 |
|---|---|---|---|
| **Purpose** | Liquidation. | Reorganization. | Adjustment. |
| **Who Can Petition** | Debtor (voluntary) or creditors (involuntary). | Debtor (voluntary) or creditors (involuntary). | Debtor (voluntary) only. |
| **Who Can Be a Debtor** | Any "person" (including partnerships, corporations, and municipalities) except railroads, insurance companies, banks, savings and loan institutions, investment companies licensed by the Small Business Administration, and credit unions. Farmers and charitable institutions cannot be involuntarily petitioned. If the court finds the petition to be a substantial abuse of the use of Chapter 7, the debtor may be required to convert to a Chapter 13 repayment plan. | Any debtor eligible for Chapter 7 relief. Railroads are also eligible. Individuals have specific rules and limitations. | **Chapter 12**—Any family farmer (one whose gross income is at least 50 percent farm dependent and whose debts are at least 50 percent farm related) or family fisherman (one whose gross income is at least 50 percent dependent on commercial fishing operations and whose debts are at least 80 percent related to commercial fishing) or any partnership or close corporation at least 50 percent owned by a family farmer or fisherman, when total debt does not exceed a specified amount ($4,031,575 for farmers and $1,868,200 for fishermen).<br><br>**Chapter 13**—Any individual (not partnerships or corporations) with regular income who owes fixed (liquidated) unsecured debts of less than $383,175 or fixed secured debts of less than $1,149,525. |
| **Procedure Leading to Discharge** | Nonexempt property is sold, and the proceeds are distributed (in order) to priority groups. Dischargeable debts are terminated. | Plan is submitted. If the plan is approved and followed, debts are discharged. | Plan is submitted and must be approved if the value of the property to be distributed equals the amount of the claims or if the debtor turns over disposable income for a three-year or five-year period. If the plan is followed, debts are discharged. |
| **Advantages** | On liquidation and distribution, most or all debts are discharged, and the debtor has an opportunity for a fresh start. | Debtor continues in business. Creditors can either accept the plan, or it can be "crammed down" on them. The plan allows for the reorganization and liquidation of debts over the plan period. | Debtor continues in business or possession of assets. If the plan is approved, most debts are discharged after the plan period. |

after the order for relief has been entered. The filing of the petition acts as an automatic stay against creditors' and co-obligors' actions against the estate.

A farmer or fisherman who has already filed a reorganization or repayment plan may convert it to a Chapter 12 plan. The debtor may also convert a Chapter 12 plan to a liquidation plan.

**Content and Confirmation of the Plan** The content of a plan under Chapter 12 is basically the same as that of a Chapter 13 repayment plan. Generally, the plan must be confirmed or denied within forty-five days of filing.

The plan must provide for payment of secured debts at the value of the collateral. If the secured debt exceeds the value of the collateral, the remaining debt is unsecured.

For unsecured debtors, the plan must be confirmed in either of the following circumstances: (1) the value of the property to be distributed under the plan equals the amount of the claim, or (2) the plan provides that all of the debtor's disposable income to be received in a three-year period (or longer, by court approval) will be applied to making payments. Disposable income is all income received less amounts needed to support the farmer or fisherman and his or her family and to continue the farming or commercial fishing operation. Completion of payments under the plan discharges all debts provided for by the plan.

## Reviewing: Creditor-Debtor Relations and Bankruptcy

Three months ago, Janet Hart's husband of twenty years died of cancer. Although he had medical insurance, he left Janet with outstanding medical bills of more than $50,000. Janet has two teenage daughters to support. She has worked at the local library for the past ten years, earning $1,500 per month. Since her husband's death, she has also received $1,500 in Social Security benefits and $1,100 in life insurance proceeds every month, for a total monthly income of $4,100. After making the mortgage payment of $1,500 and paying the amounts due on other debts, Janet has barely enough left to buy groceries for her family. She decides to file for Chapter 7 bankruptcy, hoping for a fresh start. Using the information presented in the chapter, answer the following questions.

1. What must Janet do *before* filing a petition for relief under Chapter 7?
2. How much time does Janet have after filing the bankruptcy petition to submit the required schedules? What happens if Janet does not meet the deadline?
3. Assume that Janet files a petition under Chapter 7. Further assume that the median family income in the geographic area in which Janet lives is $49,300. What steps would a court take to determine whether Janet's petition is presumed to be "substantial abuse" using the means test?
4. Suppose that the court determines that no *presumption* of substantial abuse applies in Janet's case. Nevertheless, the court finds that Janet does have the ability to pay at least a portion of the medical bills out of her disposable income. What would the court likely order in that situation?

**Debate This . . .** *Rather than being allowed to file Chapter 7 bankruptcy petitions, individuals and couples should always be forced to make an effort to pay off their debts through Chapter 13.*

## Terms and Concepts

## Issue Spotters

1. Jorge contracts with Larry of Midwest Roofing to fix Jorge's roof. Jorge pays half of the contract price in advance. Larry and Midwest complete the job, but Jorge refuses to pay the rest of the price. What can Larry and Midwest do? (See *Laws Assisting Creditors.*)

2. After graduating from college, Tina works briefly as a salesperson before filing for bankruptcy. Tina's petition states that her only debts are student loans, taxes accruing within the last year, and a claim against her based on her misuse of customers' funds during her employment. Are these debts dischargeable in bankruptcy? Explain. (See *Liquidation Proceedings.*)

• **Check your answers to the Issue Spotters against the answers provided in Appendix D at the end of this text.**

## Business Scenarios

**15–1. Liens.** Nabil is the owner of a relatively old home valued at $105,000. The home's electrical system is failing, and the wiring needs to be replaced. Nabil contracts with Kandhari Electrical to replace the electrical system. Kandhari performs the repairs, and on June 1 submits a bill of $10,000 to Nabil. Because of financial difficulties, Nabil does not pay the bill. Nabil's only asset is his home, but his state's homestead exemption is $60,000. Discuss fully Kandhari's remedies in this situation. (See *Laws Assisting Creditors.*)

**15–2. Voluntary versus Involuntary Bankruptcy.** Burke has been a rancher all her life, raising cattle and crops. Her ranch is valued at $500,000, almost all of which is exempt under state law. Burke has eight creditors and a total indebtedness of $70,000. Two of her largest creditors are Oman ($30,000 owed) and Sneed ($25,000 owed). The other six creditors have claims of less than $5,000 each. A drought has ruined all of Burke's crops and forced her to sell many of her cattle at a loss. She cannot pay off her creditors. (See *Liquidation Proceedings.*)

**(a)** Under the Bankruptcy Code, can Burke, with a $500,000 ranch, voluntarily petition herself into bankruptcy? Explain.

**(b)** Could either Oman or Sneed force Burke into involuntary bankruptcy? Explain.

## Business Case Problems

**15–3. Discharge in Bankruptcy.** Like many students, Barbara Hann financed her education partially through loans. These loans included three federally insured Stafford Loans of $7,500 each ($22,500 in total). Hann believed that she had repaid the loans, but when she filed a Chapter 13 petition, Educational Credit Management Corp. (ECMC) filed an unsecured proof of claim based on the loans. Hann objected. At a hearing at which ECMC failed to appear, Hann submitted correspondence from the lender that indicated the loans had been paid. The court entered an order sustaining Hann's objection. Despite the order, can ECMC resume its effort to collect on Hann's loans? Explain. [*In re Hann,* 711 F.3d 235 (1st Cir. 2013)] (See *Liquidation Proceedings.*)

**15–4. Discharge.** Michael and Dianne Shankle divorced. An Arkansas state court ordered Michael to pay Dianne alimony and child support, as well as half of the $184,000 in their investment accounts. Instead, Michael withdrew more than half of the investment funds and spent them. Over the next several years, the court repeatedly held Michael in contempt for failing to pay Dianne. Six years later, Michael filed for Chapter 7 bankruptcy, including in the petition's schedule the debt to Dianne of unpaid alimony, child support, and investment funds. Is Michael entitled to a discharge of this debt, or does it qualify as an exception? Explain. [*In re Shankle,* 554 Fed.Appx. 264 (5th Cir. 2014)] (See *Liquidation Proceedings.*)

**15–5. Discharge under Chapter 13.** James Thomas and Jennifer Clark married and had two children. They bought a home in Ironton, Ohio, with a loan secured by a mortgage. Later, they took out a second mortgage. On their divorce, the court gave Clark custody of the children and required Clark to pay the first mortgage. The divorce decree also required Thomas and Clark to make equal payments on the second mortgage and provided that Clark would receive all proceeds on the sale of the home. Thomas failed to make any payments, and Clark sold the home. At that point, she learned that Auto Now had a lien on the home because Thomas had not made payments on his car. Clark used all the sale proceeds to pay off the lien and the mortgages. When Thomas filed a petition for a Chapter 13 bankruptcy in a federal bankruptcy court, Clark filed a proof of claim for the mortgage and lien debts. Clark claimed that Thomas should not be able to discharge these debts because they were part of his domestic-support obligations. Are these debts dischargeable? Explain. [*In re Thomas,* 591 Fed.Appx. 443 (6th Cir. 2015)] (See *Bankruptcy Relief under Chapter 12 and Chapter 13.*)

### 15–6. Business Case Problem with Sample Answer—Liens.

 Daniel and Katherine Balk asked Jirak Construction, LLC, to remodel their farmhouse in Lawler, Iowa. Jirak provided the Balks with an initial estimate of $45,975 for the cost. Over the course of the work, the Balks made significant changes to the plan. Jirak agreed to the changes and regularly advised the Balks about the increasing costs. In mid-project, Jirak provided an itemized breakdown at their request. The Balks paid Jirak $67,000, but refused to pay more. Jirak claimed that they still owed $55,000 in labor and materials. Jirak filed a suit in an Iowa state court against the Balks to collect. Which of the liens discussed in this chapter would be most effective to Jirak in its attempt to collect? How does that type of lien work? Is the court likely to enforce it in this case? Explain. [*Jirak Construction, LLC v. Balk,* 863 N.W.2d 35 (Iowa App. 2015)] (See *Laws Assisting Creditors.*)

- For a sample answer to Problem 15–6, go to Appendix E at the end of this text.

### 15–7. Laws Assisting Creditors.

Grand Harbour Condominium Owners Association, Inc., obtained a judgment in an Ohio state court against Gene and Nancy Grogg for $45,458.86. To satisfy the judgment, Grand Harbour filed a notice of garnishment with the court, seeking funds held by the Groggs in various banks. The Groggs disputed Grand Harbour's right to garnish the funds. They claimed that the funds were exempt Social Security and pension proceeds, but they offered no proof of this claim. The banks responded by depositing $23,911.97 with the court. These funds were delivered to Grand Harbour. Later, the Groggs filed a petition for bankruptcy in a federal bankruptcy court. After they were granted a discharge, they filed a "motion to return funds to debtors" but provided no evidence that their debt to Grand Harbour had been included in the discharge. What is Grand Harbour's best argument in response to the Groggs' motion? [*Grand Harbour Condominium Owners Association, Inc. v. Grogg,* 2016 -Ohio-1386, __ Ohio App.3d __, __ N.E.2d __ (2016)] (See *Laws Assisting Creditors.*)

### 15–8. Liquidation Proceedings.

Jeffrey Krueger and Michael Torres, shareholders of Cru Energy, Inc., were embroiled in litigation in a Texas state court. Both claimed to act on Cru's behalf, and each charged the other with attempting to obtain control of Cru through fraud and other misconduct. Temporarily prohibited from participating in Cru's business, Krueger formed Kru, a company with the same business plan and many of the same shareholders as Cru. Meanwhile, to delay the state court proceedings, Krueger filed a petition for a Chapter 7 liquidation in a federal bankruptcy court. He did not reveal his interest in Kru to the bankruptcy court. Ownership of Krueger's Cru shares passed to the bankruptcy trustee, but Krueger ignored this. He called a meeting of Cru's shareholders—except Torres—and voted those shares to remove Torres from the board and elect himself chairman, president, chief executive officer, and treasurer. The Cru board then dismissed all of Cru's claims against Krueger in his suit with Torres. Are there sufficient grounds for the bankruptcy court to dismiss Krueger's bankruptcy petition? Discuss. [*In re Krueger,* 812 F.3d 365 (5th Cir. 2016)] (See *Liquidation Proceedings.*)

### 15–9. A Question of Ethics—Discharge in Bankruptcy.

*Monica Sexton filed a petition for Chapter 13 reorganization. One of her creditors was Friedman's Jewelers. Her petition misclassified Friedman's claim as $800 of unsecured debt. Within days, Friedman's filed proof of a secured claim for $300 and an unsecured claim for $462. Eventually, Friedman's was sent payments of about $300 by check. None of the checks were cashed. By then, Friedman's had filed its own petition under Chapter 11, Bankruptcy Receivables Management (BRM) had bought Friedman's unpaid accounts, and the checks had not been forwarded. Sexton received a discharge on the completion of her plan. BRM was not notified. BRM wrote to Sexton's attorney to ask about the status of her case, but received no response. BRM demanded that Sexton surrender the collateral on its claim. Sexton asked the court to impose sanctions on BRM for violating the discharge order. [*In re Sexton, 2011 WL 284180 (E.D.N.C. 2011)] (See Liquidation Proceedings.*)*

**(a)** Was Sexton's debt to Friedman's dischargeable? Discuss.

**(b)** Should BRM be sanctioned for willfully violating the discharge order? Why or why not?

## Legal Reasoning Group Activity

### 15–10. Discharge in Bankruptcy.

Cathy Coleman took out loans to complete her college education. After graduation, Coleman was irregularly employed as a teacher before filing a petition in a federal bankruptcy court under Chapter 13. The court confirmed a five-year plan under which Coleman was required to commit all of her disposable income to paying the student loans. Less than a year later, when Coleman was laid off, she still owed more than $100,000 to Educational Credit Management Corp. Coleman asked the court to discharge the debt on the ground that it would be an undue hardship for her to pay it. (See *Liquidation Proceedings.*)

**(a)** The first group will determine when a debtor normally is entitled to a discharge under Chapter 13.

**(b)** The second group will discuss whether student loans are dischargeable and when "undue hardship" is a legitimate ground for an exception to the general rule.

**(c)** The third group will outline the goals of bankruptcy law and make an argument, based on these facts and principles, in support of Coleman's request.

## UNIT THREE Application and Ethics

# Fantasy Sports—Legal Gambling?

A *fantasy sport* involves games in which the participants compile imaginary teams made up of real players in a professional sport. As in real sports, fantasy sports team owners draft, trade, and drop players. The teams are grouped into leagues and compete based on the statistical performance of the players in actual games.

Fantasy sports is a multibillion-dollar industry that includes more than three hundred companies, ranging from small start-ups to large corporations. For example, CBSSports.com, which offers fantasy sports games on its Web site, is a brand operated by CBS Interactive, a division of CBS Corporation. More than 50 million U.S. adults play fantasy sports.

One of the most important issues confronting the industry is whether participation in fantasy sports constitutes illegal gambling.

### Do Fantasy Sports Constitute Gambling under State Law?

To *gamble* is to play a game of chance or bet on the outcome of an uncertain event in the hope of winning. State laws concerning the legality of gambling vary. Even in states where most forms of gambling are illegal, however, some activities that would otherwise fall within the definition of gambling are allowed.

**Consideration, Reward, and Chance** In most states, an activity constitutes gambling if it involves consideration, reward, and chance. Most courts construe *consideration* narrowly in this context, limiting it to money or valuable property exchanged for a chance to win a prize. Some courts apply the term more broadly to any form of legal detriment exchanged for a chance to win.

A *reward* is the prize for winning. Courts generally hold that the reward, or prize, must be something tangible, regardless of its value.[1]

*Chance* requires that an activity's outcome be determined unpredictably by factors outside a participant's control, not by judgment, practice, or skill. Most states deem an activity to involve chance if greater than 50 percent of the outcome is determined by outside factors.

**Entry Fees, Prizes, and Skill** In states that apply these three elements to determine whether an activity constitutes gambling, the lack of any one of them argues in favor of an activity's lawfulness. For example, fantasy sports leagues that offer free entry for participants lack the element of consideration. Games that do not include prizes lack the element of reward.

Other fantasy sports games are not so clearly legal. For example, a game that extends for less than a full professional sports season involves a greater degree of chance and is thus less likely to qualify as legal.[2] The shorter the time, the less opportunity a participant's skill has to offset such factors as a player's health, the decisions of a team manager or coach, and weather. There is also less time for participants to negotiate trades and manage their fantasy teams.

---

**1.** See, for example, *State of Arkansas v. 26 Gaming Machines*, 356 Ark. 47, 145 S.W.3d 368 (2004).
**2.** See *Three Kings Holdings, L.L.C. v. Six*, 45 Kan.App.2d 1043, 255 P.3d 1218 (2011).

**UNIT THREE    Application and Ethics**

**Stricter Standards** The standards are stricter in some states. For example, states that apply the contract definition of *consideration*—something of legally sufficient value—to fantasy sports games will not exempt a game simply because there is no entry fee.

Some states interpret the element of chance to involve *any* chance. In those states, all fantasy sports games violate gambling laws. Other states have indicated or expressly stated that the games are illegal.[3]

### Does Federal Law Define Fantasy Sports as Gambling?

Most federal laws related to gambling were enacted to help states enforce their gambling laws. There are, however, at least two federal acts that may apply to fantasy sports.

**"Wagering Schemes"** The professional sports industry lobbied Congress to enact the Professional and Amateur Sports Protection Act (PAPSA)[4] in 1992. This act prohibits, with certain exceptions, the operation of a "wagering scheme" based on a game in which "professional or amateur athletes participate."

It is not likely that PAPSA would apply to fantasy sports generally—most professional sports leagues operate their own fantasy sports Web sites and endorse seasonal play. But the act could apply to *daily* fantasy sports games—games played over a brief period, such as a week or a single day, rather than an entire sports season. Their sponsors emphasize payouts and prizes, giving daily games the appearance of "wagering schemes."

**Skill of the Participants** The Unlawful Internet Gambling Enforcement Act (UIGEA) of 2006[5] prohibits persons "engaged in the business of betting" to "knowingly accept" funds "in connection with the participation of another person in unlawful Internet gambling." Under the act, "unlawful Internet gambling" is knowingly transmitting a bet, via the Internet, if the bet is otherwise illegal where it is "initiated, received, or . . . made." In other words, if a person places a bet in a state in which gambling is illegal, a business that accepts the bet violates the UIGEA, regardless of the business's location.[6]

The UIGEA exempts fantasy sports games in which, among other requirements, the "outcomes reflect the relative knowledge and skill of the participants and are determined predominantly by the performance of individuals . . . in multiple real-world sporting events." It is likely that *daily* fantasy sports games do not meet this requirement. Their short duration decreases the effect of a participant's skill and increases the effect of luck on the result.

### Daily Fantasy Sports—Skill or Gamble?

DraftKings and FanDuel operate daily fantasy sports (DFS) Web sites. In the fall of 2015, the two companies saturated the media with advertising, emphasizing million-dollar payouts. Then, in early October, DraftKings employee Brian Haskell allegedly used inside information to beat more than 200,000 other participants and win $350,000 in a game on FanDuel's site. DraftKings denied the allegation. Both companies announced, "Nothing is more important . . . than the integrity of the games we offer to our customers."

---

3. These states include Arizona, Iowa, Louisiana, Montana, and Washington.
4. 28 U.S.C. Sections 3701–3704.
5. 31 U.S.C. Sections 5361–5367.
6. See *Interactive Media Entertainment and Gaming Association Inc. v. Attorney General of United States*, 580 F.3d 113 (3d Cir. 2009).

Application and Ethics

Before the end of the month, the Federal Bureau of Investigation and U.S. Department of Justice opened an investigation. ESPN announced that it would stop running segments sponsored by DraftKings. The National Collegiate Athletic Association (NCAA) barred DraftKings and FanDuel from advertising at NCAA championship events and prohibited student athletes from participating in DFS. The National Football League limited the amount of money its players could win from DFS.

Meanwhile, a dozen states began considering new fantasy sports legislation. The Nevada Gaming Control Board ruled that DFS should be considered gambling and banned DFS sites from operating in the state. New York Attorney General Eric Schneiderman, characterizing DFS as games of chance rather than skill, ordered DraftKings and FanDuel to stop accepting "wagers" from New York residents.

> Daily fantasy sports companies are engaged in illegal gambling . . . , causing the same kinds of social and economic harms as other forms of illegal gambling. . . . Daily fantasy sports is neither victimless nor harmless, and it is clear that DraftKings and FanDuel are the leaders of a massive, multi-billion-dollar scheme intended to evade the law and fleece sports fans across the country.[7]

## Ethical Connection

DraftKings and FanDuel contend that they are not taking bets—that the games on their sites involve more skill than luck. They have a legal right to argue this point in a New York state court on a challenge to the order of the state's attorney general. And, in the best interest of their owners and customers, they may have an ethical duty to challenge the order.

In the meantime, do the two sites have an ethical duty to *comply* with the order? Or do they have an ethical obligation to *defy* the order to play to completion the games that New York residents started? The sites might thereby gain additional support for their argument to challenge the attorney general. Or their open defiance might undercut any sympathy a court might have for their situation. It is a judgment call—an ethical gamble—and the question for the sites might be, "Do you feel lucky?"

**Ethics Question** *Is gambling less ethical than trading in securities or funding a start-up? Why?*

**Critical Thinking** *What is the most significant factor in determining whether fantasy sports games constitute gambling? Explain.*

---

7. Press Release, New York State Office of the Attorney General, *A.G. Schneiderman Issues Cease-and-Desist Letters to FanDuel and DraftKings, Demanding That Companies Stop Accepting Illegal Wagers in New York State* (Nov. 11, 2015) (http://www.ag.ny.gov/press-release/ag-schneiderman-issues-cease-and-desist-letters-fanduel-and-draftkings-demanding).

# Answers to the *Issue Spotters*

**1. *What can Larry and Midwest do?*** Each of the parties can place a mechanic's lien on the debtor's property. If the debtor does not pay what is owed, the property can be sold to satisfy the debt. The only requirements are that the lien be filed within a specific time from the time of the work, depending on the state statute, and that notice of the foreclosure and sale be given to the debtor in advance.

**2. *Are these debts dischargeable in bankruptcy? Explain.*** No. Besides the claims listed in this problem, the debts that cannot be discharged in bankruptcy include amounts borrowed to pay back taxes, goods obtained by fraud, debts that were not listed in the petition, domestic support obligations, certain cash advances, and others.

# Sample Answers for *Business Case Problems with Sample Answer*

**Problem 15–6. *Liens.*** Among the liens discussed in this chapter, a mechanic's lien would likely be most effective to Jirak in its attempt to collect the unpaid cost of its work for the Balks. A creditor can place a mechanic's lien on the real property of a debtor who has contracted for improvements to the property and has not paid the price. When a creditor obtains a mechanic's lien, the debtor's real estate becomes security for the debt. If the debtor does not pay, the creditor can foreclose on the property and sell it to collect the amount due.

In this problem, the Balks contracted with Jirak for the remodel of their farmhouse. Due to the Balks' changes to the project during the course of the work, the costs exceeded the amount of Jirak's original estimate. Although Jirak regularly advised the Balks about the increasing costs and provided an itemized breakdown at their request, they refused to pay the price. The use of a mechanic's lien is likely the best way for Jirak to collect the unpaid amount.

In the actual case on which this problem is based, Jirak filed a suit in an Iowa state court against the Balks to foreclose on their property by way of a mechanic's lien and collect the unpaid amount. The court entered a judgment in Jirak's favor and enforced the lien. A state intermediate appellate court affirmed the judgment.

# Chapter 11

# CHAPTER

# Real Property and Land-Use Control

From the earliest times, property has provided a means for survival. Primitive peoples lived off the fruits of the land, eating the vegetation and wildlife. Later, as the wildlife was domesticated and the vegetation cultivated, property provided pastures and farmland. Throughout history, property has continued to be an indicator of family wealth and social position. In the Western world, the protection of an individual's right to his or her property has become one of our most important rights.

In this chapter, we look at the nature of real property and the ways in which it can be owned. We examine the legal requirements involved in the transfer of real property. We even consider, in this chapter's *Spotlight Case,* whether the buyer of a haunted house can rescind the sale.

Realize that real property rights are never absolute. There is a higher right—that of the government to take, for compensation, private land for public use. Later in the chapter, we discuss this right, as well as other restrictions on the ownership or use of property. We conclude the chapter with a discussion of land-use control and zoning laws.

## 26–1 The Nature of Real Property

Real property (or realty) consists of land and everything permanently attached to it, including structures and other fixtures. Real property encompasses airspace and subsurface rights, as well as rights to plants and vegetation. In essence, real property is immovable.

### 26–1a Land and Structures

Land includes the soil on the surface of the earth and the natural products or artificial structures that are attached to it. Land further includes all the waters contained on or under its surface and much, but not necessarily all, of the airspace above it. The exterior boundaries of land extend down to the center of the earth and up to the farthest reaches of the atmosphere (subject to certain qualifications).

### 26–1b Airspace and Subsurface Rights

The owner of real property has rights to both the airspace above the land and the soil and minerals underneath it. Any limitations on either airspace rights or subsurface rights, called *encumbrances,* normally must be indicated on the document that transfers title at the time of purchase.

The ways in which ownership rights in real property can be limited will be examined later in this chapter.

**Airspace Rights** Disputes concerning airspace rights may involve the right of commercial and private planes to fly over property and the right of individuals and governments to seed clouds and produce artificial rain. Flights over private land normally do not violate property rights unless the flights are so low and so frequent that they directly interfere with the owner's enjoyment and use of the land. Leaning walls or projecting eave spouts or roofs may also violate the airspace rights of an adjoining property owner.

**Subsurface Rights** In many states, ownership of land can be separated from ownership of its subsurface. In other words, the owner of the surface may sell subsurface rights to another person. When ownership is separated into surface and subsurface rights, each owner can pass title to what she or he owns without the consent of the other owner.

Subsurface rights can be extremely valuable, as these rights include the ownership of minerals, oil, or natural gas. But a subsurface owner's rights would be of little value if he or she could not use the surface to exercise those rights. Hence, a subsurface owner has a right (called a *profit*, discussed later in this chapter) to go onto the surface of the land to, for instance, find and remove minerals.

Of course, conflicts can arise between the surface owner's use of the property and the subsurface owner's need to extract minerals, oil, or natural gas. In that situation, one party's interest may become subservient (secondary) to the other party's interest either by statute or by case law. If the owners of the subsurface rights excavate, they are absolutely (strictly) liable if their excavation causes the surface to collapse. Many states have statutes that also make the excavators liable for any damage to structures on the land. Typically, these statutes set out precise requirements for excavations of various depths.

## 26–1c Plant Life and Vegetation

Plant life, both natural and cultivated, is also considered to be real property. In many instances, the natural vegetation, such as trees, adds greatly to the value of realty. When a parcel of land is sold and the land has growing crops on it, the sale includes the crops, unless otherwise specified in the sales contract. When crops are sold by themselves, however, they are considered to be personal property, or goods. Consequently, the sale of crops is a sale of goods and is governed by the Uniform Commercial Code (UCC) rather than by real property law.

## 26–1d Fixtures

Certain personal property can become so closely associated with the real property to which it is attached that the law views it as real property. Such property is known as a **fixture**—an item affixed to realty, meaning that it is attached to the real property in a permanent way. The item may be embedded in the land or permanently attached to the property or to another fixture on the property by means of cement, plaster, bolts, nails, or screws. An item, such as a statue, may even sit on the land without being attached, as long as the owner *intends* it to be a fixture.

Fixtures are included in the sale of land unless the sales contract specifies otherwise. The issue of whether an item is a fixture (and thus real estate) or not a fixture (and thus personal property) often arises with respect to land sales, real property taxation, insurance coverage, and divorces. How the issue is resolved can have important consequences for the parties involved.

**Typical Fixtures** Some items can only be attached to property permanently—such as tile floors, cabinets, and carpeting. Because such items are attached permanently,

it is assumed that the owner intended them to be fixtures. Also, when an item of property is custom-made for installation on real property, as storm windows are, the item usually is classified as a fixture.

In addition, an item that is firmly attached to the land and integral to its use may be deemed a fixture. For instance, a mobile home or a complex irrigation system bolted to a cement slab on a farm can be a fixture. The courts assume that owners, in making such installations, intend the objects to become part of their real property.

**The Role of Intent** Generally, when the courts need to determine whether a certain item is a fixture, they examine the intention of the party who placed the object on the real property. When the intent of that party is in dispute, the courts will usually deem that the item is a fixture if either or both of the following are true:

- The property attached cannot be removed without causing substantial damage to the remaining realty.
- The property attached is so adapted to the rest of the realty as to have become a part of it.

■ **CASE IN POINT 26.1** Terminal 5, a facility owned by the Port of Seattle (Port), was used in loading and unloading the shipping containers used to transport goods by ship. APL Limited entered into a long-term lease with the Port for use of Terminal 5 and for use of Port-owned container cranes. Terminal 5 was substantially rebuilt, and steel cranes were constructed and installed. The cranes were 100 feet apart, 198 feet tall, and 85 feet wide, and were mounted on rails embedded in concrete. They were hard-wired to a dedicated high-voltage electrical system built specifically for Terminal 5 and were attached to the power substation by cables.

APL later filed a lawsuit against the state of Washington for a refund of sales tax it had paid on the lease of the cranes. The state argued that the cranes were personal property and, as such, subject to sales tax. The trial court ruled in favor of the state, but a Washington appellate court reversed. The reviewing court found that the trial court had not sufficiently taken the Port's intent into account in determining that the cranes were personal property, not fixtures. "When the owner and the person that [attaches property to realty] are one and the same, a rebuttable presumption arises that the owner's intention was for the [property] to become part of the realty." The reviewing court remanded the case so the lower court could examine evidence of the Port's intent.[1] ■

---

1. *APL Limited v. Washington State Department of Revenue,* 154 Wash.App. 1020 (2010).

**Trade Fixtures Are Personal Property** Trade fixtures are an exception to the rule that fixtures are a part of the real property to which they are attached. A **trade fixture** is personal property that is installed for a commercial purpose *by a tenant* (one who rents real property from the owner, or landlord).

Trade fixtures remain the property of the tenant unless removal would irreparably damage the building or realty. A walk-in cooler, for instance, purchased and installed by a tenant who uses the premises for a restaurant, is a trade fixture. The tenant can remove the cooler from the premises when the lease terminates but ordinarily must repair any damage that the removal causes or compensate the landlord for the damage.

# 26–2 Ownership and Other Interests in Real Property

Ownership of property is an abstract concept that cannot exist independently of the legal system. No one can actually possess, or *hold,* a piece of land, the air above it, the earth below it, and all the water contained on it. One can only possess *rights* in real property.

Numerous rights are involved in real property ownership, which is why property ownership is often viewed as a bundle of rights. One who possesses the entire bundle of rights is said to hold the property in *fee simple,* which is the most complete form of ownership. When only some of the rights in the bundle are transferred to another person, the effect is to limit the ownership rights of both the transferor of the rights and the recipient.

Ownership interests in real property have traditionally been referred to as *estates in land,* which include fee simple estates, life estates, and leasehold estates. We examine these types of estates in this section, and we also discuss several forms of concurrent ownership of property. Finally, we describe certain interests in real property that is owned by others.

## 26–2a Ownership in Fee Simple

In a **fee simple absolute,** the owner has the greatest aggregation of rights, privileges, and power possible. The owner can give the property away or dispose of the property by *deed* or by *will.* When there is no will, the fee simple passes to the owner's legal heirs on her or his death. A fee simple absolute is potentially infinite in duration and is assigned forever to a person and

her or his heirs without limitation or condition.[2] The owner has the rights of *exclusive* possession and use of the property.

The rights that accompany a fee simple absolute include the right to use the land for whatever purpose the owner sees fit. Of course, other laws, including applicable zoning, noise, and environmental laws, may limit the owner's ability to use the property in certain ways. A person who uses his or her property in a manner that unreasonably interferes with others' right to use or enjoy their own property can be liable for the tort of *nuisance.*

■ **CASE IN POINT 26.2** Nancy and James Biglane owned and lived in a building next door to the Under the Hill Saloon, a popular bar that featured live music. During the summer, the Saloon, which had no air-conditioning, opened its windows and doors, and live music echoed up and down the street. The Biglanes installed extra insulation, thicker windows, and air-conditioning units in their building. Nevertheless, the noise from the Saloon kept the Biglanes awake at night. Eventually, they sued the owners of the Saloon for nuisance. The court held that the noise from the bar unreasonably interfered with the Biglanes' right to enjoy their property and prohibited the Saloon from opening its windows and doors while playing music.[3] ■

## 26–2b Life Estates

A **life estate** is an estate that lasts for the life of some specified individual. A **conveyance,** or transfer of real property, "to A for his life" creates a life estate.[4] The life tenant's ownership rights cease to exist on the life tenant's death.

The life tenant has the right to use the land, provided that he or she commits no **waste** (injury to the land). In other words, the life tenant cannot use the land in a manner that would adversely affect its value. The life tenant can use the land to harvest crops or, if mines and oil wells are already on the land, can extract minerals and oil from it, but the life tenant cannot establish new wells or mines. The life tenant can also create liens, *easements* (discussed shortly), and leases, but none can extend beyond the life

---

2. In another type of estate, the *fee simple defeasible,* ownership in fee simple automatically terminates if a stated event occurs. For instance, property might be conveyed (transferred) to a school only as long as it is used for school purposes. In addition, the fee simple may be subject to a *condition subsequent.* This means that if a stated event occurs, the prior owner of the property can bring an action to regain possession of the property.
3. *Biglane v. Under the Hill Corp.*, 949 So.2d 9 (Miss.Sup. 2007).
4. A less common type of life estate is created by the conveyance "to A for the life of B." This is known as an estate *pur autre vie*—that is, an estate for the duration of the life of another.

of the tenant. In addition, with few exceptions, the life tenant has an exclusive right to possession during his or her lifetime.

Along with these rights, the life tenant also has some duties—to keep the property in repair and to pay property taxes. In short, the owner of the life estate has the same rights as a fee simple owner except that she or he must maintain the value of the property during her or his tenancy.

In the following case, the life tenant refused to pay the taxes and the premiums for the insurance on the property. Was this waste?

Case 26.1

# Main Omni Realty Corp. v. Matus

New York Supreme Court, Appellate Division, Second Department, 124 A.D.3d 604, 1 N.Y.S.3d 319 (2015).

**Background and Facts** Craig Matus held a life estate in certain residential real property in Huntington, New York. On the termination of the life estate, title to the property was to transfer to Main Omni Realty Corporation, a wholly owned subsidiary of New York Community Bank. For a dozen years, Matus refused to pay premiums for insurance on the property. He also refused to pay the property taxes, resulting in tax liens.

To preserve its interest in the property, Main Omni paid the premiums and the liens, which avoided a foreclosure and sale of the property. Main Omni then filed a suit in a New York state court against Matus, seeking to recover the amount of the premiums and taxes on the ground of unjust enrichment. In addition, it sought to extinguish (end) the life estate on the ground of waste based on Matus's refusal to pay the taxes. The court denied Main Omni's motion for summary judgment. Main Omni appealed.

## In the Language of the Court
Ruth C. *BALKIN*, J.P. [Judge Presiding], L. Priscilla *HALL*, Leonard B. *AUSTIN*, and Betsey *BARROS*, JJ. [Judges].
     * * * *

The essential inquiry in any action for unjust enrichment or restitution is whether it is against equity and good conscience to permit the defendant to retain what is sought to be recovered. *A plaintiff must show that (1) the other party was enriched, (2) at the plaintiff's expense, and (3) that it is against equity and good conscience to permit the other party to retain what is sought to be recovered.* [Emphasis added.]

The plaintiffs established their *prima facie* entitlement to judgment as a matter of law on their first cause of action, which alleged unjust enrichment and sought restitution, and their second cause of action, which alleged waste and sought to extinguish the defendant's life estate. As life tenant, the defendant was obligated to pay the property taxes and * * * insurance on the subject property, and the intentional failure to do so constitutes waste. It is undisputed that the defendant intentionally failed to pay the property taxes and * * * insurance on the subject property, and he has clearly expressed his intention not to do so in the future. Under these circumstances, the remainder interest in the subject property is in constant danger of forfeiture in a tax lien sale, unless the plaintiffs continue paying the property taxes and * * * insurance premiums the defendant is otherwise obligated to pay. The plaintiffs therefore demonstrated, *prima facie,* that the defendant was unjustly enriched by the plaintiffs' payment of these expenses for the defendant, and that equity warrants extinguishing his life estate in the subject property.

**Decision and Remedy** *A state intermediate appellate court reversed the lower court's denial of Main Omni's motion and ordered a summary judgment in the plaintiff's favor. Because Matus continued to refuse to pay the taxes on the property, the court ended his life estate.*

**Critical Thinking**
- **Economic** *Why would the owner of a life estate refuse to pay the taxes and insurance premiums on the property of the estate? Should any reason for this refusal have influenced the court's decision in this case?*

## 26–2c Concurrent Ownership

Persons who share ownership rights simultaneously in particular property (including real property and personal property) are said to have **concurrent ownership.** There are two principal types of concurrent ownership: *tenancy in common* and *joint tenancy.* Concurrent ownership rights can also be held in a *tenancy by the entirety* or as *community property,* but these types of concurrent ownership are less common.

**Tenancy in Common** The term **tenancy in common** refers to a form of co-ownership in which each of two or more persons owns an undivided interest in the property. The interest is undivided because each tenant shares rights in the whole property. On the death of a tenant in common, that tenant's interest in the property passes to her or his heirs.

    ■ **EXAMPLE 26.3** Four friends purchase a condominium unit in Hawaii together as tenants in common. This means that each of them has a one-fourth ownership interest in the whole. If one of the four owners dies a year after the purchase, his ownership interest passes to his heirs (his wife and children, for example) rather than to the other tenants in common. ■

    Unless the co-tenants have agreed otherwise, a tenant in common can transfer her or his interest in the property to another without the consent of the remaining co-owners. In most states, it is presumed that a co-tenancy is a tenancy in common unless there is specific language indicating the intent to establish a joint tenancy.

**Joint Tenancy** In a **joint tenancy,** each of two or more persons owns an undivided interest in the property, but a deceased joint tenant's interest passes to the surviving joint tenant or tenants.

**Right of Survivorship.** The right of a surviving joint tenant to inherit a deceased joint tenant's ownership interest—referred to as a *right of survivorship*—distinguishes a joint tenancy from a tenancy in common. ■ **EXAMPLE 26.4** Jerrold and Eva are married and purchase a house as joint tenants. The title to the house clearly expresses the intent to create a joint tenancy because it refers to Jerrold and Eva as "joint tenants with right of survivorship." Jerrold has three children from a prior marriage. If Jerrold dies, his interest in the house automatically passes to Eva rather than to his children from the prior marriage. ■

**Termination of a Joint Tenancy.** A joint tenant can transfer her or his rights by sale or gift to another without the consent of the other joint tenants. Doing so terminates the joint tenancy, however. The person who purchases the property or receives it as a gift becomes a tenant in common, not a joint tenant. ■ **EXAMPLE 26.5** Three brothers, Brody, Saul, and Jacob, own a parcel of land as joint tenants. Brody is experiencing financial difficulties and sells his interest in the real property to Beth. The sale terminates the joint tenancy, and now Beth, Saul, and Jacob hold the property as tenants in common. ■

    A joint tenant's interest can also be levied against (seized by court order) to satisfy the tenant's judgment creditors. If this occurs, the joint tenancy terminates, and the remaining owners hold the property as tenants in common. (Judgment creditors can also seize the interests of tenants in a tenancy in common.)

**Tenancy by the Entirety** A less common form of shared ownership of real property by married persons is a **tenancy by the entirety.** It differs from a joint tenancy in that neither spouse may separately transfer his or her interest during his or her lifetime unless the other spouse consents. In some states in which statutes give the wife the right to convey her property, this form of concurrent ownership has effectively been abolished. A divorce, either spouse's death, or mutual agreement will terminate a tenancy by the entirety.

**Community Property** A limited number of states[5] allow married couples to own property as **community property.** If property is held as community property, each spouse technically owns an undivided one-half interest in the property. This type of ownership applies to most property acquired by the husband or the wife during the course of the marriage. It generally does *not* apply to property acquired prior to the marriage or to property acquired by gift or inheritance as separate property during the marriage. After a divorce, community property is divided equally in some states and according to the discretion of the court in other states.

## 26–2d Leasehold Estates

A **leasehold estate** is created when a real property owner or lessor (landlord) agrees to convey the right to possess and use the property to a lessee (tenant) for a certain period of time. The tenant's right to possession is

---

5. These states include Alaska, Arizona, California, Idaho, Louisiana, Nevada, New Mexico, Texas, Washington, and Wisconsin. Puerto Rico allows property to be owned as community property as well.

*temporary,* which is what distinguishes a tenant from a purchaser, who acquires title to the property.

In every leasehold estate, the tenant has a *qualified* right to exclusive possession. It is qualified because the landlord has a right to enter onto the premises to ensure that no waste is being committed. In addition, the tenant can use the land—for instance, by harvesting crops—but cannot injure it by such activities as cutting down timber to sell or extracting oil.

**Fixed-Term Tenancy** A **fixed-term tenancy,** also called a *tenancy for years,* is created by an express contract stating that the property is leased for a specified period of time, such as a month, a year, or a period of years. Signing a one-year lease to occupy an apartment, for instance, creates a fixed-term tenancy. Note that the term need not be specified by date and can be conditioned on the occurrence of an event, such as leasing a cabin for the summer or an apartment during Mardi Gras.

At the end of the period specified in the lease, the lease ends (without notice), and possession of the property returns to the lessor. If the tenant dies during the period of the lease, the lease interest passes to the tenant's heirs as personal property. Often, leases include renewal or extension provisions.

**Periodic Tenancy** A **periodic tenancy** is created by a lease that does not specify a term but does specify that rent is to be paid at certain intervals, such as weekly, monthly, or yearly. The tenancy is automatically renewed for another rental period unless properly terminated. ■ **EXAMPLE 26.6** Jewel, LLC, enters into a lease with Capital Properties. The lease states, "Rent is due on the tenth day of every month." This provision creates a periodic tenancy from month to month. ■ A periodic tenancy sometimes arises after a fixed-term tenancy ends when the landlord allows the tenant to retain possession and continue paying monthly or weekly rent.

Under the common law, to terminate a periodic tenancy, the landlord or tenant must give at least one period's notice to the other party. If the tenancy is month to month, for instance, one month's notice must be given prior to the last month's rent payment. Today, however, state statutes often require a different period of notice before the termination of a tenancy.

**Tenancy at Will** With a **tenancy at will,** either party can terminate the tenancy without notice. This type of tenancy can arise if a landlord rents property to a tenant "for as long as both agree" or allows a person to live on the premises without paying rent. Tenancy at will is rare today

because most state statutes require a landlord to provide some period of notice to terminate a tenancy. States may also require a landowner to have sufficient cause (a legitimate reason) to end a residential tenancy.

**Tenancy at Sufferance** The mere possession of land without right is called a **tenancy at sufferance.** A tenancy at sufferance is not a true tenancy because it is created when a tenant *wrongfully* retains possession of property. Whenever a tenancy for years or a periodic tenancy ends and the tenant continues to retain possession of the premises without the owner's permission, a tenancy at sufferance is created.

## 26–2e Nonpossessory Interests

In contrast to the types of property interests just described, some interests in land do not include any rights to possess the property. These interests are therefore known as **nonpossessory interests.** They include *easements, profits,* and *licenses.*

An **easement** is the right of a person to make limited use of another person's real property without taking anything from the property. The right to walk across another's property, for example, is an easement. In contrast, a **profit** is the right to go onto land owned by another and take away some part of the land itself or some product of the land. ■ **EXAMPLE 26.7** Shawn owns real property known as the Dunes. Shawn gives Carmen the right to go there and remove all of the sand and gravel that she needs for her cement business. Carmen has a profit. ■

Easements and profits can be classified as either *appurtenant* or *in gross.* Because easements and profits are similar and the same rules apply to both, we discuss them together.

**Easement or Profit Appurtenant** An easement (or profit) *appurtenant* arises when the owner of one piece of land has a right to go onto (or remove something from) an adjacent piece of land owned by another. The land that is benefited by the easement is called the *dominant estate,* and the land that is burdened is called the *servient estate.*

Because easements appurtenant are intended to *benefit the land,* they run (are conveyed) with the land when it is transferred. ■ **EXAMPLE 26.8** Owen has a right to drive his car across Green's land, which is adjacent to Owen's property. This right-of-way over Green's property is an easement appurtenant to Owen's land. If Owen sells his land, the easement runs with the land to benefit the new owner. ■

**Easement or Profit in Gross** In an easement or profit *in gross,* the right to use or take things from another's land is given to one who does not own an adjacent tract of land. These easements are intended to *benefit a particular person or business,* not a particular piece of land, and cannot be transferred.

■ **EXAMPLE 26.9** Avery owns a parcel of land with a marble quarry. Avery conveys to Classic Stone Corporation the right to come onto her land and remove up to five hundred pounds of marble per day. Classic Stone owns a profit in gross and cannot transfer this right to another. ■ Similarly, when a utility company is granted an easement to run its power lines across another's property, it obtains an easement in gross.

**Creation of an Easement or Profit** Most easements and profits are created by an express grant in a contract, deed, or will. This allows the parties to include terms defining the extent and length of time of use. In some situations, however, an easement or profit can be created without an express agreement.

An easement or profit may arise by **implication** when the circumstances surrounding the division of a parcel of property imply its creation. ■ **EXAMPLE 26.10** Barrow divides a parcel of land that has only one well for drinking water. If Barrow conveys the half without a well to Dean, a profit by implication arises because Dean needs drinking water. ■

An easement may also be created by **necessity.** An easement by necessity does not require division of property for its existence. A person who rents an apartment, for instance, has an easement by necessity in the private road leading up to it.

An easement arises by **prescription** when one person exercises an easement, such as a right-of-way, on another person's land without the landowner's consent. The use must be apparent and continue for the length of time required by the applicable statute of limitations. (In much the same way, title to property may be obtained by adverse possession, as will be discussed later in this chapter.)

■ **CASE IN POINT 26.11** Junior and Wilma Thompson sold twenty-one of their fifty acres of land in Missouri to Walnut Bowls, Inc. The deed expressly reserved an easement to the Thompsons' remaining twenty-nine acres, but it did not fix a precise location for the easement. James and Linda Baker subsequently bought the remaining acreage of the Thompsons' land.

Many years later—on learning of the easement to the Bakers' property—a potential buyer of Walnut Bowls' property refused to go through with the sale. Walnut

Bowls then put steel cables across its driveway entrances, installed a lock and chain on an access gate, and bolted a "No Trespassing" sign facing the Bakers' property. The Bakers filed a suit in a Missouri state court to determine the location of the easement. Citing the lack of an express location, the court held that there was no easement.

The Bakers appealed, and a state intermediate appellate court reversed that decision. The reviewing court held that an easement existed and instructed the trial court to determine its location. An easement can be created by deed even though its specific location is not identified. The location can later be fixed by agreement between the parties or inferred from use. If the easement is not identified in either of these ways, a court must determine the location.[6] ■

**Termination of an Easement or Profit** An easement or profit can be terminated or extinguished in several ways. The simplest way is to deed it back to the owner of the land that is burdened by it. Similarly, if the owner of an easement or profit acquires the property burdened by it, then it is merged into the property.

Another way to terminate an easement or profit is to abandon it and provide evidence of the intent to relinquish the right to use it. Mere nonuse will not extinguish an easement or profit, however, *unless the nonuse is accompanied by an overt act showing the intent to abandon.* An overt act might be, for instance, installing and using a different access road to one's property and discontinuing using an easement across the neighboring property. In any case, a court must be convinced that there was an intent to abandon the easement or profit.

**License** In the context of real property, a **license** is the revocable right of a person to come onto another person's land. It is a personal privilege that arises from the consent of the owner of the land and can be revoked by the owner. A ticket to attend a movie at a theater or a concert is an example of a license.

In essence, a license grants a person the authority to enter the land of another and perform a specified act or series of acts without obtaining any permanent interest in the land. When a person with a license exceeds the authority granted and undertakes some action on the property that is not permitted, the property owner can sue that person for the tort of trespass.

■ **CASE IN POINT 26.12** A Catholic church granted Prince Realty Management, LLC, a three-month license to use a three-foot strip of its property adjacent to

---

6. *Baker v. Walnut Bowls, Inc.,* 423 S.W.3d 293 (Mo.App. 2014).

Prince's property. The license authorized Prince to "put up plywood panels," creating a temporary fence to protect Prince's property during the construction of a new building. During the license's term, Prince installed steel piles and beams on the licensed property. When Prince ignored the church's demands that these structures be removed, the church sued Prince for trespass. The court concluded that the license allowed only temporary structures and that Prince had exceeded its authority by installing steel piles and beams. Therefore, the church was entitled to damages.[7] ■

Exhibit 26–1 illustrates the various interests in real property discussed in this chapter.

## 26–3 Transfer of Ownership

Ownership interests in real property are frequently transferred by sale, and the terms of the transfer are specified in a real estate sales contract. When real property is sold, the type of interest being transferred and the conditions of the transfer normally are set forth in a *deed* executed by the person who is conveying the property. Real property ownership can also be transferred by gift, by will or inheritance, by adverse possession, or by eminent domain.

---

7. *Roman Catholic Church of Our Lady of Sorrows v. Prince Realty Management, LLC,* 47 A.D.3d 909, 850 N.Y.S.2d 569 (2008).

### 26–3a Real Estate Sales Contracts

In some ways, a sale of real estate is similar to a sale of goods because it involves a transfer of ownership, often with specific warranties. A sale of real estate, however, is a more complicated transaction that involves certain formalities that are not required in a sale of goods. In part because of these complications, real estate brokers or agents who are licensed by the state assist the buyers and sellers during the sales transaction.

Usually, after substantial negotiation (offers, counteroffers, and responses), the parties enter into a detailed contract setting forth their agreement. A contract for a sale of land includes such terms as the purchase price, the type of deed the buyer will receive, the condition of the premises, and any items that will be included.

Unless the buyer pays cash for the property, the buyer must obtain financing through a mortgage loan. Real estate sales contracts are often contingent on the buyer's ability to obtain financing at or below a specified rate of interest. The contract may also be contingent on certain events, such as the completion of a land survey or the property's passing one or more inspections. Normally, the buyer is responsible for having the premises inspected for physical or mechanical defects and for insect infestation.

**Closing Date and Escrow** The contract usually fixes a date for performance, or **closing,** that frequently is four to twelve weeks after the contract is signed. On this day,

**EXHIBIT 26–1** Interests in Real Property

| TYPE OF INTEREST | DESCRIPTION |
|---|---|
| **Ownership Interests** | 1. *Fee simple*—The most complete form of ownership.<br>2. *Life estate*—An estate that lasts for the life of a specified individual.<br>3. *Concurrent ownership*—When two or more persons hold title to property together, concurrent ownership exists.<br>   a. Tenancy in common<br>   b. Joint tenancy<br>   c. Tenancy by the entirety<br>   d. Community property |
| **Leasehold Estates** | 1. Fixed-term tenancy (tenancy for years)<br>2. Periodic tenancy<br>3. Tenancy at will<br>4. Tenancy at sufferance |
| **Nonpossessory Interests** | 1. Easements<br>2. Profits<br>3. Licenses |

the seller conveys the property to the buyer by delivering the deed to the buyer in exchange for payment of the purchase price.

Deposits toward the purchase price normally are held in a special account, called an **escrow account,** until all of the conditions of sale have been met. Once the closing takes place, the funds in the escrow account are transferred to the seller.

**Marketable Title** The title to a particular parcel of property is especially important to the buyer. A grantor (seller) is obligated to transfer **marketable title,** or good title, to the grantee (buyer). Marketable title means that the grantor's ownership is free from encumbrances (except those disclosed by the grantor) and free of defects.

If the buyer signs a purchase contract and then discovers that the seller does not have a marketable title, the buyer can withdraw from the contract. ■ **EXAMPLE 26.13** Chan enters into an agreement to buy Fortuna Ranch from Hal. Chan then discovers that Hal has given Pearl an option to purchase the ranch and the option has not expired. In this situation, the title is not marketable, because Pearl could exercise the option and Hal would be compelled to sell the ranch to her. Therefore, Chan can withdraw from the contract to buy the property. ■

The most common way of ensuring title is through **title insurance,** which insures the buyer against loss from defects in title to real property. When financing the purchase of real property, almost all lenders require title insurance to protect their interests in the collateral for the loan.

**Implied Warranties in the Sale of New Homes**
The common law rule of *caveat emptor* ("let the buyer beware") held that the seller of a home made no warranty as to its soundness or fitness (unless the contract or deed stated otherwise). Today, however, most states imply a warranty—the **implied warranty of habitability**—in the sale of new homes.

Under this warranty, the seller of a new house warrants that it will be fit for human habitation even if the deed or contract of sale does not include such a warranty. Essentially, the seller is warranting that the house is in reasonable working order and is of reasonably sound construction. The seller can be liable if the home is defective. In some states, the warranty protects not only the first purchaser but any subsequent purchaser as well.

**Seller's Duty to Disclose Hidden Defects** In most jurisdictions, courts impose on sellers a duty to disclose any known defect that materially affects the value of the property and that the buyer could not reasonably discover. Failure to disclose such a defect gives the buyer a right to rescind the contract and to sue for damages based on fraud or misrepresentation.

There is normally a limit to the time within which the buyer can bring a suit against the seller based on the defect. Time limits run from either the date of the sale or the day that the buyer discovered (or should have discovered) the defect. ■ **EXAMPLE 26.14** Ian Newson partially renovates a house in Louisiana and sells it to Jerry and Tabitha Moreland for $87,000. Two months after the Morelands move in, they discover rotten wood behind the tile in the bathroom and experience problems with the plumbing. The state statute specifies that the Morelands have one year from the date of the sale or the discovery of the defect to file a lawsuit. Therefore, the Morelands must file suit within twelve months of discovering the defects (which would be fourteen months from the date of the sale). ■

In the following *Spotlight Case*, the court had to decide whether the buyer of a house had the right to rescind the sales contract because he was not told that the house was allegedly haunted.

## Spotlight on Sales of Haunted Houses

## Case 26.2 Stambovsky v. Ackley

Supreme Court, Appellate Division, New York, 572 N.Y.S.2d 672, 169 A.D.2d 254 (1991).

**Background and Facts** Jeffrey Stambovsky signed a contract to buy Helen Ackley's home in Nyack, New York. After the contract was signed, Stambovsky discovered that the house was widely reputed to be haunted. The Ackley family claimed to have seen poltergeists on numerous occasions over the prior nine years. The Ackleys had been interviewed and quoted in both a national publication (*Reader's Digest*) and the local newspaper. The house was described as "a riverfront Victorian (with ghost)"

**Case 26.2 Continued**

when it was part of a walking tour of Nyack, New York. When Stambovsky discovered the house's reputation, he sued to rescind the contract and recover his down payment. He alleged that Ackley and her real estate agent made material misrepresentations when they failed to disclose Ackley's belief that the home was haunted. Ackley argued that, under the doctrine of *caveat emptor,* she was under no duty to disclose to the buyer the home's haunted reputation. The trial court dismissed Stambovsky's case. Stambovsky appealed.

## In the Language of the Court

Justice *RUBIN* delivered the opinion of the court.

\* \* \* \*

While I agree with [the trial court] that the real estate broker, as agent for the seller, is under no duty to disclose to a potential buyer the phantasmal reputation of the premises and that, in his pursuit of a legal remedy for fraudulent misrepresentation against the seller, plaintiff hasn't a ghost of a chance, I am nevertheless moved by the spirit of equity to allow the buyer to seek rescission of the contract of sale and recovery of his down payment. New York law fails to recognize any remedy for damages incurred as a result of the seller's mere silence, applying instead the strict rule of *caveat emptor.* Therefore, the theoretical basis for granting relief, even under the extraordinary facts of this case, is elusive if not ephemeral [short-lived].

\* \* \* \*

*The doctrine of* caveat emptor *requires that a buyer act prudently to assess the fitness and value of his purchase and operates to bar the purchaser who fails to exercise due care from seeking the equitable remedy of rescission.* \* \* \* Applying the strict rule of *caveat emptor* to a contract involving a house possessed by poltergeists conjures up visions of a psychic or medium routinely accompanying the structural engineer and Terminix man on an inspection of every home subject to a contract of sale. It portends [warns] that the prudent attorney will establish an escrow account lest the subject of the transaction come back to haunt him and his client—or pray that his malpractice insurance coverage extends to supernatural disasters. In the interest of avoiding such untenable consequences, the notion that a haunting is a condition which can and should be ascertained upon reasonable inspection of the premises is a hobgoblin which should be exorcised from the body of legal precedent and laid quietly to rest. [Emphasis added.]

\* \* \* \*

In the case at bar [under consideration], defendant seller deliberately fostered the public belief that her home was possessed. Having undertaken to inform the public at large, to whom she has no legal relationship, about the supernatural occurrences on her property, she may be said to owe no less a duty to her contract vendee. It has been remarked that the occasional modern cases, which permit a seller to take unfair advantage of a buyer's ignorance so long as he is not actively misled are "singularly unappetizing." Where, as here, the seller not only takes unfair advantage of the buyer's ignorance but has created and perpetuated a condition about which he is unlikely to even inquire, enforcement of the contract (in whole or in part) is offensive to the court's sense of equity. Application of the remedy of rescission, within the bounds of the narrow exception to the doctrine of *caveat emptor* set forth herein, is entirely appropriate to relieve the unwitting purchaser from the consequences of a most unnatural bargain.

**Decision and Remedy** *The New York appellate court found that the doctrine of* caveat emptor *did not apply in this case. The court allowed Stambovsky to rescind the purchase contract and recover the down payment.*

**Critical Thinking**

- **Ethical** *In not disclosing the house's reputation to Stambovsky, was Ackley's behavior unethical? If so, was it unethical because she knew something he did not, or was it unethical because of the nature of the information she omitted? What if Ackley had failed to mention that the roof leaked or that the well was dry—conditions that a buyer would normally investigate? Explain your answer.*
- **Legal Environment** *Why did the court decide that applying the strict rule of* caveat emptor *was inappropriate in this case? How would applying this doctrine increase costs for the purchaser?*

## 26–3b Deeds

Possession and title to land are passed from person to person by means of a **deed**—the instrument used to transfer real property. Deeds must meet certain requirements, but unlike a contract, a deed does not have to be supported by legally sufficient consideration. Gifts of real property are common, and they require deeds even though there is no consideration for the gift.

To be valid, a deed must include the following:

1. The names of the grantor (the giver or seller) and the grantee (the donee or buyer).
2. Words evidencing the intent to convey (for instance, "I hereby bargain, sell, grant, or give"). No specific words are necessary. If the deed does not specify the type of estate being transferred, it presumptively transfers the property in fee simple absolute.
3. A legally sufficient description of the land. The description must include enough detail to distinguish the property being conveyed from every other parcel of land. The property can be identified by reference to an official survey or recorded plat map, or each boundary can be described by metes and bounds. **Metes and bounds** is a system of measuring boundary lines by the distance between two points, often using physical features of the local geography. A property description might say, for instance, "beginning at the southwesterly intersection of Court and Main Streets, then West 40 feet to the fence, then South 100 feet, then Northeast approximately 120 feet back to the beginning."
4. The grantor's (and usually his or her spouse's) signature.
5. Delivery of the deed.

Different types of deeds provide different degrees of protection against defects of title, as discussed next.

**Warranty Deeds** A **warranty deed** contains the greatest number of warranties and thus provides the most extensive protection against defects of title. In most states, special language is required to create a general warranty deed. Warranty deeds commonly include the following covenants:

1. A covenant that the grantor has the title to, and the power to convey, the property.
2. A covenant of quiet enjoyment (a warranty that the buyer will not be disturbed in her or his possession of the land).
3. A covenant that transfer of the property is made without knowledge of adverse claims of third parties.

Generally, the warranty deed makes the grantor liable for all defects of title during the time that the property was held by the grantor and previous titleholders. ■ **EXAMPLE 26.15** Sanchez sells a two-acre lot and office building by warranty deed to Fast Tech, LLC. Subsequently, Amy shows that she has better title than Sanchez had and evicts Fast Tech. Here, Fast Tech can sue Sanchez for breaching the covenant of quiet enjoyment. Fast Tech can recover the purchase price of the land, plus any other damages incurred as a result. ■

**Special Warranty Deed** A **special warranty deed,** or *limited warranty deed,* in contrast, warrants only that the grantor or seller held good title during his or her ownership of the property. In other words, the seller does not guarantee that there are no adverse claims by third parties against any previous owners of the property.

If the special warranty deed discloses all liens or other encumbrances, the seller will not be liable to the buyer if a third person subsequently interferes with the buyer's ownership. If the third person's claim arises out of, or is related to, some act of the seller, however, the seller will be liable to the buyer for damages.

**Quitclaim Deed** A **quitclaim deed** offers the least protection against defects in the title. Basically, a quitclaim deed conveys to the grantee whatever interest the grantor had. If the grantor had no interest, then the grantee receives no interest. (Naturally, if the grantor had a defective title or no title at all, a conveyance by warranty deed or special warranty deed would not cure the defect. Such a deed, however, would give the buyer a cause of action to sue the seller.)

Quitclaim deeds are often used when the seller, or grantor, is uncertain as to the extent of his or her rights in the property. They may also be used to release a party's interest in a particular parcel of property. This may be necessary, for instance, in divorce settlements or business dissolutions when the grantors are dividing up their interests in real property.

**Grant Deed** With a **grant deed,** the grantor simply states, "I grant the property to you" or "I convey, or bargain and sell, the property to you." By state statute, grant deeds carry with them an implied warranty that the grantor owns the property and has not previously transferred it to someone else or encumbered it, except as set out in the deed.

## 26–3c Recording Statutes

Once the seller delivers the deed to the buyer (at closing), legal title to the property is conveyed. Nevertheless, the buyer should promptly record the deed with the state records office. Every state has a **recording statute,** which allows deeds to be recorded in the public record for a fee. Deeds generally are recorded in the county in which the property is located. Many state statutes require that the grantor sign the deed in the presence of two witnesses before it can be recorded.

Recording a deed gives notice to the public that a certain person is now the owner of a particular parcel of real estate. By putting everyone on notice as to the true owner, recording a deed prevents the previous owners from fraudulently conveying the land to other purchasers.

### 26–3d Adverse Possession

A person who wrongfully possesses the real property of another (by occupying or using the property) may eventually acquire title to it through adverse possession. **Adverse possession** is a means of obtaining title to land without delivery of a deed and without the consent of—or payment to—the true owner. Thus, adverse possession is a method of *involuntarily* transferring title to the property from the true owner to the adverse possessor.

Essentially, when one person possesses the real property of another for a certain statutory period of time, that person acquires title to the land. The statutory period varies from three to thirty years, depending on the state, with ten years being most common.

**Requirements for Adverse Possession**  For property to be held adversely, four elements must be satisfied:

1. *Possession must be actual and exclusive.* The possessor must physically occupy the property. This requirement is clearly met if the possessor lives on the property, but it may also be met if the possessor builds fences, erects structures, plants crops, or even grazes animals on the land.

2. *The possession must be open, visible, and notorious, not secret or clandestine.* The possessor must occupy the land for all the world to see. This requirement ensures that the true owner is on notice that someone is possessing the owner's property wrongfully.

3. *Possession must be continuous and peaceable for the required period of time.* This requirement means that the possessor must not be interrupted in the occupancy by the true owner or by the courts. Continuous does not mean constant. It simply means that the possessor has continuously occupied the property in some fashion for the statutory time. Peaceable means that no force was used to possess the land.

4. *Possession must be hostile and adverse.* In other words, the possessor cannot be living on the property with the owner's permission and must claim the property as against the whole world.

■ **CASE IN POINT 26.16**  Charles Scarborough and Mildred Rollins were adjoining landowners, sharing one common boundary. Based on Rollins's survey of the property, Rollins believed that she owned a portion of a gravel road located to the south of the apartment buildings she owned. In contrast, Scarborough believed that the gravel road was located totally on his property and that he owned some property north of the gravel road toward Rollins's apartment buildings.

Scarborough filed a complaint seeking a court order stating that he had title to the property and was its sole owner. The court, however, ruled that Rollins owned a portion of the gravel road by adverse possession. She had used it openly for more than thirty-five years, it was generally thought to be part of her apartment complex, and she had paid taxes on it.[8] ■

The following case raises the question of whether a landowner next to a rail line can acquire a portion of the right-of-way by adverse possession.

---

8. *Scarborough v. Rollins,* 44 So.3d 381 (Miss.App. 2010).

---

**Case Analysis 26.3**

## Montgomery County v. Bhatt
Court of Appeals of Maryland, 446 Md. 79, 130 A.3d 424 (2016).

### In the Language of the Court
Glenn T. *HARRELL,* Jr., J. [Judge]

Driving that train, high on cocaine,
Casey Jones you better watch your speed.
Trouble ahead, trouble behind,

And you know that notion just crossed my mind.

—The Grateful Dead, *Casey Jones,* on Workingman's Dead (Warner Bros. Records 1970).

Although the record of the present case does not reflect a comparable level of drama as captured by the refrain of "Casey Jones,"

**Case 26.3 Continues**

it hints at plenty of potential trouble, both ahead and behind, for a pair of public works projects (one in place and the other incipient [in development]) cherished by the government and some citizens of Montgomery County.

The Capital Crescent Trail is a well-known hiker/biker route that runs between Georgetown in the District of Columbia and Silver Spring, Maryland. Its path was used formerly as the Georgetown Branch of the Baltimore & Ohio (B&O) Railroad. After the trains stopped running in 1985, the property was transferred in 1988 to the government of Montgomery County, Maryland, via a quitclaim deed for a consideration of $10 million. It is planned that the Maryland portion of the former rail line (and current interim hiker/biker trail) will become the proposed Purple Line, a commuter light rail project.

BACKGROUND

* * * Ajay Bhatt owns 3313 Coquelin Terrace (a subdivided, single-family residential lot—"Lot 8"—improved by a dwelling) in Chevy Chase, Montgomery County, Maryland. He purchased this property in 2006 from his aunt, who owned the property since at least the 1970s. The lot abuts the Georgetown Branch of the B&O Railroad/Capital Crescent Trail. In 1890, the right-of-way that was the rail line (and is today the hiker/biker trail) was conveyed in a fee-simple deed from George Dunlop, grantor, to the Metropolitan Southern Railroad Company ("the Railroad"), grantee.

The right-of-way was obtained by the County * * * from the Railroad pursuant to the federal Rails-to-Trails Act. [Federal regulations] allow the County to preserve the land as a hiker/biker trail until the County chooses whether and when to restore a form of rail service within the right-of-way.

On 18 October 2013, Montgomery County issued to Bhatt a civil citation asserting a violation of Section 49-10(b) of the Montgomery County Code, which prohibits a property owner from erecting or placing "any structure, fence, post, rock, or other object in a public right-of-way." The * * * claimed violation was the placement and maintenance by Bhatt's predecessors-in-interest of Lot 8 of a fence and shed within the former rail line (and current hiker/biker trail) right-of-way, without a permit. * * * The District Court of Maryland, sitting in Montgomery County, * * * found Bhatt guilty * * * and ordered him to remove the fence and shed encroaching upon the County's right-of-way.

The appeal was heard *de novo* by the [Maryland] Circuit Court. [When a court hears a case *de novo*, it decides the issues without reference to the legal conclusions or assumptions made by the previous court.]

* * * *

Bhatt's defense to the charged violation of Section 49–10(b) was that he owned the encroached-upon land by adverse possession.

Bhatt argued that, because the fence had been located beyond the property line of Lot 8 since at least 1963, the Railroad was obliged to take action to remove it prior to the maturation of the twenty-year period for adverse possession.

* * * The Circuit Court vacated the District Court's judgment and dismissed the violation citation. * * * The Circuit Court concluded ultimately that Bhatt had a creditable claim for adverse possession.

The County petitioned this Court for a writ of *certiorari.* * * * We granted the Petition.

* * * *

DISCUSSION
I. Contentions

* * * The County contends * * * that, because this Court has considered previously a railroad line to be analogous to a public highway for most purposes, the land in question is not subject to an adverse possession claim.

* * * Bhatt rejects the public highway-railroad line analogy because the land was in private, not public, use during its operation as a rail line.

II. Analysis

a. Railroads as Public Highways

A railroad is in many essential respects a public highway, and the rules of law applicable to one are generally applicable to the other. Railroads are owned frequently by private corporations, but this has never been considered a matter of any importance * * * because the function performed is that of the State. Railroad companies operate as a public use and are not viewed strictly as private corporations since they are publicly regulated common carriers. *Essentially, a railroad is a highway dedicated to the public use.* [Emphasis added.]

* * * *

b. May a public highway (or any portion of its right-of-way, no matter the type of real property interest by which it is held) be possessed adversely by an abutting private citizen?

* * * *Nothing is more solidly established than the rule that title to property held by a municipal corporation in its governmental capacity, for a public use, cannot be acquired by adverse possession.* [Emphasis added.]

* * * *

* * * Because time does not run against the state, or the public, * * * public highways are not subject to a claim for adverse possession, except in the limited circumstances of a clear abandonment by the State. By parity [equivalence] of reasoning applied to the present case, railway lines [are] also not * * * subject to a claim for adverse possession, without evidence of clear abandonment or a clear shift away from public use.

c. Use of the right-of-way

* * * We do not find in this record, however, that there is any evidence of abandonment by the rail line operator (or Montgomery County) or that the right-of-way was taken out of public use such that a claim for adverse possession could ripen within this right-of-way.

* * * *

The 1890 Dunlop Deed shows that the purchase made by the Railroad was

**Case 26.3 Continued**

from a private landowner. There was no evidence adduced [offered] by Bhatt supporting a conclusion that the right-of-way was abandoned and was not being used by the public, even during the period from 1985 when the freight service ended and 1988 when the property was conveyed to the County and became a hiker/biker trail as an interim public use.

* * * *

Because no evidence was presented by Bhatt to show that the current use of the right-of-way by Montgomery County is unreasonable or that the Railroad or the County abandoned the right-of-way, no claim for adverse possession will lie. Accordingly, we shall reverse the judgment of the Circuit Court. Bhatt's fence and shed encroached upon the right-of-way in violation of Montgomery

County Code Section 49–10(b). The District Court got it right.

JUDGMENT OF THE CIRCUIT COURT FOR MONTGOMERY COUNTY REVERSED. CASE REMANDED TO THAT COURT WITH INSTRUCTIONS TO AFFIRM THE JUDGMENT OF THE DISTRICT COURT OF MARYLAND, SITTING IN MONTGOMERY COUNTY.

### Legal Reasoning Questions

**1.** Bhatt claimed to have met all of the requirements to acquire a strip of public land through adverse possession. Which element did the court find had *not* been met? Why?

**2.** What is the "potential trouble, both ahead and behind, for a pair of public works projects" hinted at in this case? In whose favor is that "trouble" likely to be resolved?

**3.** Should a private party, by encroaching on a public right-of-way, be able to acquire title adverse to the public rights? Discuss.

---

**Purpose of the Doctrine** There are a number of public-policy reasons for the adverse possession doctrine. These include society's interest in resolving boundary disputes, in determining title when title to property is in question, and in assuring that real property remains in the stream of commerce. More fundamentally, the doctrine punishes owners who do not take action when they see adverse possession and rewards possessors for putting land to productive use.

## 26–4 Limitations on the Rights of Property Owners

No ownership rights in real property can ever really be absolute—that is, an owner of real property cannot always do whatever she or he wishes on or with the property. Nuisance and environmental laws, for instance, restrict certain types of activities. Property ownership is also conditional on the payment of property taxes. Zoning laws and building permits frequently restrict the use of realty. In addition, if a property owner fails to pay debts, the property may be seized to satisfy judgment creditors. In short, the rights of every property owner are subject to certain conditions and limitations.

### 26–4a Eminent Domain

Even ownership in fee simple absolute is limited by a superior ownership. Just as the king was the ultimate

landowner in medieval England, today the government has an ultimate ownership right in all land in the United States. This right, known as **eminent domain,** is sometimes referred to as the *condemnation power* of government to take land for public use. It gives the government the right to acquire possession of real property in the manner directed by the U.S. Constitution and the laws of the state whenever the public interest requires it.

The power of eminent domain generally is invoked through **condemnation** proceedings. ■ **EXAMPLE 26.17** When a new public highway is to be built, the government decides where to build it and how much land to condemn. After the government determines that a particular parcel of land is necessary for the highway, it will first offer to buy the property. If the owner refuses the offer, the government brings a judicial (*condemnation*) proceeding to obtain title to the land. ■

Condemnation proceedings usually involve two distinct phases. The first seeks to establish the government's right to take the property, and the second determines the fair value of the property.

**The Taking** When the government takes land owned by a private party for public use, it is referred to as a **taking.** Under the *takings clause* of the Fifth Amendment to the U.S. Constitution, the government may take private property for public use, but it must pay "just compensation" to the owner. State constitutions contain similar provisions. In the first phase of condemnation proceedings, the government must prove that it needs to acquire privately owned property for a public use.

**■ EXAMPLE 26.18** Franklin County, Iowa, engages Bosque Systems to build a liquefied natural gas pipeline that crosses the property of more than two hundred landowners. Some property owners consent to this use and accept the Bosque's offer of compensation. Others refuse the offer. A court will likely deem the pipeline to be a public use. Therefore, the government can exert its eminent domain power to "take" the land, provided that it pays just compensation to the property owners. ■

**The Compensation** The U.S. Constitution and state constitutions require that the government pay just compensation to the landowner when invoking its condemnation power. Just compensation means fair value. In the second phase of the condemnation proceeding, the court determines the fair value of the land, which usually is approximately equal to its market value.

Property may be taken by the government only for public use, not for private benefit. But can eminent domain be used to promote private development when the development is deemed to be in the public interest? See this chapter's *Ethics Today* for a discussion of this issue.

## 26–4b Inverse Condemnation

Typically, a government agency exercises the power of eminent domain in the manner just discussed. **Inverse condemnation,** in contrast, occurs when a government simply takes private property from a landowner without paying any compensation, thereby forcing the landowner to sue the government for compensation.

The taking can be physical, as when a government agency uses or occupies the land, or it may be constructive, as when an agency regulation results in loss of property value. The United States Supreme Court has held that even temporary flooding of land by the government may result in liability under the takings clause.[9]

**■ CASE IN POINT 26.19** In Walton County, Florida, water flows through a ditch from Oyster Lake to the Gulf of Mexico. When Hurricane Opal caused the water to rise in Oyster Lake, Walton County reconfigured the drainage to divert the overflow onto the nearby property of William and Patricia Hemby. The flow was eventually

---

9. *Arkansas Game and Fish Commission v. United States*, ___ U.S. ___, 133 S.Ct. 511, 184 L.Ed.2d 417 (2012).

---

## ETHICS TODAY

### Should Eminent Domain Be Used to Promote Private Development?

Issues of fairness often arise when the government takes private property for public use. One issue is whether it is fair for a government to take property by eminent domain and then convey it to private developers.

For instance, suppose a city government decides that it is in the public interest to have a larger parking lot for a local, privately owned sports stadium. Or suppose it decides that its citizens would benefit from having a manufacturing plant locate in the city to create more jobs. The government may condemn certain tracts of existing housing or business property and then convey the land to the privately owned stadium or manufacturing plant.

Such actions may bring in private developers and businesses that provide jobs and increase tax revenues, thus revitalizing communities. But is the land really being taken for "public use," as required by the Fifth Amendment to the U.S. Constitution?

#### The Supreme Court's Ruling

In 2005, the United States Supreme Court ruled that the power of eminent domain may be used to further economic development.[a] At the same time, the Court recognized that individual states have the right to pass laws that prohibit takings for economic development.

#### The States' Responses

Since then, the vast majority of the states have passed laws to curb the government's ability to take private property and subsequently give it to private developers. Nevertheless, loopholes in some state legislation still allow takings for redevelopment of slum areas. Thus, the debate over whether (and when) it is fair for the government to take citizens' property for economic development continues.

**Critical Thinking** *At what point might the predicted benefits of a new private commercial endeavor outweigh the constitutional requirement of a taking only for public use?*

---

a. *Kelo v. City of New London, Connecticut,* 545 U.S. 469, 125 S.Ct. 2655, 162 L.Ed.2d 439 (2005).

restored to pre-hurricane conditions, but during a later emergency, water was diverted onto the Hembys' property again. This diversion was not restored.

The Hembys filed a suit against the county. After their deaths, their daughter Cozette Drake pursued the claim. The court found that by allowing the water diversion to remain on Drake's property long after the emergency had passed, the county had engaged in a permanent or continuous physical invasion. This invasion rendered Drake's property useless and deprived her of its beneficial enjoyment. Drake was therefore entitled to receive compensation from the county.[10] ■

### 26–4c Restrictive Covenants

A private restriction on the use of land is known as a **restrictive covenant.** If the restriction is binding on the party who initially purchases the property and on subsequent purchasers as well, it is said to "run with the land." A covenant running with the land must be in writing (usually it is in the deed), and subsequent purchasers must have reason to know about it.

■ **EXAMPLE 26.20** In the course of developing a fifty-lot suburban subdivision, Levitt records a declaration of restrictions effectively limiting construction on each lot to one single-family house. Each lot's deed includes a reference to the declaration with a provision that the purchaser and her or his successors are bound to those restrictions. Thus, each purchaser assumes ownership with notice of the restrictions. If an owner attempts to build a duplex (or any noncompliant structure) on a lot, the other owners may obtain a court order to prevent the construction.

Alternatively, Levitt might simply have included the restrictions on the subdivision's map, filed the map in the appropriate public office, and included a reference to the map in each deed. Under these circumstances, each owner would still have been held to have constructive notice of the restrictions. ■

---

# 26–5 Land-Use Control and Zoning

The rules and regulations that collectively manage the development and use of land are known as **zoning laws.** Zoning laws were first used in the United States to segregate slaughterhouses, distilleries, kilns, and other businesses that might pose a nuisance to nearby residences. The growth of modern urban areas led to an increased need to organize uses of land. Today, zoning laws enable municipalities to control the speed and type of development within their borders by creating different zones and regulating the use of property allowed in each zone.

The United States Supreme Court has held that zoning is a constitutional exercise of a government's police powers.[11] Therefore, as long as zoning ordinances are rationally related to the health, safety, or welfare of the community, a municipal government has broad discretion to carry out zoning as it sees fit.

### 26–5a Purpose and Scope of Zoning Laws

The purpose of zoning laws is to manage the land within a community in a way that encourages sustainable and organized development while controlling growth in a manner that serves the interests of the community. One of the basic elements of zoning is the classification of land by permissible use, but zoning extends to other aspects of land use as well.

**Permissible Uses of Land** Municipalities generally divide their available land into districts according to the land's present and potential future uses. Typically, land is classified into the following types of permissible uses:

1. *Residential.* In areas dedicated for **residential use,** landowners can construct buildings for human habitation.

2. *Commercial.* Land assigned for business activities is designated as being for **commercial use,** sometimes called business use. An area with a number of retail stores, offices, supermarkets, and hotels might be designated as a commercial or business district. Land used for entertainment purposes, such as movie theaters and sports stadiums, also falls into this category, as does land used for government activities.

3. *Industrial.* Areas designated for **industrial use** typically encompass light and heavy manufacturing, shipping, and heavy transportation. For instance, undeveloped land with easy access to highways and railroads might be classified as suitable for future use by industry. Although industrial uses can be profitable for a city seeking to raise tax revenue, such uses can also result in noise, smoke, or vibrations that interfere with others' enjoyment of their property. Consequently, areas zoned for industrial use generally are kept as far as possible from residential districts and some commercial districts.

---

10. *Drake v. Walton County*, 6 So.3d 717 (Fla.App. 2009).

11. *Village of Euclid v. Ambler Realty Co.*, 272 U.S. 365, 47 S.Ct. 114, 71 L.Ed. 303 (1926).

4. *Conservation districts.* Some municipalities also establish certain areas that are dedicated to carrying out local soil and water conservation efforts. For instance, wetlands might be designated as a conservation district.

A city's residential, commercial, and industrial districts may be divided, in turn, into subdistricts. For instance, zoning ordinances may regulate the type, density, size, and approved uses of structures within a given district. Thus, a residential district may be divided into low-density (single-family homes with large lots), high-density (single- and multiple-family homes with small lots), and planned-unit (condominiums or apartments) subdistricts.

**Other Zoning Restrictions** Zoning rules extend to much more than the permissible use of land. In residential districts, for instance, an ordinance may require a house or garage to be set back a specific number of feet from a neighbor's property line.

In commercial districts, zoning rules may attempt to maintain a certain visual aesthetic. Therefore, businesses may be required to construct buildings of a certain height and width so that they conform to the style of other commercial buildings in the area.

Businesses may also be required to provide parking for patrons or take other measures to manage traffic. Sometimes, municipalities limit construction of new businesses to prevent traffic congestion.

Zoning laws may even attempt to regulate the public morals of the community. For instance, cities commonly impose severe restrictions on the location and operation of adult businesses and medical (or recreational) marijuana dispensaries.

## 26–5b Exceptions to Zoning Laws

Zoning restrictions are not absolute. It is impossible for zoning laws to account for every contingency. The purpose of zoning is to control development, not to prevent it altogether or to limit the government's ability to adapt to changing circumstances or unforeseen needs. Hence, legal processes have been developed to allow for exceptions to zoning laws, such as *variances* and *special-use permits*.

**Variances** A property owner who wants to use his or her land in a manner not permitted by zoning rules can request a **variance,** which allows an exception to the rules. The property owner making the request must demonstrate that the requested variance:

1. Is necessary for reasonable development.
2. Is the least intrusive solution to the problem.
3. Will not alter the essential character of the neighborhood.

**Hardship Situations.** Property owners normally request variances in *hardship situations*—that is, when complying with the zoning rules would be too difficult or costly due to existing property conditions. ■ **EXAMPLE 26.21** Lin, a homeowner, wants to replace her single-car garage with a two-car garage. If she does so, however, the garage will be closer to her neighbor's property than is permitted by the zoning rules. In this situation, she may ask for a variance. She can claim that the configuration of her property would make it difficult and costly to comply with the zoning code, so compliance would create a hardship for her. ■

Similarly, a church might request a variance from height restrictions in order to erect a new steeple. Or a furniture store might ask for a variance from *footprint* limitations so that it can expand its showroom. (A building's footprint is the area of ground that it covers.)

Note that the hardship may not be self-created. In other words, a person who buys property with zoning restrictions in effect cannot usually then argue that he or she needs a variance in order to use the property as intended.

**Public Hearing.** In almost all instances, before a variance is granted, there must be a public hearing with adequate notice to neighbors who may object to the exception. After the public hearing, a hearing examiner appointed by the municipality (or the local zoning board or commission) determines whether to grant the exception. When a variance is granted, it applies only to the specific parcel of land for which it was requested and does not create a regulation-free zone.

**Special-Use Permits** Sometimes, zoning laws permit a certain use only if the property owner complies with specific requirements to ensure that the proposed use does not harm the immediate neighborhood. In such instances, the zoning board can issue **special-use permits,** also called conditional-use permits.

■ **EXAMPLE 26.22** An area is designated as a residential district, but small businesses are permitted to operate there so long as they do not affect the characteristics of the neighborhood. A bank asks the zoning board for a special-use permit to open a branch in the area. At the public hearing, the bank demonstrates that the branch will be housed in a building that conforms to the style of other structures in the area. The bank also shows that adequate parking will be available and that landscaping will shield the parking lot from public view. Unless there are strong objections from the branch's prospective neighbors, the board will likely grant the permit. ■

**Special Incentives** In addition to granting exceptions to zoning regulations, municipalities may also wish to encourage certain kinds of development. To do so, they offer incentives, often in the form of lower tax rates or tax credits. For instance, to attract new businesses that will provide jobs and increase the tax base, a city may offer lower property tax rates for a period of years. Similarly, homeowners may receive tax credits for historic preservation if they renovate and maintain older homes.

## Reviewing: Real Property and Landlord-Tenant Law

Vern Shoepke purchased a two-story home from Walter and Eliza Bruster in the town of Roche, Maine. The warranty deed did not specify what covenants would be included in the conveyance. The property was adjacent to a public park that included a popular Frisbee golf course. (Frisbee golf is a sport similar to golf but using Frisbees.) Wayakichi Creek ran along the north end of the park and along Shoepke's property. The deed allowed Roche citizens the right to walk across a five-foot-wide section of the lot beside Wayakichi Creek as part of a two-mile public trail system. Teenagers regularly threw Frisbee golf discs from the walking path behind Shoepke's property over his yard to the adjacent park. Shoepke habitually shouted and cursed at the teenagers, demanding that they not throw objects over his yard. Using the information presented in the chapter, answer the following questions.

1. What is the term for the right of Roche citizens to walk across Shoepke's land on the trail?
2. What covenants would most courts infer were included in the warranty deed that was used in the property transfer from the Brusters to Shoepke?
3. Suppose that Shoepke wants to file a trespass lawsuit against some teenagers who continually throw Frisbees over his land. Shoepke discovers, however, that when the city put in the Frisbee golf course, the neighborhood homeowners signed an agreement that limited their right to complain about errant Frisbees. What is this type of promise or agreement called in real property law?

**Debate This . . .** *Under no circumstances should a local government be able to condemn property in order to sell it later to real estate developers for private use.*

## Terms and Concepts

## Issue Spotters

1. Bernie sells his house to Consuela under a warranty deed. Later, Delmira appears, holding a better title to the house than Consuela has. Delmira wants to have Consuela evicted from the property. What can Consuela do? (See *Transfer of Ownership*.)

2. Grey owns a commercial building in fee simple. Grey transfers temporary possession of the building to Haven Corporation. Can Haven transfer possession for even less time to Idyll Company? Explain. (See *Ownership and Other Interests in Real Property*.)

- **Check your answers to the Issue Spotters against the answers provided in Appendix D at the end of this text.**

## Business Scenarios

**26–1. Property Ownership.** Madison owned a tract of land, but he was not sure that he had full title to the property. When Rafael expressed an interest in buying the land, Madison sold it to Rafael and executed a quitclaim deed. Rafael properly recorded the deed immediately. Several months later, Madison learned that he had had full title to the tract of land. He then sold the land to Linda by warranty deed. Linda knew of the earlier purchase by Rafael but took the deed anyway and later sued to have Rafael evicted from the land. Linda claimed that because she had a warranty deed, her title to the land was better than that conferred by Rafael's quitclaim deed. Will Linda succeed in claiming title to the land? Explain. (See *Transfer of Ownership*.)

**26–2. Zoning.** The county intends to rezone an area from industrial use to residential use. Land within the affected area is largely undeveloped, but nonetheless it is expected that the proposed action will reduce the market value of the affected land by as much as 50 percent. Will the landowners be successful in suing to have the action declared a taking of their property, entitling them to just compensation? Why or why not? (See *Land-Use Control and Zoning*.)

**26–3. Eminent Domain.** Some Catholic organizations propose to build a private independent middle school in a run-down neighborhood in Philadelphia, Pennsylvania. They asked the Redevelopment Authority of the City of Philadelphia to acquire specific land for the project and sell it to them for a nominal price. The land included a house on North Eighth Street owned by Mary Smith, whose daughter Veronica lived there with her family. The Authority offered Smith $12,000 for the house and initiated a taking of the property.

Smith filed a suit in state court against the Authority, admitting that the house was a "substandard structure in a blighted area," but arguing that the taking was unconstitutional because its beneficiary was private. The Authority asserted that only the public purpose of the taking should be considered, not the status of the property's developer. On what basis can a government entity use the power of eminent domain to take property? What are the limits to this power? How should the court rule? Why? (See *Limitations on the Rights of Property Owners*.)

## Business Case Problems

**26–4. Zoning and Variances.** Joseph and Lois Ryan hired a contractor to build a home in Weston, Connecticut. The contractor submitted plans to the town that included a roof height of thirty-eight feet for the proposed dwelling. This exceeded the town's roof-height restriction of thirty-five feet. The contractor and the architect revised the plans to meet the restriction, and the town approved the plans and issued a zoning permit and a building permit. After the roof was constructed, a code enforcement officer discovered that it measured thirty-seven feet, seven inches high.

The officer issued a cease-and-desist order requiring the Ryans to "remove the height violation and bring the structure into compliance." The Ryans appealed to the zoning board, claiming that the error was not theirs but that of their general contractor and architect. The zoning board upheld the cease-and-desist order but later granted the Ryans a variance because "the roof height was out of compliance by approximately two feet, . . . the home [was] perched high on the land and [was] not a detriment to the neighborhood, and . . . the hardship was created by the contractor's error."

Neighbors (including Curtis Morikawa) appealed to a court. They argued that the hardship claimed was solely economic. In addition, they argued that even though it was unintended, the hardship was self-created. The trial court ruled in favor of the neighbors, and the Ryans appealed. How should the court rule? Were there legitimate grounds for granting a variance? Discuss. [*Morikawa v. Zoning Board of Appeals of Town of Weston*, 126 Conn.App. 400, 11 A.3d 735 (2011)] (See *Land-Use Control and Zoning*.)

**26–5. Business Case Problem with Sample Answer— Adverse Possession.** The McKeag family operated a  marina on their lakefront property in Bolton, New York. For more than forty years, the McKeags used a section of property belonging to their neighbors, the Finleys, as a beach for the marina's customers. The McKeags also stored a large float on the beach during the winter months, built their own retaining wall, and planted bushes and flowers there. The McKeags prevented others from using the property, including the Finleys.

Nevertheless, the families always had a friendly relationship, and one of the Finleys gave the McKeags permission to continue using the beach in 1992. He also reminded them of his ownership several times, to which they said nothing. The McKeags also asked for permission to mow grass on the property and once apologized for leaving a jet ski there. Can the McKeags establish adverse possession over the statutory period of ten years? Why or why not? [*McKeag v. Finley,* 939 N.Y.S.2d 644 (N.Y.App.Div. 2012)] (See *Transfer of Ownership.*)

- **For a sample answer to Problem 26–5, go to Appendix E at the end of this text.**

**26–6. Real Estate Sales Contracts.** A California state statute requires sellers to provide a real estate "Transfer Disclosure Statement" (TDS) to buyers of residential property consisting of one to four dwelling units. Required disclosures include information about significant defects, including hazardous materials, encroachments, easements, fill, settling, flooding, drainage problems, neighborhood noise, damage from natural disasters, and lawsuits. Mark Hartley contracted with Randall Richman to buy Richman's property in Ventura, California. The property included a commercial building and a residential duplex with two dwelling units. Richman did not provide a TDS, claiming that it was not required because the property was "mixed use"—that is, it included both a commercial building and a residential building. Hartley refused to go through with the deal. Did Hartley breach their contract, or did Richman's failure to provide a TDS excuse Hartley's nonperformance? Discuss. [*Richman v. Hartley,* 224 Cal.App.4th 1182, 169 Cal. Rptr.3d 475 (2 Dist. 2014)] (See *Transfer of Ownership.*)

**26–7. Ownership and Other Interests in Real Property.** Arthur and Diana Ebanks owned three properties in the Cayman Islands in joint tenancy. With respect to joint tenancies, Cayman law is the same as U.S. law. When the Ebanks divorced, the decree did not change the tenancy in which the properties were held. On the same day as the divorce filing, Arthur executed a will providing that "any property in my name and that of another as joint tenants . . . will pass to the survivor, and I instruct my Personal Representative to make

no claim thereto." Four years later, Arthur died. His brother Curtis, the personal representative of his estate, asserted that Arthur's interest in the Cayman properties was part of the estate. Diana said that the sole interest in the properties was hers. Who do the Cayman properties belong to? Why? [*Ebanks v. Ebanks,* __ So.3d __, 41 Fla. L. Weekly D291 (2 Dist. 2016)] (See *Ownership and Other Interests in Real Property.*)

**26–8. Special Case Analysis—Adverse Possession.** Go to Case Analysis 26.3, *Montgomery County v. Bhatt.* Read the excerpt, and answer the following questions.

**(a) Issue:** What conflict, and between which parties, did this case highlight?

**(b) Rule of Law:** On which specific requirement of what rule of law did the outcome in this case depend?

**(c) Applying the Rule of Law:** What exception to the applied rule of law might have resulted in a decision in the plaintiff's favor? Why did that exception not apply in this case?

**(d) Conclusion:** In light of the rule of law applied in this case, what was the judgment?

**26–9. A Question of Ethics—Adverse Possession.**

*Alana Mansell built a garage on her property that encroached on the property of her neighbor, Betty Hunter, by fourteen feet. Hunter knew of the encroachment and informally agreed to it, but she did not transfer ownership of the property to Mansell. A survey twenty-eight years later confirmed the encroachment, and Hunter sought the removal of the garage. Mansell asked a court to declare that she was the owner of the property by adverse possession.* [Hunter v. Mansell, *240 P.3d 469 (Colo.App. 2010)*] (See *Transfer of Ownership.*)

**(a)** Did Mansell obtain title by adverse possession? Would the open occupation of the property for nearly thirty years be in Mansell's favor? Why or why not?

**(b)** Was Mansell's conduct in any way unethical? Discuss.

# Legal Reasoning Group Activity

**26–10. Adverse Possession.** The Wallen family owned a cabin on Lummi Island in the state of Washington. A driveway ran from the cabin across their property to South Nugent Road. Floyd Massey bought the adjacent lot and built a cabin on it in 1980. To gain access to his property, Massey used a bulldozer to extend the driveway, without the Wallens' permission but also without their objection. In 2005, the Wallens sold their property to Wright Fish Company. Massey continued to use and maintain the driveway without permission or objection. In 2011, Massey sold his property to Robert Drake. Drake and his employees continued to use and maintain the driveway without permission or objection, although Drake knew it was located largely on Wright's property. In 2013, Wright sold its lot to Robert Smersh. The next year, Smersh told Drake to stop using the driveway. Drake filed a suit against Smersh, claiming an easement by prescription

(which is created by meeting the same requirements as adverse possession). (See *Transfer of Ownership.*)

**(a)** The first group will decide whether Drake's use of the driveway meets all of the requirements for adverse possession (easement by prescription).

**(b)** The second group will determine how the court should rule in this case and why. Does it matter that Drake knew the driveway was located largely on Wright's (and then Smersh's) property? Should it matter? Why or why not?

**(c)** A third group will evaluate the underlying policy and fairness of adverse possession laws. Should the law reward persons who take possession of someone else's land for their own use? Does it make sense to punish owners who allow someone else to use their land without complaint? Explain.

# Answers to the *Issue Spotters*

1. ***Delmira wants to have Consuela evicted from the property. What can Consuela do?*** This is a breach of the warranty deed's covenant of quiet enjoyment. The buyer can sue the seller and recover the purchase price of the house, plus any damages.

2. ***Can Haven transfer possession for even less time to Idyll Company? Explain.*** Yes. An owner of a fee simple has the most rights possible—he or she can give the property away, sell it, transfer it by will, use it for almost any purpose, possess it to the exclusion of all the world, or as in this case, transfer possession for any period of time. The party to whom possession is transferred can also transfer his or her interest (usually only with the owner's permission) for any lesser period of time.

# Sample Answers for *Business Case Problems with Sample Answer*

**Problem 26–5.** *Adverse Possession.* The McKeags satisfied the first three requirements for adverse possession:

1. Their possession was actual and exclusive because they used the beach and prevented others from doing so, including the Finleys.
2. Their possession was open, visible, and notorious because they made improvements to the beach and regularly kept their belongings there.
3. Their possession was continuous and peaceable for the required ten years. They possessed the property for more than four decades, and they even kept a large float there during the winter months.

Nevertheless, the McKeags' possession was *not* hostile and adverse, which is the fourth requirement. The Finleys had substantial evidence that they gave the McKeags permission to use the beach. Rather than reject the Finleys' permission as unnecessary, the McKeags sometimes said nothing and other times seemingly affirmed that the property belonged to the Finleys. Thus, because the McKeags did not satisfy all four requirements, they cannot establish adverse possession.

# Chapter 12

**CHAPTER**

# Small Businesses and Franchises

A goal of many business students is to become an **entrepreneur,** one who initiates and assumes the financial risk of a new business enterprise and undertakes to provide or control its management. One of the first decisions an entrepreneur must make is which form of business organization will be most appropriate for the new endeavor.

In selecting an organizational form, the entrepreneur will consider a number of factors. These include (1) ease of creation, (2) the liability of the owners, (3) tax considerations, and (4) the ability to raise capital. Keep these factors in mind as you read this unit and learn about the various forms of business organization. Remember, too, in considering these business forms that the primary motive of an entrepreneur is to make profits.

Traditionally, entrepreneurs have used three major business forms—the sole proprietorship, the partnership, and the corporation. In this chapter, we examine sole proprietorships and partnerships. We also look at franchises. Although the franchise is not strictly speaking a business organizational form, it is widely used today by entrepreneurs.

## 16–1 General Considerations for Small Businesses

Most small businesses begin as sole proprietorships. Once the business is under way, the sole proprietorship form may become too limited. The owner and any additional investors may then want to establish a more formal organization, such as a limited partnership (LP), a limited liability partnership (LLP), a limited liability company (LLC), or a corporation. These forms of business limit the owner's personal liability, or legal responsibility, for business debts and obligations. Each business form has its own advantages and disadvantages, but legal limited liability generally is necessary for those who wish to raise outside capital.

### 16–1a Requirements for All Business Forms

Any business, whatever its form, has to meet a variety of legal requirements, which typically relate to the following:

1. Business name registration.
2. Occupational licensing.
3. State tax registration (for instance, to obtain permits for collecting and remitting sales taxes).
4. Health and environmental permits.
5. Zoning and building codes.
6. Import/export regulations.

If the business has employees, the owner must also comply with a host of laws governing the workplace.

### 16–1b Protecting Intellectual Property

Protecting rights in intellectual property is a central concern for many small businesses. For instance, software companies and app developers depend on their copyrights and patents to protect their investments in the research and development required to create new programs. Without copyright or patent protection, a competitor or a customer could simply copy the software or app.

**Trademarks** Choosing a trademark or service mark and making sure that it is protected under trademark law can be crucial to the success of a new business venture. Indeed, a factor to consider in choosing a name for a business entity is whether the business name will be used as a trademark. The general rule is that a trademark cannot be the same as another's mark or so similar that confusion might result.

For the most protection, trademarks should be registered with the U.S. Patent and Trademark Office (PTO). If the mark is federally registered, the owner may use the symbol ® with the mark. This well-known symbol puts others on notice of the registration and helps to prevent trademark infringement. An owner who has not registered can use the symbol ™. Registration with the PTO should be renewed five years after the initial registration and at ten-year intervals thereafter.

**Trade Secrets** Much of the value of a small business may lie in its trade secrets, such as information about product development, production processes and techniques, and customer lists. Preserving the secrecy of the information is necessary for legal protection.

As a practical matter, trade secrets must be divulged to key employees. Thus, any business runs the risk that those employees might disclose the secrets to competitors—or even set up competing businesses themselves.

To protect their trade secrets, companies may require employees who have access to trade secrets to agree in their employment contracts never to divulge those secrets. A small business may also choose to include a covenant not to compete in an employment contract. A noncompete clause will help to protect against the possibility that a key employee will go to work for a competitor or set up a competing business.

### 16–1c Obtaining Loans

Raising capital is critical to the growth of most small businesses. In the early days of a business, the sole proprietor may be able to contribute sufficient capital, but as the business becomes successful, more funds may be needed. The owner may want to raise capital from external sources to expand the business. One way to do this is to borrow funds.

Obtaining a bank loan is beneficial for small businesses because it allows the owner to retain full ownership and control of the business. Note, though, that the bank may place some restrictions on future business decisions as a condition of granting the loan. In addition, bank loans may not be available for some businesses. Banks are usually reluctant to lend significant sums to businesses that are not yet established. Even if a bank is willing to make

such a loan, the bank may require personal guaranty contracts from the owner, putting the owner's personal assets at risk.

Loans with desirable terms may be available from the U.S. Small Business Administration (SBA). One SBA program provides loans of up to $25,000 to businesspersons who are women, low-income individuals, or members of minority groups. Be aware that the SBA requires business owners to put some of their own funds at risk in the business. In addition, many states offer small-business grants to individuals starting a business.

## 16–2 Sole Proprietorships

In the earliest stages, as mentioned, a small business may operate as a **sole proprietorship,** which is the simplest form of business. In this form, the owner is the business. Thus, anyone who does business without creating a separate business organization has a sole proprietorship. The law considers all new, single-owner businesses to be sole proprietorships unless the owner affirmatively adopts some other form.

More than two-thirds of all U.S. businesses are sole proprietorships. Sole proprietors can own and manage any type of business from an informal, home-office or Web-based undertaking to a large restaurant or construction firm. About 99 percent of the sole proprietorships in the United States have revenues of less than $1 million per year.

### 16–2a Advantages of the Sole Proprietorship

A major advantage of the sole proprietorship is that the proprietor owns the entire business and receives all of the profits (because she or he assumes all of the risk). In addition, starting a sole proprietorship is easier and less costly than starting any other kind of business because few legal formalities are required. Generally, no documents need to be filed with the government to start a sole proprietorship.[1]

---

1. Although starting a sole proprietorship involves fewer legal formalities than other business organizational forms, even a small sole proprietorship may need to comply with zoning requirements, obtain a state business license, and the like.

**Taxes** A sole proprietor pays only personal income taxes (including Social Security and Medicare taxes) on the business's profits. The profits are reported as personal income on the proprietor's personal income tax return. In other words, the business itself need not file an income tax return. Sole proprietors are allowed to establish retirement accounts that are tax-exempt until the funds are withdrawn.

Like any form of business enterprise, a sole proprietorship can be liable for other taxes, such as those collected and applied to the disbursement of unemployment compensation. Whether liability for the unpaid unemployment compensation taxes of a sole proprietorship remains with the seller or must be assumed by the buyer was at issue in the following case.

## Case Analysis 16.1

# A. Gadley Enterprises, Inc. v. Department of Labor and Industry Office of Unemployment Compensation Tax Services

Commonwealth Court of Pennsylvania, __ A.3d __, 2016 WL 55591 (2016).

### In the Language of the Court

*SIMPSON*, Judge.

* * * *

[Julianne Gresh (Predecessor)] operated [Romper Room Day Care (Romper Room)], a childcare center, as a sole proprietorship for 12 years. Predecessor owed the [Pennsylvania Department of Labor and Industry Office of Unemployment Compensation Tax Services (Department)] substantial unpaid UC [unemployment compensation] contributions, interest and penalties. She admitted liability and entered payment plans with the Department * * * . Pursuant to these payment plans, she made monthly payments in the minimal amount of $50. Predecessor was on the verge of losing her license to operate, and sought another entity to operate the location as a childcare facility.

[A. Gadley Enterprises, Inc. (Purchaser)] operated a childcare center, Young Environment Learning Center, in Erie, Pennsylvania. Purchaser decided to purchase assets from Predecessor in order to open a satellite location of Young Environmental Learning Center at the prior location of Romper Room. Purchaser and Predecessor executed an asset purchase agreement (Agreement).

Through the Agreement, Purchaser paid a total of $37,000 for Predecessor's tangible and intangible assets. This total was comprised of $10,000 for the use of the name "Romper Room," $10,790 for a covenant not to compete, and $17,210 for tangible assets listed on [an attached] Inventory List.

* * * The Inventory List did not include any of Predecessor's personal assets other than those used in the operation of Romper Room.

* * * Four days *after* executing the Agreement, * * * Predecessor notified the Department of the sale.

* * * The Department issued Purchaser a Notice of Assessment (Notice) in the amount of $43,370.49 for UC contributions, interest and penalties owed by Predecessor. The Notice stated Purchaser was liable because it purchased 51% or more of Predecessor's assets.

In response, Purchaser filed a petition [with the Department] for reassessment.

* * * *

Based on the evidence presented at the hearing [held on the petition], the Department issued its decision and order denying the petition for reassessment.

* * * *

Purchaser then filed a petition to review to this Court.

* * * *

[43 Pennsylvania Statutes Section 788.3(a), part of the state's Unemployment Compensation Law] provides:

(a) Every employer * * * , who shall sell in bulk fifty-one percent or more of his assets, including but not limited to, any stock of goods, wares or merchandise of any kind, fixtures, machinery, equipment, building or real estate, shall give the department ten (10) days' notice of the sale prior to completion of the transfer * * * . The employer shall present to the purchaser of such property, a certificate * * * showing that all reports have been filed and contributions, interest and penalties paid to the date of the proposed transfer. The failure of the

purchaser to require such certificate shall render such purchaser liable to the department for the unpaid contributions, interest and penalties.

* * * *

There is no dispute that Purchaser did not obtain a clearance certificate reflecting Predecessor's payment of UC liability. There is also no dispute that Predecessor owed the Department for outstanding UC contributions, interest and penalties in the amount of $43,370.49 at the time of the sale.

* * * *

Purchaser argues substantial evidence does not support the Department's finding that it purchased more than 51% of the [Predecessor's] assets.

* * * *

The Agreement establishes that the Inventory List sets forth all business assets of Predecessor. Gresh confirmed the Inventory List was a complete list of assets used in the operation of her business.

The Inventory List reflects a total value of assets equaling $19,210. * * * The parties reduced the purchase price by $2,000 to account for the reduced value of the assets when Purchaser removed certain assets from the complete Inventory List. Purchaser acquired all the assets included in the Inventory List, other than those removed, for $17,210. The amount constitutes approximately 90% of the value of the complete list of assets ($19,210 × .9 = $17,289).

The Agreement, supplemented by corroborating [supporting] testimony,

**Case 16.1 Continued**

constitutes substantial evidence to support the Department's finding that the sale qualified as a bulk sale of more than 51% of Predecessor's assets.

* * * *

Purchaser also argues the Department erred in construing the term "assets" in the bulk sales provision to include only business assets when determining whether a sale met the 51% threshold. Purchaser asserts the provision does not differentiate between business and personal assets of an employer and there is no legal distinction when the employer is a sole proprietor.

* * * *

* * * The definition of "employer" [in the UC Law] includes a sole proprietor like Predecessor.

The word "assets" is not defined in the [UC] Law.

[In Section 788.3(a)] the term "assets" precedes a list of examples, followed by the phrase "including but not limited to."

* * * *

* * * The examples * * * indicate that the term "assets" refers to business assets. This conclusion is buttressed [reinforced] by the context of the statute as a whole, which pertains to employers operating businesses and paying employees as part of their business operations.

*The factual circumstances surrounding the sale also indicate the term "assets" means "business assets." Here, the context is the sale of a business, in the childcare industry, to another business engaged in the same industry that intends to operate a childcare facility at the location of the former business. The Agreement reflects the intention of the parties that Purchaser would operate the childcare facility as a satellite location.* [Emphasis added.]

* * * *

* * * The provision does not treat sole proprietors differently than other employers. The provision contains no exemption of liability for a purchaser when an employer operates as a sole proprietorship. Nor does it contain an exemption from liability when the former employer entered a repayment plan with the Department.

Moreover, Purchaser's interpretation does not consider *the purpose of the bulk sales provision. That purpose is to ensure an employer does not divest itself of assets without satisfying outstanding liabilities, either itself or by the purchaser.* This Court agrees with the Department that Gresh's repayment agreement in the minimal amount of $50 per month does not satisfy the UC liability. [Emphasis added.]

* * * *

In sum, the Department's construction of assets as business assets is reasonable and consistent with the context and purpose of [the] bulk sales provision. Purchaser's failure to obtain a clearance certificate rendered it liable for Predecessor's unpaid UC contributions, interest and penalties, regardless of Predecessor's repayment agreement. Therefore, this Court upholds the Department's interpretation of the bulk sales provision.

* * * *

* * * For the foregoing reasons, we affirm the Department.

**Legal Reasoning Questions**

1. As is clear from the law applied in this case, and the result, the liability of a business for unpaid taxes "follows the assets." Why?

2. What action can Gadley take now to avoid suffering the loss of the funds required to cover Gresh's unpaid taxes?

3. What action should a buyer take *before* purchasing the assets of a business to avoid liability for the seller's unpaid taxes?

---

**Flexibility** A sole proprietorship offers more flexibility than does a partnership or a corporation. The sole proprietor is free to make any decision she or he wishes concerning the business—including what kind of business to pursue, whom to hire, and when to take a vacation. The sole proprietor can sell or transfer all or part of the business to another party at any time without seeking approval from anyone else. In contrast, approval is typically required from partners in a partnership and from shareholders in a corporation.

## 16–2b Disadvantages of the Sole Proprietorship

The major disadvantage of the sole proprietorship is that the proprietor alone bears the burden of any losses or liabilities incurred by the business enterprise. In other words, the sole proprietor has unlimited liability for all obligations that arise in doing business. Any lawsuit against the business or its employees can lead to unlimited personal liability for the owner of a sole proprietorship.

■ **EXAMPLE 16.1** Aaron and Melissa Klein, owners of the Sweet Cakes by Melissa bakery, refused to bake a wedding cake for a same-sex couple's wedding. They claimed that their religious beliefs did not allow them to provide services for same-sex ceremonies. The Oregon State Bureau of Labor and Industries argued that their decision violated the law. In 2015, an administrative law judge ruled against the Kleins' motion to dismiss and ordered them to pay $135,000 in damages. As sole proprietors, the Kleins were personally responsible for paying the damages. ■

**Personal Assets at Risk** Creditors can pursue the owner's personal assets to satisfy any business debts. Although sole proprietors may obtain insurance to protect the business, liability can easily exceed policy limits. This unlimited liability is a major factor to be considered in choosing a business form.

■ **EXAMPLE 16.2** Sheila Fowler operates a golf shop near a world-class golf course as a sole proprietorship. One of Fowler's employees fails to secure a display of golf clubs. They fall on Dean Maheesh, a professional golfer, and seriously injure him. If Maheesh sues Fowler's shop and wins, Fowler's personal liability could easily exceed the limits of her insurance policy. Fowler could lose not only her business, but also her house, car, and any other personal assets that can be attached to pay the judgment. ■

**Lack of Continuity and Limited Ability to Raise Capital** The sole proprietorship also has the disadvantage of lacking continuity after the death of the proprietor. When the owner dies, so does the business—it is automatically dissolved.

Another disadvantage is that in raising capital, the proprietor is limited to his or her personal funds and any loans that he or she can obtain for the business. Lenders may be unwilling to make loans to sole proprietorships, particularly start-ups, because the sole proprietor risks unlimited personal liability and may not be able to pay. (See this chapter's *Digital Update* feature for a discussion of one court's refusal to discharge a loan made to a sole proprietor who had declared bankruptcy.)

---

## DIGITAL UPDATE — A Sole Proprietorship, Facebook Poker, and Bankruptcy

One major downside of a sole proprietorship is that it is more difficult for a sole proprietor to obtain funding for start-up and expansion. Moreover, if funding is obtained through loans, the sole proprietor is exposed to personal liability.

### Personal Liability Exposure for an Online Start-up

A case in point went before the United States bankruptcy court in Massachusetts in 2015.[a] Michael Dewhurst, living in Raynham, Massachusetts, sometimes did computer work for Gerald Knappik. Dewhurst decided to start a new business venture—the commercial development of a Facebook poker–playing application. Dewhurst envisioned an application that would enable multiple individuals to play poker together over the Internet through Facebook. Dewhurst informed Knappik of his business plan and predicted that his Facebook poker application "was going to be something very big."

Knappik initially loaned $50,000 to Dewhurst for the project. The loan agreement stated, "The sole purpose of this loan agreement is to provide funds on a personal level for the startup of said business project, in conjunction with borrower's personal funds, not limited to startup costs, operating expenses, advertising costs."

That was the first of a series of personal loans that totaled $220,000.

Dewhurst had repaid only $9,000 on the total outstanding debt when he filed for bankruptcy. Ultimately, the bankruptcy court ascertained that at least $120,000 of the loans that were supposed to be used exclusively for the Facebook poker project had been used for other activities. Furthermore, Dewhurst kept "no contemporaneous records of his disbursements and uses of this cash, no cash journal, ledger, or disbursement slips of any kind."

### The Lender Objects to a Bankruptcy Discharge of Monies Owed

During bankruptcy proceedings, Knappik requested that the bankruptcy court deny discharge of Dewhurst's debts to him. Upon review, the court stated that "Dewhurst's failure to keep and preserve adequate records makes it impossible to reconstruct an accurate and complete account of financial affairs and business transactions." The bankruptcy judge ultimately denied discharge of $120,000 of the debt owed to Knappik. Thus, a sole proprietor's failed attempt to create an online poker-playing application led to personal liability even after he had filed for bankruptcy.

**Critical Thinking** *Sole proprietorships, as well as other businesses, routinely seek funding for online projects. How can the individuals involved avoid personal liability?*

a. *In re Dewhurst*, 528 Bankr. 211 (D.Mass. 2015).

## 16–3 Partnerships

A *partnership* arises from an agreement, express or implied, between two or more persons to carry on a business for a profit. Partners are co-owners of the business and have joint control over its operation and the right to share in its profits. The traditional form of partnership discussed in this chapter is commonly referred to as a general partnership now that limited liability forms of partnership exist.

### 16–3a Basic Partnership Concepts

Partnerships are governed both by common law concepts—in particular, those relating to agency—and by statutory law. As in so many other areas of business law, the National Conference of Commissioners on Uniform State Laws has drafted uniform laws for partnerships, and these have been widely adopted by the states.

**Agency Concepts and Partnership Law** When two or more persons agree to do business as partners, they enter into a special relationship with one another. Each partner is deemed to be the agent of the other partners and of the partnership, similar to an agency relationship (to be discussed in another chapter). Thus, agency concepts apply. For instance, a partner is presumed to know about and is responsible for acts carried out by another partner within the scope of the partnership relationship. In their relationships with one another, partners, like agents, are bound by fiduciary ties.

In one important way, however, partnership law differs from agency law. The partners in a partnership agree to commit funds or other assets, labor, and skills to the business with the understanding that profits and losses will be shared. Thus, each partner has an *ownership interest* in the firm. In a nonpartnership agency relationship, the agent usually does not have an ownership interest in the business and is not obligated to bear a portion of ordinary business losses.

**The Uniform Partnership Act** The Uniform Partnership Act (UPA) governs the operation of partnerships *in the absence of express agreement* and has done much to reduce controversies in the law relating to partnerships. A majority of the states have enacted the most recent version of the UPA (introduced in 1997 and last amended in 2013).

**Definition of a Partnership** The UPA defines a **partnership** as "an association of two or more persons to carry on as co-owners a business for profit" [UPA 102(11)].

Note that the UPA's definition of *person* includes corporations, so a corporation can be a partner in a partnership [UPA 102(11)]. The *intent* to associate is a key element of a partnership, and one cannot join a partnership unless all other partners consent [UPA 401(i)].

**Essential Elements of a Partnership** Conflicts sometimes arise over whether a business enterprise is a legal partnership, especially when there is no formal, written partnership agreement. To determine whether a partnership exists, courts usually look for the following three essential elements, which are implicit in the UPA's definition:

1. A sharing of profits and losses.
2. A joint ownership of the business.
3. An equal right to be involved in the management of the business.

If the evidence in a particular case is insufficient to establish all three factors, the UPA provides a set of guidelines to be used.

**The Sharing of Profits and Losses.** The sharing of both profits and losses from a business creates a presumption that a partnership exists. ■ **EXAMPLE 16.3** Syd and Drake start a business that sells fruit smoothies near a college campus. They open a joint bank account, from which they pay for supplies and expenses, and they share the proceeds (and losses) that the smoothie stand generates. If a conflict arises as to their business relationship, a court will assume that a partnership exists unless the parties prove otherwise. ■

A court will not presume that a partnership exists, however, if shared profits were received as payment of any of the following [UPA 202(c)(3)]:

1. A debt by installments or interest on a loan.
2. Wages of an employee or for the services of an independent contractor.
3. Rent to a landlord.
4. An annuity to a surviving spouse or representative of a deceased partner.
5. A sale of the **goodwill** (the valuable reputation of a business viewed as an intangible asset) of a business or property.

■ **EXAMPLE 16.4** A debtor, Mason Snopel, owes a creditor, Alice Burns, $5,000 on an unsecured debt. They agree that Mason will pay 10 percent of his monthly business profits to Alice until the loan with interest has been repaid. Although Mason and Alice are sharing profits from the business, they are not presumed to be partners. ■

**Joint Property Ownership.** Joint ownership of property does not in and of itself create a partnership [UPA 202(c)(1) and (2)]. The parties' intentions are key. ■ **EXAMPLE 16.5** Chiang and Burke jointly own farmland and lease it to a farmer for a share of the profits from the farming operation in lieu of fixed rental payments. This arrangement normally would not make Chiang, Burke, and the farmer partners. ■

**Entity versus Aggregate** At common law, a partnership was treated only as an aggregate of individuals and never as a separate legal entity. Thus, at common law a lawsuit could never be brought by or against the firm in its own name. Each individual partner had to sue or be sued.

Today, in contrast, a majority of the states follow the UPA and treat a partnership as an entity for most purposes. For instance, a partnership usually can sue or be sued, collect judgments, and have all accounting performed in the name of the partnership entity [UPA 201, 307(a)].

As an entity, a partnership may hold the title to real or personal property in its name rather than in the names of the individual partners. Additionally, federal procedural laws permit the partnership to be treated as an entity in suits in federal courts and bankruptcy proceedings.

**Tax Treatment of Partnerships** Modern law does treat a partnership as an aggregate of the individual partners rather than a separate legal entity in one situation—for federal income tax purposes. The partnership is a pass-through entity and not a taxpaying entity. A **pass-through entity** is a business entity that has no tax liability. The entity's income is passed through to the owners, who pay income taxes on it.

Thus, the income or losses the partnership incurs are "passed through" the entity framework and attributed to the partners on their individual tax returns. The partnership itself pays no taxes and is responsible only for filing an **information return** with the Internal Revenue Service.

A partner's profit from the partnership (whether distributed or not) is taxed as individual income to the individual partner. Similarly, partners can deduct a share of the partnership's losses on their individual tax returns (in proportion to their partnership interests).

## 16–3b Formation and Operation

A partnership is a voluntary association of individuals. As such, it is formed by the agreement of the partners. As a general rule, agreements to form a partnership can be *oral, written,* or *implied by conduct.* Some partnership agreements, however, such as one authorizing partners to transfer interests in real property, must be in writing to be legally enforceable.

A partnership agreement, also known as **articles of partnership,** can include almost any terms that the parties wish, unless they are illegal or contrary to public policy or statute [UPA 103]. The provisions commonly specify the amount of capital that each partner is contributing, and the percentage of the profits and losses of the business that each partner will receive.

The rights and duties of partners are governed largely by the specific terms of their partnership agreement. In the absence of provisions to the contrary in the partnership agreement, the law imposes certain rights and duties, as discussed in the following subsections. The character and nature of the partnership business generally influence the application of these rights and duties.

**Duration of the Partnership** The partnership agreement can specify the duration of the partnership by stating that it will continue until a designated date or until the completion of a particular project. This is called a *partnership for a term.* Generally, withdrawing from a partnership for a term prematurely (before the expiration date) constitutes a breach of the agreement, and the responsible partner can be held liable for any resulting losses [UPA 602(b)(2)]. If no fixed duration is specified, the partnership is a *partnership at will.* A partnership at will can be dissolved at any time without liability.

**Partnership by Estoppel** When a third person has reasonably and detrimentally relied on the representation that a nonpartner was part of a partnership, a court may conclude that a **partnership by estoppel** exists.

**Liability Imposed.** A partnership by estoppel may arise when a person who is not a partner holds himself or herself out as a partner and makes representations that third parties rely on. In this situation, a court may impose liability—but not partnership rights—on the alleged partner.

**Nonpartner as Agent.** A partnership by estoppel may also be imposed when a partner represents, expressly or impliedly, that a nonpartner is a member of the firm. In this situation, the nonpartner may be regarded as an agent whose acts are binding on the partnership [UPA 308]. ■ **CASE IN POINT 16.6** Jackson Paper Manufacturing Company made paper used by Stonewall Packaging, LLC. Jackson and Stonewall had officers and directors in common, and they shared employees, property, and equipment. In reliance on Jackson's business reputation, Best Cartage, Inc., agreed to provide transportation services for Stonewall and bought thirty-seven tractor-trailers to use in fulfilling the contract. Best provided the services until Stonewall terminated the agreement.

Best filed a suit for breach of contract against Stonewall and Jackson, seeking $500,678 in unpaid invoices and consequential damages of $1,315,336 for the tractor-trailers it had purchased. Best argued that Stonewall and Jackson had a partnership by estoppel. The court agreed, finding that "defendants combined labor, skills, and property to advance their alleged business partnership." Jackson had negotiated the agreement on Stonewall's behalf. Jackson also had bought real estate, equipment, and general supplies for Stonewall with no expectation that Stonewall would repay these expenditures. This was sufficient to prove a partnership by estoppel.[2] ∎

**Rights of Partners** The rights of partners in a partnership relate to the following areas: management, interest in the partnership, compensation, inspection of books, accounting, and property.

**Management Rights.** In a general partnership, all partners have equal rights in managing the partnership [UPA 401(f)]. Unless the partners agree otherwise, each partner has one vote in management matters *regardless of the proportional size of his or her interest in the firm.* In a large partnership, partners often agree to delegate daily management responsibilities to a management committee made up of one or more of the partners.

The majority rule controls decisions on ordinary matters connected with partnership business, unless otherwise specified in the agreement. Decisions that significantly change the nature of the partnership or that are outside the ordinary course of the partnership business, however, require the *unanimous* consent of the partners [UPA 301(2), 401(i), 401(j)]. For instance, unanimous consent is likely required for a partnership to admit new partners, to amend the partnership agreement, or to enter a new line of business.

**Interest in the Partnership.** Each partner is entitled to the proportion of business profits and losses that is specified in the partnership agreement. If the agreement does not apportion profits (indicate how the profits will be shared), the UPA provides that profits will be shared

equally. If the agreement does not apportion losses, losses will be shared in the same ratio as profits [UPA 401(b)].

■ **EXAMPLE 16.7** The partnership agreement between Rick and Brett provides for capital contributions of $60,000 from Rick and $40,000 from Brett. If the agreement is silent as to how Rick and Brett will share profits or losses, they will share both profits and losses equally.

In contrast, if the agreement provides for profits to be shared in the same ratio as capital contributions, 60 percent of the profits will go to Rick, and 40 percent will go to Brett. Unless the agreement provides otherwise, losses will be shared in the same ratio as profits. ∎

**Compensation.** Devoting time, skill, and energy to partnership business is a partner's duty and generally is not a compensable service. Rather, as mentioned, a partner's income from the partnership takes the form of a distribution of profits according to the partner's share in the business. Partners can, of course, agree otherwise.

**Inspection of the Books.** Partnership books and records must be kept accessible to all partners. Each partner has the right to receive full and complete information concerning the conduct of all aspects of partnership business [UPA 403]. The partnership books must be kept at the firm's principal business office (unless the partners agree otherwise). Every partner is entitled to inspect all books and records on demand and can make copies of the materials.

**Accounting of Partnership Assets or Profits.** An accounting of partnership assets or profits is required to determine the value of each partner's share in the partnership. An accounting can be performed voluntarily, or it can be compelled by court order. Under UPA 405(b), a partner has the right to bring an action for an accounting during the term of the partnership, as well as on the partnership's dissolution.

**Property Rights.** Property acquired *by* a partnership is the property of the partnership and not of the partners individually [UPA 203]. Partnership property includes all property that was originally contributed to the partnership and anything later purchased by the partnership or in the partnership's name (except in rare circumstances) [UPA 204].

A partner may use or possess partnership property only on behalf of the partnership [UPA 401(g)]. A partner is *not* a co-owner of partnership property and has no right to sell, mortgage, or transfer partnership property to another [UPA 501].

---

2. *Best Cartage, Inc. v. Stonewall Packaging, LLC,* 219 N.C.App. 429, 727 S.E.2d 291 (2012).

## 16-3c Duties and Liabilities of Partners

The duties and liabilities of partners are derived from agency law. Each partner is an agent of every other partner and acts as both a principal and an agent in any business transaction within the scope of the partnership agreement.

Each partner is also a general agent of the partnership in carrying out the usual business of the firm "or business of the kind carried on by the partnership" [UPA 301(1)]. Thus, every act of a partner concerning partnership business and "business of the kind" and every contract signed in the partnership's name bind the firm.

**Fiduciary Duties** The fiduciary duties that a partner owes to the partnership and to the other partners are the duty of care and the duty of loyalty [UPA 404(a)]. Under the UPA, a partner's *duty of care* is limited to refraining from "grossly negligent or reckless conduct, intentional misconduct, or a knowing violation of law" [UPA 404(c)]. A partner is not liable to the partnership for simple negligence or honest errors in judgment in conducting partnership business.

The *duty of loyalty* requires a partner to account to the partnership for "any property, profit, or benefit" derived by the partner in the conduct of the partnership's business or from the use of its property. A partner must also refrain from competing with the partnership in business or dealing with the firm as an adverse party [UPA 404(b)].

The duty of loyalty can be breached by self-dealing, misusing partnership property, disclosing trade secrets, or usurping a partnership business opportunity. The following case is a classic example.

## Meinhard v. Salmon

Court of Appeals of New York, 249 N.Y. 458, 164 N.E. 545 (1928).

**Background and Facts** Walter Salmon negotiated a twenty-year lease for the Hotel Bristol in New York City. To pay for the conversion of the building into shops and offices, Salmon entered into an agreement with Morton Meinhard to assume half of the cost. They agreed to share the profits and losses from the joint venture. (A *joint venture* is similar to a partnership but typically is created for a single project.) Salmon was to have the sole power to manage the building, however.

Less than four months before the end of the lease term, the building's owner, Elbridge Gerry, approached Salmon about a project to raze the converted structure, clear five adjacent lots, and construct a single building across the whole property. Salmon agreed and signed a new lease in the name of his own business, Midpoint Realty Company, without telling Meinhard. When Meinhard learned of the deal, he filed a suit in a New York state court against Salmon. The court ruled in Meinhard's favor, and Salmon appealed.

### In the Language of the Court

*CARDOZO,* C.J. [Chief Justice]
* * * *

Joint adventurers, like copartners, owe to one another, while the enterprise continues, the duty of the finest loyalty. Many forms of conduct permissible in a work-a-day world for those acting at arm's length are forbidden to those bound by fiduciary ties. * * * Not honesty alone, but the punctilio [strictness in observance of details] of an honor the most sensitive, is then the standard of behavior. As to this there has developed a tradition that is unbending and inveterate [entrenched]. Uncompromising rigidity has been the attitude of courts * * * when petitioned to undermine the rule of undivided loyalty.

* * * The trouble about [Salmon's] conduct is that he excluded his coadventurer from any chance to compete, from any chance to enjoy the opportunity for benefit.

* * * The very fact that Salmon was in control with exclusive powers of direction charged him the more obviously with the duty of disclosure, [because] only through disclosure could opportunity be equalized.

Case 16.2 Continued

\* \* \* Authority is, of course, abundant that one partner may not appropriate to his own use a renewal of a lease, though its term is to begin at the expiration of the partnership. The lease at hand with its many changes is not strictly a renewal. Even so, the standard of loyalty for those in trust relations is without the fixed divisions of a graduated scale. \* \* \* *A man obtaining [an] \* \* \* opportunity \* \* \* by the position he occupies as a partner is bound by his obligation to his copartners in such dealings not to separate his interest from theirs, but, if he acquires any benefit, to communicate it to them. Certain it is also that there may be no abuse of special opportunities growing out of a special trust as manager or agent.* [Emphasis added.]

\* \* \* Very likely [Salmon] assumed in all good faith that with the approaching end of the venture he might ignore his coadventurer and take the extension for himself. He had given to the enterprise time and labor as well as money. He had made it a success. Meinhard, who had given money, but neither time nor labor, had already been richly paid. \* \* \* [But] Salmon had put himself in a position in which thought of self was to be renounced, however hard the abnegation [self-denial]. He was much more than a coadventurer. He was a managing coadventurer. For him and for those like him the rule of undivided loyalty is relentless and supreme.

**Decision and Remedy** *The Court of Appeals of New York held that Salmon had breached his fiduciary duty by failing to inform Meinhard of the business opportunity and secretly taking advantage of it himself. The court granted Meinhard an interest "measured by the value of half of the entire lease."*

**Impact of This Case on Today's Law** *This classic case involved a joint venture, not a partnership. At the time, a member of a joint venture had only the duty to refrain from actively subverting the rights of the other members. The decision in this case imposed the highest standard of loyalty on joint-venture members. The duty is now the same in both joint ventures and partnerships. Courts today frequently quote the eloquent language used in this opinion when describing the standard of loyalty that applies to partnerships.*

**Critical Thinking**

• **What If the Facts Were Different?** *Suppose that Salmon had disclosed Gerry's proposal to Meinhard, who had said that he was not interested. Would the result in this case have been different? Explain.*

---

**Waiver of Fiduciary Duties** A partner's fiduciary duties may not be waived or eliminated in the partnership agreement. In fulfilling them, each partner must act consistently with the obligation of good faith and fair dealing [UPA 103(b), 404(d)]. The agreement can specify acts that the partners agree will violate a fiduciary duty.

Note that a partner may pursue his or her own interests without automatically violating these duties [UPA 404(e)]. The key is whether the partner has disclosed the interest to the other partners. ■ **EXAMPLE 16.8** Jayne Trell, a partner at Jacoby & Meyers, owns a shopping mall. Trell may vote against a partnership proposal to open a competing mall, provided that she has fully disclosed her interest in the existing shopping mall to the other partners at the firm. ■ A partner cannot make secret profits or put self-interest before his or her duty to the interest of the partnership, however.

**Authority of Partners** The UPA follows general principles of agency law that pertain to a partner's authority to bind a partnership in contract. If a partner acts within the scope of her or his authority, the partnership is legally bound to honor the partner's commitments to third parties. A partner may also subject the partnership to tort liability under agency principles.

A partnership may limit a partner's capacity to act as the firm's agent or transfer property on its behalf by filing a "statement of partnership authority" in a designated state office [UPA 105, 303]. Such limits on a partner's authority normally are effective only with respect to third parties who are notified of the limitation.

The extent of implied authority generally is broader for partners than for ordinary agents. In an ordinary partnership, the partners can exercise all implied powers reasonably necessary and customary to carry on that particular business. Some customarily implied powers include the authority to make warranties on goods in the sales business and the power to enter into contracts consistent with the firm's regular course of business.

**Liability of Partners** One significant disadvantage associated with a traditional partnership is that the partners are *personally* liable for the debts of the partnership. In most states, the liability is essentially unlimited, because the acts of one partner in the ordinary course of business subject the other partners to personal liability [UPA 305]. Note that normally the partnership's assets must be exhausted before creditors can reach the partners' individual assets, however.

**Joint Liability.** Each partner in a partnership generally is jointly liable for the partnership's obligations. **Joint liability** means that a third party must sue all of the partners as a group, but each partner can be held liable for the full amount.[3] If, for instance, a third party sues one partner on a partnership contract, that partner has the right to demand that the other partners be sued with her or him. In fact, if the third party does not name all of the partners in the lawsuit, the assets of the partnership cannot be used to satisfy the judgment.

**Joint and Several Liability.** In the majority of the states, under UPA 306(a), partners are both jointly and severally (separately, or individually) liable for all partnership obligations. **Joint and several liability** means that a third party has the option of suing all of the partners together (jointly) or one or more of the partners separately (severally). All partners in a partnership can be held liable even if a particular partner did not participate in, know about, or ratify the conduct that gave rise to the lawsuit.

A judgment against one partner severally (separately) does not extinguish the others' liability. (Similarly, a release of one partner does not discharge the partners' several liability.) Those not sued in the first action normally may be sued subsequently, unless the court in the first action held that the partnership was in no way liable. If a plaintiff is successful in a suit against a partner or partners, he or she may collect on the judgment only against the assets of those partners named as defendants.

**Indemnification.** With joint and several liability, a partner who commits a tort can be required to indemnify (reimburse) the partnership for any damages it pays. Indemnification will typically be granted *unless* the tort was committed in the ordinary course of the partnership's business.

■ **EXAMPLE 16.9** Nicole Martin, a partner at Patti's Café, is working in the café's kitchen one day when her young son suffers serious injuries to his hands from a dough press. Her son, through his father, files a negligence lawsuit against the partnership. Even if the suit is successful and the partnership pays damages to Martin's son, the firm is not entitled to indemnification. Martin would not be required to indemnify the partnership because her negligence occurred in the ordinary course of the partnership's business (making food for customers). ■

**Liability of Incoming Partners.** A partner newly admitted to an existing partnership is not personally liable for any partnership obligations incurred *before* the person became a partner [UPA 306(b)]. In other words, the new partner's liability to existing creditors of the partnership is limited to her or his capital contribution to the firm.

■ **EXAMPLE 16.10** Smartclub, an existing partnership with four members, admits a new partner, Alex Jaff. He contributes $100,000 to the partnership. Smartclub has debts amounting to $600,000 at the time Jaff joins the firm. Although Jaff's capital contribution of $100,000 can be used to satisfy Smartclub's obligations, Jaff is not personally liable for partnership debts incurred before he became a partner. If, however, the partnership incurs additional debts after Jaff becomes a partner, he will be personally liable for those amounts, along with all the other partners. ■

## 16–3d Dissociation and Termination

**Dissociation** occurs when a partner ceases to be associated in the carrying on of the partnership business. Dissociation normally entitles the partner to have his or her interest purchased by the partnership. It also terminates the partner's actual authority to act for the partnership and to participate in running its business.

Once dissociation occurs, the partnership may continue to do business without the dissociated partner.[4] If the partners no longer wish to (or are unable to) continue the business, the partnership may be terminated (dissolved).

**Events That Cause Dissociation** Under UPA 601, a partner can be dissociated from a partnership in any of the following ways:

1. By the partner's voluntarily giving notice of an "express will to withdraw." (When a partner gives notice of intent to withdraw, the remaining partners must decide whether to continue the partnership business. If they decide not to continue, the

---

3. Under the prior version of the UPA, partners were subject to joint liability on partnership debts and contracts, but not on partnership debts arising from torts.

4. Under the previous version of the UPA, when a partner withdrew from a partnership, the partnership was considered dissolved, and the business had to end. The new UPA dramatically changed the law governing partnership breakups by no longer requiring that a partnership end if one partner dissociates.

voluntary dissociation of a partner will dissolve the firm [UPA 801(1)].)

2. By the occurrence of an event specified in the partnership agreement.

3. By a unanimous vote of the other partners under certain circumstances, such as when a partner transfers substantially all of her or his interest in the partnership.

4. By order of a court or arbitrator if the partner has engaged in wrongful conduct that affects the partnership business. The court can order dissociation if a partner breached the partnership agreement or violated a duty owed to the partnership or to the other partners. Dissociation may also be ordered if the partner engaged in conduct that makes it "not reasonably practicable to carry on the business in partnership with the partner" [UPA 601(5)].

5. By the partner's declaring bankruptcy, assigning his or her interest in the partnership for the benefit of creditors, or becoming physically or mentally incapacitated, or by the partner's death.

**Wrongful Dissociation** A partner has the *power* to dissociate from a partnership at any time, but she or he may not have the *right* to do so. If the partner lacks the right to dissociate, then the dissociation is considered wrongful under the law [UPA 602]. When a partner's dissociation breaches the terms of a partnership agreement, for instance, it is wrongful.

A partner who wrongfully dissociates is liable to the partnership and to the other partners for damages caused by the dissociation. This liability is in addition to any other obligation of the partner to the partnership or to the other partners.

**Effects of Dissociation** Dissociation (rightful or wrongful) terminates some of the rights of the dissociated partner and requires that the partnership purchase his or her interest. It also alters the liability of the parties to third parties.

On a partner's dissociation, his or her right to participate in the management and conduct of the partnership business terminates [UPA 603]. The partner's duty of loyalty also ends. A partner's duty of care continues only with respect to events that occurred before dissociation, unless the partner participates in winding up the partnership's business (discussed shortly).

**Buyouts.** After a partner's dissociation, his or her interest in the partnership must be purchased according to the rules in UPA 701. The **buyout price** is based on the amount that would have been distributed to the partner if the partnership had been wound up on the date of dissociation. Offset against the price are amounts owed by the partner to the partnership, including damages for wrongful dissociation.

**Liability to Third Parties.** For two years after a partner dissociates from a continuing partnership, the partnership may be bound by the acts of the dissociated partner based on apparent authority [UPA 702]. In other words, if a third party reasonably believed at the time of a transaction that the dissociated partner was still a partner, the partnership may be liable. Similarly, a dissociated partner may be liable for partnership obligations entered into during the two-year period following dissociation [UPA 703].

To avoid this possible liability, a partnership should notify its creditors, customers, and clients of a partner's dissociation. In addition, either the partnership or the dissociated partner can file a statement of dissociation in the appropriate state office to limit the dissociated partner's authority to ninety days after the filing [UPA 704]. Filing this statement helps to minimize the firm's potential liability for the former partner and vice versa.

**Partnership Termination** The same events that cause dissociation can result in the end of the partnership if the remaining partners no longer wish to (or are unable to) continue the partnership business. A partner's departure will not necessarily end the partnership, though. Generally, the partnership can continue if the remaining partners consent [UPA 801].

The termination of a partnership is referred to as **dissolution,** which essentially means the commencement of the winding up process. **Winding up** is the actual process of collecting, liquidating, and distributing the partnership assets.

**Dissolution.** Dissolution of a partnership generally can be brought about by acts of the partners, by operation of law, or by judicial decree [UPA 801]. Any partnership (including one for a fixed term) can be dissolved by the partners' agreement.

If the partnership agreement states that it will dissolve on a certain event, such as a partner's death or bankruptcy, then the occurrence of that event will dissolve the partnership.[5] A partnership for a fixed term or a particular undertaking is dissolved by operation of law at the expiration of the term or on the completion of the undertaking.

Any event that makes it unlawful for the partnership to continue its business will result in dissolution

---

5. See, for instance, *Estate of Webster v. Thomas,* 2013 IL App (5th) 120121-U, 2013 WL 164041 (2013).

[UPA 801(4)]. Under the UPA, a court may order dissolution when it becomes obviously impractical for the firm to continue—for instance, if the business can only be operated at a loss [UPA 801(5)]

■ **CASE IN POINT 16.11** Members of the Russell family began operating Russell Realty Associates (RRA) as a partnership. Eddie Russell had decision-making authority over the partnership's business, which involved buying, holding, leasing, and selling investment properties. After several years, Eddie and his sister, Nina Russell, started having disputes, and Nina began to routinely question Eddie's business decisions. Because of their disagreements, RRA experienced two years of delays before it could sell one piece of property. Although the firm continued to profit, Eddie filed a complaint seeking a judicial dissolution of the partnership, which the court granted. Nina appealed.

The Virginia Supreme Court affirmed the lower court's decision that Russell Realty must be judicially dissolved. The partners' relationship had deteriorated to the point where the partnership was unable to function effectively. As a result, the firm had incurred substantial and unnecessary added costs, which frustrated the partnership's economic purpose and made it impracticable to continue.[6] ■

**Winding Up and Distribution of Assets.** After dissolution, the partnership continues for the limited purpose of winding up the business. The partners cannot create new obligations on behalf of the partnership and have authority only to complete unfinished transactions and wind up the business [UPA 803, 804(1)].

Winding up includes collecting and preserving partnership assets, discharging liabilities (paying debts), and accounting to each partner for the value of his or her interest in the partnership. Partners continue to have fiduciary duties to one another and to the firm during this process.

Both creditors of the partnership and creditors of the individual partners can make claims on the partnership's assets. In general, partnership creditors share proportionately with the partners' individual creditors in the partners' assets, which include their interests in the partnership.

A partnership's assets are distributed according to the following priorities [UPA 807]:

1. Payment of debts, including those owed to partner and nonpartner creditors.
2. Return of capital contributions and distribution of profits to partners.

---

6. *Russell Realty Associates v. Russell,* 724 S.E.2d 690 (Va.Sup.Ct. 2012).

If the partnership's liabilities are greater than its assets, the partners bear the losses in the same proportion in which they shared the profits unless they have agreed otherwise.

**Partnership Buy-Sell Agreements.** Before entering into a partnership, partners may agree on how the assets will be valued and divided in the event that the partnership dissolves. Such an agreement may eliminate costly negotiations or litigation later.

This agreement, called a **buy-sell agreement** or *buy-out agreement,* may provide for one or more partners to buy out the other or others should the situation warrant. Alternatively, the agreement may specify that one or more partners will determine the value of the interest being sold and that the other or others will decide whether to buy or sell.

Under UPA 701(a), if a partner's dissociation does not result in a dissolution of the partnership, a buyout of the partner's interest is mandatory. The UPA contains an extensive set of buyout rules that apply when the partners do not have a buyout agreement. Basically, a withdrawing partner receives the same amount through a buyout that he or she would receive if the business were winding up [UPA 701(b)].

---

# 16–4 Franchises

Instead of setting up a sole proprietorship to market their own products or services, many entrepreneurs opt to purchase a franchise. A **franchise** is an arrangement in which the owner of intellectual property—such as a trademark, a trade name, or a copyright—licenses others to use it in the selling of goods or services.

A **franchisee** (a purchaser of a franchise) is generally legally independent of the **franchisor** (the seller of the franchise). At the same time, the franchisee is economically dependent on the franchisor's integrated business system and obtains the advantages of a regional or national organization.

Today, franchising companies and their franchisees account for a significant portion of all retail sales in this country. Well-known franchises include McDonald's, 7-Eleven, and Holiday Inn. Franchising has also become a popular way for businesses to expand their operations internationally without violating the legal restrictions that many nations impose on foreign ownership of businesses.

## 16–4a Types of Franchises

Many different kinds of businesses sell franchises, and numerous types of franchises are available. Generally, though, franchises fall into one of three classifications: distributorships, chain-style business operations, and manufacturing arrangements.

**Distributorship** In a *distributorship,* a manufacturer (the franchisor) licenses a dealer (the franchisee) to sell its product. Often, a distributorship covers an exclusive territory. Automobile dealerships and beer distributorships are common examples.

■ **EXAMPLE 16.12** Black Bear Beer Company distributes its brands of beer through a network of authorized wholesale distributors, each with an assigned territory. Marik signs a distributorship contract for the area from Gainesville to Ocala, Florida. If the contract states that Marik is the exclusive distributor in that area, then no other franchisee may distribute Black Bear beer in that region. ■

**Chain-Style Business Operation** In a *chain-style business operation,* a franchise operates under a franchisor's trade name and is identified as a member of a select group of dealers that engage in the franchisor's business. The franchisee is generally required to follow standardized or prescribed methods of operation. Often, the franchisor insists that the franchisee maintain certain standards of performance.

In addition, the franchisee may be required to obtain materials and supplies exclusively from the franchisor. Chipotle Mexican Grill and most other fast-food chains are examples of this type of franchise. Chain-style franchises are also common in service-related businesses, including real estate brokerage firms, such as Century 21, and tax-preparing services, such as H&R Block, Inc.

**Manufacturing Arrangement** In a *manufacturing,* or *processing-plant, arrangement,* the franchisor transmits to the franchisee the essential ingredients or formula to make a particular product. The franchisee then markets the product either at wholesale or at retail in accordance with the franchisor's standards. Examples of this type of franchise include Pepsi-Cola and other soft-drink bottling companies.

## 16–4b Laws Governing Franchising

Because a franchise relationship is primarily a contractual relationship, it is governed by contract law. If the franchise exists primarily for the sale of products manufactured by the franchisor, the law governing sales contracts as expressed in Article 2 of the Uniform Commercial Code applies.

Additionally, the federal government and most states have enacted laws governing certain aspects of franchising. Generally, these laws are designed to protect prospective franchisees from dishonest franchisors and to prevent franchisors from terminating franchises without good cause.

**Federal Regulation of Franchises** The federal government regulates franchising through laws that apply to specific industries and through the Franchise Rule, created by the Federal Trade Commission (FTC).

**Industry-Specific Standards.** Congress has enacted laws that protect franchisees in certain industries, such as automobile dealerships and service stations. These laws protect the franchisee from unreasonable demands and bad faith terminations of the franchise by the franchisor.

An automobile manufacturer–franchisor cannot make unreasonable demands of dealer-franchisees or set unrealistically high sales quotas. If an automobile manufacturer–franchisor terminates a franchise because of a dealer-franchisee's failure to comply with unreasonable demands, the manufacturer may be liable for damages.[7]

Similarly, federal law prescribes the conditions under which a franchisor of service stations can terminate the franchise.[8] In addition, federal antitrust laws sometimes apply in specified circumstances to prohibit certain types of anticompetitive agreements.

**The Franchise Rule.** The FTC's Franchise Rule requires franchisors to disclose certain material facts that a prospective franchisee needs in order to make an informed decision concerning the purchase of a franchise.[9] Those who violate the Franchise Rule are subject to substantial civil penalties, and the FTC can sue on behalf of injured parties to recover damages.

The rule requires the franchisor to make numerous written disclosures to prospective franchisees (see Exhibit 16–1). All representations made to a prospective franchisee must have a reasonable basis. For instance, if a franchisor provides projected earnings figures, the franchisor must indicate whether the figures are based on actual data or hypothetical examples. If a franchisor makes sales or earnings projections based on actual data for a specific franchise location, the franchisor must disclose the number and percentage of its existing franchises that have achieved this result.

---

**7.** Automobile Dealers' Franchise Act, also known as the Automobile Dealers' Day in Court Act, 15 U.S.C. Sections 1221 *et seq.*
**8.** Petroleum Marketing Practices Act (PMPA), 15 U.S.C. Sections 2801 *et seq.*
**9.** 16 C.F.R. Section 436.1.

**EXHIBIT 16–1** The FTC's Franchise Rule Requirements

| REQUIREMENT | EXPLANATION |
| --- | --- |
| **Written (or Electronic) Disclosures** | The franchisor must make numerous disclosures, such as the range of goods and services included and the value and estimated profitability of the franchise. Disclosures can be delivered on paper or electronically. Prospective franchisees must be able to download or save any electronic disclosure documents. |
| **Reasonable Basis for Any Representations** | To prevent deception, all representations made to a prospective franchisee must have a reasonable basis at the time they are made. |
| **Projected Earnings Figures** | If a franchisor provides projected earnings figures, the franchisor must indicate whether the figures are based on actual data or hypothetical examples. The Franchise Rule does not require franchisors to provide potential earnings figures, however. |
| **Actual Data** | If a franchisor makes sales or earnings projections based on actual data for a specific franchise location, the franchisor must disclose the number and percentage of its existing franchises that have achieved this result. |
| **Explanation of Terms** | Franchisors are required to explain termination, cancellation, and renewal provisions of the franchise contract to potential franchisees before the agreement is signed. |

**State Regulation of Franchising** State legislation varies but often is aimed at protecting franchisees from unfair practices and bad faith terminations by franchisors.

**State Disclosures.** A number of states have laws similar to the federal rules that require franchisors to provide pre-sale disclosures to prospective franchisees.[10] Many state laws also require that a disclosure document (known as the Franchise Disclosure Document, or FDD) be registered or filed with a state official. State laws may also require that a franchisor submit advertising aimed at prospective franchisees to the state for approval.

To protect franchisees, a state law might require the disclosure of information such as the actual costs of operation, recurring expenses, and profits earned, along with facts substantiating these figures. State deceptive trade practices acts may also apply and prohibit certain types of actions by franchisors.

**May Require Good Cause to Terminate the Franchise.** To prevent arbitrary or bad faith terminations, a state law

may prohibit termination without "good cause" or require that certain procedures be followed in terminating a franchise. ■ **CASE IN POINT 16.13** FMS, Inc., entered into a franchise agreement with Samsung Construction Equipment North America to become an authorized dealership selling Samsung construction equipment. Samsung then sold its equipment business to Volvo Construction Equipment North America, Inc., which was to continue selling Samsung brand equipment.

Later, Volvo rebranded the construction equipment under its own name and canceled FMS's franchise. FMS sued, claiming that Volvo had terminated the franchise without "good cause" in violation of state law. Because Volvo was no longer manufacturing the Samsung brand equipment, the court found that Volvo had good cause to terminate FMS's franchise. If Volvo had continued making the Samsung equipment, though, it could not have terminated the franchise.[11] ■

## 16–4c The Franchise Contract

The franchise relationship is defined by the contract between the franchisor and the franchisee. The franchise

---

10. These states include California, Florida, Hawaii, Illinois, Indiana, Maryland, Michigan, Minnesota, New York, North Dakota, Oregon, Rhode Island, South Dakota, Texas, Utah, Virginia, Washington, and Wisconsin.

11. *FMS, Inc. v. Volvo Construction Equipment North America, Inc.*, 557 F.3d 758 (7th Cir. 2009).

contract specifies the terms and conditions of the franchise and spells out the rights and duties of the franchisor and the franchisee.

If either party fails to perform its contractual duties, that party may be subject to a lawsuit for breach of contract. If a franchisee is induced to enter into a franchise contract by the franchisor's fraudulent misrepresentation, the franchisor may be liable for damages. Generally, statutes and the case law governing franchising tend to emphasize the importance of good faith and fair dealing in franchise relationships.

**Payment for the Franchise** The franchisee ordinarily pays an initial fee or lump-sum price for the franchise license (the privilege of being granted a franchise). This fee is separate from the various products that the franchisee purchases from or through the franchisor. The franchise agreement may also require the franchisee to pay a percentage of the franchisor's advertising costs and certain administrative expenses.

In some industries, the franchisor relies heavily on the initial sale of the franchise for realizing a profit. In other industries, the continued dealing between the parties brings profit to both. Generally, the franchisor receives a stated percentage of the annual (or monthly) sales or volume of business done by the franchisee.

**Business Premises** The franchise agreement may specify whether the premises for the business must be leased or purchased outright. Sometimes, a building must be constructed to meet the terms of the agreement. The agreement will specify whether the franchisor or the franchisee is responsible for supplying equipment and furnishings for the premises.

**Location of the Franchise** Typically, the franchisor determines the territory to be served. Some franchise contracts give the franchisee exclusive rights, or "territorial rights," to a certain geographic area. Other franchise contracts, while defining the territory allotted to a particular franchise, either specifically state that the franchise is nonexclusive or are silent on the issue of territorial rights.

Many franchise disputes arise over territorial rights, and the implied covenant of good faith and fair dealing often comes into play in this area of franchising. If the contract does not grant exclusive territorial rights to the franchisee and the franchisor allows a competing franchise to be established nearby, the franchisee may suffer significant lost profits. In this situation, a court may hold that the franchisor breached an implied covenant of good faith and fair dealing.

**Business Organization** The franchisor may require that the business use a particular organizational form and capital structure. The franchise agreement may also set out standards such as sales quotas and record-keeping requirements. Additionally, a franchisor may retain stringent control over the training of personnel involved in the operation and over administrative aspects of the business.

**Quality Control by the Franchisor** The day-to-day operation of the franchise business normally is left up to the franchisee. Nonetheless, the franchise agreement may specify that the franchisor will provide some degree of supervision and control so that it can protect the franchise's name and reputation.

**Means of Control.** When the franchise prepares a product, such as food, or provides a service, such as motel accommodations, the contract often states that the franchisor will establish certain standards for the facility. Typically, the contract will state that the franchisor is permitted to make periodic inspections to ensure that the standards are being maintained.

As a means of controlling quality, franchise agreements also typically limit the franchisee's ability to sell the franchise to another party. ■ **EXAMPLE 16.14** Mark Keller, Inc., an authorized Jaguar franchise, contracts to sell its dealership to Henrique Autos West. A Jaguar franchise generally cannot be sold without Jaguar Cars' permission. Prospective franchisees must meet Jaguar's customer satisfaction standards. If Henrique Autos fails to meet those standards, Jaguar can refuse to allow the sale and can terminate the franchise. ■

**Degree of Control.** As a general rule, the validity of a provision permitting the franchisor to establish and enforce certain quality standards is unquestioned. The franchisor has a legitimate interest in maintaining the quality of the product or service to protect its name and reputation.

If a franchisor exercises too much control over the operations of its franchisees, however, the franchisor risks potential liability. A franchisor may occasionally be held liable—under the doctrine of *respondeat superior*—for the tortious acts of the franchisees' employees. ■ **EXAMPLE 16.15** The National Labor Relations Board (NLRB) received 180 employee complaints that certain McDonald's restaurants had engaged in unfair labor practices. Employees alleged that the restaurants had fired or penalized workers for participating in protests over wages and working conditions. Investigators found that at least some of the complaints had merit. The NLRB ruled that McDonald's USA, LLC, could be held jointly liable along with several of its franchisees for labor and wage violations. The NLRB reasoned that McDonald's exerts sufficient control over its franchisees to be found liable for the franchisees' employment law violations. ■

**Pricing Arrangements** Franchises provide the franchisor with an outlet for the firm's goods and services. Depending on the nature of the business, the franchisor may require the franchisee to purchase certain supplies from the franchisor at an established price.[12] A franchisor cannot, however, set the prices at which the franchisee will resell the goods. Such price setting may be a violation of state or federal antitrust laws, or both. A franchisor can suggest retail prices but cannot mandate them.

## 16–4d Franchise Termination

The duration of the franchise is a matter to be determined between the parties. Sometimes, a franchise relationship starts with a short trial period, such as a year, so that the franchisee and the franchisor can determine whether they want to stay in business with one another. At other times, the duration of the franchise contract correlates with the term of the lease for the business premises, and both are renewable at the end of that period.

**Grounds for Termination Set by Franchise Contract** Usually, the franchise agreement specifies that termination must be "for cause" and then defines the grounds for termination. Cause might include, for instance, the death or disability of the franchisee, insolvency of the franchisee, breach of the franchise agreement, or failure to meet specified sales quotas.

■ **CASE IN POINT 16.16** All Professional Realty, Inc., and All Professional Hawaii Realty, Inc., entered into four franchise agreements with Century 21 Real Estate, LLC. Century 21 (the franchisor) gave All Professional (the franchisee) the right to operate four separate offices in California and Hawaii under the name "Century 21 All Professional." The agreements required All Professional to pay royalty and advertising fees. They also permitted Century 21 to terminate the agreements for good cause, which included the franchisee's failure to operate at an approved location.

All Professional signed a note for $75,000 payable to Century 21 and agreed to make annual payments on the note. Four years later, All Professional stopped remitting the fees and making payments on the note, and it closed one of the California offices. Century 21 terminated the franchise agreements. All Professional sued, but a federal district court held in favor of Century 21, and that decision was affirmed on appeal. Century 21 did not breach the franchise agreements. All Professional did. Nonpayment of the fees and the note, and the abandonment of one of the franchisee's offices, constituted a material breach of the contract. These actions provided Century 21 with legitimate grounds for termination of the franchise agreement.[13] ■

**Notice Requirements.** Most franchise contracts provide that notice of termination must be given. If no set time for termination is specified, then a reasonable time, with notice, is implied. A franchisee must be given reasonable time to wind up the business—that is, to do the accounting and return the copyright or trademark or any other property of the franchisor.

**Opportunity to Cure a Breach.** A franchise agreement may allow the franchisee to attempt to cure an ordinary, curable breach within a certain time after notice so as to postpone, or even avoid, termination. Even when a contract contains a notice-and-cure provision, however, a franchisee's breach of the duty of honesty and fidelity may be enough to allow the franchisor to terminate the franchise.

■ **CASE IN POINT 16.17** Milind and Minaxi Upadhyaya entered into a franchise contract with 7-Eleven, Inc., to operate a store in Pennsylvania. The contract included a notice-and-cure provision. Under 7-Eleven's usual contract, franchisees lease the store and equipment, and receive a license to use 7-Eleven's trademarks and other intellectual property. 7-Eleven receives a percentage of the store's gross profit (net sales less the cost of goods sold).

A 7-Eleven manager noticed a high rate of certain questionable transactions at the Upadhyayas' store and began investigating. The investigation continued for nearly two years and revealed that the store had been misreporting its sales so as to conceal sales proceeds from 7-Eleven. Evidence indicated that nearly one-third of the store's sales transactions had not been properly recorded. 7-Eleven sent a "non-curable" notice of material breach and termination of the franchise to the Upadhyayas. The franchisees argued that they had not been given an opportunity to cure the breach. The court found there was sufficient evidence of fraud to warrant immediate termination without an opportunity to cure.[14] ■

---

12. Although a franchisor can require franchisees to purchase supplies from it, requiring a franchisee to purchase exclusively from the franchisor may violate federal antitrust laws.

13. *Century 21 Real Estate, LLC v. All Professional Realty, Inc.*, 600 Fed.Appx. 502 (9th Cir. 2015).

14. *7-Eleven, Inc. v. Upadhyaya*, 926 F.Supp.2d 614 (E.D.Penn. 2013).

**Wrongful Termination** Because a franchisor's termination of a franchise often has adverse consequences for the franchisee, much franchise litigation involves claims of wrongful termination. Generally, the termination provisions of contracts are more favorable to the franchisor than to the franchisee. This means that the franchisee, who normally invests substantial time and financial resources in making the franchise operation successful, may receive little or nothing for the business on termination. The franchisor owns the trademark and hence the business.

It is in this area that statutory and case law become important. The federal and state laws discussed earlier attempt, among other things, to protect franchisees from the arbitrary or unfair termination of their franchises by the franchisors.

**The Importance of Good Faith and Fair Dealing** Generally, both statutory law and case law emphasize the importance of good faith and fair dealing in terminating a franchise relationship. In determining whether a franchisor has acted in good faith when terminating a franchise agreement, the courts usually try to balance the rights of both parties.

If a court perceives that a franchisor has arbitrarily or unfairly terminated a franchise, the franchisee will be provided with a remedy for wrongful termination. A court will be less likely to consider a termination wrongful if the franchisor's decision was made in the normal course of business and reasonable notice was given.

The importance of good faith and fair dealing in a franchise relationship is underscored by the consequences of the franchisor's acts in the following case.

## Spotlight on Holiday Inns

## Case 16.3 Holiday Inn Franchising, Inc. v. Hotel Associates, Inc.
Court of Appeals of Arkansas, 2011 Ark.App. 147, 382 S.W.3d 6 (2011).

**Background and Facts** Buddy House was in the construction business in Arkansas and Texas. For decades, he collaborated on projects with Holiday Inn Franchising, Inc. Their relationship was characterized by good faith—many projects were undertaken without written contracts. At Holiday Inn's request, House inspected a hotel in Wichita Falls, Texas, to estimate the cost of getting it into shape. Holiday Inn wanted House to renovate the hotel and operate it as a Holiday Inn. House estimated that recovering the cost of renovation would take him more than ten years, so he asked for a franchise term longer than Holiday Inn's usual ten years. Holiday Inn refused, but said that if the hotel was run "appropriately," the term would be extended at the end of ten years. House bought the hotel, renovated it, and operated it as Hotel Associates, Inc. (HAI), generating substantial profits. He refused offers to sell it for as much as $15 million.

Before the ten years had passed, Greg Aden, a Holiday Inn executive, developed a plan to license a different local hotel as a Holiday Inn instead of renewing House's franchise license. Aden stood to earn a commission from licensing the other hotel. No one informed House of Aden's plan. When the time came, HAI applied for an extension of its franchise, and Holiday Inn asked for major renovations. HAI spent $3 million to comply with this request. Holiday Inn did not renew HAI's license, however, but instead granted a franchise to the other hotel. HAI sold its hotel for $5 million and filed a suit in an Arkansas state court against Holiday Inn, asserting fraud. The court awarded HAI compensatory and punitive damages. Holiday Inn appealed.

**In the Language of the Court**
Raymond R. *ABRAMSON*, Judge.
* * * *

Generally, a mere failure to volunteer information does not constitute fraud. But *silence can amount to actionable fraud in some circumstances where the parties have a relation of trust or confidence, where there is inequality of condition and knowledge, or where there are other attendant circumstances.* [Emphasis added.]

In this case, substantial evidence supports the existence of a duty on Holiday Inn's part to disclose the Aden [plan] to HAI. Buddy House had a long-term relationship with Holiday Inn characterized by honesty, trust, and the free flow of pertinent information. He testified that [Holiday Inn's] assurances at

**Case 16.3 Continues**

**Case 16.3 Continued**

the onset of licensure [the granting of the license] led him to believe that he would be relicensed after ten years if the hotel was operated appropriately. Yet, despite Holiday Inn's having provided such an assurance to House, it failed to apprise House of an internal business plan * * * that advocated licensure of another facility instead of the renewal of his license. *A duty of disclosure may exist where information is peculiarly within the knowledge of one party and is of such a nature that the other party is justified in assuming its non-existence.* Given House's history with Holiday Inn and the assurance he received, we are convinced he was justified in assuming that no obstacles had arisen that jeopardized his relicensure. [Emphasis added.]

Holiday Inn asserts that it would have provided Buddy House with the Aden [plan] if he had asked for it. But, Holiday Inn cannot satisfactorily explain why House should have been charged with the responsibility of inquiring about a plan that he did not know existed. Moreover, several Holiday Inn personnel testified that Buddy House in fact should have been provided with the Aden plan. Aden himself stated that * * * House should have been given the plan. * * * In light of these circumstances, we see no ground for reversal on this aspect of HAI's cause of action for fraud.

**Decision and Remedy** *The state intermediate appellate court affirmed the lower court's judgment and its award of compensatory damages. The appellate court increased the amount of punitive damages, however, citing Holiday Inn's "degree of reprehensibility."*

**Critical Thinking**

- **Legal Environment** *Why should House and HAI have been advised of Holiday Inn's plan to grant a franchise to a different hotel in their territory?*
- **Economic** *A jury awarded HAI $12 million in punitive damages. The court reduced this award to $1 million, but the appellate court reinstated the original award. What is the purpose of punitive damages? Did Holiday Inn's conduct warrant this award? Explain.*

## Reviewing: Small Businesses and Franchises

Carlos Del Rey decided to open a Mexican fast-food restaurant and signed a franchise contract with a national chain called La Grande Enchilada. The contract required the franchisee to strictly follow the franchisor's operating manual and stated that failure to do so would be grounds for terminating the franchise contract. The manual set forth detailed operating procedures and safety standards, and provided that a La Grande Enchilada representative would inspect the restaurant monthly to ensure compliance.

Nine months after Del Rey began operating his restaurant, a spark from the grill ignited an oily towel in the kitchen. No one was injured, but by the time firefighters were able to put out the fire, the kitchen had sustained extensive damage. The cook told the fire department that the towel was "about two feet from the grill" when it caught fire. This was in compliance with the franchisor's manual that required towels be placed at least one foot from the grills. Nevertheless, the next day La Grande Enchilada notified Del Rey that his franchise would terminate in thirty days for failure to follow the prescribed safety procedures. Using the information presented in the chapter, answer the following questions.

1. What type of franchise was Del Rey's La Grande Enchilada restaurant?
2. If Del Rey operates the restaurant as a sole proprietorship, who bears the loss for the damaged kitchen? Explain.
3. Assume that Del Rey files a lawsuit against La Grande Enchilada, claiming that his franchise was wrongfully terminated. What is the main factor that a court would consider in determining whether the franchise was wrongfully terminated?
4. Would a court be likely to rule that La Grande Enchilada had good cause to terminate Del Rey's franchise in this situation? Why or why not?

**Debate This . . .** *A partnership should automatically end when one partner dissociates from the firm.*

## Terms and Concepts

| | | |
|---|---|---|
| articles of partnership 356 | franchise 362 | joint liability 360 |
| buyout price 361 | franchisee 362 | partnership 355 |
| buy-sell agreement 362 | franchisor 362 | partnership by estoppel 356 |
| dissociation 360 | goodwill 355 | pass-through entity 356 |
| dissolution 361 | information return 356 | sole proprietorship 351 |
| entrepreneur 350 | joint and several liability 360 | winding up 361 |

## Issue Spotters

**1.** Frank plans to open a sporting goods store and to hire Gogi and Hap. Frank will invest only his own funds. He expects that he will not make a profit for at least eighteen months and will make only a small profit in the three years after that. He hopes to expand eventually. Would a sole proprietorship be an appropriate form for Frank's business? Why or why not? (See *Sole Proprietorships*.)

**2.** Darnell and Eliana are partners in D&E Designs, an architectural firm. When Darnell dies, his widow claims that as Darnell's heir, she is entitled to take his place as Eliana's partner or to receive a share of the firm's assets. Is she right? Why or why not? (See *Partnerships*.)

- **Check your answers to the Issue Spotters against the answers provided in Appendix D at the end of this text.**

## Business Scenarios

**16–1. Partnership Formation.** Daniel is the owner of a chain of shoe stores. He hires Rubya to be the manager of a new store, which is to open in Grand Rapids, Michigan. Daniel, by written contract, agrees to pay Rubya a monthly salary and 20 percent of the profits. Without Daniel's knowledge, Rubya represents himself to Classen as Daniel's partner and shows Classen the agreement to share profits. Classen extends credit to Rubya. Rubya defaults. Discuss whether Classen can hold Daniel liable as a partner. (See *Partnerships*.)

**16–2. Franchising.** Maria, Pablo, and Vicky are recent college graduates who would like to go into business for themselves. They are considering purchasing a franchise. If they enter into a franchising arrangement, they would have the support of a large company that could answer any questions they might have. Also, a firm that has been in business for many years would be experienced in dealing with some of the problems that novice businesspersons might encounter. These and other attributes of franchises can lessen some of the risks of the marketplace. What other aspects of franchising—positive and negative—should Maria, Pablo, and Vicky consider before committing themselves to a particular franchise? (See *Franchises*.)

## Business Case Problems

**16–3. Partnership Formation.** Patricia Garcia and Bernardo Lucero were in a romantic relationship. While they were seeing each other, Garcia and Lucero acquired an electronics service center, paying $30,000 apiece. Two years later, they purchased an apartment complex. The property was deeded to Lucero, but neither Garcia nor Lucero made a down payment. The couple considered both properties to be owned "50/50," and they agreed to share profits, losses, and management rights. When the couple's romantic relationship ended, Garcia asked a court to declare that she had a partnership with Lucero. In court, Lucero argued that the couple did not have a written partnership agreement. Did they have a partnership? Why or why not? [*Garcia v. Lucero*, 366 S.W.3d 275 (Tex. App.—El Paso 2012)] (See *Partnerships*.)

**16–4. Business Case Problem with Sample Answer—**  **Partnerships.** Karyl Paxton asked Christopher Sacco to work with her interior design business, Pierce Paxton Collections, in New Orleans. At the time, they were in a romantic relationship. Sacco was involved in every aspect of the business—bookkeeping, marketing, and design—but was not paid a salary. He was reimbursed, however, for expenses charged to his personal credit card, which Paxton also used. Sacco took no profits from the firm, saying that he wanted to "grow the business" and "build sweat equity." When Paxton and Sacco's personal relationship soured, she fired him. Sacco objected, claiming that they were partners. Is Sacco entitled to 50 percent of the profits of Pierce Paxton Collections? Explain. [*Sacco v. Paxton*, 133 So.3d 213 (La.App. 2014)] (See *Partnerships*.)

- **For a sample answer to Problem 16–4, go to Appendix E at the end of this text.**

**16–5. Formation.** Leisa Reed and Randell Thurman lived together in Spring City, Tennessee. Randell and his father, Leroy, formed a cattle-raising operation and opened a bank account in the name of L&R Farm. Within a few years, Leroy quit the operation. Leisa and Randell each wrote a personal check for $5,000 to buy his cattle. Leisa picked up supplies, fed and administered medicine to cattle, collected hay, and participated in the bookkeeping for L&R. Later, checks drawn on her personal account for $12,000 to buy equipment and $35,000 to buy cattle were deposited into the L&R account. After several years, Leisa decided that she no longer wanted to associate with Randell, but they could not agree on a financial settlement. Was Leisa a partner in L&R? Is she entitled to half of the value of L&R's assets? Explain. [*Reed v. Thurman*, 2015 WL 1119449 (Tenn.App.—Knoxville 2015)] (See *Partnerships*.)

**16–6. Quality Control.** The franchise agreement of Domino's Pizza, L.L.C., sets out operational standards, including safety requirements, for a franchisee to follow but provides that the franchisee is an independent contractor. Each franchisee is free to use its own means and methods. For example, Domino's does not know whether a franchisee's delivery drivers are complying with vehicle safety requirements. MAC Pizza Management, Inc., operates a Domino's franchise. A vehicle driven by Joshua Balka, a MAC delivery driver, hydroplaned due to a bald tire and wet pavement. It struck the vehicle of Devavaram and Ruth Christopher, killing Ruth and injuring Devavaram. Is Domino's liable for negligence? Explain. [*Domino's Pizza, L.L.C. v. Reddy*, 2015 WL 1247349 (Tex.App.—Beaumont 2015)] (See *Franchises*.)

**16–7. Formation and Operation.** FS Partners is a general partnership whose partners are Jerry Stahlman, a professional engineer, and Fitz & Smith, Inc., a corporation in the business of excavating and paving. Timothy Smith signed the partnership agreement on Fitz & Smith's behalf and deals with FS matters on Fitz & Smith's behalf. Stahlman handles the payment of FS's bills, including its tax bills, and is the designated partner on FS's federal tax return. FS was formed to buy and develop twenty acres of unoccupied, wooded land in York County, Pennsylvania. The deed to the property lists the owner as "FS Partners, a general partnership." When the taxes on the real estate were not paid, the York County Tax Claim Bureau published notice that the property would be sold at a tax sale. The bureau also mailed a notice to FS's address of record and posted a notice on the land. Is this sufficient notice of the tax sale? Discuss. [*FS Partners v. York County Tax Claim Bureau*, 132 A.3d 577 (Pa. 2016)] (See *Partnerships*.)

**16–8. Franchise Termination.** Executive Home Care Franchising, LLC, sells in-home health-care franchises. Clint, Massare,

and Greer Marshall entered into a franchise agreement with Executive Home Care. The agreement provided that the franchisees' failure to comply with the agreement's terms would likely cause irreparable harm to the franchisor, entitling it to an injunction. About two years later, the Marshalls gave up their franchise. They returned thirteen boxes of documents, stationery, operating manuals, marketing materials, and other items—everything in their possession that featured Executive Home Care trademarks. They quit operating out of the franchised location. They transferred the phone number back to the franchisor and informed their clients that they were no longer associated with Executive Home Care. They continued to engage in the home health-care business, however, under the name "Well-Being Home Care Corp." Is Executive Home Care entitled to an injunction against the Marshalls and their new company? Discuss. [*Executive Home Care Franchising, LLC v. Marshall Health Corp.*, __ Fed.Appx. __, 2016 WL 703801 (3d Cir. 2016)] (See *Franchises*.)

**16–9. A Question of Ethics—Wrongful Dissociation.** *Elliot Willensky and Beverly Moran formed a partner-*  *ship to buy, renovate, and sell a house. Moran agreed to finance the effort, which was to cost no more than $60,000. Willensky agreed to oversee the work, which was to be done in six months. Willensky lived in the house during the renovation. As the project progressed, Willensky incurred excessive and unnecessary expenses, misappropriated funds for his personal use, did not pay bills on time, and did not keep Moran informed of the costs. More than a year later, the renovation was still not completed, and Willensky walked off the project. Moran completed the renovation, which ultimately cost $311,222, and sold the house. Moran then sued to dissolve the partnership and recover damages from Willensky for breach of contract and wrongful dissociation. [Moran v. Willensky, 339 S.W.3d 651 (Tenn.App.—Nashville 2010)] (See Partnerships.)*

**(a)** Moran alleged that Willensky had wrongfully dissociated from the partnership. When did this dissociation occur? Why was his dissociation wrongful?

**(b)** Which of Willensky's actions simply represent unethical behavior or bad management, and which constitute a breach of the agreement?

# Legal Reasoning Group Activity

**16–10. Franchise Termination.** Walid Elkhatib, an Arab American, bought a Dunkin' Donuts franchise in Illinois. Ten years later, Dunkin' Donuts began offering breakfast sandwiches with bacon, ham, or sausage through its franchises. Elkhatib refused to sell these items at his store on the ground that his religion forbade the handling of pork. Elkhatib then opened a second franchise, at which he also refused to sell pork products.

The next year, at both locations, Elkhatib began selling meatless sandwiches. He also opened a third franchise. When he proposed to relocate this franchise, Dunkin' Donuts refused to approve the new location. The company also informed him that it would not renew any of his franchise agreements

because he did not carry the full sandwich line. Elkhatib filed a lawsuit against Dunkin' Donuts. (See *Franchises*.)

**(a)** The first group will argue on behalf of Elkhatib that Dunkin' Donuts wrongfully terminated his franchises.

**(b)** The second group will take the side of Dunkin' Donuts and justify its decision to terminate the franchises.

**(c)** The third group will assess whether Dunkin' Donuts acted in good faith in its relationship with Elkhatib. Consider whether Dunkin' Donuts should be required to accommodate Elkhatib's religious beliefs and allow him not to serve pork in these three locations.

# Answers to the *Issue Spotters*

**1.** *Would a sole proprietorship be an appropriate form for Frank's business? Why or why not?* Yes. When a business is relatively small and is not diversified, employs relatively few people, has modest profits, and is not likely to expand significantly or require extensive financing in the immediate future, the most appropriate form for doing business may be a sole proprietorship.

**2.** *When Darnell dies, his widow claims that as Darnell's heir, she is entitled to take his place as Eliana's partner or to receive a share of the firm's assets. Is she right? Why or why not?* No. A widow (or widower) has no right to take a dead partner's place. A partner's death causes dissociation, after which the partnership must purchase the dissociated partner's partnership interest. Therefore, the surviving partners must pay the decedent's estate (for his widow) the value of the deceased partner's interest in the partnership.

# Sample Answers for *Business Case Problems with Sample Answer*

**Problem 16–4.** *Partnerships.* Yes, Sacco is entitled to 50 percent of the profits of Pierce Paxton Collections. The requirements for establishing a partnership are (1) a sharing of profits and losses, (2) a joint ownership of the business, and (3) an equal right to be involved in the management of the business.

The effort and time that Sacco expended in the business constituted a sharing of losses, and his proprietary interest in the assets of the partnership consisted of his share of the profits, which he had expressly left in the business to "grow the company" and "build sweat equity" for the future. He was involved in every aspect of the business. Although he was not paid a salary, he was reimbursed for business expenses charged to his personal credit card, which Paxton also used. These facts arguably meet the requirements for establishing a partnership.

In the actual case on which this problem is based, Sacco filed a suit in a Louisiana state court against Paxton, and the court awarded Sacco 50 percent of the profits. A state intermediate appellate court affirmed, based generally on the reasoning stated above.

# Chapter 13

# CHAPTER

# Limited Liability Business Forms

Our government allows entrepreneurs to choose from a variety of business organizational forms. In selecting among them, businesspersons are motivated to choose organizational forms that limit their liability. Limited liability may allow them to take more business risk, which is associated with the potential for higher profits.

A relatively new and increasingly common form of business organization is the *limited liability company (LLC)*. LLCs have become the organizational form of choice among many small businesses. Other limited liability business forms include the *limited liability partnership (LLP)*, the *limited partnership (LP)*, and the *limited liability limited partnership (LLLP)*.

## 17–1 The Limited Liability Company

A **limited liability company (LLC)** is a hybrid that combines the limited liability aspects of a corporation and the tax advantages of a partnership. The LLC has been available for only a few decades, but it has become the preferred structure for many small businesses.

LLCs are governed by state statutes, which vary from state to state. In an attempt to create more uniformity, the National Conference of Commissioners on Uniform State Laws issued the Uniform Limited Liability Company Act (ULLCA). Less than one-fifth of the states have adopted it, however. Thus, the law governing LLCs remains far from uniform.

Nevertheless, some provisions are common to most state statutes. We base our discussion of LLCs on these common elements.

### 17–1a The Nature of the LLC

LLCs share many characteristics with corporations. Like corporations, LLCs must be formed and operated in compliance with state law. Like the shareholders of a corporation, the owners of an LLC, who are called **members,** enjoy limited liability [ULLCA 303].[1]

**Limited Liability of Members** Members of LLCs are shielded from personal liability in most situations. In other words, the liability of members is normally limited to the amount of their investments.

An exception arises when a member has significantly contributed to the LLC's tortious conduct. ■ **CASE IN POINT 17.1** Randy Coley, the sole member and manager of East Coast Cablevision, LLC, installed cable television systems for many hotels and resorts. Coley established a DIRECTV Satellite Master Antenna Television (SMATV) account in the name of Massanutten Resort. The system provided programming to 168 timeshare units, as well as to the resort's bar, golf shop, lobbies, and waterpark. The bill for the resort's account was sent to (and paid by) East Coast Cablevision, which in turn billed the customers.

Over time, East Coast Cablevision began providing cable services to additional customers using the resort's SMATV account but did not pay DIRECTV for these other customers. Ultimately, another cable dealer affiliated with DIRECTV sued Coley for not paying for all of the DIRECTV programming transmissions that East Coast's customers had received. The court held that because Coley had played a direct role in the unauthorized transmissions, he could be held personally liable for them.[2] ■

**When Liability May Be Imposed** The members of an LLC, like the shareholders in a corporation, can lose their limited personal liability in certain circumstances. For instance, when an individual guarantees payment of

---

1. Members of an LLC can also bring derivative actions, which you will read about in regard to corporations, on behalf of the LLC [ULLCA 101]. As with a corporate shareholder's derivative suit, any damages recovered go to the LLC, not to the members personally.

2. *Sky Cable, LLC v. Coley,* ___ F.Supp.3d ___, 2013 WL 3517337 (W.D.Va. 2013).

a business loan to the LLC, that individual is personally liable for the business's obligation. In addition, if an LLC member fails to comply with certain formalities, such as by commingling personal and business funds, a court can impose personal liability.

Under various principles of corporate law, courts may hold the owners of a business liable for its debts. On rare occasions, for instance, courts ignore the corporate structure ("pierce the corporate veil") to expose the shareholders to personal liability when it is required to achieve justice.

Similarly, courts will sometimes pierce the veil of an LLC to hold its members personally liable. Note, however, that courts have reserved piercing the veil of an LLC for circumstances that are clearly extraordinary. There must normally be some flagrant disregard of the LLC formalities, as well as fraud or malfeasance on the part of the LLC member.

■ **CASE IN POINT 17.2** Tom and Shannon Brown purchased a new home in Hattiesburg, Mississippi, from Ray Richard and Nick Welch. Richard had hired Waldron Properties, LLC (WP), to build the home. Several years later, cracks began to develop in the walls of the Browns' home as a result of defects in the construction of the foundation. The Browns sued Murray Waldron, the sole member of WP, for breach of warranty under the state's New Home Warranty Act (NHWA). Because the required NHWA notice they had received when they bought the home was signed by Waldron personally, they claimed that Waldron was liable personally.

The trial court found that WP, not Waldron individually, was the builder of the Browns' home. The Browns appealed. They contended that even if WP was the builder, the court should pierce the veil of the LLC and hold Waldron personally liable. The state appellate court disagreed and affirmed the lower court's ruling. The Browns had not entered into a contract with either Waldron or WP. There was not sufficient evidence that Waldron had disregarded LLC formalities or had engaged in fraud or other misconduct to justify piercing the LLC's veil to hold him personally liable.[3] ■

### Other Similarities to Corporations
Another similarity between corporations and LLCs is that LLCs are legal entities apart from their owners. As a legal person, the LLC can sue or be sued, enter into contracts, and hold title to property [ULLCA 201]. The terminology used to describe LLCs formed in other states or nations is also similar to that used in corporate law. For instance, an LLC formed in one state but doing business in another state is referred to in the second state as a *foreign LLC*.

### 17–1b The Formation of the LLC
LLCs are creatures of statute and thus must follow state statutory requirements.

**Articles of Organization** To form an LLC, **articles of organization** must be filed with a central state agency—usually the secretary of state's office [ULLCA 202].[4] Typically, the articles must include the name of the business, its principal address, the name and address of a registered agent, the members' names, and how the LLC will be managed [ULLCA 203]. The business's name must include the words *Limited Liability Company* or the initials *LLC* [ULLCA 105(a)]. Although a majority of the states permit one-member LLCs, some states require at least two members.

**Preformation Contracts** Businesspersons sometimes enter into contracts on behalf of a business organization that is not yet formed. Persons who are forming a corporation, for instance, may enter into contracts during the process of incorporation but before the corporation becomes a legal entity. These contracts are referred to as *preincorporation contracts.* The individual promoters who sign the contracts are bound to their terms. Once the corporation is formed and adopts the preincorporation contracts (by means of a *novation,* which substitutes a new contract for the old contract), it can enforce the contract terms.

In dealing with the preorganization contracts of LLCs, courts may apply the well-established principles of corporate law relating to preincorporation contracts. That is to say, when the promoters of an LLC enter preformation contracts, the LLC, once formed, can adopt the contracts by a novation and then enforce them.

■ **CASE IN POINT 17.3** 607 South Park, LLC, entered into an agreement to sell a hotel to 607 Park View Associates, Ltd., which then assigned the rights to the purchase to another company, 02 Development, LLC. At the time, 02 Development did not yet exist—it was legally created several months later. 607 South Park subsequently refused to sell the hotel to 02 Development, and 02 Development sued for breach of the purchase agreement.

A California appellate court ruled that LLCs should be treated the same as corporations with respect to preorganization contracts. Although 02 Development did not exist when the agreement was executed, once it came into existence, it could enforce any preorganization contract made on its behalf.[5] ■

---

4. In addition to requiring articles of organization to be filed, a few states require that a notice of the intention to form an LLC be published in a local newspaper.

5. *02 Development, LLC v. 607 South Park, LLC,* 159 Cal.App.4th 609, 71 Cal.Rptr.3d 608 (2008). See also, *Davis Wine Co. v. Vina Y Bodega Estampa, S.A.,* 823 F.Supp.2d 1159 (D.Or. 2011).

---

3. *Brown v. Waldron,* 186 So.3d 955 (Miss.App. 2016).

## 17–1c Jurisdictional Requirements

As we have seen, LLCs and corporations share several characteristics, but a significant difference between these organizational forms involves federal jurisdictional requirements. Under the federal jurisdiction statute, a corporation is deemed to be a citizen of the state where it is incorporated and maintains its principal place of business. The statute does not mention the state citizenship of partnerships, LLCs, and other unincorporated associations. The courts, however, have tended to regard these entities as citizens of every state of which their members are citizens.

The state citizenship of an LLC may come into play when a party sues the LLC based on diversity of citizenship. Remember that when parties to a lawsuit are from different states and the amount in controversy exceeds $75,000, a federal court can exercise diversity jurisdiction. *Total* diversity of citizenship must exist, however.

■ **EXAMPLE 17.4** Jen Fong, a citizen of New York, wishes to bring a suit against Skycel, an LLC formed under the laws of Connecticut. One of Skycel's members also lives in New York. Fong will not be able to bring a suit against Skycel in federal court on the basis of diversity jurisdiction because the defendant LLC is also a citizen of New York. The same would be true if Fong was bringing a suit against multiple defendants and one of the defendants lived in New York. ■

## 17–1d Advantages of the LLC

The LLC offers many advantages to businesspersons, which is why this form of business organization has become increasingly popular.

**Limited Liability** A key advantage of the LLC is the limited liability of its members. The LLC as an entity can be held liable for any loss or injury caused by the wrongful acts or omissions of its members. As we have seen, however, members themselves generally are not personally liable.

In the following case, a consumer died as a result of using an allegedly defective product made and sold by an LLC. The consumer's children sought to hold the LLC's sole member and manager personally liable for the firm's actions.

---

**Case 17.1**

# Hodge v. Strong Built International, LLC

Court of Appeal of Louisiana, Third Circuit, 159 So.3d 1159 (2015).

**Background and Facts** Donald Hodge was hunting in a deer stand when its straps—which held Hodge high up in a tree—failed. When the straps failed, Hodge and the deer stand fell to the ground, killing Hodge. Louisiana-based Strong Built International, LLC, was the maker and seller of the deer stand, and Ken Killen was Strong Built's sole member and manager.

Hodge's children, Donald and Rachel Hodge, filed a lawsuit in a Louisiana state court against Strong Built and Killen. They sought damages on a theory of product liability for the injury and death of their father caused by the allegedly defective deer stand. Killen filed a motion for summary judgment, asserting that he was not personally liable to the Hodges. The court granted the motion and issued a summary judgment in Killen's favor, dismissing the claims against him. The Hodges appealed.

**In the Language of the Court**
*AMY,* Judge.
\* \* \* \*

\* \* \* An LLC member or manager's liability to third parties is delineated in [Louisiana Revised Statute (La.R.S.)] 12:1320, which states:
\* \* \* \*

\* \* \* no member, manager, employee, or agent of a limited liability company is liable in such capacity for a debt, obligation, or liability of the limited liability company.
\* \* \* \*

\* \* \* That protection is not unlimited. Pursuant to La.R.S. 12:1320(D), *a member or manager may be subjected to personal liability for claims involving* \* \* \* *breach of a professional duty or other negligent or wrongful act.* [Emphasis added.]

\* \* \* In an affidavit, Mr. Killen asserted that he is "not an engineer, nor a licensed professional in any profession in Louisiana or any other state." Mr. Killen also asserts that he:

*Case 17.1 Continues*

**Case 17.1 Continued**

was a participant in the creation of the deer stand which * * * Strong Built International, L.L.C. manufactured and sold, but he never personally dictated or participated in the design, selection of materials used in the manufacture, or the manufacture of, or the selection of any warnings to any deer stand for the use or consumption by any consumer beyond my input and work as a manager * * * and member of * * * Strong Built International, L.L.C.

The plaintiffs offered no evidence to contradict Mr. Killen's affidavit in this regard. Accordingly, we find no basis for Mr. Killen's personal liability under the "breach of professional duty" exception.

Neither do we find sufficient evidence in the record to create a genuine issue of material fact with regard to the "other negligent or wrongful act" exception.

* * * With regard to [this exception], the member (or manager) must have a duty of care to the plaintiff. * * * That duty must be "something more" than the duties arising out of the LLC's contract with the plaintiff.

* * * *

* * * Mr. Killen states in his affidavit that not only was he not personally responsible for the design and manufacture of the deer stands while involved with Strong Built International * * * but that any involvement that he may have had was in his capacity as a member and manager. *The plaintiffs have submitted nothing to show that Mr. Killen's actions are "something more" than his duties as a member/manager of the LLC.* [Emphasis added.]

**Decision and Remedy** *A state intermediate appellate court affirmed the judgment in Killen's favor. Under the applicable Louisiana state LLC statute, no member or manager of an LLC is liable in that capacity for the liability of the company. There are exceptions, but the Hodges failed to show that Killen's actions went beyond his duties as a member and manager of Strong Built.*

**Critical Thinking**
- **Economic** *Why does the law allow—and even encourage—limits to the liability of a business organization's owners and managers for the firm's actions? Discuss.*

---

**Flexibility in Taxation** Another advantage of the LLC is its flexibility in regard to taxation. An LLC that has *two or more members* can choose to be taxed as either a partnership or a corporation. A corporate entity normally must pay income taxes on its profits, and the shareholders must then pay personal income taxes on any of those profits that are distributed as dividends. An LLC that wants to distribute profits to its members almost always prefers to be taxed as a partnership to avoid the "double taxation" that is characteristic of the corporate entity.

Unless an LLC indicates that it wishes to be taxed as a corporation, the Internal Revenue Service (IRS) automatically taxes it as a partnership. This means that the LLC, as an entity, pays no taxes. Rather, as in a partnership, profits are "passed through" the LLC to the members, who then personally pay taxes on the profits. If an LLC's members want to reinvest profits in the business rather than distribute the profits to members, however, they may prefer to be taxed as a corporation. Corporate income tax rates may be lower than personal tax rates.

An LLC that has only *one member* cannot be taxed as a partnership. For federal income tax purposes, one-member LLCs are automatically taxed as sole proprietorships unless they indicate that they wish to be taxed as corporations. With respect to state taxes, most states follow the IRS rules.

**Management and Foreign Investors** Another advantage of the LLC for businesspersons is the flexibility it offers in terms of business operations and management, as will be discussed shortly. Foreign investors are allowed to become LLC members, so organizing as an LLC can enable a business to attract investors from other countries. (Many nations—including France, Germany, Japan, and places in Latin America—have particular business forms that provide for limited liability much like an LLC.)

## 17–1e Disadvantages of the LLC

The main disadvantage of the LLC is that state LLC statutes are not uniform. Therefore, businesses that operate in more than one state may not receive consistent treatment in these states.

Generally, most states apply to a foreign LLC (an LLC formed in another state) the law of the state where the LLC was formed. Difficulties can arise, though, when one state's court must interpret and apply another state's laws.

## 17–2 LLC Management and Operation

The members of an LLC have considerable flexibility in managing and operating the business. Here, we discuss management options, fiduciary duties owed, and the operating agreement and general operating procedures of LLCs.

### 17–2a Management of an LLC

Basically, LLC members have two options for managing the firm, as shown in Exhibit 17–1. The firm can be either a "member-managed" LLC or a "manager-managed" LLC. Most state LLC statutes and the ULLCA

**EXHIBIT 17–1 Management of an LLC**

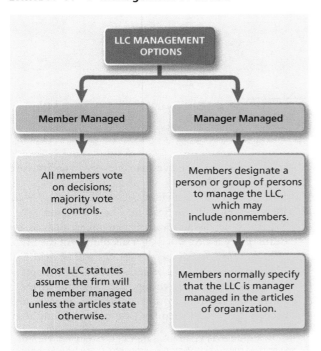

provide that unless the articles of organization specify otherwise, an LLC is assumed to be member managed [ULLCA 203(a)(6)].

In a *member-managed* LLC, all of the members participate in management, and decisions are made by majority vote [ULLCA 404(a)]. In a *manager-managed* LLC, the members designate a group of persons to manage the firm. The management group may consist of only members, both members and nonmembers, or only nonmembers.

However an LLC is managed, its managers need to be aware of the firm's potential liability under employment-discrimination laws. Those laws may sometimes extend to individuals who are not members of a protected class, as discussed in this chapter's *Managerial Strategy* feature.

### 17–2b Fiduciary Duties

Under the ULLCA, managers in a manager-managed LLC owe fiduciary duties (the duty of loyalty and the duty of care) to the LLC and its members [ULLCA 409(a), 409(h)]. (This same rule applies in corporate law—corporate directors and officers owe fiduciary duties to the corporation and its shareholders.) Because not all states have adopted the ULLCA, though, some state statutes provide that managers owe fiduciary duties only to the LLC and not to the LLC's members.

To whom the fiduciary duties are owed can affect the outcome of litigation. ■ **CASE IN POINT 17.5** Leslie Polk and his children, Yurii and Dusty Polk and Lezanne Proctor, formed Polk Plumbing, LLC, in Alabama. Dusty and Lezanne were managers of the LLC. Eventually, Yurii quit the firm. A year and a half later, Leslie "fired" Dusty and Lezanne and denied them access to the LLC's books and offices, but continued to operate the business.

Dusty and Lezanne filed a suit in an Alabama state court against Leslie, claiming breach of fiduciary duty. The trial court instructed the jury that it could not consider the plaintiffs' "firing" as part of their claim. Thus, although the jury found in their favor, it awarded only one dollar to each in damages. The plaintiffs appealed, and a state intermediate appellate court reversed and remanded the case for a new trial. Leslie did not have the authority under the terms of the LLC's operating agreement to fire two managers. The trial court had erred in not allowing the jury to consider the circumstances of Dusty and Lezanne's "firing" as part of their breach-of-fiduciary-duty claim.[6] ■

---

6. *Polk v. Polk*, 70 So.3d 363 (Ala.App. 2011).

## Can a Person Who Is Not a Member of a Protected Class Sue for Discrimination?

Under federal law and the laws of most states, discrimination in employment based on race, color, religion, national origin, gender, age, or disability is prohibited. Persons who are members of these protected classes can sue if they are subjected to discrimination. But can a person subjected to discrimination bring a lawsuit if he is not a member of a protected class, even though managers and other employees believe that he is? This somewhat unusual situation occurred in New Jersey.

### Courts in New Jersey

Myron Cowher worked at Carson & Roberts Site Construction & Engineering, Inc. For more than a year, at least two of his supervisors directed almost daily barrages of anti-Semitic remarks at him. They believed that he was Jewish, although his actual background was German-Irish and Lutheran.

Cowher brought a suit against the supervisors and the construction company, claiming a hostile work environment. The trial court, however, ruled that he did not have standing to sue under New Jersey law because he was not Jewish and, thus, was not a member of a protected class. Cowher appealed.

The appellate court disagreed with the trial court. The court ruled that if Cowher could prove that the discrimination "would not have occurred but for the perception that he was Jewish," his claim was covered by New Jersey's antidiscrimination law.[a] Thus, in the

appellate court's view, the nature of the discriminatory remarks—and not the actual characteristics of the plaintiff—determines whether the remarks are actionable.

Another New Jersey court followed the precedent set by the *Cowher* case to allow Shi-Juan Lin, a Chinese worker whose fiancé and child were black, to recover for racial discrimination. The employer created a hostile work environment by allowing Lin's supervisor to constantly use the "n" word at work. The employer knew that even though Lin was not black, she was hurt by the supervisor's remarks. Therefore, the court affirmed an administrative law judge's award of damages for pain and suffering, plus attorneys' fees.[b]

### Business Questions

1. *Should a manager for an LLC respond to employee complaints of discrimination any differently than a manager at a corporation, a partnership, or a sole proprietorship? Why or why not?*
2. *How can a company, whether an LLC or some other business form, reduce the chances of discrimination lawsuits?*

a. *Cowher v. Carson & Roberts*, 425 N.J.Super. 285, 40 A.3d 1171 (2012). See also, *Sheridan v. Egg Harbor Township Board of Education*, 2015 WL 9694404 (N.J.Sup.Ct. 2016), involving a plaintiff who alleged discrimination based on obesity.

b. *Lin v. Dane Construction Co.*, 2014 WL 8131876 (N.J.Super.A.D. 2015).

## 17–2c The LLC Operating Agreement

The members of an LLC can decide how to operate the various aspects of the business by forming an **operating agreement** [ULLCA 103(a)]. In many states, an operating agreement is not required for an LLC to exist, and if there is one, it need not be in writing. Generally, though, LLC members should protect their interests by creating a written operating agreement.

Operating agreements typically contain provisions relating to the following areas:

1. Management and how future managers will be chosen or removed. (Although most LLC statutes are silent on this issue, the ULLCA provides that members

may choose and remove managers by majority vote [ULLCA 404(b)(3)].)
2. How profits will be divided.
3. How membership interests may be transferred.
4. Whether the dissociation of a member, such as by death or departure, will trigger dissolution of the LLC.
5. Whether formal members' meetings will be held.
6. How voting rights will be apportioned. (If the agreement does not cover voting, LLC statutes in most states provide that voting rights are apportioned according to each member's capital contributions.[7]

7. In contrast, partners in a partnership generally have equal rights in management and equal voting rights unless they specify otherwise in their partnership agreement.

Some states provide that, in the absence of an agreement to the contrary, each member has one vote.)

If a dispute arises and there is no agreement covering the topic under dispute, the state LLC statute will govern the outcome. For instance, most LLC statutes provide that if the members have not specified how profits will be divided, they will be divided equally among the members. When an issue is not covered by an operating agreement or by an LLC statute, the courts often apply principles of partnership law.

Of course, LLC members are bound by the operating agreement that they make. ■ **CASE IN POINT 17.6** Green Cab Taxi and Disabled Service Association, LLC (Green Cab), is a taxi service company in King County, Washington. The operating agreement requires the members to pay weekly fees. Members who do not pay are in default and must return their taxi licenses to the company. In addition, a member in default cannot hold a seat on the board or withdraw from the company without the consent of all of the members.

When a disagreement arose among the members concerning the company's management, Shumet Mekonen and several others withdrew from the company without the other members' consent. Both sides continued to drive under the Green Cab name.

Mekonen's group filed a suit in a Washington state court against a group of members who had not withdrawn, including Dessie Zewdu. In part, the Mekonen group sought the right to operate as Green Cab. The court held that the plaintiffs could not represent themselves as Green Cab and ordered them to return their taxi licenses to the company. A state intermediate appellate court upheld the lower court's order to the plaintiffs to return their taxi licenses to Green Cab. Under the provisions of the company's operating agreement, the plaintiffs, as "defaulting members," had no right to retain and use the licenses.[8] ■

# 17–3 Dissociation and Dissolution of an LLC

Recall that in a partnership, *dissociation* occurs when a partner ceases to be associated in the carrying on of the partnership business. The same concept applies to LLCs. And like a partner in a partnership, a member of an LLC has the *power* to dissociate at any time but may not have the *right* to dissociate.

Under the ULLCA, the events that trigger a member's dissociation from an LLC are similar to the events causing a partner to be dissociated under the Uniform Partnership Act (UPA). These include voluntary withdrawal, expulsion by other members, court order, incompetence, bankruptcy, and death. Generally, if a member dies or otherwise dissociates from an LLC, the other members may continue to carry on the LLC business unless the operating agreement provides otherwise.

## 17–3a Effects of Dissociation

When a member dissociates from an LLC, he or she loses the right to participate in management and the right to act as an agent for the LLC. The member's duty of loyalty to the LLC also terminates, and the duty of care continues only with respect to events that occurred before dissociation.

Generally, the dissociated member also has a right to have his or her interest in the LLC bought out by the other members. The LLC's operating agreement may contain provisions establishing a buyout price. If it does not, the member's interest is usually purchased at fair value. In states that have adopted the ULLCA, the LLC must purchase the interest at fair value within 120 days after the dissociation.

If the member's dissociation violates the LLC's operating agreement, it is considered legally wrongful, and the dissociated member can be held liable for damages caused by the dissociation. ■ **EXAMPLE 17.7** Chadwick and Barrow are members in an LLC. Chadwick manages the accounts, and Barrow, who has many connections in the community and is a skilled investor, brings in the business. If Barrow wrongfully dissociates from the LLC, the LLC's business will suffer, and Chadwick can hold Barrow liable for the loss of business resulting from her withdrawal. ■

## 17–3b Dissolution

Regardless of whether a member's dissociation was wrongful or rightful, normally the dissociated member has no right to force the LLC to dissolve. The remaining members can opt either to continue or to dissolve the business.

Members can also stipulate in their operating agreement that certain events will cause dissolution, or they can agree that they have the power to dissolve the LLC by vote. As with partnerships, a court can order an LLC to be dissolved in certain circumstances. For instance, a court might order dissolution when the members have engaged in illegal or oppressive conduct, or when it is no longer feasible to carry on the business.

---

8. *Mekonen v. Zewdu*, 179 Wash.App. 1042 (2014).

■ **CASE IN POINT 17.8** Three men—Walter Perkins, Gary Fordham, and David Thompson—formed Venture Sales, LLC, to develop a subdivision in Petal, Mississippi. Each of them contributed land and funds, resulting in total holdings of 466 acres of land and about $158,000 in cash.

Perkins, who was working as an assistant coach for the Cleveland Browns, trusted Fordham and Thompson to develop the property. More than ten years later, however, they still had not done so, although they had formed two other LLCs and developed two other subdivisions in the area.

Fordham and Thompson claimed that they did not know when they could develop Venture's property and suggested selling it at a discounted price, but Perkins disagreed. Perkins then sought a judicial dissolution of Venture Sales. The court ordered the dissolution. Because Venture Sales was not meeting the economic purpose for which it was established (developing a subdivision), continuing the business was impracticable.[9] ■

A judge's exercise of discretion to order the dissolution of an LLC was disputed in the following case.

---

9. *Venture Sales, LLC v. Perkins*, 86 So.3d 910 (Miss.Sup. 2012).

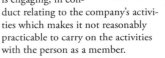

## Case Analysis 17.2

# Reese v. Newman
District of Columbia Court of Appeals, 131 A.3d 880 (2016).

### In the Language of the Court
*KING*, Senior Judge:

* * * Allison Reese and * * * Nicole Newman were co-owners of ANR Construction Management, LLC * * *. Following disputes over management of the company, Newman notified Reese in writing that she intended to * * * dissolve and wind-up the LLC. Reese did not want to dissolve the LLC but preferred that Newman simply be dissociated so that Reese could continue the business herself. Newman filed an action for judicial dissolution in [a District of Columbia court against Reese]. Reese filed a counterclaim for Newman's dissociation * * *. Following a jury trial, the jury * * * found grounds for both judicial dissolution and forced dissociation of Newman; the court, thereafter, ordered judicial dissolution of the LLC. * * * Reese appeals.

* * * *

Reese argues that the trial court erred when it purported to use discretion in choosing between dissolution of the LLC, as proposed by Newman, and forcing dissociation of Newman from the LLC, as proposed by Reese. Reese argues that the [District of Columbia (D.C.)] statute [governing dissociation from an LLC] does not allow for any discretion by the court, and that, in fact, the statute mandates that the court order

dissociation of Newman based on the jury's findings.

In matters of statutory interpretation, we review the trial court's decision *de novo*. Our analysis starts with the plain language of the statute, as the general rule of statutory interpretation is that the intent of the lawmaker is to be found in the language that he has used. To that end, *the words of the statute should be construed according to their ordinary sense and with the meaning commonly attributed to them.* [Emphasis added.]

Reese argues that the court was required to dissociate Newman from the LLC under [D.C. Code] Section 29–806.02(5) which reads:

> A person *shall* be dissociated as a member from a limited liability company when:
> * * * *
> (5) On application by the company, the person is expelled as a member by judicial order because the person has:
> (A) Engaged, or is engaging, in wrongful conduct that has adversely and materially affected, or will adversely and materially affect, the company's activities and affairs;
> (B) Willfully or persistently committed, or is willfully and persistently committing, a material breach of the operating agreement or the person's duties or obligations under Section

> 29–804.09; or
> (C) Engaged in, or is engaging, in conduct relating to the company's activities which makes it not reasonably practicable to carry on the activities with the person as a member.

Reese's interpretation of the statute is that, upon application to the court by a company, a judge shall dissociate a member of an LLC, when that member commits any one of the actions described in subsections (5)(A)-(C).

* * * While the introductory language of Section 29–806.02 does use the word "shall"—that command is in no way directed at the trial judge. It reads, "a person shall be dissociated * * * when," and then goes on to recite fifteen separate circumstances describing different occasions when a person shall be dissociated from an LLC. That is to say, when one of the events described in subparagraphs (1) through (15) occurs, the member shall be dissociated. Subparagraph (5), however, is merely one instance for which a person shall be dissociated; that is, when and if a judge has ordered a member expelled because she finds that any conditions under (5)(A)-(C) have been established. In other words, the command in the introductory language is not directed at the trial judge, it is directed at all the circumstances set forth

*Case 17.2 Continues*

**Case 17.2 Continued**

in subparagraphs (1) through (15) * * * . There is nothing in the language of Section 29–806.02(5) that strips a judge of her discretion because it does not require the judge to expel the member if any of the enumerated conditions are established. In short, Section 29–806.02(5) means: *when a judge has used her discretion to expel a member of an LLC by judicial order, under any of the enumerated circumstances in (5)(A)-(C), that member shall be dissociated.*

* * * Although Reese argues that the language of the "dissociation" section of the District's code should be read as forcing the hand of a trial judge who finds grounds for dissociation, Reese attempts to read the "dissolution" section differently.

Reese differentiates the sections by pointing to the dissolution section's express authorization to order a remedy other than dissolution in Section 29–807.01(b) which provides: "in a proceeding brought under subsection (a)(5) of this section, the * * * Court may order a remedy other than dissolution." While we are satisfied that judicial dissolution of an LLC is discretionary under this statute, Reese's attempt to buttress [reinforce] her argument that Section 29–806.02(5) is compulsory by pointing to this express provision in the dissolution section and the absence of a similar express provision in the dissociation section is unavailing. First, * * * the only "shall" in the dissociation section is in the introductory language, and the same "shall" can be found in the same place, in the dissolution section: "a limited liability company is dissolved, and its activities and affairs *shall be wound up,* upon the occurrence of any of the following." If that language does not make the rest of the section mandatory in the dissolution section, and we are persuaded that it does not, it cannot be said that the "shall" in the introduction of the dissociation section does the opposite.

* * * *

In sum, we hold that Section 29–806.02(5) can only be interpreted to mean: when a judge finds that any of the events in (5)(A)-(C) have taken place, she may (*i.e.,* has discretion to) expel by judicial order a member of an LLC, and when a judge has done so the member shall be dissociated. *Moreover, when both grounds for dissociation of a member and dissolution of the LLC exist, the trial judge has discretion to choose either alternative.* [Emphasis added.]

Here, the jury * * * found that grounds were present for either outcome. The trial judge acknowledged that both options were on the table and then exercised her discretion in ordering that dissolution take place. We find no reason to disturb that order.

* * * *

Accordingly, the judgment in this appeal is therefore affirmed.

## Legal Reasoning Questions

1. What dispute gave rise to the action filed in the court in this case? How did that dispute lead to the issue on appeal?

2. What is the role of an appellate court when reviewing the exercise of discretion by a trial court?

3. Newman alleged that after she delivered her notice to dissolve ANR, Reese locked her out of the LLC's bank accounts, blocked her access to the LLC's files and e-mail, and ended her salary and health benefits. Did any of the jury's findings support these allegations? Explain.

## 17–3c Winding Up

When an LLC is dissolved, any members who did not wrongfully dissociate may participate in the winding up process. To wind up the business, members must collect, liquidate, and distribute the LLC's assets.

Members may preserve the assets for a reasonable time to optimize their return, and they continue to have the authority to perform reasonable acts in conjunction with winding up. In other words, the LLC will be bound by the reasonable acts of its members during the winding up process.

Once all of the LLC's assets have been sold, the proceeds are distributed. Debts to creditors are paid first (including debts owed to members who are creditors of the LLC). The members' capital contributions are returned next, and any remaining amounts are then distributed to members in equal shares or according to their operating agreement.

# 17–4 Limited Liability Partnerships

The **limited liability partnership (LLP)** is a hybrid form of business designed mostly for professionals who normally do business as partners in a partnership. Almost all of the states have enacted LLP statutes.

The major advantage of the LLP is that it allows a partnership to continue as a pass-through entity for tax purposes but limits the personal liability of the partners. The LLP is especially attractive for professional service firms and family businesses. All of the "Big Four" accounting firms—the four largest international accountancy and professional services firms—are organized as LLPs, including Ernst & Young, LLP, and Pricewaterhouse Coopers, LLP.

### 17–4a Formation of an LLP

LLPs must be formed and operated in compliance with state statutes, which may include provisions of the Uniform Partnership Act (UPA). The appropriate form must be filed with a central state agency, usually the secretary of state's office, and the business's name must include either "Limited Liability Partnership" or "LLP" [UPA 1001, 1002]. An LLP must file an annual report with the state to remain qualified as an LLP in that state [UPA 1003].

In most states, it is relatively easy to convert a traditional partnership into an LLP because the firm's basic organizational structure remains the same. Additionally, all of the statutory and common law rules governing partnerships still apply, apart from those modified by the LLP statute. Normally, LLP statutes are simply amendments to a state's already existing partnership law.

### 17–4b Liability in an LLP

An LLP allows professionals, such as attorneys and accountants, to avoid personal liability for the malpractice of other partners. Of course, a partner in an LLP is still liable for her or his own wrongful acts, such as negligence. Also liable is the partner who supervised the individual who committed a wrongful act. (This generally is true for all types of partners and partnerships, not just LLPs.)

■ **EXAMPLE 17.9** Five lawyers operate a law firm as an LLP. One of the attorneys, Dan Kolcher, is sued for malpractice and loses. The firm's malpractice insurance is insufficient to pay the judgment. If the firm had been organized as a traditional (general) partnership, the personal assets of the other attorneys could be used to satisfy the obligation. Because the firm is organized as an LLP, however, no other partner at the firm can be held *personally* liable for Kolcher's malpractice, unless she or he acted as Kolcher's supervisor. In the absence of a supervisor, only Kolcher's personal assets can be used to satisfy the judgment. ■

Although LLP statutes vary from state to state, generally each state statute limits the liability of partners in some way. For instance, Delaware law protects each innocent partner from the "debts and obligations of the partnership arising from negligence, wrongful acts, or misconduct."

The UPA more broadly exempts partners in an LLP from personal liability for any partnership obligation, "whether arising in contract, tort, or otherwise" [UPA 306(c)].

**Liability outside the State of Formation** When an LLP formed in one state wants to do business in another state, it may be required to file a statement of foreign qualification in the second state [UPA 1102]. A question sometimes arises as to which law applies if the LLP statutes in the two states provide different liability protection. Most states apply the law of the state in which the LLP was formed, even when the firm does business in another state, which is also the rule under UPA 1101.

**Sharing Liability among Partners** When more than one partner in an LLP commits malpractice, there is a question as to how liability should be shared. Is each partner jointly and severally liable for the entire result, as a general partner would be in most states?

Some states provide instead for proportionate liability—that is, for separate determinations of the negligence of the partners. ■ **EXAMPLE 17.10** Accountants Zach and Lyla are partners in an LLP, with Zach supervising Lyla. Lyla negligently fails to file a tax return for a client, Centaur Tools. Centaur files a suit against Zach and Lyla. Under a proportionate liability statute, Zach will be liable for no more than his portion of the responsibility for the missed tax deadline. In a state that does not allow for proportionate liability, Zach can be held liable for the entire loss. ■

### 17–4c Family Limited Liability Partnerships

A **family limited liability partnership (FLLP)** is a limited liability partnership in which the partners are related to each other—for instance, as spouses or siblings. A person acting in a fiduciary capacity for persons so related can also be a partner. All of the partners must be natural persons or be acting in a fiduciary capacity for the benefit of natural persons.

Probably the most significant use of the FLLP form of business organization is in agriculture by family-owned farms. The FLLP offers the same advantages as other LLPs with certain additional advantages. For instance, in Iowa, FLLPs are exempt from real estate transfer taxes when partnership real estate is transferred among partners.[10]

---

10. Iowa Statutes Section 428A.2.

## 17–5 Limited Partnerships

We now look at a business organizational form that limits the liability of *some* of its owners—the **limited partnership (LP).** Limited partnerships originated in medieval Europe and have been in existence in the United States since the early 1800s. Today, most states and the District of Columbia have adopted laws based on the Revised Uniform Limited Partnership Act (RULPA).

Limited partnerships differ from traditional (general) partnerships in several ways. Exhibit 17–2 compares the characteristics of general and limited partnerships.[11]

---

11. Under the UPA, a general partnership can be converted into a limited partnership and vice versa [UPA 902, 903]. The UPA also provides for the merger of a general partnership with one or more general or limited partnerships [UPA 905].

A limited partnership consists of at least one **general partner** and one or more **limited partners**. A general partner assumes management responsibility for the partnership and has full responsibility for the partnership and for all its debts. A limited partner contributes cash or other property and owns an interest in the firm but is not involved in management responsibilities. A limited partner is not personally liable for partnership debts beyond the amount of his or her investment. If a limited partner takes part in the management of the business, however, she or he may forfeit that limited liability.

In the following case, two firms—a corporation and a limited partnership—were involved in the construction of a residential development. One individual served as the president of the corporation and the sole general partner of the partnership. In addition, he took charge of the activities at the construction site. How did this individual's status affect his responsibility for those activities?

**Case 17.3**

# DeWine v. Valley View Enterprises, Inc.

Court of Appeals of Ohio, Eleventh District, Trumbull County, 2015 –Ohio– 1222, ___ Ohio App.3d ___, ___ N.E.2d ___ (2015).

**Background and Facts** Valley View Enterprises, Inc., built Pine Lakes Golf Club and Estates in Trumbull County, Ohio, in two phases—Phase I and Phase II. Valley View Properties, Ltd., a limited partnership, cut out the roadways and constructed sewer, water, and storm-water lines with water inlets for the development. Joseph Ferrara was the owner and the president of Valley View Enterprises and the sole general partner of Valley View Properties. Ferrara failed to obtain the proper permits for the development work in a timely manner and failed to comply with their requirements once they had been obtained.

Michael DeWine, the state's attorney general, filed a lawsuit in an Ohio court against the Valley View entities and Ferrara, alleging violations of the state's water pollution control laws and seeking civil penalties. The court entered a judgment in the defendants' favor, holding with respect to Ferrara that "a corporate officer cannot be held liable merely by virtue of his status as a corporate officer." DeWine appealed.

### In the Language of the Court
Timothy J. *CANNON*, P.J. [Presiding Judge]
\* \* \* \*

Here, the state sought civil penalties from three entities: the property owner and Phase II permit holder, Valley View Properties, Ltd.; the Phase I permit holder, Valley View Enterprises, Inc.; and the sole general partner of the property owner, Mr. Ferrara.

\* \* \* The state alleges the trial court erred in its finding that "Valley View Properties is the only party against whom civil penalties can be assessed." The trial court also found Mr. Ferrara was not liable based on his "good faith" actions and Valley View Enterprises, Inc. was not liable because it had no relationship to Pine Lakes Estates; [and] the state failed to present evidence that Mr. Ferrara ordered activities that caused pollution.

\* \* \* Although the trial court found that Valley View Enterprises, Inc. had no relationship to Pine Lake Estates, the evidence establishes that Valley View Enterprises, Inc. applied for and was granted the [Phase I] Permit and, as the permittee, was required to ensure compliance with the permit. The [Phase I]

**Case 17.3 Continues**

**Case 17.3 Continued**

Permit explicitly states, "the permittee must comply with all conditions of this permit, any permit non-compliance constitutes a violation of [state law]." Additionally, * * * *the evidence demonstrates that Mr. Ferrara personally was in charge of the activities performed at the sites; authorized the construction activities at the sites; and failed to obtain necessary certifications and permits.* [Emphasis added.]

Moreover, the trial court's finding that "a corporate officer cannot be held liable merely by virtue of his status as a corporate officer" is erroneous and not supported by the evidence. Admittedly, Mr. Ferrara is the sole general partner of Valley View Properties, Ltd., an Ohio limited partnership. He is not, in relation to Valley View Properties, Ltd., a "corporate officer." Therefore, he is not, in the course of his conduct as the general partner of that limited partnership, entitled to the insulation from liability of a corporate officer.

**Decision and Remedy** *A state intermediate appellate court reversed the lower court's judgment in favor of the defendants. With respect to Ferrara's status in relation to Valley View Properties, he was the general partner and therefore not "entitled to the insulation from liability of a corporate officer." On remand, the trial court was to determine the number of violations established by the state and to issue and apportion penalties among the liable parties.*

**Critical Thinking**

- **Legal Environment** *How are the penalties likely to be apportioned among the three defendants? Explain.*

## 17–5a Formation of an LP

In contrast to the private and informal agreement that usually suffices to form a general partnership, the formation of a limited partnership is a public and formal proceeding. The partners must strictly follow statutory requirements. Not only must a limited partnership have at least one general partner and one limited partner, but the partners must also sign a **certificate of limited partnership.**

The certificate of limited partnership must include certain information, including the name, mailing address, and capital contribution of each general and limited partner. The certificate must be filed with the designated state official—under the RULPA, the secretary of state. The certificate is usually open to public inspection.

## 17–5b Liabilities of Partners in an LP

General partners are personally liable to the partnership's creditors. Thus, at least one general partner is necessary in a limited partnership so that someone has personal liability. This policy can be circumvented in states that allow a corporation to be the general partner in a partnership. Because the corporation has limited liability by virtue of corporation statutes, if a corporation is the general partner, no one in the limited partnership has personal liability.

The liability of a limited partner, as mentioned, is limited to the capital that she or he contributes or agrees to contribute to the partnership [RULPA 502]. Limited partners enjoy this limited liability only so long as they do not participate in management [RULPA 303].

A limited partner who participates in management will be just as liable as a general partner to any creditor who transacts business with the limited partnership. Liability arises when the creditor believes, based on the limited partner's conduct, that the limited partner is a general partner [RULPA 303]. The extent to which a limited partner can engage in management before being exposed to liability is not always clear, however.

## 17–5c Rights and Duties in a Limited Partnership

With the exception of the right to participate in management, limited partners have essentially the same rights as general partners. Limited partners have a right of access to the partnership's books and to information regarding partnership business.

On dissolution of the partnership, limited partners are entitled to a return of their contributions in accordance with the partnership certificate [RULPA 201(a)(10)]. They can also assign their interests subject to the certificate [RULPA 702, 704]. In addition, they can sue an

**EXHIBIT 17–2  A Comparison of General Partnerships and Limited Partnerships**

| | GENERAL PARTNERSHIP (UPA) | LIMITED PARTNERSHIP (RULPA) |
|---|---|---|
| **Creation** | By agreement of two or more persons to carry on a business as co-owners for profit. | By agreement of two or more persons to carry on a business as co-owners for profit. Must include one or more general partners and one or more limited partners. Filing of a certificate with the secretary of state is required. |
| **Sharing of Profits and Losses** | By agreement. In the absence of agreement, profits are shared equally by the partners, and losses are shared in the same ratio as profits. | Profits are shared as required in the certificate agreement, and losses are shared likewise, up to the amount of the limited partners' capital contributions. In the absence of a provision in the certificate agreement, profits and losses are shared on the basis of percentages of capital contributions. |
| **Liability** | Unlimited personal liability of all partners. | Unlimited personal liability of all general partners; limited partners liable only to the extent of their capital contributions. |
| **Capital Contribution** | No minimum or mandatory amount; set by agreement. | Set by agreement. |
| **Management** | By agreement. In the absence of agreement, all partners have an equal voice. | Only the general partner (or the general partners). Limited partners have no voice or else are subject to liability as general partners (but only if a third party has reason to believe that the limited partner is a general partner). A limited partner may act as an agent or employee of the partnership and vote on amending the certificate or on the sale or dissolution of the partnership. |
| **Duration** | Terminated by agreement of the partners, but can continue to do business even when a partner dissociates from the partnership. | Terminated by agreement in the certificate or by retirement, death, or mental incompetence of a general partner in the absence of the right of the other general partners to continue the partnership. Death of a limited partner does not terminate the partnership, unless he or she is the only remaining limited partner. |
| **Distribution of Assets on Liquidation— Order of Priorities** | 1. Payment of debts, including those owed to partner and nonpartner creditors.<br>2. Return of capital contributions and distribution of profit to partners. | 1. Outside creditors and partner creditors.<br>2. Partners and former partners entitled to distributions of partnership assets.<br>3. Unless otherwise agreed, return of capital contributions and distribution of profit to partners. |

outside party on behalf of the firm if the general partners with authority to do so have refused to file suit [RULPA 1001].

## 17–5d Dissociation and Dissolution

A general partner has the power to voluntarily dissociate, or withdraw, from a limited partnership unless the partnership agreement specifies otherwise. Under the RULPA, a limited partner can withdraw from the partnership by giving six months' notice, unless the partnership agreement specifies a term. In reality, though, most limited partnership agreements do specify a term, which eliminates the limited partner's right to withdraw. Also, some states have passed laws prohibiting the withdrawal of limited partners.

**Events That Cause Dissociation** In a limited partnership, a general partner's voluntary dissociation from the firm normally will lead to dissolution *unless* all partners agree to continue the business. Similarly, the bankruptcy, retirement, death, or mental incompetence of a general partner will cause the dissociation of that partner and the dissolution of the limited partnership unless the other members agree to continue the firm [RULPA 801].

Bankruptcy of a limited partner, however, does not dissolve the partnership unless it causes the bankruptcy of the firm. In addition, death or an assignment of the interest (right to receive distributions) of a limited partner does not dissolve a limited partnership [RULPA 702, 704, 705]. A limited partnership can be dissolved by court decree [RULPA 802].

**Distribution of Assets** On dissolution, creditors' claims, including those of partners who are creditors, take first priority. After that, partners and former partners receive unpaid distributions of partnership assets. Unless otherwise agreed, they are also entitled to a return of their contributions in the proportions in which they share in distributions [RULPA 804].

**Valuation of Assets** Disputes commonly arise about how the partnership's assets should be valued and distributed

and whether the business should be sold. ■ **CASE IN POINT 17.11** Actor Kevin Costner was a limited partner in Midnight Star Enterprises, LP, which runs a casino, bar, and restaurant in South Dakota. There were two other limited partners, Carla and Francis Caneva, who owned a small percentage of the partnership (3.25 units each) and received salaries for managing its operations. Another company owned by Costner, Midnight Star Enterprises, Limited (MSEL), was the general partner. Costner thus controlled a majority of the partnership (93.5 units).

When communications broke down between the partners, MSEL asked a court to dissolve the partnership. MSEL's accountant determined that the firm's fair market value was $3.1 million. The Canevas presented evidence that a competitor would buy the business for $6.2 million. The Canevas wanted the court to force Costner to either buy the business for that price within ten days or sell it on the open market to the highest bidder. Ultimately, the state's highest court held in favor of Costner. A partner cannot force the sale of a limited partnership when the other partners want to continue the business. The court also accepted the $3.1 million buyout price of MSEL's accountant and ordered Costner to pay the Canevas the value of their 6.5 partnership units.[12] ■

## 17–5e Limited Liability Limited Partnerships

A **limited liability limited partnership (LLLP)** differs from a limited partnership in that a general partner in an LLLP has the same liability as a limited partner in a limited partnership. In other words, the liability of all partners is limited to the amount of their investments in the firm.

A few states provide expressly for LLLPs.[13] In states that do not provide for LLLPs but do allow for limited partnerships and limited liability partnerships, a limited partnership should probably still be able to register with the state as an LLLP.

---

12. *In re Dissolution of Midnight Star Enterprises, LP*, 2006 SD 98, 724 N.W.2d 334 (S.D.Sup.Ct. 2006).
13. The states that provide for LLLPs include Colorado, Delaware, Florida, Georgia, Kentucky, Maryland, Nevada, Texas, and Virginia.

## Reviewing: Limited Liability Business Forms

The city of Papagos, Arizona, had a deteriorating bridge in need of repair on a prominent public roadway. The city posted notices seeking proposals for an artistic bridge design and reconstruction. Davidson Masonry, LLC, which was owned and managed by Carl Davidson and his wife, Marilyn Rowe, decided to submit a bid to create a decorative concrete structure that incorporated artistic metalwork. They contacted Shana Lafayette, a local sculptor who specialized in large-scale metal creations, to help them design the bridge. The city selected their bridge design and awarded them the contract for a commission of $184,000.

Davidson Masonry and Lafayette then entered into an agreement to work together on the bridge project. Davidson Masonry agreed to install and pay for concrete and structural work, and Lafayette agreed to install the metalwork at her expense. They agreed that overall profits would be split, with 25 percent going to Lafayette and 75 percent going to Davidson Masonry. Lafayette designed numerous metal sculptures of trout that were incorporated into colorful decorative concrete forms designed by Rowe. Davidson performed the structural engineering. The group worked together successfully until the completion of the project. Using the information presented in the chapter, answer the following questions.

1. Would Davidson Masonry automatically be taxed as a partnership or a corporation?
2. Is Davidson Masonry member managed or manager managed?
3. Suppose that during construction, Lafayette asked Carl Davidson to rent space in a warehouse that was close to the bridge so that she could work on her sculptures near the site where they would eventually be installed. Carl Davidson signed the rental contract in his own name rather than the name of the LLC. The other members of Davidson Masonry were not aware of the rental agreement. In this situation, would a court likely hold that Davidson Masonry was liable on the contract that Carl Davidson had entered? Why or why not?
4. Now suppose that Rowe has an argument with her husband and wants to withdraw from being a member of Davidson Masonry. What is the term for such a withdrawal, and what effect would it have on the LLC?

**Debate This** . . . *Because LLCs are essentially just partnerships with limited liability for members, all partnership laws should apply.*

## Terms and Concepts

articles of organization 372
certificate of limited
    partnership 382
family limited liability partnership
    (FLLP) 380
general partner 381

limited liability company
    (LLC) 371
limited liability limited partnership
    (LLLP) 384
limited liability partnership
    (LLP) 379

limited partner 381
limited partnership (LP) 381
member 371
operating agreement 376

## Issue Spotters

1. Gabriel, Harris, and Ida are members of Jeweled Watches, LLC. What are their options with respect to the management of their firm? (See *LLC Management and Operation*.)

2. Dorinda, Luis, and Elizabeth form a limited partnership. Dorinda is a general partner, and Luis and Elizabeth are limited partners. If Elizabeth is petitioned into involuntary bankruptcy, does that constitute a dissolution of the limited partnership? (See *Limited Partnerships*.)

• **Check your answers to the Issue Spotters against the answers provided in Appendix D at the end of this text.**

# Business Scenarios

**17–1. Limited Liability Companies.** John, Lesa, and Tabir form a limited liability company. John contributes 60 percent of the capital, and Lesa and Tabir each contribute 20 percent. Nothing is decided about how profits will be divided. John assumes that he will be entitled to 60 percent of the profits, in accordance with his contribution. Lesa and Tabir, however, assume that the profits will be divided equally. A dispute over the profits arises, and ultimately a court has to decide the issue. What law will the court apply? In most states, what will result? How could this dispute have been avoided in the first place? Discuss fully. (See *The Limited Liability Company.*)

**17–2. Diversity Jurisdiction and Limited Liability Companies.** Joe, a resident of New Jersey, wants to open a restaurant. He asks Kay, his friend, an experienced attorney and a New Yorker, for her business and legal advice in exchange for a 20 percent ownership interest in the restaurant. Kay helps Joe negotiate a lease for the restaurant premises and advises Joe to organize the business as a limited liability company (LLC).

Joe forms Café Olé, LLC, and with Kay's help, obtains financing. Then, the night before the restaurant opens, Joe tells Kay that he is "cutting her out of the deal." The restaurant proves to be a success. Kay wants to file a suit in a federal district court against Joe and the LLC. Can a federal court exercise jurisdiction over the parties based on diversity of citizenship? Explain. (See *The Limited Liability Company.*)

# Business Case Problems

**17–3. Limited Liability Companies.** Coco Investments, LLC, and other investors participated in a condominium conversion project to be managed by Zamir Manager River Terrace, LLC. The participants entered into a new LLC agreement for the project. The investors subsequently complained that Zamir had failed to disclose its plans for dramatic changes involving higher-than-expected construction costs and delays. They also claimed that Zamir had failed to provide financial information and had restructured loans in a manner that allowed Zamir representatives to avoid personal liability. The investors sued Zamir on various grounds, including breach of contract and breach of fiduciary duty. Zamir moved for summary judgment. How should the court rule? Explain. [*Coco Investments, LLC v. Zamir Manager River Terrace, LLC,* 26 Misc.3d 1231, 907 N.Y.S.2d 99 (2010)] (See *The Limited Liability Company.*)

**17–4. LLC Dissolution.** Walter Van Houten and John King formed 1545 Ocean Avenue, LLC, with each managing 50 percent of the business. Its purpose was to renovate an existing building and construct a new commercial building. Van Houten and King quarreled over many aspects of the work on the properties. King claimed that Van Houten paid the contractors too much for the work performed. As the projects neared completion, King demanded that the LLC be dissolved and that Van Houten agree to a buyout. Because the parties could not agree on a buyout, King sued for dissolution. The trial court enjoined (prevented) further work on the projects until the dispute was settled. As the ground for dissolution, King cited the fights over management decisions. There was no claim of fraud or frustration of purpose. The trial court ordered that the LLC be dissolved, and Van Houten appealed. Should either of the owners be forced to dissolve the LLC before the completion of its purpose—that is, before the building projects are finished? Explain. [*In re 1545 Ocean Avenue, LLC,* 893 N.Y.S.2d 590 (N.Y.A.D. 2 Dept. 2010)] (See *Dissociation and Dissolution of an LLC.*)

**17–5. Business Case Problem with Sample Answer— LLC Operation.** After Hurricane Katrina struck the Gulf  Coast, James Williford, Patricia Mosser, Marquetta Smith, and Michael Floyd formed Bluewater Logistics, LLC, to bid on construction contracts. Under Mississippi law, every member of a member-managed LLC is entitled to participate in managing the business. The operating agreement provided for a "super majority" 75 percent vote to remove a member who "has either committed a felony or under any other circumstances that would jeopardize the company status" as a contractor. After Bluewater had completed more than $5 million in contracts, Smith told Williford that she, Mosser, and Floyd were exercising their "super majority" vote to fire him. No reason was provided. Williford sued Bluewater and the other members. Did Smith, Mosser, and Floyd breach the state LLC statute, their fiduciary duties, or the Bluewater operating agreements? Discuss. [*Bluewater Logistics, LLC v. Williford,* 55 So.3d 148 (Miss.Sup.Ct. 2011)] (See *LLC Management and Operation.*)

- **For a sample answer to Problem 17–5, go to Appendix E at the end of this text.**

**17–6. Jurisdictional Requirements.** Fadal Machining Centers, LLC, and MAG Industrial Automation Centers, LLC, sued a New Jersey–based corporation, Mid-Atlantic CNC, Inc., in federal district court. Ten percent of MAG was owned by SP MAG Holdings, a Delaware LLC. SP MAG had six members, including a Delaware limited partnership called Silver Point Capital Fund and a Delaware LLC called SPCP Group III. In turn, Silver Point and SPCP Group had a common member, Robert O'Shea, who was a New Jersey citizen. Assuming that the amount in controversy exceeds $75,000, does the district court have diversity jurisdiction? Why or why not? [*Fadal Machining Centers, LLC v. Mid-Atlantic CNC, Inc.,* 464 Fed.Appx. 672 (9th Cir. 2012)] (See *The Limited Liability Company.*)

**17–7. Jurisdictional Requirements.** Siloam Springs Hotel, LLC, operates a Hampton Inn in Siloam Springs, Arkansas. Siloam bought insurance from Century Surety Co. to cover the hotel. When guests suffered injuries due to a leak of carbon monoxide from the heating element of an indoor swimming pool, Siloam filed a claim with Century. Century denied coverage, which Siloam disputed. Century asked a federal district court to resolve the dispute. In asserting that the federal court had jurisdiction, Century noted that the amount in controversy exceeded $75,000 and that the parties had complete diversity of citizenship. Century is "a corporation organized under the laws of Ohio, with its principal place of business in Michigan," and Siloam is "a corporation organized under the laws of Oklahoma, with its principal place of business in Arkansas." Can the court exercise diversity jurisdiction in this case? Discuss. [*Siloam Springs Hotel, L.L.C. v. Century Surety Co.*, 781 F.3d 1233 (10th Cir. 2015)] (See *The Limited Liability Company.*)

**17–8. A Question of Ethics—Limited Liability Companies.** *Blushing Brides, LLC, a publisher of wedding planning*  *magazines in Columbus, Ohio, opened an account with Gray Printing Co. in July 2000. On behalf of Blushing Brides, Louis Zacks, the firm's member-manager, signed a credit agreement that identified the firm as the "purchaser" and required payment within thirty days. Despite the agreement, Blushing Brides typically took up to six months to pay the full amount for its orders. Gray printed and shipped 10,000 copies of a fall/winter 2001 issue for Blushing Brides but had not been paid when the firm ordered 15,000 copies of a spring/summer 2002 issue. Gray refused to print the new order without an assurance of payment. On May 22, Zacks signed a promissory note payable to Gray within thirty days for $14,778,* plus interest at 6 percent per year. Gray printed the new order but by October had been paid only $7,500. Gray filed a suit in an Ohio state court against Blushing Brides and Zacks to collect the balance. [Gray Printing Co. v. Blushing Brides, LLC, 2006 -Ohio- 1656 (Ohio App. 2006)] (See The Limited Liability Company.)

**(a)** Under what circumstances is a member of an LLC liable for the firm's debts? In this case, is Zacks personally liable under the credit agreement for the unpaid amount on Blushing Brides' account? Did Zacks's promissory note affect the parties' liability on the account? Explain.

**(b)** Should a member of an LLC assume an ethical responsibility to meet the obligations of the firm? Discuss.

**(c)** Gray shipped only 10,000 copies of the spring/summer 2002 issue of Blushing Brides' magazine, waiting for the publisher to identify a destination for the other 5,000 copies. The magazine had a retail price of $4.50 per copy. Did Gray have a legal or ethical duty to "mitigate the damages" by attempting to sell or otherwise distribute these copies itself? Why or why not?

**17–9. Special Case Analysis—LLC Dissolution.** Go to Case Analysis 17.2, *Reese v. Newman*. Read the excerpt and answer the following questions.

**(a) Issue:** Which party's choice between two alternatives was at the heart of the issue on the appeal of the *Reese* case?

**(b) Rule of Law:** What rules of interpretation did the appellate court use to construe the language of the statutes that created those alternatives?

**(c) Applying the Rule of Law:** How did the court construe the language of those statutes?

**(d) Conclusion:** How did the court's construction of that language lead to the result?

## Legal Reasoning Group Activity

**17–10. Fiduciary Duties in LLCs.** Newbury Properties Group owns, manages, and develops real property. Jerry Stoker and the Stoker Group, Inc. (the Stokers), also develop real property. Newbury entered into agreements with the Stokers concerning a large tract of property in Georgia. The parties formed Bellemare, LLC, to develop various parcels of the tract for residential purposes. The operating agreement of Bellemare indicated that "no Member shall be accountable to the LLC or to any other Member with respect to any other business or activity even if the business or activity competes with the LLC's business." Later, when the Newbury group contracted with other parties to develop parcels within the tract in competition with Bellemare, LLC, the Stokers sued, alleging breach of fiduciary duty. (See *LLC Management and Operation.*)

**(a)** The first group will discuss and outline the fiduciary duties that the members of an LLC owe to each other.

**(b)** The second group will determine whether the terms of an operating agreement can alter these fiduciary duties.

**(c)** The last group will decide in whose favor the court should rule in this situation.

# Answers to the *Issue Spotters*

**1.** *What are their options with respect to the management of their firm?* The members of a limited liability company (LLC) may designate a group to run their firm, in which situation the firm would be considered a manager-managed LLC. The group may include only members, only nonmembers, or members and nonmembers. If, instead, all members participate in management, the firm would be a member-managed LLC. In fact, unless the members agree otherwise, all members are considered to participate in the management of the firm.

**2.** *If Elizabeth is petitioned into involuntary bankruptcy, does that constitute a dissolution of the limited partnership?* Bankruptcy of the limited partnership itself causes dissolution, but bankruptcy of one of the limited partners does not dissolve the partnership unless it causes the bankruptcy of the firm. Therefore, Elizabeth's involuntary bankruptcy would not dissolve the firm.

# Sample Answers for *Business Case Problems with Sample Answer*

**Problem 17–5.** *LLC Operation.* Part of the attractiveness of an LLC as a form of business enterprise is its flexibility. The members can decide how to operate the business through an operating agreement. For example, the agreement can set forth procedures for choosing or removing members or managers.

Here, the Bluewater operating agreement provided for a "super majority" vote to remove a member under circumstances that would jeopardize the firm's contractor status. Thus, one Bluewater member could not unilaterally "fire" another member without providing a reason. In fact, a majority of the members could not terminate the other's interest in the firm without providing a reason. Moreover, the only acceptable reason would be a circumstance that undercut the firm's status as a contractor.

The flexibility of the LLC business form relates to its framework, not to its members' capacity to violate its operating agreement. In the actual case on which this problem is based, Smith attempted to "fire" Williford without providing a reason. In Williford's suit, the court issued a judgment in his favor.

# Chapter 14

# CHAPTER

# Corporations

The corporation is a creature of statute. A corporation is an artificial being, existing only in law and being neither tangible nor visible. Its existence generally depends on state law, although some corporations, especially public organizations, are created under federal law. Each state has its own body of corporate law, and these laws are not entirely uniform.

The Model Business Corporation Act (MBCA) is a codification of modern corporation law that has been influential in shaping state corporation statutes. Today, the majority of state statutes are guided by the most recent version of the MBCA, often referred to as the Revised Model Business Corporation Act (RMBCA).

Keep in mind, however, that there is considerable variation among the laws of states that have used the MBCA or the RMBCA as a basis for their statutes. In addition, several states do not follow either act. Consequently, individual state corporation laws should be relied on to determine corporate law rather than the MBCA or RMBCA.

## 18–1 Nature and Classification

A corporation is a legal entity created and recognized by state law. This business entity can have one or more owners (called shareholders), and it operates under a name distinct from the names of its owners. Both individuals and other businesses can be shareholders. The corporation substitutes itself for its shareholders when conducting corporate business and incurring liability. Its authority to act and the liability for its actions, however, are separate and apart from the shareholders who own it.

A corporation is recognized under U.S. law as a person—an artificial *legal person,* as opposed to a *natural person.* As a "person," it enjoys many of the same rights and privileges under state and federal law that U.S. citizens enjoy. For instance, corporations possess the same right of access to the courts as citizens and can sue or be sued. The constitutional guarantees of due process, free speech, and freedom from unreasonable searches and seizures also apply to corporations.

### 18–1a Corporate Personnel

In a corporation, the responsibility for the overall management of the firm is entrusted to a *board of directors,* whose members are elected by the shareholders. The board of directors makes the policy decisions and hires *corporate officers* and other employees to run the daily business operations.

When an individual purchases a share of stock in a corporation, that person becomes a shareholder and an owner of the corporation. Unlike the partners in a partnership, the body of shareholders can change constantly without affecting the continued existence of the corporation. A shareholder can sue the corporation, and the corporation can sue a shareholder. Additionally, under certain circumstances, a shareholder can sue on behalf of a corporation.

### 18–1b The Limited Liability of Shareholders

One of the key advantages of the corporate form is the limited liability of its owners. Normally, corporate shareholders are not personally liable for the obligations of the corporation beyond the extent of their investments.

In certain limited situations, however, a court can *pierce the corporate veil* and impose liability on shareholders for the corporation's obligations. Additionally, creditors often will not extend credit to small companies unless the shareholders assume personal liability, as guarantors, for corporate obligations.

## 18–1c Corporate Earnings and Taxation

When a corporation earns profits, it can either pass them on to shareholders in the form of **dividends** or retain them as profits. These **retained earnings,** if invested properly, will yield higher corporate profits in the future. In theory, higher profits will cause the price of the company's stock to rise. Individual shareholders can then reap the benefits in the capital gains they receive when they sell their stock.

**Corporate Taxation** Whether a corporation retains its profits or passes them on to the shareholders as dividends, those profits are subject to income taxation by various levels of government. Failure to pay taxes can lead to severe consequences. The state can suspend the organization's corporate status until the taxes are paid and can even dissolve the corporation for failing to pay taxes.

Another important aspect of corporate taxation is that corporate profits can be subject to double taxation. The company pays tax on its profits. Then, if the profits are passed on to the shareholders as dividends, the shareholders must also pay income tax on them. (This is true unless the dividends represent distributions of capital, which are returns of holders' investments in the stock of the company.) The corporation normally does not receive a tax deduction for dividends it distributes. This double-taxation feature is one of the major disadvantages of the corporate form.

**Holding Companies** Some U.S. corporations use holding companies to reduce or defer their U.S. income taxes. At its simplest, a **holding company** (sometimes referred to as a *parent company*) is a company whose business activity consists of holding shares in another company. Typically, the holding company is established in a low-tax or no-tax offshore jurisdiction, such as the Cayman Islands, Dubai, Hong Kong, Luxembourg, Monaco, or Panama.

Sometimes, a U.S. corporation sets up a holding company in a low-tax offshore environment and then transfers its cash, bonds, stocks, and other investments to the holding company. In general, any profits received by the holding company on these investments are taxed at the rate of the offshore jurisdiction where the company is registered. Once the profits are brought "onshore," though, they are taxed at the federal corporate income tax rate. Any payments received by the shareholders are also taxable at the full U.S. rates.

## 18–1d Criminal Acts

Under modern criminal law, a corporation may be held liable for the criminal acts of its agents and employees.

Although corporations cannot be imprisoned, they can be fined. (Of course, corporate directors and officers can be imprisoned.) In addition, under sentencing guidelines for crimes committed by corporate employees, corporations can face fines amounting to hundreds of millions of dollars.

## 18–1e Tort Liability

A corporation is liable for the torts committed by its agents or officers within the course and scope of their employment under the doctrine of *respondeat superior* (to be discussed in the agency chapter). The doctrine of *respondeat superior* applies to corporations in the same way as it does to other agency relationships.

■ **CASE IN POINT 18.1** Mark Bloom was an officer and a director of MB Investment Partners, Inc. (MB), at the time that he formed North Hills, LP, a stock investment fund. Bloom and other MB employees used MB's offices and equipment to administer investments in North Hills.

Later, investors in North Hills requested a full redemption of their investments. By that time, however, most of the funds that had been invested were gone. North Hills had, in fact, been a Ponzi scheme that Bloom had used to finance his lavish personal lifestyle, taking at least $20 million from North Hills for his personal use.

Barry Belmont and other North Hills investors filed a suit in a federal district court against MB, alleging fraud. The court held that MB was liable for Bloom's fraud. MB appealed, and the appellate court affirmed. Tort liability can be attributed to a corporation for the acts of its agent that were committed within the scope of the agent's employment.[1] ■

## 18–1f Classification of Corporations

The classification of a corporation normally depends on its location, purpose, and ownership characteristics, as described in the following subsections.

**Domestic, Foreign, and Alien Corporations** A corporation is referred to as a **domestic corporation** by its home state (the state in which it incorporates). A corporation formed in one state but doing business in another is referred to in the second state as a **foreign corporation.** A corporation formed in another country (say, Mexico) but doing business in the United States is referred to in the United States as an **alien corporation.**

A corporation does not have an automatic right to do business in a state other than its state of incorporation.

---

1. *Belmont v. MB Investment Partners, Inc.,* 708 F.3d 470 (3d Cir. 2013).

In some instances, it must obtain a *certificate of authority* in any state in which it plans to do business. Once the certificate has been issued, the corporation generally can exercise in that state all of the powers conferred on it by its home state. If a foreign corporation does business in a state without obtaining a certificate of authority, the state can impose substantial fines and sanctions on that corporation.

Note that most state statutes specify certain activities, such as soliciting orders via the Internet, that are not considered "doing business" within the state. For instance, a foreign corporation normally does not need a certificate of authority to sell goods or services via the Internet or by mail.

What constitutes doing business within a state? In the following case, the court answered that question.

**Case 18.1**

# Drake Manufacturing Co. v. Polyflow, Inc.

Superior Court of Pennsylvania, 2015 PA Super 16, 109 A.3d 250 (2015).

**Background and Facts** Drake Manufacturing Company, a Delaware corporation, entered into a contract to sell certain products to Polyflow, Inc., headquartered in Pennsylvania. Drake promised to ship the goods from Drake's plant in Sheffield, Pennsylvania, to Polyflow's place of business in Oaks, Pennsylvania, as well as to addresses in California, Canada, and Holland.

When Polyflow withheld payment of about $300,000 for some of the goods, Drake filed a breach of contract suit in a Pennsylvania state court against Polyflow seeking to collect the unpaid amount. But Drake had failed to obtain a certificate of authority to do business in Pennsylvania as a foreign corporation. Polyflow asserted that this failure to register with the state deprived Drake of the capacity to bring an action against Polyflow in the state's courts. The court issued a judgment in Drake's favor. Polyflow appealed.

## In the Language of the Court

Opinion by *JENKINS*, J. [Judge]:

* * * *

[15 Pennsylvania Consolidated Statutes (Pa.C.S.)] Section 4121 provides: "A foreign business corporation, before doing business in this Commonwealth, shall procure a certificate of authority to do so from the Department of State."

* * * Typical conduct requiring a certificate of authority includes maintaining an office to conduct local intrastate business [and] entering into contracts relating to local business or sales.

*A corporation is not "doing business" solely because it resorts to the courts of this Commonwealth to recover an indebtedness.* [Emphasis added.]

* * * *

[15 Pa.C.S.] Section 4141(a) provides in relevant part that "a nonqualified foreign business corporation doing business in this Commonwealth * * * shall not be permitted to maintain any action or proceeding in any court of this Commonwealth until the corporation has obtained a certificate of authority."

* * * *

* * * The evidence demonstrates that Drake failed to submit a certificate of authority into evidence prior to the verdict in violation of 15 Pa.C.S. Section 4121. Therefore, the trial court should not have permitted Drake to prosecute its action.

The trial court contends that Drake is exempt from the certificate of authority requirement because it merely commenced suit in Pennsylvania to collect a debt * * * . Drake did much more, however, than file suit or attempt to collect a debt. Drake maintains an office in Pennsylvania to conduct local business, conduct which typically requires a certificate of authority. Drake also entered into a contract with Polyflow, and * * * shipped couplings and portable swaging machines to Polyflow's place of business in Pennsylvania * * * . In short, *Drake's conduct was * * * regular, systematic, and extensive, * * * thus constituting the transaction of business and requiring Drake to obtain a certificate of authority.* [Emphasis added.]

We also hold that Drake needed a certificate of authority to sue Polyflow in Pennsylvania for Polyflow's failure to pay for out-of-state shipments in California, Canada and Holland. A foreign corporation that

Case 18.1 Continued

"does business" in Pennsylvania * * * must obtain a certificate in order to prosecute a lawsuit in this Commonwealth, regardless of whether the lawsuit itself concerns in-state conduct or out-of-state conduct.

**Decision and Remedy** *A state intermediate appellate court reversed the judgment in Drake's favor. Under Pennsylvania state statutes, Drake was required to obtain a certificate of authority to do business in that state. Drake failed to do so. The court should not have allowed Drake to prosecute its action against Polyflow.*

**Critical Thinking**

- **Legal Environment** *Why would the appellate court permit Polyflow to get away with not paying for delivered and presumably merchantable goods?*

**Public and Private Corporations** A **public corporation** is a corporation formed by the government to meet some political or governmental purpose. Cities and towns that incorporate are common examples. In addition, many federal government organizations, such as the U.S. Postal Service, the Tennessee Valley Authority, and AMTRAK, are public corporations.

Note that a public corporation is not the same as a **publicly held corporation**. A publicly held corporation (often called a *public company*) is any corporation whose shares are publicly traded in a securities market, such as the New York Stock Exchange or the NASDAQ.

Private corporations, in contrast, are created either wholly or in part for private benefit—that is, for profit. Most corporations are private. Although they may serve a public purpose, as a public electric or gas utility does, they are owned by private persons rather than by a government.[2]

---

2. The United States Supreme Court first recognized the property rights of private corporations and clarified the distinction between public and private corporations in the landmark case *Trustees of Dartmouth College v. Woodward*, 17 U.S. (4 Wheaton) 518, 4 L.Ed. 629 (1819).

**Nonprofit Corporations** Corporations formed for purposes other than making a profit are called *nonprofit* or *not-for-profit* corporations. Private hospitals, educational institutions, charities, and religious organizations, for instance, are frequently organized as nonprofit corporations. The nonprofit corporation is a convenient form of organization that allows various groups to own property and to form contracts without exposing the individual members to personal liability.

In some circumstances, a nonprofit corporation and its members may also be immune from liability for a personal injury caused by its negligence. Whether those circumstances were present in the following case was the question before the court.

Case Analysis 18.2

## Pantano v. Newark Museum

Superior Court of New Jersey, Appellate Division, __ A.3d __, 2016 WL 528771 (2016).

### In the Language of the Court

*PER CURIAM.*

* * * *

* * * Plaintiff [Loredana Pantano] slipped and fell on icy steps at an entrance to the [Newark] Museum, suffering injuries to her back. At the time, plaintiff was employed as an immigration attorney by La Casa de Don Pedro (La Casa), a nonprofit organization located in Newark [New Jersey]. Upon arrival at her office that day, plaintiff was told by La Casa's Director of Personal Development to go to the Museum for an educational panel discussion being held as part of La Casa's fortieth anniversary celebration.

* * * The event was one of several organized to celebrate and commemorate the organization's history and role in the development of Newark. Staff members were not directly engaged in fundraising, but they were told to mingle with those attending the event, some of whom were contributors to La Casa. The Museum charged La Casa a fee for the use of the facility, specifically an auditorium to be used by the panel and those in attendance.

The Museum is a nonprofit association organized exclusively for charitable, artistic, scientific, educational, historical

Case 18.2 Continues

**Case 18.2 Continued**

and cultural purposes * * * . It does, on occasion, rent its facilities to the public in order to generate income.

Plaintiff filed suit [in a New Jersey state court against the Museum] alleging the Museum was negligent in its maintenance of the premises. * * * The Museum moved for summary judgment, contending that plaintiff was a direct beneficiary of its charitable endeavors.

* * * * The judge granted the Museum's motion, and this appeal followed.

Plaintiff contends that she was not a beneficiary of the Museum's charitable purposes at the time of her fall because she was on the premises at the direction of her employer. We agree that pursuant to the [New Jersey Supreme] Court's holding in *Mayer v. Fairlawn Jewish Center*, 38 N.J. 549, 186 A.2d 274 (1962), plaintiff was not a direct recipient of the Museum's good works.

* * * *

In pertinent part, the [state Charitable Immunity Act (CIA)] provides:

> No nonprofit corporation * * * shall * * * be liable to respond in damages to any person who shall suffer damage from the negligence * * * of such corporation * * * where such person is a beneficiary, to whatever degree, of the works of such nonprofit corporation * * * ; provided, however, that such immunity from liability shall not extend to any

person * * * where such person is one unconcerned in and unrelated to and outside of the benefactions of such corporation.

The CIA serves two primary purposes. *First, immunity preserves a charity's assets. Second, immunity recognizes that a beneficiary of the services of a charitable organization has entered into a relationship that exempts the benefactor from liability.* [Emphasis added.]

* * * The established test for determining whether a party is a beneficiary of the works of a charity has two prongs. The first is that the institution pleading the immunity, at the time in question, was engaged in the performance of the charitable objectives it was organized to advance. The second is that the injured party must have been a direct recipient of those good works.

* * * *

As to the first prong, * * * a qualifying organization does not lose its statutory immunity merely because it charges money for its services, unless it makes a profit or collects fees for services totally unrelated to its organizational pursuits. * * * Hosting an educational panel discussion in the auditorium was entirely consistent with the Museum's charitable endeavors.

The second prong of the test * * * distinguishes between persons benefiting from the charity, and persons who contribute to the charity by virtue of their attendance or participation.

* * * *

In *Mayer*, * * * an employee of the Development Corporation for Israel was promoting the sale of bonds at a dinner on the premises of [Fairlawn Jewish Center, the defendant, when he sustained an injury].

* * * *

* * * He was there in fulfillment of his function and obligation as an employee to engage in the employer's work at the direction of the employer, and not for the purpose of receiving personally the philanthropy of the Center. Under the circumstances present he was a stranger to the charity and the [CIA did] not stand in the way of recovery.

* * * *

* * * *[Thus, under the CIA,] to be a beneficiary under the second prong, the injured party must be a direct recipient of the Museum's good works. Only those unconcerned in and unrelated to the benefactions of the organization are not beneficiaries.* [Emphasis added.]

* * * *

As an intermediate appellate court, we are bound to follow and enforce the decisions of the Supreme Court. Under [*Mayer*], plaintiff, as an employee of La Casa who was ordered on the day of her fall to attend the panel discussion at the Museum, was not a direct beneficiary of the Museum's charitable endeavors.

We therefore reverse the order granting summary judgment to the Museum and remand the matter.

## Legal Reasoning Questions

1. How do the purposes of the CIA support each other?
2. Can a person be a direct beneficiary of a nonprofit's good works even though the person is on the nonprofit's premises under the direction of a third party? Explain.
3. Suppose that the museum had not been hosting an educational panel in its auditorium but instead had rented the facility to an organization for a sales conference. Would the result have been different? Discuss.

**Close Corporations** Most corporate enterprises in the United States fall into the category of close corporations. A **close corporation** is one whose shares are held by relatively few persons, often members of a family. Close corporations are also referred to as *closely held, family,* or *privately held* corporations.

Usually, the members of the small group constituting the shareholders of a close corporation are personally known to each other. Because the number of shareholders is so small, there is no trading market for the shares. In practice, a close corporation is often operated like a partnership.

The statutes in many states allow close corporations to depart significantly from certain formalities required by traditional corporation law.[3] Under the RMBCA, close corporations have considerable flexibility in determining their operating rules [RMBCA 7.32]. If all of a corporation's shareholders agree in writing, the corporation can operate without directors and bylaws. In addition, the corporation can operate without annual or special shareholders' or directors' meetings, stock certificates, or formal records of shareholders' or directors' decisions.[4]

**Management of Close Corporations.** Management of a close corporation resembles that of a sole proprietorship or a partnership, in that control is held by a single shareholder or a tightly knit group of shareholders. As a corporation, however, the firm must meet all specific legal requirements set forth in state statutes.

To prevent a majority shareholder from dominating the company, a close corporation may require that more than a simple majority of the directors approve any action taken by the board. In a larger corporation, such a requirement would typically apply only to extraordinary actions (such as selling all the corporate assets) and not to ordinary business decisions.

**Transfer of Shares in Close Corporations.** By definition, a close corporation has a small number of shareholders. Thus, the transfer of one shareholder's shares to someone else can cause serious management problems. The other shareholders may find themselves required to share control with someone they do not know or like. ■ **EXAMPLE 18.2** Three siblings, Sherry, Karen, and Henry Johnson, are the only shareholders of Johnson's Car Wash, Inc. Henry wants to sell his shares, but Sherry and Karen do not want him to sell the shares to a third person unknown to them. ■

To avoid this situation, a close corporation can restrict the transferability of shares to outside persons. Shareholders can be required to offer their shares to the corporation or to the other shareholders before selling them to an outside purchaser. In fact, in a few states close corporations must transfer shares in this manner under state statutes.

One way the close corporation can effect restrictions on transferability is by spelling them out in a **shareholder agreement.** A shareholder agreement can also provide for proportional control when one of the original shareholders dies. The decedent's shares of stock in the corporation can be divided in such a way that the proportionate holdings of the survivors, and thus their proportionate control, will be maintained.

**Misappropriation of Close Corporation Funds.** Sometimes, a majority shareholder in a close corporation takes advantage of his or her position and misappropriates company funds. In such situations, the normal remedy for the injured minority shareholders is to have their shares appraised and to be paid the fair market value for them.

**S Corporations** A close corporation that meets the qualifying requirements specified in Subchapter S of the Internal Revenue Code can choose to operate as an **S corporation.** (A corporation will automatically be taxed under Subchapter C unless it elects S corporation status.) If a corporation has S corporation status, it can avoid the imposition of income taxes at the corporate level while retaining many of the advantages of a corporation, particularly limited liability. Among the numerous requirements for S corporation status, the following are the most important:

1. The corporation must be a domestic corporation.
2. The corporation must not be a member of an affiliated group of corporations.
3. The shareholders must be individuals, estates, or certain trusts and tax-exempt organizations. Partnerships and nonqualifying trusts cannot be shareholders. Corporations can be shareholders under certain circumstances.
4. The corporation must have no more than one hundred shareholders.
5. The corporation must have only one class of stock, although it is not necessary that all shareholders have the same voting rights.
6. No shareholder of the corporation may be a nonresident alien.

An S corporation is treated differently than a regular corporation for tax purposes. An S corporation is taxed like a partnership, so the corporate income passes through to the shareholders, who pay personal income tax on it. This treatment enables the S corporation to avoid the double taxation imposed on regular corporations. In addition, the shareholders' tax brackets may be lower than the tax bracket that the corporation would have been in if the tax had been imposed at the corporate level.

In spite of these benefits, the S corporation has lost much of its appeal. The newer limited liability business forms (such as LLCs, LPs, and LLPs) offer similar tax advantages and greater flexibility.

---

3. In some states, such as Maryland, a close corporation need not have a board of directors.
4. Shareholders cannot agree, however, to eliminate certain rights of shareholders, such as the right to inspect corporate records or the right to bring *derivative actions* (lawsuits on behalf of the corporation).

**Professional Corporations** Professionals such as physicians, lawyers, dentists, and accountants can incorporate. A professional corporation is typically identified by the letters *P.C.* (professional corporation), *S.C.* (service corporation), or *P.A.* (professional association).

In general, the laws governing the formation and operation of professional corporations are similar to those governing ordinary business corporations. There are some differences in terms of liability, however, because the shareholder-owners are professionals who are held to a higher standard of conduct. For liability purposes, some courts treat professional corporations somewhat like partnerships and hold each professional liable for malpractice committed within the scope of the business by others in the firm.

**Benefit Corporations** A growing number of states have enacted legislation that creates a relatively new corporate form called a *benefit corporation*. A **benefit corporation** is a for-profit corporation that seeks to have a material positive impact on society and the environment. Benefit corporations differ from traditional corporations in the following ways:

1. *Purpose.* Although the corporation is designed to make a profit, its purpose is to benefit the public as a whole. (In contrast, the purpose of an ordinary business corporation is to provide long-term shareholder value.) The directors of a benefit corporation must, during the decision-making process, consider the impact of their decisions on society and the environment.
2. *Accountability.* Shareholders of a benefit corporation determine whether the company has achieved a material positive impact. Shareholders also have a right of private action, called a *benefit enforcement proceeding*, enabling them to sue the corporation if it fails to pursue or create public benefit.
3. *Transparency.* A benefit corporation must issue an annual benefit report on its overall social and environmental performance that uses a recognized third-party standard to assess its performance. The report must be delivered to the shareholders and posted on a public Web site.

# 18–2 Formation and Powers

Many of today's largest companies started as sole proprietorships or partnerships. They converted to corporate entities as they grew because they needed to obtain additional capital by issuing shares of stock. Incorporating a business is much simpler today than it was twenty years ago, and many states allow businesses to incorporate via the Internet.

## 18–2a Promotional Activities

In the past, preliminary steps were taken to organize and promote a business prior to incorporating. Contracts were made with investors and others on behalf of the future corporation. Today, due to the relative ease of forming a corporation in most states, persons incorporating their business rarely, if ever, engage in preliminary promotional activities.

Nevertheless, businesspersons should understand that they are personally liable for any preincorporation contracts made with investors, accountants, or others on behalf of the future corporation. Personal liability continues until the newly formed corporation assumes liability for the preincorporation contracts through a novation.

## 18–2b Incorporation Procedures

Each state has its own set of incorporation procedures. Most often, they are listed on the secretary of state's Web site. Generally, however, all incorporators follow several basic steps, discussed next.

**Select the State of Incorporation** Because state corporate laws differ, individuals seeking to incorporate a business may look for the states that offer the most advantageous tax or other provisions. Many corporations, for instance, have chosen to incorporate in Delaware because it has historically had the least restrictive laws, along with provisions that favor corporate management. For reasons of convenience and cost, though, businesses often choose to incorporate in the state in which the corporation's business will primarily be conducted.

**Secure the Corporate Name** The choice of a corporate name is subject to state approval to ensure against duplication or deception. Most state statutes require a search to confirm that the chosen corporate name is available. A new corporation's name cannot be the same as, or deceptively similar to, the name of an existing corporation doing business within the state. All states require the corporation's name to include the word *Corporation (Corp.)*, *Incorporated (Inc.)*, *Company (Co.)*, or *Limited (Ltd.).*[5]

**Prepare the Articles of Incorporation** The primary document needed to incorporate a business is the **articles of incorporation**. The articles include basic

---

5. Failure to use one of these terms to disclose corporate status may be grounds for holding an individual incorporator liable for corporate contracts under agency law.

information about the corporation and serve as a primary source of authority for its future organization and business functions. The person or persons who execute (sign) the articles are the *incorporators.*

Articles of incorporation vary widely depending on the jurisdiction and the size and type of the corporation. Generally, though, the articles *must* include the following information [RMBCA 2.02]:

1. The name of the corporation.
2. The number of shares of stock the corporation is authorized to issue [RMBCA 2.02(a)]. (Large corporations often also state a par value for each share, such as $0.20 per share, and specify the various types or classes of stock authorized for issuance.)
3. The name and street address of the corporation's initial registered agent and registered office. The registered agent is the person who can receive legal documents (such as orders to appear in court) on behalf of the corporation. The registered office is usually the main corporate office.
4. The name and address of each incorporator.

In addition, the articles *may* set forth other information, such as the names and addresses of the initial members of the board of directors and the duration and purpose of the corporation. A corporation has perpetual existence unless the articles state otherwise. A corporation can be formed for any lawful purpose. The RMBCA does not require the articles to include a specific statement of purpose. Consequently, the articles often include only a general statement of purpose. By not mentioning specifics, the corporation avoids the need for future amendments to the corporate articles [RMBCA 2.02(b) (2)(i), 3.01]. Similarly, the articles do not provide much detail about the firm's operations, which are spelled out in the company's *bylaws* (discussed shortly).

**File the Articles with the State** Once the articles of incorporation have been prepared and signed, they are sent to the appropriate state official, usually the secretary of state, along with the required filing fee. In most states, the secretary of state then stamps the articles "Filed" and returns a copy of the articles to the incorporators. Once this occurs, the corporation officially exists.

## 18–2c First Organizational Meeting to Adopt Bylaws

After incorporation, the first organizational meeting must be held. If the articles of incorporation named the initial board of directors, then the directors, by majority vote, call the meeting. If the articles did not name the directors (as is typical), then the incorporators hold the meeting to elect the directors and complete any other business necessary.

Usually, the most important function of this meeting is the adoption of **bylaws,** which are the internal rules of management for the corporation. The bylaws cannot conflict with the state corporation statute or the articles of incorporation [RMBCA 2.06]. Under the RMBCA, the shareholders may amend or repeal the bylaws. The board of directors may also amend or repeal the bylaws, unless the articles of incorporation or provisions of the state corporation statute reserve this power to the shareholders [RMBCA 10.20].

The bylaws typically describe such matters as voting requirements for shareholders, the election of the board of directors, and the methods of replacing directors. Bylaws also frequently outline the manner and time of holding shareholders' and board meetings.

## 18–2d Improper Incorporation

The procedures for incorporation are very specific. If they are not followed precisely, others may be able to challenge the existence of the corporation. Errors in incorporation procedures can become important when, for instance, a third party who is attempting to enforce a contract or bring a suit for a tort injury learns of them.

**De Jure Corporations** If a corporation has substantially complied with all conditions precedent to incorporation, the corporation is said to have *de jure* (rightful and lawful) existence. In most states and under RMBCA 2.03(b), the secretary of state's filing of the articles of incorporation is conclusive proof that all mandatory statutory provisions have been met [RMBCA 2.03(b)].

Sometimes, the incorporators fail to comply with all statutory mandates. If the defect is minor, such as an incorrect address listed on the articles of incorporation, most courts will overlook the defect and find that a *de jure* corporation exists.

**De Facto Corporations** If the defect in formation is substantial, such as a corporation's failure to hold an organizational meeting to adopt bylaws, the outcome will vary depending on the jurisdiction. Some states, including Mississippi, New York, Ohio, and Oklahoma, recognize the common law doctrine of *de facto* corporation. In those states, the courts will treat a corporation as a legal corporation despite a defect in its formation if the following three requirements are met:

1. A state statute exists under which the corporation can be validly incorporated.

**2.** The parties have made a good faith attempt to comply with the statute.

**3.** The parties have already undertaken to do business as a corporation.

Many state courts, however, have interpreted their states' version of the RMBCA as abolishing the common law doctrine of *de facto* corporations. These states include Alaska, Arizona, Minnesota, New Mexico, Oregon, South Dakota, Tennessee, Utah, and Washington, as well as the District of Columbia. In those jurisdictions, if there is a substantial defect in complying with the incorporation statute, the corporation does not legally exist, and the incorporators are personally liable.

**Corporation by Estoppel** Sometimes, a business association holds itself out to others as being a corporation when it has made no attempt to incorporate. In those situations, the firm normally will be estopped (prevented) from denying corporate status in a lawsuit by a third party. The estoppel doctrine most commonly applies when a third party contracts with an entity that claims to be a corporation but has not filed articles of incorporation. It may also apply when a third party contracts with a person claiming to be an agent of a corporation that does not in fact exist.

When justice requires, courts in some states will treat an alleged corporation as if it were an actual corporation for the purpose of determining rights and liabilities in particular circumstances. Recognition of corporate status does not extend beyond the resolution of the problem at hand.

■ **CASE IN POINT 18.3** W.P. Media, Inc., and Alabama MBA, Inc., agreed to form a wireless Internet services company. W.P. Media was to create a wireless network, and Alabama MBA was to contribute the capital. Hugh Brown signed the parties' contract on behalf of Alabama MBA as the chair of its board. At the time, however, Alabama MBA's articles of incorporation had not yet been filed. Brown filed the articles of incorporation the following year.

Later, Brown and Alabama MBA filed a suit alleging that W.P. Media had breached their contract by not building the wireless network. W.P. Media contended that Alabama MBA had not existed as a corporation when the agreement was signed and thus the agreement was void. The Supreme Court of Alabama held that because W.P. Media had treated Alabama MBA as a corporation, W.P. Media was estopped from denying Alabama MBA's corporate existence.[6] ■

---

6. *Brown v. W.P. Media, Inc.*, 17 So.3d 1167 (2009).

## 18–2e Corporate Financing

Part of the process of corporate formation involves corporate financing. Corporations normally are financed by the issuance and sale of corporate **securities**, which include stocks and bonds. **Stocks**, or *equity securities*, represent the purchase of ownership in the business firm. **Bonds**, or *debt securities*, represent the borrowing of funds by firms (and governments).

**Bonds** Bonds are issued by business firms and by governments at all levels as evidence of the funds they are borrowing from investors. Bonds normally have a designated *maturity date*—the date when the principal, or face amount, of the bond is returned to the investor. They are sometimes referred to as *fixed-income securities* because their owners (that is, the creditors) receive fixed-dollar interest payments, usually semiannually, during the period of time before maturity. Because debt financing represents a legal obligation on the part of the corporation, various features and terms of a particular bond issue are specified in a lending agreement.

Of course, not all debt is in the form of debt securities. For instance, some debt is in the form of accounts payable and notes payable, which typically are short-term debts. Bonds are simply a way for the corporation to split up its long-term debt so that it can be more easily marketed.

**Stocks** Issuing stocks is another way that corporations can obtain financing. Basically, stocks represent ownership in a business firm. The true ownership of a corporation is represented by **common stock**, which provides a proportionate interest in the corporation with regard to (1) control (voting rights), (2) earnings, and (3) net assets. A shareholder's interest is generally in proportion to the number of shares he or she owns out of the total number of shares issued.

The issuing firm is not obligated to return a principal amount per share to each holder of common stock, because no firm can ensure that the market price per share of its common stock will not decline over time. The issuing firm also does not have to guarantee a dividend. Indeed, some corporations never pay dividends. Holders of common stock are investors who assume a *residual* position in the overall financial structure of a business. In terms of receiving payment for their investments, they are last in line.

**Preferred stock** is stock with *preferences*. Holders of preferred stock usually have priority over holders of common stock as to dividends and payment on dissolution of the corporation but frequently do not have the right to vote. Holders of preferred stock have a stronger position than common shareholders with respect to dividends and claims on assets, but they will not share in the full prosperity of the firm if it grows successfully over time. Preferred stockholders do receive fixed dividends periodically, however, and they may benefit to some extent from changes in the market price of the shares.

**Venture Capital** Start-up businesses and high-risk enterprises often obtain venture capital financing. **Venture capital** is capital provided by professional, outside investors (*venture capitalists*, usually groups of wealthy investors and securities firms) to new business ventures. Venture capital investments are high risk—the investors must be willing to lose all of their invested funds—but offer the potential for well-above-average returns at some point in the future.

To obtain venture capital financing, the start-up business typically gives up a share of its ownership to the venture capitalists. Venture capitalists also may provide managerial and technical expertise, and they nearly always are given some control over the new company's decisions. Many Internet-based companies, such as Google, were initially financed by venture capital.

**Private Equity Capital** Private equity firms obtain their capital from wealthy investors in private markets. The firms use their **private equity capital** to invest in existing—often, publicly traded—corporations. Usually, they buy an entire corporation and then reorganize it. Sometimes, divisions of the purchased company are sold off to pay down debt. Ultimately, the private equity firm may sell shares in the reorganized (and perhaps more profitable) company to the public in an *initial public offering* (IPO). In this way, the private equity firm can make profits by selling its shares in the company.

**Crowdfunding** Start-up businesses can also attempt to obtain financing through *crowdfunding*. **Crowdfunding** is a cooperative activity in which people network and pool funds and other resources via the Internet to assist a cause or invest in a venture. Sometimes, crowdfunding is used to raise funds for charitable purposes, such as disaster relief, but increasingly it is being used to finance budding entrepreneurs.

In 2016, new Securities and Exchange Commission (SEC) rules went into effect to allow companies to offer and sell securities through crowdfunding. The rules removed a decades-old ban on public solicitation for private investments, which means that companies can advertise investment opportunities to the general public. According to the SEC, the new rules are intended to help

smaller companies raise capital while providing investors with additional protections. Companies are required to make specific disclosures and are limited to raising $1 million a year through crowdfunding.

### 18–2f Corporate Powers

When a corporation is created, the express and implied powers necessary to achieve its purpose also come into existence.

**Express Powers** The express powers of a corporation are found in its articles of incorporation, in the law of the state of incorporation, and in the state and federal constitutions. Corporate bylaws and the resolutions of the corporation's board of directors also establish express powers.

The following order of priority is used if a conflict arises among the various documents involving a corporation:

1. The U.S. Constitution.
2. State constitutions.
3. State statutes.
4. The articles of incorporation.
5. Bylaws.
6. Resolutions of the board of directors.

It is important that the bylaws set forth the specific operating rules of the corporation. State corporation statutes frequently provide default rules that apply if the company's bylaws are silent on an issue.

On occasion, the U.S. government steps in to challenge what a corporation may consider one of its express powers. This chapter's *Global Insight* discusses a dispute between the government and Microsoft Corporation over a demand that the company provide the government with access to e-mail stored in servers on foreign soil.

**Implied Powers** When a corporation is created, it acquires certain implied powers. Barring express constitutional, statutory, or other prohibitions, the corporation has the implied power to perform all acts reasonably necessary to accomplish its corporate purposes. For this reason, a corporation has the implied power to borrow and lend funds within certain limits and to extend credit to parties with whom it has contracts.

Most often, the president or chief executive officer of the corporation signs the necessary documents on behalf of the corporation. Corporate officers such as these have the implied power to bind the corporation in matters directly connected with the *ordinary* business affairs of the enterprise.

There is a limit to what a corporate officer can do, though. A corporate officer does not have the authority

## GLOBAL INSIGHT    Does Cloud Computing Have a Nationality?

Everyone has heard of "the cloud," and most people use it for the storage of their digital data—photos, e-mails, music, documents, and just about anything else. Not surprisingly, major global digital players like Apple, Amazon, Google, and Microsoft have spent billions to create "clouds" of servers all over the world. In the clouds are stored confidential, organized, and secure data. The revenues generated by the U.S. cloud computing industry exceed $100 billion a year. But is the long-term picture for such revenues in doubt?

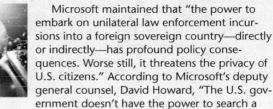

### Microsoft Battles and the Global Cloud Industry Waits

The U.S. government issued a warrant to Microsoft to produce e-mails related to a narcotics case from a Hotmail account. That account was hosted in a Microsoft cloud location in Ireland. Microsoft refused, but a magistrate judge in the Southern District of New York confirmed the government's right to the Ireland-located e-mails.[a] On appeal to a U.S. district court, Microsoft again lost.[b] Microsoft appealed to the U.S. Court of Appeals for the Second Circuit and won in 2016.[c]

---

a. *In re Warrant to Search a Certain E-Mail Account Controlled and Maintained by Microsoft Corp.*, 15 F.Supp.3d 466 (S.D.N.Y. 2014).

b. *In re Warrant to Search a Certain E-Mail Account Controlled and Maintained by Microsoft Corp.*, 2014 WL 4629624 (S.D.N.Y. 2014).

c. *In Matter of Warrant to Search a Certain E-Mail Account Controlled and Maintained by Microsoft Corp.*, ___ F.3d ___, 2016 WL 3770056 (2d Cir. 2016).

Microsoft maintained that "the power to embark on unilateral law enforcement incursions into a foreign sovereign country—directly or indirectly—has profound policy consequences. Worse still, it threatens the privacy of U.S. citizens." According to Microsoft's deputy general counsel, David Howard, "The U.S. government doesn't have the power to search a home in another country, nor should it have the power search the content of e-mails stored overseas."

A number of organizations apparently agreed with Microsoft. The ACLU, Apple, eBay, the Electronic Frontier Foundation, Fox News, the Irish government, and National Public Radio all filed "friend of the court" briefs in support of Microsoft's position. The federal appellate court was persuaded that the warrant could not be enforced extraterritorially.

### Impact on the Industry

More was at stake in this case than the issues Microsoft identified. If Microsoft had ultimately lost, some industry experts predicted that U.S. technology companies would lose up to $35 billion a year from their cloud storage business. Foreign corporations and individuals would no longer trust U.S. companies to keep their data secret.

**Critical Thinking** *The law underlying the case against Microsoft is the Electronic Communications Privacy Act, which was enacted three years before the invention of the World Wide Web. Should that law still apply today? Why or why not?*

---

to bind the corporation to an action that will greatly affect the corporate purpose or undertaking, such as the sale of substantial corporate assets.

***Ultra Vires* Doctrine** The term ***ultra vires*** means "beyond the power." In corporate law, acts of a corporation that are beyond its express or implied powers are *ultra vires* acts. In the past, most cases dealing with *ultra vires* acts involved contracts made for unauthorized purposes. Now, because the articles of incorporation of most private corporations do not state a specific purpose, the *ultra vires* doctrine has declined in importance.

Today, cases that allege *ultra vires* acts usually involve nonprofit corporations or municipal (public) corporations. ■**CASE IN POINT 18.4** Four men formed a nonprofit corporation to create the Armenian Genocide Museum & Memorial (AGM&M). The bylaws appointed them as trustees (similar to corporate directors) for life. One of the trustees, Gerard L. Cafesjian, became the chair and president of AGM&M. Eventually, the relationship among the trustees deteriorated, and Cafesjian resigned.

The corporation then brought a suit claiming that Cafesjian had engaged in numerous *ultra vires* acts, self-dealing, and mismanagement. Although the bylaws required an 80 percent affirmative vote of the trustees to take action, Cafesjian had taken many actions without the board's approval. He had also entered into contracts for real estate transactions in which he had a personal interest. Because Cafesjian had taken actions that exceeded his authority and had failed to follow rules set forth in the bylaws, the court ruled that the corporation could go forward with its suit.[7] ■

---

7. *Armenian Assembly of America, Inc. v. Cafesjian*, 692 F.Supp.2d 20 (D.C. Cir. 2010).

**Remedies for *Ultra Vires* Acts** Under Section 3.04 of the RMBCA, shareholders can seek an injunction from a court to prevent (or stop) the corporation from engaging in *ultra vires* acts. The attorney general in the state of incorporation can also bring an action to obtain an injunction against the *ultra vires* transactions or to seek dissolution of the corporation. The corporation or its shareholders (on behalf of the corporation) can seek damages from the officers and directors who were responsible for the *ultra vires* acts.

## 18–3 Piercing the Corporate Veil

Occasionally, the owners use a corporate entity to perpetrate a fraud, circumvent the law, or in some other way accomplish an illegitimate objective. In these situations, the courts will ignore the corporate structure by **piercing the corporate veil** and exposing the shareholders to personal liability [RMBCA 2.04].

Generally, courts pierce the veil when the corporate privilege is abused for personal benefit or when the corporate business is treated so carelessly that it is indistinguishable from that of a controlling shareholder. When the facts show that great injustice would result from a shareholder's use of a corporation to avoid individual responsibility, a court will look behind the corporate structure to the individual shareholders.

### 18–3a Factors That Lead Courts to Pierce the Corporate Veil

The following are some of the factors that frequently cause the courts to pierce the corporate veil:

1. A party is tricked or misled into dealing with the corporation rather than the individual.
2. The corporation is set up never to make a profit or always to be insolvent. Alternatively, it is too thinly capitalized—that is, it has insufficient capital at the time it is formed to meet its prospective debts or potential liabilities.
3. The corporation is formed to evade an existing legal obligation.
4. Statutory corporate formalities, such as holding required corporation meetings, are not followed.
5. Personal and corporate interests are mixed together, or **commingled,** to such an extent that the corporation has no separate identity.

State corporation codes usually do not prohibit a shareholder from lending funds to her or his corporation.

Courts will scrutinize such a transaction closely if the loan comes from an officer, director, or majority shareholder, however. Loans from persons who control the corporation must be made in good faith and for fair value.

■ **CASE IN POINT 18.5** Dog House Investments, LLC, operated a dog "camp" in Nashville, Tennessee. Dog House leased the property from Teal Properties, Inc., which was owned by Jerry Teal, its sole shareholder. Under the lease, Teal Properties promised to repair damage from fire or other causes that rendered the property "untenantable" (unusable). Following a flood, Dog House notified Jerry that the property was untenantable. Jerry assured Dog House that the flood damage was covered by insurance but took no steps to restore the property. The parties then agreed that Dog House would undertake the repairs and be reimbursed by Teal Properties.

Dog House spent $39,000 to repair the damage and submitted invoices for reimbursement. Teal Properties recovered $40,000 from its insurance company but did not pay Dog House. Close to bankruptcy, Dog House filed a suit in a Tennessee state court against Teal Properties and Jerry. The court pierced the corporate veil and held Jerry personally liable for the repair costs. Jerry appealed, but a state intermediate appellate court affirmed. The reviewing court found that piercing the corporate veil was appropriate because Jerry did not maintain an arms-length relationship with the corporation. Teal Properties owned no property and had no assets—it merely received rent that was immediately paid to Jerry Teal.[8] ■

### 18–3b A Potential Problem for Close Corporations

The potential for corporate assets to be used for personal benefit is especially great in a close corporation. In such a corporation, the separate status of the corporate entity and the shareholders (often family members) must be carefully preserved. Practices that invite trouble for a close corporation include the commingling of corporate and personal funds and the shareholders' continuous personal use of corporate property (for instance, vehicles).

Typically, courts are reluctant to hold shareholders in close corporations personally liable for corporate obligations unless there is some evidence of fraud or wrongdoing. ■ **CASE IN POINT 18.6** Pip, Jimmy, and Theodore Brennan are brothers and shareholders of Brennan's, Inc., which owns and operates New Orleans's famous Brennan's Restaurant. As a close corporation, Brennan's, Inc.,

---

8. *Dog House Investments, LLC v. Teal Properties, Inc.*, 448 S.W.3d 905 (Tenn.App. 2014).

did not hold formal corporate meetings with agendas and minutes, but it did maintain corporate books, hold corporate bank accounts, and file corporate tax returns.

The Brennan brothers retained attorney Edward Colbert to represent them in a family matter, and the attorney's bills were sent to the restaurant and paid from the corporate account. Later, when Brennan's, Inc., sued Colbert for malpractice, Colbert argued that the court should pierce the corporate veil because the Brennan brothers did not observe corporate formalities. The court refused to do so, however, because there was no evidence of fraud, malfeasance, or other wrongdoing by the Brennan brothers. There is no requirement for small, close corporations to operate with the formality usually expected of larger corporations.[9] ■

### 18–3c The Alter-Ego Theory

Sometimes, courts pierce the corporate veil under the theory that the corporation was not operated as a separate entity. Rather, it was just another side (the *alter ego*) of the individual or group that actually controlled the corporation. This is called the alter-ego theory.

The alter-ego theory is applied when a corporation is so dominated and controlled by an individual (or group) that the separate identities of the person (or group) and the corporation are no longer distinct. Courts use the alter-ego theory to avoid injustice or fraud that would result if wrongdoers were allowed to hide behind the protection of limited liability.

■ **CASE IN POINT 18.7** Steiner Electric Company (Steiner) is an Illinois corporation that sells electrical products. Steiner sold goods to Delta Equipment Company and Sackett Systems, Inc., on credit. Both Delta and Sackett were owned and controlled by a single shareholder—Leonard J. Maniscalco. Steiner was not fully paid for the products it sold on credit to Delta and Sackett. Eventually, Steiner sued Delta and won a default judgment, but by that time, Delta had been dissolved. Steiner then asked a state court to pierce the corporate veil and hold Maniscalco liable for the debts of the two companies, claiming the companies were merely Maniscalco's alter egos.

The court agreed and held Maniscalco liable. Delta and Sackett were inadequately capitalized, transactions were not properly documented, funds were commingled, and corporate formalities were not observed. Maniscalco had consistently treated both companies in such a manner that they were, in practice, his alter egos.[10] ■

## 18–4 Directors and Officers

Corporate directors, officers, and shareholders all play different roles within the corporate entity. Sometimes, actions that may benefit the corporation as a whole do not coincide with the separate interests of the individuals making up the corporation. In such situations, it is important to know the rights and duties of all participants in the corporate enterprise.

### 18–4a Directors

The board of directors is the ultimate authority in every corporation. Directors have responsibility for all policy-making decisions necessary to the management of all corporate affairs. No *individual* director, however, can act to bind the corporation. The directors must act as a body in carrying out routine corporate business. The board selects and removes the corporate officers, determines the capital structure of the corporation, and declares dividends. Each director has one vote, and customarily the majority rules.

Few qualifications are required for directors. Only a handful of states impose minimum age and residency requirements. A director may be a shareholder, but that is not necessary (unless the articles of incorporation or bylaws require ownership interest).

**Election of Directors** Subject to statutory limitations, the number of directors is set forth in the corporation's articles or bylaws. Historically, the minimum number of directors has been three, but today many states permit fewer. Normally, the incorporators appoint the first board of directors at the time the corporation is created, or the directors are named in the articles of incorporation. The initial board serves until the first annual shareholders' meeting. Subsequent directors are elected by a majority vote of the shareholders.

A director usually serves for a term of one year—from annual meeting to annual meeting. Most state statutes permit longer and staggered terms. A common practice is to elect one-third of the board members each year for a three-year term. In this way, there is greater management continuity.

A director can be removed *for cause*—that is, for failing to perform a required duty—either as specified in the articles or bylaws or by shareholder action. When a vacancy on the board occurs, such as if a director dies or resigns, either the shareholders or the board itself can fill the vacant position, depending on state law and the bylaws. Note that even when an election is authorized,

---

**9.** *Brennan's, Inc. v. Colbert,* 85 So.3d 787 (La.App.4th Cir. 2012).
**10.** *Steiner Electric Co. v. Maniscalco,* 51 N.E.3d 45, 2016 IL App (1st) 132023 (2016).

a court can invalidate the results if the directors have attempted to manipulate the election in order to reduce the shareholders' influence.

**Compensation of Directors** In the past, corporate directors were rarely compensated. Today, directors are often paid at least nominal sums. In large corporations, they may receive more substantial compensation because of the time, work, effort, and especially risk involved.

Most states permit the corporate articles or bylaws to authorize compensation for directors. In fact, the RMBCA states that unless the articles or bylaws provide otherwise, the board itself may set the directors' compensation [RMBCA 8.11]. Directors also receive indirect benefits, such as business contacts and prestige, and other rewards, such as stock options.

In many corporations, directors are also chief corporate officers (such as president or chief executive officer) and receive compensation in their managerial positions. A director who is also an officer of the corporation is referred to as an **inside director,** whereas a director who does not hold a management position is an **outside director.** Typically, a corporation's board of directors includes both inside and outside directors.

**Board of Directors' Meetings** The board of directors conducts business by holding formal meetings with recorded minutes. The dates of regular meetings are usually established in the articles or bylaws or by board resolution, and ordinarily no further notice is required. Special meetings can be called as well, with notice sent to all directors.

Most states allow directors to participate in board of directors' meetings from remote locations. Directors can participate via telephone, Web conferencing, or Skype, provided that all the directors can simultaneously hear one another during the meeting [RMBCA 8.20].

**Quorum of Directors.** Unless the articles of incorporation or bylaws specify a greater number, a majority of the board of directors normally constitutes a *quorum* [RMBCA 8.24]. (A **quorum** is the minimum number of members of a body of officials or other group that must be present for business to be validly transacted.) Some state statutes specifically allow corporations to set a quorum at less than a majority but not less than one-third of the directors.[11]

**Voting.** Once a quorum is present, the directors transact business and vote on issues affecting the corporation. Each director present at the meeting has one vote.[12] Ordinary matters generally require a simple majority vote, but certain extraordinary issues may require a greater-than-majority vote.

**Committees of the Board of Directors** When a board of directors has a large number of members and must deal with myriad complex business issues, meetings can become unwieldy. Therefore, the boards of large, publicly held corporations typically create committees of directors and delegate certain tasks to these committees. By focusing on specific subjects, committees can increase the efficiency of the board.

Two common types of committees are the *executive committee* and the *audit committee*. An executive committee handles interim management decisions between board meetings. It is limited to dealing with ordinary business matters and does not have the power to declare dividends, amend the bylaws, or authorize the issuance of stock. The audit committee is responsible for the selection, compensation, and oversight of the independent public accountants that audit the firm's financial records. *The Sarbanes-Oxley Act requires all publicly held corporations to have an audit committee.*

**Rights of Directors** A corporate director must have certain rights to function properly in that position, including the rights of participation, inspection, and indemnification.

**Right to Participation.** The *right to participation* means that directors are entitled to participate in all board of directors' meetings and have a right to be notified of these meetings. Because the dates of regular board meetings are usually specified in the bylaws, no notice of these meetings is required. If special meetings are called, however, notice is required unless waived by the director [RMBCA 8.23].

**Right of Inspection.** A director also has a *right of inspection,* which means that each director can access the corporation's books and records, facilities, and premises. Inspection rights are essential for directors to make informed decisions and to exercise the necessary supervision over corporate officers and employees. This right of inspection is almost absolute and cannot be restricted (by the articles, bylaws, or any act of the board of directors).

---

11. See, for example, Delaware Code Annotated Title 8, Section 141(b); and New York Business Corporation Law Section 707.

12. Except in Louisiana, which allows a director to vote by proxy under certain circumstances.

**■ CASE IN POINT 18.8** NavLink, Inc., a Delaware corporation, provides high-end data management for customers and governments in Saudi Arabia, Qatar, Lebanon, and the United Arab Emirates. NavLink's co-founders, George Chammas and Laurent Delifer, served on its board of directors.

Chammas and Delifer were concerned about the company's 2015 annual budget and three-year operating plan. Despite repeated requests, Chammas was never given the meeting minutes from several board meetings in 2015. Chammas and Delifer believed that the other directors were withholding information and holding secret "pre-board meetings" at which plans and decisions were being made without them. They filed suit in a Delaware state court seeking inspection rights.

The court ordered NavLink to provide the plaintiffs with board meeting minutes and with communications from NavLink's secretary regarding the minutes. The plaintiffs were also entitled to inspect corporate documents and communications concerning NavLink's 2015 budget and three-year plan.[13] ■

**Right to Indemnification.** When a director becomes involved in litigation by virtue of her or his position, the director may have a *right to indemnification* (reimbursement) for the legal costs, fees, and damages incurred. Most states allow corporations to indemnify and purchase liability insurance for corporate directors [RMBCA 8.51].

## 18–4b Corporate Officers and Executives

Corporate officers and other executive employees are hired by the board of directors. At a minimum, most corporations have a president, one or more vice presidents, a secretary, and a treasurer. In most states, an individual can hold more than one office, such as president and secretary, and can be both an officer and a director of the corporation.

In addition to carrying out the duties articulated in the bylaws, corporate and managerial officers act as agents of the corporation. Therefore, the ordinary rules of agency normally apply to their employment.

Corporate officers and other high-level managers are employees of the company, so their rights are defined by employment contracts. Nevertheless, the board of directors normally can remove a corporate officer at any time with or without cause. If the directors remove an officer in violation of the terms of an employment contract, however, the corporation may be liable for breach of contract.

---

13. *Chammas v. NavLink, Inc.,* 2016 WL 767714 (Del.Ch.Ct. 2016).

## 18–4c Duties and Liabilities of Directors and Officers

The duties of corporate directors and officers are similar because both groups are involved in decision making and are in positions of control. Directors and officers are considered to be fiduciaries of the corporation because their relationship with the corporation and its shareholders is one of trust and confidence. As fiduciaries, directors and officers owe ethical—and legal—duties to the corporation and to the shareholders as a group. These fiduciary duties include the duty of care and the duty of loyalty.

**Duty of Care** Directors and officers must exercise due care in performing their duties. The standard of *due care* has been variously described in judicial decisions and codified in many state corporation codes. Generally, it requires a director or officer to:

1. Act in good faith (honestly).
2. Exercise the care that an ordinarily prudent (careful) person would exercise in similar circumstances.
3. Do what she or he believes is in the best interests of the corporation [RMBCA 8.30(a), 8.42(a)].

If directors or officers fail to exercise due care and the corporation or its shareholders suffer harm as a result, the directors or officers can be held liable for negligence. (An exception is made if the *business judgment rule* applies, as will be discussed shortly.)

**Duty to Make Informed Decisions.** Directors and officers are expected to be informed on corporate matters and to conduct a reasonable investigation of the situation before making a decision. They must, for instance, attend meetings and presentations, ask for information from those who have it, read reports, and review other written materials. In other words, directors and officers must investigate, study, and discuss matters and evaluate alternatives before making a decision. They cannot decide on the spur of the moment without adequate research.

Although directors and officers are expected to act in accordance with their own knowledge and training, they are also normally entitled to rely on information given to them by certain other persons. Under the laws of most states and Section 8.30(b) of the RMBCA, such persons include competent officers or employees, professionals such as attorneys and accountants, and committees of the board of directors. (The committee must be one on which the director does not serve, however.) The reliance must be in good faith to insulate a director from liability if the information later proves to be inaccurate or unreliable.

**Duty to Exercise Reasonable Supervision.** Directors are also expected to exercise a reasonable amount of supervision when they delegate work to corporate officers and employees. ■ **EXAMPLE 18.9** Dana, a corporate bank director, fails to attend any board of directors' meetings for five years. In addition, Dana never inspects any of the corporate books or records and generally fails to supervise the activities of the bank president and the loan committee. Meanwhile, Brennan, the bank president, who is a corporate officer, makes various improper loans and permits large overdrafts. In this situation, Dana (the corporate director) can be held liable to the corporation for losses resulting from the unsupervised actions of the bank president and the loan committee. ■

**Dissenting Directors.** Directors' votes at board of directors' meetings should be entered into the minutes. Sometimes, an individual director disagrees with the majority's vote (which becomes an act of the board of directors). Unless a dissent is entered in the minutes, the director is presumed to have assented. If the directors are later held liable for mismanagement as a result of a decision, dissenting directors are rarely held individually liable to the corporation. For this reason, a director who is absent from a given meeting sometimes registers a dissent with the secretary of the board regarding actions taken at the meeting.

**The Business Judgment Rule** Directors and officers are expected to exercise due care and to use their best judgment in guiding corporate management, but they are not insurers of business success. Under the **business judgment rule,** a corporate director or officer will not be liable to the corporation or to its shareholders for honest mistakes of judgment and bad business decisions.

Courts give significant deference to the decisions of corporate directors and officers, and consider the reasonableness of a decision at the time it was made, without the benefit of hindsight. Thus, corporate decision makers are not subjected to second-guessing by shareholders or others in the corporation.

**When the Rule Applies.** The business judgment rule will apply as long as the director or officer:

1. Took reasonable steps to become informed about the matter.
2. Had a rational basis for her or his decision.
3. Did not have a conflict between her or his personal interest and the interest of the corporation.

**Provides Broad Protections.** The business judgment rule provides broad protections to corporate decision

makers. In fact, most courts will apply the rule unless there is evidence of bad faith, fraud, or a clear breach of fiduciary duties.

■ **CASE IN POINT 18.10** The board of directors of the Chugach Alaska Corporation (CAC) voted to remove Sheri Buretta as the chair and install Robert Henrichs. During his term, Henrichs acted without board approval, made decisions with only his supporters present, retaliated against directors who challenged his decisions, and ignored board rules for conducting meetings. He refused to comply with bylaws that required a special shareholders' meeting in response to a shareholder petition and personally mistreated directors, shareholders, and employees. After six months, the board voted to reinstall Buretta.

CAC filed a suit in an Alaska state court against Henrichs, alleging a breach of fiduciary duty. A jury found Henrichs liable, and the court barred him from serving on CAC's board for five years. The appellate court affirmed. Given the nature and seriousness of Henrichs's misconduct, the business judgment rule did not protect him.[14] ■

**Duty of Loyalty** *Loyalty* can be defined as faithfulness to one's obligations and duties. In the corporate context, the duty of loyalty requires directors and officers to subordinate their personal interests to the welfare of the corporation. For instance, a director should not oppose a transaction that is in the corporation's best interest simply because pursuing it may cost the director his or her position. Directors cannot use corporate funds or confidential corporate information for personal advantage and must refrain from self-dealing.

Cases dealing with the duty of loyalty typically involve one or more of the following:

1. Competing with the corporation.
2. Usurping (taking personal advantage of) a corporate opportunity.
3. Pursuing an interest that conflicts with that of the corporation.
4. Using information that is not available to the public to make a profit trading securities (insider trading).
5. Authorizing a corporate transaction that is detrimental to minority shareholders.
6. Selling control over the corporation.

The following *Classic Case* illustrates the conflict that can arise between a corporate officer's personal interest and his or her duty of loyalty.

---

14. *Henrichs v. Chugach Alaska Corp.,* 250 P.3d 531 (Alaska Sup.Ct. 2011).

# Guth v. Loft, Inc.

Supreme Court of Delaware, 23 Del.Ch. 255, 5 A.2d 503 (1939).

**Background and Facts** In 1930, Charles Guth became the president of Loft, Inc., a candy-and-restaurant chain. Guth and his family also owned Grace Company, which made syrups for soft drinks. Coca-Cola Company supplied Loft with cola syrup. Unhappy with what he felt was Coca-Cola's high price, Guth entered into an agreement with Roy Megargel to acquire the trademark and formula for Pepsi-Cola and form Pepsi-Cola Corporation. Neither Guth nor Megargel could finance the new venture, however, and Grace Company was insolvent.

Without the knowledge of Loft's board, Guth used Loft's capital, credit, facilities, and employees to further the Pepsi enterprise. At Guth's direction, a Loft employee made the concentrate for the syrup, which was sent to Grace to add sugar and water. Loft charged Grace for the concentrate but allowed forty months' credit. Grace charged Pepsi for the syrup but also granted substantial credit. Grace sold the syrup to Pepsi's customers, including Loft, which paid on delivery or within thirty days. Loft also paid for Pepsi's advertising. Finally, with profits declining as a result of switching from Coca-Cola, Loft filed a suit in a Delaware state court against Guth, Grace, and Pepsi, seeking their Pepsi stock and an accounting. The court entered a judgment in the plaintiff's favor. The defendants appealed to the Delaware Supreme Court.

## In the Language of the Court

*LAYTON,* Chief Justice, delivering the opinion of the court:
* * * *

Corporate officers and directors are not permitted to use their position of trust and confidence to further their private interests. * * * They stand in a fiduciary relation to the corporation and its stockholders. A public policy, existing through the years, and derived from a profound knowledge of human characteristics and motives, has established *a rule that demands of a corporate officer or director, peremptorily [not open for debate] and inexorably [unavoidably], the most scrupulous observance of his duty, not only affirmatively to protect the interests of the corporation committed to his charge, but also to refrain from doing anything that would work injury to the corporation* * * * . The rule that requires an undivided and unselfish loyalty to the corporation demands that there shall be no conflict between duty and self-interest. [Emphasis added.]
* * * *

* * * *If there is presented to a corporate officer or director a business opportunity which the corporation is financially able to undertake [that] is * * * in the line of the corporation's business and is of practical advantage to it * * * and, by embracing the opportunity, the self-interest of the officer or director will be brought into conflict with that of his corporation, the law will not permit him to seize the opportunity for himself.* * * *
In such circumstances, * * * the corporation may elect to claim all of the benefits of the transaction for itself, and the law will impress a trust in favor of the corporation upon the property, interests and profits so acquired. [Emphasis added.]
* * * *

* * * The appellants contend that no conflict of interest between Guth and Loft resulted from his acquirement and exploitation of the Pepsi-Cola opportunity [and] that the acquisition did not place Guth in competition with Loft * * * . [In this case, however,] Guth was Loft, and Guth was Pepsi. He absolutely controlled Loft. His authority over Pepsi was supreme. As Pepsi, he created and controlled the supply of Pepsi-Cola syrup, and he determined the price and the terms. What he offered, as Pepsi, he had the power, as Loft, to accept. Upon any consideration of human characteristics and motives, he created a conflict between self-interest and duty. He made himself the judge in his own cause. * * * Moreover, a reasonable probability of injury to Loft resulted from the situation forced upon it. Guth was in the same position to impose his terms upon Loft as had been the Coca-Cola Company.

* * * The facts and circumstances demonstrate that Guth's appropriation of the Pepsi-Cola opportunity to himself placed him in a competitive position with Loft with respect to a commodity essential to it, thereby rendering his personal interests incompatible with the superior interests of his corporation;

and this situation was accomplished, not openly and with his own resources, but secretly and with the money and facilities of the corporation which was committed to his protection.

Case 18.3 Continued

**Decision and Remedy** *The Delaware Supreme Court upheld the judgment of the lower court. The state supreme court was "convinced that the opportunity to acquire the Pepsi-Cola trademark and formula, goodwill and business belonged to [Loft], and that Guth, as its President, had no right to appropriate the opportunity to himself."*

**Impact of This Case on Today's Law** *This early Delaware decision was one of the first to set forth a test for determining when a corporate officer or director has breached the duty of loyalty. The test has two basic parts: Was the opportunity reasonably related to the corporation's line of business, and was the corporation financially able to undertake the opportunity? The court also considered whether the corporation had an interest or expectancy in the opportunity. It recognized that when the corporation had "no interest or expectancy, the officer or director is entitled to treat the opportunity as his own."*

**Critical Thinking**
- **What If the Facts Were Different?** *Suppose that Loft's board of directors had approved Pepsi-Cola's use of its personnel and equipment. Would the court's decision have been different? Discuss.*

---

**Conflicts of Interest** Corporate directors often have many business affiliations, and a director may sit on the board of more than one corporation. Of course, directors are precluded from entering into or supporting businesses that operate in direct competition with corporations on whose boards they serve. Their fiduciary duty requires them to make a full disclosure of any potential conflicts of interest that might arise in any corporate transaction [RMBCA 8.60].

Sometimes, a corporation enters into a contract or engages in a transaction in which an officer or director has a personal interest. The director or officer must make a *full disclosure* of the nature of the conflicting interest and all facts pertinent to the transaction. He or she must also abstain from voting on the proposed transaction. When these rules are followed, the transaction can proceed. Otherwise, directors would be prevented from ever having financial dealings with the corporations they serve.

■ **EXAMPLE 18.11** Ballo Corporation needs office space. Stephanie Colson, one of its five directors, owns the building adjoining the corporation's headquarters. Colson can negotiate a lease for the space to Ballo if she fully discloses her conflicting interest and any facts known to her about the proposed transaction to Ballo and the other four directors. If the lease arrangement is fair and reasonable, Colson abstains from voting on it, and the other members of the corporation's board of directors unanimously approve it, the contract is valid. ■

**Liability of Directors and Officers** Directors and officers are exposed to liability on many fronts. They can be held liable for negligence in certain circumstances, as previously discussed. They may also be held liable for the crimes and torts committed by themselves or by corporate employees under their supervision.

Additionally, if shareholders perceive that the corporate directors are not acting in the best interests of the corporation, they may sue the directors on behalf of the corporation. (This is known as a *shareholder's derivative suit,* which will be discussed later in this chapter.) Directors and officers can also be held personally liable under a number of statutes, such as statutes enacted to protect consumers or the environment.

---

## 18–5 Shareholders

The acquisition of a share of stock makes a person an owner and a shareholder in a corporation. Shareholders thus own the corporation. Although they have no legal title to corporate property, such as buildings and equipment, they do have an equitable (ownership) interest in the firm.

As a general rule, shareholders have no responsibility for the daily management of the corporation, although they are ultimately responsible for choosing the board of directors, which does have such control. Ordinarily, corporate officers and other employees owe no direct duty to individual shareholders (unless some contract or special relationship exists between them in addition to the corporate relationship).

The duty of officers and directors is to act in the best interests of the corporation and its shareholder-owners *as a whole.* In turn, as you will read later in this chapter, controlling shareholders owe a fiduciary duty to minority shareholders.

## 18–5a Shareholders' Powers

Shareholders must approve fundamental changes affecting the corporation before the changes can be implemented. Hence, shareholder approval normally is required to amend the articles of incorporation or bylaws, to conduct a merger or dissolve the corporation, and to sell all or substantially all of the corporation's assets. Some of these powers are subject to prior board approval. Shareholder approval may also be requested (though it is not required) for certain other actions, such as to approve an independent auditor.

Shareholders also have the power to vote to elect or remove members of the board of directors. As described earlier, the first board of directors is either named in the articles of incorporation or chosen by the incorporators to serve until the first shareholders' meeting. From that time on, selection and retention of directors are exclusively shareholder functions.

Directors usually serve their full terms. If the shareholders judge them unsatisfactory, they are simply not reelected. Shareholders have the inherent power, however, to remove a director from office *for cause* (breach of duty or misconduct) by a majority vote. Some state statutes (and some articles of incorporation) permit removal of directors without cause by the vote of a majority of the shareholders entitled to vote.[15]

## 18–5b Shareholders' Meetings

Shareholders' meetings must occur at least annually. In addition, special meetings can be called to deal with urgent matters. A corporation must notify its shareholders of the date, time, and place of an annual or special shareholders' meeting at least ten days, but not more than

sixty days, before the meeting date [RMBCA 7.05].[16] (The date and time of the annual meeting can be specified in the bylaws.) Notice of a special meeting must include a statement of the purpose of the meeting, and business transacted at the meeting is limited to that purpose. Most corporations specify in their bylaws the acceptable methods of notifying shareholders about meetings.

**Proxies** It usually is not practical for owners of only a few shares of stock of publicly traded corporations to attend a shareholders' meeting. Therefore, the law allows stockholders to appoint another person as their agent to vote their shares at the meeting. The agent's formal authorization to vote the shares is called a **proxy** (from the Latin *procurare,* meaning "to manage or take care of"). Proxy materials are sent to all shareholders before shareholders' meetings.

Management often solicits proxies, but any person can solicit proxies to concentrate voting power. Proxies have been used by groups of shareholders as a device for taking over a corporation. Proxies normally are revocable (can be withdrawn), unless they are specifically designated as irrevocable and coupled with an interest. A proxy is coupled with an interest when, for instance, the person receiving the proxies from shareholders has agreed to buy their shares. Under RMBCA 7.22(c), proxies are valid for eleven months, unless the proxy agreement mandates a longer period.

**Shareholder Proposals** When shareholders want to change a company policy, they can put their ideas up for a shareholder vote. They do this by submitting a shareholder proposal to the board of directors and asking the board to include the proposal in the proxy materials that are sent to all shareholders before meetings.

**Rules for Proxies and Shareholder Proposals** The Securities and Exchange Commission (SEC) regulates the purchase and sale of securities. The SEC has special provisions relating to proxies and shareholder proposals. SEC Rule 14a-8 provides that all shareholders who own stock worth at least $1,000 are eligible to submit proposals for inclusion in corporate proxy materials. The corporation is required to include information on whatever proposals will be considered at the shareholders' meeting along with proxy materials. Only those proposals that relate to significant policy considerations, not ordinary business operations, must be included.

---

15. Most states allow *cumulative voting* for directors (described later in the chapter). If cumulative voting is authorized, a director may not be removed if the number of votes against removal would be sufficient to elect a director under cumulative voting. See, for instance, California Corporations Code Section 303A. See also Section 8.08(c) of the RMBCA.

16. The shareholder can waive the requirement of notice by signing a waiver form [RMBCA 7.06]. A shareholder who does not receive notice but who learns of the meeting and attends without protesting the lack of notice is said to have waived notice by such conduct.

Under the SEC's e-proxy rules,[17] all public companies must post their proxy materials on the Internet and notify shareholders how to find that information. Although the law requires proxy materials to be posted online, public companies may also send the materials to shareholders by other means, including paper documents and DVDs sent by mail.

### 18–5c Shareholder Voting

Shareholders exercise ownership control through the power of their votes. Corporate business matters are presented in the form of *resolutions,* which shareholders vote to approve or disapprove. Each common shareholder normally is entitled to one vote per share.

The articles of incorporation can exclude or limit voting rights, particularly for certain classes of shares. For instance, owners of preferred shares are usually denied the right to vote [RMBCA 7.21]. If a state statute requires specific voting procedures, the corporation's articles or bylaws must be consistent with the statute.

**Quorum Requirements** For shareholders to act during a meeting, a quorum must be present. Generally, a quorum exists when shareholders holding more than 50 percent of the outstanding shares are present. State laws often permit the articles of incorporation to set higher or lower quorum requirements, however. In some states, obtaining the unanimous written consent of shareholders is a permissible alternative to holding a shareholders' meeting [RMBCA 7.25].

Once a quorum is present, voting can proceed. If a state statute requires specific voting procedures, the corporation's articles or bylaws must be consistent with the statute. A majority vote of the shares represented at the meeting usually is required to pass resolutions. At times, more than a simple majority vote is required, either by a state statute or by the corporate articles. Extraordinary corporate matters, such as a merger, consolidation, or dissolution of the corporation, require approval by a higher percentage of all corporate shares entitled to vote [RMBCA 7.27].

**Voting Lists** The corporation prepares a voting list before each shareholders' meeting. Ordinarily, only persons whose names appear on the corporation's stockholder records as owners are entitled to vote.

The voting list contains the name and address of each shareholder as shown on the corporate records on a given cutoff date, or *record date.* (Under RMBCA 7.07, the bylaws or board of directors may fix a record date that

is as much as seventy days before the meeting.) The voting list also includes the number of voting shares held by each owner. The list is usually kept at the corporate headquarters and must be made available for shareholder inspection [RMBCA 7.20].

**Cumulative Voting** Most states permit, and many require, shareholders to elect directors by *cumulative voting,* a voting method designed to allow minority shareholders to be represented on the board of directors.

**Formula.** With cumulative voting, each shareholder is entitled to a total number of votes equal to the number of board members to be elected multiplied by the number of voting shares that the shareholder owns. The shareholder can cast all of these votes for one candidate or split them among several nominees for director. All candidates stand for election at the same time.

**How Cumulative Voting Works.** Cumulative voting can best be understood by example. ■ **EXAMPLE 18.12** A corporation has 10,000 shares issued and outstanding. The minority shareholders hold 3,000 shares, and the majority shareholders hold the other 7,000 shares. Three members of the board are to be elected. The majority shareholders' nominees are Alvarez, Beasley, and Caravel. The minority shareholders' nominee is Dovrik. Can Dovrik be elected to the board by the minority shareholders?

If cumulative voting is allowed, the answer is yes. The minority shareholders have 9,000 votes among them (the number of directors to be elected times the number of shares, or $3 \times 3,000 = 9,000$ votes). All of these votes can be cast to elect Dovrik. The majority shareholders have 21,000 votes ($3 \times 7,000 = 21,000$ votes), but these votes must be distributed among their three nominees.

The principle of cumulative voting is that no matter how the majority shareholders cast their 21,000 votes, they will not be able to elect all three directors if the minority shareholders cast all of their 9,000 votes for Dovrik, as illustrated in Exhibit 18–1. ■ In contrast, when cumulative voting is not required, the entire board can be elected by a majority of shares.

**Other Voting Techniques** Before a shareholders' meeting, a group of shareholders can agree in writing to vote their shares together in a specified manner. Such agreements, called *shareholder voting agreements,* usually are held to be valid and enforceable. A shareholder can also vote by proxy, as noted earlier.

Another technique is for shareholders to enter into a *voting trust.* A **voting trust** is an agreement (a trust contract) under which a shareholder assigns the right to vote

---

**17.** 17 C.F.R. Parts 240, 249, and 274.

**EXHIBIT 18–1  Results of Cumulative Voting**

| Ballot | Majority Shareholder Votes | | | Minority Shareholder Votes | Directors Elected |
|---|---|---|---|---|---|
| | *Alvarez* | *Beasley* | *Caravel* | *Dovrik* | |
| 1 | 10,000 | 10,000 | 1,000 | 9,000 | Alvarez, Beasley, Dovrik |
| 2 | 9,001 | 9,000 | 2,999 | 9,000 | Alvarez, Beasley, Dovrik |
| 3 | 6,000 | 7,000 | 8,000 | 9,000 | Beasley, Caravel, Dovrik |

his or her shares to a trustee, usually for a specified period of time. The trustee is then responsible for voting the shares on behalf of all the shareholders in the trust. The shareholder retains all rights of ownership (for instance, the right to receive dividend payments) except the power to vote the shares [RMBCA 7.30].

### 18–5d Rights of Shareholders

Shareholders possess numerous rights in addition to the right to vote their shares, and we examine several here.

**Stock Certificates** In the past, corporations commonly issued **stock certificates** that evidenced ownership of a specified number of shares in the corporation. Only a few jurisdictions still require physical stock certificates, and shareholders there have the right to demand that the corporation issue certificates (or replace those that were lost or destroyed). Stock is intangible personal property, however, and the ownership right exists independently of the certificate itself.

In most states and under RMBCA 6.26, a board of directors may provide that shares of stock will be uncertificated, or "paperless"—that is, no actual, physical stock certificates will be issued. Notice of shareholders' meetings, dividends, and operational and financial reports are distributed according to the ownership lists recorded in the corporation's books.

**Preemptive Rights** Sometimes, the articles of incorporation grant preemptive rights to shareholders

[RMBCA 6.30]. With **preemptive rights,** a shareholder receives a preference over all other purchasers to subscribe to or purchase a prorated share of a new issue of stock. Generally, preemptive rights must be exercised within a specific time period (usually thirty days).

A shareholder who is given preemptive rights can purchase a percentage of the new shares being issued that is equal to the percentage of shares she or he already holds in the company. This allows each shareholder to maintain her or his proportionate control, voting power, and financial interest in the corporation. ■ **EXAMPLE 18.13** Katlin is a shareholder who owns 10 percent of a company. Because she also has preemptive rights, she can buy 10 percent of any new issue (to maintain her 10 percent position). Thus, if the corporation issues 1,000 more shares, Katlin can buy 100 of the new shares. ■

Preemptive rights are most important in close corporations because each shareholder owns a relatively small number of shares but controls a substantial interest in the corporation. Without preemptive rights, it would be possible for a shareholder to lose his or her proportionate control over the firm. Nevertheless, preemptive rights do not exist unless provided for in the articles of incorporation.

**Stock Warrants** **Stock warrants** are rights given by a company to buy stock at a stated price by a specified date. Usually, when preemptive rights exist and a corporation is issuing additional shares, it gives its shareholders stock warrants. Warrants are often publicly traded on securities exchanges.

**Dividends** As mentioned, a dividend is a distribution of corporate profits or income *ordered by the directors* and paid to the shareholders in proportion to their shares in the corporation. Dividends can be paid in cash, property, stock of the corporation that is paying the dividends, or stock of other corporations.[18]

State laws vary, but each state determines the general circumstances and legal requirements under which dividends are paid. State laws also control the sources of revenue to be used. All states allow dividends to be paid from the undistributed net profits earned by the corporation, for instance. A number of states allow dividends to be paid out of any surplus.

**Illegal Dividends.** Dividends are illegal if they are improperly paid from an unauthorized account or if their payment causes the corporation to become insolvent. Generally, shareholders must return illegal dividends only if they knew that the dividends were illegal when the payment was received (or if the dividends were paid when the corporation was insolvent). Whenever dividends are illegal or improper, the board of directors can be held personally liable for the amount of the payment.

**The Directors' Failure to Declare a Dividend.** When directors fail to declare a dividend, shareholders can ask a court to compel the directors to do so. To succeed, the shareholders must show that the directors have acted so unreasonably in withholding the dividend that their conduct is an abuse of their discretion.

Often, a corporation accumulates large cash reserves for a legitimate corporate purpose, such as expansion or research. The mere fact that the firm has sufficient earnings or surplus available to pay a dividend normally is not enough to compel the directors to declare a dividend. The courts are reluctant to interfere with corporate operations and will not compel directors to declare dividends unless abuse of discretion is clearly shown.

**Inspection Rights** Shareholders in a corporation enjoy both common law and statutory inspection rights. The RMBCA provides that every shareholder is entitled to examine specified corporate records, including voting lists [RMBCA 7.20, 16.02]. The shareholder may inspect in person, or an attorney, accountant, or other authorized assistant can do so as the shareholder's agent.

A shareholder has a right to inspect and copy corporate books and records only for a *proper purpose,* and the request to inspect must be made in advance. A shareholder who is denied the right of inspection can seek a court order to compel the inspection.

■ **CASE IN POINT 18.14** Trading Block Holdings, Inc., offers online brokerage services. On April 1, 2013, some shareholders of Trading Block, through an attorney, sent a letter asking to inspect specific items in the corporation's books and records. The letter indicated that the purpose was to determine the financial condition of the company, how it was being managed, and whether the company's financial practices were appropriate. It also stated that the shareholders wanted to know whether Trading Block's management had engaged in any self-dealing that had negatively impacted the company as a whole.

On April 30, Trading Block responded with a letter stating that the plaintiffs were on a "fishing expedition" and did not have a proper purpose for inspecting the corporate records. Eventually, the shareholders filed a motion to compel inspection in an Illinois state court. The trial court denied the plaintiffs' motion. On appeal, the reviewing court held that the plaintiffs' allegations of self-dealing by directors and officers constituted a proper purpose for their inspection request. The trial court's decision was reversed.[19] ■

**Transfer of Shares** Corporate stock represents an ownership right in intangible personal property. The law generally recognizes the owner's right to transfer stock to another person unless there are valid restrictions on its transferability, such as frequently occur with close corporation stock.

When shares are transferred, a new entry is made in the corporate stock book to indicate the new owner. Until the corporation is notified and the entry is complete, all rights—including voting rights, notice of shareholders' meetings, and the right to dividend distributions—remain with the current record owner.

**The Shareholder's Derivative Suit** When the corporation is harmed by the actions of a third party, the directors can bring a lawsuit in the name of the corporation against that party. If the corporate directors

---

**18.** On one occasion, a distillery declared and paid a dividend in bonded whiskey.

**19.** *Sunlitz Holding Co., W.L.L. v. Trading Block Holdings, Inc.,* 2014 IL App (1st) 133938, 17 N.E.3d 715, 384 Ill.Dec. 733 (4 Dist. 2014).

fail to bring a lawsuit, shareholders can do so "derivatively" in what is known as a **shareholder's derivative suit.**

The right of shareholders to bring a derivative action is especially important when the wrong suffered by the corporation results from the actions of the corporate directors and officers. For obvious reasons, the directors and officers would probably be unwilling to take any action against themselves.

**Written Demand Required.** Before shareholders can bring a derivative suit, they must submit a written demand to the corporation, asking the board of directors to take appropriate action [RMBCA 7.40]. The directors then have ninety days in which to act. Only if they refuse to do so can the derivative suit go forward. In addition, a court will dismiss a derivative suit if a majority of the directors or an independent panel determines in good faith that the lawsuit is not in the best interests of the corporation [RMBCA 7.44].

**Any Damages Awarded Go to the Corporation.** When shareholders bring a derivative suit, they are not pursuing rights or benefits for themselves personally but are acting as guardians of the corporate entity. Therefore, if the suit is successful, any damages recovered normally go into the corporation's treasury, not to the shareholders personally.

## 18–5e Duties and Liabilities of Shareholders

One of the hallmarks of the corporate form of organization is that shareholders are not personally liable for the debts of the corporation. If the corporation fails, the shareholders can lose their investments, but that generally is the limit of their liability. As discussed previously, in certain instances, a court will pierce the corporate veil (disregard the corporate entity) and hold the shareholders individually liable. But these situations are the exception, not the rule.

A shareholder can also be personally liable in certain other rare instances such as those related to illegal dividends or to *watered stock*. Finally, in certain instances, a majority shareholder who engages in oppressive conduct or attempts to exclude minority shareholders from receiving certain benefits can be held personally liable.

**Watered Stock** When a corporation issues shares for less than their fair market value, the shares are referred to as **watered stock.**[20] Usually, the shareholder who receives watered stock must pay the difference to the corporation (the shareholder is personally liable). In some states, the shareholder who receives watered stock may be liable to creditors of the corporation for unpaid corporate debts.

■ **EXAMPLE 18.15** During the formation of a corporation, Gomez, one of the incorporators, transfers his property, Sunset Beach, to the corporation for 10,000 shares of stock at a par value of $100 per share for a total price of $1 million. After the property is transferred and the shares are issued, Sunset Beach is carried on the corporate books at a value of $1 million.

On appraisal, it is discovered that the market value of the property at the time of transfer was only $500,000. The shares issued to Gomez are therefore watered stock, and he is liable to the corporation for the difference between the value of the shares and the value of the property. ■

**Duties of Majority Shareholders** In some instances, a majority shareholder is regarded as having a fiduciary duty to the corporation and to the minority shareholders. This duty arises when a single shareholder (or a few shareholders acting in concert) owns a sufficient number of shares to exercise *de facto* control over the corporation. In these situations, the majority shareholder owes a fiduciary duty to the minority shareholders.

When a majority shareholder breaches her or his fiduciary duty to a minority shareholder, the minority shareholder can sue for damages. A breach of fiduciary duties by those who control a close corporation normally constitutes what is known as *oppressive conduct*. A common example of a breach of fiduciary duty occurs when the majority shareholders "freeze out" the minority shareholders and exclude them from certain benefits of participating in the firm.

■ **EXAMPLE 18.16** Brodie, Jordan, and Barbara form a close corporation to operate a machine shop. Brodie and Jordan own 75 percent of the shares in the company, but all three are directors. After disagreements arise, Brodie asks the company to purchase his shares, but his requests are refused. A few years later, Brodie dies, and his wife, Ella, inherits his shares. Jordan and Barbara refuse to perform a valuation of the company, deny Ella access to corporate information, do not declare any dividends, and refuse to elect Ella as a director. In this situation, the majority shareholders have violated their fiduciary duty to Ella. ■

---

20. The phrase *watered stock* was originally used to describe cattle that were kept thirsty during a long drive and then were allowed to drink large quantities of water just before their sale. The increased weight of the watered stock allowed the seller to reap a higher profit.

## 18–6 Major Business Forms Compared

When deciding which form of business organization to choose, businesspersons normally consider several factors, including ease of creation, the liability of the owners, tax considerations, and the ability to raise capital. Each major form of business organization offers distinct advantages and disadvantages with respect to these and other factors.

Exhibit 18–2 summarizes the essential advantages and disadvantages of each of the forms of business organization discussed in this text.

**EXHIBIT 18–2** Major Forms of Business Compared

| | SOLE PROPRIETORSHIP | PARTNERSHIP | CORPORATION |
|---|---|---|---|
| **Method of Creation** | Created at will by owner. | Created by agreement of the parties. | Authorized by the state under the state's corporation law. |
| **Legal Position** | Not a separate entity; owner is the business. | A general partnership is a separate legal entity in most states. | Always a legal entity separate and distinct from its owners—a legal fiction for the purposes of owning property and being a party to litigation. |
| **Liability** | Unlimited liability. | Unlimited liability. | Limited liability of shareholders—shareholders are not liable for the debts of the corporation. |
| **Duration** | Determined by owner; automatically dissolved on owner's death. | Terminated by agreement of the partners, but can continue to do business even when a partner dissociates from the partnership. | Can have perpetual existence. |
| **Transferability of Interest** | Interest can be transferred, but individual's proprietorship then ends. | Although partnership interest can be assigned, assignee does not have full rights of a partner. | Shares of stock can be transferred. |
| **Management** | Completely at owner's discretion. | Each partner has a direct and equal voice in management unless expressly agreed otherwise in the partnership agreement. | Shareholders elect directors, who set policy and appoint officers. |
| **Taxation** | Owner pays personal taxes on business income. | Each partner pays pro rata share of income taxes on net profits, whether or not they are distributed. | Double taxation—corporation pays income tax on net profits, with no deduction for dividends, and shareholders pay income tax on disbursed dividends they receive. |
| **Organizational Fees, Annual License Fees, and Annual Reports** | None or minimal. | None or minimal. | All required. |
| **Transaction of Business in Other States** | Generally no limitation. | Generally no limitation.[a] | Normally must qualify to do business and obtain certificate of authority. |

**a.** A few states have enacted statutes requiring that foreign partnerships qualify to do business there.

Continues

**EXHIBIT 18–2** Major Forms of Business Compared *(Continued)*

| | LIMITED PARTNERSHIP | LIMITED LIABILITY COMPANY | LIMITED LIABILITY PARTNERSHIP |
|---|---|---|---|
| **Method of Creation** | Created by agreement to carry on a business for profit. At least one party must be a general partner and the other(s) limited partner(s). Certificate of limited partnership is filed. | Created by an agreement of the member-owners of the company. Articles of organization are filed. Charter must be issued by the state. | Created by agreement of the partners. A statement of qualification for the limited liability partnership is filed. |
| **Legal Position** | Treated as a legal entity. | Treated as a legal entity. | Generally, treated same as a general partnership. |
| **Liability** | Unlimited liability of all general partners. Limited partners are liable only to the extent of capital contributions. | Member-owners' liability is limited to the amount of capital contributions or investments. | Varies, but under the Uniform Partnership Act, liability of a partner for acts committed by other partners is limited. |
| **Duration** | By agreement in certificate, or by termination of the last general partner (retirement, death, and the like) or last limited partner. | Unless a single-member LLC, can have perpetual existence (same as a corporation). | Remains in existence until cancellation or revocation. |
| **Transferability of Interest** | Interest can be assigned, but if assignee becomes a member with consent of other partners, certificate must be amended. | Member interests are freely transferable. | Interest can be assigned same as in a general partnership. |
| **Management** | General partners have equal voice or by agreement. Limited partners may not retain limited liability if they actively participate in management. | Member-owners can fully participate in management or can designate a group of persons to manage on behalf of the members. | Same as a general partnership. |
| **Taxation** | Generally taxed as a partnership. | LLC is not taxed, and members are taxed personally on profits "passed through" the LLC. | Same as a general partnership. |
| **Organizational Fees, Annual License Fees, and Annual Reports** | Organizational fee required; usually not others. | Organizational fee required. Others vary with states. | Fees are set by each state for filing statements of qualification, statements of foreign qualification, and annual reports. |
| **Transaction of Business in Other States** | Generally no limitations. | Generally no limitations, but may vary depending on state. | Must file a statement of foreign qualification before doing business in another state. |

## Reviewing: Corporations

David Brock was on the board of directors of Firm Body Fitness, Inc., which owned a string of fitness clubs in New Mexico. Brock owned 15 percent of the Firm Body stock and was also employed as a tanning technician at one of the fitness clubs. After the January financial report showed that Firm Body's tanning division was operating at a substantial net loss, the board of directors, led by Marty Levinson, discussed terminating the tanning operations. Brock successfully convinced a majority of the board that the tanning division was necessary to market the clubs' overall fitness package. By April, the tanning division's financial losses had risen. The board hired a business analyst, who conducted surveys and determined that the tanning operations did not significantly increase membership.

A shareholder, Diego Peñada, discovered that Brock owned stock in Sunglow, Inc., the company from which Firm Body purchased its tanning equipment. Peñada notified Levinson, who privately reprimanded Brock. Shortly thereafter, Brock and Mandy Vail, who owned 37 percent of the Firm Body stock and also held shares of Sunglow, voted to replace Levinson on the board of directors. Using the information presented in the chapter, answer the following questions.

1. What duties did Brock, as a director, owe to Firm Body?
2. Does the fact that Brock owned shares in Sunglow establish a conflict of interest? Why or why not?
3. Suppose that Firm Body brought an action against Brock claiming that he had breached the duty of loyalty by not disclosing his interest in Sunglow to the other directors. What theory might Brock use in his defense?
4. Now suppose that Firm Body did not bring an action against Brock. What type of lawsuit might Peñada be able to bring based on these facts?

**Debate This** . . . *The sole shareholder of an S corporation should not be able to avoid liability for the torts of her or his employees.*

## Terms and Concepts

alien corporation 389
articles of incorporation 394
benefit corporation 394
bond 396
business judgment rule 403
bylaws 395
close corporation 392
commingle 399
common stock 396
crowdfunding 397
dividends 389
domestic corporation 389
foreign corporation 389

holding company 389
inside director 401
outside director 401
pierce the corporate veil 399
preemptive rights 408
preferred stock 396
private equity capital 397
proxy 406
public corporation 391
publicly held corporation 391
quorum 401
retained earnings 389
S corporation 393

securities 396
shareholder agreement 393
shareholder's derivative suit 410
stock 396
stock certificate 408
stock warrant 408
*ultra vires* 398
venture capital 397
voting trust 407
watered stock 410

## Issue Spotters

1. Northwest Brands, Inc., is a small business incorporated in Minnesota. Its one class of stock is owned by twelve members of a single family. Ordinarily, corporate income is taxed at the corporate and shareholder levels. Is there a way for Northwest Brands to avoid this double taxation? Explain your answer. (See *Nature and Classification*.)

2. Nico is Omega Corporation's majority shareholder. He owns enough stock in Omega that if he were to sell it, the sale would be a transfer of control of the firm. Discuss whether Nico owes a duty to Omega or the minority shareholders in selling his shares. (See *Shareholders*.)

• **Check your answers to the Issue Spotters against the answers provided in Appendix D at the end of this text.**

## Business Scenarios

**18–1. Preincorporation.** Cummings, Okawa, and Taft are recent college graduates who want to form a corporation to manufacture and sell digital tablets. Peterson tells them he will set in motion the formation of their corporation. First, Peterson makes a contract with Owens for the purchase of a piece of land for $20,000. Owens does not know of the prospective corporate formation at the time the contract is signed. Second, Peterson makes a contract with Babcock to build a small plant on the property being purchased. Babcock's contract is conditional on the corporation's formation. Peterson secures all necessary subscription agreements and capitalization, and he files the articles of incorporation. (See *Formation and Powers*.)

**(a)** Discuss whether the newly formed corporation, Peterson, or both are liable on the contracts with Owens and Babcock.

**(b)** Discuss whether the corporation is automatically liable to Babcock on formation.

**18–2. Conflicts of Interest.** Oxy Corp. is negotiating with Wick Construction Co. for the renovation of Oxy's corporate headquarters. Wick, the owner of Wick Construction Co., is also one of the five members of Oxy's board of directors. The contract terms are standard for this type of contract. Wick has previously informed two of the other directors of his interest in the construction company. Oxy's board approves the contract by a three-to-two vote, with Wick voting with the majority. Discuss whether this contract is binding on the corporation. (See *Directors and Officers*.)

## Business Case Problems

**18–3. Spotlight on Smart Inventions—Piercing the Corporate Veil.**  Thomas Persson and Jon Nokes founded Smart Inventions, Inc., to market household consumer products. The success of their first product, the Smart Mop, continued with later products, which were sold through infomercials and other means. Persson and Nokes were the firm's officers and equal shareholders. Persson was responsible for product development, and Nokes was in charge of day-to-day operations. In time, they became dissatisfied with each other's efforts. Nokes represented the firm as financially "dying," "in a grim state, . . . worse than ever," and offered to buy all of Persson's shares for $1.6 million. Persson accepted.

On the day that they signed the agreement to transfer the shares, Smart Inventions began marketing a new product—the Tap Light. It was an instant success, generating millions of dollars in revenues. In negotiating with Persson, Nokes had intentionally kept the Tap Light a secret. Persson sued Smart Inventions, asserting fraud and other claims. Under what principle might Smart Inventions be liable for Nokes's fraud? Is Smart Inventions liable in this case? Explain. [*Persson v. Smart Inventions, Inc.,* 125 Cal.App.4th 1141, 23 Cal. Rptr.3d 335 (2 Dist. 2005)] (See *Piercing the Corporate Veil*.)

**18–4. Duty of Loyalty.** Kids International Corp. produced children's wear for Walmart and other retailers. Gila Dweck was a Kids director and its chief executive officer. Because she felt that she was not paid enough, she started Success Apparel to compete with Kids. Success operated out of Kids' premises, used its employees, borrowed on its credit, took advantage of its business opportunities, and capitalized on its customer relationships. As an "administrative fee," Dweck paid Kids 1 percent of Success's total sales. Did Dweck breach any fiduciary duties? Explain. [*Dweck v. Nasser,* 2012 WL 3194069 (Del.Ch. 2012)] (See *Directors and Officers*.)

**18–5. Business Case Problem with Sample Answer—Piercing the Corporate Veil.**  Scott Snapp contracted with Castlebrook Builders, Inc., which was owned by Stephen Kappeler, to remodel a house. Kappeler estimated that the remodeling would cost around $500,000. Eventually, however, Snapp paid Kappeler more than $1.3 million. Snapp filed a suit in an Ohio state court against Castlebrook, alleging breach of contract and fraud, among other things. During the trial, it was revealed that Castlebrook had issued no shares of stock and that personal and corporate funds had been commingled. The minutes of the corporate meetings all looked exactly the same. In addition, Kappeler could not provide an accounting for the Snapp project. In particular, he could not explain evidence of double and triple billing nor demonstrate that the amount Snapp paid had actually been spent on the remodeling project.

Are these sufficient grounds to pierce the corporate veil? Explain. [*Snapp v. Castlebrook Builders, Inc.,* 2014 -Ohio- 163, 7 N.E.3d 574 (2014)] (See *Formation and Powers.*)

- **For a sample answer to Problem 18–5, go to Appendix E at the end of this text.**

**18–6. Business Judgment Rule.** Country Contractors, Inc., contracted to provide excavation services for A Westside Storage of Indianapolis, Inc., but did not complete the job and later filed for bankruptcy. Stephen Songer and Jahn Songer were Country's sole shareholders. The Songers had not misused the corporate form to engage in fraud. The firm had not been undercapitalized, personal and corporate funds had not been commingled, and Country had kept accounting records and minutes of its annual board meetings. Are the Songers personally liable for Country's failure to complete its contract? Explain. [*Country Contractors, Inc. v. A Westside Storage of Indianapolis, Inc.,* 4 N.E.3d 677 (Ind.App. 2014)] (See *Directors and Officers.*)

**18–7. Torts.** Jennifer Hoffman took her cell phone to a store owned by R&K Trading, Inc., for repairs. Later, Hoffman filed a suit in a New York state court against R&K, Verizon Wireless, Inc., and others. Hoffman sought to recover damages for a variety of torts, including infliction of emotional distress and negligent hiring and supervision. She alleged that an R&K employee, Keith Press, had examined her phone in a back room, accessed private photos of her stored on her phone, and disseminated the photos to the public. Hoffman testified that "after the incident, she learned from another R&K employee that personal information and pictures had been removed from the phones of other customers." Can R&K be held liable for the torts of its employees? Explain. [*Hoffman v. Verizon Wireless, Inc.,* 5 N.Y.S.3d 123, 125 A.D.3d 806 (2015)] (See *Nature and Classification.*)

**18–8. Rights of Shareholders.** FCR Realty, LLC, and Clifford B. Green & Sons, Inc., were co-owned by three brothers—Frederick, Clifford Jr., and Richard Green. Each brother was a shareholder of the corporation. Frederick was a controlling shareholder, as well as president. Each brother owned a one-third interest in the LLC. Clifford believed that Frederick had misused LLC and corporate funds to pay nonexistent debts and liabilities and had diverted LLC assets to the corporation. He also contended that Frederick had disbursed about $1.8 million in corporate funds to Frederick's own separate business. Clifford hired an attorney and filed an action on behalf of the two companies against Frederick for breach of fiduciary duty. Frederick argued that Clifford lacked the knowledge necessary to adequately represent the companies' interest because he did not understand financial statements. Can Clifford maintain the action against Frederick? If so, and if the suit is successful, who recovers the damages? Explain. [*FCR Realty, LLC v. Green,* __ Conn.Supp. __, __ Conn.L.Rptr. __, 2016 WL 571449 (Super. 2016)] (See *Shareholders.*)

**18–9. A Question of Ethics—Piercing the Corporate Veil.**  *In New York City, 2406-12 Amsterdam Associates LLC brought an action in a New York state court against Alianza Dominicana and Alianza LLC to recover unpaid rent. The plaintiff asserted cause to pierce the corporate veil, alleging that Alianza Dominicana had made promises to pay its rent while discreetly forming Alianza LLC to avoid liability for it. According to 2406-12, Alianza LLC was 90 percent owned by Alianza Dominicana, had no employees, and had no function but to hold Alianza Dominicana's assets away from its creditors. The defendants filed a motion to dismiss the plaintiff's claim. [2406-12 Amsterdam Associates, LLC v. Alianza, LLC, 136 A.D.3d 512, 25 N.Y.S.2d 167 (1 Dept. 2016)] (See Piercing the Corporate Veil.)*

**(a)** Assuming that 2406-12's allegations are true, are there sufficient grounds to pierce Alianza LLC's corporate veil? Discuss.

**(b)** Suppose that the parties to this dispute were small, close corporations. How might that circumstance affect the result in this case?

## Legal Reasoning Group Activity

**18–10. Corporate versus LLC Form of Business.** The limited liability company (LLC) may be the best organizational form for most businesses. For a significant number of firms, however, the corporate form or some other form of organization may be better. (See *Nature and Classification.*)

**(a)** The first group will outline several reasons why a firm might be better off as a corporation than as an LLC.

**(b)** The second group will discuss the differences between corporations and LLCs in terms of their management structures.

# Answers to the *Issue Spotters*

**1. *Is there a way for Northwest Brands to avoid this double taxation? Explain your answer.*** Yes. Small businesses that meet certain requirements can qualify as S corporations, created specifically to permit small businesses to avoid double taxation. The six requirements of an S corporation are (1) the firm must be a domestic corporation, (2) the firm must not be a member of an affiliated group of corporations, (3) the firm must have less than a certain number of shareholders, (4) the shareholders must be individuals, estates, or qualified trusts (or corporations in some cases), (5) there can be only one class of stock, and (6) no shareholder can be a nonresident alien.

**2. *Discuss whether Nico owes a duty to Omega or the minority shareholders in selling his shares.*** Yes. A single shareholder—or a few shareholders acting together—who owns enough stock to exercise *de facto* control over a corporation owes the corporation and minority shareholders a fiduciary duty when transferring those shares.

# Sample Answers for *Business Case Problems with Sample Answer*

**Problem 18–5. *Piercing the Corporate Veil.*** Yes, there are sufficient grounds in the facts of this problem to support piercing the corporate veil and holding Kappeler personally liable to Snapp. First, in a case in which a plaintiff seeks to pierce a corporate veil, there must be a fraud or other injustice to be remedied. In that situation, the factors that a court will consider in determining whether to pierce the corporate veil include (1) a party is tricked or misled into dealing with the corporation rather than the individual, (2) the corporation has insufficient capital to meet its prospective debts or other potential liabilities, (3) corporate formalities, such as holding required corporate meetings, are not followed, and (4) personal and corporate interests are commingled.

In this problem, the amount that Snapp ultimately paid the builder exceeded the original estimate by nearly $1 million—and the project was still unfinished. Kappeler could not provide an accounting for the Snapp project—he could not explain double and triple charges nor whether the amount that Snapp paid had actually been spent on the project. These facts support conclusion of fraud. And they also indicate that Kappeler may have tricked or misled Snapp into dealing with the corporation rather than with Kappeler as an individual. Castlebrook had issued no shares of stock, which indicates insufficient capitalization. The minutes of the corporate meetings "all looked exactly the same," indicating that in fact the required corporate meetings had not been held. And Kappeler had commingled personal and corporate funds.

In the actual case on which this problem is based, in Snapp's suit against the builder, the court pierced the corporate veil and held Kappeler personally liable. A state intermediate appellate court affirmed.

# Chapter 15

# CHAPTER

# Agency Relationships

One of the most common, important, and pervasive legal relationships is that of **agency.** In an agency relationship involving two parties, one of the parties, called the *agent,* agrees to represent or act for the other, called the *principal.* The principal has the right to control the agent's conduct in matters entrusted to the agent.

Agency relationships are crucial in the business world. By using agents, a principal can conduct multiple business operations at the same time in different locations. Indeed, the only way that certain business entities can function is through their agents. For instance, a corporate officer is an agent who serves in a representative capacity for the corporation. The officer has the authority to bind the corporation to a contract. Only through its officers can corporations enter into contracts.

Most employees are also considered to be agents of their employers.

Today, however, the United States is experiencing a trend toward a so-called *gig economy,* which centers on short-term, independent workers who are not employees. Companies like Uber and Lyft (discussed in this chapter's feature) provide evidence of this trend. This type of on-demand employment raises questions related to agency, making agency an increasingly important topic for students of business law and the legal environment to understand.

## 19–1 Agency Law

Section 1(1) of the *Restatement (Third) of Agency*[1] defines *agency* as "the fiduciary relation [that] results from the manifestation of consent by one person to another that the other shall act in his [or her] behalf and subject to his [or her] control, and consent by the other so to act." In other words, in a principal-agent relationship, the parties have agreed that the agent will act *on behalf and instead of* the principal in negotiating and transacting business with third parties.

The term **fiduciary** is at the heart of agency law. When this term is used as a noun, it refers to a person having a duty created by his or her undertaking to act primarily for another's benefit in matters connected with the undertaking. When used as an adjective, as in the phrase *fiduciary relationship,* it means that the relationship involves trust and confidence.

Agency relationships commonly exist between employers and employees. Agency relationships may sometimes also exist between employers and independent contractors who are hired to perform special tasks or services.

### 19–1a Employer-Employee Relationships

Normally, all employees who deal with third parties are deemed to be agents. A salesperson in a department store, for instance, is an agent of the store's owner (the principal) and acts on the owner's behalf. Any sale of goods made by the salesperson to a customer is binding on the principal. Similarly, most representations of fact made by the salesperson with respect to the goods sold are binding on the principal.

Because employees who deal with third parties generally are deemed to be agents of their employers, agency law and employment law overlap considerably. Agency relationships, however, can exist outside an employer-employee relationship, so agency law has a broader reach than employment law. Additionally, agency law is based on the common law, whereas much employment law is statutory law.

Employment laws (state and federal) apply only to the employer-employee relationship. Statutes governing

[1]. The *Restatement (Third) of Agency* is an authoritative summary of the law of agency and is often referred to by judges in their decisions and opinions.

Social Security, withholding taxes, workers' compensation, unemployment compensation, workplace safety, and employment discrimination apply only if an employer-employee relationship exists. *These laws do not apply to independent contractors.*

## 19–1b Employer–Independent Contractor Relationships

Independent contractors are not employees because, by definition, those who hire them have no control over the details of their work performance. Section 2 of the *Restatement (Third) of Agency* defines an **independent contractor** as follows:

> [An independent contractor is] a person who contracts with another to do something for him [or her] but who is not controlled by the other nor subject to the other's right to control with respect to his [or her] physical conduct in the performance of the undertaking. He [or she] may or may not be an agent.

Building contractors and subcontractors are independent contractors. A property owner who hires a contractor and subcontractors to complete a project does not control the details of the way they perform their work. Truck drivers who own their vehicles and hire out on a per-job basis are independent contractors, but truck drivers who drive company trucks on a regular basis usually are employees. See this chapter's *Ethics Today* feature for a discussion of disputes involving the classification of drivers working for Uber and Lyft.

The relationship between a principal and an independent contractor may or may not involve an agency relationship. To illustrate: A homeowner who hires a real estate broker to sell her house has contracted with an independent contractor (the broker). The homeowner has also established an agency relationship with the broker for the specific purpose of selling the property. Another example is an insurance agent, who is both an independent contractor and an agent of the insurance company for which he sells policies. (Note that an insurance *broker*, in contrast, normally is an agent of the person obtaining insurance and not of the insurance company.)

## 19–1c Determination of Employee Status

The courts are frequently asked to determine whether a particular worker is an employee or an independent contractor. How a court decides this issue can have a significant effect on the rights and liabilities of the parties.

Employers are required to pay certain taxes, such as Social Security and unemployment taxes, for employees but not for independent contractors. Therefore, workers may benefit from obtaining employee status in some situations.

**Criteria Used by the Courts** In deciding whether a worker is categorized as an employee or an independent contractor, courts often consider the following questions:

1. *How much control does the employer exercise over the details of the work?* If the employer exercises considerable control over the details of the work and the day-to-day activities of the worker, this indicates employee status. This is perhaps the most important factor weighed by the courts in determining employee status.
2. *Is the worker engaged in an occupation or business distinct from that of the employer?* If so, this points to independent-contractor, not employee, status.
3. *Is the work usually done under the employer's direction or by a specialist without supervision?* If the work is usually done under the employer's direction, this indicates employee status.
4. *Does the employer supply the tools at the place of work?* If so, this indicates employee status.
5. *For how long is the person employed?* If the person is employed for a long period of time, this indicates employee status.
6. *What is the method of payment—by time period or at the completion of the job?* Payment by time period, such as once every two weeks or once a month, indicates employee status.
7. *What degree of skill is required of the worker?* If a great degree of skill is required, this may indicate that the person is an independent contractor hired for a specialized job and not an employee.

Whether a worker is an employee or an independent contractor can affect the employer's liability for the worker's actions. An employer normally is not responsible for the actions of an independent contractor. ■ **CASE IN POINT 19.1** Terence Pershad was a tow truck driver for Five Star Auto Service. Five Star had contracted to perform towing and auto repair services for AAA North Jersey, Inc. After one of its customers was involved in a car accident, AAA called Five Star for assistance, and Five Star sent a truck driven by Pershad. Pershad got into a fight with Nicholas Coker, a passenger in the car, and assaulted Coker with a knife.

Coker filed a suit in a New Jersey state court against Pershad, Five Star, and AAA. The court determined that

## ETHICS TODAY

### Is It Fair to Classify Uber and Lyft Drivers as Independent Contractors?

The transportation-for-hire world has changed dramatically since Uber, Lyft, and other transportation-sharing companies came onto the scene. Uber started in San Francisco in 2009. Today, its services are available in one form or another in about 60 countries and more than 300 cities worldwide. Its main competitor, Lyft, was launched in 2012 and operates in more than 200 U.S. cities. The growth in transportation sharing has not been without its setbacks, though. Most of them involve laws that have prohibited Uber and Lyft from operating in certain cities, as well as lawsuits by drivers claiming that they were misclassified.

#### Classification of Workers

Workers in the United States generally fall into two categories: employees and independent contractors. Employment laws, including minimum wage and anti-discrimination statutes, cover employees. Such laws do not cover most independent contractors. Enter the digital age of on-demand workers who obtain job assignments via apps.

Workers for Lyft, Uber, and similar companies choose when and where they will perform their duties. They do not choose how much they will be paid, however. For them, employment is a take-it-or-leave-it proposition. They electronically accept the platform terms of the apps, or they obtain no work assignments.

Some critics of this contractual system argue that there should be a new category of workers with "dependent-contractor" status who receive some of the protections traditionally given only to employees. Certain aspects of current labor law would be attached to the relationships between dependent contractors and their employers.

#### Worker Misclassification Lawsuits

A number of former or current Uber and Lyft drivers have pursued legal remedies to change their job classification and to obtain better benefits. In California, for instance, two federal court judges allowed separate lawsuits to go before juries on the question of whether on-demand drivers should be considered employees rather than independent contractors.[a]

In a similar case, rather than go to court, Lyft settled a worker misclassification lawsuit for $12.25 million. The suit, which was settled in 2016, had been brought in 2013. The settlement did not achieve a reclassification of Lyft drivers as employees. Basically, Lyft agreed to change its terms of service to conform to California's independent contractor status regulations. For instance, the company can no longer deactivate drivers' accounts without reason and without warning the drivers. Drivers have to be given a fair hearing first. Even though the lawsuit and the agreement were California based, the new terms of service will apply to all Lyft's drivers nationwide.

#### Competitors Sue Uber

In many cities, competitors, especially taxi drivers, have sued Uber. These lawsuits have involved claims of unfair competition, lack of minimum wages, and unsafe vehicles. A taxi driver sued Uber in northern California, for instance, but a federal district court ruled in favor of Uber's request for summary judgment.[b]

Another suit was brought in Pennsylvania. In this one, Checker Cab of Philadelphia claimed that Uber was violating Pennsylvania's unfair competition law. Checker Cab sought a preliminary injunction to prevent Uber from taking away its customers. The federal district court refused to grant an injunction, however, because Checker Cab failed to show irreparable harm. That decision was upheld on appeal.[c]

**Critical Thinking** *What choices do disgruntled Uber and Lyft drivers have?*

a. *Cotter v. Lyft, Inc.*, 60 F.Supp.3d 1067 (N.D.Cal. 2015); *O'Connor v. Uber Technologies, Inc., et al.*, Case No. C-13-3826 EMC (N.D.Cal. 2015).
b. *Rosen v. Uber Technologies, Inc.*, __ F.Supp.3d __, 2016 WL 704078 (N.D.Cal. 2016).
c. *Checker Cab of Philadelphia v. Uber Technologies, Inc.*, __ Fed.Appx. __, 2016 WL 929310 (3d Cir. 2016).

---

Pershad was Five Star's employee and that Five Star was an independent contractor, not AAA's employee. Therefore, AAA was not liable (and Five Star was, so it entered into a settlement agreement with Coker). Coker appealed, but a state intermediate appellate court affirmed. AAA could not be held liable for the actions of Five Star, its independent contractor, because "AAA did not control the manner and means of Five Star's work."[2] ∎

**Criteria Used by the IRS** The Internal Revenue Service (IRS) has established its own criteria for determining

2. *Coker v. Pershad*, 2013 WL 1296271 (N.J.Sup.Ct. 2013).

whether a worker is an independent contractor or an employee. The most important factor is the degree of control the business exercises over the worker.

The IRS tends to closely scrutinize a firm's classification of its workers because, as mentioned, employers can avoid certain tax liabilities by hiring independent contractors instead of employees. Even when a firm has classified a worker as an independent contractor, the IRS may decide that the worker is actually an employee. If the IRS decides that an employee is misclassified, the employer will be responsible for paying any applicable Social Security, withholding, and unemployment taxes due for that employee.

**Employee Status and "Works for Hire"** Ordinarily, a person who creates a copyrighted work is the owner of it—unless it is a "work for hire." Under the Copyright Act, any copyrighted work created by an employee within the scope of her or his employment at the request of the employer is a "work for hire." The employer owns the copyright to the work.

In contrast, when an employer hires an independent contractor—such as a freelance artist, writer, or computer programmer—the independent contractor normally owns the copyright. An exception is made if the parties agree in writing that the work is a "work for hire" and the work falls into one of nine specific categories. The nine categories include audiovisual works, collective works (such as magazines), motion pictures, textbooks, tests, and translations.

■ **CASE IN POINT 19.2** As a freelance contractor, Brian Cooley created two sculptures of dinosaur eggs for the National Geographic Society for use in connection with an article in its magazine, *National Geographic.* Cooley spent hundreds of hours researching, designing, and constructing the sculptures. National Geographic hired Louis Psihoyos to photograph Cooley's sculptures for the article. Cooley and Psihoyos had separate contracts with National Geographic in which each transferred the copyrights in their works to National Geographic for a limited time.

The rights to the works were returned to the artists at different times after publication. Psihoyos then began licensing his photographs of Cooley's sculptures to third parties in return for royalties. He digitized the photographs and licensed them to various online stock photography companies, and they appeared in several books published by Penguin Group. Cooley sued Psihoyos for copyright infringement.

Psihoyos argued that he owned the photos and could license them however he saw fit, but a federal district court disagreed. The court found that Psihoyos did not have an unrestricted right to use and license the photos.

When Psihoyos reproduced an image of a Cooley sculpture, he reproduced the sculpture, which infringed on Cooley's copyright. Therefore, the court granted a summary judgment to Cooley.[3] ■

## 19–2 Formation of the Agency Relationship

Agency relationships normally are consensual. They come about by voluntary consent and agreement between the parties. Normally, the agreement need not be in writing, and consideration is not required.

A person must have contractual capacity to be a principal.[4] The idea is that those who cannot legally enter into contracts directly should not be allowed to do so indirectly through an agent. Any person can be an agent, however, regardless of whether he or she has the capacity to contract (including minors).

An agency relationship can be created for any legal purpose. An agency relationship created for a purpose that is illegal or contrary to public policy is unenforceable. ■ **EXAMPLE 19.3** Archer (as principal) contracts with Burke (as agent) to sell illegal narcotics. The agency relationship is unenforceable because selling illegal narcotics is a felony and is contrary to public policy. If Burke sells the narcotics and keeps the profits, Archer cannot sue to enforce the agency agreement. ■

An agency relationship can arise in four ways: by agreement of the parties, by ratification, by estoppel, and by operation of law.

### 19–2a Agency by Agreement

Most agency relationships are based on an express or implied agreement that the agent will act for the principal and that the principal agrees to have the agent so act. An agency agreement can take the form of an express written contract or be created by an oral agreement. ■ **EXAMPLE 19.4** Reese asks Grace, a gardener, to contract with others for the care of his lawn on a regular basis. If Grace agrees, an agency relationship exists between Reese and Grace for the lawn care. ■

An agency agreement can also be implied by conduct. ■ **CASE IN POINT 19.5** Gilbert Bishop was admitted to a nursing home, Laurel Creek Health Care Center, suffering from various physical ailments. He was not able to use his hands well enough to write but was otherwise

---

3. *Cooley v. Penguin Group (USA), Inc.,* 31 F.Supp.3d 599 (S.D.N.Y. 2014).
4. Note that some states allow a minor to be a principal. When a minor is permitted to be a principal, any resulting contracts will be voidable by the minor principal but *not* by the adult third party.

mentally competent. Bishop's sister offered to sign the admission papers for him, but it was Laurel Creek's policy to have the patient's spouse sign the forms if the patient could not.

Bishop's sister then brought his wife, Anna, to the hospital to sign the paperwork, which included a mandatory arbitration clause. Later, when the family filed a lawsuit against Laurel Creek, the nursing home sought to enforce the arbitration clause. Ultimately, a Kentucky appellate court held that Bishop was bound by the contract and the arbitration clause his wife had signed. Bishop's conduct had indicated that he was giving his wife authority to act as his agent in signing the admission papers.[5] ■

### 19–2b Agency by Ratification

On occasion, a person who is in fact not an agent (or who is an agent acting outside the scope of her or his authority) makes a contract on behalf of another (a principal). If the principal approves or affirms that contract by word or by action, an agency relationship is created by *ratification.* Ratification involves a question of intent, and intent can be expressed by either words or conduct.

### 19–2c Agency by Estoppel

Sometimes, a principal causes a third person to believe that another person is the principal's agent, and the third person acts to his or her detriment in reasonable reliance on that belief. When this occurs, the principal is "estopped to deny" (prevented from denying) the agency relationship. The principal's actions have created the *appearance* of an agency that does not in fact exist, creating an agency by estoppel.

**The Third Party's Reliance Must Be Reasonable** The third person must prove that he or she *reasonably* believed that an agency relationship existed.[6] Facts and circumstances must show that an ordinary, prudent person familiar with business practice and custom would have been justified in concluding that the agent had authority.

**Created by the Principal's Conduct** Note that the acts or declarations of a purported *agent* in and of themselves do not create an agency by estoppel. Rather,

it is the deeds or statements of the *principal* that create an agency by estoppel. ■ **CASE IN POINT 19.6** Francis Azur was president and chief executive officer of ATM Corporation of America. Michelle Vanek was Azur's personal assistant. Among other duties, she reviewed his credit-card statements. For seven years, Vanek took unauthorized cash advances from Azur's credit-card account with Chase Bank. The charges appeared on at least sixty-five monthly statements.

When Azur discovered Vanek's fraud, he fired her and closed the account. He filed a suit against Chase, arguing that the bank should not have allowed Vanek to take cash advances. The court concluded that Azur (the principal) had given the bank reason to believe that Vanek (the agent) had authority. Therefore, Azur was estopped (prevented) from denying Vanek's authority.[7] ■

### 19–2d Agency by Operation of Law

The courts may find an agency relationship in the absence of a formal agreement in other situations as well. This may occur in family relationships, such as when one spouse purchases certain basic necessaries and charges them to the other spouse's account. The courts often rule that a spouse is liable for payment for the necessaries because of either a social policy or a legal duty to supply necessaries to family members.

Agency by operation of law may also occur in emergency situations. If an agent cannot contact the principal and failure to act would cause the principal substantial loss, the agent may take steps beyond the scope of her or his authority. For instance, a railroad engineer may contract on behalf of his or her employer for medical care for an injured motorist hit by the train.

## 19–3 Duties of Agents and Principals

Once the principal-agent relationship has been created, both parties have duties that govern their conduct. As discussed previously, the principal-agent relationship is *fiduciary*—based on trust. In a fiduciary relationship, each party owes the other the duty to act with the utmost good faith.

5. *Laurel Creek Health Care Center v. Bishop,* 2010 WL 985299 (Ky.App. 2010).
6. These concepts also apply when a person who is, in fact, an agent undertakes an action that is beyond the scope of her or his authority.
7. *Azur v. Chase Bank, USA, N.A.,* 601 F.3d 212 (3d Cir. 2010).

## 19–3a Agent's Duties to the Principal

Generally, the agent owes the principal five duties—performance, notification, loyalty, obedience, and accounting (see Exhibit 19–1).

**Performance** An implied condition in every agency contract is the agent's agreement to use reasonable diligence and skill in performing the work. When an agent fails to perform his or her duties, liability for breach of contract may result.

**Standard of Care.** The degree of skill or care required of an agent is usually that expected of a reasonable person under similar circumstances. Generally, this is interpreted to mean ordinary care. If an agent has represented herself or himself as possessing special skills, however, the agent is expected to exercise the degree of skill claimed. Failure to do so constitutes a breach of the agent's duty.

**Gratuitous Agents.** Not all agency relationships are based on contract. In some situations, an agent acts gratuitously—that is, without payment. A gratuitous agent cannot be liable for breach of contract because there is no contract. He or she is subject only to tort liability. Once a gratuitous agent has begun to act in an agency capacity, he or she has the duty to continue to perform in that capacity. A gratuitous agent must perform in an acceptable manner and is subject to the same standards of care and duty to perform as other agents.

■ **EXAMPLE 19.7** Bower's friend Alcott is a real estate broker. Alcott offers to sell Bower's vacation home at no charge. If Alcott never attempts to sell the home, Bower has no legal cause of action to force her to do so. If Alcott does attempt to sell the home to Friedman, but then performs so negligently that the sale falls through, Bower can sue Alcott for negligence. ■

**Notification** An agent is required to notify the principal of all matters that come to her or his attention concerning the subject matter of the agency. This is the *duty of notification,* or the duty to inform.

■ **EXAMPLE 19.8** Perez, an artist, is about to negotiate a contract to sell a series of paintings to Barber's Art Gallery for $25,000. Perez's agent learns that Barber is insolvent and will be unable to pay for the paintings. The agent has a duty to inform Perez of Barber's insolvency because it is relevant to the subject matter of the agency, which is the sale of Perez's paintings. ■

Generally, the law assumes that the principal is aware of any information acquired by the agent that is relevant to the agency—regardless of whether the agent actually passes on this information to the principal. It is a basic tenet of agency law that notice to the agent is notice to the principal.

**Loyalty** Loyalty is one of the most fundamental duties in a fiduciary relationship. Basically, the agent has the duty to act *solely for the benefit of his or her principal* and not in the interest of the agent or a third party. For instance, an agent cannot represent two principals in the same transaction unless both know of the dual capacity and consent to it.

**EXHIBIT 19–1 Duties of the Agent**

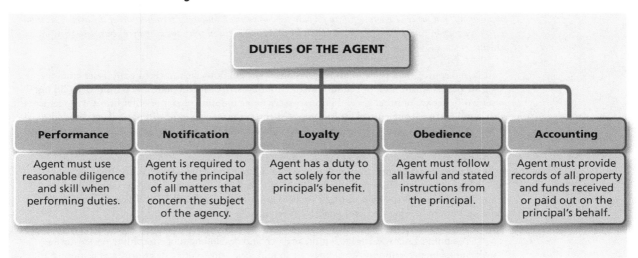

| **DUTIES OF THE AGENT** | | | | |
| --- | --- | --- | --- | --- |
| **Performance** | **Notification** | **Loyalty** | **Obedience** | **Accounting** |
| Agent must use reasonable diligence and skill when performing duties. | Agent is required to notify the principal of all matters that concern the subject of the agency. | Agent has a duty to act solely for the principal's benefit. | Agent must follow all lawful and stated instructions from the principal. | Agent must provide records of all property and funds received or paid out on the principal's behalf. |

The duty of loyalty also means that any information or knowledge acquired through the agency relationship is confidential. It is a breach of loyalty to disclose such information either during the agency relationship or after its termination. Typical examples of confidential information are trade secrets and customer lists compiled by the principal.

The agent's loyalty must be undivided. The agent's actions must be strictly for the benefit of the principal and must not result in any secret profit for the agent.

In the following case, an employer alleged that a former employee had breached his duty of loyalty by planning a competing business while still working for the employer.

## Spotlight on Taser International

## Case 19.1 Taser International, Inc. v. Ward

Court of Appeals of Arizona, Division 1, 224 Ariz. 389, 231 P.3d 921 (2010).

**Background and Facts** Taser International, Inc., develops and makes electronic control devices, commonly called stun guns, as well as accessories for electronic control devices, including a personal video and audio recording device called the TASER CAM.

Steve Ward was Taser's vice president of marketing when he began to explore the possibility of developing and marketing devices of his own design, including a clip-on camera. Ward talked to patent attorneys and a product development company and completed most of a business plan. After he resigned from Taser, he formed Vievu, LLC, to market his clip-on camera.

Ten months after Ward resigned, Taser announced the AXON, a product that provides an audio-video record of an incident from the visual perspective of the person involved. Taser then filed a suit in an Arizona state court against Ward, alleging that he had breached his duty of loyalty to Taser. The court granted Taser's motion for a summary judgment in the employer's favor. Ward appealed.

### In the Language of the Court

*PORTLEY,* Judge.

\* \* \* \*

\* \* \* An agent is under the duty to act with entire good faith and loyalty for the furtherance of the interests of his principal in all matters concerning or affecting the subject of his agency.

One aspect of this broad principle is that an employee is precluded from actively competing with his or her employer during the period of employment.

*Although an employee may not compete prior to termination, the employee may take action during employment, not otherwise wrongful, to prepare for competition following termination of the agency relationship. Preparation cannot take the form of acts in direct competition with the employer's business.* [Emphasis added.]

\* \* \* \*

It is undisputed that, prior to his resignation, Ward did not solicit or recruit any Taser employees, distributors, customers, or vendors; he did not buy, sell, or incorporate any business; he did not acquire office space or other general business services; he did not contact or enter into any agreements with suppliers or manufacturers for his proposed clip-on camera; and he did not sell any products. However, Ward did begin developing a business plan, counseled with several attorneys, explored and abandoned the concept of an eyeglass-mounted camera device, and engaged, to some extent, in the exploration and development of a clip-on camera device.

Ward argues that his pre-termination activities did not constitute active competition but were merely lawful preparation for a future business venture. Taser contends, however, that "this case is \* \* \* about developing a rival design during employment, knowing full well TASER has sold such a device and continues to develop a second-generation product."

\* \* \* \*

\* \* \* Assuming Taser was engaged in the research and development of a recording device during Ward's employment, assuming Ward knew or should have known of those efforts, and assuming Taser's device would compete with Ward's concept, substantial design and development efforts by Ward during his employment would constitute direct competition with the business activities of Taser and

**Case 19.1 Continued** | would violate his duty of loyalty. In the context of a business which engages in research, design, development, manufacture, and marketing of products, we cannot limit "competition" to just actual sales of competing products.

**Decision and Remedy** *A state intermediate appellate court agreed with Taser that an employee may not actively compete with his employer before his employment is terminated. But the parties disputed the extent of Ward's pre-termination efforts, creating a genuine issue of material fact that could not be resolved on a motion for summary judgment. The appellate court thus reversed the lower court's decision in Taser's favor and remanded the case for further proceedings.*

**Critical Thinking**

- **Legal Environment** *Did Ward breach any duties owed to his employer in addition to his alleged breach of the duty of loyalty? Discuss.*
- **What If the Facts Were Different?** *Suppose that Ward's pre-termination activities focused on a product that was not designed to compete with Taser's products. Would these efforts have breached the duty of loyalty? Why or why not?*

---

**Obedience** When acting on behalf of the principal, an agent has a duty to follow all lawful and clearly stated instructions of the principal. Any deviation from such instructions is a violation of this duty.

During emergency situations, however, when the principal cannot be consulted, the agent may deviate from the instructions without violating this duty. Whenever instructions are not clearly stated, the agent can fulfill the duty of obedience by acting in good faith and in a manner reasonable under the circumstances.

**Accounting** Unless the agent and principal agree otherwise, the agent must keep and make available to the principal an account of all property and funds received and paid out on the principal's behalf. This includes gifts from third parties in connection with the agency.

The agent has a duty to maintain a separate account for the principal's funds and must not intermingle these funds with the agent's personal funds. If a licensed professional (such as an attorney) violates this duty, he or she may be subject to disciplinary action by the licensing authority (such as the state bar association). Of course, the professional will also be liable to his or her client (the principal) for failure to account.

## 19–3b Principal's Duties to the Agent

The principal also has certain duties to the agent (as shown in Exhibit 19–2). These duties relate to compensation,

**EXHIBIT 19–2 Duties of the Principal**

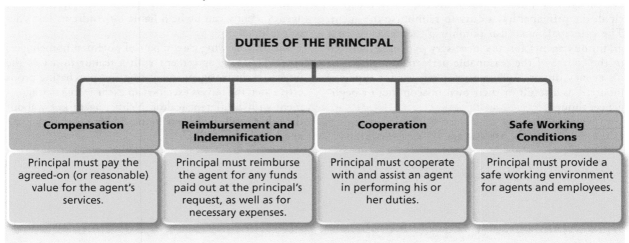

| DUTIES OF THE PRINCIPAL | | | |
|---|---|---|---|
| **Compensation** | **Reimbursement and Indemnification** | **Cooperation** | **Safe Working Conditions** |
| Principal must pay the agreed-on (or reasonable) value for the agent's services. | Principal must reimburse the agent for any funds paid out at the principal's request, as well as for necessary expenses. | Principal must cooperate with and assist an agent in performing his or her duties. | Principal must provide a safe working environment for agents and employees. |

reimbursement and indemnification, cooperation, and safe working conditions.

**Compensation** In general, when a principal requests certain services from an agent, the agent reasonably expects payment. For instance, when an accountant or an attorney is asked to act as an agent, an agreement to compensate the agent for this service is implied. The principal therefore has a duty to pay the agent for services rendered.

Unless the agency relationship is gratuitous and the agent does not act in exchange for payment, the principal must pay the agreed-on value for the agent's services. If no amount has been expressly agreed on, then the principal owes the agent the customary compensation for such services. The principal also has a duty to pay that compensation in a timely manner.

■ **CASE IN POINT 19.9** Keith Miller worked as a sales representative for Paul M. Wolff Company, a subcontractor specializing in concrete-finishing services. Sales representatives at Wolff are paid a 15 percent commission on projects that meet a 35 percent gross profit threshold. The commission is paid after the projects are completed. When Miller resigned, he asked for commissions on fourteen projects for which he had secured contracts but which had not yet been completed. Wolff refused, so Miller sued.

The court found that "an agent is entitled to receive commissions on sales that result from the agent's efforts," even after the employment or agency relationship ends. Miller had met the gross profit threshold on ten of the unfinished projects, and therefore, he was entitled to more than $21,000 in commissions.[8] ■

**Reimbursement and Indemnification** Whenever an agent disburses funds at the request of the principal, the principal has a duty to reimburse the agent. The principal must also reimburse the agent (even a gratuitous agent) for any necessary expenses incurred in the course of the reasonable performance of her or his agency duties. Agents cannot recover for expenses incurred as a result of their own misconduct or negligence, though.

8. *Miller v. Paul M. Wolff Co.*, 178 Wash.App. 957, 316 P.3d 1113 (2014).

Subject to the terms of the agency agreement, the principal has the duty to *indemnify* (compensate) an agent for liabilities incurred because of authorized and lawful acts and transactions. For instance, if the agent, on the principal's behalf, forms a contract with a third party, and the principal fails to perform the contract, the third party may sue the agent for damages. In this situation, the principal is obligated to compensate the agent for any costs incurred by the agent as a result of the principal's failure to perform the contract.

Additionally, the principal must indemnify the agent for the value of benefits that the agent confers on the principal. The amount of indemnification usually is specified in the agency contract. If it is not, the courts will look to the nature of the business and the type of loss to determine the amount. Note that this rule applies to acts by gratuitous agents as well.

**Cooperation** A principal has a duty to cooperate with the agent and to assist the agent in performing his or her duties. The principal must do nothing to prevent that performance.

For instance, when a principal grants an agent an exclusive territory, the principal creates an **exclusive agency,** in which the principal cannot compete with the agent or appoint or allow another agent to compete. If the principal does so, he or she violates the exclusive agency and is exposed to liability for the agent's lost profits.

■ **EXAMPLE 19.10** Penny (the principal) creates an exclusive agency by granting Andrew (the agent) a territory within which only Andrew may sell Penny's organic skin care products. If Penny starts to sell the products herself within Andrew's territory—or permits another agent to do so—Penny has failed to cooperate with the agent. Because she has violated the exclusive agency, Penny can be held liable for Andrew's lost sales or profits. ■

In the following case, a pair of potential homebuyers entered into an agreement with a realtor to act as the buyers' exclusive agent in locating and purchasing property. Later, the buyers executed an exclusive agency agreement with a different realtor. Neither agent knew about the other until the buyers found a home that they liked and bought it.

# NRT New England, LLC v. Jones

Appellate Court of Connecticut, 162 Conn.App. 840, 134 A.3d 632 (2016).

## In the Language of the Court

*HARPER*, J. [Judge]

* * * *

The defendant [Christopher Jones] met Andrea Woolston, a licensed realtor working as an independent contractor [for NRT New England, LLC, doing business as Coldwell Banker Residential Brokerage], in October 2010. The defendant expressed to Woolston a desire to purchase a home for himself and his then fiancée, Katherine Wiltshire. One of the first things Woolston asked the defendant was whether he was represented by another agent. The defendant responded that he was not. After a number of conversations about the defendant's needs and wishes, the parties executed an exclusive right to represent buyer agreement (agreement), which established, among other things, that Woolston was the defendant's exclusive agent for finding, negotiating, and purchasing property. Over the next several months, Woolston devoted a substantial amount of time searching for properties for the defendant to purchase. Specifically, Woolston researched available properties at six town halls in the communities in which the defendant was interested. She showcased a number of properties personally to the defendant and Wiltshire and introduced many more to them through e-mail. Woolston and the defendant had at least twenty appointments where they viewed multiple properties. Additionally, Woolston visited many properties alone to determine if they were suitable for the defendant. Altogether, Woolston spent hundreds of hours seeking a suitable home for the defendant.

The agreement was in effect from January 11, 2011 until July 11, 2011, and set forth the geographical area that the defendant was interested in and the rate of compensation for the plaintiff's services. With respect to geographical area, the parties agreed that Woolston would seek properties in Killingworth, Guilford, Essex, Old Saybrook, Deep River, Lyme, and Old Lyme [Connecticut]. With respect to compensation, the defendant agreed to pay the plaintiff a commission equal to 2.5 percent of the purchase price of the property "if the [buyer] or any person or entity acting on the [buyer's] behalf purchases, options, exchanges, leases or trades any property, through the efforts of anyone, including the [buyer]." The agreement imposed the following duties on the defendant: "The [buyer] will not deal directly with any other broker, agent or licensee during the term of this agreement. The [buyer] will notify other brokers, agents or licensees at first contact that the [buyer] is being exclusively represented by [NRT]. The [buyer] will disclose to [NRT] any past and/or current contacts for any real property or with any other real estate broker or agent."

On May 10, 2011, the defendant informed Woolston via e-mail that he and Wiltshire purchased property at 300 Vineyard Point Road in Guilford for $1,375,000. The defendant learned of this property on May 4, 2011, from Mary Jane Burt, a realtor with H. Pearce Real Estate (H. Pearce), who previously had represented Wiltshire with the sale of her house in Hamden [Connecticut]. Woolston subsequently confronted the defendant and eventually learned that he

and Wiltshire previously had executed an exclusive right to represent buyer agreement with Burt and H. Pearce. This agreement was in effect from August 1, 2010, until August 1, 2011, and contained a provision designating Burt as the exclusive agent for the defendant and Wiltshire. Thus, at the time the defendant purchased the property in Guilford, he was under contract for exclusive agency with both Woolston and Burt. The defendant never told Woolston or Burt that he had two agreements in effect at the same time. Woolston notified her superiors of what had transpired.

* * * [NRT] filed a * * * complaint [in a Connecticut state court] against the defendant [for] breach of contract * * * . After a trial * * * , the court * * * found that the plaintiff had proven * * * breach of contract * * * and damages. * * * The court awarded the plaintiff $34,375 in damages [which represented 2.5 percent of the purchase price for the Vineyard Point property] plus attorney's fees and costs. This appeal followed.

* * * *

The defendant * * * claims that the agreement was unenforceable. Specifically, he argues that the court improperly * * * found that it was inequitable to deny the plaintiff recovery.

* * * *

There is ample evidence in the record to support the court's conclusion that denying the plaintiff relief would be inequitable. Woolston testified, and the defendant himself conceded, that she rendered a significant amount of services to the defendant over several months.

**Case 19.2 Continues**

**Case 19.2 Continued**

Specifically, Woolston researched properties at town halls for availability and encumbrances, contacted property owners, arranged personal visits, prepared and presented literature to the defendant on available properties, and attended appointments with the defendant and Wiltshire. Woolston spent hundreds of hours working for the defendant in total.

The defendant, on the other hand, accepted Woolston's services while under contract with another agent in violation of the agreement. Indeed, the defendant acknowledged that he was untruthful with Woolston at the beginning of their relationship when he told her that he was not represented by another agent.

In fact, he was scheduling appointments and viewing properties with both Woolston and Burt at approximately the same time in May 2011. For example, the defendant e-mailed Woolston on May 2, 2011, thanking her for showing him a property. Approximately one week later, the defendant e-mailed Woolston to inform her that he viewed 300 Vineyard Point Road with Burt and had "put in an all cash bid that has been accepted."

The defendant nevertheless argues that it would not be inequitable to deny recovery to the plaintiff because Woolston performed no services in connection with his purchase of 300

Vineyard Point Road. We are not persuaded. *The defendant agreed to pay a commission "equal to 2.5% of the purchase price if the [buyer] or any person or entity acting on the [buyer's] behalf purchases * * * any property, through the efforts of anyone, including the [buyer], where an agreement to purchase the property was entered into during the term of this agreement."* However unjust this result may seem to the defendant in hindsight, we cannot say it is inequitable because it is precisely what he agreed to. [Emphasis added.]

\* \* \* \*

The judgment is affirmed.

**Legal Reasoning Questions**

**1.** What is the advantage to a principal of an exclusive agency agreement? What was the advantage to Jones of his agreement with Woolston? Discuss.

**2.** Why, in addition to damages, was the plaintiff awarded attorneys' fees and costs?

**3.** Jones's agreement with Woolston provided that on the purchase of the property, NRT "will, whenever feasible, seek compensation from the seller or the seller's agent." The court determined that it was not feasible. Why would it not be reasonable in this situation to ask the seller of the property to pay part of Woolston's commission?

---

**Safe Working Conditions** The common law requires the principal to provide safe working premises, equipment, and conditions for all agents and employees. The principal has a duty to inspect working areas and to warn agents and employees about any unsafe situations. When the agent is an employee, the employer's liability is frequently covered by state workers' compensation insurance. In addition, federal and state statutes often require the employer to meet certain safety standards.

### 19–3c Rights and Remedies of Agents and Principals

In general, for every duty of the principal, the agent has a corresponding right, and vice versa. When one party to the agency relationship violates his or her duty to the other party, the remedies available to the nonbreaching party arise out of contract and tort law. These remedies include monetary damages, termination of the agency relationship, an injunction, and required accountings.

The agent has the right to be compensated, to be reimbursed and indemnified, and to have a safe working

environment. An agent also has the right to perform agency duties without interference by the principal. In addition, an agent can withhold further performance and demand that the principal give an accounting.

A principal has contract remedies for an agent's breach of fiduciary duties. The principal has tort remedies if the agent engages in misrepresentation, negligence, deceit, libel, slander, or trespass. In addition, any breach of a fiduciary duty by an agent may justify the principal's termination of the agency.

## 19–4 Agent's Authority

The liability of a principal to third parties with whom an agent contracts depends on whether the agent had the authority to enter into legally binding contracts on the principal's behalf. An agent's authority can be either *actual* (express or implied) or *apparent*. If an agent contracts outside the scope of his or her authority, the principal may still become liable by ratifying the contract.

### 19–4a Express Authority

**Express authority** is authority declared in clear, direct, and definite terms. Express authority can be given orally or in writing.

**The Equal Dignity Rule** In most states, the **equal dignity rule** requires that if the contract being executed is or must be in writing, then the agent's authority must also be in writing. (Recall that a writing includes an electronic record.) Failure to comply with the equal dignity rule can make a contract voidable *at the option of the principal.* The law regards the contract at that point as a mere offer. If the principal decides to accept the offer, the acceptance must be ratified, or affirmed, in writing.

■ **EXAMPLE 19.11** Paloma (the principal) orally asks Austin (the agent) to sell a ranch that Paloma owns. Austin finds a buyer and signs a sales contract on behalf of Paloma to sell the ranch. Because a contract for an interest in realty must be in writing, the equal dignity rule applies. The buyer cannot enforce the contract unless Paloma subsequently ratifies Austin's agency status *in a writing.* Once the sales contract is ratified, either party can enforce rights under the contract. ■

Modern business practice allows several exceptions to the equal dignity rule:

1. An executive officer of a corporation normally can conduct *ordinary* business transactions without obtaining written authority from the corporation.
2. When the agent acts in the presence of the principal, the rule does not apply.
3. When the agent's act of signing is merely a formality, then the agent does not need written authority to sign. ■ **EXAMPLE 19.12** Sandra Healy (the principal) negotiates a contract but is called out of town the day it is to be signed. If Healy orally authorizes Derek Santini to sign, the oral authorization is sufficient. ■

**Power of Attorney** Giving an agent a **power of attorney** confers express authority.[9] The power of attorney is a written document and is usually notarized. (A document is notarized when a **notary public**—a person authorized to attest to the authenticity of signatures—signs, dates, and imprints the document with her or his seal of authority.) Most states have statutory provisions for creating a power of attorney.

A power of attorney can be *special* (permitting the agent to perform specified acts only), or it can be *general* (permitting the agent to transact all business for the principal). Because a general power of attorney grants extensive authority to the agent, it should be used with great caution and usually only in exceptional circumstances. Ordinarily, a power of attorney terminates on the incapacity or death of the person giving the power.[10]

### 19–4b Implied Authority

An agent has the **implied authority** to do what is reasonably necessary to carry out express authority and accomplish the objectives of the agency. Authority can also be implied by custom or inferred from the position the agent occupies.

■ **EXAMPLE 19.13** Archer is employed by Packard Grocery to manage one of its stores. Packard has not expressly stated that Archer has authority to contract with third persons. Nevertheless, authority to manage a business implies authority to do what is reasonably required (as is customary or can be inferred from a manager's position) to operate the business. This includes forming contracts to hire employees, buying merchandise and equipment, and advertising the products sold in the store. ■

Note, however, that an agent's implied authority cannot contradict his or her express authority. Thus, if a principal has limited an agent's express authority, then the fact that the agent customarily would have such authority is irrelevant.

### 19–4c Apparent Authority

Actual authority (express or implied) arises from what the principal makes clear *to the agent.* Apparent authority, in contrast, arises from what the principal causes a third party to believe. An agent has **apparent authority** when the principal, by either word or action, causes a *third party* reasonably to believe that the agent has authority to act, even though the agent has no express or implied authority.

Apparent authority usually comes into existence through a principal's pattern of conduct over time. ■ **CASE IN POINT 19.14** Gilbert Church owned Church Farm, Inc., a horse-breeding farm in Illinois, which was managed by Herb Bagley. Church Farm's advertisements for the breeding rights to one of its stallions, Imperial Guard, directed all inquiries to "Herb Bagley, Manager." Vern and Gail Lundberg contacted Bagley and executed a preprinted contract giving them breeding rights to Imperial

---

9. An agent who holds a power of attorney is called an *attorney-in-fact* for the principal. The holder does not have to be an attorney-at-law (and often is not).

10. A *durable* power of attorney, however, continues to be effective despite the principal's incapacity or death. An elderly person, for instance, might grant a durable power of attorney to provide for the handling of property and investments or specific health-care needs should he or she become incompetent.

Guard "at Imperial Guard's location." Bagley handwrote a statement on the contract that guaranteed the Lundbergs "six live foals in the first two years." He then signed it "Gilbert G. Church by H. Bagley."

The Lundbergs bred four mares, which resulted in one live foal. Church then moved Imperial Guard from Illinois to Oklahoma. The Lundbergs sued Church for breaching the contract by moving the horse. Church claimed that Bagley was not authorized to sign contracts for Church or to change or add terms but only to present preprinted contracts to potential buyers. The jury found in favor of the Lundbergs and awarded $147,000 in damages. Church appealed, but the state appellate court affirmed the judgment. The court found that "an agent may bind his principal by acts which the principal has not given him actual authority to perform, but which he appears authorized to perform." Because Church allowed circumstances to lead the Lundbergs to believe Bagley had the authority, Church was bound by Bagley's actions.[11] ∎

### 19–4d Emergency Powers

When an unforeseen emergency demands action by the agent to protect or preserve the property and rights of the principal, but the agent is unable to communicate with the principal, the agent has emergency power. ∎ **EXAMPLE 19.15** Rob Fulsom is an engineer for Pacific Drilling Company. While Fulsom is acting within the scope of his employment, he is severely injured in an accident on an oil rig many miles from home. Acosta, the rig supervisor, directs Thompson, a physician, to give medical aid to Fulsom and to charge Pacific for the medical services.

Acosta, an agent, has no express or implied authority to bind the principal, Pacific Drilling, for Thompson's medical services. Because of the emergency situation, however, the law recognizes Acosta as having authority to act appropriately under the circumstances. ∎

### 19–4e Ratification

**Ratification** occurs when the principal affirms, or accepts responsibility for, an agent's *unauthorized* act. When ratification occurs, the principal is bound to the agent's act, and the act is treated as if it had been authorized by the principal *from the outset.* Ratification can be either express or implied.

If the principal does not ratify the contract, the principal is not bound, and the third party's agreement with the agent is viewed as merely an unaccepted offer. Because the third party's agreement is an unaccepted offer, the third party can revoke it at any time, without liability, before the principal ratifies the contract. The agent, however, may be liable to the third party for misrepresenting her or his authority.

The requirements for ratification can be summarized as follows:

1. The agent must have acted on behalf of an identified principal who subsequently ratifies the action.
2. The principal must know all of the material facts involved in the transaction. If a principal ratifies a contract without knowing all of the facts, the principal can rescind (cancel) the contract.
3. The principal must affirm the agent's act in its entirety.
4. The principal must have the legal capacity to authorize the transaction at the time the agent engages in the act and at the time the principal ratifies. The third party must also have the legal capacity to engage in the transaction.
5. The principal's affirmation (ratification) must occur before the third party withdraws from the transaction.
6. The principal must observe the same formalities when ratifying the act as would have been required to authorize it initially.

## 19–5 Liability in Agency Relationships

Frequently, a question arises as to which party, the principal or the agent, should be held liable for contracts formed by the agent or for torts and crimes committed by the agent.

### 19–5a Liability for Contracts

Liability for contracts formed by an agent depends on how the principal is classified and on whether the actions of the agent were authorized or unauthorized. Principals are classified as disclosed, partially disclosed, or undisclosed.[12]

1. A **disclosed principal** is a principal whose identity is known by the third party at the time the contract is made by the agent.
2. A **partially disclosed principal** is a principal whose identity is not known by the third party. Nevertheless, the third party knows that the agent is or *may*

---

11. *Lundberg v. Church Farm, Inc.*, 502 N.E.2d 806, 151 Ill.App.3d (1986).

12. *Restatement (Third) of Agency*, Section 1.04(2).

*be* acting for a principal at the time the contract is made. ■ **EXAMPLE 19.16** Eileen has contracted with a real estate agent to sell certain property. She wishes to keep her identity a secret, but the agent makes it clear to potential buyers of the property that he is acting in an agency capacity. In this situation, Eileen is a partially disclosed principal. ■

3. An **undisclosed principal** is a principal whose identity is totally unknown by the third party. In addition, the third party has no knowledge that the agent is acting in an agency capacity at the time the contract is made.

**Authorized Acts** If an agent acts within the scope of her or his authority, normally the principal is obligated to perform the contract regardless of whether the principal was disclosed, partially disclosed, or undisclosed. Whether the *agent may also be held liable* under the contract, however, depends on the disclosed, partially disclosed, or undisclosed status of the principal.

**Disclosed or Partially Disclosed Principal.** A disclosed or partially disclosed principal is liable to a third party for a contract made by the agent. If the principal is disclosed, the agent has no contractual liability for the nonperformance of the principal or the third party. If the principal is partially disclosed, in most states the agent is also treated as a party to the contract. Thus, the third party can hold the agent liable for contractual nonperformance.[13]

■ **CASE IN POINT 19.17** Stonhard, Inc., makes epoxy and urethane flooring and installs it in industrial and commercial buildings. Marvin Sussman contracted with Stonhard to install flooring at a Blue Ridge Farms food-manufacturing facility in Brooklyn, New York. Sussman did not disclose that he was acting as an agent for the facility's owner, Blue Ridge Foods, LLC, at the time of the contract.

When Stonhard was not paid for the flooring it installed, it filed a suit against the facility, its owner, and Sussman to recover damages for breach of contract. The lower court dismissed the complaint against Sussman personally, but on appeal a reviewing court reversed that decision. The contract had been signed by Sussman "of Blue Ridge Farms." That evidence indicated that Sussman was acting as an agent for a partially disclosed principal, in that the agency relationship was known, but not the principal's identity. "As an agent for an undisclosed

[or partially disclosed] principal, Sussman became personally liable under the contract."[14] ■

**Undisclosed Principal.** When neither the fact of an agency relationship nor the identity of the principal is disclosed, the undisclosed principal is bound to perform just as if the principal had been fully disclosed at the time the contract was made.

When a principal's identity is undisclosed and the agent is forced to pay the third party, the agent is entitled to be indemnified (compensated) by the principal. The principal had a duty to perform, even though his or her identity was undisclosed, and failure to do so will make the principal ultimately liable.

Once the undisclosed principal's identity is revealed, the third party generally can elect to hold either the principal or the agent liable on the contract. Conversely, the undisclosed principal can require the third party to fulfill the contract, *unless* one of the following is true:

1. The undisclosed principal was expressly excluded as a party in the written contract.
2. The contract is a negotiable instrument signed by the agent with no indication of signing in a representative capacity.[15]
3. The performance of the agent is personal to the contract, thus allowing the third party to refuse the principal's performance.

**Unauthorized Acts** If an agent has no authority but nevertheless contracts with a third party, the *principal* cannot be held liable on the contract. It does not matter whether the principal was disclosed, partially disclosed, or undisclosed. The *agent* is liable.

■ **EXAMPLE 19.18** Chu signs a contract for the purchase of a truck, purportedly acting as an agent under authority granted by Navarro. In fact, Navarro has not given Chu any such authority. Navarro refuses to pay for the truck, claiming that Chu had no authority to purchase it. The seller of the truck is entitled to hold Chu liable for payment. ■

If the principal is disclosed or partially disclosed, and the agent contracts with a third party without authorization, the agent is liable to the third party. The agent's liability here is based on his or her breach of the *implied warranty of authority*, not on the breach of the contract

---

13. *Restatement (Third) of Agency,* Section 6.02.

14. *Stonhard, Inc. v. Blue Ridge Farms, LLC,* 114 A.D.3d 757, 980 N.Y.S.2d 507 (2 Dept. 2014).

15. Under the Uniform Commercial Code (UCC), only the agent is liable if the instrument neither names the principal nor shows that the agent signed in a representative capacity [UCC 3–402(b)(2)].

itself.[16] An agent impliedly warrants that he or she has the authority to enter a contract on behalf of the principal. If the third party knows at the time the contract is made that the agent does not have authority—or if the agent expresses to the third party *uncertainty* as to the extent of her or his authority—the agent is not personally liable.

**Actions by E-Agents** Although in the past standard agency principles applied only to *human* agents, today these same agency principles also apply to e-agents. An electronic agent, or **e-agent,** is a semiautonomous software program that is capable of executing specific tasks, such as searching through many databases and retrieving relevant information for the user.

E-agents can enter into binding agreements on behalf of their principals. Thus, if consumers place an order over the Internet, and the company (principal) takes the order via an e-agent, the company cannot later claim that it did not receive the order.

## 19–5b Liability for Torts and Crimes

Obviously, any person, including an agent, is liable for his or her own torts and crimes. Whether a principal can also be held liable for an agent's torts and crimes depends on several factors, which we examine here. In some situations, a principal may be held liable not only for the torts of an agent but also for torts committed by an independent contractor.

**Principal's Tortious Conduct** A principal who acts through an agent may be liable for harm resulting from the principal's own negligence or recklessness. Thus, a principal may be liable if he or she gives improper instructions, authorizes the use of improper materials or tools, or establishes improper rules that result in the agent's committing a tort.

■ **EXAMPLE 19.19** Parker knows that Audrey's driver's license has been suspended but nevertheless tells her to use the company truck to deliver some equipment to a customer. If someone is injured as a result, Parker will be liable for his own negligence in instructing Audrey to drive without a valid license. ■

**Principal's Authorization of Agent's Tortious Conduct** Similarly, a principal who authorizes an agent to commit a tort may be liable to persons or property injured thereby, because the act is considered to be the principal's. ■ **EXAMPLE 19.20** Pedro directs his agent, Andy, to cut the corn on specific acreage, which neither of them has the right to do. The harvest is therefore a

trespass (a tort), and Pedro is liable to the owner of the corn (Andy is also liable even if he did not know that Pedro lacked the right to harvest the corn). ■

**Liability for Agent's Misrepresentation** A principal is exposed to tort liability whenever a third person sustains a loss due to the agent's misrepresentation. The principal's liability depends on whether the agent was actually or apparently authorized to make representations and whether the representations were made within the scope of the agency.

The principal is always directly responsible for an agent's misrepresentation made within the scope of the agent's authority. ■ **EXAMPLE 19.21** Ainsley is a demonstrator for Pavlovich's products. Pavlovich sends Ainsley to a home show to demonstrate the products and to answer questions from consumers. Pavlovich has given Ainsley authority to make statements about the products. If Ainsley makes only true representations, all is fine. But if he makes false claims, Pavlovich will be liable for any injuries or damages sustained by third parties in reliance on Ainsley's false representations. ■

When a principal has placed an agent in a position of apparent authority, the principal may also be liable for the agent's fraudulent acts. For instance, partners in a partnership generally have the apparent implied authority to act as agents of the firm. Thus, if one of the partners commits a tort or a crime, the partnership itself—and often the other partners personally—can be held liable for the loss.

**Liability for Agent's Negligence** An agent is liable for his or her own torts. A principal may also be liable for harm an agent causes to a third party under the doctrine of ***respondeat superior,***[17] a Latin term meaning "let the master respond." Under the doctrine of *respondeat superior*, the principal-employer is liable for any harm caused to a third party by an agent-employee in the course or scope of employment. The doctrine imposes **vicarious liability,** or indirect liability, because the principal-employer is being held liable for torts committed by an agent-employee.

When an agent commits a negligent act in such a situation, *both* the agent and the principal are liable. ■ **EXAMPLE 19.22** Aegis hires SDI to provide landscaping services for its property. An herbicide sprayed by SDI employee David Hoggatt enters the Aegis building through the air-conditioning system and causes

---

**16.** The agent is not liable on the contract because the agent was never intended personally to be a party to the contract.

**17.** Pronounced ree-*spahn*-dee-uht soo-*peer*-ee-your. The doctrine of *respondeat superior* applies not only to employer-employee relationships but also to other principal-agent relationships in which the principal has the right of control over the agent.

Catherine Warner, an Aegis employee, to suffer a heart attack. If Warner sues, both SDI (principal) and Hoggatt (agent) can be held liable for negligence. ■

The doctrine of *respondeat superior* is similar to the theory of strict liability in that liability is imposed regardless of fault for reasons of public policy. Every person has a duty to manage his or her affairs so as not to injure another. This duty applies even when a person acts through an agent (controls the conduct of another).

**Determining the Scope of Employment.** The key to determining whether a principal may be liable for the torts of an agent under the doctrine of *respondeat superior* is whether the torts are committed within the scope of the agency. Courts may consider the following factors in determining whether a particular act occurred within the course and scope of employment:

1. Whether the employee's act was authorized by the employer.

2. The time, place, and purpose of the act.

3. Whether the act was one commonly performed by employees on behalf of their employers.

4. The extent to which the employer's interest was advanced by the act.

5. The extent to which the private interests of the employee were involved.

6. Whether the employer furnished the means or instrumentality (such as a truck or a machine) by which an injury was inflicted.

7. Whether the employer had reason to know that the employee would perform the act in question and whether the employee had done it before.

8. Whether the act involved the commission of a serious crime.

In the following case, the court had to determine whether or not a dump truck operator was the employee of a concrete services contractor.

**Case 19.3**

# Asphalt & Concrete Services, Inc. v. Perry

Court of Special Appeals of Maryland, 221 Md.App. 235, 108 A.3d 558 (2015).

**Background and Facts** Asphalt & Concrete Services, Inc. (ACS), was working on a play pad at St. John Regional Catholic School in Frederick, Maryland. ACS project manager Blake Wood contacted William Johnson at Higher Power Trucking, LLC, to arrange for a dump truck to haul material from a quarry to the job site. One day, while Johnson was driving the dump truck between the job site and the quarry, the truck struck and injured Moran Perry, who was crossing an intersection.

To recover for his injuries, Perry filed a lawsuit in a Maryland state court against ACS. Perry alleged that Johnson's negligence in operating the dump truck was the proximate cause of his injuries and that Johnson was ACS's employee. ACS, however, claimed that Johnson was an independent contractor. A jury agreed with Perry and awarded him $529,500 in damages. The court issued a judgment in Perry's favor, and ACS appealed.

### In the Language of the Court

*GRAEFF,* J. [Judge]
* * * *

* * * Pursuant to the doctrine of *respondeat superior,* an employer may be found liable for torts committed by its employee while acting in the scope of employment. ACS does not dispute this well-established rule, but it argues that the evidence showed that Mr. Johnson was not its employee.

* * * Maryland courts have traditionally considered five criteria in determining whether or not an employer/employee relationship exists between two parties. *These criteria, developed from the common law standard for determining the master/servant relationship, include (1) the power to select and hire the employee, (2) the payment of wages, (3) the power to discharge, (4) the power to control the employee's conduct, and (5) whether the work is part of the regular business of the employer.* [Emphasis added.]

Of the five factors, the factor of control stands out as the most important. * * * Whether the employer has the right to control and direct the employee in the performance of the work and in the manner in which the work is to be done is the decisive, or controlling, test.
* * * *

**Case 19.3 Continues**

Case 19.3 Continued

Here, * * * the evidence indicated as follows: (1) ACS called Mr. Johnson directly to reserve his trucking services; (2) Mr. Wood spoke only to Mr. Johnson when calling Higher Power; (3) ACS directed Mr. Johnson to go to the * * * quarry to pick up materials for the play pad project and gave him the time to be there for the pick-up; (4) Mr. Johnson was required to bring the materials directly to the job site after his truck was loaded, and if Mr. Johnson did not deliver the materials promptly, ACS had the right to dock his pay or to no longer employ him; (5) ACS paid Mr. Johnson on an hourly basis from the time he picked up his first load until ACS dismissed him from the job site; (6) after Mr. Johnson delivered his first load of materials, ACS directed him to return to the quarry to pick up and bring back additional materials; and (7) at the job site, Mr. Johnson was obligated to follow ACS's directions in terms of where to drop the materials, how much material to drop, and how many times he would need to return to the quarry. Based on that evidence, a jury could find that Mr. Johnson was subject to ACS's control, and ACS was liable for Mr. Johnson's negligence pursuant to the doctrine of *respondeat superior.*

**Decision and Remedy** *The state intermediate appellate court affirmed the jury's finding with respect to Johnson's status as ACS's employee. The court disagreed, however, with the lower court's admission of certain evidence that may have influenced the jury's finding of proximate cause for Perry's injuries. As a result, the court reversed the judgment on this ground and remanded the case for a new trial.*

**Critical Thinking**

- **Economic** *Why did ACS contend that Johnson was not its employee? Discuss.*

---

**The Distinction between a "Detour" and a "Frolic."** A useful insight into the concept of "scope of employment" can be gained from Judge Baron Parke's classic distinction between a "detour" and a "frolic" in the case of *Joel v. Morison* (1834).[18] In this case, the English court held that if a servant merely took a detour from his master's business, the master will be responsible. If, however, the servant was on a "frolic of his own" and not in any way "on his master's business," the master will not be liable.

■ **EXAMPLE 19.23** While driving his employer's vehicle to call on a customer, Mandel decides to stop at a store—which is three blocks off his route—to take care of a personal matter. As Mandel approaches the store, he negligently runs into a parked vehicle owned by Chan. In this situation, because Mandel's detour from the employer's business is not substantial, he is still acting within the scope of employment, and the employer is liable.

But suppose instead that Mandel decides to pick up a few friends in another city for cocktails and in the process negligently runs his vehicle into Chan's. In this situation, the departure from the employer's business is substantial—Mandel is on a "frolic" of his own. Thus, the employer normally will not be liable to Chan for damages. ■

An employee going to and from work or to and from meals usually is considered to be outside the scope of employment. If travel is part of a person's position, however, as it is for a traveling salesperson, then travel time is normally considered within the scope of employment.

**Liability for Agent's Intentional Torts** Most intentional torts that individuals commit have no relation to their employment, and their employers will not be held liable. Nevertheless, under the doctrine of *respondeat superior,* the employer can be liable for intentional torts that an employee commits within the course and scope of employment. For instance, a department store owner is liable when a security guard who is a store employee commits the tort of false imprisonment while acting within the scope of employment.

In addition, an employer who knows or should know that an employee has a propensity for committing tortious acts is liable for the employee's acts even if they would not ordinarily be considered within the scope of employment. ■ **EXAMPLE 19.24** Chaz, the owner of the Comedy Club, hires Alec as a bouncer for the club even though he knows that Alec has a history of arrests for criminal assault and battery. In this situation, Chaz may be liable if Alec viciously attacks a customer in the parking lot after hours. ■ An employer can also be liable for

---

**18.** 6 Car. & P. 501, 172 Eng.Rep. 1338 (1834).

permitting an employee to engage in reckless actions that can injure others.

### Liability for Independent Contractor's Torts

Generally, an employer is not liable for physical harm caused to a third person by the negligent act of an independent contractor in the performance of the contract. This is because the employer does not have *the right to control* the details of an independent contractor's performance.

Courts make an exception to this rule when the contract involves unusually hazardous activities, such as blasting operations, the transportation of highly volatile chemicals, or the use of poisonous gases. In these situations, strict liability is imposed, and an employer cannot be shielded from liability merely by using an independent contractor.

### Liability for Agent's Crimes

An agent is liable for his or her own crimes. A principal or employer normally is *not* liable for an agent's crime even if the crime was committed within the scope of authority or employment. An exception to this rule is made when the principal or employer participated in the crime by conspiracy or other action.

In addition, in some jurisdictions, a principal may be liable under specific statutes if an agent, in the course and scope of employment, violates certain regulations. For instance, a principal might be liable for an agent's violation of sanitation rules or regulations governing prices, weights, or the sale of liquor.

## 19–6 Termination of an Agency

Agency law is similar to contract law in that both an agency and a contract may be terminated by an act of the parties or by operation of law. Once the relationship between the principal and the agent has ended, the agent no longer has the right (*actual* authority) to bind the principal. For an agent's *apparent* authority to be terminated, though, third persons may also need to be notified that the agency has been terminated.

### 19–6a Termination by Act of the Parties

An agency may be terminated by certain acts of the parties, which are listed and described in Exhibit 19–3. When an agency agreement specifies the time period

**EXHIBIT 19–3** Termination by Act of the Parties

| METHOD | RULES | ILLUSTRATION |
|---|---|---|
| **1. Lapse of Time.** | Agency terminates automatically at the end of the stated time. | Page lists her property for sale with Alex, a real estate agent, for six months. The agency ends in six months. |
| **2. Purpose Achieved.** | Agency terminates automatically on the completion of the purpose for which it was formed. | Calvin, a cattle rancher, hires Abe as his agent in the purchase of fifty head of breeding stock. The agency ends when the cattle have been purchased. |
| **3. Occurrence of a Specific Event.** | Agency normally terminates automatically on the event's occurrence. | Meredith appoints Allen to handle her business affairs while she is away. The agency terminates when Meredith returns. |
| **4. Mutual Agreement.** | Agency terminates when both parties consent to end the agency relationship. | Linda and Greg agree that Greg will no longer be her agent in procuring business equipment. |
| **5. At the Option of One Party** (*revocation*, if by principal; *renunciation*, if by agent). | Either party normally has a right to terminate the agency relationship. Wrongful termination can lead to liability for breach of contract. | When Patrick becomes ill, he informs Alice that he is revoking her authority to be his agent. |

during which the agency relationship will exist, the agency ends when that time period expires. If no definite time is stated, then the agency continues for a reasonable time and can be terminated at will by either party. What constitutes a reasonable time depends on the circumstances and the nature of the agency relationship.

The parties can, of course, mutually agree to end their agency relationship. In addition, as a general rule, either party can terminate the agency relationship without the agreement of the other. The act of termination is called *revocation* if done by the principal and *renunciation* if done by the agent. Note, however, that the terminating party may face liability if the termination is wrongful.

**Wrongful Termination** Although both parties have the *power* to terminate the agency, they may not always possess the *right* to do so. Wrongful termination can subject the canceling party to a lawsuit for breach of contract. ■ **EXAMPLE 19.25** Rawlins has a one-year employment contract with Munro to act as agent in return for $65,000. Munro has the *power* to discharge Rawlins before the contract period expires. But if he does so, he can be sued for breaching the contract, because he had no *right* to terminate the agency. ■

Even in an agency at will—in which either party may terminate at any time—the principal who wishes to terminate must give the agent *reasonable* notice. The notice must be at least sufficient to allow the agent to recoup his or her expenses and, in some situations, to make a normal profit.

**Notice of Termination** When the parties terminate an agency, it is the principal's duty to inform any third parties who know of the existence of the agency that it has been terminated. No particular form is required for notice of termination to be effective. The principal can personally notify the third party, or the party can learn of the termination through some other means. Although an agent's actual authority ends when the agency is terminated, an agent's *apparent authority* continues until the third party receives notice (from any source) that such authority has been terminated.

## 19–6b Termination by Operation of Law

Certain events terminate agency authority automatically because their occurrence makes it impossible for the agent to perform or improbable that the principal would continue to want performance. Note that when an agency terminates by operation of law, there is no duty to notify third persons.

1. *Death or insanity.* The general rule is that the death or insanity of either the principal or the agent automatically and immediately terminates an ordinary agency relationship.[19] Knowledge of the death or insanity is not required.
2. *Impossibility.* When the specific subject matter of an agency is destroyed or lost, the agency terminates. Similarly, when it is impossible for the agent to perform the agency lawfully because of a change in the law, the agency terminates.
3. *Changed circumstances.* Sometimes, an event occurs that has such an unusual effect on the subject matter of the agency that the agent can reasonably infer that the principal will not want the agency to continue. In such situations, the agency terminates. ■ **EXAMPLE 19.26** Baird hires Joslen to sell a tract of land for $40,000. Subsequently, Joslen learns that there is oil under the land and that the land is therefore worth $1 million. The agency and Joslen's authority to sell the land for $40,000 are terminated. ■
4. *Bankruptcy.* If either the principal or the agent petitions for bankruptcy, the agency is *usually* terminated. In certain circumstances, such as when the agent's financial status is irrelevant to the purpose of the agency, the agency relationship may continue.
5. *War.* When the principal's country and the agent's country are at war with each other, the agency is terminated.

---

**19.** An exception to this rule exists in the bank-customer relationship. A bank, as agent, can continue to exercise specific types of authority after the customer's death or insanity and can continue to pay checks drawn by the customer for ten days after death.

## Reviewing: Agency Relationships

James Blatt hired Marilyn Scott to sell insurance for the Massachusetts Mutual Life Insurance Company. Their contract stated, "Nothing in this contract shall be construed as creating the relationship of employer and employee." The contract was terminable at will by either party. Scott financed her own office and staff, was paid according to performance, had no taxes withheld from her checks, and could legally sell products of Massachusetts Mutual's competitors. Blatt learned that Scott was simultaneously selling insurance for Perpetual Life Insurance Corporation, one of Massachusetts Mutual's fiercest competitors. Blatt therefore withheld client contact information from Scott. Scott complained to Blatt that he was inhibiting her ability to sell insurance for Massachusetts Mutual. Blatt subsequently terminated their contract. Scott filed a suit in a New York state court against Blatt and Massachusetts Mutual. Scott claimed that she had lost sales for Massachusetts Mutual—and commissions—as a result of Blatt's withholding contact information from her. Using the information presented in the chapter, answer the following questions.

1. Who is the principal and who is the agent in this scenario? By which method was an agency relationship formed between Scott and Blatt?
2. What facts would the court consider most important in determining whether Scott was an employee or an independent contractor?
3. How would the court most likely rule on Scott's employee status? Why?
4. Which of the four duties that Blatt owed Scott in their agency relationship has probably been breached?

**Debate This** . . . *The doctrine of* respondeat superior *should be modified to make agents solely liable for their tortious (wrongful) acts committed within the scope of employment.*

## Terms and Concepts

| | | |
|---|---|---|
| agency 416 | express authority 427 | power of attorney 427 |
| apparent authority 427 | fiduciary 416 | ratification 428 |
| disclosed principal 428 | implied authority 427 | *respondeat superior* 430 |
| e-agent 430 | independent contractor 417 | undisclosed principal 429 |
| equal dignity rule 427 | notary public 427 | vicarious liability 430 |
| exclusive agency 424 | partially disclosed principal 428 | |

## Issue Spotters

1. Winona contracted with XtremeCast, a broadcast media firm, to cohost an Internet-streaming sports program. Winona and XtremeCast signed a new contract for each episode. In each contract, Winona agreed to work a certain number of days for a certain salary. During each broadcast, Winona was free to improvise her performance. She had no other obligation to work for XtremeCast. Was Winona an independent contractor? (See *Agency Law.*)

2. Davis contracts with Estee to buy a certain horse on her behalf. Estee asks Davis not to reveal her identity. Davis makes a deal with Farmland Stables, the owner of the horse, and makes a down payment. Estee does not pay the rest of the price. Farmland Stables sues Davis for breach of contract. Can Davis hold Estee liable for whatever damages he has to pay? Why or why not? (See *Liability in Agency Relationships.*)

• **Check your answers to the Issue Spotters against the answers provided in Appendix D at the end of this text.**

# Business Scenarios

**19–1. Employee versus Independent Contractor.** Stephen Hemmerling was a driver for the Happy Cab Co. Hemmerling paid certain fixed expenses and followed various rules relating to the use of the cab, the hours that could be worked, and the solicitation of fares, among other things. Rates were set by the state. Happy Cab did not withhold taxes from Hemmerling's pay. While driving the cab, Hemmerling was injured in an accident and filed a claim for workers' compensation benefits in a state court. Such benefits are not available to independent contractors. On what basis might the court hold that Hemmerling was an employee? Explain. (See *Agency Law*.)

**19–2. *Respondeat Superior.*** ABC Tire Corp. hires Arnez as a traveling salesperson and assigns him a geographic area and time schedule in which to solicit orders and service customers. Arnez is given a company car to use in covering the territory. One day, Arnez decides to take his personal car to cover part of his territory. It is 11:00 A.M., and Arnez has just finished calling on all customers in the city of Tarrytown. His next appointment is at 2:00 P.M. in the city of Austex, twenty miles down the road. Arnez starts out for Austex, but halfway there he decides to visit a former college roommate who runs a farm ten miles off the main highway. Arnez is enjoying his visit with his former roommate when he realizes that it is 1:45 P.M. and that he will be late for the appointment in Austex. Driving at a high speed down the country road to reach the main highway, Arnez crashes his car into a tractor, severely injuring Thomas, the driver of the tractor. Thomas claims that he can hold ABC Tire Corp. liable for his injuries. Discuss fully ABC's liability in this situation. (See *Liability in Agency Relationships*.)

# Business Case Problems

**19–3. Liability for Contracts.** Thomas Huskin and his wife entered into a contract to have their home remodeled by House Medic Handyman Service. Todd Hall signed the contract as an authorized representative of House Medic. It turned out that House Medic was a fictitious name for Hall Hauling, Ltd. The contract did not indicate this, however, and Hall did not inform the Huskins about Hall Hauling. When a contract dispute later arose, the Huskins sued Todd Hall personally for breach of contract. Can Hall be held personally liable? Why or why not? [*Huskin v. Hall,* 2012 WL 553136 (Ohio Ct.App. 2012)] (See *Liability in Agency Relationships*.)

**19–4. Agent's Duties to Principal.** William and Maxine Miller were shareholders of Claimsco International, Inc. They filed a suit against the other shareholders, Michael Harris and Kenneth Hoxie, and the accountant who worked for all of them—John Verchota. Among other things, the Millers alleged that Verchota had breached a duty that he owed them. They claimed that at Harris's instruction, Verchota had taken various actions that placed them at a disadvantage to the other shareholders. Verchota had allegedly adjusted Claimsco's books to maximize the Millers' financial liabilities, for instance, and had falsely reported distributions of income to them without actually transferring that income. Which duty are the Millers referring to? If the allegations can be proved, did Verchota breach this duty? Explain. [*Miller v. Harris,* 2013 IL App (2d) 120512, 985 N.E.2d 671 (2 Dist. 2013)] (See *Duties of Agents and Principals*.)

**19–5. Business Case Problem with Sample Answer—Determining Employee Status.** Nelson Ovalles worked as a cable installer for Cox Rhode Island Telecom, LLC, under an agreement with a third party, M&M Communications, Inc. The agreement stated that no employer-employee relationship existed between Cox and M&M's technicians, including Ovalles. Ovalles was required to designate his affiliation with Cox on his work van, clothing, and identification badge. Cox had minimal contact with him, however, and had limited power to control how he performed his duties. Cox supplied cable wire and similar items, but the equipment was delivered to M&M, not to Ovalles. On a workday, while Ovalles was fulfilling a work order, his van rear-ended a car driven by Barbara Cayer. Is Cox liable to Cayer? Explain. [*Cayer v. Cox Rhode Island Telecom, LLC,* 85 A.3d 1140 (R.I. 2014)] (See *Agency Law*.)

- **For a sample answer to Problem 19–5, go to Appendix E at the end of this text.**

**19–6. Agent's Authority.** Terry Holden's stepmother, Rosie, was diagnosed with amyotrophic lateral sclerosis (ALS), and Terry's wife, Susan, became Rosie's primary caregiver. Rosie executed a durable power of attorney appointing Susan as her agent. Susan opened a joint bank account with Rosie at Bank of America, depositing $9,643.62 of Rosie's funds. Susan used some of the money to pay for "household expenses to keep us going while we were taking care of her." Rosie died three months later. Terry's father, Charles, as executor of Rosie's estate, filed a petition in a Texas state court against Susan for an accounting. What general duty did Susan owe Rosie as her agent? What does an agent's duty of accounting require? Did Susan breach either of these duties? Explain. [*Holden v. Holden,* 456 S.W.3d 642 (Tex.App.—Tyler 2015)] (See *Agent's Authority*.)

**19–7. Scope of Agent's Authority.** Kindred Nursing Centers East, LLC, owns and operates Whitesburg Gardens, a long-term care and rehabilitation facility, in Huntsville, Alabama. Lorene Jones was admitted to the facility following knee-replacement surgery. Jones's daughter, Yvonne Barbour, signed the admission forms required by Whitesburg Gardens as her mother's representative in her presence. Jones did not object. The forms included an "Alternative Dispute Resolution Agreement," which provided for binding arbitration in the event of a dispute between "the Resident" (Jones) and "the Facility" (Whitesburg Gardens). Six days later, Jones was transferred to a different facility. After recovering from the surgery, she filed a suit in an Alabama state court against Kindred, alleging substandard care on a claim of negligence. Can Jones be compelled to submit her claim to arbitration? Explain. [*Kindred Nursing Centers East, LLC v. Jones,* __ So.3d __, 2016 WL 762450 (Ala. 2016)] (See *Agent's Authority.*)

**19–8. Agency Relationships.** Standard Oil of Connecticut, Inc., sells home heating, cooling, and security systems. Standard schedules installation and service appointments with its customers and then contracts with installers and technicians to do the work. The company requires an installer or technician to complete a project by a certain time but to otherwise "exercise independent judgment and control in the execution of any work." The installers and technicians are licensed and certified by the state. Standard does not train them, provide instruction manuals, supervise them at customers' homes, or inspect their work. The installers and technicians use their own equipment and tools, and they can choose which days they work. Standard pays a set rate per project. According to criteria used by the courts, are these installers and technicians independent contractors or employees? Why? [*Standard Oil of*

*Connecticut, Inc. v. Administrator, Unemployment Compensation Act,* 320 Conn. 611, 134 A.3d 581 (2016)] (See *Agency Law.*)

**19–9. A Question of Ethics—Vicarious Liability.** *Jamie*

*Paliath worked as a real estate agent for Home Town Realty of Vandalia, LLC (the principal, a real estate broker). Torri Auer, a California resident, relied on Paliath's advice and assistance to buy three rental properties in Ohio. Before the sales, Paliath had represented that each property was worth approximately twice as much as what Auer would pay and that there was a waiting list of prospective tenants. Paliath also stated that all of the property needed work and agreed to do the work for a specified price. Nearly a year later, substantial work was still needed, and only a few of the units had been rented. Auer sued Paliath and Home Town Realty for fraudulent misrepresentation. [Auer v. Paliath, 140 Ohio St.3d 276, 17 N.E.3d 561, 2014-Ohio-3632 (2014)] (See Liability for Torts and Crimes.)*

**(a)** Were Paliath's representations to Auer within the scope of her employment? Explain. Will the court hold the principal (Home Town Realty) liable for the misrepresentations of the agent (Paliath)?

**(b)** What is the ethical basis for imposing vicarious liability on a principal for an agent's tort?

## Legal Reasoning Group Activity

**19–10. Agent's Duties to Principal.** John Warren wanted to buy a condominium in California. Hildegard Merrill was the agent for the seller. Because Warren's credit rating was poor, Merrill told him he needed a co-borrower to obtain a mortgage at a reasonable rate. Merrill said that her daughter Charmaine would "go on title" until the loan and sale were complete if Warren would pay her $10,000. Merrill also offered to defer her commission on the sale as a loan to Warren so that he could make a 20 percent down payment on the property. He agreed to both plans.

Merrill secured the mortgage in Charmaine's name alone by misrepresenting her daughter's address, business, and income.

To close the sale, Merrill had Warren remove his name from the title to the property. In October, Warren moved into the condominium, repaid Merrill the amount of her deferred commission, and began paying the mortgage. Within a few months, Merrill had Warren evicted. Warren subsequently filed a suit against Merrill and Charmaine. (See *Duties of Agents and Principals.*)

**(a)** The first group will determine who among these parties was in an agency relationship.

**(b)** The second group will discuss the basic duty that an agent owes a principal and decide whether that duty was breached here.

# Answers to the *Issue Spotters*

**1. *Was Winona an independent contractor?*** Yes. An independent contractor is a person who contracts with another—the principal—to do something but who is neither controlled by the other nor subject to the other's right to control with respect to the performance. Independent contractors are not employees, because those who hire them have no control over the details of their performance.

**2. *Can Davis hold Estee liable for whatever damages he has to pay? Why or why not?*** Yes. A principal has a duty to indemnify an agent for liabilities incurred because of authorized and lawful acts and transactions and for losses suffered because of the principal's failure to perform his or her duties.

# Sample Answers for *Business Case Problems with Sample Answer*

**Problem 19–5. *Determining Employee Status.*** No, Cox is not liable to Cayer for any injuries or damage that she sustained in the accident with Ovalles. Generally, an employer is not liable for physical harm caused to a third person by the negligent act of an independent contractor in the performance of a contract. This is because the employer does not have the right to control the details of the performance. In determining whether a worker has the status of an independent contractor, how much control the employer can exercise over the details of the work is the most important factor weighed by the courts.

In this problem, Ovalles worked as a cable installer for Cox under an agreement with M&M. The agreement disavowed any employer-employee relationship between Cox and M&M's installers. Ovalles was required to designate his affiliation with Cox on his van, clothing, and an ID badge. But Cox had minimal contact with Ovalles and limited power to control the manner in which he performed his work. Cox supplied cable wire and other equipment, but these items were delivered to M&M, not Ovalles. These facts indicate that Ovalles was an independent contractor, not an employee. Thus, Cox was not liable to Cayer for the harm caused to her by Ovalles when his van rear-ended Cayer's car.

In the actual case on which this problem is based, the court issued a judgment in Cox's favor. The Rhode Island Supreme Court affirmed, applying the principles stated above to arrive at the same conclusion.

# Chapter 16

# CHAPTER

# Employment Law

Until the early 1900s, most employer-employee relationships were governed by the common law. Even today, under the common law *employment-at-will doctrine,* private employers have considerable freedom to hire and fire workers at will, regardless of the employees' performance.

Numerous statutes and administrative agency regulations now also govern the workplace. Thus, to a large extent, statutory law has displaced common law doctrines. In this chapter and the next two, we look at the most significant laws regulating employment relationships.

This chapter discusses federal statutes that regulate various aspects of the workplace, including employee wages, hours, medical leave, safety, and pension and health plans.

## 20–1 Employment at Will

Employment relationships have traditionally been governed by the common law doctrine of **employment at will.** Under this doctrine, either party may terminate the employment relationship at any time and for any reason, unless doing so violates an employee's statutory or contractual rights.

Today, the majority of U.S. workers continue to have the legal status of "employees at will." In other words, this common law doctrine is still in widespread use, and only one state (Montana) does not apply it.

Nonetheless, federal and state statutes governing employment relationships prevent the doctrine from being applied in a number of circumstances. An employer may not fire an employee if doing so would violate a federal or state statute, such as a law prohibiting employment discrimination.

Note that the distinction made under agency law between employee status and independent-contractor status is important here. The employment laws that will be discussed apply only to the employer-employee relationship. They do not apply to independent contractors.

### 20–1a Common Law Exceptions to the Employment-at-Will Doctrine

As noted, statutory law has affected the application of the employment-at-will doctrine. In addition, the courts have carved out various exceptions to the doctrine based on contract theory, tort theory, and public policy.

**Exceptions Based on Contract Theory** Some courts have held that an *implied* employment contract exists between the employer and the employee. If the employee is fired outside the terms of the implied contract, he or she may succeed in an action for breach of contract even though no written employment contract exists.

■ **EXAMPLE 20.1** BDI Enterprises' employment manual and personnel bulletin both state that, as a matter of policy, workers will be dismissed only for good cause. Jing Chin is an employee at BDI. If Chin reasonably expects BDI to follow this policy, a court may find that there is an implied contract based on the terms stated in the manual and bulletin. ■ Generally, the key consideration in determining whether an employment manual creates an implied contractual obligation is the employee's reasonable expectations.

An employer's oral promises to employees regarding discharge policy may also be considered part of an implied contract. If the employer fires a worker in a manner contrary to what was promised, a court may hold that the employer has violated the implied contract and is liable for damages.

**Exceptions Based on Tort Theory** In some situations, the discharge of an employee may give rise to an action for wrongful discharge (discussed shortly) under tort theories. Abusive discharge procedures may result in a lawsuit for intentional infliction of emotional distress or defamation. In addition, some courts have permitted workers to sue their employers under the tort theory of fraud. Fraud might be alleged when an employer made false promises to a prospective employee.

■ **EXAMPLE 20.2** Goldfinch Consulting, Inc., induces Brianna to leave a lucrative job and move to another state by offering her "a long-term job with a thriving business." In fact, Goldfinch is not only having significant financial problems but is also planning a merger that will result in the elimination of the position offered to Brianna. If she takes the job in reliance on Goldfinch's representations and is fired shortly thereafter, Brianna may be able to bring an action against the employer for fraud. ■

**Exceptions Based on Public Policy** The most common exception to the employment-at-will doctrine is made on the basis that the employer's reason for firing the employee violates a fundamental public policy of the jurisdiction. Generally, the courts require that the public policy involved be expressed clearly in the statutory law governing the jurisdiction.

The public-policy exception may apply to an employee discharged for **whistleblowing**—that is, telling government authorities, upper-level managers, or the media that the employer is engaged in some unsafe or illegal activity. Normally, however, whistleblowers seek protection from retaliatory discharge under federal and state statutes, such as the Whistleblower Protection Act.[1]

---

1. 5 U.S.C. Section 1201.

■ **CASE IN POINT 20.3** Donald Waddell worked for the Boyce Thompson Institute for Plant Research. Waddell did not have an employment contract for a fixed term, and the institute's employee manual said that his job was "terminable at will." Soon after he was hired, the institute implemented a whistleblower policy designed to encourage "the highest standards of financial reporting and lawful and ethical behavior."

Waddell repeatedly told his supervisor, Sophia Darling, that she needed to file certain financial documents more promptly. Darling fired Waddell, telling him that he was disrespectful and insubordinate. Waddell then sued the institute, contending that he should not have been fired because he was acting under the company's whistleblowing policy.

A New York appellate court, however, found that Waddell could be fired. Waddell was employed at will. In addition, he was not protected under the whistleblower policy, which had been implemented after his employment. Thus, he could not have detrimentally relied on the policy in accepting the job.[2] ■

The issue in the following case was whether the at-will employment doctrine could be applied to support the discharge of an employee who brought a handgun to work and left it locked in his vehicle in plain sight.

---

2. *Waddell v. Boyce Thompson Institute for Plant Research, Inc.*, 92 A.D.3d 1172, 940 N.Y.S.2d 331 (2012).

# Caterpillar, Inc. v. Sudlow
Court of Appeals of Indiana, 52 N.E.3d 19 (2016).

### In the Language of the Court
*BAKER*, Judge.
   * * * *

          Facts
 * * * Caterpillar [Inc.,] had a Facility Firearms policy (the Firearms Policy) that read as follows:

    In accordance with Indiana State Statute 34–28–7–2, employees or suppliers legally permitted to possess and transport a firearm are authorized to store the firearm in the licensee's private means of transportation in line with state law. Any person who chooses to transport his or her firearm under this law must abide by the regulations within the law while on Caterpillar property.

    Any person found to be in violation of this policy may be subject to disciplinary action up to and including termination and/or criminal prosecution.

   Indiana Code Section 34–28–7–2(a) ("the Firearms Statute") reads as follows:

    * * * A person may not adopt or enforce an ordinance, a resolution, a policy, or a rule that:
     (1) prohibits; or
     (2) has the effect of prohibiting;
an employee of the person, including a contract employee, from possessing a firearm or ammunition that is locked in the trunk of the employee's vehicle, kept in the glove compartment of the employee's locked vehicle, or stored out of plain sight in the employee's locked vehicle.

   [One day, Caterpillar employee William] Sudlow drove to work [with] a loaded Ruger .357 Magnum handgun—for which he had a permit—stuffed down between the center console and the driver's seat. Sudlow left the gun there when he parked and exited his vehicle and entered the building to begin his workday. Another Caterpillar employee was walking through the parking lot and walked past Sudlow's vehicle. The employee noticed what appeared to be a handgun inside the vehicle. He could see the weapon's handle, the guard over the trigger, and the holster. He then reported the issue to Caterpillar's head of security. Eventually, the head of security confirmed the

**Case 20.1 Continues**

**Case 20.1 Continued**

presence of the weapon in the vehicle and told Sudlow that he was suspended indefinitely.

[Two days later,] Sudlow was fired for violating the Firearms Policy. The same day, Caterpillar posted a new firearms policy throughout the building; the new policy explicitly states that firearms in employees' vehicles must be kept "secured and out of sight."

* * * Sudlow filed a complaint [in an Indiana state court] against Caterpillar, alleging that Caterpillar had violated the Firearms Statute when it terminated his employment for violating the Firearms Policy. * * * The trial court entered an * * * order granting summary judgment in Sudlow's favor * * * . The trial court found as follows:

> 1. The Plaintiff stored a firearm in his vehicle while in the employee parking lot and said firearm was in plain sight.
> 2. The Defendant's posted policy, in effect at the time of said incident, allowed employees to store a weapon in his or her vehicle, and did not require that said firearm be kept out of sight.
> 3. The Plaintiff's actions complied with the Defendant's policy.
> * * * *
> 5. The Firearms Statute allows an employer to be more restrictive in its firearms policy, but the Defendant did not make its policy so restrictive as to prevent the Plaintiff's action in this case.

* * * A jury * * * awarded damages to Sudlow in the amount of $85,000. Caterpillar now appeals.

**Discussion and Decision**

* * * This appeal * * * calls for us to interpret statutory language, which is a pure question of law to which we apply a *de novo* standard of review [as if the reviewing court was deciding the issue for the first time].

**I. The Firearms Statute**

* * * *

Here, Caterpillar's Firearms Policy did not prohibit conduct that is protected by the Firearms Statute. * * * Indeed, * * * Caterpillar could have enacted a more restrictive policy * * * but it chose not to do so. It is readily apparent that neither the Firearms Policy nor Caterpillar's interpretation thereof violated the Firearms Statute. *As a cause of action under the Firearms Statute is authorized only when an employer violates the statute, Sudlow has no right to recover on this basis.* [Emphasis added.]

Sudlow argues that the Firearms Statute "protects a lawful possessor of firearms from adverse employment action for reasonable and responsible possession of firearms, and Caterpillar's actions had the effect of prohibiting Sudlow from lawfully keeping his firearm in his car." He similarly contends that the intent of the statute "is to protect the rights of lawful firearm possession." Sudlow essentially argues that the Firearms Statute does the following: (1) sets a default position of permitting every gun owner to be allowed to take any gun into any workplace; and (2) if the employer wants to curtail that conduct, the statute would require employers to enact a firearms policy to do so. In other words, Sudlow believes that if an employer does not have a firearms policy in place, an employee could walk into the workplace with a loaded assault rifle and face no employment consequences as a result.

It is clear that the Firearms Statute is not nearly so broad—in fact, it is written quite narrowly and specifically. According to the plain and unambiguous language of the statute, the reasonable and responsible possession of firearms—the protected activity—is defined as a firearm that is locked in the trunk, kept in the glove compartment, or stored out

of plain sight in the employee's locked vehicle. Here, Sudlow's conduct did not fall into that category; as a result, it was not protected by the Firearms Statute.

Caterpillar's Firearms Policy did not prohibit statutorily protected conduct. Furthermore, its interpretation of its Firearms Policy also did not prohibit protected conduct. Consequently, Sudlow is not entitled to relief under the Firearms Statute.

**II. Common Law**

If Sudlow does not have a cause of action under the Firearms Statute, his only recourse would be something akin to a wrongful termination claim. It is undisputed that he was an at-will employee, meaning that his employment could have been terminated by either party at will, with or without a reason. There are three exceptions to the employment-at-will doctrine, but the parties discuss only the public policy exception: we have recognized a public policy exception to the employment-at-will doctrine if a clear statutory expression of a right or duty is contravened [violated].

The Firearms Statute is the best expression of Indiana's public policy regarding the right to transport and store firearms at work. And while this statute does confer a right to store a weapon in a trunk, glove compartment, or out of sight in a locked vehicle, it simply does not confer a right to store a weapon in a vehicle in plain sight. It is apparent, therefore, that in this case, *there was no contravention [violation] of a clear statutory expression of a right*. As a result, the public policy exception to the employment-at-will doctrine does not apply, and Sudlow is not entitled to relief under the common law. [Emphasis added.]

The judgment of the trial court is reversed and remanded with instructions to enter summary judgment in favor of Caterpillar.

**Legal Reasoning Questions**

**1.** Did Caterpillar's Firearms Policy violate Indiana's public policy regarding the right to transport and store firearms at work? Explain.

**2.** On what point did the trial and appellate courts disagree? How did that difference affect the result at each level?

**3.** Is the at-will employment doctrine fair to employees? Why or why not?

### 20–1b Wrongful Discharge

Whenever an employer discharges an employee in violation of an employment contract or a statutory law protecting employees, the employee may bring an action for **wrongful discharge.** For instance, an employee who is terminated in retaliation for some protected activity, such as whistleblowing or participating in an employment-discrimination investigation, can sue for wrongful discharge.

Even if an employer's actions do not violate any provisions in an employment contract or statute, the employer may still be subject to liability. An employee can sue for wrongful discharge under a common law doctrine, such as a tort theory or agency. For instance, if while firing a female employee, an employer publicly discloses private facts about her sex life, that employee could sue for wrongful discharge based on an invasion of privacy.

# 20–2 Wages, Hours, and Layoffs

In the 1930s, Congress enacted several laws to regulate the wages and working hours of employees, including the following:

1. The Davis-Bacon Act[3] requires contractors and subcontractors working on federal government construction projects to pay "prevailing wages" to their employees.
2. The Walsh-Healey Act[4] applies to U.S. government contracts. It requires that a minimum wage, as well as overtime pay at 1.5 times regular pay rates, be paid to employees of manufacturers or suppliers entering into contracts with agencies of the federal government.
3. The Fair Labor Standards Act (FLSA)[5] extended wage-hour requirements to cover all employers engaged in interstate commerce or in producing goods for interstate commerce. Certain other types of businesses were included as well. The FLSA, as amended, provides the most comprehensive federal regulation of wages and hours today.

### 20–2a Child Labor

The FLSA prohibits oppressive child labor. Restrictions on child labor differ by age group.

Children under fourteen years of age are allowed to do only certain types of work. They can deliver newspapers, work for their parents, and be employed in entertainment and (with some exceptions) agriculture. Children aged fourteen and fifteen are allowed to work, but not in hazardous occupations. There are also restrictions on how many hours per day and per week children in these age groups can work.

Working times and hours are not restricted for persons between the ages of sixteen and eighteen, but this age group cannot be employed in hazardous jobs. None of these restrictions apply to those over the age of eighteen.

### 20–2b Minimum Wages

The FLSA provides that a **minimum wage** of $7.25 per hour must be paid to covered nonexempt employees. Most states also have minimum wages. More than half of the states have set their minimum wages above the federal minimum wage. When the state minimum wage is greater than the federal minimum wage, the employee is entitled to the higher wage.

■ **EXAMPLE 20.4** The Oakland Raiders paid $1.25 million in 2014 to settle wage claims made by the team's cheerleading squad (the Raiderettes) as a class action. The cheerleaders had complained that they were not being paid for hours that they spent attending other events and performing other tasks required of them by contract. After the time spent performing these other tasks was factored in, the cheerleaders were receiving wages that were well below California's minimum wage, persuading the Raiders to settle the dispute. ■

Are employees entitled to receive wages for all the time they spend at work, including times when they are taking a personal break? See this chapter's *Ethics Today* feature for a discussion of this issue.

### 20–2c Tipped Workers

When an employee receives tips while on the job, the FLSA gives employers a tip credit toward the minimum wage amount. The employer is required to pay only $2.13 an hour in direct wages—if that amount, plus the tips received, equals at least the federal minimum wage. If an employee's tips and direct wages do not equal the federal minimum wage, the employer must make up the difference. Note that some states have enacted laws to prevent employers from including tips in the minimum wage. In these states, tipped workers receive the regular minimum wage.

If employers pay at least the federal minimum wage, the FLSA allows them to take employee tips and make other arrangements for their distribution. ■ **CASE IN POINT 20.5** Misty Cumbie worked as a waitress at a café in Portland, Oregon, that was owned and operated by Woody Woo, Inc. Woody Woo paid its servers an hourly

---

3. 40 U.S.C. Sections 276a–276a-5.
4. 41 U.S.C. Sections 35–45.
5. 29 U.S.C. Sections 201–260.

## ETHICS TODAY

### Is It Fair to Dock Employees' Pay for Bathroom Breaks?

For some employees, "punching a time clock" means accounting for *all* of the time that they are not working. These employees must "punch in" when they arrive and "punch out" when they leave for the day, of course, but they also must clock out when they take breaks. That includes bathroom breaks, coffee breaks, and smoking breaks.

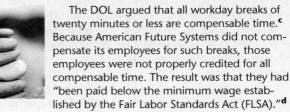

**What the Law Says**

The Fair Labor Standards Act[a] does not require that an employer offer its employees personal breaks. If an employer does offer them, though, employees must be compensated during those breaks. Otherwise, the employer may effectively be in violation of federal minimum wage laws.

**A Pennsylvania Publisher Faces Fines for Unpaid Bathroom Breaks**

The issue of unpaid bathroom breaks came to the fore when the U.S. Department of Labor (DOL) filed a lawsuit against American Future Systems, Inc. (doing business as Progressive Business Publications). The DOL alleged that American Future Systems had created a compensation system in which none of its six thousand employees were compensated for bathroom breaks.[b]

The DOL argued that all workday breaks of twenty minutes or less are compensable time.[c] Because American Future Systems did not compensate its employees for such breaks, those employees were not properly credited for all compensable time. The result was that they had "been paid below the minimum wage established by the Fair Labor Standards Act (FLSA)."[d] U.S. district court judge L. Felipe Restrepo agreed, finding American Future Systems liable for unpaid wages under the FLSA, plus damages. The company will have to pay past and current employees almost $2 million, according to DOL estimates.

**The Ethical Issue**

Irrespective of the illegality of not paying for personal breaks, there is an ethical issue. Should workers have to face the choice of taking a bathroom break or getting paid? Adam Welsh, a senior trial attorney for the Department of Labor, argued that the answer was no. "I think it's the rare employer who doesn't allow its employees to go to the bathroom," Welsh said.

**Critical Thinking** *Consider a company whose employees include both smokers and nonsmokers. The smokers take numerous paid smoking breaks, while the nonsmokers do not. Is there an ethical issue here? Discuss.*

**a.** 29 U.S.C. Sections 201 *et seq.*
**b.** *U.S. Department of Labor v. American Future Systems, Inc.*, Memorandum, Case No. 12-6171 (E.D.Pa. 2015).

**c.** 29 C.F.R. Section 785.18.
**d.** 29 U.S.C. Section 206(a)(1)(c).

---

wage that was higher than the state's minimum wage, but the servers were required to contribute their tips to a "tip pool." Approximately one-third of the tip-pool funds went to the servers, and the rest was distributed to kitchen staff members, who otherwise rarely received tips for their services. When Cumbie filed a lawsuit against Woody Woo over her tips, the court held that the tip pool did not violate the FLSA.[6] ■

## 20–2d Overtime Provisions and Exemptions

Under the FLSA, any employee who works more than forty hours per week must be paid no less than 1.5 times her or his regular pay for all hours worked over forty. The

FLSA overtime provisions apply only after an employee has worked more than forty hours per *week*. Therefore, employees who work ten hours a day, four days per week, are not entitled to overtime pay.

Certain employees are exempt from the FLSA's overtime provisions. These employees generally include executive, administrative, and professional employees, as well as outside salespersons and those who create computer code. Executive and administrative employees are those whose primary duty is management and who exercise discretion and independent judgment.

■ **CASE IN POINT 20.6** Patty Lee Smith was a pharmaceutical sales representative for Johnson and Johnson (J&J). She traveled to ten physicians' offices a day to promote the benefits of J&J's drug Concerta. Smith's work was unsupervised, she controlled her own schedule, and she received an annual salary of $66,000. When she filed a claim for overtime pay,

**6.** *Cumbie v. Woody Woo, Inc.*, 596 F.3d 577 (9th Cir. 2010).

the court held that she was an administrative employee and therefore exempt from the FLSA's overtime provisions.[7] ■

An employer can voluntarily pay overtime to ineligible employees but cannot waive or reduce the overtime requirements of the FLSA. In 2016, the Department of Labor updated its overtime regulations to allow millions more employees to receive overtime pay.[8] Whereas in the past, workers making more than $23,660 a year did not qualify for overtime pay, today, that threshold has been increased to $50,440 a year.

An employee's underreporting of hours worked can undercut his or her claim for overtime. But can an employee's underreporting *support* such a claim? That question was at the center of the following case.

---

7. *Smith v. Johnson and Johnson*, 593 F.3d 280 (3d Cir. 2010).

8. 29 C.F.R. Part 541.

---

### Case 20.2

# Bailey v. TitleMax of Georgia, Inc.
United States Court of Appeals, Eleventh Circuit, 776 F.3d 797 (2015).

**Background and Facts** Santonias Bailey was an employee of TitleMax of Georgia, Inc., in Jonesboro, Georgia. Bailey's supervisor told him that TitleMax did not pay overtime, so he regularly worked off the clock. For example, on some Saturdays, he would work from 8:30 A.M. to 5:30 P.M., but—as ordered by his supervisor—would log only seven hours despite having worked nine. His supervisor also edited Bailey's time records to report fewer hours than he actually worked by, for instance, subtracting a one-hour lunch break when there had been none.

Bailey resigned from TitleMax and filed a suit in a federal district court against the employer to recover for the unpaid overtime under the Fair Labor Standards Act (FLSA). TitleMax argued that Bailey was responsible for the unpaid time. According to TitleMax, he had never complained about his supervisor, and he had violated company policy with respect to keeping accurate time records. The court issued a judgment in the defendant's favor. Bailey appealed.

### In the Language of the Court
*MARTIN,* Circuit Judge:
* * * *

* * * The goal of the FLSA is to counteract the inequality of bargaining power between employees and employers.

In the broadest sense, this principle * * * compels our holding here. If an employer knew or had reason to know that its employee underreported his hours, it cannot escape FLSA liability by asserting [a] defense based on that underreporting. To hold otherwise would allow an employer to wield its superior bargaining power to pressure or even compel its employees to underreport their work hours.
* * * *

If an employee has worked overtime without pay, he may bring a private FLSA action for damages. An unpaid-overtime claim has two elements: (1) an employee worked unpaid overtime, and (2) the employer knew or should have known of the overtime work. *Knowledge may be imputed [attributed] to the employer when its supervisors or management encourage artificially low reporting.* [Emphasis added.]

Mr. Bailey has shown both required elements. He worked overtime without pay. TitleMax knew or should have known he worked overtime, because Mr. Bailey's supervisor both encouraged artificially low reporting and squelched truthful timekeeping.
* * * *

* * * No one disputes that his supervisor knew he was working off the clock. *The supervisor's knowledge may be imputed to TitleMax, making it liable for the FLSA violation.* * * * TitleMax argues that * * * an employee [is] deprived of his FLSA claim because he underreported his time, even if knowledge of the underreporting is imputed to the employer. [Emphasis added.]

TitleMax has identified no case in which [any federal appellate court] approved the use of [this] defense as a total bar to an employee's FLSA claim when the employer knew the employee underreported his hours.

**Case 20.2 Continues**

Case 20.2 Continued *** The dearth [scarcity] of precedent supporting TitleMax's *** argument is persuasive, if not conclusive, evidence that its argument is misguided.

**Decision and Remedy** *The U.S. Court of Appeals for the Eleventh Circuit reversed the judgment of the lower court and remanded the case for further proceedings. "Where, as here, an employer knew or had reason to know that its employee underreported his hours, it cannot invoke [a] defense based on that underreporting to bar the employee's FLSA claim."*

**Critical Thinking**
- **Legal Environment** *Congress enacted the FLSA in 1938. More than eight thousand FLSA suits are filed in federal district courts each year. How do these facts support the court's reasoning in this case?*

## 20–2e Layoffs

The Worker Adjustment and Retraining Notification (WARN) Act[9] applies to employers with at least one hundred full-time employees. The act requires these employers to provide sixty days' notice before implementing a mass layoff or closing a plant that employs more than fifty full-time workers. A mass layoff is a layoff of at least one-third of the full-time employees at a particular job site.

The WARN Act is intended to give workers advance notice so that they can start looking for new jobs while they are still employed. It is also intended to alert state agencies so that they can provide training and other resources for displaced workers. Employers thus must provide advance notice of the layoff both to the affected workers and to state and local government authorities. (An employer may notify the workers' union representative, if the workers are members of a labor union.) Even companies that anticipate filing for bankruptcy normally must provide notice under the WARN Act.

An employer that violates the WARN Act can be fined up to $500 for each day of the violation. Employees can recover back pay for each day of the violation (up to sixty days), plus reasonable attorneys' fees.

## 20–3 Family and Medical Leave

The Family and Medical Leave Act (FMLA)[10] allows employees to take time off from work for family or medical reasons or in certain situations that arise from military service. A majority of the states have similar legislation. The FMLA does not supersede any state or local law that provides more generous protection.

## 20–3a Coverage and Application

The FMLA requires employers that have fifty or more employees to provide *unpaid* leave for specified reasons. (Some employers voluntarily offer paid family leave, but this is not a requirement of the FMLA.) The FMLA expressly covers private and public (government) employees who have worked for their employers for at least a year.

An eligible employee may take up to *twelve weeks of leave* within a twelve-month period for any of the following reasons:

1. To care for a newborn baby within one year of birth.
2. To care for an adopted or foster child within one year of the time the child is placed with the employee.
3. To care for the employee's spouse, child, or parent who has a serious health condition.
4. If the employee suffers from a serious health condition and is unable to perform the essential functions of her or his job.
5. For any qualifying exigency (nonmedical emergency) arising out of the fact that the employee's spouse, son, daughter, or parent is a covered military member on active duty.[11] For instance, an employee can take leave to arrange for child care or to deal with financial or legal matters when a spouse is being deployed overseas.

In addition, an employee may take military caregiver leave to care for a family member with a serious injury or illness incurred as a result of military duty.[12] For military caregiver leave, the employee may take up to *twenty-six weeks* of leave within a twelve-month period.

In the following case, an employee asked for medical leave to care for her mother on a trip to Las Vegas, Nevada.

---

**9.** 29 U.S.C. Sections 2101 *et seq.*
**10.** 29 U.S.C. Sections 2601, 2611–2619, 2651–2654.

**11.** 29 C.F.R. Section 825.126.
**12.** 29 C.F.R. Section 825.200.

## Case 20.3

# Ballard v. Chicago Park District

United States Court of Appeals, Seventh Circuit, 741 F.3d 838 (2014).

**Background and Facts** Beverly Ballard worked for the Chicago Park District. She lived with her mother, Sarah, who suffered from end-stage congestive heart failure. Beverly served as Sarah's primary caregiver with support from Horizon Hospice & Palliative Care. The hospice helped Sarah plan and secure funds for an end-of-life goal, a "family trip" to Las Vegas. To accompany Sarah as her caretaker, Beverly asked the Park District for unpaid time off under the Family and Medical Leave Act (FMLA). The employer refused, but Beverly and Sarah took the trip as planned.

Later, the Park District terminated Beverly for "unauthorized absences." She filed a suit in a federal district court against the employer. The court issued a decision in Beverly's favor. The Park District appealed, arguing that Beverly had been absent from work on a "recreational trip."

## In the Language of the Court

*FLAUM,* Circuit Judge.

\* \* \* \*

We begin with the text of the [FMLA]: an eligible employee is entitled to leave "in order to care for" a family member with a "serious health condition."

\* \* \* \*

\* \* \* *The FMLA's text does not restrict care to a particular place or geographic location.* For instance, it does not say that an employee is entitled to time off "to care *at home* for" a family member. *The only limitation it places on care is that the family member must have a serious health condition.* We are reluctant, without good reason, to read in another limitation that Congress has not provided. [Emphasis added.]

\* \* \* \*

Sarah's basic medical, hygienic, and nutritional needs did not change while she was in Las Vegas, and Beverly continued to assist her with those needs during the trip. In fact, \* \* \* Beverly's presence proved quite important indeed when a fire at the hotel made it impossible to reach their room, requiring Beverly to find another source of insulin and pain medicine. Thus, at the very least, [Beverly] requested leave in order to provide physical care.

\* \* \* \*

\* \* \* The Park District describes [Beverly's] travel as a "recreational trip" or a "non-medically related pleasure trip." It also raises the specter that employees will help themselves to unpaid FMLA leave in order to take personal vacations, simply by bringing seriously ill family members along. So perhaps what the Park District means to argue is that the real reason Beverly requested leave was in order to take a free pleasure trip, and not in order to care for her mother. \* \* \* However, \* \* \* an employer concerned about the risk that employees will abuse the FMLA's leave provisions may of course require that requests be certified by the family member's health care provider. And any worries about opportunistic leave-taking in this case should be tempered by the fact that this dispute arises out of the hospice and palliative care context.

If Beverly had sought leave to care for her mother in Chicago, her request would have fallen within the scope of the FMLA. So too if Sarah had lived in Las Vegas instead of with her daughter, and Beverly had requested leave to care for her mother there. Ultimately, other than a concern that our straightforward reading will "open the door to increased FMLA requests," the Park District gives us no reason to treat the current scenario any differently.

**Decision and Remedy** *The U.S. Court of Appeals for the Seventh Circuit affirmed the lower court's judgment. Under the FMLA, an eligible employee is entitled to take leave from work to care for a family member with a serious health condition. The care is not restricted to a particular place (such as "at home").*

### Critical Thinking

- **What If the Facts Were Different?** *Suppose that Beverly had requested leave to make arrangements for a change in Sarah's care, such as a transfer to a nursing home. Is it likely that the result would have been different? Explain.*
- **Legal Environment** *Under the FMLA, an employee is eligible for leave when he or she is needed to care for a family member. Should "needed to care for" be interpreted to cover only ongoing physical care? Discuss.*

## 20–3b Benefits and Protections

When an employee takes FMLA leave, the employer must continue the worker's health-care coverage on the same terms as if the employee had continued to work. On returning from FMLA leave, most employees must be restored to their original position or to a comparable position (with nearly equivalent pay and benefits, for instance). An important exception allows the employer to avoid reinstating a *key employee*—defined as an employee whose pay falls within the top 10 percent of the firm's workforce.

## 20–3c Violations

An employer that violates the FMLA can be required to provide various remedies, including the following:

1. Damages to compensate the employee for lost wages and benefits, denied compensation, and actual monetary losses (such as the cost of providing care for a family member). Compensatory damages are available up to an amount equivalent to the employee's wages for twelve weeks.
2. Job reinstatement.
3. Promotion, if a promotion has been denied.

A successful plaintiff is also entitled to court costs and attorneys' fees. In addition, if the plaintiff shows that the employer acted in bad faith, the plaintiff can receive two times the amount of damages awarded by a judge or jury. Supervisors can also be held personally liable, as employers, for violations of the act.

Employers generally are required to notify employees when an absence will be counted against FMLA leave. If an employer fails to provide such notice, and that failure to notify causes harm to the employee, the employer can be sanctioned.[13]

---

# 20–4 Health, Safety, and Income Security

Under the common law, employees who were injured on the job had to file lawsuits against their employers to obtain recovery. Today, numerous state and federal statutes protect employees from the risk of accidental injury, death, or disease resulting from their employment. In addition, the government protects employees' income through Social Security, Medicare, unemployment insurance, and the regulation of pensions and health insurance plans.

## 20–4a The Occupational Safety and Health Act

At the federal level, the primary legislation protecting employees' health and safety is the Occupational Safety and Health Act,[14] which is administered by the Occupational Safety and Health Administration (OSHA). The act imposes on employers a general duty to keep the workplace safe.

To this end, OSHA has established specific safety standards that employers must follow, depending on the industry. For instance, OSHA regulations require the use of safety guards on certain mechanical equipment. It also sets maximum levels of exposure to substances in the workplace that may be harmful to workers' health.

**Notices, Records, and Reports** The act requires that employers post certain notices in the workplace, maintain specific records, and submit reports. Employers with eleven or more employees are required to keep occupational injury and illness records for each employee. Each record must be made available for inspection when requested by an OSHA compliance officer.

Whenever a work-related injury or disease occurs, employers must make reports directly to OSHA. If an employee dies or three or more employees are hospitalized because of a work-related incident, the employer must notify OSHA within eight hours. A company that fails to do so will be fined. Following the incident, a complete inspection of the premises is mandatory.

**Inspections** OSHA compliance officers may enter and inspect the facilities of any establishment covered by the Occupational Safety and Health Act. Employees may also file complaints of violations. Under the act, an employer cannot discharge an employee who files a complaint or who, in good faith, refuses to work in a high-risk area if bodily harm or death might result.

## 20–4b State Workers' Compensation Laws

State **workers' compensation laws** establish an administrative procedure for compensating workers injured on the job. Instead of suing, an injured worker files a claim

---

13. This was the United States Supreme Court's holding in *Ragsdale v. Wolverine World Wide, Inc.*, 535 U.S. 81, 122 S.Ct. 1155, 152 L.Ed.2d 167 (2002).

14. 29 U.S.C. Sections 553, 651–678.

with the state agency or board that administers local workers' compensation claims.

All states require employers to provide workers' compensation insurance, but the specific rules vary by state. Most states have a state fund that employers pay into for workers' compensation coverage. Usually, employers can purchase insurance from a private insurer as an alternative to paying into the state fund. Most states also allow certain employers to be *self-insured*—that is, employers that show an ability to pay claims do not need to buy insurance.

No state covers all employees under its workers' compensation statute. Typically, domestic workers, agricultural workers, temporary employees, and employees of common carriers (companies that provide transportation services to the public) are excluded. Minors are covered.

### Requirements for Receiving Workers' Compensation

In general, the only requirements to recover benefits under state workers' compensation laws are:

1. The existence of an employment relationship.
2. An *accidental* injury that *occurred on the job or in the course of employment,* regardless of fault. (An injury that occurs while an employee is commuting to or from work usually is not covered because it did not occur on the job or in the course of employment.)

An injured employee must notify her or his employer promptly (usually within thirty days of the accident). Generally, an employee must also file a workers' compensation claim within a certain period (sixty days to two years) from the time the injury is first noticed, rather than from the time of the accident.

### Workers' Compensation versus Litigation

If an employee accepts workers' compensation benefits, he or she may not sue for injuries caused by the employer's negligence. By barring lawsuits for negligence, workers' compensation laws also prevent employers from avoiding liability by using defenses such as contributory negligence or assumption of risk. A worker may sue an employer who *intentionally* injures the worker, however.

### 20–4c Income Security

Federal and state governments participate in insurance programs designed to protect employees and their families from the financial impact of retirement, disability, death, hospitalization, and unemployment. The key federal law on this subject is the Social Security Act.[15]

**Social Security** The Social Security Act provides for old-age (retirement), survivors', and disability insurance. The act is therefore often referred to as OASDI. Retired workers who are covered by Social Security receive monthly payments from the Social Security Administration, which administers the Social Security Act. Social Security benefits are fixed by statute but increase automatically with increases in the cost of living.

**Medicare** Medicare is a federal government health-insurance program administered by the Social Security Administration for people sixty-five years of age and older and for some under age sixty-five who are disabled. It originally had two parts, one pertaining to hospital costs and the other to nonhospital medical costs, such as visits to physicians' offices. It now offers additional coverage options and a prescription-drug plan. People who have Medicare hospital insurance can obtain additional federal medical insurance if they pay monthly premiums.

**Tax Contributions** Under the Federal Insurance Contributions Act (FICA),[16] both employers and employees contribute to Social Security and Medicare, although the contributions are determined differently. The employer withholds the employee's FICA contributions from the employee's wages and ordinarily matches the contributions.

For Social Security, the basis for the contributions is the employee's annual wage base—the maximum amount of the employee's wages that is subject to the tax. As of 2016, the maximum amount subject to the tax was $118,500, and the tax rate was 12.4 percent.

The Medicare tax rate is 2.9 percent. Unlike Social Security, Medicare has no cap on the amount of wages subject to the tax. So even if an employee's salary is well above the cap for Social Security, he or she will still owe Medicare tax on the total earned income.

For Social Security and Medicare together, typically the employer and the employee each pay 7.65 percent. This is equivalent to 6.2 percent (half of 12.4 percent) for Social Security plus 1.45 percent (half of 2.9 percent) for Medicare up to the maximum wage base. Any earned income above that threshold is taxed only for Medicare. Self-employed persons pay both the employer's and the employee's portions of the Social Security and Medicare taxes.

Under the Affordable Care Act, high-income earners are subject to an additional Medicare tax of 3.8 percent on most investment income. This additional tax applies to single wage earners making more than $200,000 and married couples making more than $250,000.

---

**15.** 42 U.S.C. Sections 301–1397e.

**16.** 26 U.S.C. Sections 3101–3125.

**Private Retirement Plans** The major federal statute that regulates employee retirement plans is the Employee Retirement Income Security Act (ERISA).[17] This act empowers a branch of the U.S. Department of Labor to enforce its provisions governing employers that have private pension funds for their employees. ERISA does *not* require an employer to establish a pension plan. When a plan exists, however, ERISA provides standards for its management.

ERISA created the Pension Benefit Guaranty Corporation (PBGC), an independent federal agency, to provide timely and uninterrupted payment of voluntary private pension benefits. The pension plans pay annual insurance premiums (at set rates adjusted for inflation) to the PBGC, which then pays benefits to participants in the event that a plan is unable to do so.

A key provision of ERISA concerns vesting. **Vesting** gives an employee a legal right to receive pension benefits when she or he stops working. Before ERISA was enacted, some employees who had worked for companies for many years received no pension benefits when their employment terminated because those benefits had not vested. Under ERISA, generally all employee contributions to pension plans vest immediately. Employee rights to employer contributions vest after five years of employment.

**Unemployment Insurance** The Federal Unemployment Tax Act (FUTA)[18] created a state-administered system that provides unemployment compensation to eligible individuals who have lost their jobs. The FUTA and state laws require employers that fall under the provisions of the act to pay unemployment taxes at regular intervals. The proceeds from these taxes are then paid out to qualified unemployed workers.

To be eligible for unemployment compensation, a worker must be willing and able to work. Workers who have been fired for misconduct or who have voluntarily left their jobs are not eligible for benefits. Normally, workers must be actively seeking employment to continue receiving benefits.

■ **EXAMPLE 20.7** Martha works for Baily Snowboards in Vermont. One day at work, Martha receives a text from her son saying that he has been taken to the hospital. Martha rushes to the hospital and does not return to work for several days. Bailey hires someone else for Martha's position, and Martha files for unemployment benefits. Martha's claim will be denied because she left her job voluntarily and made no effort to maintain contact with her employer. ■

**COBRA** The Consolidated Omnibus Budget Reconciliation Act (COBRA)[19] enables employees to continue, for a limited time, their health-care coverage after they are no longer eligible for group health-insurance plans. The workers—not the employers—pay the premiums for the continued coverage.

COBRA prohibits an employer from eliminating a worker's medical, vision, or dental insurance when the worker's employment is terminated or when a reduction in the worker's hours would affect coverage. Termination of employment may be voluntary or involuntary. Only workers fired for gross misconduct are excluded from protection. Employers, with some exceptions, must inform employees of COBRA's provisions before the termination or reduction of work hours.

A worker has sixty days (from the date that the group coverage would stop) to decide whether to continue with the employer's group insurance plan. If the worker chooses to continue coverage, the employer is obligated to keep the policy active for up to eighteen months (twenty-nine months if the worker is disabled). The coverage must be the same as that provided to the worker (and his or her family members) prior to the termination or reduction of work. An employer that does not comply with COBRA risks substantial penalties, including a tax of up to 10 percent of the annual cost of the group plan or $500,000, whichever is less.

**Employer-Sponsored Group Health Plans** The Health Insurance Portability and Accountability Act (HIPAA)[20] contains provisions that affect employer-sponsored group health plans. For instance, HIPAA restricts the manner in which employers collect, use, and disclose the health information of employees and their families. Employers must designate privacy officials, distribute privacy notices, and train employees to ensure that employees' health information is not disclosed to unauthorized parties.

Failure to comply with HIPAA regulations can result in civil penalties of up to $100 per person per violation (with a cap of $25,000 per year). Employers are also subject to criminal prosecution for certain types of HIPAA violations. An employer can face up to $250,000 in criminal fines and imprisonment for up to ten years if convicted.

**Affordable Care Act** The Affordable Care Act[21] (commonly referred to as Obamacare) requires most employers with fifty or more full-time employees to offer

---

17. 29 U.S.C. Sections 1001 *et seq*.
18. 26 U.S.C. Sections 3301–3310.
19. 29 U.S.C. Sections 1161–1169.
20. 29 U.S.C. Sections 1181 *et seq*.
21. Pub. L. No. 111-148, 124 Stat. 119, March 23, 2010, codified in various sections of 42 U.S.C.

health-insurance benefits. Under the act, any business offering health benefits to its employees (even if not legally required to do so) may be eligible for tax credits of up to 35 percent to offset the costs.

An employer who fails to provide health benefits as required under the statute can be fined up to $2,000 for each employee after the first thirty people. (This is known as the 50/30 rule: employers with fifty employees must provide insurance, and those failing to do so will be fined for each employee after the first thirty.) An employer who offers a plan that costs an employee more than 9.5 percent of the employee's income may be assessed a penalty.

## 20–5 Employee Privacy Rights

Concerns about the privacy rights of employees have arisen as employers have purportedly used invasive tactics to monitor and screen workers. Perhaps the greatest privacy concern in employment today involves electronic monitoring of employees' activities.

### 20–5a Electronic Monitoring

More than half of employers engage in some form of electronic monitoring of their employees. Many employers review employees' e-mail, as well as their social media posts and other Internet messages. Employers may also make video recordings of their employees at work, record their telephone conversations, and listen to their voice mail.

**Employee Privacy Protection** Employees of private (nongovernment) employers have some privacy protection under tort law and state constitutions. In addition, state and federal statutes may limit an employer's conduct in certain respects. For instance, the Electronic Communications Privacy Act prohibits employers from intercepting an employee's personal electronic communications unless they are made on devices and systems furnished by the employer.

Nonetheless, employers do have considerable leeway to monitor employees in the workplace. In addition, private employers generally are free to use filtering software to block access to certain Web sites, such as sites containing sexually explicit images. The First Amendment's protection of free speech prevents only *government employers* from restraining speech by blocking Web sites.

**Reasonable Expectation of Privacy** When determining whether an employer should be held liable for violating an employee's privacy rights, the courts generally weigh the employer's interests against the employee's reasonable expectation of privacy. Normally, if employees have been informed that their communications are being monitored, they cannot reasonably expect those interactions to be private. In addition, a court will typically hold that employees do not have a reasonable expectation of privacy when using a system (such as an e-mail system) provided by the employer.

If employees are *not* informed that certain communications are being monitored, the employer may be held liable for invading their privacy. Most employers that engage in electronic monitoring notify their employees about the monitoring. Nevertheless, a general policy may not sufficiently protect an employer monitoring forms of communications that the policy fails to mention. For instance, notifying employees that their e-mails and phone calls may be monitored does not necessarily protect an employer who monitors social media posts or text messages.

### 20–5b Other Types of Monitoring

In addition to monitoring their employees' online activities, employers also engage in other types of employee screening and monitoring. The practices discussed next have often been challenged as violations of employee privacy rights.

**Lie-Detector Tests** At one time, many employers required employees or job applicants to take polygraph examinations (lie-detector tests). Today, the Employee Polygraph Protection Act[22] generally prohibits employers from requiring employees or job applicants to take lie-detector tests or suggesting or requesting that they do so. The act also restricts employers' ability to use or ask about the results of any lie-detector test or to take any negative employment action based on the results.

Certain employers are exempt from these prohibitions. Federal, state, and local government employers, and certain security service firms, may conduct polygraph tests. In addition, companies that manufacture and distribute controlled substances may perform lie-detector tests. Other employers may use polygraph tests when investigating losses attributable to theft, including embezzlement and the theft of trade secrets.

**Drug Testing** In the interests of public safety and to reduce unnecessary costs, many employers, including the government, require their employees to submit to drug testing.

---

**22.** 29 U.S.C. Sections 2001 *et seq.*

**Public Employers.** Government (public) employers are constrained in drug testing by the Fourth Amendment to the U.S. Constitution, which prohibits unreasonable searches and seizures. Drug testing of public employees is allowed by statute for transportation workers, however. Courts normally uphold drug testing of certain employees when drug use in a particular job may threaten public safety. Also, when there is a reasonable basis for suspecting public employees of drug use, courts often find that drug testing does not violate the Fourth Amendment.

**Private Employers.** The Fourth Amendment does not apply to drug testing conducted by private employers. Hence, the privacy rights and drug testing of private-sector employees are governed by state law. Many states have statutes that allow drug testing by private employers but restrict when and how the testing may be performed. A collective bargaining agreement (discussed in a later chapter) may also provide protection against drug testing (or may authorize it in certain conditions).

The permissibility of testing a private employee for drugs often hinges on whether the employer's testing was reasonable. Random drug tests and even "zero-tolerance" policies (which deny a "second chance" to employees who test positive for drugs) have been held to be reasonable. It is also reasonable to require employees of private employers who are under contract with the federal government to undergo standard background investigations to disclose potential drug use.[23]

---

23. *See National Aeronautics and Space Administration v. Nelson,* 562 U.S. 134, 131 S.Ct. 746, 178 L.Ed.2d 667 (2011).

## Reviewing: Employment Law

Rick Saldona began working as a traveling salesperson for Aimer Winery in 2008. Sales constituted 90 percent of Saldona's work time. Saldona worked an average of fifty hours per week but received no overtime pay. In June 2018, Saldona's new supervisor, Caesar Braxton, claimed that Saldona had been inflating his reported sales calls and required Saldona to submit to a polygraph test. Saldona reported Braxton to the U.S. Department of Labor, which prohibited Aimer from requiring Saldona to take a polygraph test for this purpose.

In August 2018, Saldona's wife, Venita, fell from a ladder and sustained a head injury while employed as a full-time agricultural harvester. Saldona presented Aimer's Human Resources Department with a letter from his wife's physician indicating that she would need daily care for several months, and Saldona took leave until December 2018. Aimer had sixty-three employees at that time. When Saldona returned to Aimer, he was informed that his position had been eliminated because his sales territory had been combined with an adjacent territory. Using the information presented in the chapter, answer the following questions.

1. Would Saldona have been legally entitled to receive overtime pay at a higher rate? Why or why not?
2. What is the maximum length of time Saldona would have been allowed to take leave to care for his injured spouse?
3. Under what circumstances would Aimer have been allowed to require an employee to take a polygraph test?
4. Would Aimer likely be able to avoid reinstating Saldona under the *key employee* exception? Why or why not?

**Debate This** . . . *The U.S. labor market is highly competitive, so state and federal laws that require overtime pay are unnecessary and should be abolished.*

## Terms and Concepts

| | | |
|---|---|---|
| employment at will 438 | vesting 448 | workers' compensation law 446 |
| minimum wage 441 | whistleblowing 439 | wrongful discharge 441 |

## Issue Spotters

1. American Manufacturing Company (AMC) issues an employee handbook that states that employees will be discharged only for good cause. One day, Greg, an AMC supervisor, says to Larry, "I don't like your looks. You're fired." Can AMC be held liable for breach of contract? If so, why? If not, why? (See *Employment at Will*.)

2. Erin, an employee of Fine Print Shop, is injured on the job. For Erin to obtain workers' compensation, must her injury have been caused by Fine Print's negligence? Does it matter whether the action causing the injury was intentional? Explain. (See *Health, Safety, and Income Security*.)

- **Check your answers to the Issue Spotters against the answers provided in Appendix D at the end of this text.**

## Business Scenarios

**20–1. Wrongful Discharge.** Denton and Carlo were employed at an appliance plant. Their job required them to perform occasional maintenance work while standing on a wire mesh twenty feet above the plant floor. Other employees had fallen through the mesh, and one of them had been killed by the fall. When their supervisor told them to perform tasks that would likely involve walking on the mesh, Denton and Carlo refused because they feared they might suffer bodily injury or death. Because they refused to do the requested work, the two employees were fired from their jobs. Was their discharge wrongful? If so, under what federal employment law? To what federal agency or department should they turn for assistance? (See *Employment at Will*.)

**20–2. Family and Medical Leave Act.** Serge worked for Service Attendant Corporation (SAC). He requested time off under the Family and Medical Leave Act (FMLA) from April 29 through May 31 to undergo treatment for alcoholism. For the month of May, he was hospitalized as part of the treatment. When he did not return to work on June 1, SAC fired him. Did SAC violate Serge's rights under the FMLA? Explain your answer. (See *Family and Medical Leave*.)

## Business Case Problems

**20–3. Spotlight on Coca Cola—Family and Medical Leave Act.**  Jennifer Willis worked for Coca Cola Enterprises, Inc. (CCE), in Louisiana as a senior account manager. On a Monday in May 2003, Willis called her supervisor to tell him that she was sick and would not be able to work that day. She also said that she was pregnant, but she did not say she was sick because of the pregnancy. On Tuesday, she called to ask where to report to work and was told that she could not return without a doctor's release. She said that she had a doctor's appointment on "Wednesday," which her supervisor understood to be the next day. Willis meant the following Wednesday.

For more than a week, Willis did not contact CCE. When she returned to work, she was told that she had violated CCE's "No Call/No Show" policy. Under this policy "an employee absent from work for three consecutive days without notifying the supervisor during that period will be considered to have voluntarily resigned." She was fired.

Willis filed a suit in a federal district court against CCE under the Family and Medical Leave Act (FMLA). To be eligible for FMLA leave, an employee must inform an employer of the reason for the leave. Did Willis meet this requirement? Did CCE's response to Willis's absence violate the FMLA? Explain. [*Willis v. Coca Cola Enterprises, Inc.*, 445 F.3d 413 (5th Cir. 2006)] (See *Family and Medical Leave*.)

**20–4. Workers' Compensation.** As a safety measure, Dynea USA, Inc., required an employee, Tony Fairbanks, to wear steel-toed boots. One of the boots caused a sore on Fairbanks's leg. The skin over the sore broke, and within a week, Fairbanks was hospitalized with a methicillin-resistant staphylococcus aureus (MRSA) infection. He filed a workers' compensation claim. Dynea argued that the MRSA bacteria that caused the infection had been on Fairbanks's skin before he came to work. What are the requirements to recover workers' compensation benefits? Does this claim qualify? Explain. [*Dynea USA, Inc. v. Fairbanks*, 241 Or.App. 311, 250 P.3d 389 (2011)] (See *Health, Safety, and Income Security*.)

**20–5. Exceptions to the Employment-at-Will Doctrine.** Li Li worked for Packard Bioscience, and Mark Schmeizl was her supervisor. In March 2000, Schmeizl told Li to call Packard's competitors, pretend to be a potential customer, and request "pricing information and literature." Li refused to perform the assignment. She told Schmeizl that she thought the work was illegal and recommended that he contact Packard's legal department. Although a lawyer recommended against the practice, Schmeizl insisted that Li perform the calls. Moreover, he later wrote negative performance reviews because she was unable to get the requested information when she called competitors and identified herself as a Packard employee. On June 1, 2000, Li was terminated on Schmeizl's recommendation. Can Li bring a claim for wrongful discharge? Why or why not? [*Li Li v. Canberra Industries*, 134 Conn.App. 448, 39 A.3d 789 (2012)] (See *Employment at Will.*)

**20–6. Business Case Problem with Sample Answer— Unemployment Compensation.**  Fior Ramirez worked as a housekeeper for Remington Lodging & Hospitality, a hotel in Atlantic Beach, Florida. After her father in the Dominican Republic suffered a stroke, she asked her employer for time off to be with him. Ramirez's manager, Katie Berkowski, refused the request. Two days later, Berkowski received a call from Ramirez to say that she was with her father. He died about a week later, and Ramirez returned to work, but Berkowski told her that she had abandoned her position. Ramirez applied for unemployment compensation. Under the applicable state statute, "an employee is disqualified from receiving benefits if he or she voluntarily left work without good cause." Does Ramirez qualify for benefits? Explain. [*Ramirez v. Reemployment Assistance Appeals Commission*, 39 Fla.L.Weekly D317, 135 So.3d 408 (1 Dist. 2014)] (See *Health, Safety, and Income Security.*)

- **For a sample answer to Problem 20–6, go to Appendix E at the end of this text.**

**20–7. Unemployment Compensation.** Jefferson Partners LP entered into a collective bargaining agreement (CBA) with the Amalgamated Transit Union. Under the CBA, drivers had to either join the union or pay a fair share—85 percent—of union dues, which were used to pay for administrative costs incurred by the union. An employee who refused to pay was subject to discharge. Jefferson hired Tiffany Thompson to work as a bus driver. When told of the CBA requirement, she said that she thought it was unfair. She asserted that it was illegal to compel her to join the union and that it would be illegal to discharge her for not complying. She refused either to join the union or to pay the dues. More than two years later, she was fired on the ground that her continued refusal constituted misconduct. Is Thompson eligible for unemployment compensation? Explain. [*Thompson v. Jefferson Partners LP*, ___ N.W.2d ___, 2016 WL 953038 (Minn.App. 2016)] (See *Health, Safety, and Income Security.*)

**20–8. A Question of Ethics—Workers' Compensation Law.** 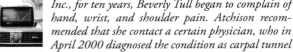 *In 1999, after working for Atchison Leather Products, Inc., for ten years, Beverly Tull began to complain of hand, wrist, and shoulder pain. Atchison recommended that she contact a certain physician, who in April 2000 diagnosed the condition as carpal tunnel syndrome "severe enough" for surgery. In August, Tull filed a claim with the state workers' compensation board. Because Atchison changed workers' compensation insurance companies every year, a dispute arose as to which company should pay Tull's claim. Fearing liability, no insurer would authorize treatment, and Tull was forced to delay surgery until December. The board granted her temporary total disability benefits for the subsequent six weeks that she missed work. On April 23, 2002, Berger Co. bought Atchison. The new employer adjusted Tull's work so that it was less demanding and stressful, but she continued to suffer pain. In July, a physician diagnosed her condition as permanent. The board granted her permanent partial disability benefits. By May 2005, bickering over the financial responsibility for Tull's claim involved five insurers—four of which had each covered Atchison for a single year and one of which covered Berger. [Tull v. Atchison Leather Products, Inc., 37 Kan.App.2d 87, 150 P.3d 316 (2007)] (See Health, Safety, and Income Security.)*

**(a)** When an injured employee files a claim for workers' compensation, a proceeding is held to assess the injury and determine the amount of compensation. Should a dispute between insurers over the payment of the claim be resolved in the same proceeding? Why or why not?

**(b)** The board designated April 23, 2002, as the date of Tull's injury. What is the reason for determining the date of a worker's injury? Should the board in this case have selected this date or a different date? Why?

**(c)** How should the board assess liability for the payment of Tull's medical expenses and disability benefits? Would it be appropriate to impose joint and several liability on the insurers (holding each of them responsible for the full amount of damages)? Or should the individual liability of each of the insurers be determined? Explain.

# Legal Reasoning Group Activity

**20–9. Wrongful Discharge.** Stefan Sorril, a health teacher at Madison Middle School and a triathlete, appeared shirtless and showed off his "ripped" body as an extra on an episode of a new reality TV show. A week after the show aired, school officials called him into the district office and asked for his resignation. Sorril later claimed that he was pressured and coerced into resigning. He said the school officials had informed him that—as a result of his appearance on the show—he would no longer be offered tenure (a senior academic's contractual right not to be terminated without just cause). Sorril subsequently sued for wrongful discharge. (See *Employment at Will.*)

**(a)** The first group will discuss whether Sorril was an employee at will and how that status would affect his claim.

**(b)** The second group will determine if Sorril can assert any of the exceptions to the employment-at-will doctrine.

**(c)** The third group will decide whether the school district should be held liable for wrongful discharge and explain their reasoning.

# Answers to the *Issue Spotters*

**1. *Can AMC be held liable for breach of contract? If so, why? If not, why not?*** Yes. Some courts have held that an implied employment contract exists between employer and employee when an employee handbook states that employees will be dismissed only for good cause. An employer who fires a worker contrary to this promise can be held liable for breach of contract.

**2. *For Erin to obtain workers' compensation, must her injury have been caused by Fine Print's negligence? Does it matter whether the action causing the injury was intentional? Explain.*** Workers' compensation laws establish a pro-cedure for compensating workers who are injured on the job. Instead of suing to collect benefits, an injured worker notifies the employer of an injury and files a claim with the appropriate state agency.

The right to recover is normally determined without regard to negligence or fault, but intentionally inflicted injuries are not covered. Unlike the potential for recovery in a lawsuit based on negligence or fault, recovery under a workers' compensation stat-ute is limited to the specific amount designated in the statute for the employee's injury.

# Sample Answers for *Business Case Problems with Sample Answer*

**Problem 20–6. *Unemployment Compensation.*** Yes, Ramirez qualifies for unemployment compensation. Generally, to be eli-gible for unemployment compensation, a worker must be willing and able to work. Workers who have been fired for misconduct or who have voluntarily left their jobs are not eligible for ben-efits. In the facts of this problem, the applicable state statute disqualifies an employee from receiving benefits if he or she vol-untarily leaves work without "good cause."

The issue is whether Ramirez left her job for "good cause." When her father in the Dominican Republic had a stroke, she asked her employer for time off to be with him. Her employer refused the request. But Ramirez left to be with her father and called to inform her employer. It seems likely that this family emergency would constitute "good cause," and Ramirez's call and return to work after her father's death indicated that she did not disregard her employer's interests.

In the actual case on which this problem is based, the state of Florida denied Ramirez unemployment compensation. On Ramirez's appeal, a state intermediate appellate court reversed, on the reasoning stated above.

# Chapter 17

# CHAPTER

# Employment Discrimination

Out of the 1960s civil rights movement to end racial and other forms of discrimination grew a body of law protecting employees against discrimination in the workplace. Legislation, judicial decisions, and administrative agency actions restrict employers from discriminating against workers on the basis of race, color, religion, national origin, gender, age, or disability. A class of persons defined by one or more of these criteria is known as a **protected class**.

Several federal statutes prohibit **employment discrimination** against members of protected classes. The most important is Title VII of the Civil Rights Act.[1] Title VII prohibits employment discrimination on the basis of race, color, religion, national origin, and gender. The Age Discrimination in Employment Act[2] and the Americans with Disabilities Act[3] pro-

hibit discrimination on the basis of age and disability, respectively. The protections afforded under these laws also extend to U.S. citizens who are working abroad for U.S. firms or for companies that are controlled by U.S. firms.

This chapter focuses on federal statutes, including the ones just mentioned. Many states have their own laws that protect employees against discrimination, however, and some provide more protection than federal laws do.

---

1. 42 U.S.C. Sections 2000e–2000e-17.
2. 29 U.S.C. Sections 621–634.
3. 42 U.S.C. Sections 12102–12118.

## 21–1 Title VII of the Civil Rights Act

Title VII of the Civil Rights Act prohibits job discrimination against employees, applicants, and union members on the basis of race, color, national origin, religion, and gender at any stage of employment. Title VII bans discrimination in the hiring process, discipline procedures, discharge, promotion, and benefits.

Title VII applies to employers with fifteen or more employees and labor unions with fifteen or more members. It also applies to labor unions that operate hiring halls (where members go regularly to be assigned jobs), employment agencies, and state and local governing units or agencies. The United States Supreme Court has ruled that an employer with fewer than fifteen employees is not automatically shielded from a lawsuit filed under Title VII.[4] In addition, the act prohibits discrimination in most federal government employment. When Title

---

4. *Arbaugh v. Y&H Corp.*, 546 U.S. 500, 126 S.Ct. 1235, 163 L.Ed.2d 1097 (2006).

VII applies to the employer, any employee—including an undocumented (alien) worker—can bring an action for employment discrimination.

### 21–1a The Equal Employment Opportunity Commission

The Equal Employment Opportunity Commission (EEOC) monitors compliance with Title VII. An employee alleging discrimination must file a claim with the EEOC before a lawsuit can be brought against the employer. The EEOC may investigate the dispute and attempt to obtain the parties' voluntary consent to an out-of-court settlement. If a voluntary agreement cannot be reached, the EEOC may file a suit against the employer on the employee's behalf.

■ **EXAMPLE 21.1** Jacqueline Cote met her wife, Diana Smithson, in Maine while they were both employees at Wal-Mart. They moved to Massachusetts and were married a few days after the state legalized same-sex marriage, and they continued working at a Wal-Mart there. Smithson eventually quit work to take care of Cote's elderly mother. Cote tried to enroll her partner in Wal-Mart's health plan, but coverage was denied. Five years later, Smithson was diagnosed with cancer.

Cote filed a claim with the EEOC arguing that Wal-Mart had intentionally discriminated against her on the basis of sex. In 2014, the commission agreed that Cote "was treated differently and denied benefits because of her sex." The EEOC ordered Wal-Mart to work with Cote to help pay Smithson's medical bills. ■

The EEOC does not investigate every claim of employment discrimination. Generally, it takes only "priority cases," such as claims that affect many workers and those involving retaliatory discharge (firing an employee in retaliation for submitting a claim to the EEOC). If the EEOC decides not to investigate a claim, the EEOC issues a "right to sue" that allows the employee to bring his or her own lawsuit against the employer.

## 21–1b Limitations on Class Actions

In an important decision, the United States Supreme Court limited the rights of employees to bring discrimination claims against their employer as a group, or class. The decision did not affect the rights of individual employees to sue under Title VII, however.

■ **CASE IN POINT 21.2** A group of female employees sued Wal-Mart, the nation's largest private employer. The employees alleged that store managers who had discretion over pay and promotions were biased against women and disproportionately favored men. The employees wished to bring a class action—a lawsuit in which a small number of plaintiffs sue on behalf of a larger group. Lower courts ruled that the employees' class-action suit could proceed, and Wal-Mart appealed. The Supreme Court ruled in favor of Wal-Mart, effectively blocking the class action. The Court held that the women had failed to prove a company-wide policy of discrimination that had a common effect on all women included in the class. Therefore, they could not maintain a class action.[5] ■

## 21–1c Intentional and Unintentional Discrimination

Title VII of the Civil Rights Act prohibits both intentional and unintentional discrimination.

**Intentional Discrimination** Intentional discrimination by an employer against an employee is known as

---

5. *Wal-Mart Stores, Inc. v. Dukes*, 564 U.S. 338, 131 S.Ct. 2541, 180 L.Ed.2d 374 (2011).

**disparate-treatment discrimination.** Because intent may sometimes be difficult to prove, courts have established certain procedures for resolving disparate-treatment cases.

***Prima Facie* Case.** A plaintiff who sues on the basis of disparate-treatment discrimination must first make out a ***prima facie* case.** *Prima facie* is Latin for "at first sight" or "on its face." Legally, it refers to a fact that is presumed to be true unless contradicted by evidence.

To establish a *prima facie* case of disparate-treatment discrimination in hiring, a plaintiff must show all of the following:

1. The plaintiff is a member of a protected class.
2. The plaintiff applied and was qualified for the job in question.
3. The plaintiff was rejected by the employer.
4. The employer continued to seek applicants for the position or filled the position with a person not in a protected class.

A plaintiff who can meet these relatively easy requirements has made out a *prima facie* case of illegal discrimination in hiring. Therefore, the plaintiff will win in the absence of a legally acceptable employer defense.

Sometimes, current and former employees make a claim of discrimination. When the plaintiff alleges that the employer fired or took some other adverse employment action against him or her, the same basic requirements apply. To establish a *prima facie* case, the plaintiff must show that he or she was fired or treated adversely for discriminatory reasons.

**Burden-Shifting Procedure.** Once the *prima facie* case is established, the burden then shifts to the employer-defendant, who must articulate a legal reason for not hiring the plaintiff. (Again, this also applies to firing and other adverse employment actions.) If the employer did not have a legal reason for taking the adverse employment action, the plaintiff wins.

If the employer can articulate a legitimate reason for the action, the burden shifts back to the plaintiff. To prevail, the plaintiff must then show that the employer's reason is a *pretext* (not the true reason) and that the employer's decision was actually motivated by discriminatory intent.

**Unintentional Discrimination** Employers often use interviews and tests to choose from among a large number of applicants for job openings. Minimum educational requirements are also common. Some employer practices, such as those involving educational requirements, may have an unintended discriminatory impact on a protected class.

**Disparate-impact discrimination** occurs when a protected group of people is adversely affected by an employer's practices, procedures, or tests, even though they do not appear to be discriminatory. In a disparate-impact discrimination case, the complaining party must first show that the employer's practices, procedures, or tests are effectively discriminatory. Once the plaintiff has made out a *prima facie* case, the burden of proof shifts to the employer to show that the practices or procedures in question were justified.

There are two ways of showing that an employer's practices, procedures, or tests are effectively discriminatory—that is, that disparate-impact discrimination exists.

**Pool of Applicants.** A plaintiff can prove a disparate impact by comparing the employer's workforce to the pool of qualified individuals available in the local labor market. The plaintiff must show that (1) as a result of educational or other job requirements or hiring procedures, (2) the percentage of nonwhites, women, or members of other protected classes in the employer's workforce (3) does not reflect the percentage of that group in the pool of qualified applicants. If the plaintiff can show a connection between the practice and the disparity, he or she has made out a *prima facie* case and need not provide evidence of discriminatory intent.

**Rate of Hiring.** A plaintiff can also prove disparate-impact discrimination by comparing the employer's *selection rates* of members and nonmembers of a protected class (nonwhites and whites, for instance, or women and men). When an educational or other job requirement or hiring procedure excludes members of a protected class from an employer's workforce at a substantially higher rate than nonmembers, discrimination occurs.

Under EEOC guidelines, a selection rate for a protected class that is less than four-fifths, or 80 percent, of the rate for the group with the highest rate of hiring generally is regarded as evidence of disparate impact. ■ **EXAMPLE 21.3** Shady Cove District Fire Department administers an exam to applicants for the position of firefighter. At the exam session, one hundred white applicants take the test, and fifty pass and are hired. At the same exam session, sixty minority applicants take the test, but only twelve pass and are hired. Because twelve is only 20 percent of sixty, the test will be considered discriminatory under the EEOC guidelines. ■

## 21–1d Discrimination Based on Race, Color, and National Origin

Title VII prohibits employers from discriminating against employees or job applicants on the basis of race, color, or national origin. Race is interpreted broadly to apply to the ancestry or ethnic characteristics of a group of persons, such as Native Americans. National origin refers to discrimination based on a person's birth in another country or his or her ancestry or culture, such as Hispanic.

If an employer's standards or policies for selecting or promoting employees have a discriminatory effect on employees or job applicants in these protected classes, then a presumption of illegal discrimination arises. To avoid liability, the employer must show that its standards or policies have a substantial, demonstrable relationship to realistic qualifications for the job in question.

■ **CASE IN POINT 21.4** Jiann Min Chang was an instructor at Alabama Agricultural and Mechanical University (AAMU). When AAMU terminated his employment, Chang filed a lawsuit claiming discrimination based on national origin. Chang established a *prima facie* case because he (1) was a member of a protected class, (2) was qualified for the job, (3) suffered an adverse employment action, and (4) was replaced by someone outside his protected class (a non-Asian instructor).

When the burden of proof shifted to the employer, however, AAMU showed that Chang had argued with a vice president and refused to comply with her instructions. The court ruled that the university had not renewed Chang's contract for a legitimate reason—insubordination—and therefore was not liable for unlawful discrimination.[6] ■

**Reverse Discrimination** Title VII also protects against *reverse discrimination*—that is, discrimination against members of a majority group, such as white males. ■ **EXAMPLE 21.5** An African American woman fires four white men from their management positions at a school district. The men file a lawsuit for reverse discrimination. They argue that the woman was trying to eliminate white males from the district administration in violation of Title VII. The woman claims that the terminations were part of a reorganization plan to cut costs.

If the judge (or jury, in a jury trial) agrees with the men that they were fired for racially discriminatory reasons, then they will be entitled to damages. If, however, the school district can show that the real reason for the terminations was a legitimate attempt to cut costs, then normally their case will be dismissed. ■

---

6. *Jiann Min Chang v. Alabama Agricultural and Mechanical University,* 355 Fed.Appx. 250 (11th Cir. 2009).

**Potential Section 1981 Claims** Victims of racial or ethnic discrimination may also have a cause of action under 42 U.S.C. Section 1981. This section, which was enacted in 1866 to protect the rights of freed slaves, prohibits discrimination on the basis of race or ethnicity in the formation or enforcement of contracts. Because employment is often a contractual relationship, Section 1981 can provide an alternative basis for a plaintiff's action and is potentially advantageous because there is no limit on the damages that can be awarded.

## 21–1e Discrimination Based on Religion

Title VII of the Civil Rights Act also prohibits government employers, private employers, and unions from discriminating against persons because of their religion. (This chapter's *Digital Update* feature discusses how employers who examine prospective employees' social media posts, including posts concerning religion, might engage in unlawful discrimination.)

Employers cannot treat their employees more or less favorably based on their religious beliefs or practices. They also cannot require employees to participate in any religious activity or forbid them from participating in one. ■ **EXAMPLE 21.6** Jason Sewell claims that his employer, a car dealership, fired him for not attending the weekly prayer meetings of dealership employees. If the dealership does require its employees to attend prayer gatherings and fired Sewell for not attending, he has a valid claim of religious discrimination. ■

**Reasonable Accommodation** An employer must "reasonably accommodate" the religious practices and sincerely held religious beliefs of its employees, unless to do so would cause undue hardship to the employer's business. An employee's religion might prohibit her or him from working on a certain day of the week, for instance, or at a certain type of job. Reasonable accommodation is required even if the belief is not based on the doctrines of a traditionally recognized religion, such as Christianity or Judaism, or of a denomination, such as Baptist.

**Undue Hardship** A reasonable attempt to accommodate does not necessarily require the employer to make every change an employee requests or to make a permanent change for an employee's benefit. An employer is not required to make an accommodation that would cause the employer undue hardship. ■ **CASE IN POINT 21.7** Miguel Sánchez-Rodríguez sold cell phones at kiosks in shopping malls for AT&T in Puerto Rico. After six years, Sánchez informed his supervisors that he had become a Seventh Day Adventist and could no longer work on Saturdays for religious reasons. AT&T responded that his position required rotating Saturday shifts and that his inability to work on Saturdays would cause the company hardship.

As a reasonable accommodation, the company suggested that Sánchez swap schedules with others and offered him two alternative positions that would not require work on Saturdays. Sánchez was unable to find workers to swap shifts with him, however, and declined the other jobs because they would result in less income. He began missing work on Saturdays. After a time, AT&T indicated that it would discipline him for any additional Saturdays that he missed. Eventually, he was placed on active disciplinary status. Sánchez resigned and filed a religious discrimination lawsuit. The court found in favor of AT&T, and a federal appellate court affirmed. The company had made adequate efforts at accommodation by allowing Sánchez to swap shifts and offering him other positions that did not require work on Saturdays.[7] ■

## 21–1f Discrimination Based on Gender

Under Title VII and other federal acts, employers are forbidden from discriminating against employees on the basis of gender. Employers are prohibited from classifying or advertising jobs as male or female unless they can prove that the gender of the applicant is essential to the job. In addition, employers cannot have separate male and female seniority lists and cannot refuse to promote employees based on their gender.

**Gender Must Be a Determining Factor** Generally, to succeed in a suit for gender discrimination, a plaintiff must demonstrate that gender was a determining factor in the employer's decision to hire, fire, or promote him or her. Typically, this involves looking at all of the surrounding circumstances.

■ **CASE IN POINT 21.8** Wanda Collier worked for Turner Industries Group, LLC, in the maintenance department. She complained to her supervisor that Jack Daniell, the head of the department, treated her unfairly. Her supervisor told her that Daniell had a problem with her gender and was harder on women. The supervisor talked to Daniell about Collier's complaint but did not take any disciplinary action.

A month later, Daniell confronted Collier, pushing her up against a wall and berating her. After this incident, Collier filed a formal complaint and kept a male co-worker with her at all times. A month later, she was

---

7. *Sánchez-Rodríguez v. AT&T Mobility Puerto Rico, Inc.*, 673 F.3d 1 (1st Cir. 2012).

## DIGITAL UPDATE — Hiring Discrimination Based on Social Media Posts

Human resource officers in most companies routinely check job candidates' social media posts when deciding whom to hire. Certainly, every young person is warned not to post photos that she or he might later regret having made available to potential employers. But a more serious issue involves standard reviewing of job candidates' social media information. Specifically, do employers discriminate based on such information?

### An Experiment in Hiring Discrimination via Online Social Networks

Two researchers at Carnegie-Mellon University conducted an experiment to determine whether social media information posted by prospective employees influences employers' hiring decisions.[a] The researchers created false résumés and social media profiles. They submitted job applications on behalf of the fictional "candidates" to about four thousand U.S. employers. They then compared employers' responses to different groups—for example, to Muslim candidates versus Christian candidates.

The researchers found that candidates whose public profiles indicated that they were Muslim were less likely to be called for interviews than Christian applicants. The difference was particularly pronounced in parts of the country with more conservative residents. In those locations, Muslims received callbacks only 2 percent of the time, compared with 17 percent for Christian applicants. According to the authors of the study, "Hiring discrimination via online searches of candidates may not be widespread, but online disclosures of personal traits can significantly influence the hiring decisions of a self-selected set of employers."

### Job Candidates' Perception of the Hiring Process

In another study, researchers at North Carolina State University looked at how job applicants view prospective employers' use of their social media profiles during the hiring process.[b] Job candidates appear to view the hiring process as unfair when they know that their social media profiles have been used in the selection process. This perception, according to the researchers, makes litigation more likely.

### The EEOC Speaks Up

Since 2014, the Equal Employment Opportunity Commission (EEOC) has investigated how prospective employers can use social media to engage in discrimination in the hiring process. Given that the Society for Human Resource Management estimates that more than three-fourths of its members use social media in employment screening, the EEOC is interested in regulating this procedure.

Social media sites, examined closely, can provide information to a prospective employer on the applicant's race, color, national origin, disability, religion, and other protected characteristics. The EEOC has reminded employers that such information—whether it comes from social media postings or other sources—may not legally be used to make employment decisions on prohibited bases, such as race, gender, and religion.

**Critical Thinking** *Can you think of a way a company could use information from an applicant's social media posts without running the risk of being accused of hiring discrimination?*

a. A. Acquisti and C. N. Fong, "An Experiment in Hiring Discrimination via Online Social Networks," *Social Service Research Network*, October 26, 2014.

b. J. W. Stoughton, L. F. Thompson, and A. W. Meade, "Examining Applicant Reactions to the Use of Social Networking Websites in Pre-Employment Screening," *Journal of Business and Psychology*, November 2013, DOI: 10.1007/s10869-013-9333-6.

---

fired. She subsequently filed a lawsuit alleging gender discrimination. The court allowed Collier's claim to go to a jury because there was sufficient evidence that gender was a determining factor in Daniell's conduct.[8] ∎

8. *Collier v. Turner Industries Group, LLC*, 797 F.Supp.2d 1029 (D. Idaho 2011).

The Federal Bureau of Investigation (FBI) requires that its applicants meet certain physical fitness standards. For women, the standards include the ability to complete a minimum of fourteen push-ups. Men must be able to complete at least thirty. Whether this difference constitutes discrimination on the basis of gender was at issue in the following case.

# Bauer v. Lynch

United States Court of Appeals, Fourth Circuit, 812 F.3d 340 (2016).

## In the Language of the Court

*KING*, Circuit Judge.

* * * *

The FBI trains its Special Agent recruits at the FBI Academy in Quantico, Virginia. * * * All Trainees must pass a physical fitness test (the "PFT").

* * * The FBI requires every Special Agent recruit to pass the PFT twice: once to gain admission to the Academy, and a second time to graduate.

* * * *

* * * Trainees * * * need to satisfy the following standards * * * :

| Event | Men | Women |
|-------|-----|-------|
| Sit-ups | 38 | 35 |
| 300-meter sprint | 52.4s | 64.9s |
| Push-ups | 30 | 14 |
| 1.5-mile run | 12m, 42s | 13m, 5s |

* * * *

After the attacks of September 11, 2001, * * * Jay Bauer resolved to contribute to the defense of our country by becoming a Special Agent in the FBI. [At the time,] he * * * served as an assistant professor at the University of Wisconsin–Milwaukee.

* * * Bauer took the PFT for the first time and failed. Although he achieved sixteen points on the test, Bauer completed only twenty-five push-ups * * * . The FBI allowed Bauer to retest [three months later] and he passed, that time completing thirty-two push-ups. With his fitness screening complete, the FBI invited Bauer to report to the Academy.

Bauer's time at the Academy largely showed great potential for a career as a Special Agent. He passed all academic tests, demonstrated proficiency in his firearms and defensive tactics training, and met all expectations for the practical applications and skills components of the Academy. Bauer's classmates also selected him as the class leader and spokesperson for the Academy graduation. Unfortunately, Bauer faced a dilemma: he was unable to pass the PFT at Quantico.

During his twenty-two weeks at the Academy, Bauer took the PFT five times. On each occasion, he would have passed but for his failure to achieve the minimum standard for push-ups. Bauer's results, and his corresponding point scores for each event, were as follows:

| Week | Sit-ups | 300-meter sprint | Push-ups | 1.5-mile run | Total Points |
|------|---------|------------------|----------|--------------|--------------|
| Week 1 | 40 (2) | 42.6 sec. (8) | 26 (0) | 10:49 (4) | 14 |
| Week 7 | 47 (4) | 43.4 sec. (7) | 25 (0) | 10:24 (5) | 16 |
| Week 14 | 50 (6) | 43.7 sec. (7) | 28 (0) | 10:45 (4) | 17 |
| Week 18 | 51 (6) | 43.8 sec. (7) | 27 (0) | 11:09 (4) | 17 |
| Week 22 | 49 (5) | 44.1 sec. (6) | 29 (0) | 10:57 (4) | 15 |

Following his final failure of the PFT, Bauer * * * was [allowed to] resign with the possibility of future employment with the FBI * * * . Bauer * * * immediately signed a resignation letter. Two weeks later, the FBI offered Bauer a position as an Intelligence Analyst in its Chicago Field Office. He accepted and has been employed in that position since.

* * * *

* * * Bauer filed this Title VII action in [a federal district court] against [Loretta Lynch,] the Attorney General. According to the claims in Bauer's complaint, the FBI's use of the gender-normed PFT standards contravened * * * Title VII * * * which prohibits sex discrimination by federal employers.

* * * *

In his summary judgment motion, Bauer maintained that the FBI's use of the gender-normed PFT standards was facially discriminatory [involving explicit categorization, such as by sex or race].

* * * *

* * * The district court agreed with Bauer, granting his motion for summary judgment.

* * * *

The Attorney General * * * filed a timely * * * appeal.

* * * *

Title VII requires that any "personnel actions affecting employees or applicants for employment" taken by federal employers "shall be made free from any discrimination based on * * * sex." * * * *A plaintiff is entitled to demonstrate discrimination by showing that the employer uses a facially discriminatory employment practice. [The Supreme Court has outlined] a "simple test" for identifying facial sex discrimination: such discrimination appears "where the evidence shows treatment of a person in a manner which but for that person's sex would be different."* [Emphasis added.]

* * * The district court applied [this] test and concluded that, because Bauer would have been held to a lower minimum number of push-ups had he been a woman, the gender-normed PFT standards constitute facial sex discrimination. The Attorney General maintains on appeal, however, that because the PFT assesses an overall level of physical fitness, and equally fit men and women possess innate physiological differences that lead to different performance outcomes, the PFT's gender-normed standards actually require the same level of fitness for all Trainees. In that way, the Attorney General contends, the PFT standards do not treat the sexes differently and therefore do not contravene Title VII.

* * * *

* * * The Attorney General * * * maintains that * * * some differential treatment of men and women based upon inherent physiological differences is not only lawful but also potentially required.

* * * *

Men and women simply are not physiologically the same for the purposes of physical fitness programs. * * * Physical fitness standards suitable for men may not always be suitable for women,

**Case 21.1 Continued**

and accommodations addressing physiological differences between the sexes are not necessarily unlawful.

* * * The physiological differences between men and women impact their relative abilities to demonstrate the same levels of physical fitness. In other words, equally fit men and women demonstrate their fitness differently. Whether physical fitness standards discriminate based on sex, therefore, depends on whether they require men and women to demonstrate different levels of fitness.

Put succinctly, *an employer does not contravene Title VII when it utilizes physical fitness standards that distinguish between the sexes on the basis of their physiological differences but impose an equal burden of compliance on both men and women, requiring the same level of physical fitness of each.* Because the FBI purports to assess physical fitness by imposing the same burden on both men and women, this rule applies to Bauer's Title VII claims. Accordingly, the district court erred in failing to apply the rule in its disposition of Bauer's motion for summary judgment. [Emphasis added.]

* * * *

Pursuant to the foregoing, we vacate the judgment of the district court and remand for * * * further proceedings.

### Legal Reasoning Questions

**1.** According to the reasoning of the court in the *Bauer* case, when do different employment standards for men and women satisfy Title VII's requirement of equality?

**2.** In what other circumstances might the rule in this case apply?

**3.** If Bauer had ultimately succeeded in his claim, what might the remedy have been? What else might have resulted?

---

**Pregnancy Discrimination** The Pregnancy Discrimination Act[9] expanded Title VII's definition of gender discrimination to include discrimination based on pregnancy. Women affected by pregnancy, childbirth, or related medical conditions must be treated the same as other persons not so affected but similar in ability to work. For instance, an employer cannot discriminate against a pregnant woman by withholding benefits available to others under employee benefit programs.

In the following case, an employer accommodated many of its employees who had lifting restrictions due to disabilities. The employer refused to accommodate a pregnant employee with a similar restriction. Did this refusal constitute a violation of the Pregnancy Discrimination Act?

_____
9. 42 U.S.C. Section 2000e(k).

**Case 21.2**

# Young v. United Parcel Service, Inc.
Supreme Court of the United States, __ U.S. __, 135 S.Ct. 1338, 191 L.Ed.2d 279 (2015).

**Background and Facts** Peggy Young was a driver for United Parcel Service, Inc. (UPS). When she became pregnant, her doctor advised her not to lift more than twenty pounds. UPS required drivers to lift up to seventy pounds and told Young that she could not work under a lifting restriction. She filed a suit in a federal district court against UPS, claiming an unlawful refusal to accommodate her pregnancy-related lifting restriction. She alleged that UPS had multiple light-duty-for-injury categories to accommodate individuals whose non-pregnancy-related disabilities created work restrictions similar to hers.

UPS responded that, because Young did not fall into any of those categories, it had not discriminated against her. The court issued a summary judgment in UPS's favor. The U.S. Court of Appeals of the Fourth Circuit affirmed the judgment. Young appealed to the United States Supreme Court.

## In the Language of the Court
Justice *BREYER* delivered the opinion of the Court.
* * * *

* * * A plaintiff alleging that the denial of an accommodation constituted disparate treatment under the Pregnancy Discrimination Act * * * may make out a *prima facie* case by showing that she belongs to

*Case 21.2 Continues*

**Case 21.2 Continued**

the protected class, that she sought accommodation, that the employer did not accommodate her, and that the employer did accommodate others similar in their ability or inability to work.

*The employer may then seek to justify its refusal to accommodate the plaintiff by relying on legitimate, non-discriminatory reasons for denying her accommodation.* [Emphasis added.]

If the employer offers an apparently legitimate, nondiscriminatory reason for its actions, the plaintiff may in turn show that the employer's proffered reasons are in fact pretextual [contrived]. We believe that the plaintiff may reach a jury on this issue by providing sufficient evidence that the employer's policies impose a significant burden on pregnant workers, and that the employer's legitimate, nondiscriminatory reasons are not sufficiently strong to justify the burden, but rather—when considered along with the burden imposed—give rise to an inference of intentional discrimination.

The plaintiff can create a genuine issue of material fact as to whether a significant burden exists by providing evidence that the employer accommodates a large percentage of nonpregnant workers while failing to accommodate a large percentage of pregnant workers. Here, for example, if the facts are as Young says they are, she can show that UPS accommodates most nonpregnant employees with lifting limitations while categorically failing to accommodate pregnant employees with lifting limitations. Young might also add that the fact that UPS has multiple policies that accommodate nonpregnant employees with lifting restrictions suggests that its reasons for failing to accommodate pregnant employees with lifting restrictions are not sufficiently strong—to the point that a jury could find that its reasons for failing to accommodate pregnant employees give rise to an inference of intentional discrimination.

\* \* \* \*

\* \* \* A party is entitled to summary judgment if there is no genuine dispute as to any material fact and the movant [that is, a person who applies to a court for a ruling in his or her favor] is entitled to judgment as a matter of law. \* \* \* *Viewing the record in the light most favorable to Young, there is a genuine dispute as to whether UPS provided more favorable treatment to at least some employees whose situation cannot reasonably be distinguished from Young's.* [Emphasis added.]

**Decision and Remedy** *The United States Supreme Court vacated the judgment of the U.S. Court of Appeals for the Fourth Circuit and remanded the case for further proceedings. Young created a genuine dispute as to whether UPS had provided more favorable treatment to employees whose situation could not reasonably be distinguished from hers. On remand, the court must determine whether Young also created a genuine issue of material fact as to whether UPS's reasons for treating Young less favorably were a pretext.*

**Critical Thinking**

- **Legal Environment** *Could UPS have succeeded in this case if it had claimed simply that it would be more expensive or less convenient to include pregnant women among those whom it accommodates? Explain.*

---

**Wage Discrimination** The Equal Pay Act[10] requires equal pay for male and female employees working at the same establishment doing similar work. To determine whether the Equal Pay Act has been violated, a court looks to the primary duties of the two jobs—the job content rather than the job description controls. If a court finds that the wage differential is due to "any factor other than gender," such as a seniority or merit system, then it does not violate the Equal Pay Act.

The 2009 Lilly Ledbetter Fair Pay Act made discriminatory wages actionable under federal law regardless of when the discrimination began.[11] Previously, plaintiffs had to file a complaint within a limited time period. Today, if a plaintiff continues to work for the employer while receiving discriminatory wages, the time period for filing a complaint is practically unlimited.

**Discrimination against Transgender Persons** In the past, most courts held that federal law (Title VII) does not protect transgender persons from discrimination. The situation may be changing, however. A growing number of federal courts are interpreting Title VII's protections against gender discrimination to apply to transsexuals.

---

10. 29 U.S.C. Section 206(d).

11. Pub. L. No. 111-2, 123 Stat. 5 (January 5, 2009), amending 42 U.S.C. Section 2000e-5[e].

■ **CASE IN POINT 21.9** Dr. Deborah Fabian applied for a position as an on-call orthopedic surgeon at the Hospital of Central Connecticut. The hospital apparently declined to hire Fabian because she disclosed her identity as a transgender woman. Fabian sued the hospital alleging violations of Title VII of the Civil Rights Act and the Connecticut Fair Employment Practices Act (CFEPA).

The hospital filed a summary judgment motion, arguing that neither Title VII nor the Connecticut statute prohibits discrimination on the basis of transgender identity. The federal district court rejected this argument, however, finding that discrimination on the basis of transgender identity is discrimination on the basis of sex for Title VII purposes. Fabian was entitled to take her case to a jury and argue violations of Title VII and the CFEPA.[12] ■

**Transgender Bathrooms** In 2016, the Obama administration issued guidance directing public schools to allow transgender students to use bathrooms matching their gender identity. The goal was to ensure a supportive and nondiscriminatory environment, but it sparked a public debate across the nation. The federal government's guidance did not have the force of law, though.

Although the federal government and its agencies have decided to treat gender identity as the person's sex for legal purposes, some states and schools (and employers) are reluctant to do so. North Carolina, for instance, has passed a law that bans individuals from using public bathrooms that do not correspond to their biological sex. Some argue that the access of transgender persons to bathrooms should be left up to individual states to address. Nevertheless, the EEOC has ruled that a transgender individual who self-identified as a woman had a right to use to use the women's bathroom at a military base in Huntsville, Alabama.[13]

**Gender-Neutral Pronouns** Another area of potential dispute in today's employment environment involves the pronouns that employers (or schools) use to refer to transgender individuals. People have traditionally said *he/him/his* when talking about a male, or *she/her/hers* when discussing a female. Some transgender people, however, prefer to be referred to using corresponding gender-neutral pronouns, such as *ze/hir/hirs*.

In fact, certain cities, including New York City, now *require* employers, landlords, and all businesses and professionals to use a transgender individual's preferred name, pronoun, and title. This allows transgender individuals to self-identify their name and gender. If an employer in New York City refuses to use the pronoun that a transgender individual (employee, client, colleague, customer, or

tenant) has expressly requested, the employer can be fined. Penalties range from $125,000 to $250,000 for violations that are deemed to be the result of malicious intent.

## 21–1g Constructive Discharge

The majority of Title VII complaints involve unlawful discrimination in decisions to hire or fire employees. In some situations, however, employees who leave their jobs voluntarily can claim that they were "constructively discharged" by the employer. **Constructive discharge** occurs when the employer causes the employee's working conditions to be so intolerable that a reasonable person in the employee's position would feel compelled to quit.

When constructive discharge is claimed, the employee can pursue damages for loss of income, including back pay. These damages ordinarily are not available to an employee who left a job voluntarily.

**Proving Constructive Discharge** To prove constructive discharge, an employee must present objective proof of intolerable working conditions. The employee must also show that the employer knew or had reason to know about these conditions yet failed to correct them within a reasonable time period. In addition, courts generally require the employee to show causation—that the employer's unlawful discrimination caused the working conditions to be intolerable. Put in a different way, the employee's resignation must be a foreseeable result of the employer's discriminatory action. Courts weigh the facts on a case-by-case basis.

Employee demotion is one of the most frequently cited reasons for a finding of constructive discharge, particularly when the employee was subjected to humiliation. ■ **EXAMPLE 21.10** Khalil's employer humiliates him by informing him in front of his co-workers that he is being demoted to an inferior position. Khalil's co-workers then continually insult him, harass him, and make derogatory remarks to him about his national origin (he is from Iran). The employer is aware of this discriminatory treatment but does nothing to remedy the situation, despite Khalil's repeated complaints. After several months, Khalil quits his job and files a Title VII claim. In this situation, Khalil will likely have sufficient evidence to maintain an action for constructive discharge in violation of Title VII. ■

**Applies to All Title VII Discrimination** Plaintiffs can use constructive discharge to establish any type of discrimination claim under Title VII, including race, color, national origin, religion, gender, and pregnancy. It is most commonly asserted in cases involving sexual harassment. Constructive discharge may also be used in cases involving discrimination based on age or disability (discussed later in this chapter).

---

**12.** *Fabian v. Hospital of Central Connecticut*, ___ F.Supp.3d ___, 2016 WL 1089178 (D.Conn. 2016).
**13.** EEOC Appeal No. 012033395, Order (E0610), April 1, 2015.

## 21–1h Sexual Harassment

Title VII also protects employees against **sexual harassment** in the workplace. Sexual harassment can take two forms:

1. *Quid pro quo* harassment occurs when sexual favors are demanded in return for job opportunities, promotions, salary increases, or other benefits. *Quid pro quo* is a Latin phrase that is often translated as "something in exchange for something else."
2. *Hostile-environment* harassment occurs when a pattern of sexually offensive conduct runs throughout the workplace and the employer has not taken steps to prevent or discourage it. Such harassment exists when the workplace is permeated with discriminatory intimidation, ridicule, and insult, and this harassment is so severe or pervasive that it alters the conditions of employment.

A court considers a number of factors when determining whether the sexually offensive conduct was sufficiently severe or pervasive to create a hostile environment. As the following case shows, these factors include the nature and frequency of the conduct and whether it unreasonably interfered with the victim's work performance.

**Case 21.3**

# Roberts v. Mike's Trucking, Ltd.

Court of Appeals of Ohio, Twelfth District, 2014 -Ohio- 766, 9 N.E.3d 483 (2014).

**Background and Facts** Teresa Roberts worked for Mike's Trucking, Ltd., in Columbus, Ohio. Her supervisor was the company's owner, Mike Culbertson. According to Roberts, Culbertson called her his "sexretary" and constantly talked about his sex life. He often invited her to sit on "Big Daddy's" lap, rubbed against her, trapped her at the door and asked her for hugs or kisses, and inquired if she needed help in the restroom. Roberts asked him to stop this conduct, but he did not. She became less productive and began to suffer anxiety attacks and high blood pressure. Roberts filed a suit in an Ohio state court against Mike's, alleging a hostile work environment through sexual harassment in violation of Title VII. A jury decided in Roberts's favor, and Mike's appealed.

### In the Language of the Court

*HENDRICKSON*, P.J. [Presiding Judge]

* * * *

* * * Conduct that is not severe or pervasive enough to create an objectively hostile or abusive work environment—an environment that a reasonable person would find hostile or abusive—is beyond Title VII's purview. Likewise, if the victim does not subjectively perceive the environment to be abusive, the conduct has not actually altered the conditions of the victim's employment, and there is no Title VII violation. Therefore, *the focus of this inquiry is: 1.) whether a reasonable person would find the environment objectively hostile; and 2.) whether the plaintiff subjectively found the conduct severe or pervasive.* [Emphasis added.]

* * * *

* * * Roberts' testimony was consistent with several witnesses affirming that Culbertson frequently engaged in a variety of conduct ranging from inappropriate discussions to groping women. The witnesses stated that Culbertson often discussed his sex life, asked Roberts and the women employees if they needed help in the bathroom * * * , referred to himself as "Big Daddy," asked Roberts and the women employees to sit in "Big Daddy's" lap, and asked them if they would give "Big Daddy" a hug.

The evidence established that the conduct occurred frequently. Roberts testified that throughout her employment, Culbertson's behavior became increasingly worse and that * * * he talked about sex hundreds of times, and attempted to corner her and hug and kiss her at least twice a week. [Former Mike's employees] testified that Culbertson talked about sex and asked the women if they needed help with the bathroom multiple times a week. The evidence also showed that the conduct became increasingly severe as Culbertson massaged Roberts [and] rubbed up against her * * * . Roberts testified that Culbertson's conduct was humiliating towards her as his remarks were in front of others and she often became "furious" with him. Other employees reported Roberts becoming angry towards Culbertson. Roberts also established that Culbertson's conduct unreasonably interfered with her work performance as she stated she did not want to go to work anymore, she became less productive, and she suffered anxiety attacks. Her fiancé testified that Roberts has lost confidence and that she is now prescribed anti-anxiety medication.

Case 21.3 Continued

Consequently, there was sufficient and substantial evidence to support the jury's finding that a reasonable person would find Culbertson's conduct created a hostile environment and Roberts found the conduct to be sufficiently severe or pervasive to affect her employment.

**Decision and Remedy** *A state intermediate appellate court affirmed the lower court's judgment in Roberts's favor. During the trial, other Mike's employees and Roberts's fiancé testified to corroborate Roberts's account. The evidence sufficiently established that Culbertson's conduct was severe or pervasive enough to create a hostile work environment for Roberts.*

**Critical Thinking**

- **Ethical** *Was Culbertson's conduct at any point unethical? Discuss.*
- **Legal Environment** *Culbertson and some other witnesses testified that he did not engage in any sexually inappropriate behavior. Should an appellate court reverse a jury's decision simply due to contrary evidence? Why or why not?*

---

**Harassment by Supervisors** For an employer to be held liable for a supervisor's sexual harassment, the supervisor normally must have taken a *tangible employment action* against the employee. A **tangible employment action** is a significant change in employment status or benefits. Such an action occurs when an employee is fired, refused a promotion, demoted, or reassigned to a position with significantly different responsibilities, for instance. Only a supervisor, or another person acting with the authority of the employer, can cause this sort of harm. A constructive discharge also qualifies as a tangible employment action.

The United States Supreme Court issued several important rulings in cases alleging sexual harassment by supervisors that established what is known as the "*Ellerth/Faragher* affirmative defense."[14] The defense has two elements:

1. The employer must have taken reasonable care to prevent and promptly correct any sexually harassing behavior (by establishing effective harassment policies and complaint procedures, for instance).
2. The plaintiff-employee must have unreasonably failed to take advantage of preventive or corrective opportunities provided by the employer to avoid harm.

An employer that can prove both elements normally will not be liable for a supervisor's harassment.

**Retaliation by Employers** Employers sometimes retaliate against employees who complain about sexual harassment or other Title VII violations. Retaliation can take many forms. An employer might demote or fire the person, or otherwise change the terms, conditions, and benefits of employment.

Title VII prohibits retaliation, and employees can sue their employers when it occurs. In a *retaliation claim,* an individual asserts that she or he has suffered harm as a result of making a charge, testifying, or participating in a Title VII investigation or proceeding.

**Requirements for Protection.** To be protected under Title VII's retaliation provisions, the plaintiff must have opposed a practice prohibited by Title VII and suffered an adverse employment action as a result of that opposition. ■ **CASE IN POINT 21.11** Myrta Morales-Cruz had a tenure-track teaching position at the University of Puerto Rico School of Law. When her probationary period was almost over, Morales-Cruz asked the university's administrative committee to grant a one-year extension for her tenure review. The dean recommended that the extension be granted but also called her "insecure," "immature," and "fragile." Another professor commented that had she shown "poor judgment" and exhibited "personality flaws."

After Morales-Cruz complained about these comments in writing to the chancellor, the dean recommended denying the one-year extension, and the administrative committee did just that. Morales-Cruz later filed a retaliation lawsuit. She claimed that the dean had retaliated

---

14. *Burlington Industries, Inc. v. Ellerth*, 524 U.S. 742, 118 S.Ct. 2257, 141 L.Ed.2d 633 (1998); and *Faragher v. City of Boca Raton*, 524 U.S. 775, 118 S.Ct. 2275, 141 L.Ed.2d 662 (1998).

against her for complaining to the chancellor about the "discriminatory" comments made in the course of her request for an extension.

The court held that Morales-Cruz had not provided a reasonable foundation for a retaliation action. Under Title VII, an employer may not retaliate against an employee because he or she has opposed a practice prohibited by Title VII. But the court found that Morales-Cruz did not allege any facts that could be construed as gender-based discrimination. Although the comments she complained about were hardly flattering, they were entirely gender-neutral. Thus, she was not engaging in protected conduct when she opposed the remarks.[15] ■

**Protection May Extend to Others.** The Supreme Court has ruled that Title VII's retaliation protection extended to an employee who spoke out about discrimination against another employee during an employer's internal investigation.[16] The Court has also held that Title VII protected an employee who was fired after his fiancée filed a gender discrimination claim against their employer.[17]

**Harassment by Co-Workers and Others** When the harassment of co-workers, rather than supervisors, creates a hostile working environment, an employee may still have a cause of action against the employer. Normally, though, the employer will be held liable only if it knew or should have known about the harassment and failed to take immediate remedial action.

Occasionally, a court may also hold an employer liable for harassment by *nonemployees* if the employer knew about the harassment and failed to take corrective action. ■ **EXAMPLE 21.12** Jordan, who owns and manages a Great Bites restaurant, knows that one of his regular customers, Dean, repeatedly harasses Kaylia, a waitress. If Jordan does nothing and permits the harassment to continue, he may be liable under Title VII even though Dean is not an employee of the restaurant. ■

**Same-Gender Harassment** In *Oncale v. Sundowner Offshore Services, Inc.,*[18] the United States Supreme Court held that Title VII protection extends to individuals who are sexually harassed by members of the same gender. Proving that the harassment in same-gender cases is "based on sex" can be difficult, though. It is easier to establish a case of same-gender harassment when the harasser is homosexual.

**Sexual-Orientation Harassment** Federal law (Title VII) does not prohibit discrimination or harassment based on a person's sexual orientation. Nonetheless, a growing number of states have enacted laws that prohibit sexual-orientation discrimination in private employment.[19] Some states, such as Oregon, explicitly prohibit discrimination based on a person's gender identity or expression. Many companies have also voluntarily established nondiscrimination policies that include sexual orientation.

### 21–1i Online Harassment

Employees' online activities can create a hostile working environment in many ways. Racial jokes, ethnic slurs, or other comments contained in e-mail, texts, blogs, or social media can lead to claims of hostile-environment harassment or other forms of discrimination. A worker who regularly sees sexually explicit images on a co-worker's computer screen may find the images offensive and claim that they create a hostile working environment. Nevertheless, employers may be able to avoid liability for online harassment by taking prompt remedial action.

### 21–1j Remedies under Title VII

Employer liability under Title VII can be extensive. If the plaintiff successfully proves that unlawful discrimination occurred, he or she may be awarded reinstatement, back pay, retroactive promotions, and damages.

Several limits apply to damages. Compensatory damages are available only in cases of intentional discrimination. Punitive damages may be recovered against a private employer only if the employer acted with malice or reckless indifference to an individual's rights. The total amount of compensatory and punitive damages that plaintiffs can recover from specific employers depends on the size of the employer. For instance, there is a $50,000 cap on damages from employers with one hundred or fewer employees.

## 21–2 Discrimination Based on Age

Age discrimination is potentially the most widespread form of discrimination because anyone—regardless of race, color, national origin, or gender—could be a victim

---

**15.** *Morales-Cruz v. University of Puerto Rico,* 676 F.3d 220 (1st Cir. 2012).

**16.** *Crawford v. Metropolitan Government of Nashville and Davidson County, Tennessee,* 555 U.S. 271, 129 S.Ct. 846, 172 L.Ed.2d 650 (2009).

**17.** See *Thompson v. North American Stainless, LP,* 562 U.S. 170, 131 S.Ct. 863, 178 L.Ed.2d 694 (2011).

**18.** 523 U.S. 75, 118 S.Ct. 998, 140 L.Ed.2d 207 (1998).

**19.** See, for instance, 775 Illinois Compiled Statutes 5/1–103.

at some point in life. The Age Discrimination in Employment Act[20] (ADEA), as amended, prohibits employment discrimination on the basis of age against individuals forty years of age or older. The act also prohibits mandatory retirement for nonmanagerial workers. In addition, the ADEA protects federal and private-sector employees from retaliation based on age-related complaints.[21]

For the act to apply, an employer must have twenty or more employees, and the employer's business activities must affect interstate commerce. The EEOC administers the ADEA, but the act also permits private causes of action against employers for age discrimination.

### 21–2a Procedures under the ADEA

The burden-shifting procedure under the ADEA differs from the procedure under Title VII. This difference resulted from a United States Supreme Court decision that dramatically changed the burden of proof in age discrimination cases.[22]

As explained earlier, if the plaintiff in a Title VII case can show that the employer was motivated, at least in part, by unlawful discrimination, the burden of proof shifts to the employer. Thus, in cases in which the employer has a "mixed motive" for discharging an employee, the employer has the burden of proving that its reason was legitimate.

Under the ADEA, in contrast, a plaintiff must show that the unlawful discrimination was not just *a* reason but *the* reason for the adverse employment action. In other words, the employee has the burden of establishing *but for* causation—that is, "but for" the employee's age, the action would not have been taken.

**Prima Facie Age Discrimination** To establish a *prima facie* case of age discrimination, the plaintiff must show that she or he was the following:

1. A member of the protected age group.
2. Qualified for the position from which she or he was discharged.
3. Discharged because of age discrimination.

Then the burden shifts to the employer to give a legitimate nondiscriminatory reason for the adverse action.

**Pretext** If the employer offers a legitimate reason for its action, then the plaintiff must show that the stated reason

is only a pretext. The plaintiff is required to prove that the plaintiff's age was the real reason for the employer's decision.

■ **CASE IN POINT 21.13** Josephine Mora, a fund-raiser for Jackson Memorial Foundation, Inc., was sixty-two years old when the foundation's chief executive officer (CEO) fired her. Mora filed an age discrimination suit against the foundation. She asserted that when she was fired, the CEO told her, "I need someone younger I can pay less." A witness heard that statement and also heard the CEO say that Mora was "too old to be working here anyway." The CEO denied making these statements, and the foundation claimed that Mora had been terminated for poor job performance.

A district court granted a summary judgment in the foundation's favor, and Mora appealed. A federal appellate court reversed, concluding that the lower court's analysis of causation was incorrect. The court held that a reasonable juror could have accepted that the CEO had made discriminatory remarks and could have found that these remarks were sufficient evidence of a discriminatory motive. If so, that could show that Mora was fired because of her age. The court therefore remanded the case to the lower court for a trial.[23] ■

### 21–2b Replacing Older Workers with Younger Workers

Numerous age discrimination cases have been brought against employers who, to cut costs, replaced older, higher-salaried employees with younger, lower-salaried workers. In such situations, whether a firing is discriminatory or simply part of a rational business decision to prune the company's ranks is not always clear.

The plaintiff must prove that the discharge was motivated by age bias. The plaintiff need not prove that she or he was replaced by a person "outside the protected class" (under the age of forty). The replacement worker need only be younger than the plaintiff. Nevertheless, the greater the age gap, the more likely the plaintiff will succeed in showing age discrimination.

### 21–2c State Employees Not Covered by the ADEA

Generally, the states are immune from lawsuits brought by private individuals in federal court (unless a state consents to such a suit). This immunity stems from the

---

20. 29 U.S.C. Sections 621–634.
21. *Gomez-Perez v. Potter,* 553 U.S. 474, 128 S.Ct. 1931, 170 L.Ed.2d 887 (2008).
22. *Gross v. FBL Financial Services, Inc.,* 557 U.S. 167, 129 S.Ct. 2343, 174 L.Ed.2d 119 (2009).

23. *Mora v. Jackson Memorial Foundation, Inc.,* 597 F.3d 1201 (11th Cir. 2010).

United States Supreme Court's interpretation of the Eleventh Amendment.

State immunity under the Eleventh Amendment is not absolute. In some situations, such as when fundamental rights are at stake, Congress has the power to abrogate (abolish) state immunity to private suits through legislation. Such legislation must unequivocally show Congress's intent to subject states to private suits.[24]

Generally, though, the Court has found that state employers are immune from private suits brought by employees under the ADEA. State employers are also immune from suits brought under the Americans with Disabilities Act[25] and the Fair Labor Standards Act.[26] They are *not* immune from the requirements of the Family and Medical Leave Act.[27]

## 21-3 Discrimination Based on Disability

The Americans with Disabilities Act (ADA)[28] prohibits disability-based discrimination in all workplaces with fifteen or more workers. An exception is state government employers, who are generally immune under the Eleventh Amendment, as just mentioned. Basically, the ADA requires that employers "reasonably accommodate" the needs of persons with disabilities unless to do so would cause the employer to suffer an "undue hardship." The ADA Amendments Act[29] broadened the coverage of the ADA's protections, as discussed shortly.

### 21-3a Procedures under the ADA

To prevail on a claim under the ADA, a plaintiff must show that he or she (1) has a disability, (2) is otherwise qualified for the employment in question, and (3) was excluded from the employment solely because of the disability. As in Title VII cases, the plaintiff must pursue the claim through the EEOC before filing an action in court for a violation of the ADA.

The EEOC may decide to investigate and perhaps sue the employer on behalf of the employee. The EEOC can bring a suit even if the employee previously signed an agreement with the employer to submit job-related disputes to arbitration.[30] If the EEOC decides not to sue, then the employee may do so.

Plaintiffs in lawsuits brought under the ADA may seek many of the same remedies that are available under Title VII. These include reinstatement, back pay, a limited amount of compensatory and punitive damages (for intentional discrimination), and certain other forms of relief. Repeat violators may be ordered to pay fines of up to $100,000.

### 21-3b What Is a Disability?

The ADA is broadly drafted to cover persons with physical or mental impairments that "substantially limit" their everyday activities. Specifically, the ADA defines a *disability* as including any of the following:

1. A physical or mental impairment that substantially limits one or more of the major life activities of the affected individual.
2. A record of having such an impairment.
3. Being regarded as having such an impairment.

Health conditions that have been considered disabilities under federal law include alcoholism, acquired immune deficiency syndrome (AIDS), blindness, cancer, cerebral palsy, diabetes, heart disease, muscular dystrophy, and paraplegia. Testing positive for the human immunodeficiency virus (HIV) has qualified as a disability, as has morbid obesity. (A morbidly obese person weighs twice the normal weight for his or her height.)

Note, however, that obesity does not qualify as a disability unless the individual's weight is outside of the normal range and occurs as the result of a physiological disorder. In other words, people who are obese (even morbidly obese), but not because of some underlying physical ailment, are not considered disabled.

■ **CASE IN POINT 21.14** Melvin Morriss applied for a machinist position at BNSF Railway Company. Because the position was safety sensitive, he was given an offer of employment conditioned upon a medical review. BNSF doctors conducted two physical examinations. In the first, Morriss weighed 285 pounds with a body mass index, or BMI, of 40.9. (BMI is a typical method of evaluating a person's weight.) In the second exam, Morriss's BMI dropped slightly to 40.4. Because BNSF had a policy of not employing workers with BMIs over 40 in safety-sensitive positions such as machinists, it rescinded its offer of employment. Morriss sued, alleging discrimination on the basis of disability, but the court found that Morriss's obesity was not a physical impairment under

24. *Tennessee v. Lane*, 541 U.S. 509, 124 S.Ct. 1978, 158 L.Ed.2d 820 (2004).
25. *Board of Trustees of the University of Alabama v. Garrett*, 531 U.S. 356, 121 S.Ct. 955, 148 L.Ed.2d 866 (2001).
26. *Alden v. Maine*, 527 U.S. 706, 119 S.Ct. 2240, 144 L.Ed.2d 636 (1999).
27. *Nevada Department of Human Resources v. Hibbs*, 538 U.S. 721, 123 S.Ct. 1972, 155 L.Ed.2d 953 (2003).
28. 42 U.S.C. Sections 12103–12118.
29. 42 U.S.C. Sections 12103 and 12205a.
30. This was the Supreme Court's ruling in *EEOC v. Waffle House, Inc.*, 534 U.S. 279, 122 S.Ct. 754, 151 L.Ed.2d 755 (2002).

the ADA. Morriss was otherwise in good health and did not suffer from any disease that would result in his being obese. A federal appellate court affirmed.[31] ■

**Association with Disabled Persons** A separate provision in the ADA prevents employers from taking adverse employment actions based on stereotypes or assumptions about individuals who associate with people who have disabilities.[32] An employer cannot, for instance, refuse to hire the parent of a child with a disability based on the assumption that the person will miss work too often or be unreliable.

■ **EXAMPLE 21.15** Joan, an employer, refuses to hire Edward, who has a daughter with a physical disability. She consciously bases her decision on the assumption that Edward will have to miss work frequently to care for his daughter. Edward can sue Joan for violating the ADA's provisions. ■

**Mitigating Measures** At one time, the courts focused on whether a person had a disability *after* the use of mitigating measures, such as corrective devices or medication. Thus, a person with severe myopia (nearsightedness) whose eyesight could be corrected by wearing glasses did not qualify as having a disability. With the corrective lenses, the person's major life activities were not substantially impaired. Then Congress amended the ADA to strengthen its protections and prohibit employers from considering mitigating measures when determining if an individual has a disability.

Disability is now determined on a case-by-case basis. A condition may fit the definition of disability in one set of circumstances, but not in another. ■ **CASE IN POINT 21.16** Larry Rohr, a welding specialist for a power district in Arizona, was diagnosed with type 2 diabetes. To keep his condition under control, Rohr was required to follow a complex regimen of daily insulin injections and blood tests, as well as a strict diet. Therefore, his physician forbade him from taking work assignments that involved overnight, out-of-town travel, which were common in his job.

Because of these limitations, the power district asked him to transfer, apply for federal disability benefits, or take early retirement. Rohr sued for disability discrimination. The lower court granted summary judgment for the employer. Rohr appealed. A federal appellate court reversed. The court held that under the amended ADA, diabetes is a disability if it significantly restricts an individual's eating (a major life activity), as it did for Rohr. Therefore, Rohr was entitled to a trial on his discrimination claim.[33] ■

**Disclosure of Confidential Medical Information** ADA provisions also require employers to keep their employees' medical information confidential.[34] An employee who discovers that an employer has disclosed his or her confidential medical information has a right to sue the employer—even if the employee was not technically disabled. The prohibition against disclosure also applies to other employees acting on behalf of the employer.

■ **CASE IN POINT 21.17** George Shoun was working at his job at Best Formed Plastics, Inc., when he fell and injured his shoulder. Another Best Formed employee, Jane Stewart, prepared an accident report for the incident and processed Shoun's workers' compensation claim. As a result of the injury, Shoun had to take several months off work and received workers' compensation.

Stewart posted on her Facebook page a statement about how Shoun's shoulder injury "kept him away from work for 11 months and now he is trying to sue us." Shoun sued Best Formed under the ADA for wrongfully disclosing confidential information about his medical condition to other people via Facebook. He claimed that the action resulted in loss of employment and impairment of his earning capacity. The court allowed Shoun's claim to go forward to trial.[35] ■

### 21–3c Reasonable Accommodation

The ADA does not require that employers accommodate the needs of job applicants or employees with disabilities who are not otherwise qualified for the work. If a job applicant or an employee with a disability, with reasonable accommodation, can perform essential job functions, however, the employer must make the accommodation.

Required modifications may include installing ramps for a wheelchair, establishing flexible working hours, creating or modifying job assignments, and designing or improving training materials and procedures. Generally, employers should give primary consideration to employees' preferences in deciding what accommodations should be made.

**Undue Hardship** Employers who do not accommodate the needs of persons with disabilities must demonstrate that the accommodations would cause *undue hardship* in terms of being significantly difficult or expensive for the employer. Usually, the courts decide whether an accommodation constitutes an undue hardship on a case-by-case basis.

■ **EXAMPLE 21.18** Bryan Lockhart, who uses a wheelchair, works for a cell phone company that provides

---

**31.** *Morriss v. BNSF Railway Co.*, 817 F.3d 1104 (8th Cir. 2016).

**32.** 42 U.S.C. Section 12112(b)(4).

**33.** *Rohr v. Salt River Project Agricultural Improvement and Power District*, 555 F.3d 850 (9th Cir. 2009).

**34.** 42 U.S.C. Sections 12112(d)(3)(B), (C), and 12112(d)(4)(C).

**35.** *Shoun v. Best Formed Plastics, Inc.*, 28 F.Supp.3d 786 (N.D.Ind. 2014).

parking for its employees. Lockhart informs his supervisor that the parking spaces are so narrow that he is unable to extend the ramp on his van that allows him to get in and out of the vehicle. Lockhart therefore requests that the company reasonably accommodate his needs by paying a monthly fee for him to use a larger parking space in an adjacent lot. In this situation, a court will likely find that it is *not* an undue hardship for the employer to pay for additional parking for Lockhart. ■

**Job Applications and Physical Exams** Employers must modify their job-application and selection process so that those with disabilities can compete for jobs with those who do not have disabilities. For instance, a job announcement might be modified to allow applicants to respond by e-mail as well as by telephone, so that it does not discriminate against potential applicants with hearing impairments.

Employers are restricted in the kinds of questions they may ask on job-application forms and during preemployment interviews. In addition, employers cannot require persons with disabilities to submit to preemployment physicals unless such exams are required of all other applicants. An employer can disqualify the applicant only if the medical problems discovered during a preemployment physical would make it impossible for the applicant to perform the job.

**Health-Insurance Plans** Workers with disabilities must be given equal access to any health insurance provided to other employees and cannot be excluded from coverage. An employer can put a limit, or cap, on health-care payments under its group health policy, but the cap must apply equally to all insured employees. Any group health-care plan that makes a disability-based distinction in its benefits violates the ADA (unless the employer can justify its actions under the business necessity defense, discussed shortly).

**Substance Abusers** Drug addiction is considered a disability under the ADA because it is a substantially limiting impairment. The act does not protect individuals who are actually using illegal drugs, however. Instead, the ADA protects only persons with *former* drug addictions—those who have completed or are now participating in a supervised drug-rehabilitation program. Individuals who have used drugs casually in the past also are not protected under the act. They are not considered addicts and therefore do not have a disability (addiction).

People suffering from alcoholism are also protected by the ADA. Employers cannot legally discriminate against employees simply because they suffer from alcoholism. Of course, employers can prohibit the use of alcohol in the workplace and require that employees not be under the influence of alcohol while working. Employers can also fire or refuse to hire a person who is an alcoholic if (1) the person poses a *substantial risk of harm* to himself or herself or to others, and (2) the risk cannot be reduced by reasonable accommodation.

Exhibit 21–1 outlines the coverage of the main employment discrimination laws discussed in this chapter.

**EXHIBIT 21–1 Coverage of Employment Discrimination Laws**

| Title VII of the Civil Rights Act | Age Discrimination in Employment Act | Americans with Disabilities Act (as Amended) |
|---|---|---|
| Prohibits discrimination based on race, color, national origin, religion, gender (including wage discrimination), and pregnancy; prohibits sexual harassment. | Prohibits discrimination against persons over forty years of age. | Prohibits discrimination against persons with a mental or physical impairment that substantially limits a major life activity now or in the past, or who are regarded as having such an impairment, or who are associated with a disabled person. |
| Applies to employers with fifteen or more employees. | Applies to employers with twenty or more employees. | Applies to employers with fifteen or more employees. |

## 21–4 Discrimination Based on Military Status

In 1994, Congress enacted the Uniformed Services Employment and Reemployment Rights Act (USERRA).[36] The USERRA protects civilian job rights and benefits for members of the military, former military personnel, and reservists. It also provides additional protections for veterans who are disabled. Most importantly, the USERRA prohibits discrimination against persons who have served in the military. In effect, it makes military service and status a protected class and gives members of this class a right to sue an employer for violations.

### 21–4a Broad Application and Provisions

The USERRA covers *all* employers, public and private, large and small. Even an employer with only one employee is subject to its provisions.[37] The act also applies to United States employers operating in foreign countries.

Under the USERRA, military plaintiffs can sue not only the employer but also individual employees who were acting in an official capacity for the employer. In other words, these employees—supervisors, for instance—can be held personally liable for violations. Additionally, there is no statute of limitations for bringing a lawsuit. The cause of action could have arisen ten weeks or ten years before the suit was filed.

The USERRA specifies that veterans can be terminated from their employment only "for cause." The employer is obligated to give employees a list of all the behaviors that would trigger a for-cause termination.

### 21–4b *Prima Facie* Case of Discrimination under the USERRA

To establish a *prima facie* case of discrimination (and retaliation) under the USERRA, the plaintiff must establish that the employer took an adverse employment action based in part on the employee's connection with the military. The connection to the military may be through the plaintiff's membership, service, or application for service, or it may be through providing testimony or statements concerning the military service of another.[38] If another similarly situated person who did not serve in the military or engage in a protected activity was treated more favorably than the plaintiff, the employer has violated the USERRA.

■ **CASE IN POINT 21.19** Baldo Bello, a staff sergeant with the United States Marine Corps Reserve, was employed by the Village of Skokie as a police officer. Police officers in Skokie normally have nine regular days off (RDO) per month and eight sick days per year. Skokie officers who are in the reserve receive two weeks of paid leave for annual training each summer, but they do not receive pay for the required weekend military training. During his first four years as an officer at Skokie, Bello always requested RDOs to cover his weekend training drills.

After that, Bello started requesting military leave for the two to four days of drills per month, in addition to his nine RDO days. Skokie at first granted Bello military leave for monthly drills but later began to deny the requests. When Skokie officials told Bello that he needed to schedule his RDOs to cover his weekend military training, Bello filed suit in a federal district court alleging violations of the USERRA. Skokie filed a motion for summary judgment, which the court denied. The court found that Bello was meeting his employer's legitimate expectations. Bello was therefore entitled to a trial on the issue of whether Skokie had treated his leave requests less favorably than requests from other employees.[39] ■

### 21–4c Plaintiffs May Be Entitled to Promotions

Under the USERRA, returning service members are to be reemployed in the jobs that they would have attained had they not been absent for military service. Reinstatement could affect their seniority, status, pay, and other rights and benefits (such as health and pension plans). In essence, this means that if a returning service member sues an employer for violations of the USERRA and is successful, she or he could receive not only damages and reinstatement but also a promotion.

## 21–5 Defenses to Employment Discrimination

The first line of defense for an employer charged with employment discrimination is to assert that the plaintiff has failed to meet his or her initial burden of proving that discrimination occurred. As noted, plaintiffs bringing age discrimination claims may find it difficult to meet this initial burden because they must prove that age discrimination was the reason for their employer's decision.

Once a plaintiff succeeds in proving that discrimination occurred, the burden shifts to the employer to

---

**36.** Pub. L. No. 103-353, codified at 38 U.S.C. Sections 4301-4335.
**37.** 20 C.F.R. Section 1002.34(a).
**38.** 38 U.S.C. Section 4311(c).

**39.** *Bello v. Village of Skokie,* 151 F.Supp.3d 849 (N.D. Ill. 2015).

justify the discriminatory practice. Possible justifications include that the discrimination was the result of a business necessity, a bona fide occupational qualification, or a seniority system. In some situations, as noted earlier, an effective antiharassment policy and prompt remedial action when harassment occurs may shield employers from liability for sexual harassment under Title VII.

### 21–5a Business Necessity

An employer may defend against a claim of disparate-impact (unintentional) discrimination by asserting that a practice that has a discriminatory effect is a **business necessity.** ■ **EXAMPLE 21.20** EarthFix, Inc., an international consulting agency, requires its applicants to be fluent in at least one foreign language. If this requirement is shown to have a discriminatory effect, EarthFix can defend it based on business necessity. That is, the company can argue that its workers must speak more than one language to perform their jobs at the required level of competence. If EarthFix can demonstrate a definite connection between foreign language fluency and job performance, it normally will succeed in this business necessity defense. ■

### 21–5b Bona Fide Occupational Qualification

Another defense applies when discrimination against a protected class is essential to a job—that is, when a particular trait is a **bona fide occupational qualification (BFOQ).** Note that race, color, and national origin can never be BFOQs.

Generally, courts have restricted the BFOQ defense to situations in which the employee's gender or religion is essential to the job. For instance, a women's clothing store might legitimately hire only female sales attendants if part of an attendant's job involves assisting clients in the store's dressing rooms.

### 21–5c Seniority Systems

An employer with a history of discrimination may have no members of protected classes in upper-level positions. Nevertheless, the employer may have a defense against a discrimination suit if promotions or other job benefits have been distributed according to a fair *seniority system*. In a **seniority system,** workers with more years of service are promoted first or laid off last.

■ **CASE IN POINT 21.21** Cathalene Johnson, an African American woman, was a senior service agent for Federal Express Corporation (FedEx) for more than seventeen years. She resigned in 2014 and filed suit against FedEx for discrimination based on race and gender, as well as for violation of the Equal Pay Act. Johnson claimed that FedEx had paid a white male co-worker about two dollars more per hour than she had received for basically the same position. FedEx argued that the man had seniority. He had worked for FedEx for seven years longer, was the most senior employee at the station where Johnson worked, and had been a courier in addition to being a service agent. The court ruled that FedEx's seniority system was fair and provided a defense to Johnson's claims.[40] ■

### 21–5d After-Acquired Evidence of Employee Misconduct

In some situations, employers have attempted to avoid liability for employment discrimination on the basis of "after-acquired evidence" of an employee's misconduct. After-acquired evidence refers to evidence that the employer discovers after a lawsuit has been filed.

■ **EXAMPLE 21.22** Pratt Legal Services fires Lucy, who then sues Pratt for employment discrimination. During pretrial investigation, Pratt discovers that Lucy made material misrepresentations on her job application. Had Pratt known of these misrepresentations, it would have had grounds to fire Lucy. ■

After-acquired evidence of wrongdoing cannot shield an employer entirely from liability for employment discrimination. It may, however, be used to limit the amount of damages for which the employer is liable.

## 21–6 Affirmative Action

Federal statutes and regulations providing for equal opportunity in the workplace were designed to reduce or eliminate discriminatory practices with respect to hiring, retaining, and promoting employees. **Affirmative action** programs go a step further and attempt to "make up" for past patterns of discrimination by giving members of protected classes preferential treatment in hiring or promotion. During the 1960s, all federal and state government agencies, private companies that contracted to do business with the federal government, and institutions that received federal funding were required to implement affirmative action policies.

Title VII of the Civil Rights Act neither requires nor prohibits affirmative action. Thus, most private companies and organizations have not been required to implement affirmative action policies, though many have done so voluntarily. Affirmative action programs have been controversial, however, particularly when they have

---

40. *Johnson v. Federal Express Corp.,* 996 F.Supp.2d 302 (M.D.Pa. 2014).

resulted in reverse discrimination against members of a majority group, such as white males.

### 21–6a Equal Protection Issues

Because of their inherently discriminatory nature, affirmative action programs may violate the equal protection clause of the Fourteenth Amendment to the U.S. Constitution. Any federal, state, or local government affirmative action program that uses racial or ethnic classifications as the basis for making decisions is subject to strict scrutiny (the highest standard to meet) by the courts.

Today, an affirmative action program normally is constitutional only if it attempts to remedy past discrimination and does not make use of quotas or preferences. Furthermore, once such a program has succeeded in the goal of remedying past discrimination, it must be changed or eliminated.

### 21–6b State Laws Prohibiting Affirmative Action Programs

Some states have enacted laws that prohibit affirmative action programs at public institutions (colleges, universities, and state agencies) within their borders. These states include California, Maryland, Michigan, New Hampshire, Oklahoma, Virginia, and Washington. The United States Supreme Court recognized that states have the power to enact such bans in 2014.

■ **CASE IN POINT 21.23**  Michigan voters passed an initiative to amend the state's constitution to prohibit publicly funded colleges from granting preferential treatment to any group on the basis of race, sex, color, ethnicity, or national origin. The law also prohibited Michigan from considering race and gender in public hiring and contracting decisions.

A lawsuit was filed challenging the initiative as a violation of the equal protection clause in the U.S. Constitution. Although a federal appellate court held that the law violated the equal protection clause, the United States Supreme Court reversed. The Court ruled that a state has the inherent power to ban affirmative action within that state, but it did not rule on the constitutionality of any specific affirmative action program.[41] ■

---

41. *Schuette v. Coalition to Defend Affirmative Action, Integration and Immigrant Rights*, ___ U.S. ___, 134 S.Ct. 1623, 188 L.Ed.2d 613 (2014).

## Reviewing: Employment Discrimination

Amaani Lyle, an African American woman, was hired by Warner Brothers Television Productions to be a scriptwriters' assistant for the writers of *Friends,* a popular adult-oriented television series. One of her essential job duties was to type detailed notes for the scriptwriters during brainstorming sessions in which they discussed jokes, dialogue, and story lines. The writers then combed through Lyle's notes after the meetings for script material. During these meetings, the three male scriptwriters told lewd and vulgar jokes and made sexually explicit comments and gestures. They often talked about their personal sexual experiences and fantasies, and some of these conversations were then used in episodes of *Friends.*

During the meetings, Lyle never complained that she found the writers' conduct offensive. After four months, Lyle was fired because she could not type fast enough to keep up with the writers' conversations during the meetings. She filed a suit against Warner Brothers, alleging sexual harassment and claiming that her termination was based on racial discrimination. Using the information presented in the chapter, answer the following questions.

1. Would Lyle's claim of racial discrimination be for intentional (disparate-treatment) or unintentional (disparate-impact) discrimination? Explain.
2. Can Lyle establish a *prima facie* case of racial discrimination? Why or why not?
3. When Lyle was hired, she was told that typing speed was extremely important to the position. At the time, she maintained that she could type eighty words per minute, so she was not given a typing test. It later turned out that Lyle could type only fifty words per minute. What impact might typing speed have on Lyle's lawsuit?
4. Lyle's sexual-harassment claim is based on the hostile working environment created by the writers' sexually offensive conduct at meetings that she was required to attend. The writers, however, argue that their behavior was essential to the "creative process" of writing for *Friends,* a show that routinely contained sexual innuendos and adult humor. Which defense discussed in the chapter might Warner Brothers assert using this argument?

**Debate This** . . . *Members of minority groups and women have made enough economic progress in the last several decades that they no longer need special legislation to protect them.*

## Terms and Concepts

affirmative action 470

bona fide occupational
    qualification (BFOQ) 470

business necessity 470

constructive discharge 461

disparate-impact
    discrimination 455

disparate-treatment
    discrimination 454

employment discrimination 453

*prima facie* case 454

protected class 453

seniority system 470

sexual harassment 462

tangible employment action 463

## Issue Spotters

1. Ruth is a supervisor for a Subs & Suds restaurant. Tim is a Subs & Suds employee. The owner announces that some employees will be discharged. Ruth tells Tim that if he has sex with her, he can keep his job. Is this sexual harassment? Why or why not? (See *Title VII of the Civil Rights Act.*)

2. Koko, a person with a disability, applies for a job at Lively Sales Corporation for which she is well qualified, but she is rejected. Lively continues to seek applicants and eventually fills the position with a person who does not have a disability. Could Koko succeed in a suit against Lively for discrimination? Explain. (See *Discrimination Based on Disability.*)

• **Check your answers to the Issue Spotters against the answers provided in Appendix D at the end of this text.**

## Business Scenarios

**21–1. Title VII Violations.** Discuss fully whether either of the following actions would constitute a violation of Title VII of the Civil Rights Act, as amended: (See *Title VII of the Civil Rights Act.*)

**(a)** Tennington, Inc., is a consulting firm with ten employees. These employees travel on consulting jobs in seven states. Tennington has an employment record of hiring only white males.

**(b)** Novo Films is making a movie about Africa and needs to employ approximately one hundred extras for this picture. To hire these extras, Novo advertises in all major newspapers in Southern California. The ad states that only African Americans need apply.

**21–2. Religious Discrimination.** Gina Gomez, a devout Roman Catholic, worked for Sam's Department Stores, Inc., in Phoenix, Arizona. Sam's considered Gomez a productive employee because her sales exceeded $200,000 per year. At the time, the store gave its managers the discretion to grant unpaid leave to employees but prohibited vacations or leave during the holiday season—October through December. Gomez felt that she had a "calling" to go on a "pilgrimage" in October to a location in Bosnia where some persons claimed to have had visions of the Virgin Mary. The Catholic Church had not designated the site an official pilgrimage site, the visions were not expected to be stronger in October, and tours were available at other times. The store managers denied Gomez's request for leave, but she had a nonrefundable ticket and left anyway. Sam's terminated her employment, and she could not find another job. Can Gomez establish a *prima facie* case of religious discrimination? Explain. (See *Title VII of the Civil Rights Act.*)

## Business Case Problems

**21–3. Spotlight on Dress Code Policies—Discrimination**  **Based on Gender.** Burlington Coat Factory Warehouse, Inc., had a dress code that required male salesclerks to wear business attire consisting of slacks, shirt, and a necktie. Female salesclerks, by contrast, were required to wear a smock so that customers could readily identify them. Karen O'Donnell and other female employees refused to wear smocks. Instead they reported to work in business attire and were suspended. After numerous suspensions, the female employees were fired for violating Burlington's dress code policy. All other conditions of employment, including salary, hours, and benefits, were the same for female and male employees. Was the dress code policy discriminatory? Why or why not? [*O'Donnell v. Burlington Coat Factory Warehouse, Inc.,* 656 F.Supp. 263 (S.D. Ohio 1987)] (See *Title VII of the Civil Rights Act.*)

**21–4. Sexual Harassment by Co-Worker.** Billie Bradford worked for the Kentucky Department of Community Based Services (DCBS). One of Bradford's co-workers, Lisa Stander, routinely engaged in extreme sexual behavior (such as touching herself and making crude comments) in Bradford's presence. Bradford and others regularly complained about Stander's conduct to their supervisor, Angie Taylor. Rather than resolve the problem, Taylor nonchalantly told Stander to stop, encouraged Bradford to talk to Stander, and suggested that Stander was just having fun. Assuming that Bradford was subjected to a hostile work environment, could DCBS be liable? Why or why not? [*Bradford v. Department of Community Based Services,* 2012 WL 360032 (E.D.Ky. 2012)] (See *Title VII of the Civil Rights Act.*)

**21–5. Business Case Problem with Sample Answer—Age Discrimination.**  Beginning in 1986, Paul Rangel was a sales professional for the pharmaceutical company sanofi-aventis U.S. LLC (S-A). Rangel had satisfactory performance reviews until 2006, when S-A issued new "Expectations" guidelines that included sales call quotas and other standards that he failed to meet. After two years of negative performance reviews, Rangel—who was then more than forty years old—was terminated. The termination was part of a nationwide reduction in force of all sales professionals who had not met the "Expectations" guidelines, including younger workers. Did S-A engage in age discrimination? Discuss. [*Rangel v. sanofi aventis U.S. LLC,* 507 Fed. Appx. 786 (10th Cir. 2013)] (See *Discrimination Based on Age.*)

- **For a sample answer to Problem 21–5, go to Appendix E at the end of this text.**

**21–6. Discrimination Based on Disability.** Cynthia Horn worked for Knight Facilities Management–GM, Inc., in Detroit, Michigan, as a janitor. When Horn developed a sensitivity to cleaning products, her physician gave her a "no exposure to cleaning solutions" restriction. Knight discussed possible accommodations with Horn. She suggested that restrooms be eliminated from her cleaning route or that she be provided with a respirator. Knight explained that she would be exposed to cleaning solutions in any situation and concluded that there was no work available within her physician's restriction. Has Knight violated the Americans with Disabilities Act by failing to provide Horn with the requested accommodations? Explain. [*Horn v. Knight Facilities Management–GM, Inc.,* 556 Fed.Appx. 452 (6th Cir. 2014)] (See *Discrimination Based on Disability.*)

**21–7. Sexual Harassment.** Jamel Blanton was a male employee at a Pizza Hut restaurant operated by Newton Associates, Inc., in San Antonio, Texas. Blanton was subjected to sexual and racial harassment by the general manager, who was female. Newton had a clear, straightforward antidiscrimination policy and complaint procedure. The policy provided that in such a situation, an employee should complain to the harasser's supervisor. Blanton alerted a shift leader and an assistant manager about the harassment, but they were subordinate to the general manager and did not report the harassment to higher-level management. When Blanton finally complained to a manager with authority over the general manager, the employer investigated and fired the general manager within four days. Blanton filed a suit in a federal district court against Newton, seeking to impose liability on the employer for the general manager's actions. What is Newton's best defense? Discuss. [*Blanton v. Newton Associates, Inc.,* 593 Fed.Appx. 389 (5th Cir. 2015)] (See *Title VII of the Civil Rights Act.*)

**21–8. Discrimination Based on Disability.** Dennis Wallace was a deputy sheriff for Stanislaus County, California, when he injured his left knee. After surgery, he was subject to limits on prolonged standing, walking, and running. The county assigned him to work as a bailiff. The sergeants who supervised him rated his performance above average. Less than a year later, without consulting those supervisors, the county placed him on an unpaid leave of absence, under the mistaken belief that he could not safely perform the essential functions of the job. Wallace filed an action in a California state court against the county, alleging discrimination based on disability. Under state law, discriminatory intent is shown by evidence that an actual or perceived disability was a "substantial motivating factor or reason" for an employer's adverse employment action. An employee is not required to show that the action was motivated by animosity or ill will. Could Wallace likely prove the "substantial motivating factor or reason" element? Explain. [*Wallace v. County of Stanislaus,* 245 Cal.App.4th 109, 199 Cal.Rptr.3d 462 (5 Dist. 2016)] (See *Discrimination Based on Disability.*)

**21–9. A Question of Ethics—Retaliation by Employers.**  *Shane Dawson, a male homosexual, worked for Entek International. Some of Dawson's co-workers, including his supervisor, made derogatory comments about his sexual orientation. Dawson's work deteriorated. He filed a complaint with Entek's human resources department. Two days later, he was fired. State law made it unlawful for an employer to discriminate against an individual based on sexual orientation.* [Dawson v. Entek International, *630 F.3d 928 (9th Cir. 2011)*] (See *Title VII of the Civil Rights Act.*)

**(a)** Could Dawson establish a claim for retaliation? Explain.

**(b)** Should homosexuals be a protected class under Title VII of the Civil Rights Act? Discuss the arguments for and against amending federal law to prohibit employment discrimination based on sexual orientation.

# Legal Reasoning Group Activity

**21–10. Racial Discrimination.** Two African American plaintiffs sued the producers of the reality television series *The Bachelor* and *The Bachelorette* for racial discrimination. The plaintiffs claimed that the shows had never featured persons of color in the lead roles. The plaintiffs also alleged that the producers did not provide people of color who auditioned for the lead roles with the same opportunities to compete as white people who auditioned. (See *Title VII of the Civil Rights Act.*)

**(a)** The first group will assess whether the plaintiffs can establish a *prima facie* case of disparate-treatment discrimination.

**(b)** The second group will consider whether the plaintiffs can establish disparate-impact discrimination.

**(c)** The third group will assume that the plaintiffs established a *prima facie* case and that the burden has shifted to the employer to articulate a legal reason for not hiring the plaintiffs. What legitimate reasons might the employer assert for not hiring the plaintiffs in this situation? Should the law require television producers to hire persons of color for lead roles in reality television shows? Discuss.

# Answers to the *Issue Spotters*

1. *Is this sexual harassment? Why or why not?* Yes. One type of sexual harassment occurs when a request for sexual favors is a condition of employment, and the person making the request is a supervisor or acts with the authority of the employer. A tangible employment action, such as continued employment, may also lead to the employer's liability for the supervisor's conduct. That the injured employee is a male and the supervisor a female, instead of the other way around, would not affect the outcome. Same-gender harassment is also actionable.

2. *Could Koko succeed in a suit against Lively for discrimination? Explain.* Yes, if she can show that Lively failed to hire her solely because of her disability. The other elements for a discrimination suit based on a disability are that the plaintiff (1) has a disability and (2) is otherwise qualified for the job. Both of these elements appear to be satisfied in this problem.

# Sample Answers for *Business Case Problems with Sample Answer*

**Problem 21–5.** *Age Discrimination.* No, sanofi-aventis U.S. LLC (S-A) does not appear to have engaged in age discrimination. The Age Discrimination in Employment Act (ADEA) prohibits employment discrimination on the basis of age against individuals forty years of age or older. For the act to apply, an employer must have twenty or more employees, and the employer's business activities must affect interstate commerce. To establish a *prima facie* case, a plaintiff must show that he or she was (1) a member of the protected age group, (2) qualified for the position from which he or she was discharged, and (3) discharged because of age discrimination. If the employer offers a legitimate reason for its action, the plaintiff must show that the stated reason is only a pretext.

In this problem, Rangel was over forty years old. But he also had negative sales performance reviews for more than two years before he was terminated as part of S-A's nationwide reduction in force of all sales professionals who had not met the "Expecta tions" guidelines, including younger workers. The facts do n indicate that a person younger than Rangel replaced him or that S-A intended to discriminate against him on the basis of age. Based on these facts, Rangel could not establish a *prima facie* case of age discrimination on the part of S-A.

In the actual case on which this problem is based, in Rangel's suit against S-A alleging age discrimination, a federal district court issued a judgment in S-A's favor. On Rangel's appeal, the U.S. Court of Appeals for the Tenth Circuit affirmed, according to the reasoning stated above.

# Chapter 18

# CHAPTER

# Intellectual Property Rights

**I**ntellectual property is any property that results from intellectual, creative processes—the products of an individual's mind. Although it is an abstract term for an abstract concept, intellectual property is nonetheless familiar to almost everyone. The apps for your iPhone, iPad, or Samsung Galaxy, the movies you see, and the music you listen to are all forms of intellectual property.

More than two hundred years ago, the framers of the U.S. Constitution recognized the importance of protecting creative works in Article I, Section 8. Statutory protection of these rights began in the 1940s and continues to evolve to meet the needs of modern society. In today's global economy, however, protecting intellectual property in one country is no longer sufficient. The United States is participating in various international agreements to secure ownership rights in intellectual property in other countries.

Whether locally or globally, businesspersons have a vital need to protect their rights in intellectual property, which may be more valuable than their physical property, such as machines and buildings. Consider, for instance, the importance of intellectual property rights to technology companies, such as Apple, Inc., and Samsung. These two companies have been involved in patent litigation over the designs of their smartphones for several years.

## 8–1 Trademarks and Related Property

A **trademark** is a distinctive mark, motto, device, or implement that a manufacturer stamps, prints, or otherwise affixes to the goods it produces so that they can be identified on the market and their origins made known. In other words, a trademark is a source indicator. At common law, the person who used a symbol or mark to identify a business or product was protected in the use of that trademark. Clearly, by using another's trademark, a business could lead consumers to believe that its goods were made by the other business. The law seeks to avoid this kind of confusion.

In the following classic case, the defendants argued that the Coca-Cola trademark was entitled to no protection under the law because the term did not accurately represent the product.

**Classic Case 8.1**

### The Coca-Cola Co. v. The Koke Co. of America
Supreme Court of the United States, 254 U.S. 143, 41 S.Ct. 113, 65 L.Ed.189 (1920).

**Company Profile** *John Pemberton, an Atlanta pharmacist, invented a caramel-colored, carbonated soft drink in 1886. His bookkeeper, Frank Robinson, named the beverage Coca-Cola after two of the ingredients, coca leaves and kola nuts. Asa Candler bought the Coca-Cola Company in 1891, and within seven years, he had made the soft drink available throughout the United States, as well as in parts of Canada and Mexico. Candler continued to sell Coke aggressively and to open up new markets, reaching Europe before 1910. In doing so, however, he attracted numerous competitors, some of which tried to capitalize directly on the Coke name.*

**Case 8.1 Continued**

**Background and Facts** The Coca-Cola Company sought to enjoin (prevent) the Koke Company of America and other beverage companies from, among other things, using the word *Koke* for their products. The Koke Company of America and other beverage companies contended that the Coca-Cola trademark was a fraudulent representation and that Coca-Cola was therefore not entitled to any help from the courts. The Koke Company and the other defendants alleged that the Coca-Cola Company, by its use of the Coca-Cola name, represented that the beverage contained cocaine (from coca leaves), which it no longer did. The trial court granted the injunction against the Koke Company, but the appellate court reversed the lower court's ruling. Coca-Cola then appealed to the United States Supreme Court.

## In the Language of the Court

Mr. Justice *HOLMES* delivered the opinion of the Court.
* * * *

* * * Before 1900 the beginning of [Coca-Cola's] good will was more or less helped by the presence of cocaine, a drug that, like alcohol or caffeine or opium, may be described as a deadly poison or as a valuable [pharmaceutical item, depending on the speaker's purposes]. The amount seems to have been very small,[a] but it may have been enough to begin a bad habit and after the Food and Drug Act of June 30, 1906, if not earlier, long before this suit was brought, it was eliminated from the plaintiff's compound.

* * * Since 1900 the sales have increased at a very great rate corresponding to a like increase in advertising. The name now characterizes a beverage to be had at almost any soda fountain. It means a single thing coming from a single source, and well known to the community. It hardly would be too much to say that the drink characterizes the name as much as the name the drink. In other words *Coca-Cola probably means to most persons the plaintiff's familiar product to be had everywhere rather than a compound of particular substances.* * * * Before this suit was brought the plaintiff had advertised to the public that it must not expect and would not find cocaine, and had eliminated everything tending to suggest cocaine effects except the name and the picture of [coca] leaves and nuts, which probably conveyed little or nothing to most who saw it. It appears to us that it would be going too far to deny the plaintiff relief against a palpable [readily evident] fraud because possibly here and there an ignorant person might call for the drink with the hope for incipient cocaine intoxication. The plaintiff's position must be judged by the facts as they were when the suit was begun, not by the facts of a different condition and an earlier time. [Emphasis added.]

**Decision and Remedy** *The district court's injunction was allowed to stand. The competing beverage companies were enjoined from calling their products Koke.*

**Impact of This Case on Today's Law** *In this early case, the United States Supreme Court made it clear that trademarks and trade names (and nicknames for those marks and names, such as the nickname "Coke" for "Coca-Cola") that are in common use receive protection under the common law. This holding is significant historically because it is the predecessor to the federal statute later passed to protect trademark rights—the Lanham Act of 1946. In many ways, this act represented a codification of common law principles governing trademarks.*

**Critical Thinking**
- **What If the Facts Were Different?** *Suppose that Coca-Cola had been trying to make the public believe that its product contained cocaine. Would the result in this case likely have been different? Why or why not?*

---

**a.** In reality, until 1903 the amount of active cocaine in each bottle of Coke was equivalent to one "line" of cocaine.

## 8–1a Statutory Protection of Trademarks

Statutory protection of trademarks and related property is provided at the federal level by the Lanham Act of 1946.[1] The Lanham Act was enacted, in part, to protect manufacturers from losing business to rival companies that used confusingly similar trademarks. The act incorporates the common law of trademarks and provides remedies for owners of trademarks who wish to enforce their claims in federal court. Many states also have trademark statutes.

**Trademark Dilution** In 1995, Congress amended the Lanham Act by passing the Federal Trademark Dilution Act,[2] which allowed trademark owners to bring suits in federal court for trademark **dilution.** In 2006, Congress further amended the law on trademark dilution by passing the Trademark Dilution Revision Act (TDRA).[3]

Under the TDRA, to state a claim for trademark dilution, a plaintiff must prove the following:

1. The plaintiff owns a famous mark that is distinctive.
2. The defendant has begun using a mark in commerce that allegedly is diluting the famous mark.
3. The similarity between the defendant's mark and the famous mark gives rise to an *association* between the marks.
4. The association is likely to impair the distinctiveness of the famous mark or harm its reputation.

Trademark dilution laws protect "distinctive" or "famous" trademarks (such as Rolls Royce, McDonald's, Starbucks, and Apple) from certain unauthorized uses. Such a mark is protected even when the use is on noncompeting goods or is unlikely to cause confusion. More than half of the states have also enacted trademark dilution laws.

**Marks Need Not Be Identical** Note that a famous mark may be diluted by the use of an *identical* mark or by the use of a *similar* mark.[4] A similar mark is more likely to lessen the value of a famous mark when the companies using the marks provide related goods or compete against each other in the same market.

■ **CASE IN POINT 8.1** Samantha Lundberg opened a business called "Sambuck's Coffeehouse," in Astoria, Oregon, even though she knew that "Starbucks" was one of the largest coffee chains in the nation. Starbucks Corporation filed a dilution lawsuit, and a federal court ruled that use of the "Sambuck's" mark constituted trademark dilution because it created confusion for consumers. Not only was there a "high degree" of similarity between the marks, but also both companies provided coffee-related services and marketed their services through "stand-alone" retail stores. Therefore, the use of the similar mark (Sambuck's) reduced the value of the famous mark (Starbucks).[5] ■

## 8–1b Trademark Registration

Trademarks may be registered with the state or with the federal government. To register for protection under federal trademark law, a person must file an application with the U.S. Patent and Trademark Office in Washington, D.C. Under current law, a mark can be registered (1) if it is currently in commerce or (2) if the applicant intends to put it into commerce within six months.

In special circumstances, the six-month period can be extended by thirty months. Thus, the applicant would have a total of three years from the date of notice of trademark approval to make use of the mark and file the required use statement. Registration is postponed until the mark is actually used. During this waiting period, any applicant can legally protect his or her trademark against a third party who previously has neither used the mark nor filed an application for it.

Registration is renewable between the fifth and sixth years after the initial registration and every ten years thereafter (every twenty years for those trademarks registered before 1990).

## 8–1c Trademark Infringement

Registration of a trademark with the U.S. Patent and Trademark Office gives notice on a nationwide basis that the trademark belongs exclusively to the registrant. The registrant is also allowed to use the symbol ® to indicate that the mark has been registered. Whenever that trademark is copied to a substantial degree or used in its entirety by another, intentionally or unintentionally, the trademark has been *infringed* (used without authorization).

When a trademark has been infringed, the owner of the mark has a cause of action against the infringer. To succeed in a trademark infringement action, the owner must show that the defendant's use of the mark created a likelihood of confusion about the origin of the defendant's goods or services. The owner need not prove that

---

1. 15 U.S.C. Sections 1051–1128.
2. 15 U.S.C. Section 1125.
3. Pub. L. No. 103-312, 120 Stat. 1730 (2006).
4. See *Louis Vuitton Malletier S.A. v. Haute Diggity Dog, LLC*, 507 F.3d 252 (4th Cir. 2007); and *Moseley v. V Secret Catalogue, Inc.*, 537 U.S. 418, 123 S.Ct. 1115, 155 L.Ed.2d 1 (2003).
5. *Starbucks Corp. v. Lundberg*, 2005 WL 3183858 (D.Or. 2005).

the infringer acted intentionally or that the trademark was registered (although registration does provide proof of the date of inception of the trademark's use).

The most commonly granted remedy for trademark infringement is an *injunction* to prevent further infringement. Under the Lanham Act, a trademark owner that successfully proves infringement can recover actual damages, plus the profits that the infringer wrongfully received from the unauthorized use of the mark. A court can also order the destruction of any goods bearing the unauthorized trademark. In some situations, the trademark owner may also be able to recover attorneys' fees.

At the center of the following case was an injunction granted in an earlier dispute between two brothers prohibiting one of them from using trademarks owned by the other, including a mark featuring their shared last name.

## Case 8.2

# LFP IP, LLC v. Hustler Cincinnati, Inc.
United States Court of Appeals, Sixth Circuit, 810 F.3d 424 (2016).

**Background and Facts** Brothers Jimmy and Larry Flynt owned "The Hustler Club," a bar and nightclub in Cincinnati, Ohio. Larry opened Hustler clubs in other Ohio cities. Within a few years, he also began publishing *Hustler,* a sexually explicit magazine. Larry formed LFP IP, Inc., and other corporations to conduct his enterprises. Many of them used the trademarks "HUSTLER" and "LARRY FLYNT," which LFP owned. Jimmy opened his own store, Hustler Cincinnati, and paid LFP licensing fees to use the "HUSTLER" mark.

When the store stopped paying the fees, LFP filed a suit in a federal district court against the store's corporate owner, alleging trademark infringement. The court issued an injunction prohibiting Jimmy from using the "HUSTLER" mark. Later, he opened a store called "FLYNT Sexy Gifts." LFP claimed that this name was likely to cause confusion with the "LARRY FLYNT" mark. The court modified the injunction to limit Jimmy's use of the "Flynt" name without "Jimmy." Jimmy appealed.

### In the Language of the Court
*SUTTON,* Circuit Judge.
* * * *

Courts * * * may exercise their sound judicial discretion to modify an injunction if the circumstances, whether of law or fact, obtaining at the time of its issuance have changed, or new ones have since arisen.

* * * The [district] court * * * applied the traditional test for trademark infringement under federal law, asking whether (1) Larry and his companies owned the LARRY FLYNT trademark, (2) Jimmy used the mark in commerce, and (3) the use was likely to cause confusion. The court found all three elements satisfied * * * . Because the original injunction was tailored to prevent trademark infringement by [Jimmy] and because Jimmy had committed new violations, the district court acted appropriately when it modified its initial grant of relief to cover Jimmy's conduct at the [new] outlet.

The district court's modified injunction was also suitably tailored to the changed circumstances. Balancing the competing interests of Larry and Jimmy, the court permitted Jimmy to use his full name while protecting Larry's interest in the LARRY FLYNT trademark.
* * * *

Jimmy * * * takes issue with some of the factual findings that the district court used to justify the modified injunction.

But none of the district court's factual findings is clearly erroneous. * * * Larry * * * presented evidence that he used the mark in connection with a wide range of adult entertainment products, including the kinds of products sold at Jimmy's store. Because *product use * * * marks the salient [most noticeable] indicator of ownership in trademark-infringement actions*, the district court reasonably found that Larry * * * owned the LARRY FLYNT trademark with respect to retail goods. The court also reasonably found that Larry began using the mark on adult entertainment products before Jimmy did. * * * And * * * Larry's company * * * continued to use that mark in commerce. [Emphasis added.]

In claiming an absence of evidence of consumer confusion, Jimmy missteps. Some of the evidence comes from Jimmy himself. When asked about instances where a consumer has been confused, in terms of whether or not Jimmy was the owner of the store, Jimmy responded, "I have experienced the

*Case 8.2 Continues*

**Case 8.2 Continued**

confusion in the names, you know. Jimmy and Larry Flynt, in this market area, is somewhat synonymous with Hustler or with Flynt. You're not going to get around that."

**Decision and Remedy** *The U.S. Court of Appeals for the Sixth Circuit affirmed the lower court's modification of the injunction. The injunction was initially tailored to prevent Jimmy's infringement of his brother's marks. When Jimmy committed a new violation by opening "FLYNT Sexy Gifts," the district court acted appropriately in modifying the injunction to cover this conduct.*

**Critical Thinking**
- **E-Commerce** *Could Jimmy use his last name—the name that he shares with his brother—as a domain name? Why or why not?*
- **What If the Facts Were Different?** *Suppose that Jimmy had used the marks at the center of this case on an entirely different line of goods, not adult entertainment products. Would the result have been the same? Explain.*

## 8–1d Distinctiveness of the Mark

A trademark must be sufficiently distinctive to enable consumers to identify the manufacturer of the goods easily and to distinguish between those goods and competing products.

**Strong Marks** Fanciful, arbitrary, or suggestive trademarks are generally considered to be the most distinctive (strongest) trademarks. These marks receive automatic protection because they serve to identify a particular product's source, as opposed to describing the product itself.

**Fanciful and Arbitrary Trademarks.** Fanciful trademarks use invented words, such as "Xerox" for one manufacturer's copiers and "Google" for a search engine. Arbitrary trademarks use common words in an uncommon way that is not descriptive of the product, such as "Dutch Boy" as a name for paint.

Even a single letter used in a particular style can be an arbitrary trademark. ■ **CASE IN POINT 8.2** Sports entertainment company ESPN sued Quiksilver, Inc., a maker of youth-oriented clothing, alleging trademark infringement. ESPN claimed that Quiksilver's clothing used the stylized "X" mark that ESPN uses in connection with the "X Games" ("extreme" sports competitions).

Quiksilver filed counterclaims for trademark infringement and dilution, arguing that it had a long history of using the stylized X on its products. ESPN had created the X Games in the mid-1990s, and Quiksilver had been using the X mark since 1994. ESPN asked the court to dismiss Quiksilver's counterclaims, but the court refused, holding that the X on Quiksilver's clothing is clearly an arbitrary mark. The court found that the two Xs are

"similar enough that a consumer might well confuse them." Therefore, Quicksilver could continue its claim for trademark infringement.[6] ■

**Suggestive Trademarks.** Suggestive trademarks indicate something about a product's nature, quality, or characteristics, without describing the product directly. These marks require imagination on the part of the consumer to identify the characteristic.

"Dairy Queen," for instance, suggests an association between its products and milk, but it does not directly describe ice cream. "Blu-ray" is a suggestive mark that is associated with the high-quality, high-definition video contained on a particular type of optical data storage disc. Although blue-violet lasers are used to read blu-ray discs, the term *blu-ray* does not directly describe the disc.

**Secondary Meaning** Descriptive terms, geographic terms, and personal names are not inherently distinctive and do not receive protection under the law until they acquire a secondary meaning. A secondary meaning may arise when customers begin to associate a specific term or phrase (such as *London Fog*) with specific trademarked items (coats with "London Fog" labels) made by a particular company.

Whether a secondary meaning becomes attached to a name usually depends on how extensively the product is advertised, the market for the product, the number of sales, and other factors. ■ **CASE IN POINT 8.3** Unity Health Plans Insurance Corporation has been a health maintenance organization (HMO) insurer in Wisconsin since 1955. In 2013, another health-care provider, Iowa

---

6. *ESPN, Inc. v. Quiksilver, Inc.*, 586 F.Supp.2d 219 (S.D.N.Y. 2008).

Health System, began rebranding itself (changing its name and marketing) as UnityPoint Health. When the company expanded into Wisconsin, where Unity Health already had an established presence, Unity Health filed a trademark infringement suit in federal court.

The court found that Unity Health was a descriptive mark, and thus not inherently distinctive. But the court also held that the Unity Health mark had acquired a secondary meaning, largely because it had been used for so long and so exclusively by one health insurer in Wisconsin. It made no difference to the court that only one part of the mark (Unity) was common to both trademarks. To allow Iowa Health Systems to use the mark UnityPoint Health in Wisconsin would likely create confusion for consumers. Therefore, the court issued an injunction and blocked Iowa Health from using the trademark Unity-Point Health.[7] ■

Once a secondary meaning is attached to a term or name, a trademark is considered distinctive and is protected. Even a color can qualify for trademark protection, as did the color schemes used by some state university sports teams, including Ohio State University and Louisiana State University.[8]

■ **CASE IN POINT 8.4** Federal Express Corporation (FedEx) provides transportation and delivery services worldwide using the logo FedEx in a specific color combination. FedEx sued a competitor, JetEx Management Services, Inc., for using the same color combination and a similar name and logo. JetEx also mimicked FedEx's trademarked slogan ("The World on Time" for FedEx, and "Keeping the World on Time" for JetEx). FedEx alleged trademark infringement and dilution, among other claims. A federal district court in New York granted a permanent injunction to block JetEx from using the infringing mark in FedEx colors.[9] ■

**Generic Terms** Generic terms that refer to an entire class of products, such as *bicycle* and *computer,* receive no protection, even if they acquire secondary meanings. A particularly thorny problem arises when a trademark acquires generic use. For instance, *aspirin* and *thermos* were originally the names of trademarked products, but today the words are used generically. Other trademarks that have acquired generic use are *escalator, trampoline, raisin bran, dry ice, lanolin, linoleum, nylon,* and *cornflakes.*

A trademark does not become generic simply because it is commonly used, however. ■ **CASE IN POINT 8.5** In 2014, David Elliot and Chris Gillespie sought to register numerous domain names, including "googledisney.com" and "googlenewstvs.com." (A *domain name* is part of an Internet address, such as "cengage.com.") They were unable to register the names because all of them used the word *google,* a trademark of Google, Inc.

Elliot and Gillespie brought an action in federal court to have the Google trademark cancelled because it had become a generic term. They argued that because most people now use *google* as a verb ("to google") when referring to searching the Internet with any search engine (not just Google), the term should no longer be protected. The court held that even if people do use the word *google* as a verb, it is still a protected trademark if consumers associate the noun with one company. The court concluded that "the primary significance of the word *google* to a majority of the public who utilize Internet search engines is a designation of the Google search engine."[10] ■

## 8–1e Service, Certification, and Collective Marks

A **service mark** is essentially a trademark that is used to distinguish the *services* (rather than the products) of one person or company from those of another. For instance, each airline has a particular mark or symbol associated with its name. Titles and character names used in radio and television are frequently registered as service marks.

Other marks protected by law include certification marks and collective marks. A **certification mark** is used by one or more persons, other than the owner, to certify the region, materials, mode of manufacture, quality, or other characteristic of specific goods or services. Certification marks include "Good Housekeeping Seal of Approval" and "UL Tested."

When used by members of a cooperative, association, or other organization, a certification mark is referred to as a **collective mark.** ■ **EXAMPLE 8.6** Collective marks appear at the ends of motion picture credits to indicate the various associations and organizations that participated in the making of the films. The union marks found on the tags of certain products are also collective marks. ■

## 8–1f Trade Dress

The term **trade dress** refers to the image and overall appearance of a product. Trade dress is a broad concept

---

**7.** *Unity Health Plans Insurance Co. v. Iowa Health System,* 995 F.Supp.2d 874 (W.D.Wis. 2014).

**8.** *Board of Supervisors of Louisiana State University v. Smack Apparel Co.,* 438 F.Supp.2d 653 (E.D.La. 2006). See also *Abraham v. Alpha Chi Omega,* 781 F.Supp.2d 396 (N.D.Tex. 2011).

**9.** *Federal Express Corp. v. JetEx Management Services, Inc.,* 2014 WL 4628983 (E.D.N.Y. 2014).

**10.** *Elliot v. Google,* 45 F.Supp.3d 1156 (D.Ariz. 2014).

and can include either all or part of the total image or overall impression created by a product or its packaging.

■ **EXAMPLE 8.7** The distinctive decor, menu, layout, and style of service of a particular restaurant may be regarded as trade dress. Trade dress can also include the layout and appearance of a catalogue, the use of a lighthouse as part of the design of a golf hole, the fish shape of a cracker, or the G-shaped design of a Gucci watch. ■

Basically, trade dress is subject to the same protection as trademarks. In cases involving trade dress infringement, as in trademark infringement cases, a major consideration is whether consumers are likely to be confused by the allegedly infringing use.

## 8–1g Counterfeit Goods

Counterfeit goods copy or otherwise imitate trademarked goods, but they are not the genuine trademarked goods. The importation of goods that bear counterfeit (fake) trademarks poses a growing problem for U.S. businesses, consumers, and law enforcement. In addition to the negative financial effects on legitimate businesses, certain counterfeit goods, such as pharmaceuticals and nutritional supplements, can present serious public health risks.

**The Stop Counterfeiting in Manufactured Goods Act** The Stop Counterfeiting in Manufactured Goods Act[11] (SCMGA) was enacted to combat counterfeit goods. The act makes it a crime to traffic intentionally in or attempt to traffic in counterfeit goods or services, or to knowingly use a counterfeit mark on or in connection with goods or services.

Before this act, the law did not prohibit the creation or shipment of counterfeit labels that were not attached to any product. Therefore, counterfeiters would make labels and packaging bearing another's trademark, ship the labels to another location, and then affix them to an inferior product to deceive buyers. The SCMGA closed this loophole by making it a crime to knowingly traffic in counterfeit labels, stickers, packaging, and the like, regardless of whether the items are attached to any goods.

**Penalties for Counterfeiting** Persons found guilty of violating the SCMGA may be fined up to $2 million or imprisoned for up to ten years (or more if they are repeat offenders). If a court finds that the statute was violated, it must order the defendant to forfeit the counterfeit products (which are then destroyed), as well as any property

used in the commission of the crime. The defendant must also pay restitution to the trademark holder or victim in an amount equal to the victim's actual loss.

■ **CASE IN POINT 8.8** Charles Anthony Jones pleaded guilty to trafficking of counterfeit prescription erectile dysfunction drugs. The court sentenced Jones to thirty-seven months in prison and ordered him to pay $633,019 in restitution. Jones appealed, arguing that the amount awarded was more than the pharmaceutical companies' actual losses. The court agreed. The pharmaceutical companies were entitled only to their lost net profits rather than the retail price of the genuine drugs.[12] ■

**Combating Foreign Counterfeiters** Although Congress has enacted statutes against counterfeit goods, the United States cannot prosecute foreign counterfeiters because our national laws do not apply to them. One effective tool that U.S. officials have used to combat online sales of counterfeit goods is to obtain a court order to close down the domain names of Web sites that sell such goods. For instance, U.S. agents have shut down hundreds of domain names on the Monday after Thanksgiving ("Cyber Monday"). Shutting down the Web sites, particularly on key shopping days, prevents some counterfeit goods from entering the United States. Europol, an international organization, has also used this tactic.

## 8–1h Trade Names

Trademarks apply to *products*. A **trade name** indicates part or all of a business's name, whether the business is a sole proprietorship, a partnership, or a corporation. Generally, a trade name is directly related to a business and its goodwill.

A trade name may be protected as a trademark if the trade name is also the name of the company's trademarked product—for example, Coca-Cola. Unless it is also used as a trademark or service mark, a trade name cannot be registered with the federal government. Trade names are protected under the common law, but only if they are unusual or fancifully used. The word *Safeway*, for example, was sufficiently fanciful to obtain protection as a trade name for a grocery chain.

## 8–1i Licensing

One way to avoid litigation and still make use of another's trademark or other form of intellectual property is to obtain a license to do so. A **license** in this context is an agreement, or contract, permitting the use of a

---

11. Pub. L. No. 109-181 (2006), which amended 18 U.S.C. Sections 2318–2320.

12. *United States v. Jones*, 616 Fed.Appx. 726 (5th Cir. 2015).

trademark, copyright, patent, or trade secret for certain purposes. The party that owns the intellectual property rights and issues the license is the *licensor,* and the party obtaining the license is the *licensee.* The licensee generally pays fees, or *royalties,* for the privilege of using the intellectual property.

A license grants only the rights expressly described in the license agreement. A licensor might, for example, allow the licensee to use the trademark as part of its company or domain name, but not otherwise use the mark on any products or services. Disputes frequently arise over licensing agreements, particularly when the license involves Internet uses.

■ **CASE IN POINT 8.9**   George V Restauration S.A. and others owned and operated the Buddha Bar Paris, a restaurant with an Asian theme in Paris, France. One of the owners allowed Little Rest Twelve, Inc., to use the Buddha Bar trademark and its associated concept in New York City under the name *Buddha Bar NYC.* Little Rest paid royalties for its use of the Buddha Bar mark and advertised Buddha Bar NYC's affiliation with Buddha Bar Paris. This connection was also noted on its Web site and in the media.

When a dispute arose, the owners of Buddha Bar Paris withdrew their permission for Buddha Bar NYC's use of their mark, but Little Rest continued to use it. The owners of the mark filed a suit in a New York state court against Little Rest. The court granted an injunction to prevent Little Rest from using the mark.[13] ■

# 8–2 Patents

A **patent** is a grant from the government that gives an inventor the exclusive right to make, use, or sell his or her invention for a period of twenty years. Patents for designs, as opposed to those for inventions, are given for a fourteen-year period. The applicant must demonstrate to the satisfaction of the U.S. Patent and Trademark Office that the invention, discovery, process, or design is novel, useful, and not obvious in light of current technology.

Until recently, U.S. patent law differed from the laws of many other countries because the first person to invent a product obtained the patent rights rather than the first person to file for a patent. It was often difficult to prove who invented an item first, however, which prompted Congress to change the system in 2011 by passing the America Invents Act.[14] Now the first person to file an application for a patent on a product or process will receive patent protection. In addition, the new law established a nine-month limit for challenging a patent on any ground.

The period of patent protection begins on the date the patent application is filed, rather than when the patent is issued, which may sometimes be years later. After the patent period ends (either fourteen or twenty years later), the product or process enters the public domain, and anyone can make, sell, or use the invention without paying the patent holder.

## 8–2a Searchable Patent Databases

A significant development relating to patents is the availability online of the world's patent databases. The Web site of the U.S. Patent and Trademark Office (www.uspto.gov) provides searchable databases covering U.S. patents granted since 1976. The Web site of the European Patent Office (www.epo.org) provides online access to 50 million patent documents in more than seventy nations through a searchable network of databases.

Businesses use these searchable databases in many ways. Companies may conduct patent searches to list or inventory their patents, which are valuable assets. Patent searches may also be conducted to study trends and patterns in a specific technology or to gather information about competitors in the industry.

## 8–2b What Is Patentable?

Under federal law, "[w]hoever invents or discovers any new and useful process, machine, manufacture, or composition of matter, or any new and useful improvement thereof, may obtain a patent therefor, subject to the conditions and requirements of this title."[15] Thus, to be patentable, the applicant must prove that the invention, discovery, process, or design is *novel, useful,* and *not obvious* in light of current technology.

In sum, almost anything is patentable, except the laws of nature, natural phenomena, and abstract ideas (including algorithms[16]). Even artistic methods and works of art, certain business processes, and the struc-

---

13. *George V Restauration S.A. v. Little Rest Twelve, Inc.,* 58 A.D.3d 428, 871 N.Y.S.2d 65 (2009).

14. The full title of this law is the Leahy-Smith America Invents Act, Pub. L. No. 112-29 (2011), which amended 35 U.S.C. Sections 1, 41, and 321.

15. 35 U.S.C. Section 101.

16. An *algorithm* is a step-by-step procedure, formula, or set of instructions for accomplishing a specific task. An example is the set of rules used by a search engine to rank the listings contained within its index in response to a query.

tures of storylines are patentable, provided that they are novel and not obvious.[17]

Plants that are reproduced asexually (by means other than from seed), such as hybrid or genetically engineered plants, are patentable in the United States, as are genetically engineered (or cloned) microorganisms and animals. ■ **CASE IN POINT 8.10** Monsanto, Inc., sells its patented genetically modified (GM) seeds to farmers to help them achieve higher yields from crops using fewer pesticides. It requires farmers who buy GM seeds to sign licensing agreements promising to plant the seeds for only one crop and to pay a technology fee for each acre planted. To ensure compliance, Monsanto has many full-time employees whose job is to investigate and prosecute farmers who use the GM seeds illegally. Monsanto has filed nearly 150 lawsuits against farmers in the United States and has been awarded more than $15 million in damages (not including out-of-court settlement amounts).[18] ■

## 8–2c Patent Infringement

If a firm makes, uses, or sells another's patented design, product, or process without the patent owner's permission, that firm commits the tort of patent infringement. Patent infringement may occur even though the patent owner has not put the patented product into commerce. Patent infringement may also occur even though not all features or parts of a product are copied. (To infringe the patent on a process, however, all steps or their equivalent must be copied.) To read about an important issue in patent infringement today, see this chapter's *Digital Update* feature.

**Patent Infringement Lawsuits and High-Tech Companies** Obviously, companies that specialize in developing new technology stand to lose significant profits if someone "makes, uses, or sells" devices that incorporate their patented inventions. Because these firms are the holders of numerous patents, they are frequently involved in patent infringement lawsuits (as well as other types of intellectual property disputes).

■ **CASE IN POINT 8.11** Apple sued Samsung in federal court alleging that Samsung's Galaxy smartphones and tablets that use Google's HTC Android operating system infringe on Apple's patents. Apple has design patents that

cover its devices' graphical user interface (the display of icons on the home screen), shell, and screen and button design. Apple has also patented the way information is displayed on iPhones and other devices, the way windows pop open, and the way information is scaled and rotated.

A jury found that Samsung had willfully infringed five of Apple's patents and awarded damages. The parties appealed. A judge later reduced the amount of damages awarded on the patent claims, but litigation between the two companies has continued. In 2015, a federal appellate court held that elements of the physical design of these two manufacturers' mobile devices and their on-screen icons were functional and thus not protected under the Lanham Act. A product feature is functional and not protected as trade dress if it is essential to the article's use or purpose or affects the cost or quality of the article.[19] ■

**Patent Infringement and Foreign Sales** Many companies that make and sell electronics and computer software and hardware are based in foreign nations (for instance, Samsung Electronics Company is a Korean firm). Foreign firms can apply for and obtain U.S. patent protection on items that they sell within the United States. Similarly, U.S. firms can obtain protection in foreign nations where they sell goods.

In the United States, the Supreme Court has narrowly construed patent infringement as it applies to exported software, however. As a general rule, under U.S. law, no patent infringement occurs when a patented product is made and sold in another country. ■ **CASE IN POINT 8.12** AT&T Corporation holds a patent on a device used to digitally encode, compress, and process recorded speech. AT&T brought an infringement case against Microsoft Corporation, which admitted that its Windows operating system incorporated software code that infringed on AT&T's patent.

The United States Supreme Court held that Microsoft was liable only for infringement in the United States and not for the Windows-based computers produced in foreign locations. The Court reasoned that Microsoft had not "supplied" the software for the computers but had only electronically transmitted a master copy, which the foreign manufacturers copied and loaded onto the computers.[20] ■

---

**17.** For a United States Supreme Court case discussing the obviousness requirement, see *KSR International Co. v. Teleflex, Inc.*, 550 U.S. 398, 127 S.Ct. 1727, 167 L.Ed.2d 705 (2007).

**18.** See, for example, *Monsanto Co. v. Bowman*, 657 F.3d 1341 (Fed.Cir. 2011); and *Monsanto Co. v. Scruggs*, 2009 WL 1228318 (Fed.Cir. 2009).

**19.** *Apple, Inc. v. Samsung Electronics Co.*, 926 F.Supp.2d 1110 (N.D.Cal. 2013); 786 F.3d 983 (Fed. Cir. 2015).

**20.** *Microsoft Corp. v. AT&T Corp.*, 550 U.S. 437, 127 S.Ct. 1746, 167 L.Ed.2d 737 (2007).

## DIGITAL UPDATE — The Problem of Patent Trolls

In recent years, a huge number of patent infringement lawsuits have been filed against software and technology firms. Many patent cases involve companies defending real innovations, but some lawsuits are "shakedowns" by patent trolls.

*Patent trolls*—more formally called nonpracticing entities (NPEs) or patent assertion entities (PAEs)—are firms that do not make or sell products or services but are in the business of patent litigation. These firms buy patents and then try to enforce them against companies that *do* sell products or services, demanding licensing fees and threatening infringement lawsuits. Patent trolls usually target online businesses.

### "I'm Going to Sue You Unless You Pay Me to Go Away"

Patent trolls literally bank on the fact that when threatened with infringement suits, most companies would rather pay to settle than engage in costly litigation, even if they believe they could win.

Consider an example. Soverain Software, LLC, sued dozens of online retailers, including Amazon, Avon, Home Depot, Macy's, Nordstrom, Kohl's, RadioShack, The Gap, and Victoria's Secret. Soverain claimed that it owned patents that covered nearly any use of online shopping-cart technology and that all these retailers had infringed on its patents. Amazon paid millions to settle with Soverain, as did most of the other defendants.

Interestingly, one online retailer, Newegg, Inc., refused to pay Soverain and ultimately won in court. In 2013, a federal appellate court held that the shopping-cart patent claim was invalid on the ground of obviousness because the technology for it had already existed before Soverain obtained its patent.[a]

### The Role of Software Patents

The patent troll problem is concentrated in software patents, which often include descriptions of what the software does rather than the computer code involved. Many software patents are vaguely worded and overly broad. In the United States, both the patent system and the courts have had difficulty evaluating and protecting such patents.

As a result, nearly any business that uses basic technology can be a target of patent trolls. In fact, *more than 60 percent of all new patent cases* are filed by patent trolls. The firms most commonly targeted by patent trolls are large technology companies, including AT&T, Google, Apple, Samsung, Amazon, and Verizon. In one recent year, "AT&T was sued for patent infringement by patent trolls 54 times—more than once a week."[b]

**Critical Thinking** *Some argue that the best way to stop patent trolls from taking advantage of the system would be to eliminate software patents completely and pass a law that makes software unpatentable. Would this be fair to software and technology companies? Why or why not?*

a. *Soverain Software, LLC v. Newegg, Inc.*, 728 F.3d 1332 (Fed. Cir. 2013), *cert.* denied, 134 S.Ct. 910 (2014).
b. Roger Parloff, "Taking on the Patent Trolls," *Fortune*, February 27, 2014.

## 8–2d Remedies for Patent Infringement

If a patent is infringed, the patent holder may sue for relief in federal court. The patent holder can seek an injunction against the infringer and can also request damages for royalties and lost profits. In some cases, the court may grant the winning party reimbursement for attorneys' fees and costs. If the court determines that the infringement was willful, the court can triple the amount of damages awarded (treble damages).

In the past, permanent injunctions were routinely granted to prevent future infringement. Today, however, according to the United States Supreme Court, a patent holder must prove that it has suffered irreparable injury and that the public interest would not be *disserved* by a permanent injunction.[21] Thus, courts have discretion to decide what is equitable in the circumstances and to consider what is in the public interest rather than just the interests of the parties.

■ **CASE IN POINT 8.13** Cordance Corporation developed some of the technology and software that automates Internet communications. Cordance sued Amazon.com, Inc., for patent infringement, claiming that Amazon's one-click purchasing interface infringed on one of Cordance's patents. After a jury found Amazon guilty of infringement, Cordance requested the court to issue a permanent injunction against Amazon's infringement or,

21. *eBay, Inc. v. MercExchange, LLC*, 547 U.S. 388, 126 S.Ct. 1837, 164 L.Ed.2d 641 (2006).

alternatively, to order Amazon to pay Cordance an ongoing royalty.

The court refused to issue a permanent injunction because Cordance had not proved that it would otherwise suffer irreparable harm. Cordance and Amazon were not direct competitors in the relevant market. Cordance had never sold or licensed the technology infringed by Amazon's one-click purchasing interface and had presented no market data or evidence to show how the infringement negatively affected Cordance. The court also refused to impose an ongoing royalty on Amazon.[22] ■

# 8–3 Copyrights

A **copyright** is an intangible property right granted by federal statute to the author or originator of a literary or artistic production of a specified type. The Copyright Act of 1976,[23] as amended, governs copyrights. Works created after January 1, 1978, are automatically given statutory copyright protection for the life of the author plus 70 years. For copyrights owned by publishing houses, the copyright expires 95 years from the date of publication or 120 years from the date of creation, whichever comes first. For works by more than one author, the copyright expires 70 years after the death of the last surviving author.[24]

When copyright protection ends, works enter into the *public domain*. Intellectual property, such as songs and other published works, that have entered into the public domain belong to everyone and are not protected by copyright or patent laws.

■ **CASE IN POINT 8.14** The popular character Sherlock Holmes originated in stories written by Arthur Conan Doyle and published from 1887 through 1927. Over the years, elements of the characters and stories created by Doyle have appeared in books, movies, and television series, including *Elementary* on CBS and *Sherlock* on BBC.

Before 2013, those who wished to use the copyrighted Sherlock material had to pay a licensing fee to Doyle's estate. Then, in 2013, the editors of a book of Holmes-related stories filed a lawsuit in federal court claiming that the basic Sherlock Holmes story elements introduced before 1923 should no longer be protected. The court agreed and ruled that these elements have entered the public domain—that is, the copyright has expired, and they can be used without permission.[25] ■

## 8–3a Registration

Copyrights can be registered with the U.S. Copyright Office (www.copyright.gov) in Washington, D.C. Registration is not required, however. A copyright owner no longer needs to place the symbol © or the term *Copr.* or *Copyright* on the work to have the work protected against infringement. Chances are that if somebody created it, somebody owns it.

Generally, copyright owners are protected against the following:

1. Reproduction of the work.
2. Development of derivative works.
3. Distribution of the work.
4. Public display of the work.

## 8–3b What Is Protected Expression?

Works that are copyrightable include books, records, films, artworks, architectural plans, menus, music videos, product packaging, and computer software. To be protected, a work must be "fixed in a durable medium" from which it can be perceived, reproduced, or communicated. As noted, protection is automatic, and registration is not required.

Section 102 of the Copyright Act explicitly states that it protects original works that fall into one of the following categories:

1. Literary works (including newspaper and magazine articles, computer and training manuals, catalogues, brochures, and print advertisements).
2. Musical works and accompanying words (including advertising jingles).
3. Dramatic works and accompanying music.
4. Pantomimes and choreographic works (including ballets and other forms of dance).
5. Pictorial, graphic, and sculptural works (including cartoons, maps, posters, statues, and even stuffed animals).
6. Motion pictures and other audiovisual works (including multimedia works).
7. Sound recordings.
8. Architectural works.

---

22. *Cordance Corp. v. Amazon.com, Inc.*, 730 F.Supp.2d 333 (D.Del. 2010).
23. 17 U.S.C. Sections 101 *et seq.*
24. These time periods reflect the extensions of the length of copyright protection enacted by Congress in the Copyright Term Extension Act of 1998, 17 U.S.C. Section 302. The United States Supreme Court upheld the constitutionality of the act in 2003. See *Eldred v. Ashcroft*, 537 U.S. 186, 123 S.Ct. 769, 154 L.Ed.2d 683 (2003).

25. *Klinger v. Conan Doyle Estate, Ltd.*, 988 F.Supp.2d 879 (N.D.Ill. 2013).

**Section 102 Exclusions** Generally, anything that is not an original expression will not qualify for copyright protection. Facts widely known to the public are not copyrightable. Page numbers are not copyrightable because they follow a sequence known to everyone. Mathematical calculations are not copyrightable.

Furthermore, it is not possible to copyright an *idea*. Section 102 of the Copyright Act specifically excludes copyright protection for any "idea, procedure, process, system, method of operation, concept, principle, or discovery, regardless of the form in which it is described, explained, illustrated, or embodied." Thus, anyone can freely use the underlying ideas or principles embodied in a work.

What is copyrightable is the particular way in which an idea is *expressed*. Whenever an idea and an expression are inseparable, the expression cannot be copyrighted. An idea and its expression, then, must be separable to be copyrightable. Thus, for the design of a useful item to be copyrightable, the way it looks must be separate from its utilitarian (functional) purpose.

■ **CASE IN POINT 8.15** Inhale, Inc., registered a copyright on a hookah—a device for smoking tobacco by filtering the smoke through water held in a container at the base. Starbuzz Tobacco, Inc., sold hookahs with water containers shaped exactly like the Inhale containers.

Inhale filed a suit in a federal district court against Starbuzz for copyright infringement. The court determined that the shape of the water container on Inhale's hookahs was not copyrightable. The U.S. Court of Appeals for the Ninth Circuit affirmed the judgment. "The shape of a container is not independent of the container's utilitarian function—to hold the contents within its shape—because the shape accomplishes the function."[26] ■

---

26. *Inhale, Inc. v. Starbuzz Tobacco, Inc.*, 755 F.3d 1038 (2014).

**Compilations of Facts** Unlike ideas, *compilations* of facts are copyrightable. Under Section 103 of the Copyright Act, a compilation is "a work formed by the collection and assembling of preexisting materials or data that are selected, coordinated, or arranged in such a way that the resulting work as a whole constitutes an original work of authorship."

The key requirement in the copyrightability of a compilation is originality. If the facts are selected, coordinated, or arranged in an original way, they can qualify for copyright protection. Therefore, the White Pages of a telephone directory do not qualify for copyright protection, because they simply list alphabetically names and telephone numbers. The Yellow Pages of a directory can be copyrightable, provided the information is selected, coordinated, or arranged in an original way. Similarly, a compilation of information about yachts listed for sale has qualified for copyright protection.[27]

## 8–3c Copyright Infringement

Whenever the form or expression of an idea is copied, an infringement of copyright has occurred. The reproduction does not have to be exactly the same as the original, nor does it have to reproduce the original in its entirety. If a substantial part of the original is reproduced, the copyright has been infringed.

In the following case, rapper Curtis Jackson—better known as "50 Cent"—was the defendant in a suit that claimed his album *Before I Self-Destruct*, and the film of the same name, infringed the copyright of Shadrach Winstead's book *The Preacher's Son—But the Streets Turned Me into a Gangster.*

---

27. *BUC International Corp. v. International Yacht Council, Ltd.*, 489 F.3d 1129 (11th Cir. 2007).

---

**Case Analysis 8.3**

# Winstead v. Jackson
United States Court of Appeals, Third Circuit, 509 Fed.Appx. 139 (2013).

### In the Language of the Court
PER CURIAM. [By the Whole Court]
* * * *

* * * Winstead filed his * * * complaint in the United States District Court for the District of New Jersey, claiming that Jackson's album/CD and film derived their contents from, and infringed the copyright of, his book.
* * * *

* * * The District Court dismissed Winstead's * * * complaint * * *, concluding that Jackson * * * did not improperly copy protected aspects of Winstead's book.
* * * *

Winstead appeals.
* * * *

Here, it is not disputed that Winstead is the owner of the copyrighted

property * * *. However, *not all copying is copyright infringement, so even if actual copying is proven, the court must decide, by comparing the allegedly infringing work with the original work, whether the copying was unlawful. Copying may be proved inferentially by showing that the allegedly infringing work is substantially similar to the copyrighted*

**Case 8.3 Continues**

**Case 8.3 Continued**

*work.* A court compares the allegedly infringing work with the original work, and considers whether a "lay-observer" would believe that the copying was of protectable aspects of the copyrighted work. The inquiry involves distinguishing between the author's expression and the idea or theme that he or she seeks to convey or explore, because the former is protected and the latter is not. The court must determine whether the allegedly infringing work is similar because it appropriates the unique expressions of the original work, or merely because it contains elements that would be expected when two works express the same idea or explore the same theme. [Emphasis added.]

* * * A lay observer would not believe that Jackson's album/CD and film copied protectable aspects of Winstead's book. Jackson's album/CD is comprised of 16 individual songs, which explore drug-dealing, guns and money, vengeance, and other similar clichés of hip hop gangsterism. Jackson's fictional film is the story of a young man who turns to violence when his mother is killed in a drive-by shooting. The young man takes revenge by killing the man who killed his mother, and then gets rich by becoming an "enforcer" for a powerful criminal. He takes up with a woman who eventually betrays him, and is shot to death by her boyfriend, who has just been released from prison. The movie ends with his younger brother vowing to seek vengeance. Winstead's book purports to be autobiographical and tells the story of a young man whose beloved father was a Bishop in the church. The protagonist was angry as a child because his stepmother abused him, but he found acceptance and self-esteem on the streets of Newark because he was physically

powerful. He earned money robbing and beating people, went to jail, returned to crime upon his release, and then made even more money. The protagonist discusses his time at Rahway State Prison in great and compelling detail. The story ends when the protagonist learns that his father has passed away; he conveys his belief that this tragedy has led to his redemption, and he hopes that others might learn from his mistakes.

* * * Although Winstead's book and Jackson's works share similar themes and setting, the story of an angry and wronged protagonist who turns to a life of violence and crime has long been a part of the public domain [and is therefore not protected by copyright law]. Winstead argues * * * that a protagonist asking for God's help when his father dies, cutting drugs with mixing agents to maximize profits, and complaining about relatives who are addicts and steal the product, are protectable, but these things are not unique. To the extent that Jackson's works contain these elements, they are to be expected when two works express the same idea about "the streets" or explore the same theme. Winstead argues that not every protagonist whose story concerns guns, drugs, and violence in an urban setting winds up in prison or loses a parent, but this argument only serves to illustrate an important difference between his book and Jackson's film. Jackson's protagonist never spends any time in prison, whereas Winstead's protagonist devotes a considerable part of his story to his incarcerations.

In addition, Winstead's book and Jackson's works are different with respect to character, plot, mood, and sequence of events. Winstead's protagonist embarks on a life of crime at a very young age, but is redeemed by the death of his beloved

father. Jackson's protagonist turns to crime when he is much older and only after his mother is murdered. He winds up dead at a young age, unredeemed. Winstead's book is hopeful; Jackson's film is characterized * * * by moral apathy. It is true that both works involve the loss of a parent and the protagonist's recognition of the parent's importance in his life, but nowhere does Jackson appropriate anything unique about Winstead's expression of this generic topic.

Winstead contends that direct phrases from his book appear in Jackson's film. * * * He emphasizes these phrases: "Yo, where is my money at," "I would never have done no shit like that to you," "my father, my strength was gone," "he was everything to me," and "I did not know what to do," but, like the phrases "putting the work in," "get the dope, cut the dope," "let's keep it popping," and "the strong take from the weak but the smart take from everybody," they are either common in general or common with respect to hip hop culture, and do not enjoy copyright protection. The average person reading or listening to these phrases in the context of an overall story or song would not regard them as unique and protectable. Moreover, words and short phrases do not enjoy copyright protection. The similarity between Winstead's book and the lyrics to Jackson's songs on the album/CD is even more tenuous. "Stretching the dope" and "bloodshot red eyes" are common phrases that do not enjoy copyright protection. A side-by-side comparison of Winstead's book and the lyrics from Jackson's album/CD do not support a claim of copyright infringement.

For the foregoing reasons, we will affirm the order of the District Court dismissing [Winstead's] complaint.

**Legal Reasoning Questions**

**1.** Which expressions of an original work are protected by copyright law?

**2.** Is all copying copyright infringement? If not, what is the test for determining whether a creative work has been unlawfully copied?

**3.** How did the court in this case determine whether the defendant's work infringed on the plaintiff's copyright?

**Remedies for Copyright Infringement** Those who infringe copyrights may be liable for damages or criminal penalties. These range from actual damages or statutory damages, imposed at the court's discretion, to criminal proceedings for willful violations.

Actual damages are based on the harm caused to the copyright holder by the infringement, while statutory damages, not to exceed $150,000, are provided for under the Copyright Act. Criminal proceedings may result in fines and/or imprisonment. A court can also issue a permanent injunction against a defendant when the court deems it necessary to prevent future copyright infringement.

■ **CASE IN POINT 8.16** Rusty Carroll operated an online term paper business, R2C2, Inc., that offered up to 300,000 research papers for sale at nine Web sites. Individuals whose work was posted on these Web sites without their permission filed a lawsuit against Carroll for copyright infringement. Because Carroll had repeatedly failed to comply with court orders regarding discovery, the court found that the copyright infringement was likely to continue unless an injunction was issued. The court therefore issued a permanent injunction prohibiting Carroll and R2C2 from selling any term paper without sworn documentary evidence that the paper's author had given permission.[28] ■

**The "Fair Use" Exception** An exception to liability for copyright infringement is made under the "fair use" doctrine. In certain circumstances, a person or organization can reproduce copyrighted material without paying royalties. Section 107 of the Copyright Act provides as follows:

> [T]he fair use of a copyrighted work, including such use by reproduction in copies or phonorecords or by any other means specified by [Section 106 of the Copyright Act], for purposes such as criticism, comment, news reporting, teaching (including multiple copies for classroom use), scholarship, or research, is not an infringement of copyright. In determining whether the use made of a work in any particular case is a fair use the factors to be considered shall include—
>
> (1) the purpose and character of the use, including whether such use is of a commercial nature or is for nonprofit educational purposes;
> (2) the nature of the copyrighted work;
> (3) the amount and substantiality of the portion used in relation to the copyrighted work as a whole; and
> (4) the effect of the use upon the potential market for or value of the copyrighted work.

**What Is Fair Use?** Because these guidelines are very broad, the courts determine whether a particular use is fair on a case-by-case basis. Thus, anyone who reproduces copyrighted material may be committing a violation. In determining whether a use is fair, courts have often considered the fourth factor to be the most important.

■ **CASE IN POINT 8.17** A number of research universities, in partnership with Google, Inc., agreed to digitize books from their libraries and create a repository for them. Eighty member institutions (including many colleges and universities) contributed more than ten million works into the HathiTrust Digital Library. Some authors complained that this book scanning violated their rights and sued the HathiTrust and several associated entities for copyright infringement.

The court, however, sided with the defendants and held that making digital copies for the purposes of online search was a fair use. The library's searchable database enabled researchers to find terms of interest in the digital volumes—but not to read the volumes online. Therefore, the court concluded that the digitization did not provide a substitute that damaged the market for the original works.[29] ■

**The First Sale Doctrine** Section 109(a) of the Copyright Act provides that the owner of a particular item that is copyrighted can, without the authority of the copyright owner, sell or otherwise dispose of it. This rule is known as the first sale doctrine.

Under this doctrine, once a copyright owner sells or gives away a particular copy of a work, the copyright owner no longer has the right to control the distribution of that copy. Thus, for instance, a person who buys a copyrighted book can sell it to someone else. The first sale doctrine also applies to a person who receives promotional CDs, such as a music critic or radio programmer.[30]

■ **CASE IN POINT 8.18** Supap Kirtsaeng, a citizen of Thailand, was a graduate student at the University of Southern California. He enlisted friends and family in Thailand to buy copies of textbooks there and ship them to him in the United States. Kirtsaeng resold the textbooks on eBay, where he eventually made about $100,000.

John Wiley & Sons, Inc., had printed eight of those textbooks in Asia. Wiley sued Kirtsaeng in federal district court for copyright infringement. Kirtsaeng argued that Section 109(a) of the Copyright Act allows the first purchaser-owner of a book to sell it without the copyright owner's permission. The trial court held in favor of Wiley, and that decision was affirmed on appeal. Kirtsaeng then appealed to the United States Supreme Court, which ruled

---

**28.** *Weidner v. Carroll,* 2010 WL 310310 (S.D.Ill. 2010).

**29.** *Authors Guild, Inc., v. HathiTrust,* 755 F.3d 87 (2d Cir. 2014).
**30.** See, for example, *UMG Recordings, Inc. v. Augusto,* 628 F.3d 1175 (9th Cir. 2011).

in Kirtsaeng's favor. The first sale doctrine applies even to goods purchased abroad and resold in the United States.[31] ■

### 8–3d Copyright Protection for Software

The Computer Software Copyright Act amended the Copyright Act to include computer programs in the list of creative works protected by federal copyright law.[32] Generally, copyright protection extends to those parts of a computer program that can be read by humans, such as the "high-level" language of a source code. Protection also extends to the binary-language object code, which is readable only by the computer, and to such elements as the overall structure, sequence, and organization of a program.

Not all aspects of software are protected, however. Courts typically have not extended copyright protection to the "look and feel"—the general appearance, command structure, video images, menus, windows, and other screen displays—of computer programs. (Note that copying the "look and feel" of another's product may be a violation of trade dress or trademark laws, however.) Sometimes it can be difficult for courts to decide which particular aspects of software are protected.

■ **CASE IN POINT 8.19** Oracle America, Inc., is a software company that owns numerous application programming interfaces, or API packages. Oracle grants licenses to others to use these API packages to write applications in the Java programming language. Java is open and free for anyone to use, but using it requires an interface. When Google began using some of Oracle's API packages to run Java on its Android mobile devices, Oracle sued for copyright infringement. Google argued that the software packages were command structure and, as such, not protected under copyright law. Ultimately, a federal appellate court concluded that the API packages were source code and were entitled to copyright protection.[33] ■

---

# 8–4 Trade Secrets

The law of trade secrets protects some business processes and information that are not, or cannot be, patented, copyrighted, or trademarked. A **trade secret** is basically information of commercial value, such as customer lists, plans, and research and development. Trade secrets may also include pricing information, marketing methods, production techniques, and generally anything that makes an individual company unique and that would have value to a competitor.

Unlike copyright and trademark protection, protection of trade secrets extends to both ideas and their expression. For this reason, and because there are no registration or filing requirements for trade secrets, trade secret protection may be well suited for software.

Of course, a company's trade secrets must be disclosed to some persons, particularly to key employees. Businesses generally attempt to protect their trade secrets by having all employees who use a protected process or information agree in their contracts, or in confidentiality agreements, never to divulge it.

### 8–4a State and Federal Law on Trade Secrets

Under Section 757 of the *Restatement of Torts,* those who disclose or use another's trade secret, without authorization, are liable to that other party if either of the following is true:

1. They discovered the secret by improper means.
2. Their disclosure or use constitutes a breach of a duty owed to the other party.

Stealing confidential business data by industrial espionage, such as by tapping into a competitor's computer, is a theft of trade secrets without any contractual violation and is actionable in itself.

Trade secrets have long been protected under the common law. Today, nearly every state has enacted trade secret laws based on the Uniform Trade Secrets Act.[34] Additionally, the Economic Espionage Act[35] makes the theft of trade secrets a federal crime.

### 8–4b Trade Secrets in Cyberspace

Computer technology is undercutting many business firms' ability to protect their confidential information, including trade secrets. For example, a dishonest employee could e-mail trade secrets in a company's computer to a competitor or a future employer. If e-mail is not an option, the employee might walk out with the information on a flash drive.

Misusing a company's social media account is yet another way in which employees may appropriate trade secrets. ■ **CASE IN POINT 8.20** Noah Kravitz worked for a company called PhoneDog for four years as a product reviewer and video blogger. PhoneDog provided him with the Twitter account "@PhoneDog_Noah." Kravitz's popularity grew, and he had approximately 17,000

---

**31.** *Kirtsaeng v. John Wiley & Sons, Inc.,* ___ U.S. ___, 133 S.Ct. 1351, 185 L.Ed.2d 392 (2013).
**32.** Pub. L. No. 96-517 (1980), amending 17 U.S.C. Sections 101, 117.
**33.** *Oracle America, Inc. v. Google Inc.,* 750 F.3d 1339 (Fed.Cir. 2014).

**34.** The Uniform Trade Secrets Act, as drafted by the National Conference of Commissioners on Uniform State Laws (NCCUSL), can be found at uniformlaws.org.
**35.** 18 U.S.C. Sections 1831–1839.

followers by the time he quit. PhoneDog requested that Kravitz stop using the Twitter account. Although Kravitz changed his handle to "@noahkravitz," he continued to use the account. PhoneDog subsequently sued Kravitz for misappropriation of trade secrets, among other things. Kravitz moved for a dismissal, but the court found that the complaint adequately stated a cause of action for misappropriation of trade secrets and allowed the suit to continue.[36] ■

Exhibit 8–1 outlines trade secrets and other forms of intellectual property discussed in this chapter.

36. *PhoneDog v. Kravitz*, 2011 WL 5415612 (N.D.Cal. 2011). See also *Mintel Learning Technology, Inc. v. Ambrow Education Holding Ltd.*, 2012 WL 762126 (N.D.Cal. 2012).

**EXHIBIT 8–1** Forms of Intellectual Property

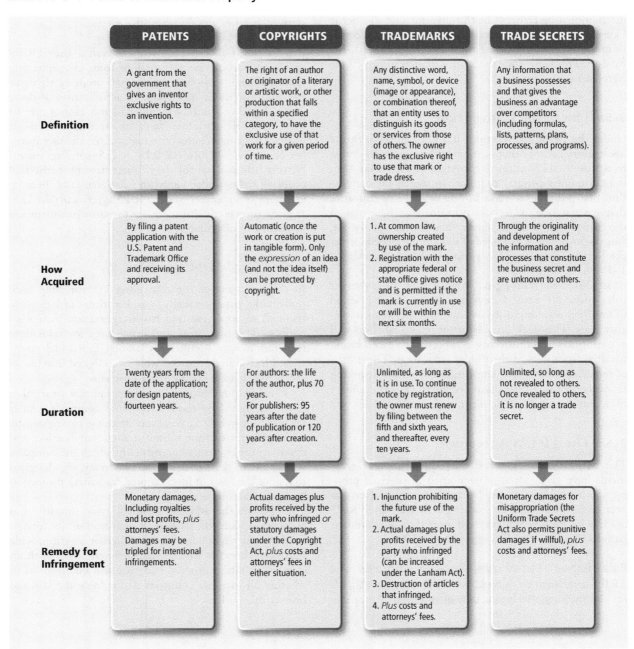

| | PATENTS | COPYRIGHTS | TRADEMARKS | TRADE SECRETS |
|---|---|---|---|---|
| **Definition** | A grant from the government that gives an inventor exclusive rights to an invention. | The right of an author or originator of a literary or artistic work, or other production that falls within a specified category, to have the exclusive use of that work for a given period of time. | Any distinctive word, name, symbol, or device (image or appearance), or combination thereof, that an entity uses to distinguish its goods or services from those of others. The owner has the exclusive right to use that mark or trade dress. | Any information that a business possesses and that gives the business an advantage over competitors (including formulas, lists, patterns, plans, processes, and programs). |
| **How Acquired** | By filing a patent application with the U.S. Patent and Trademark Office and receiving its approval. | Automatic (once the work or creation is put in tangible form). Only the *expression* of an idea (and not the idea itself) can be protected by copyright. | 1. At common law, ownership created by use of the mark. 2. Registration with the appropriate federal or state office gives notice and is permitted if the mark is currently in use or will be within the next six months. | Through the originality and development of the information and processes that constitute the business secret and are unknown to others. |
| **Duration** | Twenty years from the date of the application; for design patents, fourteen years. | For authors: the life of the author, plus 70 years. For publishers: 95 years after the date of publication or 120 years after creation. | Unlimited, as long as it is in use. To continue notice by registration, the owner must renew by filing between the fifth and sixth years, and thereafter, every ten years. | Unlimited, so long as not revealed to others. Once revealed to others, it is no longer a trade secret. |
| **Remedy for Infringement** | Monetary damages, Including royalties and lost profits, *plus* attorneys' fees. Damages may be tripled for intentional infringements. | Actual damages plus profits received by the party who infringed *or* statutory damages under the Copyright Act, *plus* costs and attorneys' fees in either situation. | 1. Injunction prohibiting the future use of the mark. 2. Actual damages plus profits received by the party who infringed (can be increased under the Lanham Act). 3. Destruction of articles that infringed. 4. *Plus* costs and attorneys' fees. | Monetary damages for misappropriation (the Uniform Trade Secrets Act also permits punitive damages if willful), *plus* costs and attorneys' fees. |

# 8–5 International Protection for Intellectual Property

For many years, the United States has been a party to various international agreements relating to intellectual property rights. For instance, the Paris Convention of 1883, to which almost 180 countries are signatory, allows parties in one country to file for patent and trademark protection in any of the other member countries. Other international agreements in this area include the Berne Convention, the Trade-Related Aspects of Intellectual Property Rights (known as the TRIPS agreement), the Madrid Protocol, and the Anti-Counterfeiting Trade Agreement.

## 8–5a The Berne Convention

Under the Berne Convention, if a U.S. citizen writes a book, every country that has signed the convention must recognize the U.S. author's copyright in the book. Also, if a citizen of a country that has not signed the convention first publishes a book in one of the 169 countries that have signed, all other countries that have signed the convention must recognize that author's copyright. Copyright notice is not needed to gain protection under the Berne Convention for works published after March 1, 1989.

In 2011, the European Union altered its copyright rules under the Berne Convention to extend the period of royalty protection for musicians from fifty years to seventy years. This decision aids major record labels as well as performers and musicians who previously faced losing royalties from sales of their older recordings. The profits of musicians and record companies have been shrinking for years because of the sharp decline in sales of compact discs and the rise in illegal downloads.

## 8–5b The TRIPS Agreement

The Berne Convention and other international agreements have given some protection to intellectual property on a worldwide level. None of them, however, has been as significant and far reaching in scope as the TRIPS agreement. Representatives from more than one hundred nations signed the TRIPS agreement in 1994.

**Establishes Standards and Procedures** The TRIPS agreement established, for the first time, standards for the international protection of intellectual property rights, including patents, trademarks, and copyrights for movies, computer programs, books, and music. Each member country of the World Trade Organization must include in its domestic laws broad intellectual property rights and effective remedies (including civil and criminal penalties) for violations of those rights.

Each member nation must also ensure that legal procedures are available for parties who wish to bring actions for infringement of intellectual property rights. Additionally, a related document established a mechanism for settling disputes among member nations.

**Prohibits Discrimination** Generally, the TRIPS agreement forbids member nations from discriminating against foreign owners of intellectual property rights in the administration, regulation, or adjudication of those rights. In other words, a member nation cannot give its own nationals (citizens) favorable treatment without offering the same treatment to nationals of all other member countries. ■ **EXAMPLE 8.21** A U.S. software manufacturer brings a suit for the infringement of intellectual property rights under Germany's national laws. Because Germany is a member of the TRIPS agreement, the U.S. manufacturer is entitled to receive the same treatment as a German manufacturer. ■

## 8–5c The Madrid Protocol

In the past, one of the difficulties in protecting U.S. trademarks internationally was the time and expense required to apply for trademark registration in foreign nations. The filing fees and procedures for trademark registration vary significantly among individual countries. The Madrid Protocol, which was signed into law in 2003, may help to resolve these problems.

The Madrid Protocol is an international treaty that has been signed by about a hundred countries. Under its provisions, a U.S. company wishing to register its trademark abroad can submit a single application and designate other member countries in which the company would like to register its mark. The treaty was designed to reduce the costs of international trademark protection by more than 60 percent.

Although the Madrid Protocol may simplify and reduce the cost of trademark registration in foreign countries, it remains to be seen whether it will provide significant benefits to trademark owners. Even with an easier registration process, there are still questions as to whether all member countries will enforce the law and protect the mark.

### 8-5d The Anti-Counterfeiting Trade Agreement

In 2011, Australia, Canada, Japan, Korea, Morocco, New Zealand, Singapore, and the United States signed the Anti-Counterfeiting Trade Agreement (ACTA), an international treaty to combat global counterfeiting and piracy. Other nations have since signed the agreement.

**Goals and Provisions** The goals of the treaty are to increase international cooperation, facilitate the best law enforcement practices, and provide a legal framework to combat counterfeiting. ACTA applies not only to counterfeit physical goods, such as medications, but also to pirated copyrighted works being distributed via the Internet. The idea is to create a new standard of enforcement for intellectual property rights that goes beyond the TRIPS agreement and encourages international cooperation and information sharing among signatory countries.

**Border Searches** Under ACTA, member nations are required to establish border measures that allow officials, on their own initiative, to search commercial shipments of imports and exports for counterfeit goods. The treaty neither requires nor prohibits random border searches of electronic devices, such as laptops, tablet devices, and smartphones, for infringing content.

If border authorities reasonably believe that any goods in transit are counterfeit, the treaty allows them to keep the suspect goods unless the owner proves that the items are authentic and noninfringing. The treaty allows member nations, in accordance with their own laws, to order online service providers to furnish information about suspected trademark and copyright infringers, including their identities.

## Reviewing: Intellectual Property Rights

Two computer science majors, Trent and Xavier, have an idea for a new video game, which they propose to call Hallowed. They form a business and begin developing their idea. Several months later, Trent and Xavier run into a problem with their design and consult a friend, Brad, who is an expert in designing computer source codes. After the software is completed but before Hallowed is marketed, a video game called Halo 2 is released for both the Xbox and the Playstation systems. Halo 2 uses source codes similar to those of Hallowed and imitates Hallowed's overall look and feel, although not all the features are alike. Using the information presented in the chapter, answer the following questions.

1. Would the name *Hallowed* receive protection as a trademark or as trade dress? Explain.
2. If Trent and Xavier had obtained a patent on Hallowed, would the release of Halo 2 have infringed on their patent? Why or why not?
3. Based only on the facts described above, could Trent and Xavier sue the makers of Halo 2 for copyright infringement? Why or why not?
4. Suppose that Trent and Xavier discover that Brad took the idea of Hallowed and sold it to the company that produced Halo 2. Which type of intellectual property issue does this raise?

**Debate This** . . . *Congress has amended copyright law several times so that copyright holders now have protection for many decades. Was Congress right in extending these copyright time periods?*

## Terms and Concepts

| | | |
|---|---|---|
| certification mark 155 | intellectual property 150 | trade dress 155 |
| collective mark 155 | license 156 | trade name 156 |
| copyright 160 | patent 157 | trade secret 164 |
| dilution 152 | service mark 155 | trademark 150 |

## Issue Spotters

1. Roslyn, a food buyer for Organic Cornucopia Food Company, decides to go into business for herself as Roslyn's Kitchen. She contacts Organic's suppliers, offering to buy their entire harvest for the next year. She also contacts Organic's customers, offering to sell her products at prices lower than Organic's prices. Has Roslyn violated any of the intellectual property rights discussed in this chapter? Explain. (See *Trade Secrets*.)

2. Global Products develops, patents, and markets software. World Copies, Inc., sells Global's software without the maker's permission. Is this patent infringement? If so, how might Global save the cost of suing World for infringement and at the same time profit from World's sales? (See *Patents*.)

• **Check your answers to the Issue Spotters against the answers provided in Appendix D at the end of this text.**

## Business Scenarios

**8–1. Fair Use.** Professor Wise is teaching a summer seminar in business torts at State University. Several times during the course, he makes copies of relevant sections from business law texts and distributes them to his students. Wise does not realize that the daughter of one of the textbook authors is a member of his seminar. She tells her father about Wise's copying activities, which have taken place without her father's or his publisher's permission. Her father sues Wise for copyright infringement. Wise claims protection under the fair use doctrine. Who will prevail? Explain. (See *Copyrights*.)

**8–2. Patent Infringement.** John and Andrew Doney invented a hard-bearing device for balancing rotors. Although they obtained a patent for their invention from the U.S. Patent and Trademark Office, it was never used as an automobile wheel balancer. Some time later, Exetron Corp. produced an automobile wheel balancer that used a hard-bearing device with a support plate similar to that of the Doneys' device. Given that the Doneys had not used their device for automobile wheel balancing, does Exetron's use of a similar device infringe on the Doneys' patent? Why or why not? (See *Patents*.)

## Business Case Problems

### 8–3. Spotlight on Macy's—Copyright Infringement.

 United Fabrics International, Inc., bought a fabric design from an Italian designer and registered a copyright to it with the U.S. Copyright Office. When Macy's, Inc., began selling garments with a similar design, United filed a copyright infringement suit against Macy's. Macy's argued that United did not own a valid copyright to the design and so could not claim infringement. Does United have to prove that the copyright is valid to establish infringement? Explain. [*United Fabrics International, Inc. v. C&J Wear, Inc.*, 630 F.3d 1255 (9th Cir. 2011)] (See *Copyrights*.)

**8–4. Theft of Trade Secrets.** Hanjuan Jin, a citizen of China, worked as a software engineer for Motorola for many years in a division that created proprietary standards for cellular communications. Contrary to Motorola's policies, Jin also secretly began working as a consultant for Lemko Corp., as well as with Sun Kaisens, a Chinese software company, and with the Chinese military. She started corresponding with Sun Kaisens's management about a possible full-time job in China. Jin took several medical leaves of absence from Motorola to return to Beijing and work with Sun Kaisens and the military.

After one of these medical leaves, Jin returned to Motorola. Over a period of several days, Jin accessed and downloaded thousands of documents on her personal laptop and on pen drives. When, later, she attempted to board a flight to China from Chicago, she was randomly searched by U.S. Customs and Border Protection officials at the airport. U.S. officials discovered the downloaded Motorola documents. Are there any circumstances under which Jin could avoid being prosecuted for theft of trade secrets? If so, what are these circumstances? Discuss fully. [*United States v. Hanjuan Jin*, 833 F.Supp.2d 977 (N.D.Ill. 2012)] (See *Trade Secrets*.)

**8–5. Copyright Infringement.** SilverEdge Systems Software hired Catherine Conrad to perform a singing telegram. SilverEdge arranged for James Bendewald to record Conrad's performance of her copyrighted song to post on its Web site. Conrad agreed to wear a microphone to assist in the recording, told Bendewald what to film, and asked for an additional fee only if SilverEdge used the video for a commercial purpose. Later, the company chose to post a video of a different performer's singing telegram instead. Conrad filed a suit in a federal district court against SilverEdge and Bendewald for copyright infringement. Are the defendants liable? Explain. [*Conrad v. Bendewald*, 500 Fed.Appx. 526 (7th Cir. 2013)] (See *Copyrights*.)

### 8–6. Business Case Problem with Sample Answer— Patents.

The U.S. Patent and Trademark Office (PTO)  denied Raymond Gianelli's application for a patent for a "Rowing Machine"—an exercise machine on which a user *pulls* on handles to perform a rowing motion against a selected resistance. The PTO considered the device obvious in light of a previously patented "Chest Press Apparatus for Exercising

Regions of the Upper Body"—an exercise machine on which a user *pushes* on handles to overcome a selected resistance. On what ground might this result be reversed on appeal? Discuss. [*In re Gianelli*, 739 F.3d 1375 (Fed. Cir. 2014)] (See *Patents.*)

- **For a sample answer to Problem 8–6, go to Appendix E at the end of this text.**

**8–7. Patents.** Rodney Klassen was employed by the U.S. Department of Agriculture (USDA). Without the USDA's authorization, Klassen gave Jim Ludy, a grape grower, plant material for two unreleased varieties of grapes. For almost two years, most of Ludy's plantings bore no usable fruit, none of the grapes were sold, and no plant material was given to any other person. The plantings were visible from publicly accessible roads, but none of the vines were labeled, and the variety could not be identified by simply viewing the vines. Under patent law, an applicant may not obtain a patent for an invention that is in public use for more than one year before the date of the application. Could the USDA successfully apply for patents on the two varieties given to Ludy? Explain. [*Delano Farms Co. v. California Table Grape Commission*, 778 F.3d 1243 (Fed. Cir. 2015)] (See *Patents.*)

**8–8. Copyright.** Savant Homes, Inc., is a custom home designer and builder. Using what it called the "Anders Plan," Savant built a model house in Windsor, Colorado. This was a ranch house with two bedrooms on one side and a master suite on the other, separated by a combined family room, dining room, and kitchen. Ron and Tammie Wagner toured the Savant house. The same month, the Wagners hired builder Douglas Collins and his firm, Douglas Consulting, LLC, to build a house for them in Windsor. After it was built, Savant filed a suit in a federal district court against Collins for copyright infringement, alleging that the builder had copied the Anders Plan in the design and construction of the Wagner house. Collins showed that the Anders Plan consisted of standard elements and standard arrangements of elements. In these circumstances, has infringement occurred? Explain.

[*Savant Homes, Inc. v. Collins*, 809 F.3d 1133 (10th Cir. 2016)] (See *Copyrights.*)

**8–9. A Question of Ethics—Copyright Infringement.**

 *Custom Copies, Inc., prepares and sells coursepacks, which contain compilations of readings for college courses. A teacher selects the readings and delivers a syllabus to the copy shop, which obtains the materials from a library, copies them, and binds the copies. Blackwell Publishing, Inc., which owns the copyright to some of the materials, filed a suit, alleging copyright infringement. Custom Copies filed a motion to dismiss for failure to state a claim. [Blackwell Publishing, Inc. v. Custom Copies, Inc., 2006 WL 1529503 (N.D.Fla. 2006)] (See Copyrights.)*

**(a)** Custom Copies argued, in part, that creating and selling did not "distribute" the coursepacks. Does a copy shop violate copyright law if it only copies materials for coursepacks? Does the copying fall under the "fair use" exception? Should the court grant the defendant's motion? Why or why not?

**(b)** What is the potential impact of copying and selling a book or journal without the permission of, and the payment of royalties or a fee to, the copyright owner? Explain.

**8–10. Special Case Analysis—Copyright Infringement.** Go to Case Analysis 8.3, *Winstead v. Jackson*. Read the excerpt, and answer the following questions. (See *Copyrights.*)

**(a) Issue:** This case focused on an allegation of copyright infringement involving what parties and which creative works?

**(b) Rule of Law:** What is the test for determining whether a creative work infringes the copyright of another work?

**(c) Applying the Rule of Law:** How did the court determine whether the claim of copyright infringement was supported in this case?

**(d) Conclusion:** Was the defendant liable for copyright infringement? Why or why not?

## Legal Reasoning Group Activity

**8–11. Patents.** After years of research, your company develops a product that might revolutionize the green (environmentally conscious) building industry. The product is made from relatively inexpensive and widely available materials combined in a unique way that can substantially lower the heating and cooling costs of residential and commercial buildings. The company has registered the trademark it intends to use on the product and has filed a patent application with the U.S. Patent and Trademark Office. (See *Patents.*)

**(a)** One group should provide three reasons why this product does or does not qualify for patent protection.

**(b)** Another group should develop a four-step procedure for how your company can best protect its intellectual property rights (trademark, trade secret, and patent) and prevent domestic and foreign competitors from producing counterfeit goods or cheap knockoffs.

**(c)** Another group should list and explain three ways your company can utilize licensing.

# Answers to the *Issue Spotters*

**1.** *Has Roslyn violated any of the intellectual property rights discussed in this chapter? Explain.* Yes, Roslyn has committed theft of trade secrets. Lists of suppliers and customers cannot be patented, copyrighted, or trademarked, but the information they contain is protected against appropriation by others as trade secrets. And most likely, Roslyn signed a contract agreeing not to use this information outside her employment by Organic. But even without this contract, Organic could make a convincing case against its ex-employee for a theft of trade secrets.

**2.** *Is this patent infringement? If so, how might Global save the cost of suing World for infringement and at the same time profit from World's sales?* This is patent infringement. A software maker in this situation might best protect its product, save litigation costs, and profit from its patent by the use of a license. In the context of this problem, a license would grant permission to sell a patented item. (A license can be limited to certain purposes and to the licensee only.)

# Sample Answers for *Business Case Problems with Sample Answer*

**Problem 8–6.** *Patents.* One ground on which the denial of the patent application in this problem could be reversed on appeal is that the design of Raymond Gianelli's "Rowing Machine" is *not obvious* in light of the design of the "Chest Press Apparatus for Exercising Regions of the Upper Body."

To obtain a patent, an applicant must demonstrate to the satisfaction of the U.S. Patent and Trademark Office (PTO) that the invention, discovery, process, or design is novel, useful, and not obvious in light of current technology. In this problem, the PTO denied Gianelli's application for a patent for his "Rowing Machine"—an exercise machine on which a user *pulls* on handles to perform a rowing motion against a selected resistance to strengthen the back muscles. The PTO considered the device obvious in light of a patented "Chest Press Apparatus for Exercising Regions of the Upper Body"—a chest press exercise machine on which a user *pushes* on handles to overcome a selected resistance. But it can be easily argued that it is *not* obvious to modify a machine with handles designed to be *pushed* into one with handles designed to be *pulled*. In fact, anyone who has used exercise machines knows that a way to cause injury is to use a machine in a manner not intended by the manufacturer.

In the actual case on which this problem is based, the U.S. Court of Appeals for the Federal Circuit reversed the PTO's denial of Gianelli's application for a patent, based on the reasoning stated above.

# Chapter 19

# CHAPTER

# Internet Law, Social Media, and Privacy

The Internet has changed our lives and our laws. Technology has put the world at our fingertips and now allows even the smallest business to reach customers around the globe. At the same time, the Internet presents a variety of challenges for the law.

Courts are often in uncharted waters when deciding disputes that involve the Internet, social media, and online privacy. Judges may have no common law precedents to rely on when resolving a case. Long-standing principles of justice may be inapplicable. New rules are evolving, but often not as quickly as technology.

For instance, Facebook is confronting lawsuits over its facial recognition software, which scans the faces in uploaded photos and identifies them in other photos across the site. As a result of this technology, Facebook has collected and stored a huge amount of facial recognition data— data that some users claim violates their privacy. The situation has been complicated by DeepFace, a sophisticated new technology developed by Facebook that can recognize faces almost as well as humans. In fact, Facebook has already agreed not to use the facial recognition software in Europe due to privacy complaints. In the United States, however, privacy rights generally hinge on whether the person has a reasonable expectation of privacy, which might be lacking in photos posted online.

## 9–1 Internet Law

A number of laws specifically address issues that arise only on the Internet. Three such issues are unsolicited e-mail, domain names, and cybersquatting, as we discuss here. We also discuss how the law is dealing with problems of trademark infringement and dilution online.

### 9–1a Spam

Businesses and individuals alike are targets of **spam.**[1] Spam is the unsolicited "junk e-mail" that floods virtual mailboxes with advertisements, solicitations, and other messages. Considered relatively harmless in the early days of the Internet, by 2017 spam accounted for roughly 75 percent of all e-mails.

**State Regulation of Spam** In an attempt to combat spam, thirty-seven states have enacted laws that prohibit or regulate its use. Many state laws that regulate spam require the senders of e-mail ads to instruct the recipients on how they can "opt out" of further e-mail ads from the same sources. For instance, in some states, an unsolicited e-mail must include a toll-free phone number or return e-mail address that the recipient can use to ask the sender to send no more unsolicited e-mails.

**The Federal CAN-SPAM Act** In 2003, Congress enacted the Controlling the Assault of Non-Solicited Pornography and Marketing (CAN-SPAM) Act.[2] The legislation applies to any "commercial electronic mail messages" that are sent to promote a commercial product or service. Significantly, the statute preempts state antispam laws except for those provisions in state laws that prohibit false and deceptive e-mailing practices.

Generally, the act permits the sending of unsolicited commercial e-mail but prohibits certain types of spamming activities. Prohibited activities include the use of a false return address and the use of false, misleading, or deceptive information when sending e-mail. The statute also prohibits the use of "dictionary attacks"—sending messages to randomly generated e-mail addresses—and the "harvesting" of e-mail addresses from Web sites through the use of specialized software.

■ **EXAMPLE 9.1** Sanford Wallace, known as the "Spam King," is considered to be one of the world's most prolific

---

1. The term *spam* is said to come from the lyrics of a Monty Python song that repeats the word *spam* over and over.

2. 15 U.S.C. Sections 7701 *et seq.*

spammers. He has operated several businesses over the years that used *botnets* (automated spamming networks) to send out hundreds of millions of unwanted e-mails. Wallace also infected computers with spyware and then sold consumers the software to fix it. He infiltrated Facebook accounts to spam 27 million of its users. He has been sued by the Federal Trade Commission, Facebook, and MySpace, and ordered to pay millions of dollars in fines. The Federal Bureau of Investigation ultimately arrested Wallace and brought criminal charges. In 2015, he pleaded guilty to fraud, spam, and violating a court order not to access Facebook. ■

Arresting prolific spammers, however, has done little to curb spam, which continues to flow at a rate of 70 billion messages per day. In effect, this means that the federal CAN-SPAM act has done little or nothing to reduce the amount of spam.

**The U.S. Safe Web Act** After the CAN-SPAM Act prohibited false and deceptive e-mails originating in the United States, spamming from servers located in other nations increased. These cross-border spammers generally were able to escape detection and legal sanctions because the Federal Trade Commission (FTC) lacked the authority to investigate foreign spamming.

Congress sought to rectify the situation by enacting the U.S. Safe Web Act (also known as the Undertaking Spam, Spyware, and Fraud Enforcement with Enforcers Beyond Borders Act).[3] The act allows the FTC to cooperate and share information with foreign agencies in investigating and prosecuting those involved in spamming, spyware, and various Internet frauds and deceptions.

The Safe Web Act also provides a "safe harbor" for **Internet service providers (ISPs)**—that is, organizations that provide access to the Internet. The safe harbor gives ISPs immunity from liability for supplying information to the FTC concerning possible unfair or deceptive conduct in foreign jurisdictions.

### 9–1b Domain Names

As e-commerce expanded worldwide, one issue that emerged involved the rights of a trademark owner to use the mark as part of a domain name. A **domain name** is part of an Internet address, such as "cengage.com."

**Structure of Domain Names** Every domain name ends with a top-level domain (TLD), which is the part of the name to the right of the period. The TLD often indicates the type of entity that operates the site. For instance, *com* is an abbreviation for *commercial,* and *edu* is short for *education.*

The second-level domain (SLD)—the part of the name to the left of the period—is chosen by the business entity or individual registering the domain name. Competition for SLDs among firms with similar names and products has led to numerous disputes. By using an identical or similar domain name, parties have attempted to profit from a competitor's **goodwill** (the nontangible value of a business).

**Distribution System** The Internet Corporation for Assigned Names and Numbers (ICANN), a nonprofit corporation, oversees the distribution of domain names and operates an online arbitration system. Due to numerous complaints, ICANN recently overhauled the domain name distribution system.

In 2012, ICANN started selling new generic top-level domain names (gTLDs) for an initial price of $185,000 plus an annual fee of $25,000. Whereas TLDs were limited to only a few terms (such as *com, net,* and *org*), gTLDs can take any form. By 2017, many companies and corporations had acquired gTLDs based on their brands, such as *aol, bmw, canon, target,* and *walmart.* Some companies have numerous gTLDs. Google's gTLDs, for instance, include *android, bing, chrome, gmail, goog,* and *YouTube.*

Because gTLDs have greatly increased the potential number of domain names, domain name registrars have proliferated. Registrar companies charge a fee to businesses and individuals to register new names and to renew annual registrations (often through automated software). Many of these companies also buy and sell expired domain names.

### 9–1c Cybersquatting

One of the goals of the new gTLD system was to address the problem of *cybersquatting.* **Cybersquatting** occurs when a person registers a domain name that is the same as, or confusingly similar to, the trademark of another and then offers to sell the domain name back to the trademark owner.

■ **CASE IN POINT 9.2** Apple, Inc., has repeatedly sued cybersquatters that registered domain names similar to its products, such as iphone4s.com and ipods.com. Apple won a judgment in litigation at the World Intellectual Property Organization against a company that was squatting on the domain name iPhone6s.com.[4] ■

---

3. Pub. L. No. 109-455, 120 Stat. 3372 (2006), codified in various sections of 15 U.S.C. and 12 U.S.C. Section 3412.

4. WIPO Case No. D2012-0951.

**Anticybersquatting Legislation** Because cybersquatting has led to so much litigation, Congress enacted the Anticybersquatting Consumer Protection Act (ACPA),[5] which amended the Lanham Act—the federal law protecting trademarks. The ACPA makes cybersquatting illegal when both of the following are true:

1. The domain name is identical or confusingly similar to the trademark of another.
2. The one registering, trafficking in, or using the domain name has a "bad faith intent" to profit from that trademark.

Despite the ACPA, cybersquatting continues to present a problem for businesses.

**Frequent Changes in Domain Name Ownership Facilitates Cybersquatting** All domain name registrars are supposed to relay information about their transactions to ICANN and other companies that keep a master list of domain names, but this does not always occur. The speed at which domain names change hands and the difficulty in tracking mass automated registrations have created an environment in which cybersquatting can flourish.

■ **CASE IN POINT 9.3** OnNet USA, Inc., owns the English-language rights to 9Dragons, a game with a martial arts theme, and operates a Web site for its promotion. When a party known as "Warv0x" began to operate a pirated version of the game at Play9D.com, OnNet filed an action under the ACPA in a federal court. OnNet was unable to obtain contact information for the owner of Play9D.com through its Australian domain name registrar, however, and thus could not complete service of process. Therefore, the federal court allowed OnNet to serve the defendant by publishing a notice of the suit in a newspaper in Gold Coast, Australia.[6] ■

**Typosquatting** **Typosquatting** is registering a name that is a misspelling of a popular brand, such as googl.com or appple.com. Because many Internet users are not perfect typists, Web pages using these misspelled names receive a lot of traffic. More traffic generally means increased profit (advertisers often pay Web sites based on the number of unique visits, or hits).

Typosquatting may sometimes fall beyond the reach of the ACPA. If the misspelling is significant, the trademark owner may have difficulty proving that the name is identical or confusingly similar to the trademark of another, as the ACPA requires.

---

5. 15 U.S.C. Section 1129.
6. *OnNet USA, Inc. v. Play9D.com*, 2013 WL 120319 (N.D.Cal. 2013).

Typosquatting adds costs for businesses seeking to protect their domain name rights. Companies must attempt to register not only legitimate variations of their domain names but also potential misspellings. Large corporations may have to register thousands of domain names across the globe just to protect their basic brands and trademarks.

**Applicability and Sanctions of the ACPA** The ACPA applies to all domain name registrations of trademarks. Successful plaintiffs in suits brought under the act can collect actual damages and profits, or they can elect to receive statutory damages ranging from $1,000 to $100,000.

Although some companies have been successful suing under the ACPA, there are roadblocks to pursuing such lawsuits. Some domain name registrars offer privacy services that hide the true owners of Web sites, making it difficult for trademark owners to identify cybersquatters. Thus, before bringing a suit, a trademark owner has to ask the court for a subpoena to discover the identity of the owner of the infringing Web site. Because of the high costs of court proceedings, discovery, and even arbitration, many disputes over cybersquatting are settled out of court.

To facilitate dispute resolution, ICANN now offers the Uniform Rapid Suspension (URS) system. URS allows trademark holders with clear-cut infringement claims to obtain rapid relief. ■ **EXAMPLE 9.4** In the first dispute filed involving gTLDs, IBM filed a complaint with URS against an individual who registered the domain names IBM.guru and IBM.ventures in February 2014. A week later, the URS panel decided in IBM's favor and suspended the two domain names. ■

### 9–1d Meta Tags

*Meta tags* are key words that give Internet browsers specific information about a Web page. Meta tags can be used to increase the likelihood that a site will be included in search engine results, even if the site has nothing to do with the key words. In effect, one site can appropriate the key words of other sites with more frequent hits so that the appropriating site will appear in the same search engine results as the more popular sites.

Using another's trademark in a meta tag without the owner's permission normally constitutes trademark infringement. Some uses of another's trademark as a meta tag may be permissible, however, if the use is reasonably necessary and does not suggest that the owner authorized or sponsored the use.

■ **CASE IN POINT 9.5** Farzad and Lisa Tabari are auto brokers—the personal shoppers of the automotive world. They contact authorized dealers, solicit bids, and arrange for customers to buy from the dealer offering the best combination of location, availability, and price. The Tabaris offered this service at the Web sites buy-a-lexus.com and buyorleaselexus.com.

Toyota Motor Sales U.S.A., Inc., the exclusive distributor of Lexus vehicles and the owner of the Lexus mark, objected to the Tabaris' practices. The Tabaris removed Toyota's photographs and logo from their site and added a disclaimer in large type at the top, but they refused to give up their domain names. Toyota sued for infringement. The court forced the Tabaris to stop using any "domain name, service mark, trademark, trade name,

meta tag or other commercial indication of origin that includes the mark LEXUS."[7] ■

## 9–1e Trademark Dilution in the Online World

Trademark *dilution* occurs when a trademark is used, without authorization, in a way that diminishes the distinctive quality of the mark. Unlike trademark infringement, a claim of dilution does not require proof that consumers are likely to be confused by a connection between the unauthorized use and the mark. For this reason, the products involved need not be similar, as the following *Spotlight Case* illustrates.

---

7. *Toyota Motor Sales, U.S.A., Inc. v. Tabari*, 610 F.3d 171 (9th Cir. 2011).

---

## Spotlight on Internet Porn

# Case 9.1 Hasbro, Inc. v. Internet Entertainment Group, Ltd.

United States District Court, Western District of Washington, 1996 WL 84853 (1996).

**Background and Facts** In 1949, Hasbro, Inc.—then known as the Milton Bradley Company—published its first version of Candy Land, a children's board game. Hasbro is the owner of the trademark "Candy Land," which has been registered with the U.S. Patent and Trademark Office since 1951. Over the years, Hasbro has produced several versions of the game, including Candy Land puzzles, a travel version, a computer game, and a handheld electronic version. In the mid-1990s, Brian Cartmell and his employer, the Internet Entertainment Group, Ltd., used the term *candyland.com* as a domain name for a sexually explicit Internet site. Anyone who performed an online search using the word *candyland* was directed to this adult Web site. Hasbro filed a trademark dilution claim in a federal court, seeking a permanent injunction to prevent the defendants from using the Candy Land trademark.

**In the Language of the Court**
*DWYER*, U.S. District Judge
* * * *

2. Hasbro has demonstrated a probability of proving that defendants Internet Entertainment Group, Ltd., Brian Cartmell and Internet Entertainment Group, Inc. (collectively referred to as "defendants") have been diluting the value of Hasbro's CANDY LAND mark by using the name CANDYLAND to identify a sexually explicit Internet site, and by using the name string "candyland.com" as an Internet domain name which, when typed into an Internet-connected computer, provides Internet users with access to that site.
* * * *

4. Hasbro has shown that defendants' use of the CANDY LAND name and the domain name candyland.com in connection with their Internet site is causing irreparable injury to Hasbro.

5. *The probable harm to Hasbro from defendants' conduct outweighs any inconvenience that defendants will experience if they are required to stop using the CANDYLAND name.* [Emphasis added.]
* * * *

THEREFORE, IT IS HEREBY ORDERED that Hasbro's motion for preliminary injunction is granted.

*Case 9.1 Continues*

**Case 9.1 Continued**

**Decision and Remedy** *The federal district court granted Hasbro an injunction against the defendants, agreeing that the domain name* candyland *was "causing irreparable injury to Hasbro." The judge ordered the defendants to immediately remove all content from the* candyland.com *Web site and to stop using the Candy Land mark.*

**Critical Thinking**

- **Economic** *How can companies protect themselves from others who create Web sites that have similar domain names, and what limits each company's ability to be fully protected?*
- **What If the Facts Were Different?** *Suppose that the site using* candyland.com *had not been sexually explicit but had sold candy. Would the result have been the same? Explain.*

## 9–1f Licensing

A company may permit another party to use a trademark (or other intellectual property) under a license. A licensor might grant a license allowing its trademark to be used as part of a domain name, for instance.

Another type of license involves the use of a product such as software. This sort of licensing is ubiquitous in the online world. When you download an application on your smartphone, tablet, or other mobile device, for instance, you are typically entering into a license agreement. You are obtaining only a *license* to use that app and not ownership rights in it. Apps published on Google Play, for instance, may use its licensing service to prompt users to agree to a license at the time of installation and use.

Licensing agreements frequently include restrictions that prohibit licensees from sharing the file and using it to create similar software applications. The license may also limit the use of the application to a specific device or give permission to the user for a certain time period.

## 9–2 Copyrights in Digital Information

Copyright law is probably the most important form of intellectual property protection on the Internet. This is because much of the material on the Internet (including software and database information) is copyrighted, and in order to transfer that material online, it must be "copied." Generally, whenever a party downloads software or music into a computer's random access memory, or RAM, without authorization, a copyright is infringed.

Initially, criminal penalties for copyright violations could be imposed only if unauthorized copies were exchanged for financial gain. Then, Congress amended the law and extended criminal liability for the piracy of copyrighted materials to persons who exchange unauthorized copies of copyrighted works without realizing a profit.

## 9–2a Digital Millennium Copyright Act

In 1998, Congress enacted the Digital Millennium Copyright Act (DMCA).[8] The DMCA gave significant protection to owners of copyrights in digital information. Among other things, the act established civil and criminal penalties for anyone who circumvents (bypasses) encryption software or other technological antipiracy protection. Also prohibited are the manufacture, import, sale, and distribution of devices or services for circumvention.

**Allows Fair Use** The DMCA provides for exceptions to fit the needs of libraries, scientists, universities, and others. In general, the law does not restrict the "fair use" of circumvention methods for educational and other noncommercial purposes. For instance, circumvention is allowed to test computer security, to conduct encryption research, to protect personal privacy, and to enable parents to monitor their children's use of the Internet. The exceptions are to be reconsidered every three years.

One federal appellate court extended the situations in which the fair use doctrine applies. ■ **CASE IN POINT 9.6** Stephanie Lenz posted a short video on YouTube of her toddler son dancing with the Prince song "Let's Go Crazy" playing in the background. Universal Music Group (UMG) sent YouTube a take-down notice that stated that the video violated copyright law under the DMCA. YouTube removed the "dancing baby" video and

---

**8.** 17 U.S.C. Sections 512, 1201–1205, 1301–1332; and 28 U.S.C. Section 4001.

notified Lenz of the allegations of copyright infringement, warning her that repeated incidents of infringement could lead it to delete her account.

Lenz filed a lawsuit against UMG claiming that accusing her of infringement constituted a material misrepresentation (fraud) because UMG knew that Lenz's video was a fair use of the song. The district court held that UMG should have considered the fair use doctrine before sending the take-down notice. UMG appealed, and the U.S. Court of Appeals for the Ninth Circuit affirmed. Lenz was allowed to pursue nominal damages from UMG for sending the notice without considering whether her use was fair.[9] ■

### Limits Liability of Internet Service Providers

The DMCA also limits the liability of Internet service providers (ISPs). Under the act, an ISP is not liable for copyright infringement by its customer *unless* the ISP is aware of the subscriber's violation. An ISP may be held liable only if it fails to take action to shut down the subscriber after learning of the violation. A copyright holder must act promptly, however, by pursuing a claim in court, or the subscriber has the right to be restored to online access.

### 9–2b File-Sharing Technology

Soon after the Internet became popular, a few enterprising programmers created software to compress large data files, particularly those associated with music. The best-known compression and decompression system is MP3, which enables music fans to download songs or entire CDs onto their computers or onto portable listening devices, such as smartphones and tablets. The MP3 system also made it possible for music fans to access other fans' files by engaging in file-sharing via the Internet.

**Methods of File-Sharing** File-sharing is accomplished through **peer-to-peer (P2P) networking.** The concept is simple. Rather than going through a central Web server, P2P networking uses numerous personal computers (PCs) that are connected to the Internet. Individuals on the same network can access files stored on one another's PCs through a **distributed network.** Parts of the network may be distributed all over the country or the world, which offers an unlimited number of uses. Persons scattered throughout the country or the world can work together on the same project by using file-sharing programs.

A newer method of sharing files via the Internet is **cloud computing,** which is essentially a subscription-based or pay-per-use service that extends a computer's software or storage capabilities. Cloud computing can deliver a single application through a browser to multiple users. Alternatively, cloud computing might be a utility program to pool resources and provide data storage and virtual servers that can be accessed on demand. Amazon, Facebook, Google, IBM, and Sun Microsystems are using and developing more cloud computing services.

**Sharing Stored Music and Movies** When file-sharing is used to download others' stored music files, copyright issues arise. Recording artists and their labels stand to lose large amounts of royalties and revenues if relatively few digital downloads or CDs are purchased and then made available on distributed networks. Anyone can get the music for free on these networks, which has prompted recording companies to pursue individuals for file-sharing copyrighted works.

■ **CASE IN POINT 9.7** Maverick Recording Company and other recording companies sued Whitney Harper in federal court for copyright infringement. Harper had used a file-sharing program to download a number of copyrighted songs from the Internet and had then shared the audio files with others via a P2P network. The plaintiffs sought $750 per infringed work—the minimum amount of statutory damages available under the Copyright Act.

Harper claimed that she was an "innocent" infringer because she was unaware that her actions constituted copyright infringement. Under the act, innocent infringement can result in a reduced penalty. The court, however, noted that a copyright notice appeared on all the songs that Harper had downloaded. She therefore could not assert the innocent infringer defense, and the court ordered her to pay damages of $750 per infringed work.[10] ■

**Pirated Movies and Television** File-sharing also creates problems for the motion picture and television industries, which lose significant amounts of revenue annually as a result of piracy. Numerous Web sites offer software that facilitates the illegal copying of movies and television programs. BitTorrent, for instance, is a P2P protocol that enables users to download and transfer high-quality files from the Internet. Popcorn Time is a BitTorent site that offers streaming services that enable users to watch pirated movies and television shows without downloading them.

---

9. *Lenz v. Universal Music Group*, 801 F.3d 1126 (9th Cir. 2015).

10. *Maverick Recording Co. v. Harper*, 598 F.3d 193 (2010).

# 9–3 Social Media

**Social media** provide a means by which people can create, share, and exchange ideas and comments via the Internet. Social networking sites, such as Facebook, Google+, LinkedIn, Pinterest, and Tumblr, have become ubiquitous. Studies show that Internet users spend more time on social networks than at any other sites. The amount of time people spend accessing social networks on their smartphones and other mobile devices has been increasing every year (by nearly 30 percent in 2016 alone).

■ **EXAMPLE 9.8** Facebook has more than 1.6 billion active monthly users. Individuals use Facebook to maintain social contacts, update friends on events, and distribute images to others. Facebook members often share common interests based on their school, location, or recreational affiliation, such as a sports team. ■

## 9–3a Legal Issues

The emergence of Facebook and other social networking sites has created a number of legal and ethical issues for businesses. For instance, a firm's rights in valuable intellectual property may be infringed if users post trademarked images or copyrighted materials on these sites without permission. Various aspects of the legal process may involve the content of social media, as discussed next. Employers' social media policies may also be at issue.

**Impact on Litigation** Social media posts now are routinely included in discovery in litigation because they can provide damaging information that establishes a person's intent or what she or he knew at a particular time. Like e-mail, posts on social networks can be the smoking gun that leads to liability.

Tweets and other social media posts can also be used to reduce damages awards. ■ **EXAMPLE 9.9** Jill Daniels sued for injuries she sustained in a car accident, claiming that her injuries made it impossible for her to continue working as a hairstylist. The jury initially determined that her damages were $237,000, but when the jurors saw tweets and photographs of Daniels partying in New Orleans and vacationing on the beach, they reduced the final award to $142,000. ■

**Impact on Settlement Agreements** Social media posts have been used to invalidate settlement agreements that contain confidentiality clauses. ■ **CASE IN POINT 9.10** Patrick Snay was the headmaster of Gulliver Preparatory School in Florida. When Gulliver did not renew

Snay's employment contract, Snay sued the school for age discrimination. During mediation, Snay agreed to settle the case for $80,000 and signed a confidentiality clause that required him and his wife not to disclose the "terms and existence" of the agreement. Nevertheless, Snay and his wife told their daughter, Dana, that the dispute had been settled and that they were happy with the results.

Dana, a college student, had recently graduated from Gulliver and, according to Snay, had suffered retaliation at the school. Dana posted a Facebook comment that said "Mama and Papa Snay won the case against Gulliver. Gulliver is now officially paying for my vacation to Europe this summer. SUCK IT." The comment went out to 1,200 of Dana's Facebook friends, many of whom were Gulliver students, and school officials soon learned of it. The school immediately notified Snay that he had breached the confidentiality clause and refused to pay the settlement amount. Ultimately, a state intermediate appellate court held that Snay had breached the confidentiality clause and therefore could not enforce the settlement agreement.[11] ■

**Criminal Investigations** Law enforcement uses social media to detect and prosecute criminals. A surprising number of criminals boast about their illegal activities on social media. ■ **EXAMPLE 9.11** A nineteen-year-old posts a message on Facebook bragging about how drunk he was on New Year's Eve and apologizing to the owner of the parked car that he hit. The next day, police officers arrest him for drunk driving and leaving the scene of an accident. ■

Some police departments now authorize officers to go undercover on social media sites. ■ **EXAMPLE 9.12** As part of Operation Crew Cut, New York Police Department (NYPD) officers routinely pretend to be young women in order to "friend" suspects on Facebook. Using these fake identities, officers are able to avoid the social media site's privacy settings and gain valuable information about illegal activities. ■

**Administrative Agency Investigations** Federal regulators also use social media posts in their investigations into illegal activities. ■ **EXAMPLE 9.13** Reed Hastings, the top executive of Netflix, stated on Facebook that Netflix subscribers had watched a billion hours of video the previous month. As a result, Netflix's stock price rose, which prompted a federal agency investigation. Under securities laws, such a statement is considered to be material information to investors. Thus, it must be disclosed to

---

11. *Gulliver Schools, Inc. v. Snay*, 137 So.3d 1045 (Fla.App. 2014).

all investors, not just a select group, such as those who had access to Hastings's Facebook post.

The agency ultimately concluded that it could not hold Hastings responsible for any wrongdoing because the agency's policy on social media use was not clear. The agency then issued new guidelines that allow companies to disclose material information through social media if investors have been notified in advance. ■

In addition, an administrative law judge can base her or his decision on the content of social media posts. ■ **CASE IN POINT 9.14** Jennifer O'Brien was a tenured teacher at a public school in New Jersey when she posted two messages on her Facebook page. "I'm not a teacher—I'm a warden for future criminals!" and "They had a scared straight program in school—why couldn't I bring first graders?" Not surprisingly, outraged parents protested. The deputy superintendent of schools filed a complaint against O'Brien with the state's commissioner of education, charging her with conduct unbecoming a teacher.

After a hearing, an administrative law judge (ALJ) ordered that O'Brien be removed from her teaching position. O'Brien appealed to a state court, claiming that her Facebook postings were protected by the First Amendment and could not be used by the school district to discipline or discharge her. The court found that O'Brien had failed to establish that her Facebook postings were protected speech and that the seriousness of O'Brien's conduct warranted removal from her position.[12] ■

**Employers' Social Media Policies** Many large corporations have established specific guidelines on using social media in the workplace. Employees who use social media in a way that violates their employer's stated policies may be disciplined or fired from their jobs. Courts and administrative agencies usually uphold an employer's right to terminate a person based on his or her violation of a social media policy.

■ **CASE IN POINT 9.15** Virginia Rodriquez worked for Wal-Mart Stores, Inc., for almost twenty years and had been promoted to management. Then she was disciplined for violating the company's policies by having a fellow employee use Rodriquez's password to alter the price of an item that she purchased. Under Wal-Mart's rules, another violation within a year would mean termination.

Nine months later, on Facebook, Rodriquez publicly chastised employees under her supervision for calling in sick to go to a party. The posting violated Wal-Mart's "Social Media Policy," which was "to avoid public comment that adversely affects employees." Wal-Mart

terminated Rodriquez. She filed a lawsuit, alleging discrimination, but the court issued a summary judgment in Wal-Mart's favor.[13] ■

## 9–3b The Electronic Communications Privacy Act

The Electronic Communications Privacy Act (ECPA)[14] amended federal wiretapping law to cover electronic forms of communications. Although Congress enacted the ECPA many years before social media networks existed, it nevertheless applies to communications through social media.

The ECPA prohibits the intentional interception of any wire, oral, or electronic communication. It also prohibits the intentional disclosure or use of the information obtained by the interception.

**Exclusions** Excluded from the ECPA's coverage are any electronic communications through devices that an employer provides for its employee to use "in the ordinary course of its business." Consequently, if a company provides the electronic device (cell phone, laptop, tablet) to the employee for ordinary business use, the company is not prohibited from intercepting business communications made on it. This "business-extension exception" permits employers to monitor employees' electronic communications made in the ordinary course of business. It does not, however, permit employers to monitor employees' personal communications.

Another exception to the ECPA allows an employer to avoid liability under the act if the employees consent to having their electronic communications monitored by the employer.

**Stored Communications** Part of the ECPA is known as the Stored Communications Act (SCA).[15] The SCA prohibits intentional and unauthorized access to *stored* electronic communications and sets forth criminal and civil sanctions for violators. A person can violate the SCA by intentionally accessing a stored electronic communication. The SCA also prevents "providers" of communication services (such as cell phone companies and social media networks) from divulging private communications to certain entities and individuals.

■ **CASE IN POINT 9.16** Two restaurant employees, Brian Pietrylo and Doreen Marino, were fired after their manager uncovered their password-protected MySpace group. The group's communications, stored on MySpace's

12. *In re O'Brien*, 2013 WL 132508 (N.J. Sup. 2013).

13. *Rodriquez v. Wal-Mart Stores, Inc.*, 2013 WL 102674 (N.D. Tex. 2013).
14. 18 U.S.C. Sections 2510–2521.
15. 18 U.S.C. Sections 2701–2711.

Web site, contained sexual remarks about customers and management, as well as comments about illegal drug use and violent behavior. One employee said the group's purpose was to "vent about any BS we deal with out of work without any outside eyes spying on us."

The restaurant learned about the private MySpace group when a hostess showed it to a manager who requested access. The hostess was not explicitly threatened with termination but feared she would lose her job if she did not comply.

After they were fired, Pietrylo and Marino filed a lawsuit against the restaurant. They claimed that their former employer had gained unauthorized access to their MySpace group communications in violation of the SCA. The court allowed the employees' SCA claim, and the jury awarded them $17,003 in compensatory and punitive damages.[16] ■

### 9–3c Protection of Social Media Passwords

In recent years, employees and applicants for jobs or colleges have sometimes been asked to divulge their social media passwords. An employer or school may look at an individual's Facebook or other account to see if it includes controversial postings such as racially discriminatory remarks or photos of drug parties. Such postings can have a negative effect on a person's prospects even if they were made years earlier or are taken out of context.

By 2017, about half of the states had enacted legislation to protect individuals from having to disclose their social media passwords. Each state's law is slightly different. Some states, such as Michigan, prohibit employers from taking adverse action against an employee or job applicant based on what the person has posted online. Michigan's law also applies to e-mail and cloud storage accounts.

Legislation will not completely prevent employers and others from taking actions against a person based on his or her social network postings, though. Management and human resources personnel are unlikely to admit that they looked at someone's Facebook page and that it influenced their decision. They may not even have to admit to looking at the Facebook page if they use private browsing, which enables people to keep their Web browsing activities confidential. How, then, would a rejected job applicant be able to prove that she or he was rejected because the employer accessed social media postings? See this chapter's *Digital Update* feature for a discussion of employer monitoring of social media.

---

16. *Pietrylo v. Hillstone Restaurant Group*, 2009 WL 3128420 (D.N.J. 2009).

### 9–3d Company-wide Social Media Networks

Many companies, including Dell, Inc., and Nikon Instruments, form their own internal social media networks. Software companies offer a variety of systems, including Salesforce.com's Chatter, Microsoft's Yammer, and Cisco Systems' WebEx Social. Posts on these internal networks, or *intranets,* are quite different from the typical posts on Facebook, LinkedIn, and Twitter. Employees use these intranets to exchange messages about topics related to their work, such as deals that are closing, new products, production flaws, how a team is solving a problem, and the details of customer orders. Thus, the tone is businesslike.

**Protection of Trade Secrets** An important advantage to using an internal system for employee communications is that the company can better protect its trade secrets. The company usually decides which employees can see particular intranet files and which employees will belong to each specific "social" group within the company. Companies providing internal social media networks often keep the resulting data on their own servers in secure "clouds."

**Other Advantages** Internal social media systems also offer additional benefits. They provide real-time information about important issues, such as production glitches. Additionally, posts can include tips on how to best sell new products or deal with difficult customers, as well as information about competitors' products and services. Another major benefit is a significant reduction in e-mail. Rather than wasting fellow employees' time reading mass e-mailings, workers can post messages or collaborate on presentations via the company's social network.

---

## 9–4 Online Defamation

**Cyber torts** are torts that arise from online conduct. One of the most prevalent cyber torts is online defamation. Defamation is wrongfully hurting a person's reputation by communicating false statements about that person to others. Because the Internet enables individuals to communicate with large numbers of people simultaneously (via a blog or tweet, for instance), online defamation has become a problem in today's legal environment.

■ **EXAMPLE 9.17** Singer-songwriter Courtney Love was sued for defamation based on remarks she posted

## DIGITAL UPDATE — Monitoring Employees' Social Media—Right or Wrong?

Just about everyone seems to be using some form of social media. That, of course, includes employees. Increasingly, employees' social media use is being monitored by their employers. Sometimes, employees are even being fired over their social media posts.

### Monitoring of Employees' Social Media Use

Employers have monitored their employees' Internet use for years. According to Gartner, Inc., an information technology advisory company, employers are now using the same technology to examine workers' social media use.

Companies have a number of concerns about how their employees use social media. For one thing, they may worry about security problems, such as employees' posting unauthorized videos of company activities. In addition, they do not wish to have their clients discussed on employees' social media posts. Finally, some companies are concerned that certain posts may violate the law. For instance, if hospital employees discuss patients, they not only are disregarding hospital regulations, but also are violating the federal Health Insurance Portability and Accountability Act (HIPAA).[a]

### Restrictions on Access to Employees' Social Media Records

In disputes over discrimination, hostile work environment, and other employment situations, employers typically seek access to certain employees' complete social media records. The courts have not uniformly accepted such access.[b] The general rule is that during any dispute, courts require employers to demonstrate a "reasonable" need for social media evidence. So-called fishing expeditions are rarely allowed.

But what about regular monitoring of employee online behavior? As long as an employee has no expectation of privacy on the social media site and is not part of a protected class, courts will side with employers. After all, social media posts are public, even when privacy settings are enabled. Note, though, that whenever employer monitoring involves obtaining information about religious affiliation, sexual orientation, or pregnancies, litigation may ensue.

The rule of thumb is that the more personal the information about any employee, the more problematic social media monitoring becomes. As one expert in the field stated, "Recent cases teach that when a company decides to monitor employee behavior online, uncertainty takes over."[c]

**Critical Thinking** *Some companies use internal social media networks for work-related employee communications. Would the same legal rules that apply to monitoring public social media platforms, such as Twitter and Facebook, also apply to company-provided social media platforms?*

a. Pub. L. No. 104-191 (1996); 29 U.S.C. Sections 1181 *et seq.*

b. *Ogden v. All-State Career School*, 299 F.R.D. 446 (2014). See also *Appler v. Mead Johnson & Co., LLC*, 2015 WL 5615038, and *In re Milo's Kitchen Dog Treats Consol*, 307 F.R.D. 177 (2015).

c. Rodney Satterwhite, "'Friend' or Foe? Balancing the Litigation Risks of Monitoring Employees' Social Media Profiles at Various Stages of Employment," 2014 WL 5465794 (2014).

about fashion designer Dawn Simorangkir on Twitter. Love claimed that her statements were statements of opinion (rather than statements of fact, as required) and therefore were not actionable as defamation. Nevertheless, Love ended up paying $430,000 to settle the case out of court. ∎

## 9–4a Identifying the Author of Online Defamation

An initial issue raised by online defamation is simply discovering who is committing it. In the real world, identifying the author of a defamatory remark generally is an easy matter. It is more difficult if a business firm discovers that defamatory statements about its policies and products are being posted in an online forum, because the postings are anonymous. Therefore, a threshold barrier to anyone who seeks to bring an action for online defamation is discovering the identity of the person who posted the defamatory message.

An Internet service provider (ISP) can disclose personal information about its customers only when ordered to do so by a court. Consequently, businesses and individuals are increasingly bringing lawsuits against "John Does" (John Doe, Jane Doe, and the like are fictitious names used in lawsuits when the identity of a party is not known or when a party wishes to conceal his or her name for privacy reasons). Then, using the authority of the courts, the plaintiffs can obtain from the ISPs the identity of the persons responsible for the defamatory messages.

■ **CASE IN POINT 9.18** Seven users of Yelp, Inc.—a social networking Web site for consumer reviews—posted negative reviews of Hadeed Carpet Cleaning, Inc., in Alexandria, Virginia. Hadeed brought a defamation suit against the "John Doe" reviewers in a Virginia state court, claiming that because these individuals were not actual customers, their comments were false and defamatory. Yelp failed to comply with a court order to reveal the users' identities and was held in contempt.

Yelp appealed, claiming that releasing the identities would violate the defendants' First Amendment right to free speech. A state intermediate appellate court affirmed the lower court's judgment, noting that Hadeed could not move forward with its defamation lawsuit unless it knew the identities of the defendants. Revealing the identities of Yelp reviewers was not a violation of their First Amendment rights.[17] ■

### 9–4b Liability of Internet Service Providers

Recall that under tort law those who repeat or otherwise republish a defamatory statement are normally subject to liability. Thus, newspapers, magazines, and television and radio stations are subject to liability for defamatory content that they publish or broadcast, even though the content was prepared or created by others. Applying this rule to cyberspace, however, raises an important issue: Should ISPs be regarded as publishers and therefore be held liable for defamatory messages that are posted by their users?

**General Rule** The Communications Decency Act (CDA) states that "[n]o provider or user of an interactive computer service shall be treated as the publisher or speaker of any information provided by another information content provider."[18] Thus, under the CDA, ISPs usually are treated differently from publishers in print and other media and are not liable for publishing defamatory statements that come from a third party.

**Exceptions** Although the courts generally have construed the CDA as providing a broad shield to protect ISPs from liability for third party content, some courts have started establishing limits to this immunity. ■ **CASE IN POINT 9.19** Roommate.com, LLC, operates an online roommate-matching Web site that helps individuals find roommates based on their descriptions of themselves and their roommate preferences. Users respond to a series of online questions, choosing from answers in drop-down and select-a-box menus.

Some of the questions asked users to disclose their sex, family status, and sexual orientation—which is not permitted under the federal Fair Housing Act. When a nonprofit housing organization sued Roommate.com, the company claimed it was immune from liability under the CDA. A federal appellate court disagreed and ruled that Roommate.com was not immune from liability. By creating the Web site and the questionnaire and answer choices, Roommate.com prompted users to express discriminatory preferences and matched users based on these preferences in violation of federal law.[19] ■

## 9–5 Other Actions Involving Online Posts

Online conduct can give rise to a wide variety of legal actions. E-mails, tweets, posts, and every sort of online communication can form the basis for almost any type of tort. For example, in addition to defamation, suits relating to online conduct may involve allegations of wrongful interference or infliction of emotional distress.

Besides actions grounded in the common law, online conduct may give rise to a cause of action directed expressly at online communications by a statute. In the following case, the court was asked to issue an injunction to prohibit speech that was alleged to constitute *cyberstalking*. The applicable statute defined this term to require, in part, "substantial emotional distress."

---

**17.** *Yelp, Inc. v. Hadeed Carpet Cleaning, Inc.*, 62 Va.App. 678, 752 S.E.2d 554 (2014).

**18.** 47 U.S.C. Section 230.

**19.** *Fair Housing Council of San Fernando Valley v. Roommate.com, LLC*, 666 F.3d 1216 (9th Cir. 2012).

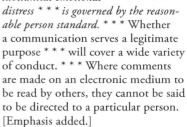

# David v. Textor

District Court of Appeal of Florida, Fourth District, 41 Fla.L.Weekly D131, __ So.3d __ (2016).

## In the Language of the Court

WARNER, J. [Judge].

\* \* \* \*

[Alkiviades] David and [John] Textor both have companies which produce holograms used in the music industry. \* \* \* Shortly before the Billboard Music Awards show, it was announced that Textor's company, Pulse Entertainment, would show a Michael Jackson hologram performance. Immediately thereafter, David's company, Hologram USA, Inc., \* \* \* filed suit for patent infringement against Pulse in the U.S. District Court in Nevada \* \* \*. Pulse countered by filing a business tort suit against David in California.

[One month later,] Textor filed a petition [in a Florida state court against David under Florida Statutes] Sections 784.046 and 784.0485, which concern cyberstalking.

The alleged acts of cyberstalking were (1) a \* \* \* text from David to Textor, demanding that Textor give credit to David's company at the Billboard Awards show for the hologram, for which David would drop his patent infringement suit; otherwise, he threatened to increase damages in that suit and stated, "You will be ruined I promise you"; (2) an e-mail from David to business associates (other than Textor) that he had more information about Textor that would be released soon, but not specifying what that information was; (3) an online article from July 2014 on Entrepreneur.com, in which David was quoted as saying that he "would have killed [Textor] if he could"; and (4) articles about Textor that David posted and reposted in various online outlets.

\* \* \* \*

The trial court [issued an injunction] prohibiting David from communicating with Textor or posting any information about him online, and ordering that

he remove any materials he already had posted.

David \* \* \* moved to dissolve the \* \* \* injunction. \* \* \* The court denied the motion to dissolve and amended its order to prohibit David from communicating with Textor either through electronic means, in person, or through third parties. The amended order also provided:

> Respondent David shall immediately cease and desist from sending any text messages, e-mails, posting any tweets (including the re-tweeting or forwarding), posting any images or other forms of communication directed at John Textor without a legitimate purpose. Threats or warnings of physical or emotional harm or attempts to extort Textor or any entity associated with Textor by Respondent David, personally or through his agents, directed to John Textor, directly or by other means, are prohibited.

From this order, David appeals. David claims that none of the allegations in the petition constitute cyberstalking, but are merely heated rhetoric over a business dispute. Further, he claims that the injunction constitutes a prior restraint on speech, which violates the First Amendment.

[Florida Statutes] Section 784.0485 allows an injunction against \* \* \* cyberstalking. \* \* \* Section 784.048 defines \* \* \* cyberstalking:

> \* \* \* "Cyberstalk" means to engage in a course of conduct to communicate, or to cause to be communicated, words, images, or language by or through the use of electronic mail or electronic communication, directed at a specific person, causing substantial emotional distress to that person and serving no legitimate purpose.

*Whether a communication causes substantial emotional distress \* \* \* is governed by the reasonable person standard.* \* \* \* Whether a communication serves a legitimate purpose \* \* \* will cover a wide variety of conduct. \* \* \* Where comments are made on an electronic medium to be read by others, they cannot be said to be directed to a particular person. [Emphasis added.]

In this case, Textor alleged that two communications came directly from David to him, both of which were demands that Textor drop his lawsuit. In neither of them did David make any threat to Textor's safety. From the full e-mail, David's threats that Textor would be "sorry" if he didn't settle must be taken in the context of the lawsuit and its potential cost to Textor. Because of the existence of the various lawsuits and the heated controversy over the hologram patents, these e-mails had a legitimate purpose in trying to get Textor to drop what David considered a spurious lawsuit. Moreover, nothing in the e-mails should have caused substantial emotional distress to Textor, himself a sophisticated businessman. Indeed, that they did not is reflected in Textor's refusal to settle or adhere to their terms.

The postings online are also not communications which would cause substantial emotional distress. Most of them are simply re-tweets of articles or headlines involving Textor. That they may be embarrassing to Textor is not at all the same as causing him substantial emotional distress sufficient to obtain an injunction.

Even the alleged physical threat made by David in an online interview, that David would have killed Textor if he could have, would not cause a reasonable person substantial emotional distress.

**Case 9.2 Continues**

**Case 9.2 Continued**

In the online article the author stated that "David joked" when stating that he would have killed Textor. Spoken to a journalist for publication, it hardly amounts to an actual and credible threat of violence to Textor.

In sum, none of the allegations in Textor's petition show acts constituting cyberstalking, in that a reasonable person would not suffer substantial emotional distress over them. Those communications made directly to Textor served a legitimate purpose.

An injunction in this case would also violate [the freedom of speech under the U.S. Constitution's First Amendment. An] injunction directed to speech is a classic example of prior restraint on speech triggering First Amendment concerns. * * * *Prior restraints on speech and publication are the most serious and the least tolerable infringement on First Amendment rights.* [Florida Statutes] Section 784.048 itself recognizes the First Amendment rights of individuals by concluding that a "course of conduct" for

purposes of the statute does not include protected speech. [Emphasis added.]

Here, the online postings simply provide information, gleaned from other sources, regarding Textor and the many lawsuits against him. The injunction prevents not only communications *to* Textor, but also communications *about* Textor. Such prohibition by prior restraint violates the Constitution.

For the foregoing reasons, we reverse the * * * injunction and remand with directions to dismiss the petition.

**Legal Reasoning Questions**

1. How is *cyberstalking* defined by the statute in this case, and what conduct by the defendant allegedly fit this definition?

2. What standard determines whether certain conduct meets the requirements of the cyberstalking statute? What law or legal principle limits an injunction that is directed at speech?

3. Why did the court in this case "reverse the . . . injunction and remand with directions to dismiss the petition"? Explain.

## 9–6 Privacy

Online businesses have been accused of violating users' privacy rights. The courts have held that the right to privacy is guaranteed by the Bill of Rights and some state constitutions. To maintain a suit for the invasion of privacy, though, a person must have a reasonable expectation of privacy in the particular situation.

### 9–6a Reasonable Expectation of Privacy

People clearly have a reasonable expectation of privacy when they enter their personal banking or credit-card information online. They also have a reasonable expectation that online companies will follow their own privacy policies. But it is probably not reasonable to expect privacy in statements made on Twitter—or photos posted on Twitter, Flickr, or Instagram, for that matter.

Sometimes, to be sure, people mistakenly believe that they are making statements or posting photos in a private forum. ■ **EXAMPLE 9.20** Randi Zuckerberg, the older sister of Mark Zuckerberg (the founder of Facebook), used a mobile app called "Poke" to post a "private" photo on Facebook of their family gathering during the holidays. Poke allows the sender to decide how long the photo can be seen by others. Facebook allows users to configure their privacy settings to limit access to photos, which Randi thought she had done. Nonetheless, the photo showed up in the Facebook feed of Callie Schweitzer, who then put it on Twitter, where it eventually "went viral." Schweitzer apologized and removed the photo, but it had already gone public for the world to see. ■

In the following case, the court considered whether a Facebook user's expectation of privacy in photos that she posted on the site was reasonable.

Case 9.3

## Nucci v. Target Corp.

District Court of Appeal of Florida, Fourth District, 162 So.3d 146 (2015).

**Background and Facts** Maria Nucci filed a suit in a Florida state court against Target Corporation, alleging that she suffered an injury when she slipped and fell on a "foreign substance" on the floor of a Target store. Target filed a motion to compel an inspection of Nucci's Facebook profile, which

**Case 9.3 Continued**

included 1,249 photos. Target argued that it was entitled to view the profile because Nucci's lawsuit put her physical and mental condition at issue.

Nucci responded that her Facebook page's privacy setting prevented the general public from having access to it. She claimed that she had a reasonable expectation of privacy in the profile and that Target's access would invade that privacy right. The court issued an order to compel discovery of certain photos, including some on Nucci's Facebook page, that were relevant to her physical and mental condition before and following the alleged injury. Nucci petitioned a state intermediate appellate court for relief from the order.

## In the Language of the Court

*GROSS*, J. [Judge]
* * * *

*In a personal injury case* * * * *, the fact-finder is required to examine the quality of the plaintiff's life before and after the accident to determine the extent of the loss.* From testimony alone, it is often difficult for the fact-finder to grasp what a plaintiff's life was like prior to an accident. It would take a great novelist, a Tolstoy, a Dickens, or a Hemingway, to use words to summarize the totality of a prior life. If a photograph is worth a thousand words, *there is no better portrayal of what an individual's life was like than those photographs the individual has chosen to share through social media before the occurrence of an accident causing injury.* Such photographs are the equivalent of a "day in the life" slide show produced by the plaintiff before the existence of any motive to manipulate reality. [Emphasis added.]
* * * *

The Florida Constitution expressly protects an individual's right to privacy. * * * The right to privacy in the Florida Constitution ensures that individuals are able to determine for themselves when, how and to what extent information about them is communicated to others.

Before the right to privacy attaches, there must exist a legitimate expectation of privacy. * * *

* * * Social networking sites, such as Facebook, are free websites where an individual creates a "profile" which functions as a personal Web page and may include, at the user's discretion, numerous photos and a vast array of personal information including age, employment, education, religious and political views and various recreational interests. Once a user joins a social networking site, he or she can use the site to search for "friends" and create linkages to others based on similar interests.
* * * *

* * * *Generally, the photographs posted on a social networking site are neither privileged nor protected by any right of privacy, regardless of any privacy settings that the user may have established.* Such posted photographs are unlike medical records or communications with one's attorney, where disclosure is confined to narrow, confidential relationships. Facebook itself does not guarantee privacy. By creating a Facebook account, a user acknowledges that her personal information would be shared with others. Indeed, that is the very nature and purpose of these social networking sites else they would cease to exist. [Emphasis added.]

* * * The expectation that such information is private, in the traditional sense of the word, is not a reasonable one.

**Decision and Remedy** *The state intermediate appellate denied Nucci's petition for relief from the order to compel discovery of her Facebook photos. The court concluded that "the photographs sought were reasonably calculated to lead to the discovery of admissible evidence, and Nucci's privacy interest in them was minimal."*

### Critical Thinking

- **What If the Facts Were Different?** *Suppose that Target had asked for a much broader range of Facebook material that concerned not just Nucci's physical and mental condition at the time of her alleged injury but also her personal relationships with her family, romantic partners, and significant others. Would the result have been the same? Discuss.*
- **Ethical** *Would a court also allow Target discovery of Facebook photos that were posted by Nucci's friends and family? Why or why not?*

## 9–6b Data Collection and Cookies

Whenever a consumer purchases items online from a retailer, such as Amazon.com or Best Buy, the retailer collects information about the consumer. **Cookies** are invisible files that computers, smartphones, and other mobile devices create to track a user's Web browsing activities. Cookies provide detailed information to marketers about an individual's behavior and preferences, which is then used to personalize online services.

Over time, a retailer can amass considerable data about a person's shopping habits. Does collecting this information violate a consumer's right to privacy? Should retailers be able to pass on the data they have collected to their affiliates? Should they be able to use the information to predict what a consumer might want and then create online "coupons" customized to fit the person's buying history?

■ **EXAMPLE 9.21** Facebook, Inc., once used a targeted advertising technique called "Sponsored Stories." An ad would display a Facebook friend's name and profile picture, along with a statement that the friend "likes" the company sponsoring the advertisement. A group of plaintiffs filed suit, claiming that Facebook had used their pictures for advertising without their permission. When a federal court refused to dismiss the case, Facebook agreed to settle. ■

## 9–6c Internet Companies' Privacy Policies

The Federal Trade Commission (FTC) investigates consumer complaints of privacy violations. The FTC has forced many companies, including Google, Facebook, Twitter, and MySpace, to enter a consent decree that gives the FTC broad power to review their privacy and data practices. It can then sue companies that violate the terms of the decree.

■ **EXAMPLE 9.22** In 2012, Google settled a suit brought by the FTC alleging that it had misused data from Apple's Safari users. Google allegedly had used cookies to trick the Safari browser on iPhones and iPads so that Google could monitor users who had blocked such tracking. This violated the company's consent decree with the FTC. Google agreed to pay $22.5 million to settle the suit without admitting liability. ■

Facebook has faced a number of complaints about its privacy policy and has changed its policy several times to satisfy its critics and ward off potential government investigations. Other companies, including mobile app developers, have also changed their privacy policies to provide more information to consumers. Consequently, it is frequently the companies, rather than courts or legislatures, that are defining the privacy rights of their online users.

## Reviewing: Internet Law, Social Media, and Privacy

While he was in high school, Joel Gibb downloaded numerous songs to his smartphone from an unlicensed file-sharing service. He used portions of the copyrighted songs when he recorded his own band and posted videos on YouTube and Facebook. Gibb also used BitTorrent to download several movies from the Internet. Now he has applied to Boston University. The admissions office has requested access to his Facebook password, and he has complied. Using the information presented in the chapter, answer the following questions.

1. What laws, if any, did Gibb violate by downloading the music and videos from the Internet?
2. Was Gibb's use of portions of copyrighted songs in his own music illegal? Explain.
3. Can individuals legally post copyrighted content on their Facebook pages? Why or why not?
4. Did Boston University violate any laws when it asked Joel to provide his Facebook password? Explain.

**Debate This** . . . *Internet service providers should be subject to the same defamation laws as newspapers, magazines, and television and radio stations.*

## Terms and Concepts

| | | |
|---|---|---|
| cloud computing 175 | distributed network 175 | peer-to-peer (P2P) networking 175 |
| cookie 184 | domain name 171 | social media 176 |
| cybersquatting 171 | goodwill 171 | spam 170 |
| cyber tort 178 | Internet service provider (ISP) 171 | typosquatting 172 |

## Issue Spotters

1. Karl self-publishes a cookbook titled *Hole Foods*, in which he sets out recipes for donuts, Bundt cakes, tortellini, and other foods with holes. To publicize the book, Karl designs the Web site holefoods.com. Karl appropriates the key words of other cooking and cookbook sites with more frequent hits so that holefoods.com will appear in the same search engine results as the more popular sites. Has Karl done anything wrong? Explain. (See *Internet Law*.)

2. Eagle Corporation began marketing software in 2007 under the mark "Eagle." In 2017, Eagle.com, Inc., a different company selling different products, begins to use *eagle* as part of its URL and registers it as a domain name. Can Eagle Corporation stop this use of *eagle*? If so, what must the company show? (See *Internet Law*.)

• **Check your answers to the Issue Spotters against the answers provided in Appendix D at the end of this text.**

## Business Scenarios

**9–1. Internet Service Providers.** CyberConnect, Inc., is an Internet service provider (ISP). Pepper is a CyberConnect subscriber. Market Reach, Inc., is an online advertising company. Using sophisticated software, Market Reach directs its ads to those users most likely to be interested in a particular product. When Pepper receives one of the ads, she objects to the content. Further, she claims that CyberConnect should pay damages for "publishing" the ad. Is the ISP regarded as a publisher and therefore liable for the content of Market Reach's ad? Why or why not? (See *Online Defamation*.)

**9–2. Privacy.** SeeYou, Inc., is an online social network. SeeYou's members develop personalized profiles to interact and share information—photos, videos, stories, activity updates, and other items—with other members. Members post the information that they want to share and decide with whom they want to share it. SeeYou launched a program to allow members to share with others what they do elsewhere online. For example, if a member rents a movie through Netflix, SeeYou will broadcast that information to everyone in the member's online network. How can SeeYou avoid complaints that this program violates its members' privacy? (See *Privacy*.)

## Business Case Problems

**9–3. Business Case Problem with Sample Answer—Privacy.**  Using special software, South Dakota law enforcement officers found a person who appeared to possess child pornography at a specific Internet address. The officers subpoenaed Midcontinent Communications, the service that assigned the address, for the personal information of its subscriber. With this information, the officers obtained a search warrant for the residence of John Rolfe, where they found a laptop that contained child pornography. Rolfe argued that the subpoenas violated his "expectation of privacy." Did Rolfe have a privacy interest in the information obtained by the subpoenas issued to Midcontinent? Discuss. [*State of South Dakota v. Rolfe*, 825 N.W.2d 901 (S.Dak. 2013)] (See *Privacy*.)

• **For a sample answer to Problem 9–3, go to Appendix E at the end of this text.**

**9–4. File-Sharing.** Dartmouth College professor M. Eric Johnson, in collaboration with Tiversa, Inc., a company that monitors peer-to-peer networks to provide security services, wrote an article titled "Data Hemorrhages in the Health-Care Sector." In preparing the article, Johnson and Tiversa searched the networks for data that could be used to commit medical or financial identity theft. They found a document that contained the Social Security numbers, insurance information, and treatment codes for patients of LabMD, Inc. Tiversa notified LabMD of the find in order to solicit its business. Instead of hiring Tiversa, however, LabMD filed a suit in a federal district court against the company, alleging trespass, conversion, and violations of federal statutes. What do these facts indicate about the security of private information? Explain. How should the court rule? [*LabMD, Inc. v. Tiversa, Inc.*, 2013 WL 425983 (11th Cir. 2013)] (See *Copyrights in Digital Information*.)

**9–5. Social Media.** Mohammad Omar Aly Hassan and nine others were indicted in a federal district court on charges of conspiring to advance violent jihad (holy war against enemies of Islam) and other offenses related to terrorism. The evidence at Hassan's trial included postings he made on Facebook concerning his adherence to violent jihadist ideology. Convicted, Hassan appealed, contending that the Facebook items had not been properly authenticated (established as his own comments). How might the government show the connection between postings on Facebook and those who post them? Discuss. [*United States v. Hassan*, 742 F.3d 104 (4th Cir. 2014)] (See *Social Media*.)

**9–6. Social Media.** Kenneth Wheeler was angry at certain police officers in Grand Junction, Colorado, because of a driving-under-the-influence arrest that he viewed as unjust. While in Italy, Wheeler posted a statement to his Facebook page urging his "religious followers" to "kill cops, drown them in the blood of their children, hunt them down and kill their entire bloodlines" and provided names. Later, Wheeler added a post to "commit a massacre in the

Stepping Stones preschool and day care, just walk in and kill everybody." Could a reasonable person conclude that Wheeler's posts were true threats? How might law enforcement officers use Wheeler's posts? Explain. [*United States v. Wheeler,* 776 F.3d 736 (10th Cir. 2015)] (See *Social Media.*)

**9–7. Social Media.** Irvin Smith was charged in a Georgia state court with burglary and theft. Before the trial, during the selection of the jury, the state prosecutor asked the prospective jurors whether they knew Smith. No one responded affirmatively. Jurors were chosen and sworn in, without objection. After the trial, during deliberations, the jurors indicated to the court that they were deadlocked. The court charged them to try again. Meanwhile, the prosecutor learned that "Juror 4" appeared as a friend on the defendant's Facebook page and filed a motion to dismiss her. The court replaced Juror 4 with an alternate. Was this an appropriate action, or was it an "abuse of discretion"? Should the court have admitted evidence that Facebook friends do not always actually know each other? Discuss. [*Smith v. State of Georgia,* 335 Ga.App. 497, 782 S.E.2d 305 (2016)] (See *Social Media.*)

**9–8. A Question of Ethics—Criminal Investigations.**

*After the unauthorized release and posting of classified U.S. government documents to WikiLeaks.org, allegedly involving Bradley Manning, a U.S. Army private first class, the U.S. government began a criminal investigation. The government obtained a court order to require Twitter, Inc., to turn over subscriber information and communications to and from the e-mail addresses of Birgitta Jonsdottir and others. The court sealed the order and the other documents in the case, reasoning that "there exists no right to public notice of all the types of documents filed in a . . . case." Jonsdottir and the others appealed this decision. [*In re* Application of the United States of America for an Order Pursuant to 18 U.S.C. Section 2703(d), 707 F.3d 283 (4th Cir. 2013)] (See *Social Media.*)*

**(a)** Why would the government want to "seal" the documents of an investigation? Why would the individuals under investigation want those documents to be "unsealed"? What factors should be considered in striking a balance between these competing interests?

**(b)** How does law enforcement use social media to detect and prosecute criminals? Is this use of social media an unethical invasion of individuals' privacy? Discuss.

## Legal Reasoning Group Activity

**9–9. File-Sharing.** James, Chang, and Sixta are roommates. They are music fans and frequently listen to the same artists and songs. They regularly exchange MP3 music files that contain songs from their favorite artists. (See *Copyrights in Digital Information.*)

**(a)** One group of students will decide whether the fact that the roommates are transferring files among themselves for

no monetary benefit precludes them from being subject to copyright law.

**(b)** The second group will consider an additional fact. Each roommate regularly buys CDs and rips (copies) them to his or her hard drive. Then the roommate gives the CDs to the other roommates to do the same.

# Answers to the *Issue Spotters*

**1. *Has Karl done anything wrong? Explain.*** Karl may have committed trademark infringement. A site that appropriates the key words of other sites with more frequent hits will appear in the same search engine results as the more popular sites. But using another's trademark as a key word without the owner's permission normally constitutes trademark infringement. Of course, some uses of another's trademark as a meta tag may be permissible if the use is reasonably necessary and does not suggest that the owner authorized or sponsored the use.

**2. *Can Eagle Corporation stop this use of* eagle*? If so, what must the company show?*** Yes. This may be an instance of trademark dilution. Dilution occurs when a trademark is used, without permission, in a way that diminishes the distinctive quality of the mark. Dilution does not require proof that consumers are likely to be confused by the use of the unauthorized mark. The products involved do not have to be similar. Dilution does require, however, that a mark be famous when the dilution occurs.

# Sample Answers for *Business Case Problems with Sample Answer*

**Problem 9–3. *Privacy.*** No, Rolfe did not have a privacy interest in the information obtained by the subpoenas issued to Midcontinent Communications. The right to privacy is guaranteed by at least one interpretation of the U.S. Constitution's Bill of Rights and by some state constitutions. A person must have a reasonable expectation of privacy, though, to maintain a suit or to assert a successful defense for an invasion of privacy. People clearly have a reasonable expectation of privacy when they enter their personal banking or credit card information online. They also have a reasonable expectation that online companies will follow their own privacy policies. But people do not have a reasonable expectation of privacy in statements made on Twitter and other data that they publicly disseminate. In other words, there is no violation of a subscriber's right to privacy when a third-party Internet provider receives a subpoena and discloses the subscriber's information.

Here, Rolfe supplied his e-mail address and other personal information, including his Internet protocol address, to Midcontinent. In other words, Rolfe publicly disseminated this information. Law enforcement officers obtained this information from Midcontinent through the subpoenas issued by the South Dakota state court. Rolfe provided his information to Midcontinent—he had no legitimate expectation of privacy in that information.

In the actual case on which this problem is based, Rolfe was charged with, and convicted of, possessing, manufacturing, and distributing child pornography, as well as other crimes. As part of the proceedings, the court found that Rolfe had no expectation of privacy in the information that he made available to Midcontinent. On appeal, the South Dakota Supreme Court upheld the conviction.

# Chapter 20

# CHAPTER

# Consumer Protection

All statutes, agency rules, and common law judicial decisions that serve to protect the interests of consumers are classified as **consumer law.** Traditionally, in disputes involving consumers, it was assumed that the freedom to contract carried with it the obligation to live by the deal made. Over time, this attitude has changed considerably.

Today, countless federal and state laws attempt to protect consumers

from unfair trade practices, unsafe products, discriminatory or unreasonable credit requirements, and other problems related to consumer transactions. Nearly every agency and department of the federal government has an office of consumer affairs, and most states have one or more such offices to help consumers. Also, typically the attorney general's office assists consumers at the state level.

In recent years, there has been a renewed interest in attempting to protect consumers in their dealings with credit-card companies, financial institutions, and insurance companies. Congress has enacted new credit-card regulations and financial reforms to regulate the nation's largest banks. It has also enacted health-care reforms and revised food safety laws.

## 24–1 Advertising, Marketing, and Sales

Numerous federal laws have been passed to define the duties of sellers and the rights of consumers. Exhibit 24–1 shows many of the areas of consumer law that are regulated by federal statutes. We begin our discussion of this legislation by examining some of the laws and regulations relating to advertising, marketing, and sales. Although we focus on federal law, realize that state consumer protection laws in these and other areas often provide more sweeping and significant protections than do federal laws.

### 24–1a Deceptive Advertising

One of the most important federal consumer protection laws is the Federal Trade Commission Act.[1] The act created the Federal Trade Commission (FTC) to carry out the broadly stated goal of preventing unfair and deceptive trade practices, including deceptive advertising.

Generally, **deceptive advertising** occurs if a reasonable consumer would be misled by the advertising claim. Vague generalities and obvious exaggerations are permissible. These claims are known as *puffery*. When a claim

takes on the appearance of authenticity, however, it may create problems.

**Claims That Appear to Be Based on Factual Evidence** Advertising that *appears* to be based on factual evidence but, in fact, is not reasonably supported by evidence will be deemed deceptive. ■ **CASE IN POINT 24.1** MedLab, Inc., advertised that its weight-loss supplement ("The New Skinny Pill") would cause users to lose substantial amounts of weight rapidly. The ads claimed that "clinical studies prove" that people who take the pill lose "as much as 15 to 18 pounds per week and as much as 50 percent of all excess weight in just 14 days, without dieting or exercising." The FTC sued MedLab for deceptive advertising.

An expert hired by the FTC to evaluate the claim testified that to lose this much weight, "a 200-pound individual would need to run between 57 and 68 miles every day"—the equivalent of more than two marathons per day. The court concluded that the advertisement was false and misleading, granted the FTC a summary judgment, and issued a permanent injunction to stop MedLab from running the ads.[2] ■

The following case involved an advertising claim based on limited scientific evidence.

---

1. 15 U.S.C. Sections 41–58.

2. *Federal Trade Commission v. MedLab, Inc,* 615 F.Supp.2d 1068 (N.D.Cal. 2009).

**EXHIBIT 24-1** Selected Areas of Consumer Law Regulated by Statutes

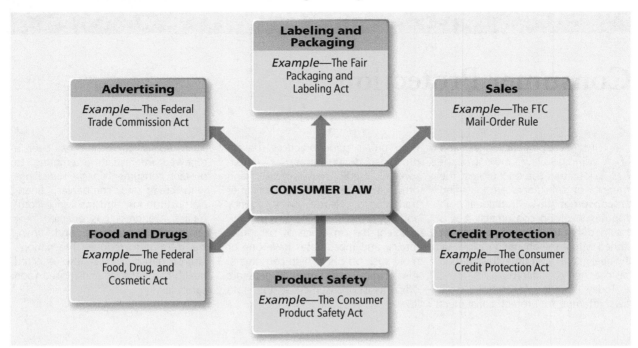

**Labeling and Packaging**

*Example*—The Fair Packaging and Labeling Act

**Advertising**

*Example*—The Federal Trade Commission Act

**Sales**

*Example*—The FTC Mail-Order Rule

**CONSUMER LAW**

**Food and Drugs**

*Example*—The Federal Food, Drug, and Cosmetic Act

**Credit Protection**

*Example*—The Consumer Credit Protection Act

**Product Safety**

*Example*—The Consumer Product Safety Act

**Case 24.1**

# POM Wonderful, LLC v. Federal Trade Commission

United States Court of Appeals, District of Columbia Circuit, 777 F.3d 478 (2015).

**Background and Facts** POM Wonderful, LLC, makes and sells pomegranate-based products. In ads, POM touted medical studies claiming to show that daily consumption of its products could treat, prevent, or reduce the risk of heart disease, prostate cancer, and erectile dysfunction. These ads mischaracterized the scientific evidence.

The Federal Trade Commission (FTC) charged POM with, and held POM liable for, making false, misleading, and unsubstantiated representations in violation of the FTC Act. POM was barred from running future ads asserting that its products treat or prevent any disease unless "randomized, controlled, human clinical trials" (RCTs, for "randomized controlled trials") demonstrated statistically significant results. POM petitioned the U.S. Court of Appeals for the District of Columbia Circuit to review this injunctive order.

## In the Language of the Court

*SRINIVASAN*, Circuit Judge:

* * * *

* * * POM's ads * * * convey the net impression that clinical studies or trials show that a causal relation has been established between the consumption of the challenged POM products and its efficacy to treat, prevent or reduce the risk of the serious diseases in question. The Commission found that experts in the relevant fields would require RCTs * * * to establish such a causal relationship.

The Commission examined each of the studies invoked by petitioners in their ads, concluding that the referenced studies fail to qualify as RCTs of the kind that could afford adequate substantiation. Petitioners' claims therefore were deceptive.

Case 24.1 Continued

* * * *

* * * The Commission's finding is supported by substantial record evidence. That evidence includes written reports and testimony from medical researchers stating that experts in the fields of cardiology and urology require randomized, double-blinded, placebo-controlled clinical trials to substantiate any claim that a product treats, prevents, or reduces the risk of disease.

The Commission drew on that expert testimony to explain why the attributes of well-designed RCTs are necessary to substantiate petitioners' claims. A control group, for example, allows investigators to distinguish between real effects from the intervention, and other changes, including those due to the mere act of being treated (placebo effect) and the passage of time. Random assignment of a study's subjects to treatment and control groups increases the likelihood that the treatment and control groups are similar in relevant characteristics, so that any difference in the outcome between the two groups can be attributed to the treatment. And when a study is double-blinded ([that is,] when neither the study participants nor the investigators know which patients are in the treatment group and which patients are in the control group), it is less likely that participants or investigators will consciously or unconsciously take actions potentially biasing the results.

* * * *

* * * The need for RCTs is driven by the claims petitioners have chosen to make. * * * *An advertiser* * * *may assert a health-related claim backed by medical evidence falling short of an RCT if it includes an effective disclaimer disclosing the limitations of the supporting research.* Petitioners did not do so. [Emphasis added.]

**Decision and Remedy** *The U.S. Court of Appeals for the District of Columbia Circuit enforced the FTC's order with respect to POM's ads. The court pointed out that "An advertiser who makes express representations about the level of support for a particular claim must possess the level of proof claimed in the ad and must convey that information to consumers in a non-misleading way."*

**Critical Thinking**

- **Ethical** *POM claimed that it is unethical to require RCTs to substantiate disease-related claims about food products. It argued that, for instance, "doctors cannot . . . ethically deprive a control group of patients of all Vitamin C for a decade to determine whether Vitamin C helps prevent cancer." Is this a valid argument? Why or why not?*

---

**Claims Based on Half-Truths** Some advertisements contain "half-truths," meaning that the presented information is true but incomplete and may therefore lead consumers to a false conclusion. ■ **EXAMPLE 24.2** The maker of Campbell's soups advertised that "most" Campbell's soups are low in fat and cholesterol and thus helpful in fighting heart disease. What the ad did not say was that many Campbell's soups are high in sodium and that high-sodium diets may increase the risk of heart disease. Hence, the FTC ruled that Campbell's claims were deceptive. ■ In addition, advertising that contains an endorsement by a celebrity may be deemed deceptive if the celebrity does not actually use the product.

**Bait-and-Switch Advertising** The FTC has issued rules that govern specific advertising techniques. One of the most important rules is contained in the FTC's "Guides Against Bait Advertising."[3]

Some retailers systematically advertise merchandise at low prices to get customers into their stores. But when the customers arrive, they find that the merchandise is not in stock. Salespersons then encourage them to purchase more expensive items instead. This practice, known as **bait-and-switch advertising,** is a form of deceptive advertising. The low price is the "bait" to lure the consumer into the store. The salesperson is instructed to "switch" the consumer to a different, more expensive item.

Under the FTC guidelines, bait-and-switch advertising occurs if the seller does any of the following:

1. Refuses to show the advertised item.
2. Fails to have a reasonable quantity of the item in stock.
3. Fails to promise to deliver the advertised item within a reasonable time.
4. Discourages employees from selling the advertised item.

---

3. 16 C.F.R. Part 238.

**Online Deceptive Advertising** Deceptive advertising occurs in the online environment as well as offline. The FTC actively monitors online advertising. It has identified hundreds of Web sites that have made false or deceptive claims for products and services ranging from medical treatments to exercise equipment and weight-loss aids.

The FTC has issued guidelines to help online businesses comply with existing laws prohibiting deceptive advertising. These guidelines include the following requirements:

1. All ads—both online and offline—must be truthful and not misleading.

2. The claims made in an ad must be substantiated—that is, advertisers must have evidence to back up their claims.

3. Ads cannot be unfair, which the FTC defines as "likely to cause substantial consumer injury that consumers could not reasonably avoid and that is not outweighed by the benefit to consumers or competition."

4. Ads must disclose relevant limitations and qualifying information concerning the claims advertisers are making.

5. Required disclosures must be "clear and conspicuous." For instance, because consumers may not read an entire Web page, an online disclosure should be placed as close as possible to the claim being qualified. Generally, hyperlinks to a disclosure are recommended only for lengthy disclosures. If hyperlinks are used, they should be obvious and should be placed as close as possible to the relevant information it qualifies.

The FTC creates additional guidelines as needed to respond to new issues that arise with online advertising. One new issue involves so-called native ads, which are discussed in this chapter's *Digital Update* feature.

**Federal Trade Commission Actions** The FTC receives complaints from many sources, including competitors of alleged violators, consumers, trade associations, Better Business Bureaus, and government organizations and officials. When the agency receives numerous and widespread complaints about a particular problem, it will investigate.

**Formal Complaint.** If the FTC concludes that a given advertisement is unfair or deceptive, it drafts a formal complaint, which is sent to the alleged offender. The company may agree to settle the complaint without further proceedings. If not, the FTC can conduct a hearing in which the company can present its defense.

**FTC Orders and Remedies.** If the FTC succeeds in proving that an advertisement is unfair or deceptive, it usually issues a **cease-and-desist order** requiring the company to stop the challenged advertising. In some circumstances, it may also impose a sanction known as **counteradvertising.** This requires the company to advertise anew—in print, on the Internet, on radio, and on television—to inform the public about the earlier misinformation. The FTC sometimes institutes a **multiple product order,** which requires a firm to stop false advertising for all of its products, not just the product involved in the original action.

**Damages When Consumers Are Injured.** When a company's deceptive ad involves wrongful charges to consumers, the FTC may seek other remedies, including damages. ■ **CASE IN POINT 24.3** The FTC sued Bronson Partners, LLC, for deceptively advertising two products—Chinese Diet Tea and Bio-Slim Patch. Bronson's ads claimed that the diet tea "eliminates 91 percent of absorbed sugars," "prevents 83 percent of fat absorption," and "doubles your metabolic rate to burn calories fast." The Bio-Slim Patch ads promised "lasting weight loss" and claimed that "ugly fatty tissue will disappear at a spectacular rate" as product users wear the patch while carrying on their normal lifestyle.

Eventually, Bronson conceded that it had engaged in deceptive advertising, and the FTC sought damages. The court awarded the FTC $1,942,325, which was the amount of Bronson's revenues from the two products.[4] ■

**Restitution Possible.** When a company's deceptive ad leads to wrongful payments by consumers, the FTC may seek other remedies, including restitution. ■ **CASE IN POINT 24.4** Verity International, Ltd., billed phone-line subscribers who accessed certain online pornography sites at the rate for international calls to Madagascar. When consumers complained about the charges, Verity told them that the charges were valid and had to be paid, or the consumers would face further collection actions. A federal appellate court held that this representation of "uncontestability" was deceptive and a violation of the FTC act. The court ordered Verity to pay nearly $18 million in restitution to consumers.[5] ■

---

4. *Federal Trade Commission v. Bronson Partners, LLC,* 664 F.3d 359 (2d Cir. 2011).
5. *Federal Trade Commission v. Verity International, Ltd.,* 443 F.3d 48 (2d Cir. 2006).

**Regulating "Native" Ads on the Internet**

Sponsored content on the Internet—content that someone pays to put there—is everywhere. One particular type of sponsored content is the "native" ad. Here, *native* describes advertisements that follow the natural form and function of the user experience into which they are placed. Thus, such an ad matches the rest of a Web page's content, including the visual design, as if it were "native" to the page.

### Native Ad Integration on Desktops and Mobile Devices

Perhaps the most obvious native ads are in search engine results. When you type "native ads" in a Google search box, you will find that the first several "hits" listed in the search results are actually sponsored ads. Yet they have the look and feel of the rest of the search results.

Additionally, native ads are often placed within stories in online publications. Suppose, for instance, that you are reading a story on new fashions on your smartphone. You will likely see a native ad that looks as if it is part of the story but that is actually sponsored and perhaps written by a clothing company.

Some native ads are delivered via "recommendation widgets." Usually, the widgets are integrated into a page but do not mimic the appearance of the page. Rather, they direct you to a different Web page—perhaps telling you that "you might like" that site. Clicking the widget takes you to the site.

Native ads have become increasingly popular because desktop, smartphone, and tablet users have figured out how to block traditional online ads. Moreover, native ads are less intrusive than traditional online ads—important because of the increasing number of consumers who most often access small screens, such as those on smartphones.

### The Federal Trade Commission Takes Action

In response to the growth in native advertising, the Federal Trade Commission (FTC) has issued guidelines.[a] The FTC starts out with the basic question "[A]s native advertising evolves, are consumers able to differentiate advertising from other content?" In its guidance document,[b] the FTC suggests the following:

- Disclosures should be placed where consumers will notice them.
- Disclosures should be placed not after the native ad, but before or above it.
- Disclosures should remain with native ads if the ads are republished.
- Once consumers arrive on a click- or tap-into page where the complete native ad appears, disclosures should be placed as close as possible to where consumers will look first.
- Disclosures should stand out and should be understandable.

**Critical Thinking** *What is the equivalent of native advertising in commercially released movies?*

**a.** Federal Trade Commission, *Native Advertising: A Guide to Business,* December 2015.

**b.** Federal Trade Commission, *.com Disclosures: How to Make Effective Disclosures in Digital Advertising,* March 2013, available at www.ftc.gov/tips-advice/business-center/guidance/com-disclosures-how-make-effective-disclosures-digital.

---

**False Advertising Claims under the Lanham Act** The Lanham Act[6] protects trademarks, as discussed elsewhere. The act also covers false advertising claims. To state a successful claim for false advertising under this act, a business must establish each of the following elements:

**1.** An injury to a commercial interest in reputation or sales.

**2.** Direct causation of the injury by false or deceptive advertising.

**3.** A loss of business from buyers who were deceived by the advertising.

The dispute between the parties in the following case focused initially on a mimicked microchip. When the case reached the United States Supreme Court, the question was whether Static Control Components, Inc., could sue Lexmark International, Inc., for false advertising under the Lanham Act.

**6.** 15 U.S.C. Sections 1051–1128.

# Lexmark International, Inc.
# v. Static Control Components, Inc.

Supreme Court of the United States, __ U.S. __, 134 S.Ct. 1377, 188 L.Ed.2d 392 (2014).

**Background and Facts** Lexmark International, Inc., sells the only style of toner cartridges that work with the company's laser printers. Other businesses—known as remanufacturers—acquire and refurbish used Lexmark cartridges to sell in competition with the cartridges sold by Lexmark. To deter remanufacturing, Lexmark introduced a program that gave customers a 20 percent discount on new toner cartridges if they agreed to return the empty cartridges to Lexmark. Static Control Components, Inc., makes and sells components for the remanufactured cartridges, including microchips that mimic the chips in Lexmark's cartridges.

Lexmark released ads that claimed Static Control's microchips illegally infringed Lexmark's patents. Lexmark then filed a suit in a federal district court against Static Control, alleging violations of intellectual property law. Static Control counterclaimed, alleging that Lexmark had engaged in false advertising in violation of the Lanham Act. The court dismissed the counterclaim. It held that Static Control lacked standing to bring that claim. On Static Control's appeal, the U.S. Court of Appeals for the Sixth Circuit reversed the dismissal. Lexmark appealed to the United States Supreme Court.

## In the Language of the Court

Justice *SCALIA* delivered the opinion of the Court.

* * * *

First, * * * a statutory cause of action extends only to plaintiffs whose interests fall within the zone of interests protected by the law invoked.

* * * *

* * * To come within the zone of interests in a suit for false advertising under [the Lanham Act,] a plaintiff must allege an injury to a commercial interest in reputation or sales.

* * * *

Second, * * * a statutory cause of action is limited to plaintiffs whose injuries are proximately caused by violations of the statute.

* * * *

* * * A plaintiff suing under [the Lanham Act] ordinarily must show economic or reputational injury flowing directly from the deception wrought by the defendant's advertising; and that occurs when deception of consumers causes them to withhold trade from the plaintiff.

* * * *

Applying those principles to Static Control's false-advertising claim, we conclude that Static Control comes within the class of plaintiffs whom Congress authorized to sue under [the Lanham Act].

To begin, Static Control's alleged injuries—lost sales and damage to its business reputation—are injuries to precisely the sorts of commercial interests the Act protects. *Static Control is suing not as a deceived consumer, but [in the words of the statute] as a "person engaged in * * * commerce within the control of Congress" whose position in the marketplace has been damaged by Lexmark's false advertising.* There is no doubt that it is within the zone of interests protected by the statute. [Emphasis added.]

Static Control also sufficiently alleged that its injuries were proximately caused by Lexmark's misrepresentations.

First, Static Control alleged that Lexmark disparaged its business and products by asserting that Static Control's business was illegal. *When a defendant harms a plaintiff's reputation by casting aspersions [abuse] on its business, the plaintiff's injury flows directly from the audience's belief in the disparaging statements.* [Emphasis added.]

* * * *

The District Court emphasized that Lexmark and Static Control are not direct competitors [since Static Control is not itself a remanufacturer]. But when a party claims reputational injury from disparagement, competition is not required for proximate cause; and that is true even if the defendant's aim was to harm its immediate competitors, and the plaintiff merely suffered collateral damage.

**Case 24.2 Continued**

In addition, Static Control adequately alleged proximate causation by alleging that it designed, manufactured, and sold microchips that both (1) were necessary for, and (2) had no other use than, refurbishing Lexmark toner cartridges. It follows from that allegation that any false advertising that reduced the remanufacturers' business necessarily injured Static Control as well.

**Decision and Remedy** *The United States Supreme Court affirmed the lower court's ruling. Static Control had adequately pleaded the elements of a cause of action under the Lanham Act for false advertising. The Court's decision clarified that businesses do not need to be direct competitors to bring an action for false advertising under the act.*

**Critical Thinking**
- **What If the Facts Were Different?** *Suppose that Lexmark had issued a retraction of its advertising claims before this case reached the Supreme Court. Would the outcome have been different? Discuss.*
- **Legal Environment** *Under the Court's ruling in this case, is Static Control now entitled to relief? Explain your answer.*

## 24–1b Marketing

In addition to regulating advertising practices, Congress has passed several laws to protect consumers against other marketing practices.

**Telephone Solicitation** The Telephone Consumer Protection Act (TCPA)[7] prohibits telephone solicitation using an automatic telephone dialing system or a prerecorded voice. In addition, most states have statutes regulating telephone solicitation. The TCPA also makes it illegal to transmit ads via fax without first obtaining the recipient's permission.

The Federal Communications Commission (FCC) enforces the TCPA. The FCC imposes substantial fines ($11,000 each day) on companies that violate the junk fax provisions of the act.[8] The TCPA also gives consumers a right to sue for either $500 for each violation of the act or for the actual monetary losses resulting from a violation, whichever is greater. If a court finds that a defendant willfully or knowingly violated the act, the court has the discretion to treble (triple) the amount of damages awarded.

**Fraudulent Telemarketing** The Telemarketing and Consumer Fraud and Abuse Prevention Act[9] directed the FTC to establish rules governing telemarketing and to bring actions against fraudulent telemarketers.

The FTC's Telemarketing Sales Rule (TSR)[10] requires a telemarketer to identify the seller's name, describe the product being sold, and disclose all material facts related to the sale (such as the total cost). The TSR makes it illegal for telemarketers to misrepresent information or facts about their goods or services. A telemarketer must also remove a consumer's name from its list of potential contacts if the customer so requests.

An amendment to the TSR established the national Do Not Call Registry. Telemarketers must refrain from calling those consumers who have placed their names on the list. Significantly, the TSR applies to any offer made to consumers in the United States—even if the offer comes from a foreign firm. Thus, the TSR helps to protect consumers from illegal cross-border telemarketing operations.

## 24–1c Sales

A number of statutes protect consumers by requiring the disclosure of certain terms in sales transactions and providing rules governing unsolicited merchandise. The FTC has regulatory authority in this area, as do some other federal agencies.

Many states and the FTC have **"cooling-off" laws** that permit the buyers of goods sold door to door to cancel their contracts within three business days. The FTC rule also requires that consumers be notified in Spanish of this right if the oral negotiations for the sale were in that language.

The contracts that fall under these cancellation rules include trade show sales contracts, contracts for home

---

7. 47 U.S.C. Sections 227 *et seq.*
8. See, for instance, *Imhoff Investment, LLC v. Alfoccinio, Inc.,* 792 F.3d 627 (6th Cir. 2015).
9. 15 U.S.C. 6101–6108.

---

10. 16 C.F.R. Sections 310.1–310.8.

equity loans, Internet purchase contracts, and home (door-to-door) sales contracts. In addition, certain states have passed laws allowing consumers to cancel contracts for dating services, gym memberships, and weight loss programs.

The FTC Mail or Telephone Order Merchandise Rule[11] protects consumers who purchase goods via mail, Internet, phone, or fax. Merchants are required to ship orders within the time promised in their advertisements and to notify consumers when orders cannot be shipped on time. If the seller does not give an estimated shipping time, it must ship within thirty days. Merchants must also issue a refund within a specified period of time when a consumer cancels an order.

## 24–2 Labeling and Packaging Laws

A number of federal and state laws deal specifically with the information given on labels and packages. In general, labels must be accurate, and they must use words that are easily understood by the ordinary consumer. In some instances, labels must specify the raw materials used in the product, such as the percentage of cotton, nylon, or other fiber used in a garment. In other instances, the product must carry a warning, such as those required on cigarette packages and advertising.[12]

### 24–2a Automobile Fuel Economy Labels

The Energy Policy and Conservation Act (EPCA)[13] requires automakers to attach an information label to every new car. The label must include the Environmental Protection Agency's fuel economy estimate for the vehicle. ■ **CASE IN POINT 24.5** Gaetano Paduano bought a new Honda Civic Hybrid in California. The information label on the car included the fuel economy estimate from the Environmental Protection Agency (EPA). Honda's sales brochure added, "Just drive the Hybrid like you would a conventional car and save on fuel bills."

When Paduano discovered that the car's fuel economy was less than half of the EPA's estimate, he sued Honda for deceptive advertising under a California law. The automaker claimed that the federal law (the EPCA) preempted the state's deceptive advertising law. The court held in Paduano's favor, finding that the federal statute did not preempt a claim for deceptive advertising made under state law.[14] ■

### 24–2b Food Labeling

Because the quality and safety of food are so important to consumers, several statutes deal specifically with food labeling. The Fair Packaging and Labeling Act requires that food product labels identify (1) the product, (2) the net quantity of the contents (and, if the number of servings is stated, the size of a serving), (3) the manufacturer, and (4) the packager or distributor. The act includes additional requirements concerning descriptions on packages, savings claims, components of nonfood products, and standards for the partial filling of packages.

**Nutritional Content of Food Products** Food products must bear labels detailing the nutritional content, including the number of calories and the amounts of various nutrients that the food contains. The Nutrition Labeling and Education Act[15] requires food labels to provide standard nutrition facts and regulates the use of such terms as *fresh* and *low fat*.

The U.S. Food and Drug Administration (FDA) and the U.S. Department of Agriculture (USDA) are the primary agencies that issue regulations on food labeling. These rules are published in the *Federal Register* and updated annually.

**Caloric Content of Restaurant Foods** The health-care reforms enacted in 2010 (the Affordable Care Act, or Obamacare) included provisions aimed at combating the problem of obesity in the United States. All restaurant chains with twenty or more locations are now required to post the caloric content of the foods on their menus so that customers will know how many calories the foods contain.[16] Foods offered through vending machines must also be labeled so that their caloric content is visible to would-be purchasers.

In addition, restaurants must post guidelines on the number of calories that an average person requires daily so that customers can determine what portion of a day's calories a particular food will provide. The hope is that consumers, armed with this information, will consider the number of calories when they make their food choices. The federal law on menu labeling supersedes all previous state and local laws in this area.

11. 16 C.F.R. Sections 435.1–435.2.
12. 15 U.S.C. Sections 1331–1341.
13. 49 U.S.C. Section 32908(b)(1).
14. *Paduano v. American Honda Motor Co.*, 169 Cal.App.4th 1453, 88 Cal. Rptr.3d 90 (2009).
15. 21 U.S.C. Section 343.1.
16. See Section 4205 of the Patient Protection and Affordable Care Act, Pub. L. No. 111-148, 124 Stat. 119 (March 23, 2010).

## 24–3 Protection of Health and Safety

Although labeling and packaging laws promote consumer health and safety, there is a significant distinction between regulating the information dispensed about a product and regulating the actual content of the product. The classic example is tobacco products. Producers of tobacco products must use labels that warn consumers about the health hazards associated with their use, but the sale of tobacco products has not been subjected to significant restrictions. We now examine various laws that regulate the actual products made available to consumers.

### 24–3a The Federal Food, Drug, and Cosmetic Act

The most important federal legislation regulating food and drugs is the Federal Food, Drug, and Cosmetic Act (FDCA).[17] The act protects consumers against adulterated (contaminated) and misbranded foods and drugs. The FDCA establishes food standards, specifies safe levels of potentially hazardous food additives, and provides classifications of foods and food advertising. Most of these statutory requirements are monitored and enforced by the Food and Drug Administration (FDA).

Interestingly, the European Union and a number of other countries, such as Canada, have banned some foods that the FDA assumes to be safe. These foods include brominated vegetable oil (a common ingredient in sports drinks, such as Gatorade) and Olestra/Olean (a cholesterol-free fat substitute found in certain potato chips). Food products containing such substances may not be sold in the European Union. Similarly, certain food colorings found in processed foods in the United States (in M&Ms and Kraft macaroni and cheese, for instance) are not allowed in foods in some other countries.

**Tainted Foods** In the last twenty years or so, many people in the United States have contracted food poisoning from eating foods that were contaminated, often with salmonella or *E. coli* bacteria. ■ **EXAMPLE 24.6** During 2015 and 2016, hundreds of people across the United States were sickened by eating tainted food at the popular restaurant chain Chipotle Mexican Grill. Causes of illness in these outbreaks included *E-coli* and salmonella, as well as the highly contagious norovirus. ■

In response to the problem of food contamination, Congress enacted the Food Safety Modernization Act (FSMA)[18] to provide greater government control over the U.S. food safety system. The act gives the FDA authority to directly recall any food products that it suspects are tainted, rather than relying on the producers to recall items.

The FSMA requires anyone who manufactures, processes, packs, distributes, receives, holds, or imports food products to pay a fee and register with the U.S. Department of Health and Human Services. (There are some exceptions for small farmers.) Owners and operators of such facilities are required to analyze and identify food safety hazards, implement preventive controls, monitor effectiveness, and take corrective actions. The FSMA places additional restrictions on importers of food and requires them to verify that imported foods meet U.S. safety standards.

**Drugs and Medical Devices** The FDA is also responsible under the FDCA for ensuring that drugs are safe and effective before they are marketed to the public. Because the FDA must ensure the safety of new medications, there is always a delay before drugs are available to the public, and this sometimes leads to controversy.

■ **CASE IN POINT 24.7** A group of citizens petitioned the FDA to allow everyone access to "Plan B"—the morning-after birth control pill—without a prescription. The FDA denied the petition and continued to require women under the age of seventeen to obtain a prescription. The group appealed to a federal district court, claiming that the prescription requirement can delay access to the pill. The pill should be taken as soon as possible after sexual intercourse, preferably within twenty-four hours. The court ruled in favor of the plaintiffs and ordered the FDA to make the morning-after pill available to people of any age without a prescription.[19] ■

### 24–3b The Consumer Product Safety Act

The Consumer Product Safety Act[20] created a comprehensive regulatory scheme over consumer safety matters and established the Consumer Product Safety Commission (CPSC).

**The CPSC's Authority** The CPSC conducts research on the safety of individual consumer products and maintains a clearinghouse on the risks associated with various products. The Consumer Product Safety Act authorizes the CPSC to do the following:

---

17. 21 U.S.C. Sections 301–393.
18. Pub. L. No. 111-353, 124 Stat. 3885 (January 4, 2011). This statute affected numerous parts of Title 21 of the U.S.C.
19. *Tummino v. Hamburg,* 936 F.Supp.2d 162 (E.D.N.Y. 2013).
20. 15 U.S.C. Sections 2051–2083.

1. Set safety standards for consumer products.
2. Ban the manufacture and sale of any product that the commission believes poses an "unreasonable risk" to consumers. (Products banned by the CPSC have included various types of fireworks, cribs, and toys, as well as many products containing asbestos or vinyl chloride.)
3. Remove from the market any products it believes to be imminently hazardous. The CPSC frequently works in conjunction with manufacturers to conduct voluntary recalls of defective products from stores. ■ **EXAMPLE 24.8** In cooperation with the CPSC, the Scandinavian company IKEA recalled three million baby bed canopies and thirty million wall-mounted children's lamps because they posed a strangulation risk to children. ■
4. Require manufacturers to report on any products already sold or intended for sale if the products have proved to be hazardous.
5. Administer other product-safety legislation, including the Child Protection and Toy Safety Act[21] and the Federal Hazardous Substances Act.[22]

**Notification Requirements** The Consumer Product Safety Act requires the distributors of consumer products to notify the CPSC immediately if they receive information that a product "contains a defect which . . . creates a substantial risk to the public" or "an unreasonable risk of serious injury or death."

■ **EXAMPLE 24.9** A company that sells juicers receives twenty-three letters from customers complaining that during operation the juicer suddenly exploded, sending pieces of glass and razor-sharp metal across the room. The company must immediately notify the CPSC because the alleged defect creates a substantial risk to the public. ■

### 24-3c Health-Care Reforms

The health-care reforms enacted in 2010 gave Americans new rights and benefits with regard to health care.[23] The legislation also prohibited certain insurance company practices.

**Expanded Coverage for Children and Seniors**
The reforms enabled more children to obtain health-insurance coverage and allowed young adults (under age twenty-six) to remain on their parents' health insurance policies. The legislation also ended lifetime limits and most annual limits on care, and gave insured persons access to recommended preventive services (such as cancer screening and vaccinations) without cost. People can no longer be denied insurance because of preexisting conditions. Medicare recipients now receive a 50 percent discount on name-brand drugs, and the reforms will eliminate a gap in Medicare's prescription drug coverage by 2020.

**Controlling Costs of Health Insurance** In an attempt to control the rising costs of health insurance, certain restrictions were placed on insurance companies. Insurance companies must spend at least 85 percent of all premium dollars collected from large employers (80 percent of the premiums collected from individuals and small employers) on benefits and quality improvement. If insurance companies do not meet these goals, they must provide rebates to consumers. Additionally, states can require insurance companies to justify any premium increases to be eligible to participate in the new health-insurance exchanges. In spite of the legislation, health insurance costs have continued to increase.

## 24-4 Credit Protection

Credit protection is one of the more important aspects of consumer protection legislation. Many U.S. consumers have credit cards, and most carry a balance on these cards—a total of about $2.5 trillion of debt nationwide. The Consumer Financial Protection Bureau (CFPB) is the agency that oversees the credit practices of banks, mortgage lenders, and credit-card companies.[24]

### 24-4a The Truth-in-Lending Act

A key statute regulating the credit and credit-card industries is the Truth-in-Lending Act (TILA), the name commonly given to Title I of the Consumer Credit Protection Act, as amended.[25] The TILA is basically a *disclosure law*. It is administered by the Federal Reserve Board and requires sellers and lenders to disclose credit terms and loan terms so that individuals can shop around for the best financing arrangements.

---

21. 15 U.S.C. Section 1262(e).
22. 15 U.S.C. Sections 1261–1273.
23. Patient Protection and Affordable Health Care Act of 2010, Pub. L. No.111-148, 124 Stat. 119 (March 23, 2010); and the Health Care and Education Reconciliation Act of 2010, Pub. L. No. 111-152, 124 Stat. 1029 (March 30, 2010).

24. Title 10 of the Restoring American Financial Stability Act of 2010, S.B. 3217, April 15, 2010.
25. 15 U.S.C. Sections 1601–1693r.

**Application** TILA requirements apply only to those who, in the ordinary course of business, lend funds, sell on credit, or arrange for the extension of credit. Thus, sales or loans made between two consumers do not come under the protection of the act. Additionally, this law protects only debtors who are natural persons (as opposed to the artificial "person" of a corporation). It does not extend to other legal entities.

**Disclosure Requirements** The TILA's disclosure requirements are contained in **Regulation Z,** issued by the Federal Reserve Board of Governors. If the contracting parties are subject to the TILA, the requirements of Regulation Z apply to any transaction involving an installment sales contract that calls for payment to be made in more than four installments. Transactions subject to Regulation Z typically include installment loans, retail and installment sales, car loans, home-improvement loans, and certain real estate loans if the amount of financing is less than $25,000.

Under the provisions of the TILA, all of the terms of a credit instrument must be clearly and conspicuously disclosed. A lender must disclose the annual percentage rate (APR), finance charge, amount financed, and total payments (the sum of the amount loaned, plus any fees, finance charges, and interest). If a creditor fails to follow the *exact* procedures required by the TILA, the creditor risks contract rescission (cancellation) under the act.

**Equal Credit Opportunity** Congress enacted the Equal Credit Opportunity Act (ECOA)[26] as an amendment to the TILA. The ECOA prohibits the denial of credit solely on the basis of race, religion, national origin, color, gender, marital status, or age. The act also prohibits credit discrimination on the basis of whether an individual receives certain forms of income, such as public-assistance benefits.

Under the ECOA, a creditor may not require a cosigner on a credit instrument if the applicant qualifies under the creditor's standards of creditworthiness for the amount and terms of the credit request. ■ **CASE IN POINT 24.10** T.R. Hughes, Inc., and Summit Pointe, LLC, obtained financing from Frontenac Bank to construct two real estate developments near St. Louis, Missouri. The bank also required the builder, Thomas R. Hughes, and his wife, Carolyn Hughes, to sign personal guaranty agreements for the loans.

When the borrowers failed to make the loan payments, the bank sued the two companies and Thomas and Carolyn Hughes personally, and foreclosed on the properties. Carolyn claimed that the personal guaranty contracts that she signed were obtained in violation of the ECOA. The court held that because the applicant, Thomas R. Hughes, was creditworthy, the personal guarantys of Carolyn Hughes were obtained in violation of the ECOA and therefore unenforceable.[27] ■

**Credit-Card Rules** The TILA also contains provisions regarding credit cards. One provision limits the liability of a cardholder to $50 per card for unauthorized charges made before the creditor is notified that the card has been lost. If a consumer receives an *unsolicited* credit card in the mail that is later stolen, the company that issued the card cannot charge the consumer for any unauthorized charges.

Another provision requires credit-card companies to disclose the balance computation method that is used to determine the outstanding balance and to state when finance charges begin to accrue. Other provisions set forth procedures for resolving billing disputes with the credit-card company. These procedures are used if, for instance, a cardholder thinks that an error has occurred in billing or wishes to withhold payment for a faulty product purchased by credit card.

**Amendments to Credit-Card Rules** Amendments to the TILA's credit-card rules added the following protections:

1. A company may not retroactively increase the interest rates on existing card balances unless the account is sixty days delinquent.
2. A company must provide forty-five days' advance notice to consumers before changing its credit-card terms.
3. Monthly bills must be sent to cardholders twenty-one days before the due date.
4. The interest rate charged on a customer's credit-card balance may not be increased except in specific situations, such as when a promotional rate ends.
5. A company may not charge over-limit fees except in specified situations.
6. When the customer has balances at different interest rates, payments in excess of the minimum amount due must be applied first to the balance with the highest rate. (For instance, a higher interest rate is commonly charged for cash advances.)
7. A company may not compute finance charges based on the previous billing cycle (a practice known as double-cycle billing). This practice hurts consumers because they are charged interest for the previous cycle even if they have paid the bill in full.

---

26. 15 U.S.C. Sections 1691–1691f.

27. *Frontenac Bank v. T.R. Hughes, Inc.,* 404 S.W.3d 272 (Mo.App. 2012).

## 24-4b The Fair Credit Reporting Act

The Fair Credit Reporting Act (FCRA)[28] protects consumers against inaccurate credit reporting and requires that lenders and other creditors report correct, relevant, and up-to-date information. The act provides that consumer credit reporting agencies may issue credit reports to users only for specified purposes. Legitimate purposes include the extension of credit, the issuance of insurance policies, and responding to the consumer's request.

Whether an Internet service provider had a legitimate purpose to pull a customer's credit report was at issue in the following case.

---

**28.** 15 U.S.C. Sections 1681–1681t.

---

**Case Analysis 24.3**

# Santangelo v. Comcast Corporation

United States District Court, Northern District of Illinois, Eastern Division, __ F.Supp.3d __, 2016 WL 464223 (2016).

### In the Language of the Court
John Z. *LEE*, United States District Judge
  * * * *

I. Factual and Procedural Background
  [Keith Santangelo filed a complaint in a federal district court against Comcast Corporation, alleging a violation of the Fair Credit Reporting Act (FCRA).] Santangelo alleges * * * that he contacted Comcast through the company's online customer service "Chat" function * * * and requested Internet service for his new apartment. During the chat session, a Comcast representative asked Santangelo for permission to run a credit inquiry. Santangelo asked if any option was available to avoid the credit inquiry. The Comcast representative told him that the company would forgo the inquiry if he paid a $50 deposit.

The option to pay a $50 deposit in order to avoid a credit inquiry was an explicit part of Comcast's official Risk Management Policy * * * .The policy also required a $50 deposit from any prospective customer who agreed to a credit inquiry but whose credit score proved to be unsatisfactory. According to Santangelo, the deposit policy "reflects Comcast's calculated business decision and belief that the collection of a $50 deposit is sufficient to cover the risk presented by a person with bad credit and is sufficient to cover the risk presented by a person who refuses a credit pull."

Santangelo opted to pay the $50 deposit in lieu of a credit inquiry. * * * Nevertheless, Comcast, without Santangelo's authorization, pulled his credit report * * * . This credit inquiry depleted [lowered] Santangelo's credit score.
  * * * *

  * * * Comcast now moves to dismiss the * * * complaint.
II. Analysis
  * * * *

*FCRA prohibits the obtaining of a "consumer report," commonly known as a credit report, except for purposes authorized by that statute. The statute lists specific permissible purposes, such as * * * any * * * "legitimate business need * * * in connection with a business transaction that is initiated by the consumer."* These limitations are intended to produce a balance between consumer privacy and the needs of a modern, credit-driven economy. [Emphasis added.]

Santangelo contends that Comcast did not have a permissible purpose for obtaining his credit report after he paid the $50 deposit in exchange for the company's promise not to check his credit. If he is correct and the company's violation was willful, he would be entitled to recover attorney's fees and either actual damages or statutory damages between $100 and $1,000. If the company's violation was merely negligent, Santangelo would be permitted to recover only attorney's fees and actual damages.
1. Standing
  Comcast first argues that Santangelo lacks standing to bring his FCRA claim. To establish standing * * * a plaintiff must show * * * the injury is fairly traceable to the challenged action of the defendant.

According to Comcast, Santangelo has not alleged an injury-in-fact that is fairly traceable to the FCRA violation he claims. Santangelo responds that he has sustained three injuries-in-fact: the loss of the $50 he paid as a deposit, the violation of his legal right not to have his credit report pulled without a permissible purpose, and the resulting depletion of his credit score.
  * * * *

  * * * It was the very fact that Comcast received the $50 from Santangelo before it performed the credit check that made it illegal. * * * And once Comcast checked Santangelo's credit, it should have refunded the deposit immediately, rather than keeping it. Comcast's receipt and withholding of the $50, therefore, is inextricable [inseparable] from the FCRA violation and can be said to be fairly traceable to the FCRA violation. * * * Even if the $50.00 deposit were fully refundable, Santangelo still has standing based on the lost time-value of the money.

  * * * Santangelo also has sufficiently alleged an injury-in-fact by alleging that Comcast obtained his credit report without a permissible purpose in violation of the FCRA.

*Because the FCRA grants consumers a legally protected interest in limiting access to their credit reports and provides redress for violations, * * * Santangelo's allegations about Comcast's interference with that legally protected interest are sufficient*

**Case 24.3 Continued**

*to establish* * * * *standing.* [Emphasis added.]

* * * Santangelo also alleges that the FCRA violation in this case depleted his credit score. In response, Comcast contends that a reduced credit score, without resulting damages, does not constitute an injury.

* * * The Court agrees with Santangelo that a depleted credit score is sufficient to constitute an injury * * * . Credit scores are of great importance in our economy, and a depleted credit score could affect a consumer in numerous ways, inflicting harm that often may be difficult to prove or quantify. Congress has the power to discourage the needless depletion of consumers' credit scores even when the depleted score cannot be neatly tied to a financial harm.

2. Sufficiency of Santangelo's allegations

Comcast next argues that Santangelo's allegations do not state an FCRA claim.

* * * *

In his * * * complaint, Santangelo * * * alleges that Comcast's deposit policies demonstrate its lack of a legitimate need to run credit checks with respect

to consumers who paid a $50 deposit. According to the * * * complaint, Comcast's established policy is to forgo a credit check in exchange for a $50 deposit. The company also has a policy of accepting a $50 deposit from consumers who opt for a credit check but prove to have poor credit. Santangelo compares this situation to that of a car dealer who accepts a cash payment for the full purchase price of a car. * * * The car dealer * * * does not have a legitimate need to obtain the purchaser's credit report. Similarly, a landlord does not have a legitimate need to obtain a tenant's credit report if the tenant is entitled to a lease renewal without regard to creditworthiness.

In response, Comcast * * * argues that it had a legitimate business need to establish Santangelo's creditworthiness despite his deposit because—unlike in the car dealer example—his $50 deposit would cover less than two months of service in a long-term contract. * * * [Santangelo] contends that, under company policy, his creditworthiness was irrelevant to Comcast's determination of his eligibility for service once the deposit

was collected, much like the tenants in [the landlord example].

* * * *

* * * Comcast's mere violation of its alleged agreement not to pull Santangelo's credit report does not support an FCRA claim. But the possibility that the company itself believed that its customers' creditworthiness was irrelevant if they paid a deposit is enough.

Comcast's final argument for dismissing Santangelo's FCRA claim is that he neither explicitly alleges that the company's actions were willful, which is necessary to trigger statutory damages, nor identifies any actual damages that he could recover if Comcast acted only negligently. Although [Santangelo] does not use the word willful in his complaint, he alleges that the company obtained his credit report despite that it "knew that it did not have a legitimate business need." This allegation implies recklessness at the very least, and reckless conduct qualifies as willful conduct under the FCRA.

* * * *

III. Conclusion

* * * The Court denies Comcast's motion to dismiss.

**Legal Reasoning Questions**

1. Comcast argued that it had refunded Santangelo's $50, plus interest in the amount of $10, four months after pulling his credit report. Does this argument undercut the plaintiff's claim to have standing? Why or why not?

2. What might discovery reveal that would affect the outcome in this case? Explain.

3. What damages might Santangelo be able to prove based on the depletion of his credit score?

---

**Consumer Notification and Inaccurate Information** Any time a consumer is denied credit or insurance on the basis of her or his credit report, the consumer must be notified of that fact. The notice must include the name and address of the credit-reporting agency that issued the report. The same notice must be sent to consumers who are charged more than others ordinarily would be for credit or insurance because of their credit reports.

Under the FCRA, consumers may request the source of any information used by the credit agency, as well as the identity of anyone who has received an agency's report.

Consumers are also permitted to access the information about them contained in a credit reporting agency's files.

If a consumer discovers that an agency's files contain inaccurate information, he or she should report the problem to the agency. On the consumer's written (or electronic) request, the agency must conduct a systematic examination of its records. Any unverifiable or erroneous information must be deleted within a reasonable period of time.

**Remedies for Violations** A credit reporting agency that fails to comply with the act is liable for actual damages, plus additional damages not to exceed $1,000 and attorneys' fees.[29] Creditors and other companies that use information from credit reporting agencies may also be liable for violations of the FCRA. The United States Supreme Court has held that an insurance company's failure to notify new customers that they were paying higher insurance rates as a result of their credit scores was a *willful* violation of the FCRA.[30]

■ **CASE IN POINT 24.11** Branch Banking & Trust Company of Virginia (BB&T) gave Rex Saunders an auto loan but failed to give him a payment coupon book and refused his attempts to make payments on the loan. In fact, BB&T told him that it had not extended a loan to him. Eventually, BB&T discovered its mistake and demanded full payment, plus interest and penalties.

When payment was not immediately forthcoming, BB&T declared that Saunders was in default. It then repossessed the car and forwarded adverse credit information about Saunders to credit reporting agencies, without noting that Saunders disputed the information. Saunders filed a lawsuit alleging violations of the FCRA and was awarded $80,000 in punitive damages. An appellate court found that the damages award was reasonable, given BB&T's willful violation.[31] ■

## 24–4c The Fair and Accurate Credit Transactions Act

Congress passed the Fair and Accurate Credit Transactions (FACT) Act in an effort to combat identity theft.[32] The act established a national fraud alert system. Consumers who suspect that they have been or may be victimized by identity theft can place an alert on their credit files. When a consumer establishes that identify theft has occurred, the credit reporting agency must stop reporting allegedly fraudulent account information.

The act also requires the major credit reporting agencies to provide consumers with free copies of their own credit reports every twelve months. Another provision requires account numbers on credit-card receipts to be truncated (shortened). Merchants, employees, or others who may have access to the receipts can no longer obtain the consumers' names and full credit-card numbers. Financial institutions must work with the FTC to identify

"red flag" indicators of identity theft and to develop rules for the disposal of sensitive credit information.

## 24–4d The Fair Debt Collection Practices Act

The Fair Debt Collection Practices Act (FDCPA)[33] attempts to curb perceived abuses by collection agencies. The act applies only to specialized debt-collection agencies and attorneys who regularly attempt to collect debts on behalf of someone else, usually for a percentage of the amount owed. Creditors attempting to collect debts are not covered by the act unless, by misrepresenting themselves, they cause debtors to believe they are collection agencies.

**Requirements of the Act** Under the FDCPA, a collection agency may not do any of the following:

1. Contact the debtor at the debtor's place of employment if the debtor's employer objects.
2. Contact the debtor at inconvenient or unusual times (such as three o'clock in the morning), or at any time if the debtor is being represented by an attorney.
3. Contact third parties other than the debtor's parents, spouse, or financial adviser about payment of a debt unless a court authorizes such action.
4. Harass or intimidate the debtor (by using abusive language or threatening violence, for instance) or make false or misleading statements (such as posing as a police officer).
5. Communicate with the debtor at any time after receiving notice that the debtor is refusing to pay the debt, except to advise the debtor of further action to be taken by the collection agency.

The FDCPA also requires a collection agency to include a **validation notice** when it initially contacts a debtor for payment of a debt or within five days of that initial contact. The notice must state that the debtor has thirty days in which to dispute the debt and to request a written verification of the debt from the collection agency.

**Enforcement of the Act** The Federal Trade Commission is primarily responsible for enforcing the FDCPA. A debt collector who fails to comply with the act is liable for actual damages, plus additional damages not to exceed $1,000 and attorneys' fees.

---

29. 15 U.S.C. Section 1681n.
30. *Safeco Insurance. Co. of America v. Burr,* 551 U.S. 47, 127 S.Ct. 2201, 167 L.Ed.2d 1045 (2007).
31. *Saunders v. Branch Banking & Trust Co. of Virginia,* 526 F.3d 142 (4th Cir. 2008).
32. Pub. L. No. 108-159, 117 Stat. 1952.

33. 15 U.S.C. Section 1692.

Debt collectors who violate the act are exempt from liability if they can show that the violation was not intentional and resulted from a bona fide error. Furthermore, the error must have occurred in spite of procedures the company had already put in place to avoid such errors. The "bona fide error" defense typically has been applied to mistakes of fact or clerical errors. A few courts have gone further and allowed the good faith error defense in other circumstances.[34]

**34.** See, for instance, *Zortman v. J.C. Christensen & Associates, Inc.,* 2012 WL 1563918 (D.Minn. 2012); see also *Mbaku v. Bank of America, N.A.,* 2013 WL 425981 (D.Colo. 2013).

## Reviewing: Consumer Protection

Leota Sage saw a local motorcycle dealer's newspaper advertisement offering a MetroRider EZ electric scooter for $1,699. When she went to the dealership, however, she learned that the EZ model had been sold out. The salesperson told Sage that he still had the higher-end MetroRider FX model in stock for $2,199 and would sell her one for $1,999. Sage was disappointed but decided to purchase the FX model.

When Sage said that she wished to purchase the scooter on credit, she was directed to the dealer's credit department. As she filled out the credit forms, the clerk told Sage, who is an Asian American, that she would need a cosigner to obtain a loan. Sage could not understand why she would need a cosigner and asked to speak to the store manager. The manager apologized, told her that the clerk was mistaken, and said that he would "speak to" the clerk. The manager completed Sage's credit application, and Sage then rode the scooter home. Seven months later, Sage received a letter from the manufacturer informing her that a flaw had been discovered in the scooter's braking system and that the model had been recalled. Using the information presented in the chapter, answer the following questions.

1. Did the dealer engage in deceptive advertising? Why or why not?
2. Suppose that Sage had ordered the scooter through the dealer's Web site but the dealer was unable to deliver it by the date promised. What would the FTC have required the merchant to do in that situation?
3. Assuming that the clerk required a cosigner based on Sage's race or gender, what act prohibits such credit discrimination?
4. What organization has the authority to ban the sale of scooters based on safety concerns?

**Debate This** . . . *Laws against bait-and-switch advertising should be abolished because no consumer is ever forced to buy anything.*

## Terms and Concepts

| | | |
|---|---|---|
| bait-and-switch advertising 517 | "cooling-off" laws 521 | multiple product order 518 |
| cease-and-desist order 518 | counteradvertising 518 | Regulation Z 525 |
| consumer law 515 | deceptive advertising 515 | validation notice 528 |

## Issue Spotters

1. United Pharmaceuticals, Inc., believes that it has developed a new drug that will be effective in the treatment of patients with AIDS. The drug has had only limited testing, but United wants to make the drug widely available as soon as possible. To market the drug, what must United prove to the U.S. Food and Drug Administration? (See *Protection of Health and Safety.*)

2. Gert buys a notebook computer from EZ Electronics. She pays for it with her credit card. When the computer proves defective, she asks EZ to repair or replace it, but EZ refuses. What can Gert do? (See *Credit Protection.*)

- **Check your answers to the Issue Spotters against the answers provided in Appendix D at the end of this text.**

# Business Scenarios

**24–1. Unsolicited Merchandise.** Andrew, a resident of California, received an advertising circular in the U.S. mail announcing a new line of regional cookbooks distributed by the Every-Kind Cookbook Co. Andrew didn't want any books and threw the circular away. Two days later, Andrew received in the mail an introductory cookbook entitled *Lower Mongolian Regional Cookbook*, as announced in the circular, on a "trial basis" from Every-Kind. Andrew was not interested but did not go to the trouble to return the cookbook. Every-Kind demanded payment of $20.95 for the *Lower Mongolian Regional Cookbook*. Discuss whether Andrew can be required to pay for the book. (See *Advertising, Marketing, and Sales.*)

**24–2. Credit-Card Rules.** Maria Ochoa receives two new credit cards on May 1. She has solicited one of them from Midtown Department Store, and the other arrives unsolicited from High-Flying Airlines. During the month of May, Ochoa makes numerous credit-card purchases from Midtown Department Store, but she does not use the High-Flying Airlines card. On May 31, a burglar breaks into Ochoa's home and steals both credit cards, along with other items. Ochoa notifies the Midtown Department Store of the theft on June 2, but she fails to notify High-Flying Airlines. Using the Midtown credit card, the burglar makes a $500 purchase on June 1 and a $200 purchase on June 3. The burglar then charges a vacation flight on the High-Flying Airlines card for $1,000 on June 5. Ochoa receives the bills for these charges and refuses to pay them. Discuss Ochoa's liability for the charges. (See *Credit Protection.*)

# Business Case Problems

**24–3. Spotlight on McDonald's—Food Labeling.**

McDonald's Corp.'s Happy Meal® meal selection consists of an entrée, a small order of french fries, a small drink, and a toy. In the early 1990s, McDonald's began to aim its Happy Meal marketing at children aged one to three. In 1995, McDonald's began making nutritional information for its food products available in documents known as "McDonald's Nutrition Facts." Each document lists the food items that the restaurant serves and provides a nutritional breakdown, but the Happy Meal is not included.

Marc Cohen filed a suit against McDonald's in an Illinois state court. Among other things, Cohen alleged that McDonald's had violated a state law prohibiting consumer fraud and deceptive business practices by failing to adhere to the Nutrition Labeling and Education Act (NLEA). The NLEA sets out different requirements for products specifically intended for children under the age of four—for instance, the products' labels cannot declare the percent of daily value of nutritional components. Does it make sense to have different requirements for children of this age? Why or why not? Should a state court impose such regulations? Explain. [*Cohen v. McDonald's Corp.*, 347 Ill.App.3d 627, 808 N.E.2d 1, 283 Ill.Dec. 451 (1 Dist. 2004)] (See *Labeling and Packaging Laws.*)

**24–4. Deceptive Advertising.** Brian Cleary and Rita Burke filed a suit against cigarette maker Philip Morris USA, Inc., seeking class-action status for a claim of deceptive advertising. Cleary and Burke claimed that "light" cigarettes, such as Marlboro Lights, were advertised as safer than regular cigarettes, even though the health effects are the same. They contended that the tobacco companies concealed the true nature of light cigarettes. Philip Morris correctly claimed that it was authorized by the government to advertise cigarettes, including light cigarettes. Assuming that is true, should the plaintiffs still be able to bring a deceptive advertising claim against the tobacco company? Why or why not? [*Cleary v. Philip Morris USA, Inc.*, 683 F.Supp.2d 730 (N.D.Ill. 2010)] (See *Advertising, Marketing, and Sales.*)

**24–5. Business Case Problem with Sample Answer—Fair Debt-Collection Practices.** Bank of America hired

Atlantic Resource Management, LLC, to collect a debt from Michael E. Engler. Atlantic called Engler's employer and asked his supervisor about the company's policy concerning the execution of warrants. The caller then told the supervisor that, to stop process of the warrant, Engler needed to call Atlantic about "Case Number 37291 NY0969" during the first three hours of his next shift. When Engler's supervisor told him about the call, Engler feared that he might be arrested, and he experienced discomfort, embarrassment, and emotional distress at work. Can Engler recover under the Fair Debt Collection Practices Act? Why or why not? [*Engler v. Atlantic Resource Management, LLC*, 2012 WL 464728 (W.D.N.Y. 2012)] (See *Credit Protection.*)

- **For a sample answer to Problem 24–5, go to Appendix E at the end of this text.**

**24–6. Deceptive Advertising.** Innovative Marketing, Inc. (IMI), sold "scareware"—computer security software. IMI's Internet ads redirected consumers to sites where they were told that a scan of their computers had detected dangerous files—viruses, spyware, and "illegal" pornography. In fact, no scans were conducted. Kristy Ross, an IMI cofounder and vice president, reviewed and edited the ads, and was aware of the many complaints that consumers had made about them. An individual can be held liable under the Federal Trade Commission Act's prohibition of deceptive practices if the person (1) participated directly in the deceptive practices or had the authority to control them and (2) had or should have had knowledge of them. Were IMI's ads deceptive? If so, can Ross be held liable?

Explain. [*Federal Trade Commission v. Ross*, 743 F.3d 886 (4th Cir. 2014)] (See *Advertising, Marketing, and Sales.*)

### 24–7. A Question of Ethics—Fair Debt-Collection Practices.

 *Barry Sussman graduated from law school, but also served time in prison for attempting to collect debts by posing as an FBI agent. He theorized that if a debt-collection business collected only debts that it owned as a result of buying checks written on accounts with insufficient funds (NSF checks), it would not be subject to the Fair Debt Collection Practices Act (FDCPA). Sussman formed Check Investors, Inc., to act on his theory. Check Investors bought more than 2.2 million NSF checks, with an estimated face value of about $348 million, for pennies on the dollar. Check Investors added a fee of $125 or $130 (more than the legal limit in most states) to the face amount of each check and aggressively pursued its drawer to collect. The firm's employees were told to accuse drawers of being criminals and to threaten them with arrest and prosecution. The threats were false. Check Investors never took steps to initiate a prosecution. The employees contacted the drawers' family members and used "saturation phoning"—phoning a drawer numerous times in a short period. They used abusive language, referring to drawers as "deadbeats," "retards," "thieves," and "idiots." Between January 2000 and January 2003, Check Investors netted more than $10.2 million from its efforts. [Federal Trade Commission v. Check Investors, Inc., 502 F.3d 159 (3d Cir. 2007)]* (See *Credit Protection.*)

**(a)** The Federal Trade Commission filed a suit in a federal district court against Check Investors and others, alleging, in part, violations of the FDCPA. Was Check Investors a "debt collector," collecting "debts," within the meaning of the FDCPA? If so, did its methods violate the FDCPA? Were its practices unethical? What might Check Investors argue in its defense? Discuss.

**(b)** Are "deadbeats" the primary beneficiaries of laws such as the FDCPA? If not, how would you characterize debtors who default on their obligations?

## Legal Reasoning Group Activity

**24–8. Consumer Protections.** Many states have enacted laws that go even further than federal law to protect consumers. These laws vary tremendously from state to state. (See *Advertising, Marketing, and Sales.*)

**(a)** The first group will decide whether having different laws is fair to sellers who may be prohibited from engaging in a practice in one state that is legal in another.

**(b)** The second group will consider how these different laws might affect a business.

**(c)** A third group will determine whether it is fair that residents of one state have more protection than residents of another.

# Answers to the *Issue Spotters*

**1. *To market the drug, what must United prove to the U.S. Food and Drug Administration?*** Under an extensive set of procedures established by the U.S. Food and Drug Administration, which administers the federal Food, Drug, and Cosmetic Act, drugs must be shown to be effective as well as safe before they may be marketed to the public. In general, manufacturers are responsible for ensuring that the drugs they offer for sale are free of any substances that could injure consumers.

**2. *What can Gert do?*** Under the Truth-in-Lending Act, a buyer who wishes to withhold payment for a faulty product purchased with a credit card must follow specific procedures to settle the dispute. The credit card issuer then must intervene and attempt to settle the dispute.

# Sample Answers for *Business Case Problems with Sample Answer*

**Problem 24–5. *Fair Debt-Collection Practices.*** Engler may recover under the Fair Debt Collection Practices Act (FDCPA). Atlantic is subject to the FDCPA because it is a debt-collection agency and was attempting to collect a debt on behalf of Bank of America. Atlantic used offensive tactics to collect from Engler. After all, Atlantic gave Engler's employer the false impression that Engler was a criminal, had a pending case, and was about to be arrested. Finally, Engler suffered harm because he experienced discomfort, embarrassment, and distress as a result of Atlantic's abusive conduct. Engler may recover actual damages, statutory damages, and attorneys' fees from Atlantic.

# Chapter 21

# CHAPTER

# Antitrust Law

After the Civil War (1861–1865), the American public became increasingly concerned about declining competition in the marketplace. Large corporate enterprises were attempting to reduce or eliminate competition by legally tying themselves together in *business trusts*.

The most famous trust was the Standard Oil trust of the late 1800s. Participants in the trust transferred their stock to a trustee. The trustee then fixed prices, controlled production, and established exclusive geographic markets for all of the oil companies that were members of the trust. Some observers began to argue that the trust wielded so much economic power that corporations outside the trust could not compete effectively.

Eventually, legislators at both the state and the federal level began to enact laws to rein in the trusts. Hence, the laws regulating economic competition in the United States today are referred to as **antitrust laws.**

At the national level, antitrust legislation began when Congress passed the Interstate Commerce Act[1] in 1887, followed by the Sherman Antitrust Act[2] in 1890. In 1914, Congress passed the Clayton Act[3] and the Federal Trade Commission Act.[4] The purpose of antitrust legislation was—and still is—to foster competition. Behind these laws lies our society's belief that competition leads to lower prices, better products, a wider selection of goods, and more product information.

---

1. 49 U.S.C. Sections 501–526

2. 15 U.S.C. Sections 1–7.
3. 15 U.S.C. Sections 12–27.
4. 15 U.S.C. Sections 41–58a.

## 27–1 The Sherman Antitrust Act

The author of the Sherman Antitrust Act, Senator John Sherman, was the brother of the famed Civil War general William Tecumseh Sherman. He was also a recognized financial authority. He had been concerned for years about what he saw as diminishing competition within U.S. industry and the emergence of monopolies. He told Congress that the Sherman Act "does not announce a new principle of law, but applies old and well-recognized principles of the common law."[5]

Indeed, today's antitrust laws are the direct descendants of common law actions intended to limit **restraints of trade** (agreements between or among firms that have the effect of reducing competition in the marketplace). Such actions date to the fifteenth century in England. The common law was not always consistent, however, and had not been effective in curbing the trusts. That is why Sherman proposed the Sherman Antitrust Act, often simply called the Sherman Act.

---

5. 21 *Congressional Record* 2456 (1890).

### 27–1a Major Provisions of the Sherman Act

Sections 1 and 2 contain the main provisions of the Sherman Act:

1. Every contract, combination in the form of trust or otherwise, or conspiracy, in restraint of trade or commerce among the several States, or with foreign nations, is hereby declared to be illegal [and is a felony punishable by fine and/or imprisonment].
2. Every person who shall monopolize, or attempt to monopolize, or combine or conspire with any other person or persons, to monopolize any part of the trade or commerce among the several States, or with foreign nations, shall be deemed guilty of a felony [and is similarly punishable].

### 27–1b Differences between Section 1 and Section 2

The two sections of the Sherman Act are quite different. Section 1 requires two or more persons, because a person cannot contract, combine, or conspire alone. Thus, the essence of the illegal activity is *the act of joining together.* Section 2, though, can apply either to one person or to two or more persons because it refers to "every person." Thus, unilateral conduct can result in a violation of Section 2.

It follows that the cases brought to the courts under Section 1 of the Sherman Act differ from those brought under Section 2. Section 1 cases are often concerned with whether an agreement (written or oral) leads to a restraint of trade. Section 2 cases deal with the structure of a monopoly that exists in the marketplace.

The term **monopoly** generally is used to describe a market in which there is a single seller or a very limited number of sellers. Whereas Section 1 focuses on agreements that are restrictive—that is, agreements that have a wrongful purpose—Section 2 looks at the so-called misuse of **monopoly power** in the marketplace. Monopoly power exists when a firm has an extreme amount of **market power**—the ability to affect the market price of its product.

Both Section 1 and Section 2 seek to curtail market practices that result in undesired monopoly pricing and output behavior. For a case to be brought under Section 2, however, the "threshold" or "necessary" amount of monopoly power must already exist. We illustrate the different requirements for violating these two sections of the Sherman Act in Exhibit 27–1.

### 27–1c Jurisdictional Requirements

The Sherman Act applies only to restraints that have a significant impact on interstate commerce. Courts have generally held that any activity that substantially affects interstate commerce falls within the scope of the Sherman Act. As will be discussed later in this chapter, the Sherman Act also extends to U.S. nationals abroad who are engaged in activities that affect U.S. foreign commerce.

Federal courts have exclusive jurisdiction over antitrust cases brought under the Sherman Act. State laws regulate local restraints on competition, and state courts decide claims brought under those laws.

---

## 27–2 Section 1 of the Sherman Act

The underlying assumption of Section 1 of the Sherman Act is that society's welfare is harmed if rival firms are permitted to join in an agreement that consolidates their market power or otherwise restrains competition. The types of trade restraints that Section 1 of the Sherman Act prohibits generally fall into two broad categories: *horizontal restraints* and *vertical restraints,* both of which will be discussed shortly. First, though, we look at the rules that the courts may apply when assessing the anticompetitive impact of alleged restraints of trade.

### 27–2a *Per Se* Violations versus the Rule of Reason

Some restraints are so substantially anticompetitive that they are deemed ***per se* violations**—illegal *per se* (inherently)—under Section 1. Other agreements, however, even though they result in enhanced market power, do not *unreasonably* restrain trade and are therefore lawful. Using the **rule of reason,** the courts analyze anticompetitive agreements that allegedly violate Section 1 of the Sherman Act to determine whether they actually constitute reasonable restraints of trade.

**Rationale for the Rule of Reason** The need for a rule-of-reason analysis of some agreements in restraint of trade is obvious. If the rule of reason had not been

**EXHIBIT 27–1** Required Elements of a Sherman Act Violation

| SECTION 1 VIOLATION REQUIREMENTS | SECTION 2 VIOLATION REQUIREMENTS |
|---|---|
| 1. An agreement between two or more parties that<br>2. Unreasonably restrains competition and<br>3. Affects interstate commerce. | 1. The possession of monopoly power in the relevant market, and<br>2. The willful acquisition or maintenance of that power as distinguished from its growth or development as a consequence of a superior product, business acumen, or historic accident. |

developed, almost any business agreement could conceivably be held to violate the Sherman Act. United States Supreme Court Justice Louis Brandeis effectively phrased this sentiment in *Chicago Board of Trade v. United States,* a case decided in 1918:

> Every agreement concerning trade, every regulation of trade, restrains. To bind, to restrain, is of their very essence. The true test of legality is whether the restraint imposed is such as merely regulates and perhaps thereby promotes competition or whether it is such as may suppress or even destroy competition.[6]

**Factors That Courts Consider** When analyzing an alleged Section 1 violation under the rule of reason, a court will consider the following factors:

1. The purpose of the agreement.
2. The parties' ability to implement the agreement to achieve that purpose.
3. The effect or potential effect of the agreement on competition.
4. Whether the parties could have relied on less restrictive means to achieve their purpose.

**■ CASE IN POINT 27.1** A group of consumers sued NBC Universal, the Walt Disney Company, and other broadcasters, as well as cable and satellite distributors. The consumers claimed that the bundling together of high-demand and low-demand television channels in cable and satellite programming packages violates the Sherman Act. Bundling forces consumers to pay for channels they do not watch to have access to channels they watch regularly.

The consumers argued that the defendants, through their control of high-demand programming, exercised market power that made it impossible for any distributor to offer unbundled programs. A federal appellate court ruled in favor of the defendants and dismissed the case. The court reasoned that the Sherman Act applies to actions that diminish competition and that the bundling of channels does not injure competition.[7] ■

## 27–2b Horizontal Restraints

The term **horizontal restraint** is encountered frequently in antitrust law. A horizontal restraint is any agreement that in some way restrains competition between rival firms competing in the same market. Horizontal restraints may include price-fixing, group boycotts, market divisions, and trade associations.

**Price Fixing** Any **price-fixing agreement**—an agreement among competitors to fix prices—constitutes a *per se* violation of Section 1. The agreement on price need not be explicit. As long as it restricts output or artificially fixes price, it violates the law.

**The Reason Behind the Agreement Is Not a Defense.** A price-fixing agreement is always a violation of Section 1, even if there are good reasons behind it. **■ CASE IN POINT 27.2** In a classic price-fixing case, independent oil producers in Texas and Louisiana were caught between falling demand due to the Great Depression of the 1930s and increasing supply from newly discovered oil fields. A group of the major refining companies agreed to buy "distress" gasoline (excess supplies) from the independents so as to dispose of it in an "orderly manner." Although there was no explicit agreement as to price, it was clear that the purpose of the agreement was to limit the supply of gasoline on the market and thereby raise prices.

There may have been good reasons for the agreement. Nonetheless, the United States Supreme Court recognized the potentially adverse effects that such an agreement could have on open and free competition. The Court held that the reasonableness of a price-fixing agreement is never a defense. Any agreement that restricts output or artificially fixes price is a *per se* violation of Section 1.[8] ■

**Price-Fixing Cartels Today.** Price-fixing cartels (groups) are still commonplace in today's business world, particularly among global companies. The U.S. government actively pursues companies that it suspects of being involved in price-fixing cartels. International price-fixing cartels have been alleged in numerous industries, including air freight, auto parts, computer monitors, digital commerce, and drug manufacturers.

**■ CASE IN POINT 27.3** After Amazon.com released the Kindle e-book reader, it began selling e-book downloads at $9.99 (lower than the actual cost) and made up the difference by selling more Kindles. When the iPad entered the e-book scene, Apple and some book publishers agreed to use Apple's "agency" model, which Apple was already using for games and apps. The agency model allowed the book publishers to set their own prices while Apple kept 30 percent as a commission.

The U.S. government sued Apple and the publishers for price fixing. Because the publishers involved in the arrangement chose prices that were relatively similar, the government argued that price fixing was evident

---

6. 246 U.S. 231, 38 S.Ct. 242, 62 L.Ed. 683 (1918).
7. *Brantley v. NBC Universal, Inc.,* 675 F.3d 1192 (9th Cir. 2012).

8. *United States v. Socony-Vacuum Oil Co.,* 310 U.S. 150, 60 S.Ct. 811, 84 L.Ed. 1129 (1940).

and "would not have occurred without the conspiracy among the defendants." Ultimately, a federal appellate court held that Apple's agreement with publishers to raise e-book prices was a *per se* illegal price-fixing conspiracy. As a result, Apple was ordered to pay $400 million to consumers and $50 million in attorneys' fees.[9] ■

**Group Boycotts** A **group boycott** is an agreement by two or more sellers to refuse to deal with (that is, to boycott) a particular person or firm. Because they involve concerted action, group boycotts have been held to constitute *per se* violations of Section 1 of the Sherman Act.

To prove a violation of Section 1, the plaintiff must demonstrate that the boycott or joint refusal to deal was undertaken with the intention of eliminating competition or preventing entry into a given market. Although most boycotts are illegal, a few, such as group boycotts against a supplier for political reasons, may be protected under the First Amendment right to freedom of expression.

**Horizontal Market Division** It is a *per se* violation of Section 1 of the Sherman Act for competitors to divide up territories or customers. ■ **EXAMPLE 27.4** Axm Electronics Basics, Halprin Servo Supplies, and Aicarus Prime Electronics compete against each other in the states of Kansas, Nebraska, and Oklahoma. The three firms agree that Axm will sell products only in Kansas, Halprin will sell only in Nebraska, and Aicarus will sell only in Oklahoma.

This concerted action violates Section 1 of the Sherman Act. It reduces marketing costs and allows all three firms (assuming there is no other competition) to raise the price of the goods sold in their respective states. The same violation would take place if the three firms divided up their customers by class rather than region. They might agree that Axm would sell only to institutional purchasers (such as governments and schools) in all three states, Halprin only to wholesalers, and Aicarus only to retailers. The result would be the same. ■

**Trade Associations** Businesses in the same general industry or profession frequently organize trade associations to pursue common interests. A trade association may engage in various joint activities, such as exchanging information, representing the members' business interests before governmental bodies, and conducting advertising campaigns. Trade associations also frequently are involved in setting regulatory standards to govern the industry or profession.

Generally, the rule of reason is applied to many of these horizontal actions. If a court finds that a trade association practice or agreement that restrains trade is sufficiently beneficial both to the association and to the public, it may deem the restraint reasonable.

In *concentrated industries,* however, trade associations can be, and have been, used as a means to facilitate anticompetitive actions, such as fixing prices or allocating markets. A **concentrated industry** is one in which either a single firm or a small number of firms control a large percentage of market sales. When trade association agreements have substantially anticompetitive effects, a court will consider them to be in violation of Section 1 of the Sherman Act.

**Joint Ventures** Joint ventures undertaken by competitors are also subject to antitrust laws. If a joint venture does not involve price fixing or market divisions, the agreement will be analyzed under the rule of reason. Whether the joint undertaking violates Section 1 will then depend on the factors stated earlier in this chapter. A court will look at the venture's purpose, the potential benefits relative to the likely harms, and whether there are less restrictive alternatives for achieving the same goals.

## 27–2c Vertical Restraints

A **vertical restraint** of trade results from an agreement between firms at different levels in the manufacturing and distribution process. In contrast to horizontal relationships, which occur at the same level of operation, vertical relationships encompass the entire chain of production.

The chain of production normally includes the purchase of inventory, basic manufacturing, distribution to wholesalers, and eventual sale of a product at the retail level. For some products, these distinct phases are carried on by different firms. In other instances, a single firm carries out two or more of the separate functional phases. Such enterprises are said to be **vertically integrated firms.**

Even though firms operating at different functional levels are not in direct competition with one another, they are in competition with other firms. Thus, agreements between firms standing in a vertical relationship may affect competition. Some vertical restraints are *per se* violations of Section 1. Others are judged under the rule of reason.

**Territorial or Customer Restrictions** In arranging for the distribution of its products, a manufacturing firm often wishes to insulate dealers from direct

---

9. *United States v. Apple, Inc.,* 791 F.3d 290 (2d Cir. 2015). Apple had previously agreed to settle the case for these amounts if its appeal was unsuccessful.

competition with other dealers selling its products. To do so, the manufacturer may institute territorial restrictions or attempt to prohibit wholesalers or retailers from reselling the products to certain classes of buyers, such as competing retailers.

**May Have Legitimate Purpose.** A firm may have legitimate reasons for imposing territorial or customer restrictions. For instance, an electronics manufacturer may wish to prevent a dealer from reducing costs and undercutting rivals by offering its products without promotion or customer service. In this situation, the cost-cutting dealer reaps the benefits (sales of the product) paid for by other dealers who undertake promotion and arrange for customer service. By not providing customer service (and relying on a nearby dealer to provide these services), the cost-cutting dealer may also harm the manufacturer's reputation.

**Judged under the Rule of Reason.** Territorial and customer restrictions were once considered *per se* violations of Section 1.[10] In 1977, the United States Supreme Court held that they should be judged under the rule of reason. ■ **CASE IN POINT 27.5** The Supreme Court case involved GTE Sylvania, Inc., a manufacturer of television sets. Sylvania limited the number of retail franchises that it granted in any given geographic area. It also required each franchisee to sell only Sylvania products from the location at which it was franchised. Sylvania retained sole discretion to increase the number of retailers in an area.

When Sylvania decided to open a new franchise, it terminated the franchise of Continental T.V., Inc., an existing franchisee in that area that would have been in competition with the new franchise. Continental filed a lawsuit claiming that Sylvania's vertically restrictive franchise system violated Section 1 of the Sherman Act. The United States Supreme Court found that "vertical restrictions promote interbrand competition by allowing the manufacturer to achieve certain efficiencies in the distribution of his products." Therefore, Sylvania's vertical system, which was not price restrictive, did not constitute a *per se* violation of Section 1 of the Sherman Act.[11] ■

The decision in the *Continental* case marked a definite shift from rigid characterization of territorial and customer restrictions to a more flexible, economic analysis

of these vertical restraints under the rule of reason. This rule is still applied in most vertical restraint cases.

**Resale Price Maintenance Agreements** An agreement between a manufacturer and a distributor or retailer in which the manufacturer specifies what the retail prices of its products must be is known as a **resale price maintenance agreement.** Such agreements were once considered to be *per se* violations of Section 1 of the Sherman Act.

Today, however, both *maximum* resale price maintenance agreements and *minimum* resale price maintenance agreements are judged under the rule of reason.[12] The setting of a maximum price that retailers and distributors can charge for a manufacturer's products may sometimes increase competition and benefit consumers.

## 27–3 Section 2 of the Sherman Act

Section 1 of the Sherman Act proscribes certain concerted, or joint, activities that restrain trade. In contrast, Section 2 condemns "every person who shall monopolize, or attempt to monopolize." Thus, two distinct types of behavior are subject to sanction under Section 2: *monopolization* and *attempts to monopolize.*

One tactic that may be involved in either offense is predatory pricing. **Predatory pricing** occurs when one firm (the predator) attempts to drive its competitors from the market by selling its product at prices substantially *below* the normal costs of production. Once the competitors are eliminated, the predator presumably will raise its prices far above their competitive levels to recapture its losses and earn higher profits.

### 27–3a Monopolization

The United States Supreme Court has defined **monopolization** as involving the following two elements:

1. The possession of monopoly power in the relevant market.
2. "The willful acquisition or maintenance of the power as distinguished from growth or development as a

---

10. See *United States v. Arnold, Schwinn & Co.*, 388 U.S. 365, 87 S.Ct. 1856, 18 L.Ed.2d 1249 (1967).
11. *Continental T.V., Inc. v. GTE Sylvania, Inc.*, 433 U.S. 36, 97 S.Ct. 2549, 53 L.Ed.2d 568 (1977).

12. The United States Supreme Court ruled that maximum resale price agreements should be judged under the rule of reason in *State Oil Co. v. Khan*, 522 U.S. 3, 118 S.Ct. 275, 139 L.Ed.2d 199 (1997). In *Leegin Creative Leather Products, Inc. v. PSKS, Inc.*, 551 U.S. 877, 127 S.Ct. 2705, 168 L.Ed.2d 623 (2007), the Supreme Court found that the rule of reason also applies to minimum resale price agreements.

consequence of a superior product, business acumen, or historic accident."[13]

To establish a violation of Section 2, a plaintiff must prove both of these elements—monopoly power and an *intent* to monopolize.

**Defining Monopoly Power** The Sherman Act does not define *monopoly.* In economic theory, monopoly refers to control of a specific market by a single entity. It is well established in antitrust law, however, that a firm may be a monopolist even though it is not the sole seller in a market.

Additionally, size alone does not determine whether a firm is a monopoly. ■ **EXAMPLE 27.6** A "mom and pop" grocery located in the isolated town of Happy Camp, Idaho, is a monopolist if it is the only grocery serving that particular market. Size in relation to the market is what matters, because monopoly involves the power to affect prices. ■

**Proving Monopoly Power** Monopoly power can be proved by direct evidence that the firm used its power to control prices and restrict output.[14] Usually, though, there is not enough evidence to show that the firm intentionally controlled prices, so the plaintiff has to offer indirect, or circumstantial, evidence of monopoly power.

To prove monopoly power indirectly, the plaintiff must show that the firm has a dominant share of the relevant market and that there are significant barriers for new competitors entering that market. ■ **CASE IN POINT 27.7** DuPont manufactures and sells para-aramid fiber, a synthetic fiber used to make body armor, fiber-optic cables, and tires, among other things. Although several companies around the world manufacture this fiber, only three sell in the U.S. market—DuPont (based in the United States), Teijin (based in the Netherlands), and Kolon Industries, Inc. (based in Korea). DuPont is the industry leader, and at times has produced 60 percent of all para-aramid fibers purchased in the United States.

After DuPont brought suit against Kolon for theft and misappropriation of trade secrets, Kolon counterclaimed that DuPont had illegally monopolized and attempted to monopolize the U.S. para-aramid market in violation of Section 2. Kolon claimed that, to deter competition, DuPont had illegally used multiyear supply agreements for all of its high-volume para-aramid customers. A federal appellate court, however, found that there was insufficient proof that DuPont had possessed monopoly power in the U.S. market during the relevant time period (between 2006 and 2009). Additionally, the court concluded that Kolon had not shown that the supply agreements foreclosed competition. Therefore, the court held in favor of DuPont on the antitrust claims.[15] ■

**Relevant Market** Before a court can determine whether a firm has a dominant market share, it must define the relevant market. The relevant market consists of two elements: (1) a relevant product market and (2) a relevant geographic market.

**Relevant Product Market.** The relevant product market includes all products that have identical attributes (all brands of tea, for instance), as well as products that are reasonably interchangeable with them. Products are considered reasonably interchangeable if consumers treat them as acceptable substitutes. For instance, tea and coffee are reasonably interchangeable, so they may be included in the same relevant product market.

Establishing the relevant product market is often the key issue in monopolization cases because the way the market is defined may determine whether a firm has monopoly power. When the product market is defined narrowly, the degree of a firm's market power appears greater.

■ **EXAMPLE 27.8** White Whale Apps acquires Springleaf Apps, its main competitor in nationwide Android-based mobile phone apps. White Whale maintains that the relevant product market consists of all online retailers of mobile phone apps. The Federal Trade Commission (FTC), however, argues that the relevant product market consists of retailers that sell only apps for Android mobile phones. Under the FTC's narrower definition, White Whale can be seen to have a dominant share of the relevant product market. Thus, the FTC can take appropriate actions against White Whale. ■

In the following case, the FTC alleged that the leading U.S. producer of domestic ductile iron pipe fittings sought to maintain monopoly power in violation of antitrust law. The FTC filed this action under Section 5 of the Federal Trade Commission Act. Section 5, like Section 2 of the Sherman Act, requires proof of both the possession of monopoly power in the relevant market and the willful acquisition or maintenance of that power.

---

**13.** *United States v. Grinnell Corp.,* 384 U.S. 563, 86 S.Ct. 1698, 16 L.Ed.2d 778 (1966).

**14.** See, for instance, *Broadcom Corp. v. Qualcomm, Inc.,* 501 F.3d 297 (3d Cir. 2007).

**15.** *Kolon Industries, Inc. v. E.I. DuPont de Nemours & Co.,* 748 F.3d 160 (4th Cir. 2014).

# McWane, Inc. v. Federal Trade Commission

United States Court of Appeals, Eleventh Circuit, 783 F.3d 814 (2015).

## In the Language of the Court

*MARCUS,* Circuit Judge:

\* \* \* \*

\* \* \* Pipe fittings join together pipes and help direct the flow of pressurized water in pipeline systems. They are sold primarily to municipal water authorities and their contractors. Although there are several thousand unique configurations of fittings (different shapes, sizes, coatings, etc.), approximately 80% of the demand is for about 100 commonly used fittings.

Fittings are commodity products produced to American Water Works Association ("AWWA") standards, and any fitting that meets AWWA specifications is interchangeable, regardless of the country of origin.

\* \* \* Certain municipal, state, and federal laws require [government] waterworks projects to use domestic-only fittings. Domestic fittings sold for use in projects with domestic-only specifications command higher prices than imported fittings.

\* \* \* \*

\* \* \* In late 2009, McWane [Inc., headquartered in Birmingham, Alabama,] was the only supplier of domestic fittings.

\* \* \* Looking to take advantage of the increased demand for domestic fittings prompted by [the passage of the American Recovery and Reinvestment Act of 2009 (ARRA), which provided a large infusion of money for waterworks projects that required domestic pipe fittings, Star Pipe Products] decided to enter the market for domestic [fittings].

In response to Star's forthcoming entry into the \* \* \* market, McWane implemented its "Full Support Program" in order "to protect its domestic brands and market position." \* \* \* McWane informed customers that if they did not "fully support McWane branded

products for their domestic fitting and accessory requirements," they "may forgo participation in any unpaid rebates they had accrued for domestic fittings and accessories or shipment of their domestic fitting and accessory orders of McWane products for up to 12 weeks."

\* \* \* \*

\* \* \* The FTC issued a \* \* \* complaint charging \* \* \* that McWane's \* \* \* Full Support Program constituted unlawful maintenance of a monopoly over the domestic fittings market.

\* \* \* \*

\* \* \* The Commission found that the relevant market was the supply of domestically manufactured fittings for use in domestic-only waterworks projects, because imported fittings are not a substitute for domestic fittings for such projects. The Commission noted that this conclusion was bolstered by the higher prices charged for domestic fittings used in domestic-only projects. The Commission also found that McWane had monopoly power in that market, with 90–95% market share \* \* \* and [that there were] substantial barriers to entry in the form of major capital outlays required to produce domestic fittings.

The Commission [also found] that McWane's Full Support Program \* \* \* foreclosed Star's access to distributors for domestic fittings and harmed competition, thereby contributing significantly to the maintenance of McWane's monopoly power in the market. It noted that \* \* \* the country's two largest waterworks distributors (with a combined 60% market share), prohibited their branches from purchasing domestic fittings from Star after the Full Support Program was announced \* \* \*. Unable to attract [customers], Star was prevented from generating the revenue needed to acquire its own foundry, a

more efficient means of producing domestic fittings; thus, its growth into a rival that could challenge McWane's monopoly power was artificially stunted.

Moreover, the Commission found that \* \* \* McWane's \* \* \* conduct had an impact on price: after the Full Support Program was implemented, McWane raised domestic fittings prices and increased its gross profits despite flat production costs, and it did so across states, regardless of whether Star had entered the market as a competitor.

\* \* \* \*

[The Commission issued an order directing McWane to stop requiring exclusivity from its customers.] McWane filed a timely petition in this Court seeking review of the Commissioner's order.

\* \* \* \*

\* \* \* *Given the identification of persistent price differences between domestic fittings and imported fittings, the distinct customers, and the lack of reasonable substitutes in this case, there was sufficient evidence to support the Commission's market definition.* [Emphasis added.]

\* \* \* \*

\* \* \* The evidence of McWane's overwhelming market share (90%), the large capital outlays required to enter the domestic fittings market, and McWane's undeniable continued power over domestic fittings prices amount to sufficient evidence that a reasonable mind might accept as adequate to support the Commission's conclusion [that McWane possessed monopoly power in the relevant market].

\* \* \* \*

\* \* \* We agree that [McWane's] conduct amounts to a violation of Section 5 of the Federal Trade Commission Act.

Accordingly, we AFFIRM.

Case 27.1 Continued

### Legal Reasoning Questions

**1.** How did McWane's Full Support Program harm competition? Explain.

**2.** What did the Federal Trade Commission conclude? What "factual and economic" evidence supported this conclusion?

**3.** Instead of imposing an exclusivity policy, what action might McWane have taken to benefit its customers and compete with Star?

---

**Relevant Geographic Market.** The second component of the relevant market is the geographic extent of the market in which the firm and its competitors sell the product or services. For products that are sold nationwide, the geographic boundaries of the market can encompass the entire United States.

If transportation costs are significant or a producer and its competitors sell in only a limited area (one in which customers have no access to other sources of the product), then the geographic market is limited to that area. A national firm may thus compete in several distinct areas and have monopoly power in one geographic area but not in another.

Generally, the geographic market is that section of the country within which a firm can increase its price a bit without attracting new sellers or losing many customers to alternative suppliers outside that area. Of course, the Internet is changing perceptions of the size and limits of a geographic market. It may become difficult to perceive any geographic market as local, except for products that are not easily transported, such as concrete.

**The Intent Requirement** Monopoly power, in and of itself, does not constitute the offense of monopolization under Section 2 of the Sherman Act. The offense also requires an *intent* to monopolize.

A dominant market share may be the result of good business judgment or the development of a superior product. It may simply be the result of a historical accident. In these situations, the acquisition of monopoly power is not an antitrust violation. Indeed, it would be contrary to society's interest to condemn every firm that acquired a position of power because it was well managed and efficient and marketed a product desired by consumers.

If a firm possesses market power as a result of carrying out some purposeful act to acquire or maintain that power through anticompetitive means, then it is in violation of Section 2. In most monopolization cases, intent may be inferred from evidence that the firm had monopoly power and engaged in anticompetitive behavior.

**Unilateral Refusals to Deal** As discussed previously, joint refusals to deal (group boycotts) are subject to close scrutiny under Section 1 of the Sherman Act. A single manufacturer acting unilaterally, though, normally is free to deal, or not to deal, with whomever it wishes.[16]

Nevertheless, in some instances, a unilateral refusal to deal will violate Section 2 of the Sherman Act. These instances occur only if (1) the firm refusing to deal has—or is likely to acquire—monopoly power and (2) the refusal is likely to have an anticompetitive effect on a particular market.

■ **EXAMPLE 27.9** Clark Industries owns three of the four major downhill ski areas in Blue Hills, Idaho. Clark refuses to continue participating in a jointly offered six-day "all Blue Hills" lift ticket. Clark's refusal to cooperate with its smaller competitor is a violation of Section 2 of the Sherman Act. Because Clark owns three-fourths of the local ski areas, it has monopoly power. Thus, its unilateral refusal to deal has an anticompetitive effect on the market. ■

## 27–3b Attempts to Monopolize

Section 2 also prohibits **attempted monopolization** of a market, which requires proof of the following three elements:

**1.** Anticompetitive conduct.

**2.** The specific intent to exclude competitors and garner monopoly power.

---

16. For a classic case in this area, see *United States v. Colgate & Co.*, 250 U.S. 300, 39 S.Ct. 465, 63 L.Ed. 992 (1919). See also *Pacific Bell Telephone Co. v. Linkline Communications, Inc.*, 555 U.S. 438, 129 S.Ct. 1109, 172 L.Ed.2d 836 (2009).

3. A "dangerous" probability of success in achieving monopoly power. The probability cannot be dangerous unless the alleged offender possesses some degree of market power. Only serious threats of monopolization are condemned as violations.

As mentioned earlier, predatory pricing is a form of anticompetitive conduct that, in theory, could be used by firms that are attempting to monopolize. Related to predatory pricing is *predatory bidding*. This practice involves the acquisition and use of *monopsony power*, which is market power on the *buy* side of a market. Predatory bidding occurs when a buyer bids up the price of an input too high for its competitors to pay, causing them to leave the market. The predatory bidder then attempts to drive down input prices to reap above-competitive profits and recoup any losses it suffered in bidding up the input prices.

The question in the following *Spotlight Case* was whether a claim of predatory bidding was sufficiently similar to a claim of predatory pricing that the same antitrust test should apply to both.

## Spotlight on Weyerhaeuser

## Case 27.2 Weyerhaeuser Co. v. Ross-Simmons Hardwood Lumber Co.
Supreme Court of the United States, 549 U.S. 312, 127 S.Ct. 1069, 166 L.Ed.2d 911 (2007).

**Background and Facts** Weyerhaeuser Company entered the Pacific Northwest's hardwood lumber market in 1980. By 2000, Weyerhaeuser owned six mills processing 65 percent of the red alder logs in the region. Meanwhile, Ross-Simmons Hardwood Lumber Company operated a single competing mill. When the prices of the logs rose and those for the lumber fell, Ross-Simmons suffered heavy losses. Several million dollars in debt, the mill closed in 2001.

Ross-Simmons filed a suit in a federal district court against Weyerhaeuser, alleging attempted monopolization under Section 2 of the Sherman Act. Ross-Simmons claimed that Weyerhaeuser used its dominant position in the market to bid up the prices of logs and prevent its competitors from being profitable. Weyerhaeuser argued that the antitrust test for predatory pricing applies to a claim of predatory bidding and that Ross-Simmons had not met this standard. The district court ruled in favor of the plaintiff, the U.S. Court of Appeals for the Ninth Circuit affirmed, and Weyerhaeuser appealed to the United States Supreme Court.

### In the Language of the Court
Justice *THOMAS* delivered the opinion of the Court.
* * * *

Predatory-pricing and predatory-bidding claims are analytically similar. This similarity results from the close theoretical connection between monopoly and monopsony. The kinship between monopoly and monopsony suggests that similar legal standards should apply to claims of monopolization and to claims of monopsonization.

* * * Both claims involve the deliberate use of unilateral pricing measures for anticompetitive purposes. And both claims logically require firms to incur short-term losses on the chance that they might reap supracompetitive [above-competitive] profits in the future.
* * * *

* * * *"Predatory pricing schemes are rarely tried, and even more rarely successful." Predatory pricing requires a firm to suffer certain losses in the short term on the chance of reaping supracompetitive profits in the future. A rational business will rarely make this sacrifice.* The same reasoning applies to predatory bidding. [Emphasis added.]
* * * *

* * * A failed predatory-pricing scheme may benefit consumers. * * * Failed predatory-bidding schemes can also * * * benefit consumers.

In addition, predatory bidding presents less of a direct threat of consumer harm than predatory pricing. A predatory-pricing scheme ultimately achieves success by charging higher prices to consumers. By

Case 27.2 Continued

contrast, a predatory-bidding scheme could succeed with little or no effect on consumer prices because a predatory bidder does not necessarily rely on raising prices in the output market to recoup its losses.

* * * *

* * * [Thus,] our two-pronged [predatory pricing] test should apply to predatory-bidding claims.

* * * A plaintiff must prove that the alleged predatory bidding led to below-cost pricing of the predator's outputs. That is, the predator's bidding on the buy side must have caused the cost of the relevant output to rise above the revenues generated in the sale of those outputs. * * * Given the multitude of procompetitive ends served by higher bidding for inputs, the risk of chilling procompetitive behavior with too lax a liability standard is * * * serious * * *. Consequently, only higher bidding that leads to below-cost pricing in the relevant output market will suffice as a basis for liability for predatory bidding.

A predatory-bidding plaintiff also must prove that the defendant has a dangerous probability of recouping the losses incurred in bidding up input prices through the exercise of monopsony power. Absent proof of likely recoupment, a strategy of predatory bidding makes no economic sense because it would involve short-term losses with no likelihood of offsetting long-term gains.

Ross-Simmons has conceded that it has not satisfied [this] standard. Therefore, its predatory-bidding theory of liability cannot support the jury's verdict.

**Decision and Remedy** *The United States Supreme Court held that the antitrust test that applies to claims of predatory pricing also applies to claims of predatory bidding. Because Ross-Simmons conceded that it had not met this standard, the Court vacated the lower court's judgment and remanded the case.*

**Critical Thinking**

- **Social** *Do predatory-bidding schemes ever benefit consumers? Explain your answer.*
- **Economic** *Why does a plaintiff alleging predatory bidding have to prove that the defendant's "bidding on the buy side caused the cost of the relevant output to rise above the revenues generated in the sale of those outputs"?*

## 27–4 The Clayton Act

Congress enacted the Clayton Act to strengthen federal antitrust laws. The act was aimed at specific anticompetitive or monopolistic practices that the Sherman Act did not cover. The substantive provisions of the act—set out in Sections 2, 3, 7, and 8—deal with four distinct forms of business behavior, which are declared illegal but not criminal. For each provision, the act states that the behavior is *illegal only if it tends to substantially lessen competition or to create monopoly power.*

### 27–4a Section 2—Price Discrimination

Section 2 of the Clayton Act prohibits **price discrimination,** which occurs when a seller charges different prices to competing buyers for identical goods or services. Congress strengthened this section by amending it with the passage of the Robinson-Patman Act in 1936. As amended, Section 2 prohibits price discrimination that cannot be justified by differences in production costs, transportation costs, or cost differences due to other reasons. In short, a seller cannot charge one buyer a lower price than it charges that buyer's competitor.

**Requirements** To violate Section 2, the seller must be engaged in interstate commerce, the goods must be of like grade and quality, and the goods must have been sold to two or more purchasers. In addition, the effect of the price discrimination must be to substantially lessen competition, tend to create a monopoly, or otherwise injure competition. Without proof of an actual injury resulting from the price discrimination, the plaintiff cannot recover damages.

Note that price discrimination claims can arise from discounts, offsets, rebates, or allowances given to one buyer over another. Moreover, giving favorable credit terms, delivery, or freight charges to some buyers, but not others, can also lead to allegations of price discrimination. For instance, when a seller offers goods to different customers at the same price but includes free delivery for certain buyers, it may violate Section 2 in some circumstances.

**Defenses** There are several statutory defenses to liability for price discrimination.

1. *Cost justification.* If the seller can justify the price reduction by demonstrating that a particular buyer's purchases saved the seller costs in producing and selling the goods, the seller will not be liable for price discrimination.

2. *Meeting a competitor's prices.* If the seller charged the lower price in a good faith attempt to meet an equally low price of a competitor, the seller will not be liable for price discrimination. ■ **EXAMPLE 27.10** Rogue, Inc., is a retail dealer of Mercury Marine outboard motors in Shady Cove, Oregon. Mercury Marine also sells its motors to other dealers in the Shady Cove area. When Rogue discovers that Mercury is selling its outboard motors at a substantial discount to Rogue's largest competitor, it files a price discrimination lawsuit. Mercury Marine can defend itself by showing that the discounts given to Rogue's competitor were made in good faith to meet the low price charged by another manufacturer of marine motors. ■

3. *Changing market conditions.* A seller may lower its price on an item in response to changing conditions affecting the market for or the marketability of the goods concerned. Sellers are allowed to readjust their prices to meet the realities of the market without liability for price discrimination. Thus, if an advance in technology makes a particular product less marketable than it was previously, a seller can lower the product's price.

## 27–4b Section 3—Exclusionary Practices

Under Section 3 of the Clayton Act, sellers or lessors cannot condition the sale or lease of goods on the buyer's or lessee's promise not to use or deal in the goods of the seller's competitor. In effect, this section prohibits two types of vertical agreements involving exclusionary practices—exclusive-dealing contracts and tying arrangements.

**Exclusive-Dealing Contracts** A contract under which a seller forbids a buyer to purchase products from the seller's competitors is called an **exclusive-dealing contract.** A seller is prohibited from making an exclusive-dealing contract under Section 3 if the effect of the contract is "to substantially lessen competition or tend to create a monopoly."

In the past, courts were more inclined to find that exclusive-dealing contracts substantially lessened competition. ■ **CASE IN POINT 27.11** In one classic case, Standard Oil Company, the largest gasoline seller in the nation in the late 1940s, made exclusive-dealing contracts with independent stations in seven western states.

The contracts involved 16 percent of all retail outlets, whose sales were approximately 7 percent of all retail sales in that market. The United States Supreme Court ruled that the market was substantially concentrated because the seven largest gasoline suppliers all used exclusive-dealing contracts with their independent retailers and together controlled 65 percent of the market.

Looking at market conditions after the arrangements were instituted, the Court found that market shares were extremely stable and that entry into the market was apparently restricted. Thus, the Court held that the Clayton Act had been violated because competition was "foreclosed in a substantial share" of the relevant market.[17] ■ Note that since the Supreme Court's 1949 decision, a number of subsequent decisions have called the holding in this case into doubt.

Today, it is clear that to violate antitrust law, an exclusive-dealing agreement (or a tying arrangement, discussed next) must qualitatively and substantially harm competition. To prevail, a plaintiff must present affirmative evidence that the performance of the agreement will foreclose competition and harm consumers.

**Tying Arrangements** When a seller conditions the sale of a product (the tying product) on the buyer's agreement to purchase another product (the tied product) produced or distributed by the same seller, a **tying arrangement** results. The legality of a tying arrangement (or *tie-in sales agreement*) depends on several factors, such as the purpose of the agreement. Courts also focus on the agreement's likely effect on competition in the relevant markets (the market for the tying product and the market for the tied product).

Section 3 of the Clayton Act has been held to apply only to commodities, not to services. Tying arrangements, however, can also be considered agreements that restrain trade in violation of Section 1 of the Sherman Act. Thus, cases involving tying arrangements of services have been brought under Section 1 of the Sherman Act. Although earlier cases condemned tying arrangements as illegal *per se*, courts now evaluate tying agreements under the rule of reason.[18]

■ **CASE IN POINT 27.12** James Batson bought a nonrefundable ticket from Live Nation Entertainment, Inc., to attend a rock concert at the Charter One Pavilion in Chicago. The front of the ticket noted that the

---

17. *Standard Oil Co. of California v. United States*, 337 U.S. 293, 69 S.Ct. 1051, 93 L.Ed. 1371 (1949).
18. *Illinois Tool Works, Inc. v. Independent Ink, Inc.*, 547 U.S. 28, 126 S.Ct. 1281, 164 L.Ed.2d 26 (2006). This decision was the first time the Supreme Court recognized that tying arrangements can have legitimate business justifications.

price included a nine-dollar parking fee. Batson did not have a car to park, however. In fact, he had walked to the concert venue and had bought the ticket just before the performance.

Frustrated at being charged for parking that he did not need, Batson filed a suit in a federal district court against Live Nation. He argued that the bundled parking fee was unfair because consumers were forced to pay it or forego the concert. He asserted that this was a tying arrangement in violation of Section 1 of the Sherman Act. The court dismissed the suit, and a federal appellate court affirmed. The court was unable to identify a product (or service) market in which Live Nation had sufficient power to force consumers who wanted to attend a concert (the tying product) to buy "useless parking rights" (the tied product). While such bundles may be annoying, there was no evidence that Live Nation's parking tie-in restrained competition for parking in Chicago.[19] ∎

### 27–4c Section 7—Mergers

Under Section 7 of the Clayton Act, a person or business organization cannot hold stock or assets in more than one business when "the effect . . . may be to substantially lessen competition." Section 7 is the statutory authority for preventing mergers or acquisitions that could result in monopoly power or a substantial lessening of competition in the marketplace. Section 7 applies to both horizontal and vertical mergers, as discussed in the following subsections.

A crucial consideration in most merger cases is **market concentration.** Determining market concentration involves allocating percentage market shares among the various companies in the relevant market. When a small number of companies share a large part of the market, the market is concentrated. ∎ **EXAMPLE 27.13** If the four largest grocery stores in Chicago account for 80 percent of all retail food sales, the market is concentrated in those four firms. If one of these stores absorbs the assets and liabilities of another, so that the other ceases to exist, the result is a merger that further concentrates the market and possibly diminishes competition. ∎

Competition is not necessarily diminished solely as a result of market concentration, however. Courts will consider other factors in determining if a merger violates Section 7. One factor of particular importance is whether the merger will make it more difficult for *potential* competitors to enter the relevant market.

**Horizontal Mergers** Mergers between firms that compete with each other in the same market are called **horizontal mergers.** If a horizontal merger creates an entity with a significant market share, the merger may be considered illegal because it increases market concentration. The Federal Trade Commission (FTC) and the U.S. Department of Justice (DOJ) have established guidelines for determining which mergers will be challenged.[20]

When analyzing the legality of a horizontal merger, the courts consider three additional factors. The first factor is the overall concentration of the relevant market. The second is the relevant market's history of tending toward concentration. The final factor is whether the merger is apparently designed to establish market power or restrict competition.

**Vertical Mergers** A **vertical merger** occurs when a company at one stage of production acquires a company at a higher or lower stage of production. An example of a vertical merger is a company merging with one of its suppliers or retailers.

Whether a vertical merger will be deemed illegal generally depends on several factors, such as whether the merger creates a single firm that controls an undue percentage share of the relevant market. The courts also analyze the concentration of firms in the market, barriers to entry into the market, and the apparent intent of the merging parties. If a merger does not prevent competitors of either of the merging firms from competing in a segment of the market, the merger will not be condemned as foreclosing competition and thus is legal.

### 27–4d Section 8— Interlocking Directorates

Section 8 of the Clayton Act deals with *interlocking directorates*—that is, the practice whereby individuals serve as directors on the boards of two or more competing companies simultaneously. Specifically, no person may be a director for two or more competing corporations at the same time if either of the corporations has capital, surplus, or undivided profits aggregating more than $31,841,000 or competitive sales of $3,184,100 or more. The Federal Trade Commission adjusts these threshold amounts each year. (The amounts given here are those announced by the commission in 2016.)

---

19. *Batson v. Live Nation Entertainment, Inc.,* 746 F.3d 827 (7th Cir. 2014).

20. These guidelines include a formula for assessing the degree of concentration in the relevant market called the *Herfindahl-Hirschman Index* (HHI), which is available at www.justice.gov/atr/public/guidelines/hmg-2010.html.

## 27–5 Enforcement and Exemptions

The federal agencies that enforce the federal antitrust laws are the U.S. Department of Justice (DOJ) and the Federal Trade Commission (FTC), which was established by the Federal Trade Commission Act.[21] Section 5 of that act condemns all forms of anticompetitive behavior that are not covered under other federal antitrust laws.

### 27–5a Agency Actions

Only the DOJ can prosecute violations of the Sherman Act, which can be either criminal or civil offenses. Violations of the Clayton Act are not crimes, but the act can be enforced by either the DOJ or the FTC through civil proceedings.

The DOJ or the FTC may ask the courts to impose various remedies, including **divestiture** (making a company give up one or more of its operations) and dissolution. A meatpacking firm, for instance, might be forced to divest itself of control or ownership of butcher shops.

The FTC has sole authority to enforce violations of Section 5 of the Federal Trade Commission Act. FTC actions are effected through administrative orders, but if a firm violates an FTC order, the FTC can seek court sanctions for the violation.

### 27–5b Private Actions

A private party who has been injured as a result of a violation of the Sherman Act or the Clayton Act can sue for **treble damages** (three times the actual damages suffered) and attorneys' fees. In some instances, private parties may also seek injunctive relief to prevent antitrust violations. A party wishing to sue under the Sherman Act must prove that:

1. The antitrust violation either caused or was a substantial factor in causing the injury that was suffered.
2. The unlawful actions of the accused party affected business activities of the plaintiff that were protected by the antitrust laws.

Additionally, the United States Supreme Court has held that to pursue antitrust lawsuits, private parties must present some evidence suggesting that an illegal agreement was made.[22]

A private party can bring an action under Section 2 of the Sherman Act based on the attempted enforcement of a fraudulently obtained patent. This is called a *Walker Process* claim.[23] To prevail, the plaintiff must first show that the defendant obtained the patent by fraud on the U.S. Patent and Trademark Office and enforced the patent with knowledge of the fraud. The plaintiff must then establish all the other elements of a Sherman Act monopolization claim—anticompetitive conduct, an intent to monopolize, and a dangerous probability of achieving monopoly power.

In the following case, a respiratory filter maker was accused of patent infringement. The maker sought a declaratory judgment of non-infringement, asserting a *Walker Process* claim. One of the primary issues was whether attorney fees were an appropriate basis for damages.

---

21. 15 U.S.C. Sections 41–58.

22. *Bell Atlantic Corp. v. Twombly*, 550 U.S. 544, 127 S.Ct. 1955, 167 L.Ed.2d 929 (2007).
23. The name of the claim comes from the title of the case in which the claim originated—*Walker Process Equipment v. Food Machine and Chemical Corp.*, 382 U.S. 172, 86 S.Ct. 347, 15 L.Ed.2d 247 (1965).

---

**Case 27.3**

# TransWeb, LLC v. 3M Innovative Properties Co.

United States Court of Appeals, Federal Circuit, 812 F.3d 1295 (2016).

**Background and Facts** TransWeb, LLC, makes respirator filters made of nonwoven fibrous material to be worn by workers at contaminated worksites. At a filtration industry exposition, TransWeb's founder, Kumar Ogale, handed out samples of TransWeb's filter material. At the time, 3M Innovative Products Company was experimenting with filter materials. At the expo, 3M employees obtained the TransWeb samples.

Case 27.3 Continued

More than a year later, 3M obtained patents for its filter products and filed a suit against TransWeb, claiming infringement. 3M asserted that it had not received the TransWeb samples until after its patent application had been filed. The suit was dismissed.

TransWeb then filed a suit in a federal district court, seeking a declaratory judgment of non-infringement and asserting a *Walker Process* claim. A jury found that 3M had obtained its patents through fraud, that its assertion of the patents against TransWeb violated antitrust law, and that Trans-Web was entitled to attorney fees as damages. TransWeb had incurred $7.7 million defending against 3M's infringement suit. The court trebled this to $23 million. 3M appealed.

## In the Language of the Court

*HUGHES,* Circuit Judge.
\* \* \* \*

3M argues that the district court erred in awarding the $23 million of attorney-fees damages, because TransWeb failed to show any link between those attorney fees and an impact on competition. 3M argues that those attorney fees had no effect on competition because they did not force TransWeb out of the market or otherwise affect prices in the market.
\* \* \* \*

3M's argument focuses on the fact that the harmful effect on competition proven by TransWeb at trial never actually came about. TransWeb proved at trial that increased prices for fluorinated filter \* \* \* respirators would have resulted had 3M succeeded in its suit.
\* \* \* \*

\* \* \* 3M's unlawful act was \* \* \* aimed at reducing competition and would have done so had the suit been successful. 3M's unlawful act was the bringing of suit based on a patent known to be fraudulently obtained. What made this act unlawful under the antitrust laws was its attempt to gain a monopoly based on this fraudulently obtained patent. TransWeb's attorney fees flow directly from this unlawful aspect of 3M's act. \* \* \* The attorney fees are precisely the type of loss that the claimed violations would be likely to cause.
\* \* \* \*

\* \* \* *It is the abuse of the legal process by the antitrust-defendant that makes the attorney fees incurred by the antitrust-plaintiff during that legal process a relevant antitrust injury.* [Emphasis added.]

No assertion of a patent known to be fraudulently obtained can be a proper use of legal process. No successful outcome of that litigation, regardless of how much the patentee subjectively desires it, would save that suit from being improper due to its tainted origin.

\* \* \* The antitrust laws exist to protect competition. If we were to hold that TransWeb can seek antitrust damages only [by] forfeiture of competition, but not [by] defending the anticompetitive suit, then we would be incentivizing the former over the latter. \* \* \* This is not in accord with the purpose of those very same antitrust laws.

Furthermore, it furthers the purpose of the antitrust laws to encourage TransWeb to bring its antitrust suit \* \* \* instead of waiting to be excluded from the market \* \* \* . If TransWeb proceeds only after being excluded from the market \* \* \* , then the [injury] will no longer be borne by TransWeb alone, but rather would be shared by all consumers in the relevant markets.

**Decision and Remedy** *The U.S. Court of Appeals for the Federal Circuit affirmed the lower court's judgment and award of trebled attorney fees. "TransWeb's attorney fees appropriately flow from the unlawful aspect of 3M's antitrust violation and thus are an antitrust injury that can properly serve as the basis for antitrust damages."*

## Critical Thinking

- **Legal Environment** *How would TransWeb's injury have been "shared by all consumers in the relevant markets" if TransWeb had not sued until* after *it had been driven out of those markets by 3M's actions?*
- **Ethical** *What does 3M's conduct suggest about its corporate ethics?*

## 27–5c Exemptions from Antitrust Laws

There are many legislative and constitutional limitations on antitrust enforcement. Most of the statutory and judicially created exemptions to the antitrust laws apply only in certain areas (see Exhibit 27–2). One of the most significant exemptions covers joint efforts by businesspersons to obtain legislative, judicial, or executive action. Under this exemption, for instance, music producers and record companies can jointly lobby Congress to change the copyright laws without being held liable for attempting to restrain trade. Another exemption covers professional baseball teams.

**EXHIBIT 27–2  Exemptions to Antitrust Enforcement**

| EXEMPTION | SOURCE AND SCOPE |
|---|---|
| Labor | The Clayton Act—Permits unions to organize and bargain without violating antitrust laws and specifies that strikes and other labor activities normally do not violate any federal law. |
| Agricultural Associations | The Clayton Act and the Capper-Volstead Act—Allow agricultural cooperatives to set prices. |
| Fisheries | The Fisheries Cooperative Marketing Act—Allows the fishing industry to set prices. |
| Insurance Companies | The McCarran-Ferguson Act—Exempts the insurance business in states in which the industry is regulated. |
| Exporters | The Webb-Pomerene Act—Allows U.S. exporters to engage in cooperative activity to compete with similar foreign associations.<br>The Export Trading Company Act—Permits the U.S. Department of Justice to exempt certain exporters. |
| Professional Baseball | The United States Supreme Court—Has held that professional baseball is exempt because it is not "interstate commerce."[a] |
| Oil Marketing | The Interstate Oil Compact—Allows states to set quotas on oil to be marketed in interstate commerce. |
| Defense Activities | The Defense Production Act—Allows the president to approve, and thereby exempt, certain activities to further the military defense of the United States. |
| Small Businesses' Cooperative Research | The Small Business Administration Act—Allows small firms to undertake cooperative research. |
| State Actions | The United States Supreme Court—Has held that actions by a state are exempt if the state clearly articulates and actively supervises the policy behind its action.[b] |
| Regulated Industries | Federal Agencies—Industries (such as airlines) are exempt when a federal administrative agency (such as the Federal Aviation Administration) has primary regulatory authority. |
| Businesspersons' Joint Efforts to Seek Government Action | The United States Supreme Court—Cooperative efforts by businesspersons to obtain legislative, judicial, or executive action are exempt unless it is clear that an effort is "objectively baseless" and is an attempt to make anticompetitive use of government processes.[c] |

a. *Federal Baseball Club of Baltimore, Inc. v. National League of Professional Baseball Clubs,* 259 U.S. 200, 42 S.Ct. 465, 66 L.Ed. 898 (1922). See *City of San Jose v. Office of the Commissioner of Baseball,* 776 F.3d 686 (9th Cir. 2015).
b. See *Parker v. Brown,* 317 U.S. 341, 63 S.Ct. 307, 87 L.Ed. 315 (1943).
c. *Eastern Railroad Presidents Conference v. Noerr Motor Freight, Inc.,* 365 U.S. 127, 81 S.Ct. 523, 5 L.Ed.2d 464 (1961); and *United Mine Workers of America v. Pennington,* 381 U.S. 657, 89 S.Ct. 1585, 14 L.Ed.2d 626 (1965). These two cases established the exception often referred to as the *Noerr-Pennington* doctrine.

# 27–6 U.S. Antitrust Laws in the Global Context

U.S. antitrust laws have a broad application. Not only may persons in foreign nations be subject to their provisions, but the laws may also be applied to protect foreign consumers and competitors from violations committed by U.S. business firms. Consequently, *foreign persons,* a term that by definition includes foreign governments, may sue under U.S. antitrust laws in U.S. courts.

## 27–6a The Extraterritorial Application of U.S. Antitrust Laws

Section 1 of the Sherman Act provides for the extraterritorial effect of the U.S. antitrust laws. Any conspiracy that has a *substantial effect* on U.S. commerce is within the reach of the Sherman Act. The violation may even occur outside the United States, and foreign governments as well as individuals can be sued for violation of U.S. antitrust laws.

Before U.S. courts will exercise jurisdiction and apply antitrust laws, it must be shown that the alleged violation had a substantial effect on U.S. commerce. U.S. jurisdiction is automatically invoked, however, when a *per se* violation occurs.

If a domestic firm, for instance, joins a foreign cartel to control the production, price, or distribution of goods, and this cartel has a *substantial effect* on U.S. commerce, a *per se* violation may arise. Hence, both the domestic firm and the foreign cartel could be sued for violation of the U.S. antitrust laws.

Likewise, if a foreign firm doing business in the United States enters into a price-fixing or other anticompetitive agreement to control a portion of U.S. markets, a *per se* violation may exist. ■ **CASE IN POINT 27.14** Carrier Corporation is a U.S. firm that manufactures air-conditioning and refrigeration (ACR) equipment. To make these products, Carrier uses ACR copper tubing it buys from Outokumpu Oyj, a Finnish company. Carrier is one of the world's largest purchasers of ACR copper tubing.

After the Commission of the European Communities found that Outokumpu had conspired with other companies to fix ACR tubing prices in Europe, Carrier filed a suit in a U.S. court. Carrier alleged that the cartel had also conspired to fix prices in the United States by agreeing that only Outokumpu would sell ACR tubing in the U.S. market. The district court dismissed the case for lack of jurisdiction, but a federal appellate court reversed. The reviewing court found that the alleged anticompetitive conspiracy had a substantial effect on U.S. commerce. Therefore, the U.S. courts had jurisdiction over the Finnish defendant.[24] ■

## 27–6b The Application of Foreign Antitrust Laws

Large U.S. companies increasingly must be concerned about the application of foreign antitrust laws. The European Union (EU), in particular, has stepped up its enforcement actions against antitrust violators.

**European Union Enforcement** The EU's laws promoting competition are stricter in many respects than those of the United States and define more conduct as anticompetitive. The EU actively pursues antitrust violators, especially individual companies and cartels that allegedly engage in monopolistic conduct. EU investigations of possible antitrust violations often take years. See this chapter's *Digital Update* feature for a discussion of how the EU is pursuing Google, Inc., for antitrust violations.

**Increased Enforcement in Asia and Latin America** Many other nations also have laws that promote competition and prohibit trade restraints. Japanese antitrust laws forbid unfair trade practices, monopolization, and restrictions that unreasonably restrain trade. China's antitrust rules restrict monopolization and price fixing (except that the Chinese government can set prices on exported goods). Indonesia, Malaysia, South Korea, and Vietnam all have statutes protecting competition. Argentina, Brazil, Chile, Peru, and several other Latin American countries have adopted modern antitrust laws as well.

Most of the antitrust laws apply extraterritorially, as U.S. antitrust laws do. This means that a U.S. company may be subject to another nation's antitrust laws if the company's conduct has a substantial effect on that nation's commerce. For instance, in 2015, China fined the U.S. chipmaker Qualcomm, Inc., $975 million for violating antitrust laws. China has also targeted Microsoft, Inc., in its antitrust investigations and has searched Microsoft's company servers in China for evidence of violations.

---

24. *Carrier Corp. v. Outokumpu Oyj,* 673 F.3d 430 (6th Cir. 2012).

## DIGITAL UPDATE

# Google Faces an Antitrust Complaint from the European Union

"Just google it." Google's search engine is so dominant that the company name has become a verb synonymous with conducting an Internet search. According to the European Commissioner for Competition, Margrethe Vestager, Google has become too dominant, at least with respect to comparison shopping and product search. For that reason, the European Union (EU) has formally charged Google with an antitrust violation. The charges relate specifically to Google operations in the EU.

### The EU's Antitrust Objections

According to the EU, Google is abusing a dominant position—a breach of EU antitrust rules. The EU has alleged that Google promotes its own comparison shopping service at the expense of competitors. It does this by "positioning and prominently displaying its comparison shopping service in its general search result pages, irrespective of its merits." As a result, "users do not necessarily see the most relevant results in response to queries—to the detriment of consumers and rival comparison shopping services." Presumably, this conduct started in 2008.

### What the EU Wants Google to Do and Google's Response

Now that the EU has established its complaint against Google, here is what it wants Google to do: change the way it displays search results in the EU. When Google shows comparison shopping services in response to a user's query, the search results should show the most relevant services first.

In response to both the complaint and the suggested remedy, Google offered a 130-page rebuttal. It contends that it cannot change its core software. It also claims that the results in its search algorithms are based on relevance. In addition, Google contends that it has actually boosted traffic to its Web competitors. Therein lies the major argument against the EU's antitrust complaint. Search engines have proliferated on the Web, suggesting that Google's success has not eliminated competition.

### The Compartmentalization of Search on the Web

More and more frequently, Internet users do not engage in general searches. Rather, they know exactly where to go to obtain product information. When they want information on movies, for instance, they go to the Internet Movie Data Base (IMDB) rather than Google. When they want information on music, they go to iTunes. When they want to search for the cheapest airfares, they go to Kayak or similar sites. When they want to find the best rates on hotels, they go to sites such as hotels.com. And when they are interested in buying a product, they frequently go to Amazon or eBay. Amazon, in particular, has fine-tuned its ability to generate advertising revenues through its Amazon-sponsored links.

And, of course, social media must be considered. More people are on social media sites than ever before, particularly on their mobile devices. Users spend four times more time on Facebook than they do on Google. These users often "crowdsource"—that is, look for answers from Facebook friends rather than search on Google. Facebook is also becoming increasingly competitive with Google in the services it offers, including mobile payments and the Facebook Messenger instant messaging service.

Whether the European Antitrust Commission accepts Google's arguments will determine Google's fate. Will it pay billions of dollars in fines and be forced to make significant changes in how it does business? That probably will not be decided any time soon. Experts estimate that the case could go on for years.

**Critical Thinking** *Which companies in Europe do you think may have pressured the European Union to lodge its antitrust complaint against Google?*

---

# Reviewing: Antitrust Law

The Internet Corporation for Assigned Names and Numbers (ICANN) is a nonprofit entity that organizes Internet domain names. It is governed by a board of directors elected by various groups with commercial interests in the Internet. One of ICANN's functions is to authorize an entity to serve as a registry for certain "Top Level Domains" (TLDs). ICANN and VeriSign entered into an agreement that authorized VeriSign to serve as a registry for the ".com" TLD and provide registry services in accordance with ICANN's specifications. VeriSign complained that ICANN was restricting the services that it could make available as a registrar, blocking new services, imposing unnecessary conditions on those services, and setting the prices at which the services were offered. VeriSign claimed that ICANN's control of the registry services for domain names violated Section 1 of the Sherman Act. Using the information presented in the chapter, answer the following questions.

1. Should ICANN's actions be judged under the rule of reason or be deemed *per se* violations of Section 1 of the Sherman Act? Why?
2. Should ICANN's actions be viewed as a horizontal or a vertical restraint of trade? Why?
3. Does it matter that ICANN's directors are chosen by groups with a commercial interest in the Internet? Explain.
4. If the dispute is judged under the rule of reason, what might be ICANN's defense for having a standardized set of registry services that must be used?

**Debate This** . . .    *The Internet and the rise of e-commerce have rendered our current antitrust concepts and laws obsolete.*

## Terms and Concepts

antitrust law 568
attempted monopolization 575
concentrated industry 571
divestiture 580
exclusive-dealing contract 578
group boycott 571
horizontal merger 579
horizontal restraint 570
market concentration 579
market power 569

monopolization 572
monopoly 569
monopoly power 569
*per se* violation 569
predatory pricing 572
price discrimination 577
price-fixing agreement 570
resale price maintenance
   agreement 572

restraint of trade 568
rule of reason 569
treble damages 580
tying arrangement 578
vertical merger 579
vertical restraint 571
vertically integrated firm 571

## Issue Spotters

1. Under what circumstances would Pop's Market, a small store in a small, isolated town, be considered a monopolist? If Pop's is a monopolist, is it in violation of Section 2 of the Sherman Act? Why or why not? (See *Section 2 of the Sherman Act*.)

2. Maple Corporation conditions the sale of its syrup on the buyer's agreement to buy Maple's pancake mix. What factors would a court consider to decide whether this arrangement violates the Clayton Act? (See *The Clayton Act*.)

• **Check your answers to the Issue Spotters against the answers provided in Appendix D at the end of this text.**

## Business Scenarios

**27–1. Group Boycott.** Jorge's Appliance Corp. was a new retail seller of appliances in Sunrise City. Because of its innovative sales techniques and financing, Jorge's attracted many customers. As a result, the appliance department of No-Glow Department Store, a large chain store with a great deal of buying power, lost a substantial number of sales. No-Glow told a number of appliance manufacturers from whom it made large-volume purchases that if they continued to sell to Jorge's, No-Glow would stop buying from them. The manufacturers immediately stopped selling appliances to Jorge's. Jorge's filed a suit against No-Glow and the manufacturers, claiming that their actions constituted an antitrust violation. No-Glow and the manufacturers were able to prove that Jorge's was a small retailer with a small market share. They claimed that because the relevant market was not substantially affected, they were not guilty of restraint of trade. Discuss fully whether there was an antitrust violation. (See *Section 1 of the Sherman Act*.)

**27–2. Antitrust Laws.** Allitron, Inc., and Donovan, Ltd., are interstate competitors selling similar appliances, principally in the states of Illinois, Indiana, Kentucky, and Ohio. Allitron and Donovan agree that Allitron will no longer sell in Indiana and Ohio and that Donovan will no longer sell in Illinois and Kentucky. Have Allitron and Donovan violated any antitrust laws? If so, which law? Explain. (See *Section 1 of The Sherman Act.*)

## Business Case Problems

**27–3. Section 2 of the Sherman Act.** While Deer Valley Resort Co. (DVRC) was developing its ski resort in the Wasatch Mountains near Park City, Utah, it sold parcels of land in the resort village to third parties. Each sales contract reserved the right of approval over the conduct of certain businesses on the property, including ski rentals. For fifteen years, DVRC permitted Christy Sports, LLC, to rent skis in competition with DVRC's ski rental outlet. Then DVRC opened a new midmountain ski rental outlet and revoked Christy's permission to rent skis. This meant that most skiers who flew into Salt Lake City and shuttled to Deer Valley had few choices. They could carry their ski equipment with them on their flights, take a shuttle into Park City and look for cheaper ski rentals there, or rent from DVRC. Christy filed a suit in a federal district court against DVRC. Was DVRC's action an attempt to monopolize in violation of Section 2 of the Sherman Act? Why or why not? [*Christy Sports, LLC v. Deer Valley Resort Co.*, 555 F.3d 1188 (10th Cir. 2009)] (See *Section 2 of the Sherman Act.*)

**27–4. Price Fixing.** Together, EMI, Sony BMG Music Entertainment, Universal Music Group Recordings, Inc., and Warner Music Group Corp. produced, licensed, and distributed 80 percent of the digital music sold in the United States. The companies formed MusicNet to sell music to online services that sold the songs to consumers. MusicNet required all of the services to sell the songs at the same price and subject to the same restrictions. Digitization of music became cheaper, but MusicNet did not change its prices. Did MusicNet violate the antitrust laws? Explain. [*Starr v. Sony BMG Music Entertainment*, 592 F.3d 314 (2d Cir. 2010)] (See *Section 1 of the Sherman Act.*)

**27–5. Business Case Problem with Sample Answer—Price Discrimination.** Dayton Superior Corp. sells its  products in interstate commerce to several companies, including Spa Steel Products, Inc. The purchasers often compete directly with each other for customers. From 2005 to 2007, one of Spa Steel's customers purchased Dayton Superior's products from two of Spa Steel's competitors. According to the customer, Spa Steel's prices were always 10 to 15 percent higher for the same products. As a result, Spa Steel lost sales to at least that customer and perhaps others. Spa Steel wants to sue Dayton Superior for price discrimination. Which requirements for such a claim under Section 2 of the Clayton Act does Spa Steel satisfy? What additional facts will it need to prove? [*Dayton Superior Corp. v. Spa Steel Products, Inc.*, 2012 WL 113663 (N.D.N.Y. 2012)] (See *The Clayton Act.*)

• For a sample answer to Problem 27–5, go to Appendix E at the end of this text.

**27–6. Section 1 of the Sherman Act.** The National Collegiate Athletic Association (NCAA) and the National Federation of State High School Associations (NFHS) set a new standard for non-wood baseball bats. Their goal was to ensure that aluminum and composite bats performed like wood bats in order to enhance player safety and reduce technology-driven home runs and other big hits. Marucci Sports, LLC, makes non-wood bats. Under the new standard, four of Marucci's eleven products were decertified for use in high school and collegiate games. Marucci filed suit against the NCAA and the NFHS under Section 1 of the Sherman Act. At trial, Marucci's evidence focused on injury to its own business. Did the NCAA and NFHS's standard restrain trade in violation of the Sherman Act? Explain. [*Marucci Sports, L.L.C. v. National Collegiate Athletic Association*, 751 F.3d 368 (5th Cir. 2014)] (See *Section 1 of the Sherman Act.*)

**27–7. Mergers.** St. Luke's Health Systems, Ltd., operated an emergency clinic in Nampa, Idaho. Saltzer Medical Group, P.A., had thirty-four physicians practicing at its offices in Nampa. Saint Alphonsus Medical Center operated the only hospital in Nampa. St. Luke's acquired Saltzer's assets and entered into a five-year professional service agreement with the Saltzer physicians. This affiliation resulted in a combined share of two-thirds of the Nampa adult primary care provider market. Together, the two entities could impose a significant increase in the prices charged to patients and insurers, and correspondence between the parties indicated that they would. Saint Alphonsus filed a suit against St. Luke's to block the merger. Did this affiliation violate antitrust law? Explain. [*Saint Alphonsus Medical Center-Nampa, Inc. v. St. Luke's Health System, Ltd.*, 778 F.3d 775 (9th Cir. 2015)] (See *The Clayton Act.*)

**27–8. Section 1 of the Sherman Act.** Manitou North America, Inc., makes and distributes telehandlers (forklifts with extendable telescopic booms) to dealers throughout the United States. Manitou agreed to make McCormick International, LLC, its exclusive dealer in the state of Michigan. Later, Manitou entered into an agreement with Gehi Company, which also makes and sells telehandlers. The companies agreed to allocate territories within Michigan among certain dealers for each manufacturer, limiting the dealers' selection of competitive products to certain models. Under this agreement, McCormick was precluded from buying or selling Gehi telehandlers. What type of trade restraint did the agreement between Manitou and Gehi represent? Is this a violation of antitrust law? If so, who was injured, and how were they injured? Explain. [*Manitou North America, Inc. v. McCormick International, LLC*, __ N.W.2d __, 2016 WL 439354 (2016)] (See *Section 1 of the Sherman Act.*)

**27–9. A Question of Ethics—Section 1 of the Sherman Act.**  *In the 1990s, DuCoa, L.P., made choline chloride, a B-complex vitamin essential for the growth and development of animals. DuCoa, Bioproducts, Inc., and Chinook Group, Ltd., each had one-third of the U.S. market for choline chloride. To stabilize the market and keep the price of the vitamin higher than it would otherwise have been, the companies took action. They agreed to fix the price and allocate market share by deciding which of them would offer the lowest price to each customer. At times, however, the companies disregarded the agreement.*

*During an increase in competitive activity in August 1997, Daniel Rose became president of DuCoa. The next month, a subordinate advised him of the conspiracy. By February 1998, Rose had begun to implement a strategy to persuade DuCoa's competitors to rejoin the conspiracy. By April, the three companies had reallocated their market shares and increased their prices. In June,* *the U.S. Department of Justice began to investigate allegations of price fixing in the vitamin market. Ultimately, a federal district court convicted Rose of conspiracy to violate Section 1 of the Sherman Act. [United States v. Rose, 449 F.3d 627 (5th Cir. 2006)] (See Section 1 of the Sherman Act.)*

**(a)** The court "enhanced" Rose's sentence to thirty months' imprisonment, one year of supervised release, and a $20,000 fine. Among other things, the court based this enhancement on Rose's role as "a manager or supervisor" in the conspiracy. Rose appealed the enhancement to the U.S. Court of Appeals for the Fifth Circuit. Was it fair to increase Rose's sentence on this ground? Why or why not?

**(b)** Was Rose's participation in the conspiracy unethical? If so, how might Rose have behaved ethically instead? If not, could any of the participants' conduct be considered unethical? Explain.

## Legal Reasoning Group Activity

**27–10. Antitrust Violations.** Residents of the city of Madison, Wisconsin, became concerned about overconsumption of liquor near the campus of the University of Wisconsin (UW). The city initiated a new policy, imposing conditions on area bars to discourage reduced-price "specials" that were believed to encourage high-volume and dangerous drinking. Later, the city began to draft an ordinance to ban all drink specials. Bar owners responded by announcing that they had "voluntarily" agreed to discontinue drink specials on Friday and Saturday nights after 8:00 P.M. The city put its ordinance on hold. Several UW students filed a lawsuit against the local bar owners' association, alleging violations of antitrust law. (See *Section 1 of the Sherman Act.*)

**(a)** The first group will identify the grounds on which the plaintiffs might base their claim for relief and formulate an argument on behalf of the plaintiffs.

**(b)** The second group will determine whether the defendants are exempt from the antitrust laws.

**(c)** The third group will decide how the court should rule in this dispute and provide reasons for the ruling.

# Answers to the *Issue Spotters*

**1.** *Under what circumstances would Pop's Market, a small store in a small, isolated town, be considered a monopolist? If Pop's is a monopolist, is it in violation of Section 2 of the Sherman Act? Why or why not?* Size alone does not determine whether a firm is a monopoly—size in relation to the market is what matters. A small store in a small, isolated town is a monopolist if it is the only store serving that market. Monopoly involves the power to affect prices and output. If a firm has sufficient market power to control prices and exclude competition, that firm has monopoly power. Monopoly power in itself is not a violation of Section 2 of the Sherman Act. The offense also requires that the defendant intended to acquire or maintain that power through anticompetitive means.

**2.** *What factors would a court consider to decide whether this arrangement violates the Clayton Act?* This agreement is a tying arrangement. The legality of a tying arrangement depends on the purpose of the agreement, the agreement's likely effect on competition in the relevant markets (the market for the tying product and the market for the tied product), and other factors. Tying arrangements for commodities are subject to Section 3 of the Clayton Act. Tying arrangements for services can be agreements in restraint of trade in violation of Section 1 of the Sherman Act.

# Sample Answers for *Business Case Problems with Sample Answer*

**Problem 27–5.** *Price Discrimination.* Spa Steel satisfies most of the requirements for a price discrimination claim under Section 2 of the Clayton Act. Dayton Superior is engaged in interstate commerce, and it sells goods of like grade and quality to at least three purchasers. Moreover, Spa Steel can show that, because it sells Dayton Superior's products at a higher price, it lost business and thus suffered an injury. To recover, however, Spa Steel will also need to prove that Dayton Superior charged Spa Steel's competitors a lower price for the same product. Spa Steel cannot recover if its prices were higher for reasons related to its own business, such as having higher overhead expenses or seeking a larger profit.

# Index